Eichmann Before Jerusalem

EICHMANN
BEFORE
JERUSALEM

THE UNEXAMINED LIFE OF A MASS MURDERER

Bettina Stangneth

TRANSLATED FROM THE GERMAN BY
RUTH MARTIN

THE BODLEY HEAD
LONDON

First published in Great Britain in 2014 by
The Bodley Head
20 Vauxhall Bridge Road,
London SW1V 2SA

A Penguin Random House company

Penguin
Random House
UK

www.penguinrandomhouse.com

www.vintage-books.co.uk

A CIP catalogue record for this book
is available from the British Library

ISBN 9781847923233 (Hardback)
ISBN 9781847923257 (Trade Paperback)

Printed and bound in Great Britain by Clays Ltd, St Ives plc

MIX
Paper from
responsible sources
FSC
www.fsc.org   FSC® C018179

Penguin Random House is committed to a sustainable future for
our business, our readers and our planet. This book is made from
Forest Stewardship Council® certified paper.

For Dieter, the guiding star on my journey through the night.

Contents

Selected Cast of Characters

These are some of the less familiar people associated with Adolf Eichmann (aka Otto Heninger on the Lüneberg Heath and Ricardo Klement in Argentina) in the postwar period.

Principal Participants in the Sassen Discussions

ALVENSLEBEN, LUDOLF VON: Himmler's former chief adjutant; higher SS and police leader; after the war, the highest-ranking Nazi in Argentina

FRITSCH, EBERHARD: Head of Dürer Verlag from 1946, publishing Nazi texts and owning a bookstore that became a focal point for Nazis in Argentina; publisher of *Der Weg—El Sendero,* the most extremist postwar Nazi magazine

LANGER, DR.: Former SD officer from Vienna; other details unknown

SASSEN, WILLEM: Dutch Nazi collaborator and member of SS journalist corps; propagandist, correspondent, author, and ghostwriter for Nazis in Argentina; organizer and host of the interviews and discussion group with Eichmann

Adolf Eichmann's Family

EICHMANN, HORST ADOLF; Dieter Helmut; Ricardo Francisco: Younger sons of Adolf and Vera Eichmann

EICHMANN, KARL ADOLF: Adolf Eichmann's father

EICHMANN, KLAUS: Eldest son of Adolf and Vera Eichmann

EICHMANN, OTTO: Adolf Eichmann's brother; with Robert, organized and supported the defense in Eichmann's trial

EICHMANN, ROBERT: Adolf Eichmann's stepbrother; a lawyer who organized and supported his brother's defense, 1960–62; large portions of the Argentina Papers were stolen from his office

EICHMANN, VERA: Adolf Eichmann's wife; postwar, she used her birth surname, Liebl

Involved with Eichmann's Escape from Justice and Journey to Argentina

FREIESLEBEN, HANS: SS member who arranged a hiding place for Eichmann on Lüneberg Heath

FULDNER, HORST CARLOS: German-Argentine SS member; helped Nazis escape on behalf of Juan Perón

HUDAL, BISHOP ALOIS: Roman bishop and Hitler sympathizer who helped falsify identity papers for Nazi fugitives, including Eichmann

KRAWIETZ, NELLY: Sister of SS member Kurt Bauer; hid Eichmann on his escape from a prisoner-of-war camp; later visited him when he was in hiding on Lüneberg Heath

KUHLMANN, HERBERT, AKA PEDRO GELLER: Former member of SS panzer corps; traveled from Europe to Argentina with Eichmann; in 1953, was guarantor for Eichmann's apartment in Chacabuco Street; worked at CAPRI

SCHINTLHOLZER, LUIS (ALOIS): Austrian SS officer involved in 1938 pogrom in Innsbruck and war crimes in Italy; helped Eichmann escape Germany

Members of the Dürer Circle and Other Associated Nazis in Argentina

HAGEL, HERBERT: SS member; former secretary to the gauleiter of Linz; employed by CAPRI

HEILIG, BERTHOLD: Former NSDAP district leader in Brunswick; worked for CAPRI in Tucumán

KLINGENFUß, KARL: Worked in Nazi Foreign Office's "Jewish Department"; head of German-Argentine Chamber of Commerce until 1967

KOPPS, REINHARD, AKA JUAN MALER: Prolific writer, fanatical Nazi, and rival of Sassen's; worked for Dürer Verlag in the early days of *Der Weg*

LEERS, JOHANN VON: SS officer and prominent ideologue employed in the Ministry of Propaganda; in Argentina 1950–54; wrote for *Der Weg*

MENGE, DIETER: SS member; Luftwaffe pilot; in Argentina became a scrap-metal magnate; Sassen's patron

NEURATH, CONSTANTIN VON: Son of Germany's former foreign minister; with Rudel, founder of Kameradenwerk, a fund to assist fugitive Nazis legally and financially; from 1958, director of Siemens Argentina S.A.

OVEN, WILFRED VON: Press adjutant to Goebbels in the Ministry of Propaganda; author of a book on Goebbels, published by Dürer Verlag

PFEIFFER, FRANZ WILHELM: Wehrmacht colonel and rumored guardian of Nazi gold; owner of the rabbit farm in Joaquín Gorina managed by Eichmann; friend of Sassen and Rudel

POBIERZYM, PEDRO: Polish Wehrmacht soldier; did business with Nazis in Argentina, including Dieter Menge and Willem Sassen

RUDEL, HANS-ULRICH: Luftwaffe bomber pilot, the most highly decorated serviceman under Hitler; with Neurath, founded Kameradenwerk, a fund to assist Nazis legally and financially; friend of Fritsch and admirer of Sassen, who ghostwrote Rudel's books, published by Dürer Verlag

SCHWAMMBERGER, JOSEF: SS member and camp commandant in Krakow, 1942–44; employed by Siemens Argentina S.A.

VOLLMER, DIETER: Close colleague of Fritsch who worked on *Der Weg;* returned to Germany in 1954 but remained in contact with Dürer

VÖTTERL, JOSEF: Member of the criminal and border police with Einsatzkommando 10A of Einsatzgruppe D; fled to Buenos Aires but moved back to Germany in 1955; found employment with BfV; returned to Argentina in 1958

Connected to Eichmann's Pursuit, Arrest, and Trial

AHARONI, ZVI: Mossad agent who found out Eichmann's Argentine address and positively identified "Ricardo Klement" as Eichmann

BAUER, FRITZ: Attorney general of Hesse, 1956–68; prosecutor of Nazi war criminals; located Eichmann in Argentina and provided the information to Israeli authorities

FRIEDMAN, TUVIAH: Holocaust survivor whose family was murdered; Nazi hunter; creator of the Haifa Institute for the Documentation of Nazi War Crimes

GENOUD, FRANÇOIS: Swiss financier, Hitler admirer, and dedicated Nazi; profited from the commercializing writings of Nazis such as Martin Bormann and Joseph Goebbels; involved in a deal to sell Eichmann's writings for profit and to finance Eichmann's defense

HAREL, ISSER: Head of Mossad, 1952–63; author of a controversial account of Eichmann's capture

HAUSNER, GIDEON: Israeli attorney general, 1960–63; led the prosecution of Eichmann

HERMANN, LOTHAR: Lawyer; survivor of Dachau whose family died in the Holocaust; legal adviser, first in Buenos Aires, then in the German-Jewish community in Coronel Suárez; alerted Bauer and others that Eichmann was in Argentina

LESS, AVNER W.: Chief inspector in the Israeli police; interrogated Eichmann after his capture

MAST, HEINRICH: German and American intelligence officer; associate of Höttl; said to have informed Wiesenthal in 1953 that Eichmann was in Argentina

SERVATIUS, ROBERT: West German attorney; defended Nazis at the Nuremberg Trials and later was Eichmann's defense counsel

TARRA, VALENTIN: Altaussee criminal investigator who observed Eichmann's family while Eichmann was in hiding

WIESENTHAL, SIMON: Holocaust survivor and, after the war, the most famous Nazi hunter; found the first photograph of Eichmann; prevented the Eichmann family's every attempt to have him declared dead

Others

HARLAN, THOMAS: Son of Veit Harlan, the notorious anti-Semitic film director; author, devoted to revealing Nazi war crimes; friend of Fritz Bauer; in 1961, published one of the first articles based on the Argentina Papers (obtained from Langbein) in the Polish weekly *Polityka*

HÖTTL, WILHELM: Austrian SS officer; postwar, was a prosecution witness at the Nuremberg Trials, quoting Eichmann on the number of six million Holocaust victims; later an "intelligence" agent providing much false information to intelligence services, the press, and historians

KASZTNER, RUDOLF (REZSÖ): Austro-Hungarian Jew; executive vice president of the Budapest Rescue Committee; with Brand, negotiated the 1944 "blood for goods" proposal with Eichmann, an attempt to save Hungarian Jewry; after the war, accused of collaborating with Nazis; assassinated in 1957

LANGBEIN, HERMANN: Concentration camp survivor; first general secretary of the International Auschwitz Committee in Vienna; brought criminal charges against Eichmann in Austria in 1959; in 1961, obtained and disseminated the most complete copy of the Argentina Papers

ORMOND, HENRY: Dachau survivor; lawyer for Nazi victims; friend of Bauer and Harlan; helped to make the Argentina Papers available in 1961

PASSENT, DANIEL: Editor of Polish weekly *Polityka;* in 1961, published a five-part series based on Langbein's copy of the Argentina Papers, with commentary by Harlan and himself

RAKOWSKI, MIECZYSŁAW F.: Editor-in-chief of *Polityka;* verified the authenticity of the Argentina Papers

SASSEN, MIEP: Second wife of Willem

SASSEN, SASKIA: Daughter of Willem and Miep

SCHNEIDER, INGE: Family friend of the Sassens; daughter of the captain of the ship on which the Sassens fled Europe

WISLICENY, DIETER: SS officer who was Eichmann's subordinate, close friend, and acolyte; postwar, a prosecution witness at the Nuremberg Trials; blamed Eichmann in an attempt to save his own life; tried and hanged in 1948 in Bratislava; his Nuremberg testimony would help the prosecution of Eichmann in 1961

Introduction

This business is not really clear to me at all.

—Hannah Arendt[1]

We cannot speak of the systematic extermination of millions of men, women, and children without mentioning his name—and yet people are no longer even sure what his first name *was:* Karl Adolf? Otto? It's the simplest of questions yet it can still surprise us, long after we thought we'd established who he was. But are there really still such large gaps in our knowledge of a man who has been so thoroughly investigated for so many years, by both academics and the media? Adolf Eichmann's fame surpasses even that of Heinrich Himmler and Reinhard Heydrich. So why write another book? It was the simplest of questions: I wanted to find out who knew Adolf Eichmann before Mossad famously snatched him from Argentina and put him before a court in Israel.

Eichmann's answer, given in Israel, is not hard to find: "Until 1946, I had next to no public profile, until Dr. Hoettl . . . branded me the murderer of 5 or 6 million Jews."*[2] We should not be surprised to hear these words from an accused man—and this one in particular. Eichmann, after all, is famous for saying that he had been "just a small cog in Adolf Hitler's extermination machine." What *is* surprising is that, until now, the secondary literature on Eichmann has dutifully parroted this view. Other great controversies might surround the man behind the genocide, but everyone is agreed that until his trial in Jerusalem, the name Eichmann was known only to a small circle of people.[3]

The suspicion that something was amiss, both in Eichmann's story and in the research, arose when I started to read old newspapers. On May 23, 1960, the Israeli prime minister, David Ben-Gurion, unexpectedly announced to the world that Adolf Eichmann had been captured

---

* In all quotations, old or incorrect spellings of names remain uncorrected. The customary note [*sic*] is omitted.

and was to stand trial. What followed was not a puzzled silence but pages and pages of detailed articles describing a man about whom, supposedly, very little was known, by very few people. A glance at some even older publications confirmed my suspicion unequivocally. Long before the start of his trial, this "unknown" man already had more nicknames than most other Nazis: Caligula; Czar of the Jews; Manager of the Holocaust; Grand Inquisitor; Engineer of the Jewish Genocide; the Final Solutionist; the Bureaucrat; the Mass Murderer. All these epithets were applied to Eichmann between 1939 and 1960. They didn't arise after his arrest— they appeared long before that, in newspapers, pamphlets, and books. You have only to read these materials to find out exactly what people knew and thought about Eichmann, and when. During this period, only one group claimed, with equal unanimity, to know nothing about him. They were the postwar Nazis, his former colleagues, who were desperate to play down what they knew. But the evidence raises the questions: How did this knowledge come to be lost? How could a man cause himself to disappear, retrospectively, from the eyes of the world? The answer leads us to the problematic heart of the singular crime against humanity that we call the Holocaust, the Shoah, the extermination of the Jews.

We like to imagine criminals as shady figures, committing their crimes in secret, fearful of public judgment. When they are unmasked, we like to imagine a consistent reaction from the public, an instinctive wish to ostracize them and bring them to justice. The first attempts to consider the perpetrators of the disenfranchisement, expulsion, and murder of the European Jews were wholly in line with this cliché of shady characters, terrorizing their victims while society's back was turned. But we have long since moved on from this vision of a small group of pathological, asocial freaks within an upstanding population who would have mounted a collective resistance, if only they had known what was going on. We now know a lot about how the National Socialist worldview functioned. We know about the dynamics of collective behavior and the impact of totalitarian regimes. We understand the influence that an atmosphere of violence can have, even on people with no particular inclination toward sadism, and we have explored the disastrous effect of the division of labor on people's sense of individual responsibility. Of course, huge disagreement remains about where and how we should classify a perpetrator like Adolf Eichmann. Depending on whose account you read, he comes across variously as an ordinary man who was turned into a thoughtless murderer by a totalitarian regime; a radical anti-Semite whose aim was the extinction of the Jewish people, or a mentally ill man whose innate sadism was legitimated by the regime. We have a multitude of irreconcilable images of Eichmann, made even more so by the controversy around Hannah Arendt's *Eichmann in Jerusalem: A Report on the Banality of Evil*. The public view, however, largely remains an empty shell. We are still missing a view of the "Eichmann phenomenon" before Jerusalem: the way Eichmann was perceived during the different periods of his life.

Jean-Jacques Rousseau tells us that in every assumption that leads to injustice, two parties are always involved: the person making the claim, and all the others who believe him.[4] We can learn a good deal about the danger inherent in this curious collaboration by looking at the public perception of Adolf Eichmann. The greatest danger arises when someone has as clear an understanding of this collaboration as did the notorious "Adviser for Jewish Affairs." For this reason, my book tells Eichmann's story not as a chronological account of his crimes or his actions as they developed, but as a study of the impact he made: who knew Eichmann and when; what people thought of him and when; and how he reacted to what they thought and said. To what extent, I ask, was the Eichmann phenomenon shaped by his talent for self-dramatization? What did this role-playing contribute to his murderous career, and what can it contribute now to our understanding of his story?

Our ability to reconstruct these perspectives today rests on an exceptional body of source material: there are more documents, testimonials and eyewitness reports on Eichmann than on any other leading Nazi. Not even Hitler or Goebbels has occasioned more material. And the reason is not simply Eichmann's survival for seventeen years after the end of the war, nor the impressive efforts of the Israeli police in collecting evidence for the trial: the reason is primarily his own passion for speaking and writing. Eichmann acted out a new role for every stage of his life, for each new audience and every new aim. As subordinate, superior officer, perpetrator, fugitive, exile, and defendant, Eichmann kept a close eye on the impact he was having at all times, and he tried to make every situation work in his favor. And there was a method to his behavior, as a comparison of the many roles he played will reveal.

The only one of Eichmann's roles to have become really well known is the one he performed in Jerusalem. The intention is obvious: he was doing his best to stay alive and to justify his actions. If we want to discover how Eichmann's performance in Jerusalem relates to the perpetrator and to his deadly success, we must go back to Eichmann *before* Jerusalem and take a look behind the interpretations that rely solely on his appearance there.

If we are to believe what Eichmann said in Israel, his real life—the one he had always longed for—began only in 1945, when the madness of the Thousand Year Reich lay in ruins. That was when the Adviser for Jewish Affairs became a harmless rabbit breeder, as he always had been at the bottom of his heart. It was the regime that had been evil, and other people, and his stellar career under Adolf Hitler had really been just a bizarre twist of fate. But because Eichmann was aware that a lot of other people might see things differently, he carefully avoided using the name Adolf Eichmann, even making his wife call him by his first forename, Otto, which had also been his grandfather's name.[5] While the others were capitulating, he disappeared among the prisoners of war, becoming "Adolf Karl Barth." Before he managed to escape, he was tried as "Otto Eckmann." Then he was "Otto Heninger," a forester on the Lüneberg Heath in northern Germany, working alongside other men who had new names. After that, he bred chickens, enchanting the female population of his rural backwater in the evenings with his violin playing. The life of Otto Heninger, which was already so very like that of the Argentine rabbit breeder, had only two distinct disadvantages: he couldn't contact his family and he was wanted for war crimes. "In the five years I spent underground, living as a 'mole,' it became second nature to me, whenever I saw a new face, to ask myself a few questions, like: Do you know this face? Does this person look like he has seen you before? Is he trying to recall when he might have met you? And during these years, the fear never left me that somebody could come up behind me and suddenly cry: 'Eichmann!'"[6] His hope that, in time, grass would grow over the National Socialist genocide, just as it does over other graves, remained unfulfilled. Ultimately he could see no solution but to flee the country, and so in 1950 Otto Heninger disappeared as well. Ricardo Klement left Europe from Genoa, receiving a new identity and new papers in Argentina. He was then able to begin the life he had always wanted: he found work on a hydroelectric power station project, and led a troop of surveyors across Tucumán, a subtropical area in the north of

Argentina where the mountains and valleys are reminiscent of the Alps. He had plenty of time to make trips on horseback too, exploring the mountains, crossing the pampas, and even twice attempting to climb Aconcagua, the Americas' highest mountain. Two years later, when his wife and their three sons were finally able to join him, he began taking the boys with him on his expeditions, teaching them to ride and fish and imparting to them his own love of nature. For a while, the collapse of the project's firm somewhat dampened the family's blissful existence: Ricardo Klement had to look for work, and he wasn't always successful, but by 1955 at the latest, his happiness must have been complete. He was handed not only the manager's job at a rabbit farm but also a fourth son, even though his wife was over forty. Little "Hasi" was the apple of his father's eye. No wonder Klement then decided to build his own house, to accommodate his lovely wife, his four sons, Fifi the dachshund, Rex the German shepherd, the cuckoo clock, and the paintings of alpine scenes.[7] And if he hadn't been kidnapped by Mossad, he would still be living the harmless life of Ricardo Klement. . . .

This moving tale had just one major flaw: Ricardo Klement might have been the name on his passport, but the reformed Nazi and nature lover, a man who was now entirely apolitical, had never arrived in Argentina. Rural idylls were not Eichmann's thing. For him, the war—his war— had never ended. The SS *Obersturmbannführer* might have been retired from service, but the fanatical National Socialist was still on active duty. He might have lost his totalitarian state, in which you could murder millions of people without so much as raising your hand against one of them, but he was still far from defenseless. This man might sit on the veranda of the rabbit farm at the end of his working day, a glass of red wine in his hand, thirty miles away from his family. He might even play the violin. But none of that could convince him that his life was as idyllic as it seemed. On the thirty-fifth parallel, dusk and sunset don't really exist; it gets dark at a stroke—night falls more suddenly and dramatically than northern Europeans are used to. In the evenings, he read and wrote, and his work was anything but introspective. This was no contented man in his fifties, reading for pleasure: the peaceable rabbit farmer was capable of throwing books against the wall and tearing them to pieces, filling them with aggressive marginalia, insults, and invectives, and covering mountains of paper with his commentaries, writing like a man possessed. Pencils snapped under the force of his scribbling;

his fighting spirit was unbroken. The ideological warrior had not been defeated, and he was by no means alone.

The reason we know so much about his life in Argentina today is due to a happy coincidence. Over the last two years, documents have surfaced in several archives and are now available to researchers. For the first time, the Argentina Papers—Eichmann's own notes made in exile—can be examined in conjunction with the taped and transcribed conversations known (slightly misleadingly) as the Sassen interviews. At a combined total of more than thirteen hundred pages, these sources do more than just present Eichmann's life and thought before his arrest. This first attempt to summarize and interpret them is also a challenge to others, to engage with these documents as the most important postwar material on National Socialist crimes against humanity. Suddenly we are able to make connections that could never have been made before. And one thing in particular stands out: not once during his escape and exile did Eichmann seek the shadows or try to act in secrecy. He wanted to be visible in Argentina, and he wanted to be viewed as he once had been: as the symbol of a new age.

Those who seek out the light will be seen. Clearly more people had dealings with Eichmann after 1945 than was previously thought. Tracing his route into the underground and into exile, we come across not only Nazi hunters and hit squads, but people who helped and sympathized with him and even became his friends—though for a long time afterward, they denied ever having known him, or said they had met him only briefly. Willem Sassen, a Dutch volunteer in the Waffen-SS and a war propagandist, spent decades claiming only to have been Eichmann's "ghostwriter." Like him, most of Eichmann's friends denied most of their contact with the wanted man. Their denials no longer carry any weight. The Argentina Papers reveal the names of the people who sought Eichmann out to talk about old times and, more important, to discuss political plans for the future. In Argentina, Eichmann was no more a failure and a pariah than Willem Sassen was merely an inquisitive journalist, or Himmler's chief adjutant, Ludolf von Alvensleben, a reformed Nazi. For in spite of all attempts to ignore them, there they were: the Nazis in Argentina. They had escaped the Allied courts and were regrouping, with much bigger plans than to be left in peace to start new lives. From a safe distance, the men around Eichmann used their freedom in exile to comment on developments in Germany and the rest of the world. They pursued ambitious plans for political over-throw, busily putting together a network of like-minded people. They even started counterfeiting documents designed to defend their view of glorious National Socialism against reality. And in their midst was Adolf Eichmann: self-assured, dedicated, and in demand as a specialist (with millions of murders to prove his expertise)—exactly what a man who had had his own department in the Head Office for Reich Security was used to.

"Eichmann in Argentina" is not a one-man play but a chronicle of the ex-*Obersturmbannführer*'s astonishing second career—as an expert on history and on the "Jewish question." As much as he later tried to per-suade everyone that the German defeat had altered and reformed him, a study of his thought and his social life in Argentina reveals something else entirely. If Eichmann ever really wanted to be the placid, harm-less Ricardo Klement, it was not until he was sitting in an Israeli prison cell. In Argentina, he proudly signed photos for his comrades "Adolf Eichmann—SS-*Obersturmbannführer* (retired)."

But Eichmann after 1945 is much more than an Argentine affair. In West Germany, his name had been burned into people's memories, even if later they denied all knowledge of him. A plethora of witness state-ments, press articles, and publications on Eichmann demonstrates how preoccupied the Germans were with his name and what it stood for, even before 1960. But in our search for the "Eichmann phenomenon," we can also draw on an indirect source, the importance of which cannot be overestimated: the testimonies of his victims and pursuers and, above all, his former colleagues and confidants. There was no way they could forget him: they must have been afraid he would remember them just as well as they remembered him. Nobody who knew this man, or even just knew who he was, wanted to be caught remembering him. American intelligence service documents, "wanted" lists, and the few files released by the Public Prosecutor's Office, by the Bundesamt für Verfassungss-chutz (BfV, or Federal Office for the Protection of the Constitution), and by the German Foreign Office, allow us to create a preliminary sketch of Adolf Eichmann's importance in the period immediately after the war, particularly in the new West Germany and Austria. Eichmann—or rather, the image people had of him—gradually became a political prob-lem. The fact that the key witness to the Nazis' crimes against humanity was still at large undermined the German strategy for overcoming the past, which was to try to forget it had ever happened. And the fact that Eichmann had no desire to live a quiet, low-profile life in Argentina, even writing an open letter to West German chancellor Konrad Adenauer, meant that he was becoming a risk. Could anybody really want this man, who knew so much, to speak out in the Federal Republic?

All this made the hunt for Eichmann a much more complex story than previously published tales of love, betrayal, and death would have us believe. The story wasn't just about the millions of victims and the Nazi hunters determined to track down their murderer, or about one government or another doing a more or less skillful job of it. Plenty of people were determined to prevent the past from returning from exile along with the man. Overcoming their desperate need to stay silent required much more than giving credence to the observant blind man in Argentina who realized that his daughter's boyfriend was the son of a war criminal. The story of Eichmann before Jerusalem is a series of missed opportunities to hold the trial in Germany and create a genuine new beginning. This is the story we must investigate if we want to understand the extent to which the structures of that unspeakable age survived beyond the war's end. They were supposed to have been replaced by a new state, though there were no new people to administer it. Scandalously, the German authorities still hold files on Eichmann that have not been released to the public because their contents are deemed to be a danger to the common good. Acceptance of the fact that Adolf Eichmann, SS-*Obersturmbannführer* (retired), is a chapter of German history is long overdue.

Ever since *Eichmann in Jerusalem: A Report on the Banality of Evil* was published in 1963, every essay on Adolf Eichmann has also been a dialogue with Hannah Arendt.[8] A Jew from Königsberg who had studied philosophy under Karl Jaspers and Martin Heidegger until National Socialism drove her out of Germany, Arendt went to Jerusalem in 1961 for Eichmann's trial. Like all philosophers, she wanted to understand. But our understanding is always mediated by our context: we bring to the task our own thoughts and experiences and our own images of the past. Hannah Arendt read about Adolf Eichmann in the newspapers for the first time in 1943 at the latest, and eighteen years later she was familiar with all the research on him. What she expected to find in Jerusalem was something she had already described in detail: a diabolical, highly intelligent mass murderer who commanded a kind of horrified fascination, the kind of murderer seen in great works of literature. "He was one of the most intelligent of the lot," she wrote in 1960. Anyone who dared to understand him would be taking a great leap toward understanding the Nazis' crimes. "Am very tempted."[9]

Arendt, a philosopher with a gift for acute observation, was not the only person who was puzzled by Eichmann in the flesh. Regardless of where they came from, almost all the trial observers received the same impression: Eichmann-in-Jerusalem was a wretched creature, with none of the scintillating, satanic charisma they had expected. The SS *Obersturmbannführer* who had spread fear and terror and death for millions exhausted the observers' attention with his endless sentences, and his talk of acting on orders and taking oaths of allegiance. Shouldn't the fact that he was so astoundingly good at doing so have aroused suspicions, even in 1961? Voices of doubt were present, but they were very quiet and not at all popular. The crucial difference between these voices and the trial observers was that the doubters all had access to at least part of the Argentina Papers.

In 1960 Holocaust research was in its infancy, documentary evidence was scarce, and the desire to extract information from perpetrators who were brought to trial made people incautious. Hannah Arendt chose the method of understanding that she was familiar with: repeatedly reading Eichmann's words and conducting a detailed analysis of the person speaking and writing, on the assumption that someone speaks and writes only when they want to be understood. She read the transcripts of his hearing and the trial more thoroughly than almost anyone else. And for this very reason, she fell into his trap: Eichmann-in-Jerusalem was little more than a mask. She didn't recognize it, although she was acutely aware that she had not understood the phenomenon as well as she had hoped.

No other book on Adolf Eichmann—and probably on National Socialism as a whole—has occasioned more debate than *Eichmann in Jerusalem*. The book achieved the primary goal of philosophers since Socrates: controversy for the sake of understanding. However, since at least the end of the 1970s, reference to Hannah Arendt has served to distract us from the matter at hand. One cannot help but feel that the story of the trial has stopped being about Eichmann, and that we would rather talk about the debate and various theories of evil than try to discover more about the man himself than a thinker in 1961 could possibly have known. And yet a major development has given us access to other sources entirely—at least in theory.

Since 1979 large parts of the so-called Sassen interviews have become available, and we can now see what Hannah Arendt and all the other trial observers were not allowed to see: Eichmann *before* Jerusalem, chatting in his friend's front room, surrounded by former comrades—Nazis in Argentina, just like him. Historians' engagement with this wealth of information has, however, remained worryingly brief. They have displayed some reluctance and a notable lack of curiosity regarding this source, even after some of the original tapes surfaced in 1998. A thorough reading of the transcripts alone confirms that more happened in Argentina than just a journalist on the lookout for a story meeting up with a washed-up Nazi on the lookout for a bottle of whiskey, and reveling in their memories. If anyone was of a mind to actually argue against Hannah Arendt, rather than continue to lament the success of her book, they could have found plenty of ammunition here. Instead, we go on retelling Eichmann's stories from Israel, referring to the dates he gave, quoting from an insupportable pseudoedition of the transcripts from a tendentious publisher, and leaving unexamined material on Eichmann sitting in archives, wrongly labeled—material that could put even the legendarily reactionary stance of historians to the test. And so there is at least one thing we should learn from Hannah Arendt: when faced with the unknown, we should let ourselves be tempted.

My book is, first, an attempt to present all the available material, as well as the challenges that come with it. Even the story of how the Argentina Papers came to be distributed among several archives, like pieces of a monstrous jigsaw puzzle, gives us an unexpected insight into the "Eichmann phenomenon." And any controversy about this phenomenon is worthwhile. My book presents these sources in detail for the first time, and the route they have taken through history, in the hope that it will enable further research and prompt more questions.

Eichmann Before Jerusalem is also a dialogue with Hannah Arendt, and not simply because I first came to this topic many years ago through *Eichmann in Jerusalem*. Our understanding of history is so dependent on our own time and circumstances that we cannot ignore a perspective like Arendt's. She had the courage to form a clear judgment, even at the risk of knowing too little in spite of all her meticulous work. And one of the most significant insights to be gained from studying Adolf Eichmann is reflected in Arendt: even someone of average intelligence can induce a highly intelligent person to defeat herself with her own weapon: her desire to see her expectations fulfilled. We will be able to recognize this mechanism only if thinkers deal bravely enough with their expectations and judgments to see their own failure.

Having written this book, it remains for me to preface it with a warning, in the same words that Hannah Arendt wrote to a good friend before flying to Jerusalem for the Eichmann trial: "It could be interesting—apart from being horrible."[10]

"MY NAME BECAME A SYMBOL"

They knew me wherever I went.
                    —Adolf Eichmann to Willem Sassen, 1957

To this day, we don't know exactly when Eichmann decided to live in Argentina, but he once explained why he was drawn there: "I knew that in this 'promised land' of South America I had a few good friends, to whom I could say openly, freely and proudly that I am Adolf Eichmann, former SS *Obersturmbannführer*."[1]

Proud to be Adolf Eichmann? What an extraordinary remark! The fact that Eichmann saw this as a realistic possibility was as grotesque then as it seems now. His name had become a byword for the Nazis' extermination of the Jews, as he was all too aware. Nobody goes to great lengths to live under a false name, among strangers, without good reason. And when Adolf Eichmann was planning his escape, he had an excellent reason: he was simply too well known to remain undiscovered for long.

Too many people knew him and knew about his part in the disenfranchisement, expulsion, and mass murder of the Jews. If this fact is not as clear to us today as it was to Eichmann in the late 1940s, it is due to his extraordinary success in presenting himself in Jerusalem. After being kidnapped in 1960, he did his utmost to paint himself as an unimportant head of department, one among many, a "small cog in the machine" of the murderous Third Reich. He was ultimately an anonymous man who had been "made a scapegoat" through error, chance, and the cowardice of others, an unknown SS officer with no influence to speak of. But Eichmann knew very well that this image was a lie. By no means had his name been known only to a very limited circle of people; nor did it become common currency only during the trial. On the contrary, his reputation played a fundamental part in the enormity of the crime for which Eichmann remains notorious to this day.

As his name developed into a symbol of the Holocaust, Adolf Eichmann kept a close watch on it; indeed, both he and his superiors specifically encouraged the development. He wanted to be anything but the "man in the shadows" that he sometimes claimed to be. Only before the court in Israel did he try to give the impression that he had been a nameless, faceless, disposable minor official—but then, who wouldn't want to be invisible when threatened with the death penalty? Still, the idea that Eichmann had been a man in the shadows seemed plausible to many people. Some even saw his invisibility as the key to his murderous success.[2] Yet obvious clues tell us that by 1938 at the very latest, Eichmann was neither unknown nor interested in operating behind the scenes. As we follow these clues, a far more colorful picture of this shady character will emerge.

1

The Path into the Public Eye

He was popular and welcomed everywhere.
—Rudolf Höß on Eichmann

In 1932 in Linz, Austria, Adolf Eichmann joined the National Socialist German Workers' Party (NSDAP) and the SS. His family had moved from Germany to Austria when he was a child: his father knew that in Linz, he could make a nice, middle-class career for himself. His son's career took a very different path: not for him a place on the parish council or a position in his father's firm. In 1933 the National Socialist movement was outlawed in Austria, and Eichmann seized the opportunity to accompany a senior party functionary back to Germany, the center of this new political power. Whether by intent, good advice, or a sure instinct for gaining power, he found his way into the SS security service in 1934. The Sicherheitsdienst, or SD, was small but already notorious. The organization behind the acronym was already known to have played a significant part in the Night of the Long Knives. Eichmann's later attempt to explain his transfer to the SD as a "mix-up" is absurd: if that were so, he would have been the only person in Germany unaware of the aura around the SD's secretive employees and their charismatic leader Reinhard Heydrich.[1] People who joined the SD in mid-1934 were well compensated—not with a high salary but with a mixture of respect and dread from their fellow party members. They also gained an impressive office: the majestic palace at 102 Wilhelmstraße in Berlin, the capital and power center of the Reich. For a man of not yet thirty, who two years previously had been a moderately successful gasoline salesman in Upper Austria, this was a big step up in the world. Eichmann felt he had established himself, a fact reflected in his decision to marry and start a family (which, within the SS, was also a good career move). He married Vera Liebl, a woman from Mladé, in Bohemia, four years his junior. She and her two brothers, who worked for the Gestapo, would come to profit from her husband's social climbing.

The men of the SD held a special position from the beginning. They were the NSDAP's internal intelligence service, and therefore certain regulations didn't apply to them. They were not required to participate in military drills, and their SS uniforms mostly stayed in the closet. After April 1935, when off-duty contact with Jews was forbidden to normal party members, the SD's intelligence function allowed its members to interpret the rules a little more freely: they defined themselves as always being on duty. Incognito investigation was one of the tasks that Eichmann most relished, and he remembered it fondly decades later. He visited Jewish organizations, making contacts who thought him liberal-minded and eager to learn.[2] He found a Jewish Hebrew teacher (whom his superior officer then twice forbade him from actually engaging) and immersed himself in Jewish literature, as all his colleagues did, studying everything from six-hundred-page tomes to the daily newspapers. He fostered international relationships, and a Jewish man even invited him on a trip to Palestine. Later Eichmann would speak of a "course of study that took three years."[3] He didn't mention that his superiors occasionally had to reprimand him for disorganization and tardiness.[4] It would be easy to mistake his lifestyle for that of a scientifically inclined aesthete with somewhat crude political views except that, between coffeehouse chats, memos, lectures, and evening conferences with his colleagues, he was meticulously keeping denunciation files and writing anti-Semitic propaganda, making arrests, and carrying out joint interrogations with the Gestapo. The SD was both an ideological elite and an instrument of power, a combination that made it highly attractive for the self-declared "new and different" generation.

The first image we have of Eichmann as perceived by a wider (and in this case Jewish) public comes from mid-1937. He was a "smart and brisk" young man who became unfriendly when addressed by his name rather than by his title. "He loved to remain anonymous," wrote Ernst Marcus, looking back on 1936–37, "and he took the mention of his name next to his official title of 'Herr Kommissar' as an insult."[5] It seems Eichmann was unable to resist the cliché of faceless power in a long leather coat—an image formed as much by the SD as by the Gestapo, organizations that their victims found difficult to tell apart. But he did not cling to this anonymity for long. When he traveled to the Middle East with his colleague Herbert Hagen, the British Secret Intelligence Service observed them and prevented them from entering Palestine.

Photos of the trip were kept on file.[6] By the end of 1937, the name of this "SD Kommissar" was known in Berlin circles. Eichmann was said to be "inexplicably well informed" when it came to topics that Nazis usually preferred to ignore: Zionism, problems with money transfers during forced emigration, discussions among Jews, and a huge variety of interest groups, people, and associations.

It's difficult to pinpoint exactly when Eichmann began to turn from a silent, discreet observer into the blustering voice of the master race. In Berlin, at least, his reputation for anonymity was conclusively quashed in June 1937, when he almost broke up Rabbi Joachim Prinz's farewell party, creating such a scene that the two thousand guests were unable to ignore the SS man.[7] People knew exactly who was meant by "a repulsive, unpleasant fellow, you shake hands with him and you want to wash your hands afterward." Erring on the side of caution, Eichmann corrected this denunciation for his superiors: "I make sure I never shake hands with these Jews."[8] The time for discreetly acquiring information was evidently over.

This transformation was in line with the SD's new self-image: it wanted to stop working behind the scenes and stake its claim on implementing anti-Jewish policy. This was a prestigious issue, close to Hitler's heart, and following the establishment of the Nuremberg race laws, new opportunities opened up.[9] Eichmann played a substantial role in helping the SD take advantage of these the very next year. He and his organization were impatient for their new age, impatient to take a stand and to show their "enemy" which way the wind was blowing. As Eichmann's idiosyncratic phraseology would have it: "They are finally realizing a bomb is beginning to strike."[10] At the start of 1938, Eichmann was known to Berlin's Jewish community and seemed entirely unconcerned about his growing reputation with "the enemy."

The Creation of an Elite Unit

With the ascendency of the SD, Eichmann's reputation also grew within Nazi circles. At first, only the lower ranks knew him, from the lectures he gave on training days, but he quickly made a wider circle of contacts. For a start, he collaborated with other departments, such as the Foreign Office, the Gestapo, and the Reich Department of Commerce—though this didn't always go smoothly. Forcing the emigration of Jews involved working with numerous different authorities. Then there was Heydrich's advertising strategy, through which he deftly publicized his SD, and the SD's Jewish Department, II 112. In January 1937 alone, more than three hundred people visited Department II 112. They were not only officers from the War Academy and the Reich War Ministry but also the future foreign minister Joachim von Ribbentrop and the head of the Yugoslav secret police.[11] The department's calendar included lectures to the party's youth organizations and trips to Upper Silesia[12] and the Nuremberg Rally. Eichmann was there as a guest of Julius Streicher, publisher of the Nazi newspaper *Der Stürmer,* whose colleague had taken pains to make contact with Eichmann.[13] Even though the British had denied him entry to Palestine and the trip had been a failure, in 1937 this still made Eichmann a "recognized expert" on the "Jewish question."

At this early stage, he already possessed a talent for using even failed projects to build his reputation. Later, in Israel, Eichmann would still claim to know the country: after all, he had visited before. In the mid-1930s his "expert knowledge" made a considerable impression among National Socialists, and his pride was evident: "I was an apprentice in the years 1934/35/36. . . . But by the time I went to Palestine, I had already become a Bachelor. And when I came back, they made me a Master."[14] Not everyone who met Eichmann in his first years in Berlin, from 1934 to 1938, remembered his name or his face, but a great number of people knew what the SD's Jewish Department was and what it did. Its staff garnered attention merely for being members of the department. Given Eichmann's considerable talent for self-promotion, he must have made excellent use of this opportunity.

The Little Prime Minister

In mid-March 1938 Austria was "annexed," and Eichmann was transferred to Vienna as head of a special unit under Department II 112. This move put him firmly in the public gaze. From the outset, he made no secret of how he viewed his place in history. Before a subpoenaed gathering of all notable representatives of Judaism in Vienna, Eichmann flaunted his black SS uniform, his riding crop, and his knowledge of Judaism and Zionism. Adolf Böhm, who had just completed the second volume of *Die Zionistische Bewegung* (The History of the Zionist Movement), learned that Eichmann was one of his most avid readers, who knew whole pages of the first volume from memory. Böhm realized that the SS was going to use the knowledge he had painstaking gathered as its access point to the world of Jewish organizations, and as a weapon against the Jews. Eichmann then explained what he expected from the third volume: a lengthy chapter about himself. Adolf Eichmann as a pioneer of Zionism? The fact that Adolf Böhm couldn't bear this thought, and never wrote another word, tells us all we need to know, without even thinking about what happened next.[15]

Eichmann's self-image no longer seems that of a shy, retiring, and subordinate person. He claimed a place in world history for himself, on the basis of nothing but membership in a fledgling SS organization. It is difficult to overstate the self-confidence of the master race's "ideological elite." Here is the impression he made on one eyewitness: "And then Eichmann entered, like a young god; he was very good-looking at that time, tall, black, shining."[16] His behavior, too, was godlike: he was master of arresting and then releasing people, of banning institutions and then allowing them to resume. He initiated and censored a Jewish newspaper and eventually even got to decide who could access the Jewish community's bank accounts.[17] The lines of authority among the National Socialists in Vienna were by no means clearly defined—there was wrangling over jurisdiction from the start[18]—but Eichmann nonetheless proclaimed his power to the outside world. "I have them completely in hand here, they dare not take a step without first consulting me," he wrote to his superiors in Berlin. His pride is obvious: "I have brought the leaders, at least, up to speed, as you can imagine." He was similarly proud of what he had done with the *Zionistische Rundschau* (Zionist Review), which was soon to be launched: "To some extent, it will be 'my' newspaper."[19]

His fame spread rapidly. From the end of March, Eichmann's name can be found in letters and reports written by Jews both in Austria and abroad.[20] He declared to everyone "that he had been chosen to steer and lead Jewish affairs in Vienna."[21] He was the most senior National Socialist to have contact with the representatives of Jewish communities and organizations. "The Jews," Tom Segev writes, "looked upon him and Hitler as the two Adolfs who perpetrated the Holocaust."[22] Eichmann was the face of Hitler's anti-Jewish policy—and not only to the

Jews. The contacts that he made with international Jewish organizations strengthened this impression: they had to provide cooperation and, more important, money to increase the emigration numbers, and some forced émigrés took the name Eichmann with them into exile. His name appeared in David Ben-Gurion's diary only three months after the start of the war.[23]

When Eichmann officially took up leadership of the newly founded Central Office for Jewish Emigration in Vienna, he suddenly achieved fame in Nazi circles as well. Soon Heydrich invited him to Berlin to attend a meeting with Göring, allowing him to dazzle influential men like Goebbels, Frick, Funk, and Stuckart with his "experience ... of practical implementation"[24] and the impressive accuracy of his emigration figures. His performance gained him a reputation in these circles as a master of "unconventional organization," one of the era's key phrases. As an interagency institution, the Central Office caused quite a stir, and numerous ministers and Nazi bigwigs sent their representatives to Vienna to see this experiment for themselves.[25] It was a perfect fit for National Socialist ideology, smashing conventional bureaucracy and replacing it with something new, faster, and more effective: "This is how I became the famous Eichmann, all the way up to the RF [*Reichsführer*-SS Heinrich Himmler] and the other ministries."[26] The idea was so attractive that Göring wanted to adopt it across the Reich, and Eichmann justifiably hoped to have a hand in it. Not even Heydrich passed up the opportunity to visit Vienna. With his characteristically ambiguous combination of praise, irony, and an eye for a slogan, he called Eichmann his "little prime minister."[27]

Eichmann was fully aware that a reputation within the National Socialist system equated to direct power: "All this has now given me an enormous boost."[28] The thirty-two-year-old had made it into the Nazi elite: he was invited to the film industry ball in Vienna, took part in the parade on the invasion of Bohemia and Moravia, and received tokens of respect from Nazi leaders.[29] His position was so assured that he was granted permission to initiate experiments, such as the first forced-labor camps for Jews in Austria (Doppl and Sandhof), using his own staff.[30] His superiors were so pleased with their innovative man in Vienna that they even turned a blind eye to an abuse of power.[31]

At this point, he would recall in 1957, "I was poised to become *Reichskommissar* for the control of Jewish affairs." But envy of his career had "thwarted" this plan.[32] The fact that other people's input and ideas had also gone into the creation of the Viennese institution[33] didn't stop Eichmann from grandstanding, particularly since the people with the ideas were Jews. He would remember them only decades later, when he was called upon in court to answer for his part in the murders and expulsions. In Vienna and in the years afterward, he did an excellent job of painting himself as the man of the moment, and at the end of 1938, his "unique institution" was celebrated in the Sunday picture supplement of the *Völkische Beobachter*[34] and even in *Pester Loyd*.[35] His name may not have appeared there, but the articles were littered with phrases typical of Eichmann, who worked busily on public relations from the outset.

The Czar of the Jews

In early March 1939, the representatives of the Jewish community in Berlin were called to appear before Eichmann. What happened at this meeting can be surmised from the accounts of the surviving participants. Benno Cohn,[36] Paul Eppstein, Heinrich Stahl, Philipp Koczower, and (probably) Arthur Lilienthal met Eichmann, wearing civilian clothes, along with a high-ranking uniformed SS officer. Cohn reported that the meeting was unpleasant, to say the least: Eichmann attacked them energetically, shouting and screaming, and threatened to send them to a concentration camp. He then announced the opening of the Central Office for Jewish Emigration in Berlin for the following day. Cohn, who would give evidence at the trial in 1961, remembered the start of the conversation: "It began with a forceful attack by Eichmann on the representatives of the German Jews. He had a folder of press cuttings in front of him, foreign of course, in which Eichmann was portrayed as a bloodhound who wanted to kill the Jews. He read us excerpts from the *Pariser Tageblatt,* asked us if this was correct, and said the information had to come from our circles. 'Who spoke to Landau from the ITA? It must have been one of you!'" Finding his own name in the so-called "emigrant press" seems not to have pleased Eichmann. But at the start of 1939, what article about him in one of his "enemy's" exile newspapers had prompted such an aggressive reaction?

In Argentina, and even during his imprisonment in Israel, Eichmann would recount the story of the first time he read his name in a newspaper with some pride. It had been "a leading article, with the headline 'The Czar of the Jews.'"[37] Eichmann's memory of this experience tells us how excited he was, since the piece was not, in fact, about him; nor did the headline refer to him; and it wasn't a leading article but the last line of a side article on the front page of the *Pariser Tageszeitung* (the successor to the *Pariser Tageblatt*), a German-language exile paper published in France.[38] On February 15, 1939, the column entitled "From the Reich" read:

GESTAPO PUSHES FOR EMIGRATION

Berlin, February 14

The "Ita" reports that in the last week, 300 Jews in Breslau suddenly received the order from the Gestapo to charter a ship immediately, and emigrate to Shanghai within the week. When the Jewish community in Breslau explained that they did not have the money required to hire the ship, the Gestapo told them that "this was now a legal requirement." On the same day, the Gestapo confiscated the necessary funds from the three wealthiest Jews in Breslau. The forced emigration plan has temporarily foundered because the shipping company demanded a guarantee in foreign currency for the return journey, in case the transport was not admitted to Shanghai.

The Gestapo's pressure on the Jews released from concentration camps to emigrate quickly has not lessened. Thousands of recently released people are besieging foreign consulates and the offices of Jewish organizations, particularly in Berlin and Vienna, in the hope of being offered an opportunity to emigrate, no matter to where and under what circumstances. They are all threatened with repeated arrest and internment in a concentration camp if they do not succeed in leaving Germany within a set period—which is often extremely short.

It is reported that the Central Emigration Office for Jews being set up in Berlin will open in the coming week. It will be contained in the large building that once housed the Jewish "Brethren Society" and is to be headed by SS Officer Eichmann, known from Vienna by the nickname "Czar of the Jews."

Current research shows that the "Ita" (JTA, the Jewish Telegraphic Agency, founded by Jacob Landau and Meir Grossmann) had been well informed. From Eichmann's point of view—judging by his reaction in March 1939—it was rather too well informed. At this exact moment at the beginning of 1939, the Nazis were holding discussions with the Japanese and Chinese consulates to ascertain the likelihood of resistance in those countries to mass Jewish immigration. Eichmann had tasked an old acquaintance, Heinrich Schlie,[39] with making these inquiries (bypassing the Foreign Office in a most unbureaucratic way). Schlie, who headed the "Hanseatic Travel Agency," had been cultivating a close working relationship with the Jewish Office since July 1937, in the expectation of getting a considerable amount of business from it. These diplomatic consultations were a delicate matter: it was vital not to lose this newly discovered way of getting rid of Jews before it could be used, and to use it before competing offices got wind of it. The article's other details are also correct: Jews were released from concentration camps only if they could show they were able to emigrate, and they were immediately rearrested once the time limit had expired. This procedure was no secret in Nazi circles; on the contrary, it was an effective method of expulsion: intimidation, keeping people "on their toes," was a consciously chosen strategy. During the Nazi period, the only people propounding the view that forced emigration was a humanitarian campaign, with the full agreement of both sides, worked for the Ministry of Propaganda. The article's reference to Eichmann's fame in Vienna is also correct: he certainly hadn't kept a low profile there.

So what did Eichmann find so very troubling about this article? It couldn't have been the epithet *Czar of the Jews:* such nicknames were openly coveted in Nazi circles. The term *bloodhound,* cited by Eichmann at the meeting with the Jewish representatives, was one of the most widely used. Alois Brunner and Josef Weiszl, two of Eichmann's friends and colleagues from the end of 1938, were also known as "bloodhounds." In Hungary in 1944, Eichmann even introduced himself this way: "Do you know who I am? I am a bloodhound!"[40] The sobriquet was even attached to Heydrich, and it was a perfect fit for the SS's image, which was full of hunting metaphors. The Nazis let their imaginations run wild with these nicknames: in Vienna, Brunner also liked to call himself "Jud Süß."[41] Josef Weiszl, one of the Eichmann group's most brutal thugs, was in charge of the first Jewish camp, in Doppl, for the Vienna Central Office: he wrote his wife in amusement that he was now being called the "Jews' emperor of Doppl,"[42] while Camp Commandant

Amon Göth was the "Emperor of Krakow."[43] In this context, the "czar" nickname suited the tone of the period much better than the "little prime minister." In the 1950s, Eichmann would indulge in his own flight of fancy: he told Sassen on several occasions that he had been called the "Jews' pope," and he also said: "The men in my command had the kind of respect for me that prompted the Jews to effectively set me on a throne."[44] Anyone comparing himself to the king of the Jews has some real issues to work through. To be called the "Czar of the Jews" by the "enemy" was a welcome piece of flattery for Eichmann, not an offense worth getting upset about. Later, Eichmann would admit that he had used the article to preen in front of the Jewish representatives.[45]

However, the Reich Central Office in Berlin, whose opening Eichmann announced to the representatives that same day, was a different matter. On January 24, 1939, Göring had given Heydrich the task of setting up a Reich Central Office for Jewish Emigration, to be headed by Heydrich. In the quarterly report of the Head Office for Reich Security (RSHA) dated March 1939, February 27 was named as the official founding date, with work beginning there from the start of March. The article in the Pariser Tageszeitung appeared on February 15, giving the correct address: Eichmann's future workplace would be the large Jewish Brethren Society building at 116 Kurfürstenstraße. In other words, the small article was announcing Eichmann's appointment to a position originally envisaged for Heydrich—the head of the RSHA—at a time when, apart from those directly involved, hardly anyone knew Eichmann had been transferred to Berlin.

A personnel matter such as this was an exceptionally delicate thing for a Nazi careerist. Eichmann's superiors doubtless asked him why he had been so reckless as to boast to the enemy about a position he had not yet even been given. An episode like that would have been embarrassing enough to prompt Eichmann's aggression at the subpoenaed meeting, especially as another of his superiors was present. The pressure he was under made him overreact and focus on the first part of the article (the circumstances of the forced emigration) in his attack on the Jewish representatives, reading into it typical Nazi images like the "bloodhound" and the "Enemy of the Jews, with bloodshot eyes,"[46] which the reporter didn't even mention. It had touched a raw nerve: his reputation within his own camp.

This press affair casts further doubt on Eichmann's later assertion in

Israel that he had not wanted to leave Vienna and had had to be forced into accepting the transfer to Berlin. It also undermines the witnesses who said (based on what Eichmann had told them) that he had thought of Vienna as the most successful period of his life. His reluctance to return to Berlin cannot have been all that great, if pride and ambition overcame his sense of caution and made him boast about his transfer to people in Vienna. The original source of the information may well have been the Jewish Religious Community in Vienna and not the Jewish community in Berlin. True, Landau at the JTA had just returned from Berlin,[47] but the *Pariser Tageszeitung* also had a source based in Vienna, as later articles reveal. Eichmann must have leaked the information there himself: he then accused Heinrich Stahl and the other Jewish representatives in Berlin of having been on unauthorized visits to Vienna and having spoken to members of the Jewish Religious Community there.

A Man of Importance

Eichmann would never tire of talking about his memories, though as is often the case, he recalled only the flattering and the anti-Semitic parts. The "Czar of the Jews" had made it onto the front pages of the international press, achieving the sort of fame that many people still dream of today—even if the "Paris hacks" had "smeared" his "work" rather than celebrating it. And from then on, his file of press cuttings grew steadily: "In this time of peace before 1939, the number of articles about me in the foreign press was so great that Wurm at *Der Stürmer* (a former teacher) collected them up and gave them to me as a present."[48] We may doubt whether it was really Paul Wurm who compiled the collection, as Eichmann had brought their close working relationship to an end in 1937.[49] And Eichmann really had no need of such a source: many departments, including the Jewish Office, collected press articles. Inspecting the "Jewish world press" was one of its daily tasks. Quite likely, Eichmann didn't want people to suspect that he had created this collection himself, before apparently destroying it in the last months of the war. But you can hear the pride in his voice when he gushes: "Nobody else was such a household name in Jewish political life at home and abroad in Europe as little old me."[50] Among Eichmann's staff, the prominence of their superior, who was even mentioned in the Reich's hate sheet, was obviously no secret.[51]

According to Eichmann, the next newspaper article about him appeared in relation to the Prague Central Office,[52] as he would tell Sassen: "When I was detailed to the Protectorate, some other foreign rag wrote about me."[53] This time the "rag" was *Aufbau,* the monthly publication for the Jews of the German-Jewish Club in New York. The September 1939 issue carried a small announcement on page 8:

> Prague: The "Emigration Service" headed by *Sturmtruppführer* Eichmann has commenced the transfer of all Jews in the Protectorate to Prague. 200 Jews must leave the occupied region every day, by any means necessary.

At this point, Eichmann was an SS *Hauptsturmführer.* The article's reference to *Sturmtruppführer*—which was not a Nazi rank but a military position—was probably one of the mistakes commonly made in other countries in identifying the imaginatively named SS ranks; Eichmann was never deployed as a *Sturmtruppführer.* Otherwise, this article also comes from a reliable source. After Eichmann finished setting up the Reich Central Office in Berlin, and while still overseeing Vienna, he also became involved with the organization of the Prague Central Office. By this point, Bohemia and Moravia had been incorporated into the German Reich as a "protectorate," and Eichmann even moved his family to Prague. Adolf and Vera Eichmann, who was heavily pregnant with her second son at the end of 1939, moved into an apartment formerly owned by the Jewish Communist writer Egon Erwin Kisch. Some of her family moved to the same building. Being the wife of a careerist could have unforeseen consequences. There is incontrovertible evidence of Eichmann's activity in Prague from July 14, 1939, the day he appeared as Walter Stahlecker's "representative" at negotiations with the protectorate's government.[54] Stahlecker, an SS *Gruppenführer* and a personal friend of Eichmann's, introduced Eichmann not only as his representative but as the head of the institutions on which the Prague Central Office was to be modeled: the "Reich paradigm," based on the examples of Berlin and Vienna. He also invited those present to visit Vienna.[55] The representatives of the Jewish community in Prague were aware of who they were dealing with from the outset, and the "exchange" that they were ordered to undertake with their "colleagues" in Vienna would have left no room for doubt.[56] In August 1939, barely a month after the founding of the Prague Central Office for Jewish Emigration under Eichmann's official leadership, the Czechoslovakian intelligence service in London received a detailed and well-informed report on the situation of the Jewish population in the protectorate. It presented a powerful image of Eichmann.

> In July, *Oberstuf.* Eichmann took over the leadership of the Gestapo department for Jewish questions. He had previously been the official responsible for Jewish questions in Vienna and the Eastern March. Eichmann has been granted extraordinary powers, and is said to report directly to Himmler. After Prague, his next aim is to rid the entire Protectorate of Jews.
>
> Herr Eichmann immediately threw himself into the fulfillment of this task. Since, as he says himself, he cannot deal with every individual Jew, he has identified a total of 4 people as speakers for Jewry in the Protectorate: these are the people to whom he gives his orders and grants audiences. They are the head of the Jewish Religious Community in Prague, Dr. Emil Kafka, the Community's secretary, Dr. František Weidmann, and two representatives of the Palestine Office, Dr. Kahn and Secretary Edelstein. The first thing he did was to send Dr. Weidmann to Vienna for 24 hours, to visit the facilities . . . there. On his return, Herr Eichmann gave the order to establish immediately the emigration department for the Jewish Religious Community in Prague.[57]

The "Central Office" was "an office headed by the Gestapo: Herr Eichmann and his colleagues Günther, Bartl, Novak and Fuchs." Representatives of the individual Czech authorities also worked there, "because Eichmann has decreed that from now on no other office can hand out any sort of permit to the Jews. . . . The Jewish Religious Community in Prague . . . vouches to Herr Eichmann that 250 Jews per day will go to the Central Office to apply for permission to emigrate." This quota was a huge problem, and so, the article continued,

> the Jews are threatened with a real catastrophe, as Herr Eichmann is sure that every Jew will find some way to emigrate once he has been arrested two or three times. Herr Eichmann's aim is to create a feeling among the Jews that their chance of hap-

piness means being allowed to leave the country, even if they're almost naked. Support is therefore being given to people and "travel agencies" dealing with the export of Jews *en gros*. Herr Eichmann has allowed a number of suspicious persons who arrange expensive transport . . . for a living to move their offices to Prague. These are the notorious, sad, illegal transports to Palestine, South America etc. Detailed reports have appeared in the world press. . . .

As well as organizing emigrations, Herr Eichmann is taking all other steps necessary to rid the Protectorate of Jews. The required mood is being created among the Jews so that they become "inclined to emigrate." First and foremost, he has decreed that all Jews must move to Prague. . . . This means that their livelihoods are destroyed. Herr Eichmann works on the principle that what these people live on and where they will live is not his concern. If there are 10 or 15 Jews to a room in Prague, they will make more of an effort to move abroad. Herr Eichmann is using the same strategy here in the Protectorate that he used in the Eastern March. . . .

Any intervention or explanation is pointless. Whatever verbal order Herr Eichmann gives becomes statutory regulation. And the execution is under way.[58]

Whoever the author of this report was, he seems to have been personally acquainted with Eichmann. The extent of the description here shows just how important he thought this SS man was. In contrast to Eichmann-in-Jerusalem, this Eichmann had not the slightest difficulty in saying "I" when it came to giving orders and making decisions. He dispatched, decreed, allowed, took steps, issued orders, and gave audiences. The report leaves his demeanor in no doubt. The resettlement of all Czech Jews to Prague, also reported in the *Aufbau* article, was part of the same pattern that Eichmann had already followed so effectively in Vienna: all Jews had to relocate to the capital so that they could emigrate from there as quickly as possible. In Prague, he didn't even try to conceal the reason for this move: the more straitened their living conditions and the more threatening their situation, the greater the pressure on them to emigrate.

By late summer 1939, Eichmann's strenuous efforts to expel and disenfranchise the Jews had made him conspicuous to the Jewish communities of Austria, Bohemia, Moravia, and the so-called "Old Reich." His steady acquisition of power had not gone unnoticed in his own circles, either: here too he quickly became the man who had "started up the Central Emigration Offices in Vienna and Prague."[59] Eichmann also profited from Heydrich's career, which was unsurprising in a system built less on rank than on protection. He later gave a memorable description of this "anteroom authority": "I never had to wait long in Heydrich's anteroom either. Although it would have been very interesting, because one met all kinds of people there, and once somebody had been seen in Heydrich's anteroom . . . , it didn't matter what his rank was, you knew he was a man of importance."[60] A man like Adolf Eichmann.

Victory from the Jaws of Defeat

On the day the little article appeared in *Aufbau,* the invasion of Poland began, which not only altered the press's priorities but also resulted in a significant extension of Eichmann's field of activity. The much-cited *Lebensraum* to the east would contribute more than three million Polish Jews to the "Jewish question" and open up new possibilities for the Nazis' resettlement plans: now the Jews could not only be blackmailed, robbed, and hounded out—they could also be transported from the margins of society to the still more inhospitable margins of the newly enlarged Reich. Thanks to thorough research, we now know a great deal about the first deportation of Jews from Vienna to Ostrava in October 1939, under Eichmann's leadership. The plan for a "Jewish reservation" in the east attracted international attention. On October 23 and 24 the London *Daily Telegraph* and the *Pariser Tageszeitung* reported a planned "Jewish reservation" in Lublin "to which Jews are to be brought from all over Poland." The papers also followed "Hitler's plans for a Jewish state" in their next issues.[61] The first articles about the deportation of Jews from Vienna to Ostrava appeared on November 18, 1939, long after the campaign had become mired in teething problems and had been abandoned—but surprisingly early for information that would ordinarily be strictly classified.[62]

Eichmann was involved in spreading the news: he had ordered leading representatives of the Viennese and Prague Jewish communities to accompany the first transports into the marshlands, to Nisko on the river San. Benjamin Murmelstein, Julius Boshan, Berthold Storfer, Jakob Edelstein, and Richard Friedman were not to be deported (yet): they had to watch as the murderous project was carried out.[63] They therefore became witnesses to Eichmann's entry into Ostrava and Nisko, where he delivered at least one "welcome address." In addition to the postwar descriptions of this self-aggrandizing, arrogant performance, we have an article in the *Pariser Tageszeitung* from November 25, 1939, under the headline "Reservation Guarded by Death's Head SS," which ended with the paragraph:

> In Warsaw it is reported that the Gestapo agent Ehrmann [!] has arrived. He was previously the "Expert on Jewish Affairs" in Vienna and later in Prague. He was born in the German colony of Sarona in Palestine, speaks Yiddish and Hebrew, and is an intimate friend of Julius Streicher. In Prague, he threatened the Jews with a massacre if they did not emigrate quickly, though he also created the greatest difficulties for those applying for emigration permits.

Even the typist's mangling of the name cannot disguise the subject of this article.[64] There is only one man (as we will see in more detail over the following chapters) to whom this erroneous description could apply. The reference to a friendship with Streicher is incorrect, and Eichmann must have found it irritating. The rest of the article gives an impression of the press outcry caused by the Nisko campaign, naming Danish, Swiss, and Polish papers. The first deportation attempt attracted such a lot of media attention that it is difficult to see why additional eyewitnesses were invited along. It is unlikely that the National Socialists had simply underestimated the campaign's public profile, particularly as they believed that every little Jewish community leader possessed more international influence than even the important ones had in reality. Perhaps Eichmann and his superiors were initially trying to reassure the public by sending Jewish authorities to accompany the transports. The presence of prominent people, in their experience, gave the impression of respectability, and respectability was vital here. This was the first attempt to put thousands of the Reich's inhabitants onto trains whose destinations were unknown, in full view of the public. The National Socialists were particularly concerned about public opinion in this test case and compiled detailed notes on every public reaction to what was going on.[65] Conversely, it is entirely possible that the witnesses to this doomed experiment were principally there to increase the pressure to emigrate, which had begun to falter.

Now the alternative to emigration was no longer life in Vienna under straitened circumstances, with violence and harassment; it was life in a swamp, with no contact with the outside world. As Eichmann explained to Jakob Edelstein on his return to Prague, "the daily contingent of emigrants gathering at the Prague Central Office for Jewish Emigration" had to grow, "otherwise the Prague Central Office for Jewish Emigration will be closed." At the same time, he allowed Edelstein to leave the protectorate for negotiations abroad.[66] If the Nazis' project had really been a complete failure (or as Eichmann phrased it, using one of his awful formulations, a "deadly disgrace"[67]), then once again Eichmann managed to make the best of it: he used the swamps of the San as the ultimate threat. Edelstein traveled to Trieste and took the opportunity to smuggle his report on Nisko abroad. The resultant article in the London *Times* ran to nearly three hundred lines. Appearing under the headline "The Nazi Plan: A Stony Road to Extermination," it made no bones about what had happened, giving a conservative estimate of ten thousand people dead in Poland and hundreds of thousands expelled. It reported that Jewish communities "are forced to cooperate in this gruesome work." The article gave full details of the deportation process, using the German terms "Judenreservat," "Lebensraum," and Polish "Reststaat."[68]

We don't know how the Nazis reacted to this article, but they doubtless read it. It did no harm to Eichmann's career, which continued to progress rapidly. Not even the rage of Governor General Hans Frank, who tried to stop the transport from entering his jurisdiction, could touch Eichmann. When word got out that Frank had issued an arrest warrant for Eichmann if he should ever set foot in the General Government of occupied Polish territories again, Eichmann took it as an extremely childish joke. "He gave the order," Eichmann would explain in Argentina, "to arrest a member of the RSHA, an adviser at the highest level. You see how high-handed he was. That was Frank's manner . . . he was a megalomaniac, starting to behave like a dictator—imagine, arresting me just like that." And Eichmann's reasoning for this flagrant presumption? "He obviously saw me as competition."[69] Eichmann is the one exploding with megalomania here, claiming that Hans Frank,

Hitler's lawyer and the governor general of the occupied eastern territories, stood no chance in a power struggle against Adolf Eichmann. Neither Frank, nor the people who laughed at Frank's faux pas, could have taken Eichmann for a little man with a bureaucratic soul, acting under orders, with no influence of his own.

The Perfect Hebraist

Three days after the article appeared in the *Times,* Eichmann was put in charge of Special Department R, in Office IV (otherwise known as the Gestapo) of the Head Office for Reich Security (RSHA). On January 30, 1940, this department was amalgamated with the Reich Central Office for Jewish Emigration and became Department IV D 4 in the Office for Occupied Territories (Office IV D). The change broadened Eichmann's remit considerably: in addition to forced Jewish emigration, he was now responsible for coordinating plans to relocate Jews to the east. There was no doubt about Eichmann's talent for organizing large-scale population displacements, as his subsequent promotion shows. From April 1940, he and one of his colleagues also took over the Central Resettlement Office in Posen, responsible for implementing Himmler's plan to "evacuate foreigners from the Warthegau." Poles and Jews were forcibly relocated, to the advantage of ethnic German settlers from Volhynia and Bessarabia. Interestingly, by this time Eichmann's fame must already have spread to Poland. Frieda Mazia, who lived in Sosnowiec at this time, would testify at the trial in 1961:

> By about the start of 1940, we knew that if a senior German functionary or an officer arrived, it was best to stay hidden, and not show your face on the street. . . . People were saying you should have no contact with them, because there was one among them who was born in a German colony in Palestine, and spoke Yiddish and Hebrew, and was familiar with all the Jewish customs.[70]

Frau Mazia was not simply projecting what she discovered after the war onto her experience at the time: her memory is corroborated both by the *Pariser Tageszeitung* article quoted above and by one of the most potent articles ever written about Eichmann. On December 6, 1940,

Aufbau in New York ran a small piece on its front page, this time entirely focused on Eichmann:

THE PERFECT HEBRAIST

The Gestapo's new informer and hangman in Romania is Kommissar Eichmann, who arrived in Bucharest this week. Eichmann comes from Palestine, and was born in the Templar settlement of Sarona, near Tel Aviv. He is fluent in Hebrew and is familiar with the history of Zionism, as well as all the personalities, influences and tendencies of the Zionist movement's various groups.

Almost nothing in this article is accurate, and Eichmann may have found it flattering for that very reason, since the source of the fairy tales was none other than himself. Eichmann came from Solingen, in the Rhineland, but he had heard of the exotic-sounding Templar settlement (though it wasn't even in *Meyer's Lexicon*). It was probably Leopold von Mildenstein (one of his first commanding officers and an expert on the Middle East) or his acquaintance Otto von Bolschwing who told him about Sarona. A mob of radically anti-Semitic Germans who had settled near Tel Aviv in 1871, the people of Sarona were still clinging to their aim of being the last bastion of Christianity in the Holy Land.[71] Alternatively, Eichmann may have stumbled across the name while searching through Jewish newspapers.[72] He is known to have used Sarona very early on, both to impress people in his own camp and to intimidate the Jewish representatives and their milieu. In 1940 Heinrich Grüber, the pastor in Berlin who advocated for Jews who no longer practiced their faith, asked Eichmann directly about the place where he was supposed to have been born. It's not entirely clear what Eichmann told him, but Grüber was certainly convinced of the legend afterward.[73]

Eichmann even told the Jews in Vienna about it. He chatted with feigned fluency about Vladimir Jabotinsky and Chaim Weizmann and their differences over Zionism, and he mentioned names that would be of little interest to anyone who wasn't Jewish.[74] According to Benjamin Murmelstein's statement, he also heard this story from Eichmann.[75] Dieter Wisliceny (Eichmann's colleague and friend, bound to him by a complicated, jealous love-hate relationship) gave several different versions, which can all be summarized as: Eichmann told the story and was tickled pink that people believed him. He was well aware of how useful this legend could be: it explained, for example, why he (supposedly) spoke Hebrew and knew so much about the Jews.[76]

The story is a common thread winding through the public's perception of Eichmann: in 1943 people were talking about it in Holland;[77] in 1944 Eichmann used it offensively in Hungary to underpin his authority. Wisliceny used it to make the Jewish community afraid of his commander, who knew everything, could read everything, and—a masterstroke of caricature—looked so Jewish himself that he could move undetected among the Jews at any time. This terrifying scenario made such a lasting impression that after the war, people were frightened Eichmann might secretly have gone to Palestine, posing as a Jew, and could be hiding there among the survivors.[78] Apparently Eichmann also told the Sarona fairy tale in passing to Richard Glücks, the concentration camp inspector from SS Leadership Main Office, who was considerably higher ranking than Eichmann. It helped his reputation in many respects.

A glance at the modest means with which Eichmann managed to present himself as a perfect Hebraist, even to his colleagues, teaches us something about his use of role-playing and image-making.[79] Eichmann spoke no Hebrew and only a little Yiddish. He had attempted to learn—probably inspired by his admiration for Mildenstein, who was at home in both languages—but had quickly reached his limits. He dated his first attempts back to his honeymoon, in March 1935.[80] In summer 1936 he submitted an application for a Jewish teacher, but Heydrich rejected it, recommending an "Aryan" language teacher who had also applied to his office, but nothing came of the offer.[81] Mildenstein left at around the same time, and over the following year the department's language problem became increasingly apparent, as no one else was able to read Hebrew. In spite of his "self-study," Eichmann failed to learn—and yet his second application for a teacher in June 1937 was also rejected.[82] Eichmann said he then bought a textbook: *Hebräisch für Jedermann* (Hebrew for Everyone) by Saul Kaléko.[83] Contrary to the title—and to Eichmann's version of the story—this book was not exactly straightforward, even for proficient autodidacts. It must, however, have made an impressive desk ornament in Eichmann's office.

In 1938 Eichmann paid for a few hours of instruction out of his own pocket, with Benjamin Murmelstein in Vienna. This didn't get him any further.[84] Witnesses in both Austria and Hungary were convinced that

Eichmann was just a skilled bluffer, using a few set phrases in both languages.[85] In Israel in 1960, he would show himself to be unable to read or understand any Hebrew. But the few nuggets he had gleaned, and the ability to hold a Hebrew book the right way round, proved to be enough for him to play the role of an "insider."

He achieved this success thanks to his gift for role-playing and his good memory, but also because German Jews were entirely unused to this sort of interest from National Socialists. The fact that Eichmann's knowledge was so remarked upon must mean that he was already a particularly interesting and well-known character in the Nazi regime—otherwise these legends could not have grown and spread.

Eichmann always kept a close eye on his public image and did his best to influence it. Even his last notes were prompted by other people's books and depictions of him. In 1961 his anti-Semitic paranoia would make him overestimate what he saw as the closed nature of academia and journalism, just as in 1939 he overestimated the impact of the foreign press in his own country and screamed at the Jewish representatives in Berlin. It was forbidden to bring these newspapers into Germany, and even owning one was dangerous. The unbroken chain of information between "international Jewry," the "international press," and "Jewish-infiltrated academia" existed only in the Nazis' nightmares.

However, the public image of Eichmann in the European and American press was no fantasy, dreamed up at a safe distance. The sources were informants from Nazi-occupied Europe, meaning that even inaccurate articles show us something of the effect this man created.

The Ideal Symbol

Adolf Eichmann was not the first person to realize how useful a public image can be. The use of ideals and symbolism was one of the secrets for the Nazi Party's success. Hitler's *Mein Kampf* also provides a warning never to underestimate the effect of a symbolic figure. Speaking in the 1950s in Argentina, Eichmann would say that wartime was when he had finally become famous: "They knew me wherever I went."[86] He even turned up in a book published by some of his comrades in Vienna,[87] though his name was spread largely through his visibility to his victims: "Through the press, the name Eichmann had emerged as a symbol. . . . In any case, the word Jew . . . was irreversibly linked with the word Eichmann."[88] And his various official departments with their nondescript and frequently changing names soon just became known as "Eichmann's office."[89] These concepts were so powerful that they can be found in witness statements from the Nuremberg trials, along with the term "Eichmann's special commando" for his representatives abroad.[90] This usage cannot be wholly explained by the fact that Eichmann, unlike many officials in the RSHA, remained in his post throughout the war. He would never have gained this reputation without the public performance that went with it, and without that reputation, "Eichmann's office" would not have had the position of power that it achieved over the years. A single person's influence extends only as far as his arm or his commands can reach. His image, however, can have an impact in places he never goes, provided he finds someone to carry it there—even if that someone is his enemy. "Much more power . . . was attributed to me than I actually had," Eichmann explained. And "this fear" of his presumed power meant that "everyone felt he was being watched."[91]

The Nazi Party's concept of power was very personalized, and the rapid success of this concept was repeated further down the organization. Eichmann and his colleagues quickly learned how useful a Führer-like figure can be, as a focal point for gathering power. This was one of his fundamental reasons for not hiding in the shadows or shying away from public displays. The Nazis needed a shop-front sign to which the Jewish question could be "irreversibly linked," and Eichmann was the name to fulfill that symbolic function. Eichmann would later try to make this choice look like pure chance—a view that surfaces occasionally in books and articles on his role. But what other name could even have been considered for the position?

Eichmann kept a close watch on his growing reputation, and it could not have escaped him that his exploits were becoming increasingly notorious. The international press reported on them, and the Nazis went over the press of "international Jewry" with a fine-tooth comb. Reviewing the press was a reconnaissance mission in a war that was partly being fought with "intellectual weapons." Eichmann's significance, both in his own estimation and for his colleagues, grew in direct proportion to the number of plans and campaigns to which he managed to link his name. By this time, many people were also familiar with Eichmann from his appearances at interministry meetings and planning conferences. With all due caution about viewing history through an individual biography, it is surprising how many of the participant lists for important meetings feature Eichmann's name. He was involved right from the start, leading experiments—like the Vienna Central Office, Doppl, Nisko, the Szczecin deportations, ghettoization, and even the first attempts at mass extermination—which can now be seen as prototypes for practices that later became standard. At the notorious Wannsee Conference, Heydrich officially enthroned Eichmann as the coordinator of all interministerial efforts toward the "final solution of the Jewish question." It was the logical next step for his career. A lunatic project like this required someone who had experience in unconventional solutions, someone who wouldn't get caught up in the usual bureaucratic formalities. Eichmann's leadership of the Vienna Central Office, and everything that came after, proved he could do just that. He had a talent for organization, and for making possible things that had never been done before. When others were at a loss, he was the man they called on. For example, a professor at Strasbourg University was adamant that he wanted the "skulls of Jewish-Bolshevist Commissars" to add to a collection of skeletons, despite the fact they were still alive. With Eichmann on board, this too could be organized.[92]

Eichmann enjoyed his reputation for being the man for tricky assignments. Even when he was neither the initiator nor the driving force of a project, he still managed to convince others he had originated it. The so-called Madagascar Plan is still linked to his name today, although the original idea was verifiably not his, and he never worked on its details.[93] But still he triumphed: in spite of all evidence to the contrary, even today no one can talk about this resettlement plan without mentioning his name. In later years, when circumstances had changed, Eichmann would make an immense effort to divert attention away from himself and play down his role. But that effort only provides further evidence of the position he had really held during the Nazis' glory years. No one would do that unless they had something to hide, and Eichmann did it surprisingly effectively.

It has therefore taken some time for historians to recognize the significance of the gigantic eviction and resettlement plans in which Eichmann played a substantial part. As head of Special Department IV R, he was responsible for "the central processing of Security Police matters during the implementation of the eviction in the East." The connections were clearer to Eichmann's contemporaries, as we can see from a report by the Ministry of the Interior, claiming that in September 1941 Eichmann advocated extending the definition of Jews to include half Jews. He was "strongly in favor of the new ruling, though with no real view on the form it should take." The biographical note on him read: "Eichmann set up the Central Offices in Vienna and Prague, and led the deportation of Jews from Szczecin etc. to the General Government."[94]

The expulsion of the Jews from Szczecin on the night of February 13, 1940, and the deportations from Posen and Schneidemühl that followed, were the overture to the planned reordering of occupied Eastern Europe in its entirety. These events caused worldwide press attention, which was closely monitored by the Reich and made a lot of people nervous.[95] But Eichmann used the attention, just as he had the failure of Nisko, to build up pressure in meetings with Jewish representatives in the months afterward, and to threaten them with a similar "resettlement" program if the emigration quotas were not met.[96] Eichmann's public persona made the press inflate his role in the resettlement. He liked to give the impression he was behind everything and everyone. Newspaper coverage of the affair created a threatening picture, which only those watching from a distance could afford to underestimate. At this point in time, reports of excessive violence, and even propagandist exaggeration in the international press, served to help Eichmann rather than hurt him. The more reports went around that "this Eichmann did that," and the more incidents were "attributed [to him] out of pure habit," the greater his reputation became.[97] Eichmann not only saw through this mechanism; he used it to further his own interests.

Public Relations

As coordinator for the resettlement in Eastern Europe, Eichmann's self-confidence was apparent to his victims and his fellow officers alike. In January 1941 Himmler ordered an exhibition to be prepared for March of that year, celebrating the *Heimholung* campaign. "The Great Homecoming" would be partly a promotional event, and partly Himmler blowing his own trumpet. It was designed to present the success of the resettlement policies, and Eichmann was desperate to be in on it. He fought doggedly and successfully for "the evacuation to be given a special hall in the resettlement exhibition," fulfilling his desire to present his "achievements" to the German public. The Main Welfare Office for Ethnic Germans objected, preferring to leave this section out for fear of a negative public reaction.[98] Pictures of happy new settlers were one thing; numbers and images of people who had been expelled were another. But Eichmann's pressure was for nothing. The exhibition was postponed until June 1941, and having viewed it, Himmler canceled it at the last minute, putting off the experts who had provided the content until March 1942. The exhibition never took place, in part because the "success" that was hoped for was never achieved. The plan shows, however, that a life in the shadows was never a Nazi ideal, and that the country's leaders even had to curtail their subordinates' compulsion to show off when they thought it wiser to draw a veil over particular events.

At the start of 1941, "Eichmann's office" expanded again, and for the next three years it would be known as Department IV B 4, a designation whose fame would last well beyond the war years. The extent to which Eichmann's reputation must have grown over the subsequent months can be judged from an article that appeared in the London exile newspaper *Die Zeitung* on October 24, 1941, in reference to an article in a Swedish paper:

MASS MURDER OF BERLIN JEWS

The Stockholm paper *Social Democraten* reports the following details regarding the transport of over 5,000 Berlin Jews to the east:

The campaign began on the night of October 17. People were pulled from their beds by the SS and ordered to get dressed and pack a suitcase. Then they were immediately taken away, their apartments sealed, and everything in them confiscated. Those who had been arrested were taken to railroad freight depots and ruined synagogues and transported east on October 19. They were all old men between 50 and 80, women and children. They will be "used for useful work" in the east, which means drying out the Rokitno Marshes. The work will be done during the Russian winter, by old men, women, and children, in the clothes in which they were arrested. There can now be no doubt that this campaign is premeditated mass murder. The campaign leader is SS *Gruppenführer* Eichmann.[99]

A *Gruppenführer* in the SS was equivalent to a lieutenant general in the Wehrmacht, a rank to which Eichmann never even came close. At this point, he was an SS *Sturmbannführer*. In court, Eichmann would try to claim that he had been just a petty official in the RSHA, but twenty years earlier this was clearly not how he was seen, and it seemed logical that he should hold a higher rank.[100] Documents from the time show that Eichmann played a significant part in the deportation of the Berlin Jews: in summer 1941 Goebbels requested "the transfer of all 62,000 Jews still living in Berlin to Poland within a maximum of eight weeks," following the end of the war, which he expected shortly.[101] In a meeting at the Ministry of Propaganda on March 20, 1941, Eichmann announced that it would be possible to deport 15,000 Jews from Berlin, if they were joined up with the 60,000 Jews that Hitler had approved for deportation from Vienna. According to the minutes, "the result of the statement was that Party comrade Eichmann was asked to work up a suggestion for the evacuation of the Jews for *Gauleiter* Dr. Goebbels."[102] Originally, the evacuation was envisaged as a long-term plan, because it was still thought "that current manufacturing requires every Jew capable of working," but Eichmann was involved in the deliberations from the beginning. The Russian campaign put things in a different light, and the violent atmosphere of a "war of extermination" made options that few would have dared even to consider previously seem like acceptable "solutions." Goebbels recognized the opportunity right away, and as early as August 18, 1941, he began to discuss the issue of the Berlin Jews again, both with Hitler and in the weeks-long anti-Semitic press campaign that followed. The first wave of deportations from the Reich territories began on October 15, 1941, and the first transport from Berlin took 1,013 Jews to Lodz on October 18.

News spread immediately, making the front page of *Aufbau* once again. The article made such a deep impression on Max Horkheimer that he cut it out, showed it to his friend Theodor W. Adorno, and filed it away.[103] And the events found such widespread attention from the press over the next few days that on October 28 Goebbels noted in his diary: "The modestly-sized preliminary evacuations of Jews from Berlin are still a major theme in enemy propaganda."[104] The Stockholm paper *Social Democraten* was well informed, even if the figure of five thousand deportees was not the number from the Berlin transports, but the approximate total of all those deported between October 18 and the date of the article, including Jews from Vienna, Frankfurt, Prague, and Cologne.[105] These events were so unprecedented that the person charged with organizing them was assumed to be high-ranking, and Eichmann's public demeanor did nothing to contradict that assumption. When he later protested that he had only been in charge of "purely technical transport matters," he was clearly just trying to protect himself. Technical matters would have been far too small a role for the Eichmann of 1941.

The Devil Himself

In the winter of 1941–42, the meaning of the term *Final Solution* moved inexorably toward "extermination." Eichmann claimed to have "coined" the term *Final Solution* himself[106] and even bragged about Göring's orders allowing him to "brush aside all objections and influences from other ministries and authorities," so the change of meaning was also associated with his name.[107] Eichmann traveled east early on, to see the methods of extermination for himself, and his presence was of course recorded. The picture he would later paint, of a pen pusher's secret, lonely business trips, bore little relation to the truth. In an incautious moment, he caricatured this idea himself. In Argentina he said he had always been afraid of losing his composure when faced with this horror, "because there would be some low-ranking little prick standing behind us, who would have interpreted it as a sign of weakness, and it would have spread like wildfire." Lowly subordinates could falter, but *Obersturmbannführer* Eichmann? "That couldn't happen!"[108] To be or not to be—a symbol.

And his own people were not the only ones watching him. Although the rest of the world's initial reaction to the mass murders was one of disbelief and was therefore muted, that didn't mean his activities weren't reflected in the newspapers. The international press was already reporting accurately on the plans for Theresienstadt by March 1942,[109] and on the mass murders from May onward. That spring the papers warned that the perpetrators' names were being collected.[110] The exile press documented the large number of death sentences visited on the Baum resistance group, a decision in which Eichmann has been proven to have had a hand.[111] The papers pilloried conditions in Warsaw,[112] and the terrible circumstances surrounding the deportations from France, including the *Kindertransporte* (transports of children), which we now know Eichmann ordered to "roll" to their deaths.[113] The first reports on Chelmno, and the gas vans that Eichmann saw there, appeared in November 1942.[114] The numbers that were quoted in relation to the Nazis' murder plans were so frightening (and in retrospect so accurate)[115] that the Joint Declaration by Members of the United Nations of December 17, 1942, threatened all the people responsible with retribution.

This development in anti-Jewish policy meant the press had lost its usefulness for Eichmann: as long as he was still negotiating with Jews on emigration quotas and financing, and thus required cooperation from international organizations, a threatening image was advantageous. Now that murder had become the aim, negotiation was no longer required, and the image that had once aided discussions was preventing the Nazis from concealing their lethal intentions. They no longer needed to threaten; they needed to reassure, soothe, distract, and appease. Otherwise mass deportations would be impossible to organize. People who have to be taken somewhere so they can be killed as discreetly as possible must have at least a little faith in the people transporting them or they won't get on a train. Without the grain of hope that, in the end, it might not be so bad, all motivation vanishes. Hannah Arendt called it "the logic of the lesser evil."

Eichmann continually managed to inveigle his Jewish negotiating partners into making concessions and cooperating, using nothing but their hope that by "negotiating" with him, they could prevent something worse from happening. How terrible their realization must have been that they were caught in a trap. On the transports, in the camps, and in direct sight of the apparatus of extermination, the Nazis' involuntary collaborators realized what they had been involved in. If they did not feel then, in this moment of realization, that they had fallen victim to a diabolical perpetrator, Satan in human form, then when? The terrible visions that emerged later of "Caligula" and "Grand Inquisitor Eichmann," the heartless monster, were rooted in these moments of unavoidable insight into the true aims of National Socialist anti-Jewish policies.[116] But the roots of these visions also lay in the victim's insight into the psychological mechanisms by which they had been manipulated, and which play just as significant a part in making people into victims as the actual threat of violence.

When a person is acting from a secure position of power, the question of whether he really is the thing you take him for is largely irrelevant: his reputation will determine your expectations and also your behavior. If you are made to view an SS man as the master over life and death, you have little room for doubt. Your expectation will turn him into the thing you are most afraid of, and everything you see will confirm the rumor and make the legend into reality. Encountering someone who can utilize this dynamic, consciously reflecting your expectations back to you, will render your human powers of judgment useless. For his part, playing out this cycle of dependency, fear, and expectation with his victims can take a man from head of department to Czar of the Jews. Eichmann and those like him were well aware that this form of manipulation could give them "an enormous boost."

"Eichmann" became the embodiment of this mechanism: it was the name the Jewish community representatives knew, and people trusted them. So the name walked abroad among the Nazis' victims, though the man himself was nowhere to be seen and was not immediately responsible for their suffering. This explains the memories of many Holocaust survivors of encounters with *Obersturmbannführer* Adolf Eichmann, when in all likelihood they never met him. It seems to be part of our instinct for self-preservation that we cannot and will not imagine the person largely responsible for our fate as a lame, puny figure.

People who have experienced suffering, humiliation, and loss do not want to have been the victims of someone mediocre: that a mere nobody has power over us is even more unbearable than the idea that someone has power over us. This mechanism blocks our view of the perpetrator. It gives more power to the dynamic of symbol creation and strengthens the sphere of power by limiting our capacity for making clear judgments. In the end, a desperate desire at least to have sight of their tormentor leads people to create false memories. Eichmann was "seen" in meetings, institutions, and concentration camps where he is proven never to have been, or to have been only at a different time. But the value of these memories lies in the element of projection involved: the victims were able to see Eichmann in every jackbooted Nazi or arrogant inspector who screamed at them only because "Eichmann" had become much more than just a person. The name was the symbol and the guarantor of the power that was crushing people, and it no longer mattered who actually embodied and exploited it. The threat inherent in that name went far beyond what a faceless, nameless bureaucracy could ever have achieved.

Good Press, Bad Press

Eichmann's part in what came to be known as the Fiala press affair proves how concerned the Germans now were about unwanted publicity, and how very aware Eichmann was of international opinion. The Nazis might have kept telling themselves that the extermination of the Jews was the only means for their own survival, but they lacked sufficient faith in this view to share it with the rest of the world. The Nazi police state was born of the fear that not even its own population would understand its campaign of murder. Himmler guessed early on that this "glorious chapter of our history" could never be written, and he prevented Odilo Globocnik from sinking a memorial plaque into the earth for the heroes of Operation Reinhard. This plan to get rid of the Polish Jews in the General Government had seen the start of large-scale murder in concentration camps, and Himmler already had enough on his plate with evidence that had been sunk into the earth. In summer 1942 he ordered his commanders to find a way to avoid digging any more mass graves and to clear up the old ones.[117] Any form of publicity would be harmful.

The threshold between the German population and the rest of the world was where the press posed the greatest threat, in the nations that were bound to Germany by occupation or affinity but that still had a semi-intact government. When terms like *mass murder* and *extermination* were bandied about, Eichmann's colleagues increasingly encountered unpleasant questions, even resistance. This gave rise to the idea of using press reports to counteract these concerns. According to Wisliceny, Eichmann recommended a Slovakian journalist named Fritz Fiala, who had taken over as editor-in-chief of the German-language newspaper *Der Grenzbote* when it had been expropriated from the German-Jewish owner. Fiala was also the Slovakian correspondent for several other newspapers in Europe.[118] As an investigative journalist, Fiala had offered to look into the "true conditions" in the camps and set the murky picture straight in the public eye.

In summer 1942, as Himmler's concern was growing about world opinion in the international press, Eichmann remembered Fiala's offer. On Himmler's orders (Eichmann later claimed), he arranged a tour of visits for Fiala in high summer. Wisliceny traveled with him to a Slovakian concentration camp, then on to Katowice the following morning, where a criminal commissar from the State Police Authority joined them. He accompanied them to Sosnowiec-Bedzin. There he led them through the ghetto to the forced-labor factories and, after lunch and a conversation with the Jewish elders, on to Auschwitz, where they arrived at two p.m. In Auschwitz they were personally received by Commandant Rudolf Höß. He showed Fiala the commandant's office and some select sections of the camp, then drove on with them to a laundry staffed by female forced laborers from Slovakia and France, whom Fiala was allowed to question and photograph. It seems Wisliceny managed to politely decline an invitation to dine with Höß, though afterward he wrote of scheduling issues. They left the camp at around four p.m., "or perhaps even earlier," according to Wisliceny's recollections.

Fiala wrote several reports including photos on the German camps and the Jews deported from Slovakia, in full knowledge that Eichmann and Himmler would censor these texts. Why the articles appeared only in November is difficult to establish.[119] Perhaps Himmler wanted to time the good press for his visit to Prague;[120] perhaps the Nazis were waiting to see how public opinion developed; or perhaps they lost faith in the plan—the articles did, after all, contain names of places that people usually avoided mentioning. The fact is that on November 7, 8, and 10, 1942, three long articles appeared in *Der Grenzbote,* illustrated with photos of laughing, white-clad girls, in clean surroundings, singing hymns of praise to conditions in the German camps.[121] Fiala mentioned names that could be verified in Slovakia, while the quotes attributed to the women reveal the whole cruel circus for what it was. One apparently not only laughed at the reporter when he told her about the "atrocity propaganda" that had appeared in other countries; she also told him that life in Auschwitz was considerably better than that in Palestine. The part Fiala (who was also an SD informant) played in this perfidious game remains unclear, and we still don't know whether he was really shown "only smiling faces in Auschwitz," or if he just painted them that way. Abbreviated versions of the articles appeared in other newspapers,[122] and they later served Eichmann as grounds for refusing all attempts by officials to view a concentration camp for themselves. He was fighting the ideological war with the weapons of the unfree press, where propaganda was countered with propaganda.

The attempts to influence public opinion by launching an alternative image of the camps were not without success, but live "demonstrations" still had more of an effect than Fiala's pseudoreportage. Given the tightly state-controlled press in the German sphere of influence, this could only have come as a surprise to a Nazi who was certain that the foreign press was controlled by that great enemy, the Jewish world conspiracy. From the racial theorists' point of view, the possibility that freedom of the press might actually function was unimaginable. Eichmann found other ways to sell Theresienstadt as a model ghetto, in spite of people's initial mistrust. The first media reports from March 1942 saw what was happening there as "the martyrdom of the Jews in the protectorate," the next step in a "diabolical scheme" that would end in extermination.[123] However, a visit to Theresienstadt arranged for the German Red Cross in June 1943 managed to sway public opinion. In a masterful piece of theater, Eichmann and his colleagues managed to present an entirely different, spruced-up camp to the visitors, where conditions were peaceful and no one was being deported. The visitors' criticisms about overcrowding and malnourishment took a backseat, and the fact that the visit had been allowed spoke strongly in the camp's favor.[124] Even if this performance wasn't enough to offset the growing accusations of extermination and mass murder in other camps, Theresienstadt inspired sufficient doubt that even critical journalists, who were aware of the camp's token status, allowed themselves to be seduced. As planned, they saw Theresienstadt in a more positive light than it deserved: as a "terminus" camp in relatively good condition, with standards acceptable for wartime. The detailed front-page story in the New York *Aufbau* of August 27, 1943, "Theresienstadt: A 'Model Ghetto,'" ended with this paragraph:

> When Theresienstadt was "created," the Nazis' power was already in decline. Some Nazi leaders were haunted by the fear of the unavoidable retribution that the future holds for them. They started searching for alibis. Eichmann, the Hebrew and Yiddish-speaking Gestapo Kommissar who terrorized the Jewish community in Prague, must have gotten nervous. The atmosphere in Theresienstadt is in sharp contrast to the pogrom mentality of

Goebbels and Rosenberg. When the day of retribution comes for the Nazi "protectors," they will use it in their defense: "in a time of extreme despotism, we were as humane as possible. Theresienstadt is our alibi."[125]

Instead of questioning the facts with which they were presented, people doubted the Germans' motives, thereby fundamentally underestimating the extent of their violence and lies. The idea that Eichmann and his colleagues could go to such lengths to make an entire town look presentable for just one day, only to return to gruesome normality the next, lay far beyond the outside world's powers of imagination. It was Hannah Arendt, incidentally, who argued against the interpretation of Theresienstadt as an alibi, in a reader's letter to *Aufbau* in September 1943 (the latest date at which she might have heard Eichmann's name for the first time). However, even Arendt did not guess at the true magnitude of the crime.[126] "The real reasons for Theresienstadt," she tried to explain, lay somewhere else entirely, because even this so-called model ghetto was part of the deportation policy.[127] It belonged to "a unified political line": Jews were tolerated, and even quite well treated, only where they could either be used to stir up anti-Semitism, or where they had to be spared because there were too many witnesses around. "In Czechoslovakia and Germany, the Nazis have just tried to reassure the population once again that they intend to segregate the Jews, not annihilate them. This is the purpose Theresienstadt serves, in the middle of the protectorate, an area that the civilian population can check up on. Massacres are only undertaken in areas that are either empty of people, like the Russian steppes, or where at least some of the indigenous population can be persuaded to participate, at least to some extent." Arendt saw this situation with astonishing clarity, even from exile. A plausible description of what was really going on in Hitler's domain required one thing above all: "an explanation of the relationship between the persecution of the Jews and the Nazi state apparatus." The idea of an "alibi" had no place there.

Hannah Arendt's voice remained an exception, however. The report from the International Committee of the Red Cross, following its next official visit to Theresienstadt in 1944, sounds so starry-eyed that it's hard not to admire Eichmann's PR work. The delegate from the German Red Cross claimed: "The settlement made a very good overall impression on everybody."[128] Theresienstadt's overseers learned from the grievances raised by the first delegation, such as overcrowding. These had been resolved in time for the second visit, by the most brutal means, so that this time nothing spoiled the camp's good impression. Eichmann and his colleagues created an illusion that rendered the horror almost invisible—and it is easier to deceive someone who doesn't expect hell than someone who fears the worst. In 1943 and at the start of 1944, public attention was drawn to other issues, largely due to the way the war was going, but the strategy of drawing attention from the extermination of the Jews through targeted deployment of the press was hugely successful. Eichmann's skill in this regard exceeded anything that Goebbels's clumsy propaganda could have achieved with its rabble-rousing articles. He was even able to inveigle the "enemy press" into spreading his lies for him.

"I Was Here, There and Everywhere"

But even the most skilled PR work could prevent the facade from slipping only for a little while. The Nazis were slowly starting to doubt the certainty of final victory; and only their faith in victory had stopped them worrying about covering their tracks. The hope that they would have time to tidy up later gradually vanished, and those involved started to fear for their postwar reputations and their personal futures in the event of a German defeat.[129]

While others were turning their thoughts to the postwar period, Eichmann's reputation was spreading across the whole of occupied Europe and the countries adjacent to it. This was thanks not only to the "advisers on Jewish affairs" from "Eichmann's office," but also to the boss himself, who traveled tirelessly among them. "I was here, there and everywhere, you never knew when I was going to show up," Eichmann would say later.[130] His official travel itinerary was impressive: conferences in Amsterdam; receptions in Bratislava; negotiations on diamond trading in The Hague; diplomatic receptions in Nice and trips to Monaco; interministry meetings in Paris and flying visits to Copenhagen, alongside visits to the ghettoes, Theresienstadt, the extermination camps, and offices in the east, all the way to Kiev and Königsberg.[131] "I was a traveler,"[132] Eichmann always emphasized. "I was able to creep into every territory of our corner of Europe."[133] "The famous name Eichmann"[134] opened doors everywhere. It was better than his red official passport—even if many of the countless people whose doorbells he and his colleagues rang came to wish later that they hadn't been in when he called.

But by this point, Eichmann's career was no longer progressing as smoothly as it once had. In 1943 two incidents in particular hampered it: the uprising in the Warsaw ghetto, which went completely against Eichmann's notion of Jewry, and the successful resistance to deportations from Denmark, the failure of which he took as a personal defeat.[135] The Nazis simply had no plan in place for opposition: for physical violence from Jews, who had not been thought of as willing to fight, and for sabotage by nations whose Jewish problem the Nazis were trying to solve. This turn of events posed a real threat to someone whose entire arsenal consisted of tricks, deceit, and pitting institutions against one another. Eichmann had to respond to a change in behavior from both sides: his fellow perpetrators and confidants, and their opponents. He had to maintain control on the one side and authority on the other. During this period, he fostered and spread another self-image, with help from his colleagues: this Eichmann was not only an influential man; he also had many influential friends.

Heydrich's sudden death in June 1942 lost Eichmann one of his most important backers, both in administrative and emotional terms. The assassination of his superior was something he also had to take as a personal threat. Fearing for his own safety, Eichmann surrounded himself with bulletproof glass, traveled with a mobile arsenal in the trunk of his car, and began ensuring that no one took his photograph.[136] His family's personal security detail was increased, and his children had a bodyguard on their way to school.[137] Retaining his former power proved more problematic. At first, Himmler tried to take over Heydrich's responsibilities, but Himmler was a busy man and famously fickle, which caused some difficulties. From an outsider's perspective, Eichmann became closer to Himmler, but in practice he was not always able to rely on Himmler's backing. Heinrich "Gestapo" Müller, the head of RSHA's Department IV, was not a careerist who forced himself into the public eye, which didn't make it any easier for Eichmann to orient himself.

Nonetheless Eichmann's close contact with Himmler became something that he and his colleagues could parade in front of their enemies, and competitors in their own camp. The "advisers on Jewish affairs" that

Eichmann sent into every occupied territory came from "Eichmann's office" and called themselves "Eichmann's special commando." And as Eichmann traveled among them and negotiated with offices all over the Reich, he invoked the *Reichsführer*-SS. Eichmann's real legitimation was actually much higher, since he was ultimately deployed "on the Führer's special mission"; but in a regime governed by relationships, only personal access to someone in power carried any real influence. The backing of the Reich Chancellery might have made an impression in negotiations with the Ministry of the Interior,[138] but the implication that you could report an incident to Himmler in person evidently had a greater impact. Seen from the outside, the threat Eichmann constantly repeated from 1943 onward—to fly off to see Himmler every time negotiations stalled—looks a little like a child's "I'll tell my mom on you." But the National Socialist leadership was a system dependent on personalities, and the potential of this threat should not be underestimated.

In more than one case, a single decision by Hitler or Himmler unexpectedly threw everything into confusion and ended careers that had previously appeared untouchable. In Argentina, Eichmann would claim to Sassen that in 1943 he once gave SS *Obergruppenführer* Karl Wolff, Himmler's chief of staff, a dressing-down on the telephone. This claim could just be the fantasy of a notorious show-off, but it shows how hierarchies were founded in National Socialism and how they functioned.[139] Anyone with real access to Himmler had the potential to completely destabilize other people's plans, and was therefore a powerful man. It's important to recognize exactly what Eichmann was claiming when he said he would fly off to see Himmler about something: in the middle of the war's final phase, with the Red Army already within earshot, and in spite of fuel and material shortages, Eichmann thought it plausible that he, an *Obersturmbannführer* (and even the lower-ranking Wisliceny), might have a plane at his disposal at all times and would be allowed in to see Himmler without an appointment.

If the people around Eichmann, including close colleagues, imagined he wielded this kind of power, then all his grandstanding must have paid off. Which is by no means to say that he actually had this power, or that his conduct was in keeping with his position, but this was clearly the impression he managed to give. Eichmann was aware of the connection: it was only his colleagues treating him "with such respect" that allowed him to appear more than he was.

Gustaf Gründgens, one of the greatest stage actors and most astute observers of that period in which SD officers, too, made a show of themselves, explained this mechanism to the actors in his company with potent simplicity: "The king is always played by others." The powerful king himself doesn't need to be an exceptional actor: well-played subjects can turn a shadow on the stage into a monarch through their behavior toward him. Power is a phenomenon created by group dynamics, never solely by the "powerful man." *It* calls *him* into being. Once you have seen through this phenomenon, you can use the helpless behavior of your victims to increase the effect. Eichmann's colleagues certainly had a talent for doing so, and he himself was very well cast for his role. He gave an impressive performance as a powerful man among the most powerful of men. Toward the end, Wisliceny (and also Eichmann, if we believe what Wisliceny said) even started claiming to be personally related to Himmler, in a final escalation of their attempts to find a foothold in this slippery network.[140] And people were willing to swallow it: such claims had an impact on their victims as well as their colleagues, and finally also on postwar historians.

The Grand Mufti's Friend

Eichmann also managed to claim a relationship of an altogether different sort, one that appealed to his pride as much as to his weakness for fantastical stories: his close personal friendship with the "Grand Mufti of Jerusalem."[141] The idea's public appeal can be gauged by how the story developed, even helping Eichmann to cover up his escape after the war. The way Eichmann rendered credible the lie of this friendship reveals the interplay between his boasting, his skillful handling of information, and the public's response.

During the 1930s Haj Mohammed Amin al-Husseini, the mufti of Jerusalem, opened doors to all kinds of negotiations in the Middle East. A former soldier, he was granted his religious position by the British in 1921. He was a sought-after contact for trading partners, from an economic as well as a political perspective, and so he had more than one connection with the German Reich. One of these connections was via Reichert from the German intelligence service in Jerusalem to the SD's Jewish office. Otto von Bolschwing, an undercover agent who was

friends with Leopold von Mildenstein, Eichmann's commanding officer
from his early years in the SS, also played a role here. There is speculation that Eichmann and Hagen were supposed to meet al-Husseini, or at
least people close to him, on their trip to the Middle East in 1937. This
speculation is partly founded on Eichmann's application for a clothing
allowance. He wanted new suits and a light coat, based on the fact that
"my trip [will involve] negotiations with Arab princes, among others."[142]

Shortly before the SD men arrived, al-Husseini made a hurried exit
from Palestine, having incited an Arab uprising against the British occupying forces. Later people reasoned that the meeting was prevented only
by this coincidence. Regardless of whether that was true, al-Husseini had
sent Hitler his congratulations when Hitler gained power in 1933, and
he had intensified the contact in 1937. After making his escape through
Ankara and Rome, the mufti found asylum in Berlin on November 6,
1941. He remained there until the end of the war, causing a few colorful
headlines and running up a vast expense account. Hitler granted him an
audience on November 28, 1941, and again on December 9.[143] The mufti
was also active elsewhere in the Nazi Reich: on December 18, 1942, he
gave a speech to open the Central Islamic Institute in Berlin; he founded
the Croatian "13th Waffen Mountain Division of the SS *Handschar*," a
multiethnic SS unit of Muslim and other soldiers; and he took a particular interest in the "Jewish question." Hitler's radical anti-Semitism
fell on friendly ears with the mufti. He broadcast his flaming diatribes
over the German radio, spreading his hatred from Cairo to Tehran and
Bombay: "Kill the Jews wherever you find them. This pleases God, history and the Faith."[144]

His presence in Germany brought with it exotic pictures for the press
and, for the book trade, a colorful biography of a man with a henna-
red beard and blue eyes.[145] Al-Husseini had his own liaison officer in
Department IV of the RSHA (Hans-Joachim Weise), who accompanied
him on his trips around Germany, Italy, and the occupied territories and
was responsible for his personal security. Werner Otto von Hentig in the
Foreign Office was also responsible for his well-being. Al-Husseini's staff
took part in at least one SD training conference in summer 1942,[146] and
in the first half of 1942, there was at least one long discussion between
al-Husseini and Friedrich Suhr, head of Subdepartment IV B 4b (Jewish
and Property Affairs, Foreign Affairs) under Eichmann.[147] Like Adolf
Hitler and Joseph Goebbels, Eichmann was deeply impressed by the for-

eign guest. Wisliceny (who once again was not there) would recall the enthusiastic account Eichmann gave of al-Husseini's visit to his office, dating it to the start of 1942. According to Wisliceny's statement, made in prison in 1946, Eichmann told him that the grand mufti had first been to see Himmler.

> A short time later the Grand Mufti visited the Head of the Jewish Department, . . . Adolf Eichmann, in his offices in Berlin at 116 Kurfürstenstraße. . . . I happened to see Eichmann in Berlin a few days later, and he told me about this visit in detail. Eichmann had given the Grand Mufti a detailed presentation on the "solution to the Jewish question in Europe" in his "Card Room," where he had collected statistics on the Jewish populations of the various European countries. The Grand Mufti was apparently very impressed. He told Eichmann he had already asked Himmler—who had agreed—to send one of Eichmann's people to Jerusalem as his personal adviser, when he, the Grand Mufti, returned there after the victory of the Axis powers. During this conversation, Eichmann asked me whether I might want to do this, but I declined an "oriental adventure" of this sort unequivocally. Eichmann was very much impressed by the Grand Mufti. He told me then, and repeated it later, that the Grand Mufti had also made a strong impression on Himmler, and had an influence in Jewish-Arab matters. Eichmann saw and spoke to the Grand Mufti often, as far as I know. At least, he mentioned this in conversation in Budapest, in summer 1944.[148]

The more Wisliceny tried to offload onto Eichmann in order to exonerate himself, the more colorful his stories about Eichmann and the grand mufti became. The two of them had been best friends, he said; Eichmann had told him that al-Husseini watched Jews being exterminated in Auschwitz "incognito" (which, given al-Husseini's appearance, is rather unlikely). Wisliceny's final statements have an obvious air of desperation. He told Moshe Pearlman, who was hunting for Eichmann on behalf of the Israeli intelligence service: "The Mufti was also reported to have told Himmler, at the height of Germany's military successes, that after the Nazi victory he hoped Himmler would lend him Eichmann, so that his methods for 'solving the Jewish question' could be implemented in Palestine."[149]

The source of all these stories was a man sitting in jail in Bratislava, who would have sold anyone down the river in order to escape the hangman's noose. They carry little weight. Wisliceny and Eichmann said similar things during the war to intimidate and pressure their Jewish negotiating partners. When Wisliceny needed to take a hard line with Jewish representatives or politicians from occupied countries, he would assure them that "the mufti is very closely connected to Eichmann, and works with him."[150] During a negotiation over the possibility of allowing Slovakian children to emigrate, Wisliceny explained that "the mufti was a merciless arch-enemy of the Jews. . . . He constantly aired these thoughts in his meetings with Eichmann, who was famously a Palestinian-born German. The mufti also helped initiate the Germans' systematic extermination of European Jewry, and he was a constant collaborator with and adviser to Eichmann and Himmler in the implementation of these plans." Confronted with this statement after the war, Wisliceny argued he had never said "that Eichmann was born in Palestine, or that the mufti was a 'constant collaborator' of Himmler's." In other words, he didn't take back the claim that the mufti had collaborated with Eichmann—a claim that would serve only to imply his international commitments in anti-Jewish policy.

Eichmann was by no means cautious about this story; in fact, he used press articles and office gossip to support it. Al-Husseini's escape to the German Reich, and his popular public appearances with Hitler, were closely observed by the *Wochenschau* and the other major newspapers. Numerous public offices also noted Amin al-Husseini's attempts to involve himself in the Jewish question. As soon as the grand mufti heard that an emigration of Jewish refugees to Palestine was even being considered, he wrote piles of protest letters and made personal appearances at the ministries responsible. These actions did not go unreported and became a topic of conversation within the government offices.[151] Eichmann reacted by claiming he had informed his friend personally.[152] Even his colleagues in other institutions thought this was possible, and they heeded the warning that he could do the same again. In Hungary in 1944, when negotiations stalled over yet more deportations, he claimed several times that he was meeting al-Husseini in Linz.[153] Al-Husseini really was in Linz at the end of 1944, and Eichmann did go there on occasion; but then, it was also where his family lived. It was, of course, possible to discover that such an illustrious guest was visiting without having a personal invitation from him. Official-sounding duties were also a good excuse for Eichmann to absent himself from Budapest for a few days, where by this point the Red Army could be heard in the distance. During this period at the latest, Eichmann must have begun to talk to his wife, and his father in Linz, about what they would do if the Axis powers were defeated and he had to go underground. A series of highly discreet visits to the grand mufti provided the perfect cover.

In Argentina, when Eichmann would mention al-Husseini, he did not talk of these visits—though he was hardly reticent about his contact with other powerful people, inflating the most fleeting of encounters into full-scale working relationships.[154] Within Sassen's group, however, he would stress that he had only ever met the mufti once, and it had not been during the visit to his department. Three of the grand mufti's officers had come instead, asking for explanations of everything the department did. Eichmann met al-Husseini once, at a reception, and otherwise always dealt with his entourage, whom he called "my Arab friends." Eichmann's notable reserve within the Sassen circle had a simple reason: the publisher Eberhard Fritsch, who was Sassen's friend, was in contact with al-Husseini himself. And al-Husseini was a reader of Fritsch's magazine *Der Weg—El Sendero,* which sometimes printed his explicitly anti-Semitic messages and, once, even a facsimile of his autograph.

Eichmann was as little able to gauge the true nature of this relationship as he was the real remuneration of the Middle Eastern businesses that men like Otto Skorzeny (a fellow exile and former SS officer) boasted about. So when speaking to members of the Sassen group, he had good reason to hedge his bets and hold back on stories of his colorful friendship. In Israel in 1960, Eichmann finally recognized the great danger posed by his own fabrications and tried to understate the contact even more:

> I believe the grand mufti came to Berlin in 1942 or 1943, with an entourage. Department IV held an evening reception in the RSHA's guesthouse on the Wannsee to mark his stay in Berlin, to which I was invited. Three gentlemen from the entourage—they were introduced as "Iraqi majors," and I have long forgotten the names, or rather did not retain them in the first place—came to the Head Office for Reich Security for information. One of the majors, so I was told (by Department IV, no doubt, since

where else would I have heard it from) was later to function as the "Heydrich of the Middle East." He was—so they said, at least— the grand mufti's nephew. The grand mufti himself neither visited Department IV B 4, nor did I ever speak to him, apart from a brief formal introduction by one of the Department IV hosts, on the occasion of the aforementioned evening in Wannsee.[155]

In his interrogation, Eichmann claimed he had been nowhere near the office when al-Husseini visited his department. He had, admittedly, encountered al-Husseini at the reception, but they had not spoken to each other there, the difference in rank between the state guest and the departmental head being too great.[156] We cannot rule out the possibility that this was the truth, and everything else the fabrications of a talented con man. But this doesn't change the fact that the relationship Eichmann claimed to have with al-Husseini was very convincing during the Nazi period. It's easy to imagine Eichmann, the head of the Jewish Office, being friends with al-Husseini, the Middle Eastern prince. They both wanted the same thing from an anti-Semitic war, though this wasn't why people believed the stories. Their effect was achieved purely through the skillful shaping of public opinion and through the self-confidence with which Eichmann cultivated his image. A subservient, eager officer, who made sure his back was covered every time he had to make a decision, would never have gotten away with this story. Eichmann was well served by clichés, both in his stories and his posturing.

The success of this story can be gauged from what happened immediately after the war. When he announced to his fellow inmates in the prisoner of war camp that he was going to escape to the Middle East, to seek refuge with the grand mufti, people believed him right away. A short time later rumors began to circulate of Eichmann's new career in the Middle East, and not even his arrest managed to quash them. His "personal friendship" with the grand mufti developed a life of its own, and when Eichmann's life was almost over, it proved stronger even than Eichmann himself. At the trial, the prosecution suddenly produced a pocket diary, apparently taken from the possession of Amin al-Husseini, in which the name Eichmann was clearly written under November 9, 1944. The liar was inextricably trapped in his own lie.[157] Nobody will believe anything a person says after he has declared the perfect evidence of his lie to be a forgery.

The Madman

During the final years of the Nazi regime, Eichmann was already start-ing to sense the dangerous repercussions of his image making. If he had been largely unknown at this time, he would not have needed to worry about his postwar reputation. But any hopes Eichmann might have had of being forgotten or overlooked were obviously unrealistic, for two reasons: first, his reputation was far from unfounded—he had not become a symbol of anti-Jewish policy by chance; and second, this reputation made him the perfect surface onto which other people could project their own guilt. Eichmann had always pushed himself forward, and now it was all too easy to hide behind him. This tendency showed itself even in 1944. His department had expanded again, in spite of all the staffing problems caused by fighting a war on several fronts. It was now called IV A 4 and included what had originally been the most pres-tigious area of responsibility: "sects and churches." By this time, Eich-mann was far from unknown in church circles. His cocky approach had even earned him a mention in a report to the representatives of both Christian denominations. Gerhard Lehfeldt, a lawyer and a Protestant, had made contact with Eichmann in 1942–43 and was convinced that the planned law on *Mischlinge* or "half Jews" was "a suggestion from *Ob.Sturmbannführer* Eichmann," as was the Nazis' reaction to the pro-tests in Rosenstraße. When Aryan women demonstrated outside the Berlin community center where their Jewish husbands were being detained, the regime eventually gave in and released the men rather than deporting them to Auschwitz. It was better to let a handful of Jews go free than risk the negative publicity of continuing dissent. The Lehfeldt Report was passed on to the head of the Fulda bishops' conference, Adolf Bertram, and was expressly disclosed to the pope.[158] Word got out that Eichmann was now officially responsible for churches, and his reputa-tion spread even further. From March 1944, there were for all intents and purposes two Eichmanns: Eichmann himself, who now visited Ber-lin only occasionally, and his fanatically loyal deputy Rolf Günther, who ran "Eichmann's office" entirely in accordance with his boss's wishes. "Eichmann" could therefore be in two places at once.[159]

But during this period, an enemy was emerging in his own house. Eichmann was away in Hungary, personally overseeing a deportation for the first time with terrifying efficiency and taking his dubious fame to another level at the head of "Eichmann's special commando." Meanwhile his colleagues and staff (including those who had been closest to him) were beginning to put out feelers in another direction. Dieter Wisliceny, Hermann Krumey, Kurt Becher, and even Heinrich Himmler were seeking contact with people they had avoided for ten years, people whom they had wanted to wipe off the face of the earth. Wisliceny and Krumey held long conversations with influential Jews, in which they portrayed Eichmann as an evil monster. They, meanwhile, had just been helplessly following orders and had really wanted to stop it all. Himmler attempted to negotiate with international representatives; and Ernst Kaltenbrunner sounded out the possibilities for a separate Austrian peace agreement or at least a special position for himself after the war. Wilhelm Höttl, the Austrian SS officer whose Nuremberg testimony first mentioned the figure of six million dead, was recruited as a spy for the other side. Above all, people were building brand-new cliques, equipping themselves for future lines of questioning, and spreading the name Eichmann for very different reasons.[160]

Eichmann's special place in the public eye proved useful to all these efforts. Since people already believed that the SS *Obersturmbannführer* had more power than other men of his rank, it was logical for his colleagues to emphasize his influence even more, while understating their own. It didn't always work: for someone like Kaltenbrunner to claim he had been constantly overruled by Eichmann sounded ridiculous. But this too is an indication of Eichmann's elevated position: even Kaltenbrunner saw the sliver of a chance that someone might believe him. And for many people who held posts less influential than the leader of the RSHA, the strategy actually worked. In 1944–45, Eichmann's image was determined by several factors. First was his own behavior, which appeared more and more self-confident as his independence increased, as his position in Budapest was strengthened, and as the war began to take a catastrophic course. Second was the behavior of his coworkers, who began to take a different tone in their dealings with Jewish victims, distancing themselves from their boss and stressing his power over them. Finally, the Jewish representatives were once more being sent abroad for negotiations, and they talked about Eichmann there, writing letters or reports about their contact with him.

Having first made a brief (and astonishingly dishonest) show of diplomacy,[161] Eichmann's actions in Hungary were driven by a combination of megalomania and desperation: "As my chief, *Gruppenführer* Mueller, expressed it, they were sending in the master himself, so I wanted to behave like a master."[162] And so "an SS [*Obersturmbannführer*] Eichmann came to Hungary."[163] The result was a terrible burst of activity, with no trace of restraint or caution. Again, Eichmann boasted about anything that seemed at all plausible to him: his genuinely close ties to the highest powers in Hungary; his somewhat indirect contact with the powers of the Third Reich; his access to everything from a "personal aircraft" to direct control of the gas chambers at Auschwitz. "I am a bloodhound!," "I'll set the mills of Auschwitz grinding!,"[164] "I'll give you the Jews you want," "Blood for goods," "I'll inform Himmler," "I'll do away with all the Jewish filth of Budapest."[165] He was not always calm and businesslike: he argued with foreign diplomats; he threatened to have "friends of the Jews," like the "Jewish dog [Raoul] Wallenberg," assassinated;[166] he claimed he was going to see the grand mufti (who then really did interfere in Nazi policies); he went to Auschwitz to deal with problems personally; he received visits from the Foreign Office and from Camp Commandant Höß; he seemed to be everywhere and nowhere at once. Eichmann talked so much and for so long that the people around him—ignorant of what was really going on—believed he might actually have been involved in the overthrow of the Hungarian Reich administrator Miklós Horthy.[167] They thought he was being held personally responsible for leaking pictures of the Majdanek extermination camp being liberated,[168] and that he would eventually have a public showdown with Himmler. His showing-off in front of his subordinates reached new heights—at least, if we believe Wisliceny's later testimony. Wisliceny claimed that in Hungary, Eichmann boasted that he and Otto Globocnik were behind the whole idea of exterminating the Jews.[169] Eichmann inflated his murderous lifetime achievement to crazy proportions and believed there was "certain to be a monument erected to me in Budapest."[170] He threatened his victims with the prospect that after the "final victory," Hitler would make him "World Commissar of the Jews."[171] If Eichmann's record of terror in Hungary were not so sobering, we might be tempted to mistake the show he put on there for theater of the absurd. But his performance was effective, ultimately garnering him a reputation for hunting Jews with the "obsession of a madman."[172] The official number of deportees—437,402 men, women, and children—makes even this phrase sound like an understatement.

While Eichmann was screaming at his Jewish negotiating partners Joel Brand and Rezsö Kasztner, his colleagues were taking a more measured approach to their conversations. Good cop, bad cop acts were nothing new; but this time Eichmann's colleagues were playing the good guys in earnest. Wisliceny didn't hesitate to lie about the extermination of Jews being "Eichmann's dream,"[173] and he bragged about his own influence to prove how much he had been helping the victims.[174] With Kasztner, he even started styling himself as the victim of Eichmann's threats, intimidation, and blackmail—someone worthy of Kasztner's pity. Wisliceny claimed he had always done what he could to combat his all-powerful superior, with no thought for himself.[175] Krumey tried to present himself as a reliable informant on the horror, who just wanted the truth to be known. Kurt Becher, Eichmann's rival for Himmler's favor, who was deployed on another special operation, used Eichmann as a threat when his own negotiations over Jewish assets stalled. "Every department," Eichmann explained later, was "trying to squeeze everything possible out of the Jews, to winkle it out by threatening them with the big bad Eichmann."[176] Kurt Becher used this tactic both to arrange one of the Holocaust's biggest thefts and to construct a successful alibi for Nuremberg.[177] The Hungarian perpetrators started using the same strategy and tried to befriend the Jewish representatives.[178] Their overestimation of the Jews' importance was shaped by the same crazed antiSemitism that had made them persecute the Jews in the first place. In any case, the hope that a single Jewish advocate would make people forget a decade of persecution was fulfilled in only a few, isolated cases. In the end, all Wisliceny's discussions with Kasztner were of no benefit: not even a good word from Kasztner was enough to save him. However, these conversations did lay the groundwork for a highly influential image of Eichmann. Kurt Becher had more luck: changing sides proved to be his salvation. Moreover, despite the millions of thefts chalked up to his account, he was able to obliterate all traces of his involvement in murder. In the final months of the war, many others followed his example, taking every chance they could to distance themselves from the Holocaust in public and, in the process, defining Eichmann's special role. This precaution was to prove extremely useful for their defense once the war was over.

Rezsö Kasztner and Joel Brand also spread the image of "the monster Adolf Eichmann"[179] beyond the Reich's borders. Before and after his arrest in Turkey, and while he was being held in Cairo, Brand reported on Eichmann and his role in the extermination of the Jews to Ira Hirschmann and the British intelligence service.[180] This indirectly precipitated reports of the notorious "blood for goods" offer in the world press.[181] Kasztner's wartime diary formed the basis of the Kasztner Report, which appeared immediately after the war. This, together with his other statements (all strongly influenced by Wisliceny and Becher) formed a substantial part of the material the British and American authorities used to prepare for the Nuremberg Trials.[182] Eichmann's earlier public image, which he had so proudly helped to construct, was developing into something over which he no longer had control. Ultimately, he was left with no choice but to use this reputation to further his murderous ends for as long as he could—and then to change his name.

Most Wanted No. 14 . . . 9 . . . 1

Eichmann was aware of the increasingly unpleasant effect his name had on people. When Himmler temporarily pulled him out of Budapest, he saw it as a reaction to his reputation—if he had stayed, there would have been "difficulties because of my name."[183] But to some extent, Eichmann viewed the hopelessness of his situation as a mark of distinction, as we can tell from the way he started flaunting a new rank: his position on the list of most-wanted war criminals. And Eichmann was not alone. Nazi perpetrators openly vied with one another over their positions on the list. Ever since the Allies first threatened to start collecting names, speculations had been circulating about who would be on the most-wanted list. People were named on illegal radio stations in the occupied territories and were warned against any further involvement in mass murder. Wilhelm Höttl described both Eichmann and Kaltenbrunner talking about their "war-criminal rank."[184] Even if Höttl is among the least trustworthy of all witnesses, in this case his version of events is corroborated by others. Eichmann didn't deny the showboating, and in Argentina he said: "I found the war criminals in a press review once, I was no. 9, and I had a bit of a laugh about it all."[185] In his interrogation in Israel, he claimed he was number 14. Horst Theodor Grell, the adviser on Jewish affairs in the Budapest embassy, was Eichmann's go-between; in the fall of 1944, he remembered Eichmann proudly telling him that the enemy considered him "war criminal number 1," because he had six million people on his conscience. Grell didn't take it seriously and thought Eichmann was exaggerating his own importance: as the saying goes, *"viel Feind, viel Ehr"* ("many enemies, much honor").[186] Although Grell's disbelief and surprise at the mass extermination is a brazen lie, the implication about Eichmann is clear: his pride in his "career" and his penchant for exaggeration remained undefeated, even in the face of the war's approaching conclusion. Grell's testimony even seems prophetic: by 1947 Eichmann really was being sought as the "No.1 Enemy of the Jews," by David Ben-Gurion and Simon Wiesenthal.[187]

As the war's end grew ever closer, Eichmann's colleagues increasingly avoided appearing in public with him. The "Czar of the Jews" was the last person they wanted to be seen having lunch with, even though the canteen in Eichmann's office building was one of the few to have remained untouched by the air raids. The man of the house at 116 Kurfürstenstraße was to be shunned wherever possible. The careerist of the glory years had become a nonperson, and Eichmann was not oblivious to the insult. As he complained in 1957, at first "people couldn't do enough [to] invite me to ministers' meetings, or to unofficial meetings, private dinners and suchlike," but afterward everyone pretended they hadn't known him.[188] Over the following years, Eichmann managed to spread the story that during these last months of 1945, he did nothing more than oversee the food supplies and the defensive measures for his department's building. The numerous people who knew better wisely refrained from correcting him, but during the last chapter of the Nazi regime, Eichmann was certainly not engaged in a rearguard action.

Historians are only just starting to reconstruct these final months of the war without relying on Eichmann's fairy tale, but the little we do know shows how hard the murderers of the Jews worked to keep their extermination factories operating right up to the end. On Heinrich Himmler's orders, Eichmann traveled through what was left of the Reich, collecting prominent Jews and taking them hostage. Himmler promised, in all seriousness, that they would function as a life insurance policy in negotiations with the Allies. The evidence also suggests Eichmann was involved in the very last extermination campaign: the gassing at Ravensbrück concentration camp. On January 26, 1945, Otto Moll's notorious special commando was sent to the camp with its gas vans, and gas chambers were also erected there.[189] Women who had been transferred from Ravensbrück to Theresienstadt at the start of February that year, and survived the war there, remembered being interrogated by Eichmann. He asked what they knew about these murders and threatened to punish them if they spoke of what they had seen to anyone in Theresienstadt.[190]

According to Charlotte Salzberger, who had been deported from Holland in January 1943, she, her sister, and three other women were interrogated by Eichmann, Günther, Ernst Moes, and Karl Rahm. They were questioned "in a very polite manner," in order "to find out what we knew about the extermination." All the women realized at once who was conducting the interrogation, and why: "We knew who Eichmann was, even in Holland. We knew he was a man who used a lot of Yiddish and Hebrew expressions—and there was also a rumor he spoke Hebrew and was born in Sarona. This was very clear from the way he spoke. He was interested in our history, our background, our life in Holland. He asked very specific questions about synagogues, Zionist matters, certificates, our membership of youth movements." The women recognized this as a diversion from the real issue. "He told us we now had the right to go to the Theresienstadt ghetto, but if we said anything there about our experiences in Ravensbrück, or about anything we knew, 'then you will'—this was the phrase he used—'be going up the chimney.'"

Nonetheless the fear quickly spread through Theresienstadt that gas chambers might be erected there, too, and everyone who lived to talk about it cited Eichmann as the driving force behind these plans.[191] Eichmann was in Theresienstadt at this point, preparing for the next visit of the International Committee of the Red Cross, and could not afford any talk of gassing. At the start of April, however, when he accompanied Hans G. P. Dunant through Theresienstadt, along with Foreign Office representatives and other Nazi functionaries, he made his position clear. At the closing reception in Prague, he introduced himself as "the direct agent of the *Reichsführer* SS for all Jewish questions." "In the course of the evening," Otto Lehner from the International Committee of the

Red Cross remembers, "Eichmann expounded his theories on the Jewish problem." In front of the gathering of international diplomats, he rambled on about plans for a Jewish reservation. And "as regards the overall problem of the Jews, Eichmann maintained that Himmler was in favor of humane methods. He himself was not completely in agreement with these methods, but as a good soldier he of course followed the commands of the *Reichsführer* with total obedience."[192] However, in his report Lehner noted hopefully that Eichmann had promised him that nothing would happen to the Jews in Theresienstadt.

On Eichmann's frequent visits to Schloss Ziethen, near Berlin, Heinrich Himmler's official residence, Rudolf Höß remembers him being similarly up-front about his plans. Eichmann was not even able to take pleasure in the prospect of a promotion to SS *Standartenführer* and chief of police.[193] This had less to do with Germany's looming defeat, as he often said later, than with the fact that he now trusted the people offering to promote him as little as he did his immediate colleagues. The extent of this mistrust became clear from his well-planned, dramatic exit. Eichmann gave various triumphal accounts of his own actions in this period. Partly because his office at 116 Kurfürstenstraße still had a roof and a well-stocked kitchen, it became a meeting place for senior Nazi functionaries. It also offered them a chance to create new identities: by this point counterfeiters were based there, churning out false papers on demand. Eichmann liked to pose in front of his superiors with his service revolver. He needed no papers: his gun was his new identity. Heinrich Müller responded just as Eichmann hoped: "If we had 50 Eichmanns, we would have won the war."[194] An Eichmann would follow his Führer anywhere, even into death. He expressed this idea to his colleagues as well, giving a final address that remains his most famous quote to this day: he would leap laughing into the pit, because millions of Jews would be lying there with him.

This ghoulish show-off told no one in Berlin of the preparations he was really making for life after the Führer. He had long since made sure that new papers, bearing a new identity, would be deposited for him in a safe place. He had also lied to Dieter Wisliceny and Wilhelm Höttl, saying that he had broken off contact with his family, and described a different escape plan to them. Both men promptly started spreading the lie.[195] His caution was well founded: his fellow officers had made their own plans for emerging into the new era as cleanly as possible, at

Eichmann's expense. Even Ernst Kaltenbrunner, a superior with whom Eichmann was on first-name terms, and who had brought Eichmann into the party back in Austria, did everything he could to rid himself of this undesirable company prior to his arrest. He sent Eichmann off to the nonexistent "Alpine Fortress" national redoubt, to defend Germany with his life from a little hut on a mountaintop. Eichmann's supervisor undoubtedly hoped he would give his life for the Fatherland by falling into a crevasse. In the end, even his long-standing colleagues begged him to leave, because their proximity to a "wanted war criminal" put them in too much danger.[196] And when people started removing pictures of Hitler from walls all over the Reich, burying copies of *Mein Kampf* in their gardens, and chiseling swastikas from the facades of all the buildings that were still standing, the symbol of the Nazis' greatest scandal was left with no option but to disappear as quickly as he could.

2

The Postwar Career of a Name

Adolf was always the black sheep of the family.

—Karl Adolf Eichmann,
U.S. Army Counter Intelligence Corps (CIC) statement[1]

When a person discards his name, he ultimately loses control over it. This might be one of the ground rules of modern marketing, but it came as a surprise to Eichmann, who was usually such a master of self-promotion. Eichmann had long since given up on the idea of the "final victory" that people were still promising and had considered his escape options in good time. Even so, he failed to foresee just how quickly everyone around him would manage to repurpose their "Heil Hitler" salute, pointing their outstretched arms right at him and using the "famous name Eichmann" to open some rather different doors.

By 1944 at the latest, Eichmann knew he was a wanted war criminal. Very few of these wanted lists have been investigated—but the name Eichmann appears on every list that has surfaced. In the Jewish Agency for Palestine's "wanted" card file of June 8, 1945, Eichmann is 6/94: the highest-ranking name in the file.[2] On June 27, 1945, the World Jewish Congress asked the American prosecutor in the first Nuremberg trial to find Adolf Eichmann and try him as one of the principal war criminals.[3] In August, Wisliceny gave detailed reports on Eichmann during his interrogation by the Americans.[4] The police authority in Vienna had also put Eichmann on their wanted list, which led to an arrest warrant being issued the following year.[5] In September 1945 Eichmann appeared on the "Black List of German Police, SS and Miscellaneous Party and Paramilitary Personalities" created by the British intelligence division MI4. On June 17, 1946, a three-page report on Eichmann was produced by the U.S. Army Counter Intelligence Corps (CIC), which relied largely on Höttl, Becher, and statements by Eichmann's family (which were clearly intended to cause confusion). This report corrected the Sarona legend. By 1960, Eichmann's CIA file contained well over one hundred reports and documents.[6] The organization that would later become the UN War Crimes Commission had been collecting the names of perpetrators since fall 1943, and of course Eichmann's name could also be found in the Central Registry of War Criminals and Security Suspects (CROWCASS) lists, which became famous as the *Nazi Hunter's Bible*.[7]

Nevertheless, after the German capitulation it was not the omnipresent Allied military units that caused him the greatest concern. The Americans arrested him, but all they had were names—and following a total defeat, names could easily be changed. At first Eichmann became the low-ranking Adolf Karl Barth (in the prisoner of war camps in Ulm and Weiden/Oberpfalz), but he swiftly turned into SS *Untersturmführer* Otto Eckmann, from Breslau. This sounded enough like his real name that if someone were to recognize him and call out to him, no one would notice. Otto Eckmann was also an officer and therefore exempt from the work details. His choice was well thought through: all the records in Breslau had been destroyed, and he had moved his date of birth "forward by 1 year ... it was easier to remember these numbers, my signature had become natural, so that even in a moment of absent-mindedness if I had to sign something, I would not fall victim to any kind of frasaco [fiasco]."[8] He kept this name and rank even when he was transferred to Oberdachstetten in Bavaria.[9]

Eichmann, who of course had experience in conducting interrogations, had no concerns about the interrogators seeing through his disguise. The prisoner of war camp was huge, and proving anyone's identity was nearly impossible. The men who might recognize his face, however, posed a much greater threat: the concentration camp survivors and the Jews Eichmann had encountered in his role as an "emigration expert." These people occasionally visited the prison camps, searching for their tormentors and the people who had murdered their families. "Jewish commissions came to the camps," Eichmann would later boast, "and we had to line up. They sized me up, yes, seeing if they could spot any mugs they recognized. ... We had to line up by company, and ... there was a commission of maybe 15 of these Hymies. ... They went carefully up and down the rows, staring each of us right in the kisser, yes, me too, right in the mug, all smiles. We weren't allowed to speak, or we'd have called them all kinds of names, and when they were done—two steps forward, and on to the next line."[10]

Eichmann did, however, say that it was quite easy to avoid these searches, as long as the prisoners stuck together and were not particularly eager for anyone to be found out. It was a difficult task to spot the smooth face of a uniformed SS officer among thousands of scruffy, unshaven men, especially when this group of inmates was united in defeat. But their unity rapidly began to crumble as more and more details of the Nazi war crimes became known, shocking and shaking the faith of even devoted National Socialists. There is a limit to the burden that can be borne by even the closest of comradeships. They tend to collapse when people start worrying about their individual futures—when they are confronted with interrogators from the U.S. Counter Intelligence Corps, for example, or placed on trial in Nuremberg. At that point, it became impossible to vanish into the crowd. Eichmann quickly realized he was under threat from people he counted as friends as well as from enemies. The National Socialists' fear of the gallows suddenly made them tell the authorities they would know Eichmann's face anywhere, keen as they were for people to forget exactly why this was.

After the regime change, someone who had spent many years proclaiming his special role would inevitably become the surface onto which others tried to project their own guilt. Eichmann was no innocent scapegoat, but testimonies made during war crimes trials ascribed power to him that he never possessed: of course Eichmann hadn't murdered six million Jews by himself. People knew exactly who Eichmann was, and for this very reason they started claiming they never knew him, had never met him, and had at best a rudimentary understanding of what he had done. They claimed the extermination of the Jews had been so top secret that no one even knew the names of the people involved. But when Eichmann's name was mentioned, they didn't say, "Who? Never heard of him!" Defendants and witnesses instead replied: "Him? Never met him!" They explained at length why they couldn't have known exactly who and what he was, let alone encountered him in person. And so this surprising fact—the sheer number of people who knew Eichmann's name, whether Nazis, regime opponents, or victims—vanished from sight.

"I Would Leap Laughing into the Pit . . ."

At the Nuremberg Trials, perpetrating the Holocaust was just one of many charges to be answered, and not even one of the more prominent ones. The authorities' underestimation of the crime is apparent from the preparations the American prosecutor made for this section. In the end, only one man was assigned to it, and he was so overstretched that he relied almost entirely on Kasztner's report.[11] Given the monstrous scale of this crime against humanity, the endless list of those responsible, and the incredible task of trying to comprehend how things worked within a Reich that was under attack from all sides—something today's researchers are still attempting to reconstruct—this can come as no surprise. The prosecution was also cautious about placing too much emphasis on Jewish affairs, for fear of being criticized by their own countries, and this too played its part in ensuring that the genocide did not become the International Military Tribunal's most important theme. Images were shown of the piles of corpses at Bergen-Belsen, Buchenwald, and Auschwitz, but the true magnitude of the horror emerged only at the end of 1945, in the testimonies of Rudolf Höß, Wilhelm Höttl, and Dieter Wisliceny. The first trial had been running for three months by this point (though it should be noted that all these statements had been available to the investigating authorities for months). If you run a computer search on the transcripts of the first Nuremberg trial for Eichmann's name, you quickly get the impression that very little was said about him.[12] This impression is strengthened by the fact that the name was incorrectly spelled (as Aichmann) in the edition of the Kasztner Report that was used as evidence. But if you look at how often the name occurs within the limited space granted to the topic, and count the sworn statements, only snippets of which were read out in court, things look rather different: when discussion turns to the extermination of the Jews, Eichmann is one of the most important names.[13]

In July 1945, Eichmann was still stuck in an American prisoner of war camp in Oberpfalz, living under the name Adolf Karl Barth. Meanwhile at Nuremberg, Rudolf Mildner, who until recently had been the commander of the Security Police and the SD in Vienna, was hiding behind the picture he had painted of the chain of command there: "*Gruppenführer* Müller discussed the implementation verbally with *Obersturm-*

bannführer Eichmann, the head of Department IV A 4 and a member of the Security Service (SD) from Office III, who had been seconded to Office IV for these purposes."[14] The strategy is plain: with no documents and no witnesses, an outsider has no way of discovering the truth—and unfortunately, no one asked exactly how Mildner knew about the chain of command. In the lead-up to the war crimes trials in Nuremberg, and in many of the Nazis' crime scenes, a multitude of reports and statements about Eichmann was produced. They stemmed from former opponents (Roswell McClelland, Switzerland, August 2, 1945), allies (Vajna Gabór, minister of the interior under Ferenc Szálasi in Hungary, August 28, 1945), and colleagues or friends. A month or so after the start of the first Nuremberg trial, the prosecution produced Wilhelm Höttl's notorious testimony, which spoke of the six million victims that Eichmann had mentioned to him (November 26, 1945). In mid-December there were readings from Kasztner's affidavit, and shortly afterward from Höttl's sworn statement, which unleashed a flood of press articles with headlines like "Murder of Six Million Jews." The numbers—four million dead in the concentration camps, and another two million killed by the *Einsatzkommandos* (special operations units)—were suddenly known all over the world, and their author was named in the same breath: Adolf Eichmann.

On December 19, 1945, the *Fuldaer Volkszeitung* told readers that "Höttl bases his information on the statement of one Adolf Eichmann, a senior SS officer who played a significant role in the extermination campaign." "Höttl believes Eichmann's information is correct as, in his position, he would have had the best overview of the numbers of murdered Jews. Eichmann directed the extermination camps via special commandos, and he also had a senior position in the Gestapo, giving him an insight into the number of Jews killed in other ways." From this moment on, there was no doubt in anyone's mind: Eichmann was the crucial witness when it came to victim numbers. In Argentina, this reputation would open the door to the Sassen circle for him. On December 20 the tribunal made an initial attempt to map out how the Gestapo was organized, including Eichmann's department, though this effort became hopelessly tangled up in the constantly changing department names. At the start of January 1946, the testimonies of Dieter Wisliceny and Otto Ohlendorf, the leader of Einsatzgruppe D, prompted more press articles featuring Eichmann's name. Eichmann's former friend and colleague painted a picture of a despotic superior officer who had victimized him, and quoted the now-famous words: "He said he would leap laughing into the pit, because the feeling that he had six million people on his conscience would be a source of extraordinary satisfaction for him."[15] Göring, the highest-ranking defendant in the trial, commented: "This Wisliceny is just a little swine, who looks like a big one because Eichmann isn't here"[16]—a sympathetic stance from a man who had known Eichmann personally since the conference following the November pogrom.

Cool-headed Escape Plans

Eichmann often said it was these witness statements that prompted his escape from the prisoner of war camp. People had even started to mention his name inside the prison camps, and the CIC interrogations in Ansbach were becoming increasingly unpleasant for the man who was now Prisoner Otto Eckmann. He knew it could only be a matter of time before someone unmasked him. Some of his fellow prisoners in the Oberdachstetten camp either knew or had guessed who Otto Eckmann really was. It had become a risk, and they must have been relieved when he told them about his escape plans. Even being caught in the vicinity of Adolf Eichmann could have endangered their futures. And as he would do again and again in the years that followed, Eichmann skillfully laid a false trail. He was planning, he told the other officers, to go "to the grand mufti."[17] Only a few weeks later this news got out, and it ensured, until his capture in Argentina, that people would suspect he had gone to the Middle East. In reality, he was calmly and cunningly making an entirely different plan, in collaboration with a low-ranking SS man, Kurt Bauer, whose sister Nelly had promised to help him. Most important, Eichmann found a contact in a place where not even his closest friends would have thought to look: northern Germany. While he was still interned in the camp, another SS man, Hans Freiesleben,[18] arranged a hiding place for him: with Hans's brother, Woldemar. He was the forester for a district near Celle, in Lower Saxony, and his discretion could be relied upon. Eichmann's fellow officers were the first to be questioned on his whereabouts, and they said that Eichmann—an intrepid, seasoned traveler—was trying to reach his Muslim friend in

the Middle East. Meanwhile their comrade had used less talkative helpers to organize his new life.

In January, Otto Eckmann donned a chamois hat and an old Wehrmacht coat altered in a "Bavarian" style. He and Bauer found a hiding
place on a farm, with the help of Bauer's widowed sister, Nelly Krawietz.
According to eyewitnesses, she was a very nice-looking young lady. She
accompanied him to Hamburg by train. Couples attracted less attention than men traveling alone, and their papers were seldom checked.
But before he went on to Celle, Eichmann had another destination: the
Rhineland.[19] Though there is no concrete evidence, he may even have
thought there might be better accommodation there, about which Nelly
was to know nothing. One thing we do know is that he was collecting
his new identity papers, "the documents I had arranged for Otto Heninger."[20] The identity of the counterfeiter is unknown, but we can guess
who was keeping them for him: his father's brother was still living in
the area where Eichmann was born, in the Bergisches Land, near Düsseldorf. Eichmann's father had such complete faith in his brother that,
over the years that followed, he kept him informed of his son's whereabouts, even writing to him about Eichmann's escape and his new life
in Argentina.[21] Adolf Eichmann had been to visit his uncle there before.
The address was an obvious depository for a new identity and probably
also one of the ways Eichmann kept in touch with his father.[22] In any
case, Eichmann had planned his escape well in advance, and he had had
ample time to commission convincingly forged papers and hide them in
the Rhineland. Given the chaos that followed the German capitulation,
when all the transport and postal networks collapsed, Eichmann must
have made his emergency preparations very early on.

Barely three months after Otto Eckmann's disappearance from the
camp in Bavaria, Otto Heninger[23] was officially registered as a resident
of the Lüneberg Heath. It was March 20, 1946—the day after Adolf
Eichmann's fortieth birthday. Heninger was a salesman from Breslau,
born on March 1, 1906, and he is resident number 1,757 in the records.
His entry contains the additional information: "married, evangelical,
refugee," previous place of residence Prien am Chiemsee. Woldemar
Freiesleben gave Heninger a helping hand. He had fled to the area himself in June 1945, with his wife and children, and he now lived in the
Kohlenbach forester's house, as the area forester in the service of the
Abbey forestry commission.[24] Like a number of other men registered

as living "at Freiesleben's" during this period, Heninger's refuge was a hut in the woods, affectionately named "the Island." He was employed collecting wood and felling trees for a company called Burmann & Co.

Eichmann remained cool-headed and calculating. Not even Wisliceny, who knew him better than most, would have imagined a hiding place like this. When he offered to hunt down his former colleague for the Allies, the list of possible hideouts Wisliceny put together betrayed an intimate knowledge of Eichmann's habits. "Anyone who knows Eichmann," said Wisliceny confidently, "knows he's too cowardly to be alone."[25] Clearly no one knew Eichmann well enough. The list contained no hint of the hiding place in northern Germany or even the Rhineland. Wisliceny believed his superior was capable of anything, but not of deceiving him. And Eichmann was correct in his estimation of the danger that the Nuremberg Trials represented for him.

The Nuremberg Ghost

. . . the sinister figure who had charge of the extermination program.
> —Robert H. Jackson, chief U.S. prosecutor at Nuremberg

Eichmann did not immediately become the subject of the Nuremberg Trials' press coverage. On January 10, 1946, a few days after Wisliceny's testimony, a circular was sent to all CIC offices containing the order to find and arrest Adolf Eichmann, the man jointly responsible for the murder of six million Jews. It came with a warning, describing him as a "desperate type who, if cornered, will try to shoot it out."[26] In February, Eichmann's name turned up in documents on the persecution of Jews in France. On March 4, 1946, Kaltenbrunner's defense counsel assumed that everyone would know who Eichmann was when he said, "Eichmann, as is well known, was the man who carried out the whole extermination operation against the Jews." On April 5, while Dömö Sztójay was busy testifying against Eichmann in Budapest, Rudolf Höß submitted his declaration under oath to the tribunal in Nuremberg. It contained a lecture on Eichmann's symbolic role in recent years, which had given him "an enormous boost," though this was still only partially correct in 1946, just as it had been in 1942. This development supported the old clique's line of defense, and they were quick to make use of it. Höttl lied for Kaltenbrunner, confirming under oath that Eichmann had had no "direct official contact" with his comrades in Austria.[27] Kaltenbrunner in turn claimed that Eichmann usually reported directly to Himmler, going over his head and bypassing Gestapo chief Müller. By this point, Müller had to all intents and purposes vanished, and Himmler was dead. Kaltenbrunner told a brazen lie about having seen Eichmann only twice in his life.[28] Wilhelm Bruno Waneck, Höttl's superior and a close acquaintance of Kaltenbrunner's, leaped to defend this version of events, saying that Kaltenbrunner had often been criticized for "paying too little attention to Department IV, and leaving everything to Müller." After Heydrich's death, Himmler had handed over "the solution to the Jewish question . . . entirely to Eichmann." "Even when Heydrich was alive, Eichmann assumed a dominant position, an absolutely exceptional post which continually grew and broadened in scope, and he acted completely independently in the whole Jewish sector [meaning within the RSHA]. After Heydrich's death, he was answerable to Himmler directly. Within the RSHA, this fact was generally known, to my knowledge" (April 15, 1946). Kaltenbrunner's defense counsel referred to Auschwitz as having been "under the spiritual leadership of the infamous Eichmann."[29]

Höß's first appearance before the court on April 15, 1946, finally cemented the image of the "men in the shadows" in everyone's minds— not least because of his ghostly appearance. Höß had been commandant of the concentration camp with the most horrific record of all. He stated that Eichmann had not only been involved in the building of the camp and the decision to use Zyklon B, but that he had also conveyed orders to Höß and was an even more fervent anti-Semite than Höß himself. On April 29, 1946, Julius Streicher mumbled that he had never heard of this Eichmann (whom he had invited to the party congress in 1937). On June 17, 1946, Helmut Knochen, who was responsible for the deportation of Jews from Paris, explained that direct orders came to him from Eichmann or Himmler. On June 28, Werner Best spoke about "Eichmann's office." Kaltenbrunner's defense counsel made a logical plea for acquittal on July 9, since "only to the knowledge of Bormann, Himmler and Eichmann was a mass crime plotted and carried out from 1941." It had been "Himmler's and Eichmann's anti-Jewish campaign." On July 13, 1946, Konrad Morgen explained why he had brought a lawsuit against Eichmann when he was an SS judge, thus strengthening the picture of Eichmann as having been a special case even in the SS. Three days later Robert H. Jackson, the chief U.S. prosecutor, called Eichmann "the sinister figure who had charge of the extermination program"—a formulation that Eichmann found particularly provoking when he read it afterward.[30] On July 18, 1946, Walter Huppenkothen, a Gestapo *Gruppenleiter* in the RSHA and a member of the July 20 special commission, said: "The Jewish Office (IV B 4, later IV A 4b) and its leader, SS *Obersturmbannführer* Eichmann, assumed a special position in Department IV. It was accommodated in a house in Kurfürstenstraße, in which Eichmann and most of the other members of his office also lived." Eichmann had "traveled frequently." Officially Müller had been his "immediate superior." Intending to publicly place some distance between himself and Eichmann, Huppenkothen added: "Eichmann and his colleagues never spoke about their assignments. But from conversations with my comrades, I know that Eichmann often met with Himmler."[31]

Karl Heinz Hoffmann, the former head of the Gestapo in Denmark, took this line and ran with it: "The treatment of the Jewish question was at that time in the hands of Eichmann, who had not come out of the State Police, but had been transferred from the SD to the State Police. He and his personnel were located in a building set aside for that purpose and had no contact with the other officials. . . . Theoretically he was attached to Department IV, but he conducted a very intense activity of his own and I also emphasized that this may be traced back largely to the fact that he did not come from the Police" (August 1, 1946).

Rudolf Merkel, the defense counsel in the case against the Gestapo, summed up: "In April 1942, Hitler ordered the 'final solution of the Jewish question,' that is, the physical extermination, the murder, of the Jews. . . . The tool which was used by Hitler and Himmler for the carrying out of that order was SS *Obersturmbannführer* Adolf Eichmann who with his department was attached to the organization of Amt IV of the RSHA; however, he actually had an entirely independent and autonomous position, which above all was wholly independent of the Gestapo." Merkel talked about "Eichmann's organization" and claimed there were only two people responsible for the persecution of the Jews: Eichmann and Christian Wirth, one of the architects of Operation Reinhard (August 23, 1946). In his defense of the SS, Horst Pelckmann explained that the Foreign Office also became a helpless victim of Eichmann's lies, "through his skillful juggling of truth and untruth" (August 26, 1946). Finally, even the SD's defense tried to cut all ties between Eichmann's office and the SD, claiming that the "Eichmann Department" was outside its jurisdiction. This trend even reached a point where a former Waffen-SS general and a former police general,[32] who were both SS *Obergruppenführers*, ended up arguing about who had been more afraid of the lowly SS *Obersturmbannführer* Eichmann. They were supporting each other's statements, which explained that they would dearly have liked to do something about the deportations and foot marches out of Hungary, but it had been completely impossible for them to act against Eichmann in his position of power. In 1945 Kasztner had termed this "Eichmannism."[33]

The prosecutors and judges could see exactly what was going on here. The American prosecutor Thomas J. Dodds set the record straight on August 29, 1946: "There was no 'Department Eichmann' as such. Eichmann was simply the head of the department of the Gestapo which was charged with matters pertaining to the Churches and to the Jews. It was this department of the Gestapo which had primary executive responsibility for the rounding-up of the Jews of Europe and the committing of them to concentration camps. The Eichmann Department, so-called, within the Gestapo, was no more independent of the Gestapo than any other department under Mueller." And his Russian colleague agreed: "Eichmann's plan to exterminate the Jews in Europe with the help of the death camps came from the Gestapo system" (August 30, 1946). But this portrayal of Eichmann still had an impact, and traces of it remained in the final judgment. Eichmann was mentioned by name three times. "A special section of the Gestapo office of the RSHA under *Standartenführer* Eichmann was set up with responsibility for Jewish matters, which employed its own agents to investigate the Jewish problem in occupied territory."[34] Eichmann's name was then linked to the term that was to become a synonym for the extermination of the Jews: "This 'final solution' meant the extermination of the Jews, which early in 1939 Hitler had threatened would be one of the consequences of an outbreak of war, and a special section in the Gestapo under Adolf Eichmann, as head of Section B4 of the Gestapo, was formed to carry out the policy. The plan for exterminating the Jews was developed shortly after the attack on the Soviet Union." And Eichmann's legitimation for it was clearly stated: he "had been put in charge of this program by Hitler."[35]

Whenever Eichmann is discussed in the context of the Nuremberg Trials, sooner or later a particular quote from Francis Biddle appears.[36] Next to the name Eichmann in the margin of one of the trial documents, the U.S. judge wrote: "Who is he?" It is generally assumed that, rather than this being a philosophical or psychological question, Biddle simply didn't know to whom the document referred. But it's easy to overlook the time when this note was made: the very short period before the trial started, when a handful of (mostly non-German) jurists were struggling to come to grips with the Nazi regime and the scale of its crimes. Even today no one can seriously claim to have a complete and thorough overview of this subject. And the Allied list of wanted war criminals contained more than sixty thousand names. So it isn't surprising that a judge was unfamiliar with one of them, which appeared in a draft document: on the contrary, his note shows how seriously he was taking these preparations. But it is rather surprising to learn *where* Francis Biddle read this name, because there it was, on the document that Biddle was reading when he drew his question mark next to it. The document was an early draft of the "frame of the judgment," a highly classified counterpart to the indictments.[37] A year later, when the panel of judges decided to include this name among a mere eighty mentioned in the text of the judgment, and to refer to it no fewer than three times, Biddle's question had obviously been answered.

Eichmann became the "Nuremberg Ghost," ever present but impossible to lay hands on.[38] His name haunted all the war crimes trials that followed. In a manner of speaking, Nuremberg in 1946 was no different from Vienna in spring 1939: Eichmann's name was once again being dropped by his superiors and associates, and it was inextricably linked with anti-Jewish policy. But times had changed, and (at least initially) Adolf Eichmann could take no pleasure in it. There was no more "work" to which he and his prominence could have given "an enormous boost." He was no longer surrounded by admirers; he was an outcast, someone it was better not to have known, and the only way to profit from him was by sending him to his doom. Eichmann was now, for the most part, alone in the forest. Later he would manage to muster some understanding for his former comrades and their efforts to offload their guilt onto him: "I possibly wouldn't have done anything different."[39] Of course, if the boot had been on the other foot, it would have been difficult for Eichmann to find someone half as well suited to the role of scapegoat.

As it was, there was nothing he could do about it, and he had no choice but to read his famous name in the papers and in the first pamphlets he was able to get hold of in northern Germany. As he put it years later, he had now finally been dragged into "the international limelight,"[40] and he made the logical decision to remain invisible—something he would never have countenanced during the previous decade.

Was Eichmann ever really the "man in the shadows"?[41] Perhaps only during the short time he spent playing the SD commissar in a long leather coat, as feared and mysterious as a film noir villain. But by 1937 at the latest, other roles had become more tempting, and they soon also turned out to be more useful. Eichmann became a symbol for anti-Jewish policy, exactly as he had planned. The symbol was perpetuated by other people's perception and by his own behavior, but it was also how he saw himself. The only difference in the postwar period was that he was elevated even further and held up as an isolated perpetrator. This was thanks to his associates and accomplices' efforts to defend themselves, and to all the people who took comfort in the fact that it had only been a small group, a secret society made up of a few insiders, all of them strange and sinister even among the National Socialists, who had committed the greatest crime in history. The more closed this society of murderers appeared to be, the more plausible were the claims of the "others" to have known nothing about it.

Only in Israel in 1960 would it dawn on Eichmann: being thought of as a man in the shadows could have its advantages. At that point, he would agree with Wisliceny's description only too willingly, though as the head of the Jewish Office he would have found it incredibly insulting. Sitting in his cell in Israel, he wanted nothing more than to be able to prove that no one knew him—not because of his vast, mysterious power, but because he was so unobtrusive and unimportant. Eichmann's incomprehension, bewilderment, and personal disappointment over the lies told by people who had once been his friends and comrades was so pitiful, you might almost think he believed it himself some of the time. How did he manage to talk away his own prominence so successfully that the world began to ignore Eichmann's image before 1960–61? A brief glance at this pretrial image quickly teaches us that he could not have been both a symbol and an unknown.

The fact is that none of the colleagues with whom Eichmann tried to compare himself during his trial had ever reached his level of prominence, either in the literature up until 1960 or in the public eye during the Nazi period, whether among perpetrators or victims. In magazines that were riddled with Eichmann's name, you would search in vain for the names of Rademacher, Thadden, Wisliceny, Brunner, or even Six, and his colleagues weren't mentioned in the Nuremberg judgment either. In 1951, when the State of Israel formulated its claim for reparations from Germany before the whole world, it named only five perpetrators in the original document. Eichmann was one of them,[42] and none of the newspapers that reported it asked why.

3

Detested Anonymity

He was probably bored to death.
　　—Hannah Arendt, on Eichmann in his North German hideout

At first glance, there was nothing on the Lüneberg Heath to serve as a reminder of a glittering SS career. The lifestyles of Otto Heninger and Adolf Eichmann could hardly have been more different. Instead of a uniform and gleaming boots, an office and an orderly, he was left with a secondhand Wehrmacht coat and a hut in the forest. No plenipotentiary powers, no carte blanche, no trips in his own official car around half of Europe, no new ways to exterminate the "enemy." In the space of a few months, Eichmann's existence had become entirely unremarkable—you might even call it tranquil. As a prisoner of war and a fugitive, his life had been in danger, and all his energy was focused on survival. Now, the peace of the forest, his plentiful rations,[1] and an unchanging daily routine provided a certain security and an opportunity for reflection. In Argentina, Eichmann claimed: "In the year 1946 I made a first attempt to set my recollections down in writing, using the figures which at that time were quite freshly lodged in my memory."[2] Considering his circumstances and the timing of his later bouts of writing, this wasn't out of character. Still, it's impossible to imagine this activity as particularly contemplative: Eichmann might have lost his desk, but he had lost none of his attitude. His writing was not an attempt to comprehend his own actions; it arose from the fact that people were condemning the crimes he felt to be his life's work. Eichmann wasn't going in search of the truth; he was looking for a plausible justification of his actions in case the worst should happen.

He must have started formulating this view of his incredible career—a story that would exonerate him as far as possible—when he was still a prisoner of war, constantly threatened with interrogations. News of the numerous cases against his superiors and colleagues made him consider how he would look to a tribunal, be it as witness or as defendant. Eichmann had played the role of interrogator often enough to know that he wouldn't get away with an outright lie. But the truth was too monstrous to be mitigated. Eichmann might have agreed with the commandant of Auschwitz that the murder of millions of Jews was nothing more than the "battles" that "the next generation will no longer have to fight."[3] But he was intelligent enough to know that most other people wouldn't see it that way. They were busy trying to forget or repress who and what they had spent the previous twelve years following—but for dedicated National Socialists who were wanted for crimes against humanity, the war was by no means over.

Eichmann always claimed that from the very beginning, he read everything that was written about the Nazis' extermination of the Jews. "In the forested heathland," he explained somewhat incautiously to Willem Sassen, "I was given a whole pile of old newspapers with articles about me. The headlines were Mass Murderer Eichmann, where is the mass murderer, where is Eichmann and similar."[4] His later conversations and statements show that he really was familiar with the major texts and events of the time, although it isn't entirely clear when he first read them. We only know *what* he might have read during this period, without being able to rule out the possibility that he might only have had sight of the material at a later date. The first book, which he later would quote repeatedly, was *Der SS-Staat* (The SS State) by Eugen Kogon, a work based on the Buchenwald Report, a group effort by former inmates of the camp, commissioned by the U.S. military authorities.[5] The book, published in 1946, contributed to the image of the Nazi perpetrators as a few asocial, perverse sadists, which Eichmann must have found insulting and provoking. It bore no relation to his vision of the Nazi leadership as a new elite, of which he had been a member. Eichmann would also have been able to read about Höttl's and Wisliceny's statements in early postwar newspapers and pamphlets, as they were widely covered in the press. He said he also read *Das Urteil von Nürnberg* (The Judgment of Nuremberg) while he was still in northern Germany. The book was published in fall 1946, in Robert M. W. Kempner's edition.[6] Fundamentally, nothing speaks against Eichmann having read these publications during his forestry period: nostalgic political conversations were evidently not unusual on "the Island." People from the local area recall that the house, inhabited by the woodsmen and by Ruth, the Red Cross sister who lived with them, was a popular meeting place for anyone who fancied a beer and a chat about old times. The pamphlets were certainly not costly to obtain either, since the British occupying forces distributed them as part of the "reeducation" effort. In any case, by the time Eichmann moved out of the woods in 1948, to run a chicken farm in the little hamlet of Altensalzkoth, his interest would have been apparent. Looking back on his life at that time, however, he claims the opposite: "Life went on peacefully on this beautiful heathland. On Sundays I cycled to the village inn near Celle. . . . It sometimes made me smile when the landlord told me what the local paper was saying about Eichmann. 'It's probably all lies and made-up stories,' he would say—and this made me very glad and content."[7]

But Eichmann's special role in history did not confront him only in the newspaper articles and books he read. His new home lay just a couple of miles from the former concentration camp of Bergen-Belsen, which was now a displaced persons' (DP) camp, temporary accommodation for the people who had survived the National Socialists' deportations. Eichmann was living right next to his victims—only now his business was eggs, not execution. In Argentina he used this spectral scenario to tell Sassen what he wanted to hear: "On the Lüneberg Heath, it was near where Bergen-Belsen had been, and everything round there smelled of garlic and it was all Jews, because who was buying anything at that time? Only the Jews, and then I said to myself, I, I who was bargaining with Jews over wood and eggs, I was amazed and astounded, and I thought you see—goddammit! They all should have been killed, and there those fellas are, doing deals with me, you know?"[8] In spite of this repugnant Nazi bluster among friends, the proximity of Bergen-Belsen posed a genuine problem for Eichmann (though he mentioned it only in passing): "Throughout these years the fear never left me that someone might come up behind me and suddenly cry: 'Eichmann!'"[9] Taking a good look in the mirror clearly didn't cause him the same level of concern.

We don't know which of his thoughts Eichmann wrote down on the Lüneberg Heath, because—so he claimed in Argentina, at least—he burned first his recollections, and then even the statistics, not wishing to travel with them once he left his hiding place.[10] The people who met Otto Heninger in the Miele-Kohlenberg district forestry, and then in Altensalzkoth, had no idea about his fears and his inner turmoil. They met a pleasant man who didn't drink or gamble, organized a fair distribution of rations, knew his way around the "red tape," was intelligent and polite, and paid his rent on time. This charming man with the slight Viennese accent clearly didn't have a provincial upbringing. "He was such a quiet, unassuming person. On warm summer evenings he often played his violin for us. He played Mozart, Schubert, Bach and Beethoven," one of the village women told journalists in 1960.[11] The men of the area also thought highly of the newcomer: his general technical knowledge meant he could fix broken equipment, and he was the only one in the area with a radio, on which he particularly liked to follow the news. Otto Heninger was a sort of man for all seasons, and although it sounds like a terrible cliché, even the children loved him: he helped tutor them and gave them chocolate.[12] It is unlikely that anyone knew who Otto Heninger really was. The members of this little village community let him into their lives, rented him rooms and fields, drove his chickens to market, bought his eggs, and respected his reserved manner. At this time, shortly after the war, nobody liked to ask too many questions.[13] Eichmann, however, had none too high an opinion of the villagers. "I wasn't able to read anything more challenging than a children's story without making the simple folk around me suspicious."[14] Although Hannah Arendt had not heard this striking statement, she was nevertheless quite right to suppose that Eichmann must have been "bored to death" on the Lüneberg Heath.[15] One distinct advantage was that at least he wasn't making attempts on other people's lives.

Festung Nord

Eichmann portrayed himself as a man alone among strangers, and in later years, he always avoided mentioning his contacts from this period by name. But even out on the Lüneberg Heath, a former SS man was not so very isolated. He wasn't the only person with a past to choose this part of the country as a hiding place. Before the war's end, the Nazis in Berlin had considered possible emergency meeting places. While some people fantasized about imaginary defensive positions in the Alpenfestung (Alpine Fortress) and Festung Nord (North Fortress), men like Eichmann were probably aware of what these national redoubts were really for: in case of defeat, a coterie of like-minded people could quickly be gathered there, to allow the exchange of important information. The area around Celle in the north, and the Salzkammergut in the Austrian Alps, were strategically favorable. Both were remote but also close to national borders. It would be possible to repopulate networks there without being noticed, and in an emergency, people could make a quick exit: Altausee, in the geographical center of Austria, was a stone's throw from the Italian part of South Tyrol, and from Altensalzkoth it was easy to reach the major German ports. Eichmann, who had spent so many years as an emigration expert, must have seen the advantages of these "fortresses" immediately. It was no coincidence that he located himself and his family, respectively, in these exact spots. Contemporaries in the Altensalzkoth area remembered visits from SS men like Willi Koch,[16] who in all likelihood knew precisely who Otto Heninger was. One of Eichmann's other guests certainly knew: Luis Schintlholzer, the man who afterward liked to brag about having been part of the circle that had helped Eichmann escape—and whose words reached the ears of an informant for the West German intelligence service.[17]

Luis (Alois) Schintlholzer was one of the brutal criminals and SS thugs whose involvement in the 1938 November pogrom in Innsbruck made them notorious.[18] But this was only the beginning of the young Austrian's career as a killer. He was born in 1914, and as a young man, he was famed throughout the city as a boxer. Schintlholzer was heavily involved in the Waffen-SS's so-called reprisals against the Italian civilian population and in the destruction of the village of Caviola in 1943, during which forty people were murdered—a few of them burned alive in their houses. He was also active in the persecution of the Jews, becoming leader of the Trient Gestapo in February 1945. Even his retreat at the end of the war was accompanied by murder and lethal beatings.[19] Despite repeated arrests after the war, Schintlholzer always managed to get away scot-free, although an Italian court sentenced him to life imprisonment in absentia. In the late 1940s, the unrepentant SS man was living in Bielefeld with his wife (and later children). He kept his real name, though he had a forged German passport, because there was a warrant out for his arrest in Austria. We don't know the circumstances of Schintlholzer and Eichmann's meeting in northern Germany. They may have made contact through a circle of Austrian SS comrades, of which Schintlholzer was a committed member until his death in 1989. However they met, they both doubtless knew who they were dealing with. Schintlholzer would later say that Eichmann told him about documents and notes on the "Final Solution to the Jewish Question" that he had hidden in northern Germany. There were statistics there too and, most important, background information on those responsible.[20] Schintlholzer was Otto Heninger's final guest on the Lüneberg Heath: he was there to make sure Eichmann reached the Austrian border undetected. Speaking to Willem Sassen, Eichmann hinted: "On the Lüneberg Heath I got around a fair bit, you know. You see, I had been on the move constantly, I didn't just go and hide in a hole somewhere."[21] Given that he even managed to meet up with an old comrade from Bielefeld, we can guess what he might have meant by this remark.

In time, plenty of men returned from the prisoner of war camps. At least one of them took up with Eichmann again: Hans Freiesleben, who came to live in Altensalzkoth after his release. SS comradeship proved lasting. Old associations that, at first, had been useful for pure survival, and the provision of hiding places, developed into a network of escape routes over the following years. The sheer number of former National Socialist officials who found their way to northern Germany points to something more than a collection of individual escape plans. And some of these men would meet Eichmann again in Argentina.

Family Ties

We cannot assume that Eichmann intended to settle permanently on the Lüneberg Heath. But over time he came to feel so comfortable there that, in 1947, he accepted an invitation to the wedding of one of his fellow foresters. Nor did he shy away from the wedding photo, standing quite close to the bride. If he had stayed in this area, he would most likely never have been found. But safety was no substitute for his family. Much to the delight of the village gossips,[22] Otto Heninger received the occasional visit from Nelly Krawietz, the pretty straw-blond lady from the south who prepared exotic dishes like *Kaiserschmarrn* for him. People also spoke of him having a couple of relationships in the local area— but this didn't stop Eichmann from wanting to go back to his family.

It was Vera Eichmann who made the first attempt to return to their old life. Her behavior following her infamous husband's disappearance betrays the fact that the Eichmanns had discussed their emergency plans in advance. She was not only cautious but showed surprising strength, enduring interrogations, house searches, and surveillance by the Allies and survivor groups. It was thanks to Eichmann's wife that for a number of years not a single photograph of him was to be found. Like his family in Linz, Vera must have kept all her papers very well hidden, bringing them out only in 1952, shortly before her departure for Argentina. When she was questioned by the CIC in November 1946, she told them she had divorced her husband in March 1945 and had seen him for the last time in April, when he had wanted to say good-bye to the children in Altaussee. She seemed clueless about her husband's crimes and gave a statement that bore a striking resemblance to those given by Eichmann's parents and siblings the month before.[23]

Everyone repeated the legend that Eichmann was the black sheep of the family, which Eichmann himself put about among his comrades before the end of the war. The fact that Vera Eichmann received support from her husband's family doesn't seem to have raised any eyebrows.[24] Nor did it occur to anyone that Karl Adolf Eichmann would never have fallen out with his son over the latter's National Socialist worldview, because he himself was a committed Nazi. Eichmann's father had joined the NSDAP at the end of the 1930s, which as Vera Eichmann later said caused him some difficulties in 1945. But it wasn't simply "because he was a Nazi": there were also items in his possession for which he had no proof of ownership, and the things that obviously didn't belong to him were subsequently confiscated. David Cesarani is right to warn us not to underestimate the "dynamic interplay between father and son."[25]

In April 1947 Eichmann's wife took the next step, attempting to have her husband declared dead in Bad Ischl. She claimed he had fallen in Prague in 1945. This may have been done in collaboration with Eichmann's father, who had also discussed escape plans with his son early on. If it had been successful, Adolf Eichmann might really have managed to spend his life undiscovered in Europe, particularly given how adaptable we know he was. It would also have given his wife the right to a pension. At first glance, Vera Eichmann's evidence looked convincing: she brought Lisa Kals, who was married to a man from Altaussee and was also resident there, with her as a witness. She was able to produce a letter from a Czech captain by the name of Karl Lukas, giving a report of Eichmann's death. But Simon Wiesenthal immediately realized he had heard the name before: it belonged to Vera's sister's husband, who now lived with her mother near Linz. Alerted by Wiesenthal, the Altaussee

police spotted a further inconsistency: Lisa Kals, the recipient of the letter from Vera's brother-in-law, had been born Lisa Liebl.[26] Vera Eichmann had tried to obtain a death certificate for her husband with the aid
of her two sisters and her brother-in-law.[27]

When Wiesenthal produced two sworn statements proving that Eichmann had been seen alive in Altaussee in May, Vera Eichmann withdrew the application, having achieved the exact opposite of what she
had intended. It was now clear to everyone that Eichmann was still
alive; otherwise this subterfuge on the part of his family would not have
been necessary. The CIC made another search of the Eichmann family's
houses, and the house of one of his lovers. An Israeli spy even managed
to secure a photo of Eichmann through Maria Mösenbacher, another
of his female acquaintances.[28] Wisliceny had put the investigator on to
a man who claimed to have been Eichmann's driver and could therefore provide him with a substantial list of these female acquaintances. In
truth, this man was Josef Weiszl, the "Jews' emperor of Doppl," a notorious sadist whose dog whip had become his trademark; he was also Wilhelm Höttl's brother-in-law.[29] Weiszl appeared before a military court
in Paris a short time later, where he told more tales on his boss; Weiszl,
of course, had practiced sadism only under orders. Although the Eichmanns were probably unaware of the photo, Adolf Eichmann would
surely have heard about the house searches from his father. During conversations with his associates in Argentina, it emerged that Eichmann
even knew about the arrest warrant that had been issued in Vienna.[30] All
the members of the Eichmann family could see there was no alternative
for Adolf Eichmann. He would have to resort to his emergency plan:
escape from Germany. For Vera Eichmann, this would mean more years
of waiting, doing nothing to alert suspicion. When she finally met her
husband again in Buenos Aires, she had not seen him for seven years.

Eichmann's Hesitation

We can make an educated guess at how Eichmann came to consider
Argentina as a possible destination. He would later say he had read "that
the former National Socialist *Gauleiter* of Carinthia was living in Argentina."[31] Eichmann was obviously referring to Siegfried Uiberreither,
who, strictly speaking, had been the gauleiter of Styria. He had managed

to escape from Dachau in May 1947, before he could be handed over to Yugoslavia along with the real gauleiter of Carinthia, Friedrich Rainer. The Austrian papers were full of this matter, and speculations soon surfaced that Uiberreither had fled to Argentina.[32] By the end of the 1940s, a surprising number of people knew that former Nazi bigwigs were living in Argentina. Rumors were not the only things circulating; books and magazines from the Dürer publishing house were also making the rounds. Based in Buenos Aires, Dürer spread extreme National Socialist ideas, openly peddling authors with very familiar names. Germans with far-right leanings also eagerly read Der Weg—El Sendero, the most right-wing of all the postwar Nazi magazines, which was published by Dürer from 1947. It was as openly anti-Semitic, racist, and National Socialist as if the Third Reich had never collapsed.

Eberhard Fritsch, Dürer's young publisher, relied on the huge publicity he received in Germany. He was so aggressive and self-confident that the ever-increasing circulation of this fascist propaganda sheet from abroad unleashed a wave of warnings and exposés in the German media. People wrote of "Nazi resistance cells" in Argentina and "the Hitlers of South America"; they warned readers about "the Weg that leads into the abyss." Munich's Neue Zeitung called Fritsch the "up-and-coming man of the Fourth Reich."[33] The Hamburg-based Der Spiegel also claimed that prominent Nazis had been ordered to flee to Argentina by the Wehrmacht's high command.[34] Der Weg also ran ads for travel agencies and for a trustworthy-sounding club called Kameradenwerk (Comrade Work). For a devoted National Socialist like Eichmann, these must have sounded like messages from the Promised Land.

Wilfred von Oven, a former subordinate of Goebbels's and an unrepentant National Socialist, also ended up in northern Germany after the war. He made no secret of the fact that it was the Dürer publications that had first made him curious about Argentina. Eberhard Fritsch published Oven's book on Goebbels while he was still living in Schleswig-Holstein, using communication networks between Germany and Buenos Aires that were clearly already fully functioning.[35] In Argentina, Eichmann would come to value this network.

Argentina didn't just sound good; it was a realistic destination for Nazi fugitives. Thanks to groundbreaking source studies by the Argentine author Uki Goñi, we now know a great deal about the networks that made escape possible for those who were keen to emigrate. For someone with a biography like Eichmann's, improvisation in this area was not advisable. At first, the established escape route went via harbors in Sweden, which from northern Germany were practically on Eichmann's doorstep. But after this route was exposed in 1948, people had to rely on the southern alternative. A chain of German helpers, Argentine public officials, Austrian border guards, Italian records offices, the Red Cross, men from Vatican circles, and influential shipping magnates allowed people to escape. In order to start down this route, it was imperative to have two documents. The first was a short-term visa for Argentina, provided by Horst Carlos Fuldner, a people smuggler who had the blessing of the Argentine caudillo Juan Perón. The second was identity papers in the same name, which in Eichmann's case were issued by the commune of Termeno, in South Tyrol. Eichmann, the concentration camp "doctor" Josef Mengele, and Himmler's chief adjutant, Ludolf von Alvensleben (all particularly problematic cases), were issued papers there at the same time in 1948. Eichmann's paper was dated June 11, numbered 131, and made out in the name of Riccardo Klement.[36] Bishop Alois Hudal, the self-appointed protector of persecuted and tortured persons—by which he meant Nazis—would later become famous for having arranged papers from Rome for this particular fugitive.[37]

Almost two years elapsed between these papers being issued and Eichmann's actual escape. He made use of the visa only at the last minute, just before it expired. What could have made him hesitate? One possible answer is the political upheaval in Germany between 1947 and 1950. At the London Conference of Foreign Ministers in December 1947, it became obvious that differences with the Soviet Union were continuing to grow, and a split between the Allies was no longer to be avoided. A lot of Nazis had speculated about this east-west conflict before the end of the war. They hoped that the Western powers' anti-Bolshevism would ultimately prove stronger than their desire to bring down Hitler's Germany. Germany could then reemerge as a sovereign state. "Eichmann firmly believed in the dispute between the Western powers and Russia, and saw it as his last chance," one of his close colleagues later reported.[38] Göring also expressed this belief several times in Nuremberg, hoping that it might even return him to power.[39]

The year 1948 saw the gradual realization of this split. With it came the hope of a new beginning for Germany and, more important, of a general amnesty. Another development came as a more unpleasant surprise to Eichmann: on June 20, 1948, the currency reform came into effect. It meant the loss of his job, as the company he worked for after Burmann & Co. promptly went bankrupt. The currency reform also threatened the money that Eichmann had been carefully putting aside. For someone living illegally, the introduction of the Deutschmark posed a serious problem. Avoiding all contact with officials meant receiving neither the so-called bounty allowance of forty Deutschmarks nor the new currency. It would also be impossible for him to exchange his old Reichsmarks without help: for this exchange you needed a bank account and the correct documentation for the Finance Office's checks. Eichmann had neither. Although he had a legitimate resident's permit and valid papers, he had carefully avoided any contact with officials. People living illegally would now have to rely on money launderers, which didn't make the exchange rate particularly favorable. He would also have no protection against any misappropriation of funds. Someone like Eichmann, who had used unfair exchange rates in Vienna to generate millions for the Reich, knew this only too well.

When he wasn't "quartered" in confiscated villas with well-stocked wine cellars, Eichmann had always made a conscious effort to live frugally, and the currency reform was a setback to his plans to find a new life overseas. Even old comrades wouldn't provide help for free. His investment in the chicken farm should possibly be seen in this light. In the 1930s, when Jews were routinely robbed of everything they owned before being allowed to leave the country, Eichmann had learned that if you wanted to safeguard your funds, you had to invest in material assets—as long as a criminal state didn't set out laws prohibiting the purchase of material assets for this very reason.

No one prevented Eichmann from investing in chickens, and no one would have stopped him from exchanging his poultry for the new currency a few weeks later. However, once this new, stable currency had been introduced, the earning potential of his investment became apparent. As the children of the village remembered, Eichmann kept more than one hundred chickens and charged a steep twenty pfennigs for an egg. For comparison, his monthly rent was ten Deutschmarks.[40] And so he was able to put some money aside, and wait a little while, hoping that the milestone of five years after the end of the war might lead to an amnesty after all. But another event might also have played a role in Eichmann's hesitation: a failed attempt by the police, Israeli "guests," and a Nazi hunter to arrest him in Austria, in the winter of 1948.

A Family Visit?

During a press conference in 1960, Simon Wiesenthal explained to an astonished audience that he had tried to catch Adolf Eichmann on his planned Christmas visit to Altaussee in 1949: "The house was surrounded, but Eichmann didn't come. He was warned off, or became suspicious, and disappeared again."[41] This was not just one of Wiesenthal's dramatic stories but a genuine operation, even if his dates were not entirely accurate.

In the fall of 1948, there were clues that Eichmann was going to try to visit his family between Christmas and the New Year. Reports on the operation that followed have been written by several of the people involved; their details don't always tally, but they can be reduced to a common core and a set of dates.[42] In December 1948, representatives of the Austrian police force from Linz (including Leo Frank-Maier[43]), together with Israeli agents (including Michael Bloch[44])and Simon Wiesenthal, were lying in wait in Altaussee. The plan was to arrest Eichmann and hand him over to the Israelis, for which the chief of police in Linz would receive five thousand dollars in addition to the operation's costs. And so they attempted to distribute themselves as unobtrusively as possible through the sparsely populated area—in the middle of a cold winter, when nighttime temperatures fell to -4 degrees F. The team all spoke of interruptions in their surveillance but couldn't agree on who was ultimately to blame for Eichmann being warned off. The most likely explanation is that in a place as small as Altaussee, it simply wasn't possible to conduct an operation on this scale without being discovered. The reports even mention rumors circulating in the town that Israelis were there, or the Nazi hunter Simon Wiesenthal, who was not unknown in Austria.

Did Eichmann really attempt to visit his family in the period between Christmas and New Year 1948? Did he run the costly risk of traveling across Germany and crossing the border under a false name? We know from later years that despite being *gottgläubig* (adhering to a racially based Nazi religion), Eichmann associated Christmas with a strong

sense of family. And his papers were waiting for him in Italy, so the visit
to his family could have been a stopping point along an escape route
that he actually took later. But in that case, Eichmann would have disappeared from Altensalzkoth without selling his property there, incurring
a huge financial loss. Neither Vera Eichmann nor the children would
speak of such a plan in later years; nor did Eichmann's observant neighbors in Altensalzkoth notice any long absence. Eichmann later indicated
that the possibility had crossed his mind, though he was talking about
1950, when his escape route took him within a few miles of his wife and
children as he traveled across Austria. He briefly considered whether to
run the risk of meeting his family but, with great self-discipline, decided
against it.[45] It is unlikely that Eichmann was less disciplined in 1948. In
any case, he thought too much like an investigator to make the error
of arriving on such a significant date, especially after Vera Eichmann's
failed attempt to have him declared dead.

But something else speaks against Eichmann having been close to
his family at this time: at the end of September 1948, an interview in
Linz gave rise to a series of newspaper articles. "Eichmann's parents,"
the Vienna *Welt am Abend* reported, "have heard nothing from their
son since the end of the war." Investigations in the area had, however,
brought to light the rumor that Adolf Eichmann had been an American
prisoner of war until 1946. He had taken the name Eckermann and was
now said to be in the Middle East, "as an adviser to the grand mufti of
Jerusalem, El Husseini, helping him to rid Palestine of its Jewish problem." The stories, with headlines like "The Reich Commissar for the
Jews" and "A Member of the Arab Legion," persisted stubbornly in the
press throughout October 1948.[46] Curt Riess, who had just finished his
biography of Goebbels, went to Altaussee as a "special correspondent"
to try to track Eichmann down. This trip resulted in nothing more than
a somewhat labored and sensationalistic series of articles on "the merry
wives of Altaussee," which also managed to tap into legends of hidden
Nazi gold. *Die Neue Welt* did at least provide a revealing document on
Eichmann: his two-page, handwritten CV from 1937, taken from his
service record, which pinpointed exactly when and where he was born,
and how he began his murderous career. Riess also described exactly
where Eichmann's family now lived. One piece of information in particular came up again and again in the articles and must have caused the
Eichmann family grave concern: "Eichmann is first on all the lists of war

criminals." Whatever travel plans Eichmann might have made, the end of 1948 was not a good time to put them into action. Clearly the man who had dreamed of becoming the "Reich Commissar for the Jews" was still on everyone's mind.

A few years later the Gehlen Organization (the predecessor of the German Federal Intelligence Service, the BND) discovered that in 1949, a year after the failed Christmas operation, the Israeli consul in Vienna had set aside fifty thousand schillings for a campaign to find and arrest Eichmann.[47] There was even talk of a vast bounty of a million schillings on his head. Gehlen's informant said that an Israeli unit had taken up residence in Austria, to kidnap Eichmann when he visited his family at Christmas. It had even chartered a plane from Salzburg airport. Was there another attempt to catch Eichmann, a year later?

Gehlen's informant, according to the files, was Josef Adolf Urban. He was a man of many talents, born in 1920, and had been arrested in 1948 in a Linz coffeehouse that served as a trading center for fake passports. He had a bag full of counterfeit documents on him, which was enough for the Linz police to take him into custody. Leo Frank-Maier, one of the police officers involved, reported on Urban's interrogation. He had allowed Simon Wiesenthal to listen in, because the man they had apprehended was clearly helping war criminals escape. In spite of the hard evidence, they were forced to release Josef Adolf Urban after two days. According to Frank-Maier, two American CIC agents turned up and demanded that the suspect be released: Urban was a vital coordinator in a spy network being deployed against the Soviet Union. Frank-Maier quickly discovered that in reality, Urban was feeding the U.S. agency made-up "information" from his also largely made-up "field agents." He had even invented a number of weapons factories in the East.[48]

What Frank-Maier could not know was that the Americans weren't the only ones keen to avoid Urban being put on trial. The intelligence fabricator was also an informant for the national security division of the Austrian Ministry of the Interior, and this fact would inevitably have come to light if he were put on trial.[49] Urban actually supplied pretty much every agency going, from the Deuxième Bureau to the Israeli intelligence service and of course the Gehlen Organization.[50] He was, as the authors of a comprehensive study on the BND put it, a "roving secret-service mercenary."[51] Reinhard Gehlen commissioned Urban, who he thought was well connected, together with Bruno Kauschen, to expand the Austrian branch of the German secret service.[52] It is not known whether Gehlen was aware of how Urban sometimes came up with his explosive information and where he had learned to do so.

Was the information on the Israelis' planned kidnap genuine? It wouldn't have been difficult to find out about the failed operation in Altaussee in winter 1948–49, details of which had not escaped the local barkeeper. We cannot rule out the possibility that there was more fiction than truth in the insider knowledge that Urban passed on in 1952: at this point, as we will see, Gehlen was very interested in Eichmann. Urban then also claimed he had personally helped Eichmann escape—a confession that seems not to have harmed his career in the postwar West German intelligence service.[53] As is usually the case with intelligence service information, the publicly available files reveal very little. But we do know where Josef Adolf Urban learned the art of manipulation: first in the SD, then with Adolf Eichmann in Hungary.[54]

The young careerist joined the NSDAP at eighteen (membership no. 6312927), and quickly became an SD leader in Vienna. He was one of Walter Schellenberg's Balkan experts and finished up as head of the SD control center in Budapest, where Adolf Eichmann was proving to the world just how many people you could "transport to extermination" in the space of six weeks. Even Wiesenthal was taken aback by Urban's stories about Rudolf Kasztner.[55] Reinhard Gehlen certainly had an eye for well-trained people.

Urban would have been one of the last people with an interest in Eichmann's reappearance. Urban knew what Eichmann had done before 1945, and Eichmann knew Urban's history. If Eichmann *had* turned up, Urban would have given him false papers for free (although Eichmann would never have relied on a petty criminal like Urban). But the former Budapest SD boss had another reason for not betraying Eichmann: he would remain a committed National Socialist as long as he lived. Colleagues reported that he always swore his employees into office "on the Führer Adolf Hitler, as he had reliable information that he was still alive and, according to Urban, living in a warm oasis in the South Polar region." An insufficient knowledge of geography was clearly the least of Urban's problems.[56] But his political views didn't stop Reinhard Gehlen from continuing to employ Josef Adolf Urban in the BND as late as 1956. He remained on the BND's payroll until the 1970s.

However, there is more evidence of a second attempt to smuggle

Eichmann out of Austria besides that in the Gehlen Organization's files. In addition to Simon Wiesenthal, two other men reported on a possible operation over the New Year period of 1949–50: the tireless Nazi hunter Tuviah Friedman, and Asher Ben Natan, who at that time was still the head of the Israeli Foreign Office's political department, the forerunner of Mossad. But this plan also failed when Eichmann didn't arrive.[57]

The Gehlen Organization files contain more than just Urban's finagling, due to a crucial development during the year between the two kidnap attempts. The bounty on the head of the "number one enemy of the Jews" had grown, according to Urban, though it had also shifted. The transformation from five thousand dollars into fifty thousand schillings would, in spite of the extra zero, have more than halved its value—but the huge sum of a million Austrian schillings was also mentioned. Discrepancies like these do not exactly speak in favor of the information's reliability.

Twelve years later Eichmann really would be abducted by plane, after an Israeli unit finally managed to apprehend the man who had been hunted for so long. The CIA was certain that the plan must have originated with Simon Wiesenthal.[58] It had obviously got wind of the failed abduction attempts in the late 1940s.

We don't know whose tip-off alerted Simon Wiesenthal to Eichmann's visit to Altaussee, or why so many people believed an arrest operation would prove successful. We may doubt that this was a serious announcement about a planned visit. Whether it was a misunderstanding, a case of mistaken identity, or even a test by the family to find out how closely they were being observed, it served to let Eichmann know that people's interest in him was undiminished. If the rumor of Israelis in Altaussee reached him after the fact, he must have found it extremely unsettling. After he was kidnapped in 1960, he spoke of his fear that the Jews, having lost so many of their own children, might now exact revenge on the children of the man who was (at least partly) to blame.[59] But because the list of war criminals was generally known, and because the Austrian police were on the alert, he had good reason to stay as far away from danger as possible. No wonder Eichmann decided to remain in remote Altensalzkoth a little longer, living the life of harmless Otto Heninger, farming chickens and selling expensive eggs to the people he had failed to deport to their deaths. But by 1950, Eichmann had money, and he had to face the fact that the founding of West Germany had not brought him immunity from prosecution. His visa for Argentina was about to expire. It was high time he was on his way.

An Orderly Escape

But even as he left Altensalzkoth, Eichmann kept a cool head. Absconding in the middle of the night would have aroused suspicion and led to stories that could have reached the wrong ears. But moving on, or even emigrating, was not a rare occurrence during these years. The war and its aftermath—escape, abduction, eviction, DP camps, and a shortage of accommodation—had created conditions in which a great number of people were looking for somewhere to call home. Eichmann managed to place Otto Heninger in their ranks. He sold his chickens to Forester Frei-esleben, explained to his landlady that he wanted to go to work in Scandinavia as a mechanical engineer, and wrote a farewell letter to Nelly that laid a false trail for her as well.[60] He told her he was turning himself over to the Russians, which didn't sound as absurd then as it might to our ears: there was a lot of speculation at the time about senior Gestapo officials, like Eichmann's old boss Müller, escaping to the Soviet-occupied zone; who chose this escape route has still not been systematically investigated. The story had the added advantage of not exactly being simple to check out. In any case, Otto Heninger didn't vanish like a thief in the night: he paid his outstanding rent and bade a proper farewell to Altensalzkoth. Nobody asked questions, and nobody informed the police. The neighbors retained a memory of him as a pleasant incomer. If they missed his reserved manner or his violin playing, they had only to look at him in the wedding photo. It might have been nice to hear from him occasionally and learn how he was doing out there in the big wide world. But nobody anticipated a postcard from Israel.

One of the questions that remains unanswered is whether Eichmann somehow managed to make contact with the escape network, or whether it sought him out. We can't rule out help from his father in Linz: if an article from an Austrian newspaper about Uiberreither's escape really made it all the way to northern Germany, Eichmann must have been in close contact with Austria. He himself gave contradictory accounts of these events. In one version, he found the people smugglers by placing carefully coded advertisements in local newspapers.[61]

According to the wildly romantic story he told at the start of 1961, the contact was the result of some risk-taking on his part, and thanks to a trustworthy comrade: "So I confessed to one of my closer friends on the Heath my intention to go overseas, and asked him if he knew anyone who knew about things to do with making this journey. In this way I came into contact with a man in Hamburg in 1950, a former SS man, who traveled a lot between Germany and Italy. I gave him 300 Marks out of my savings (2500 Deutschmarks of profit from the egg business), and obtained from him the most precise information about the 'U-boat route' to South America. He gave me every detail, every stopping place, every contact point."[62]

All his versions have one thing in common: they aim to deflect attention away from the people involved. Eichmann maintained this grateful solidarity with the people who had helped him right up until his execution. Today we can see that one basic element of his story simply doesn't make sense: the papers necessary for the first part of his escape were produced at the start of June 1948, before the currency reform, and even before Eichmann lost his forestry job and became a chicken farmer. He deliberately gave a later date in his stories. Giving false dates was a disinformation tactic he described in detail to Sassen.[63] He perfected it to a frightening degree and used it at various points in his life.[64] During his trial, he managed to persuade the world that his role was less than it had really been by giving later dates for his activities. A man who is present for the first time at the opening of a new institution has a very different role from someone who visited the future site of that institution in the planning stages. He applied this tactic to places like the Central Emigration Offices and to the death camps. Similarly, a person who plans his escape carefully over the course of two years is very different from a person who makes a snap decision to travel to Italy, with nothing but a few addresses in his pocket, trusting he'll be able to find out where to go from there. This sort of redating can draw a veil over large periods of time. All kinds of unpleasant questions can be avoided, like how Eichmann had the money and the connections to find out about an escape route in 1948, immediately before the currency reform; and how he came by the contact for the church offices that helped him obtain identity papers from South Tyrol and a short-term visa for Argentina. There was no way Eichmann could have traveled there in person. And Nelly Krawietz was out of the question, as he evidently didn't trust her.

The path to constructing a new identity was complex, and obtaining the identity papers and the short-term visa was just the first step. With these papers, photos, and a character reference from the Franciscan priest Edoardo Dömöter, Eichmann could apply for a passport with the Red Cross in Genoa. Once he had the passport and the short-term visa, he could apply for a long-term visa at the Argentine embassy, and this, together with a doctor's reference and another proof of identity, was what Eichmann needed in order to apply for personal documents in Buenos Aires. And then he needed passage on a ship. This whole process took a good two weeks in Genoa. Even Eichmann, the seasoned emigration specialist, could not have improvised such an efficient use of tiny bureaucratic loopholes across several countries and institutions—let alone men like Josef Mengele and Ludolf von Alvensleben, who had no experience at all in the flexible handling of exit arrangements.

The escape organization was a highly professional affair, as can be seen from the photographs that are still in the International Red Cross's passport application files. Adolf Eichmann is surprisingly well dressed in his photo. With his carefully clipped hair, round glasses, beard, suit, and bow tie, he not only looks much older but is also the very model of an engineer, nothing like an officer. And Eichmann's photos are no exception. Ludolf von Alvensleben, Himmler's former chief adjutant, stood almost six feet tall and had a pronounced receding hairline, but here he appears in a curly toupee, with a little beard and drooping shoulders. There was a costumer at work here who knew exactly what he was doing.

Like many others going into exile, Eichmann used a system supported by a number of different parties, not least the professional people smugglers employed by the Argentine president Juan Domingo Perón. Argentina had an interest in German professionals who could help to drive forward the transformation of an agrarian country into an industrialized nation, and assisting their escape seemed like a solid investment. Conditions in postwar Europe were favorable for tempting these people overseas: the whole region had been reduced to rubble, everyone had to find a new place for himself, and people were open to offers. Argentina was not the only country trying to convince well-educated men to emigrate, but it was one of the few that also provided this opportunity to criminals like Eichmann. On the Argentine side, aid for fugitives was organized by the German-Argentine Rudolfo Freude, who had close connections to emigration officials. Another German-Argentine, the aforementioned Horst Carlos Fuldner, traveled to Europe in 1948 to provide papers and organizational structures to help people escape; he was assisted by the Argentine consulate. Fuldner was the man whom, years later, Eichmann's son would call "Father's best friend."[65]

The myth of ODESSA has obscured our view of reality for a long time. It was said to be a tightly run *"Organization der ehemaligen SS-Angehörigen"* (organization of former SS members), established after the fall of the Third Reich, that continued to run like clockwork in the underground. Initially, *Odessa* was just a code word in the prison camps, by which SS members could identify one another in order to provide mutual support.[66] Myths survive because they feed our imagination, and the myth of this organization fed the minds of two traumatized groups at once: the Nazi hunters, who over time began to overestimate their opponents the way hunters tend to do, and who were fond of conspiracy theories; and the National Socialists, who had idealized the efficiency of an organization like the SS when they had been in power and were comforted by the idea that it might still exist in some way following Germany's capitulation. The notion that an association existed underground, to which all SS men were automatically given membership after 1945 and that continued to exist as if nothing had happened that May, was obviously a fantasy born variously of fear or hope. But just as obviously, people who are committed to an ideology don't lose faith in it, or stop feeling a certain bond with one another, just because the state that sustained it and them has collapsed. On the contrary: Germany's defeat created an omnipresent new enemy at home—the Allied forces— and having a common enemy strengthened Nazi solidarity. Romantic notions of the SS did not become nostalgic memories; they created a network suited to the new era. No large underground organization of former SS members ever existed, but there were former SS members in the underground who needed help and obtained it more easily from people for whom the SS had positive associations. Alliances like these are based on recommendations and relationships, especially when they are operating illegally. Membership in a strongly ideological organization served as a "recommendation" when it came to securing accommodations, contacts, a mailing address, or something more significant. The basic structure, like that of other National Socialist institutions such as the RSHA, changed in response to new developments. A rigid organization for aiding fugitives, if such a thing were possible, could never have been as effective as this flexible common-interest group, which allowed complete strangers to rely on one another for help. It shaped Eichmann's escape through Europe just as it would shape his life in Argentina and even his behavior in the Jerusalem District Court. If we want to understand the context of Eichmann's life in Argentina, we will get nowhere unless we look at how his escape was organized. Old comrades and their new sympathizers provided a kind of mutual aid that didn't readily reveal itself: their network was oriented toward discretion. Help had to be given silently, because the enemy was everywhere, and maintaining the value of seemingly loose connections rested on never revealing how they worked. Eichmann still believed this in 1962 and always expressed his gratitude when he spoke of "the organization" to which he and his family owed their escape and their new life.[67]

The Emigration Expert

Although Adolf Eichmann's escape would not have been possible without the help of church institutions close to the Vatican, his road did not lead to Rome. Nevertheless the idea of Eichmann in the Eternal City persisted for a long time. In 1961 Moshe Pearlman named Genoa as Eichmann's point of departure as well as the Franciscan priest who helped him there—he had had special access to the statements Eichmann made during his interrogation.[68] Hannah Arendt brought Pearlman's information to a wider audience, but this still didn't dispel the tenacious rumor that Eichmann had met Alois Hudal in Rome and had been made to take a test of faith with Anton Weber, the padre of the St. Raphael Society. Hudal may have had a hand in organizing Eichmann's false papers, but we can rule out a personal encounter in Rome. Still, the name Hudal had been associated with efforts to help Nazi fugitives leave Europe since the early 1950s. So what could have been more natural, once Eichmann was arrested, than to fabricate a connection between Eichmann's escape via Italy, aided by the church, and the only name people had heard in that context, Alois Hudal?

Although Bishop Hudal personally welcomed Nazis to Rome and looked after them during their escape, Eichmann was not one of them. His escape route took him out of Altensalzkoth in May 1950 and south to the border with Austria. The journey was easy and comfortable. Luis Schintlholzer from Bielefeld drove his old comrade from Celle to Bad Reichenhall on the Austrian border—at least, this is the story that got the former SS officer from Innsbruck into trouble in later years.[69] It was only a day's drive, so no accommodation was necessary. From there a people smuggler took Eichmann along the back roads to Kufstein in Austria, and he went from there to Innsbruck, where he had a contact address, by taxi. In Nazi circles, Innsbruck was well known as a stopping place for people on the run from their past. There is much to suggest that Eichmann met his father there, or at least a middleman, as he left part of his savings behind in Austria.[70] From Innsbruck, he went south to the Vinaders guesthouse, in Gries am Brenner, and people smugglers helped him cross the border into Italy. Johann Corradini, the vicar of Sterzing, met Eichmann there and gave him back his luggage, which the man of God had personally taken across the border by bicycle. He also arranged a "taxi driver." This wasn't a one-off job for Corradini, and it's safe to assume that the taxi driver was also in the know, earning good money from driving special passengers. In any case, he drove the fugitive to Bolzano, where, according to Eichmann's new CV, he had been born in 1913, as the illegitimate child of Anna Klement. This was where Eichmann said he received a free short-term visa from the Argentine immigration authority. He must also have been given the identity papers from Termeno that had been deposited for him there, which declared him "stateless."

From Bolzano, Eichmann's journey continued through Verona to Genoa, where he found refuge in a Franciscan monastery. We are still largely ignorant of which of his former comrades he met there. Eichmann mentioned only Pedro Geller, a former officer in a tank regiment whose real name was Herbert Kuhlmann. Eichmann claimed to have lent him money for the crossing. We can assume that Kuhlmann, alias Geller, was not the only person Eichmann met on his journey; he made contacts during this period for his new life overseas. Eichmann spent his last weeks in Europe in the monastery, passing the time by attending various appointments at the Red Cross offices and the outpost of the Argentine immigration authority in Genoa (DAIA) or playing chess and discussing worldviews with the "old monk Franciscus." Rumors that Eichmann officially converted to Catholicism and was baptized at this point are not to be believed.[71] Baptism would have been neither smart nor necessary, as his false papers from Termeno already said he was a Catholic. Eichmann would later consistently describe himself as *gott-gläubig* and took up his host's request for him to attend the morning service with his usual self-importance: "On the day before my departure the monk, Pater Franciscus, urged me to come to mass, as he wanted to bless me. 'It can't hurt,' he said. I put my arm around his shoulders and called him 'my good old Pharisee.'"[72] The fake religion in his passport didn't trouble his conscience, and he described his attitude with an astonishing lack of tact: "Without hesitation I called myself [not: I became!] a Catholic. In reality I belonged to no church, but the help bestowed on me by the Catholic priests remained deep in my memory, and so I decided to honor the Catholic Church by becoming an honorary member."[73] The men around Himmler had a slightly idiosyncratic idea of honor.

Eichmann's relief, as the *Giovanna C* finally left Genoa's harbor with about fifteen refugees on board, could still be heard in his voice when he recalled the crossing in Israel.[74] Reveling in the pathos of his salvation, he was struck by a particularly tasteless parallel between himself and earlier refugees: "Once it was the Jews, now it was—Eichmann!"[75] This comparison is revealing as well as offensive: in 1960 Eichmann was trying to convince everyone that he had been a complete unknown, but here he was, using the name Eichmann with all its symbolic meaning. On a first reading, it sounds like an incredible liberty, a perpetrator trying to rank himself alongside his victims—but on second glance, it reveals Eichmann as exactly what he was: a man who stood in irreconcilable opposition to the Jews, and who knew that other people saw him that way too. They would immediately understand the juxtaposition of Jews with Eichmann, which rested on "the famous name Eichmann." It was surely no coincidence that Eichmann remembered these feelings as he cast his mind back to the last leg of his escape. He felt that the power of his old name promised the opportunity to make a new start in his new homeland: "I knew that in this 'promised land' of South America I had a few good friends, to whom I could say openly, freely and proudly that I am Adolf Eichmann."[76] Friends who would help him precisely *because* of who he was. From the start, Ricardo Klement had been just a name on an identity document. The crossing to Argentina would give Eichmann back his freedom and his name.

INTERLUDE

A False Trail in the Middle East

Eichmann (M) Adolf currently Damascus.
—Heading of the West German intelligence
service file on Eichmann, 1952

"When the ship, the *Giovanna C.*, left the harbor at Genoa," Eichmann would write in Israel, "I felt like a hunted deer that has finally managed to shake off its pursuer. I was overcome by a wave of the sense of freedom."[1] If this really was how Eichmann felt on his Atlantic crossing in summer 1950, his hope was justified. He was being hunted, but none of his pursuers suspected he was on his way to Latin America. Eichmann had played such a canny game of hide-and-seek that, prior to his arrest ten years later, no one had hit upon his refuge in northern Germany. Speculations about his initial hideout all centered on the region most often associated with Eichmann: Austria. They could imagine him there, near his family and in close contact with his old comrades. After Eichmann's actual escape route became known in 1960, people were quick to pour scorn on Simon Wiesenthal[2] for his conviction that Eichmann was "in close contact with the underground movements '*Edelweiss*,' '*Sechsgestirn*' [Constellation of Six] and '*Spinne*' [Spider]." He believed these secret Nazi cells were the pillars that supported ODESSA, because *Spinne* "had its headquarters in the Syrian embassy in Rome."[3] But Wiesenthal was by no means the only person to fall for this rumor. Even the CIC agents were familiar with it,[4] and the same stories featured in confidential reports from the Upper Austrian Security Agency in Linz. A former SS man had given them a detailed story about Eichmann financing a transnational organization, but the story was so overblown, it would have made anyone suspicious. The informant claimed that SS general Paul Hausser was one of the underground's ringleaders—a slight problem with this idea being that Hausser remained interned in a prisoner of war camp until 1949. Notes on these stories were entered into the files of the West German intelligence service[5] and the CIA,[6] but there was no hint of northern Germany as Eichmann's hideout anywhere before 1960. Disguising himself as Otto Heninger on the Lüneberg Heath was an undeniable masterstroke by the fugitive Adolf Eichmann.

In 1950, with the exception of Eichmann's family and the people who had provided him with direct help (most of whom claimed not to have known exactly whom they were helping), no one guessed that Eichmann was now bound for Argentina. His consistency and self-discipline, staying in the underground and trusting only the right people, helped him remain undiscovered; but the key to his success was the false trails he had started to lay at the end of 1944, as he bade farewell to his comrades. In 1946 he disappeared from a prisoner of war camp and vanished into thin air. When rumors that he was in Austria turned out to be false, everyone assumed he had put his plans into action and found refuge in the Middle East, with Amin al-Husseini, the grand mufti of Jerusalem.

Everything that people had heard about Eichmann up to this point seemed to point to this plan: his supposed gift for languages; the friendship he claimed to have with the grand mufti and the Arabs; the legend of his birth in the Templar colony of Sarona. There was also his fanatical hatred of Jews, and his oft-repeated willingness to fight "Jewry" to his last breath, using every means at his disposal. Eichmann made clever use of clichés, in the stories he told as well as in the image of himself he presented. The traveling murder expert had simply moved on, going where the work took him. The first attempts to track him down show just how convincingly Eichmann had promoted these fantasies.

The first lengthy article appeared in *Der Weg*, the Berlin journal for Jewish questions, on August 16, 1946, headed "No Trace of Karl Eichmann."[7] The article, sections of which were subsequently reprinted in newspapers, not only contained that famous confusion of Eichmann's forenames (Otto Adolf) with those of his father (Karl Adolf); it also gave a detailed history of the Adviser on Jewish Affairs. It mentioned Eichmann's typical patterns of speech and his changing appearance. (The text was based on several different reports from his contemporaries.) He was suspected of being in a DP camp, where he could disguise himself as a victim; people even thought he could have had plastic surgery to alter his face. The article announced that it was the task of Jewish survivors to find Eichmann and bring him to trial.

In January 1947 the *Jüdisches Gemeindeblatt für die britische Zone* (Jewish Community Paper for the British Zone) carried an equally detailed article under the programmatic headline "The Man We Are Looking For."[8] "Karl Eichmann," it said, was a man of around thirty-five, "young, slim, tall, blonde, blue-eyed, studied theology." He had been "the Nazis' most capable tool in their persecution of the Jews." The article repeated the legend of the perfect Hebraist: born in Sarona, he returned there in 1936 to establish contact among the mufti, Himmler, and Hitler. He had been seen for the last time in Theresienstadt. He was now suspected of "masquerading as a Jew" in order to hide among them. "He may also have returned to Palestine to continue playing his games there as an illegal immigrant, perhaps as a Jewish terrorist?" After the end of the war, the fear was widespread that the murderer Eichmann might have found refuge among his victims. Even Simon Wiesenthal expressed that fear in his short book *Großmufti—Großagent der Achse* (Grand Mufti—Great Agent of the Axis Powers). Its lengthy chapter on Eichmann closed with the speculation: "Eichmann, the number-one enemy of the Jews, has still not been arrested. We cannot rule out the possibility that this greatest of all criminals used his knowledge of Yiddish and Hebrew to disguise himself as a Jew in a DP camp, or to flee to his Arab friends in the Middle East, posing as an illegal Zionist immigrant."[9] The illustrated volume also contained a photo that Wiesenthal mistakenly believed depicted Eichmann.

Léon Poliakov published the first real photo in 1949, in his article "Adolf Eichmann ou le rêve de Caligula" (Adolf Eichmann or Caligula's Dream).[10] The French text was hardly discussed in Germany—which makes it all the more surprising that Eichmann was aware he had been compared to a Roman emperor who was a notorious madman and a rabid anti-Semite. Eichmann claimed to be either flattered or insulted by the comparison, depending who he was talking to. Poliakov refuted the Sarona legend and quoted witness statements and documents from the first Nuremberg trial, but the most important thing was the photo. For the first time, people were able to see what Eichmann looked like—or rather, what he looked like before he entered the SS. This image of a languorous youth, not wearing a uniform or striking an arrogant pose, fired speculation about what people saw as his typically Jewish appearance. When Willem Sassen later asked him about it, Eichmann insisted the picture had been retouched: he had never worn a tie like that, and the facial expression was not his either.[11]

The suspicion that Eichmann's escape route might have taken him south was given weight by a number of SS men who really did arrive in the Middle East, seeking not just refuge but a new assignment. In summer 1948 the *Jüdisches Gemeindeblatt* published an article about an "SS general in Arab service" whose name was Hans Eichmann and who was born in Palestine.[12] In addition to the transatlantic escape network, people were helping Nazis reach the Middle East.

The Jewish survivors naturally felt far more threatened by the idea of Nazis in North Africa than in South America. The survivors still had vivid memories of the moment when Rommel, Hitler's "Desert Fox," had positioned his units outside Jerusalem, and they sensed danger in a German-Arab alliance. Simon Wiesenthal admitted that this fear had prompted him to make a knowingly false announcement to the world, about Eichmann's phone call to his family from Cairo. Wiesenthal, and a friend who was a correspondent for the United Press news agency, decided the time had come "to give the Arabs a fitting accomplice." The news was given to the Israeli press via Radio Austria, and from there it reached the rest of the world, serving as "propaganda for the Jewish side."[13] An article in the New York newspaper *Aufbau* on August 27, 1948, shows the impact of this move, but also what it owed to rumors that had been circulating for some time.

EICHMANN IN CAIRO

Even before the attacks [on Jews] began in Cairo, news came from Vienna that the notorious Gestapo agent Adolf Karl Eichmann had fled to Egypt and was living in Cairo under a false name, with false papers. Eichmann escaped from a camp in Regensburg and vanished without trace. One day Eichmann's relatives, living in Linz (Upper Austria), received a message that made them suspect the wanted criminal must be in Cairo.

According to reports from Wolfgang Bretholz, . . . several hundred Jews were killed during the days of terror in Cairo. The pogroms were planned, and there had clearly been lengthy preparations for them.

It is possible that Eichmann had a hand in this. Eichmann, born in Sarona near Tel Aviv, speaks fluent Arabic and is familiar enough with Arab customs that he is able to pass himself off as an Arab without arousing suspicion. As you will recall, it was also Eichmann who brokered the first connection between the mufti and Hitler. The mufti lives in Cairo, and has arranged accommodation and employment for other former Gestapo people, as the report from Vienna also says. Cairo has become a haven for numerous wanted Nazi criminals.

Eichmann, who also speaks Yiddish and Hebrew, is famed as a "specialist" in Jewish questions. He organized the deportation of Jews from Berlin, Vienna, and Prague, and is one of the principal people responsible for the murder of six million Jews in the death camps.

This story reflects more than the usual paranoia of former victims, or pro-Israeli propaganda. The false trail that Eichmann laid was the route that some of his former subordinates, like Alois Brunner, really took. In spring 1952 the German press began discussing the role played by German National Socialists in Egypt—again, with reference to Eichmann.[14] Although further research is needed, this role is now undeniable. Similar claims were made in reports by the German and American intelligence services, alleging that Eichmann, whom a local informant had confused with other Nazis on the run, had converted to Islam.[15] The root of these suspicions lay in the fact that no one knew where Eichmann was or where he was heading. And this was unsettling, because people's interest in seeing him arrested had not diminished. They were following every finger that was pointed, and Eichmann had seen to it that one of them pointed toward the Arab world. Without this deliberate misdirection, Wiesenthal's Cairo story would not have had such an impact.

Speculations about Eichmann's supposed escape to the Middle East were so persistent that they can be found even in early books written about Eichmann after 1960. Alternative escape stories have continued to surface, according to which Eichmann left Germany in 1948 and went either to Spain or to the Middle East before finally fleeing to Argentina. In 1959 the German journalist Hans Weibel-Altmeyer was offered the mass murderers Alois Brunner and Adolf Eichmann "for sale." The reporter, who had his photo taken with Amin al-Husseini, said that the former grand mufti had claimed to know exactly where both these gentlemen were.[16] After Eichmann was kidnapped, Quentin Reynolds reported that he had initially gone to Syria under the name Karl Brinkmann, stayed with Alois Brunner and Walter Rauff, and then traveled through Lebanon, Iraq, Egypt, Jordan, North Africa, and Saudi Arabia, where he had used the names Eckmann and Hirth. Only then had he fled to Buenos Aires, via Spain and Genoa.[17] As clearly false as these stories were, they demonstrate that traumatized victims of the Nazi regime were not the only people who believed them.[18]

If something positive can be taken from the many pages of erroneous escape stories, it is that in the end, even these false trails contributed to Eichmann's downfall. In late 1959, when the right people had finally discovered Eichmann's whereabouts and were plotting his abduction from Argentina, it was vital that Eichmann and his friends believed they were safe. With the help of his Israeli allies, Fritz Bauer, the attorney general from Frankfurt who had tracked Eichmann down, reignited the old rumors: new articles about Eichmann appeared in the press, now claiming he was in Kuwait. Eichmann was ultimately caught out using one of his own lies.

Nevertheless, during those first five years after the war, no trace of Eichmann could be found anywhere. Not that people weren't following up every lead—the need for revenge was too great. Vengeance squads were busy compiling hit lists and going in search of the people who had tortured them. "The method of those seeking revenge was simple," Tom Segev observed, having spoken to former members of these hit squads. "They disguised themselves as British military policemen and appeared at their victims' houses in a military pickup truck, its license plates obscured with mud. They would knock on the door, ascertain the identity of the man, and ask him to come with them for some sort of routine procedure. In general, there were no problems. They would take their victim to a predesignated location, identify themselves, and shoot him."[19]

Naturally, Eichmann was also on a hit list. In 1966 Michael Bar-Zohar, an Israeli author who had excellent relationships with David Ben-Gurion and Moshe Dayan, managed to speak to the leader of the unit that had hunted Eichmann. As they were carrying out surveillance on Vera Eichmann, the men noticed that she and her brother-in-law often went to a secluded villa. They followed her and Eichmann's brother to this house, in which four men were living a decidedly secretive life. The four men left the premises only at night and received provisions covertly. One evening the team accosted the man they took to be Eichmann as he was taking a walk, and said they were from Palestine. He replied arrogantly, "You can't do anything to me," whereupon he

was shot and fatally wounded.[20] Many years later Tom Segev spoke to
Shimon Avidan, who had been part of that team. Avidan told him that
everyone was convinced they had caught the Adviser on Jewish Affairs,
but Avidan had been less sure.[21] Eichmann, who read about the incident
later in a magazine sent from Austria, always spoke of this execution
with a strange pride.

Argentina afforded Eichmann temporary protection. The reason he
had avoided detection thus far was not only his clever choice of hiding
places but also the fact that no one thought him capable of living in
the shadows for long. The agile, grandiloquent, and ambitious image
maker that Eichmann's colleagues and victims had encountered during
his glory days was sure to seek out a new "task." He was entirely unsuited
to a sedate, anonymous existence. The vehemence with which he had
always propounded his National Socialist ideology made it seem highly
implausible that he could just resign himself to the new era and its legal
norms. Eichmann's need for action and admiration was imprinted so
clearly on people's memories that from 1946 on, rumors circulated of
him having plastic surgery on his face, so that he could take up a prominent position once again without being recognized by his surviving victims.[22] People kept a particular lookout for an identifying scar above his
left eye,[23] the result of a motorcycle accident in his youth.[24] It seemed
unlikely that Eichmann would want to remain in the underground.
How could someone who had been a member of the master race, over-
stepping the boundaries of human nature to such a degree, be satisfied
with a nameless existence in some little town somewhere? Could Adolf
Eichmann ever really stop fighting for his insane ideals? However far
Eichmann's pursuers were from discovering him in those first years, this
estimation of his character was ultimately proved correct. Sitting in an
Israeli cell in 1961, pondering what had caused him the most suffering
after 1945, his answer was clear: "the mental burden resulting from the
anonymity of my person."[25]

EICHMANN IN ARGENTINA

Vera, think of it this way: what would have happened if one of the many bombs had got me during the war. This way, Fate gave us all those extra years. We must be grateful to him for that.
— Adolf Eichmann, farewell letter to his wife, May 31, 1962

1

Life in the "Promised Land"

On July 14, 1950, the *Giovanna C* reached Buenos Aires harbor with its cargo of Third Reich imports, and Adolf Eichmann set foot on Argentine soil for the first time. Years later he would still have a vivid memory of the moment: "My heart was filled with joy. The fear that someone could denounce me vanished. I was there, and in safety!"[1] From his observation, one might almost think he was a prodigal son returning home, not a man stepping out into an unknown land. Where other émigrés—particularly those traveling on false papers—might have been contending with feelings of uncertainty, or at best curiosity and a sense of expectation, Eichmann remembered feeling nothing of the sort. He had it far easier than most, of course: he was not only traveling with old comrades, but was greeted at the harbor by yet more willing helpers and was immediately absorbed into the exile community. At first, he stayed in a guesthouse that was used to accommodate newly arrived Nazis. On August 3 he presented his proof of identity, along with his application for Argentine personal documents. He was now officially seven years younger, and his name (spelled the Hispanic way, with one c) was Ricardo Klement. He had been born in Bolzano on May 23, 1913, was unmarried, Catholic, a technician by trade, and stateless. Before long Horst Carlos Fuldner, the German-Argentine people smuggler who had arranged papers for him in 1948, found him an apartment in Florida, a well-to-do part of the city. Eichmann moved in with another new Argentine, Fernando Eifler. A stopgap job in a metalwork shop provided him with an income. He worked under an engineer who, in an earlier life, had been a specialist adviser to SS *Obergruppenführer* Hans Kammler, the leader of the SS's civil engineering department; he had also been responsible for building concentration camps and extermination facilities.[2] The engineer offered to keep Eichmann on, but like many other German fugitives, Eichmann had set his sights on something better. "One day," as he would later recount, "a former *Untersturmbannführer* from the Waffen-SS contacted me to let me know that 'the organization' had found a position for me. A new company, headed by Argentines and Germans, was going to build a hydroelectric plant to provide electricity in the city of Tucumán, at the foot of the Andes, in the north of the country. And I was to take up a management position, as a lead organizer."[3] The new company, which had coincidentally been registered a week after Eichmann's arrival, was called CAPRI—Compañia Argentina para Proyectos y Realizaciones Industriales, Fuldner y Cía. As Uki Goñi reports, the Argentines joked about the "Capri Fisherman," playing on the lyrics of a contemporary German song. They referred to the firm as the Compañia Alemana para Recièn Immigrados (the German Company for Recent Immigrants).[4] The company was, as they suspected, a Perón-sponsored cover organization for Third Reich technocrats, which existed thanks mainly to a large government contract for developing hydroelectric plants. It was a kind of occupational therapy for those who had recently arrived, only very few of whom were qualified for their jobs.[5]

Eichmann worked for the company's project office, as part of a surveying team that, over the following years, would employ up to three hundred people in the remote province of Tucumán. Geographically speaking, Tucumán was an ideal location for a plant, and until 1955, it was governed by Fernando Riera and Luis Cruz, members of Perón's party. During this period, the province had just over seven hundred thousand inhabitants. It lies in the northwest of Argentina and stretches to the eastern mountain range of the Andes. From the savannah-like Sierras Subandinas, the landscape becomes first hilly, then mountainous. Apart from the subtropical climate, with average temperatures ranging from 77 degrees F in the summer to 55 degrees F in the winter, it must have reminded Eichmann a little of Austria. The living conditions, however, were not quite as middle class as his family's in Linz. Tucumán's principal industry was sugarcane; hydroelectricity would bring modern technology to the region and take advantage of its high levels of precipitation. It was a simple life but not without comfort. At first Eichmann lived in the south of the region, in La Cocha, where CAPRI's project office was located and where the company had rented a house and two housekeepers for him.[6] This was no solitary existence: trips to the capital city, eight hundred miles away, were also part of his new life. Whenever he stayed in Buenos Aires, he had use of a desk in the firm's office at 374 Avenida de Córdoba. Hans Fischböck, a former SS *Brigadeführer* who had been the Nazis' finance minister in Austria, overseeing the systematic theft of Jewish property, worked in the same building, one floor up.[7] Elsewhere, Eichmann may well have been reunited with many more old acquaintances than we know about. Berthold Heilig, for example, also found work with CAPRI, through Karl Klingenfuß. He had initially sought help from Ludolf von Alvensleben, Himmler's former chief adjutant and the highest-ranking Nazi in Argentina, and Eduard Roschmann, who a few short years previously had been in charge of the Riga Ghetto.[8] In expat circles, finding the right people was easy. Klingenfuß had worked in the German Foreign Office's "Jewish Department," and until 1967 he would be the head of the German-Argentine Chamber of Commerce. Within the Sassen circle, Eichmann referred to him succinctly as "[Eberhard von] Thadden's representative."[9] He was involved in the deportation of ten thousand Jews from Belgium—though after the war, he claimed that he had begged to be given a different position to avoid it. Klingenfuß, who was friends with Johann von Leers, was well aware of who Eichmann was and what he looked like.[10]

Eichmann would later tell the Sassen circle about meeting Erich Rajakowitsch in Buenos Aires in 1952. He had been a close colleague, whom Eichmann personally recruited for the Vienna Central Office in 1938. A lawyer, he had previously distinguished himself in the commercial exploitation of passports for Jews, and he had seemed like the ideal SS man and legal mind for Eichmann's department.[11] Eichmann was proved right: as his "adviser on Jewish affairs" in Holland, Rajakowitsch had been jointly responsible for the "successful" deportation of around one hundred thousand people. A lot of German was spoken on the streets of Buenos Aires.[12]

Eichmann also met old colleagues and associates in Tucumán. Armin Schoklitsch had been the former director of the Polytechnic in Graz, as well as an SS man and an SD informer. He was now the scientific head of the Tucumán project. A civilian once more, he wasn't the only fugitive from Styria: several other members of its former *Gauleitung* were working in Tucumán. The NSDAP district leader in Brunswick, Berthold Heilig, and several regular SS men had also settled down there.[13] Heilig's children still remember Eichmann, with whom their father occasionally had a beer and made plans for the future—though Heilig's position at CAPRI was never as good as Eichmann's.[14] Herbert Hagel, former secretary to the gauleiter of Linz, was also employed there. In 1944–45, it had been his job to transport valuables stolen from Hungarian Jews to Altaussee. In an interview in 1999, Hagel said quite openly that, in Tucumán, he had asked Eichmann about the real number of Jews killed. Eichmann answered: "I don't know how many died—half a million maximum."[15]

The episode has a far more interesting aspect than Eichmann lying about figures: during this period, he was quite clearly using his true identity. He was able to do so because he was surrounded by people who would have recognized him anyway. Men like Hagel knew Eichmann was the right person to talk to if you wanted to find out about the extermination of the Jews and the number of victims involved. Eichmann's reputation as the one surviving insider with an overview of the murder quotas preceded him to Argentina. Another CAPRI employee, Heinz Lühr, who seems to have socialized with the major figures of the Third Reich without being initiated into their circles, described the CAPRI community in Tucumán as a place where "everyone was hiding from his own past." But Eichmann's reserved manner piqued Lühr's curiosity, and he asked rather too many questions. Schoklitsch's wife took him aside and admonished him: "Herr Lühr, leave the past alone, that man has had troubles enough in his life."[16] People in this community weren't alone in hiding from their pasts; they were sympathetic and provided mutual protection against curious but clueless outsiders. CAPRI was the ideal retreat for oppressed mass murderers.

Eichmann's traveling companion Herbert Kuhlmann oversaw the equipment for the project and quickly ascended the firm's hierarchy. Meanwhile Eichmann's work lay in raising water levels, which meant traveling long distances on horseback with a troop of men. Someone always had a camera, and he stopped shying away from pictures. "Tucumán was a happy time," he would later recall. "I also had the opportunity to indulge one of my greatest pleasures: riding. I spent many hours in the saddle, on horseback treks."[17] Eichmann looks relaxed as he poses in the countryside, in a cable car, and even on his horse. Wearing a poncho, surrounded by colleagues; climbing to a plateau with Argentina's highest mountain in the background; working in the rain; clad in white and riding a galloping gray horse in the sun—the images could have come from a cigarette ad. Life in Argentina had taken away his horror of being seen and recognized. He liked his new life and the recognition he got from the people around him.

Holding the position of "management expert" didn't just mean lead-ing a troop of men on a surveying expedition; Eichmann also paid reg-ular visits to Tucumán University. Here he met better-qualified fellow fugitives and new associates, like the professor José Darmanín.[18] In 1993 Darmanín would still remember the man who had regularly brought his colleague Schoklitsch the survey results, and had so enjoyed chatting about the country and its people "in good French." Eichmann clearly hadn't lost the knack of winning people over and dazzling them with his linguistic abilities. He had last studied French at school and in reality spoke and understood only a few words of the language.[19] This talent would doubtless have proved useful in his efforts to learn Spanish as quickly as possible. He was eager to belong in this country, where (with a little more help from "my friends") he had been issued his first Argen-tine identity card, and permanent residency, on October 2, 1950.[20] Eich-mann was deeply impressed by Argentina's hospitality. As a National Socialist, he wasn't used to a country treating foreigners this way.

A Christmas Card from Uncle Ricardo

Friends both old and new; a new identity; a job; financial security—the conditions were now in place for Eichmann to take the next step back toward regaining his old life. He found a house in Tucumán and wrote a letter to Austria. "Six years had passed," he would later recall, "since I said goodbye to my wife and three sons, whom I had to leave behind in the little lakeside town in the Alps of my Fatherland. I had not forgotten that they would be closely watched for any clue as to where I was. But by now it might be possible to risk making contact with them. Using a ring-exchange that had also been built up by 'the organization,' my wife and I were able to send letters to each other. In 1952 the leading National Socialists in Buenos Aires arranged for my wife to be issued money by certain contacts in Germany, for the journey to South America."[21]

Eichmann wrote these words in Israel, hinting at an extensive net-work whose operations went beyond mere communication. The large population of German refugees had created not only a courier service but travel agencies, money transfer routes, a kind of welfare system, and services for problems with all kinds of papers.

Providing aid to would-be escapees was a big business in Argentina, and many immigrants derived a large part of their income from it. Hans-Ulrich Rudel was an internationally admired flying ace and the most highly decorated serviceman under Hitler, with medals including the Knight's Cross of the Iron Cross. He went into the aid business shortly after his arrival in Buenos Aires, in June 1948. He teamed up with Constantin von Neurath, a doctor of law who was named after his father (Germany's former foreign minister, who had been tried and imprisoned for war crimes in Nuremberg), to found Kameradenwerk (Comrade Work). This was a fund for legal and emergency aid, to help those who had been brought low by the failure of the Reich's final victory. His services included sending parcels, arranging money transfers, and organizing legal representation. Rudel's work was made easier by the friendship he cultivated with President Perón and the fact that he could provide expert assistance in building up the Argentine air force, which gave him government contracts and import licenses. Neurath went on to become director of Siemens Argentina S.A. and used this position to continue helping his comrades.[22] Others did what they could, taking on courier duties or donating money.

Rudel was also quick to make contact with the most successful German network in Argentina: the Dürer House. It was the front for a multilayered organization, led by a man of German descent who had been born in Buenos Aires in 1921. Eberhard Ludwig Cäsar Fritsch was a radical National Socialist, though he had never had the opportunity to put his beliefs into criminal practice, having experienced the rise and fall of Nazi Germany only at a distance, from Argentina. He had been allowed into the German Reich only once, for the World Congress of the Hitler Youth, which took place in 1935, on a huge campsite near Berlin, when Hitler-land was still eager to appear fresh and open to the world.[23] You can imagine how impressed the fourteen-year-old leader of the Argentine Hitler Youth must have been by this advertisement for the party. But instead of going to war, Fritsch had to go back to school on the other side of the world. Afterward he worked as a German teacher at the Fredericus School. He gained some publishing experience as the editor of a youth magazine before taking over Dürer in 1946.[24] With the help of financiers, he bought up the remainder of a German bookstore and opened a business that was simultaneously a lending library, an antiquarian bookstore, and an arts-and-crafts store.[25] Most important, it became a focal point for stranded, homesick Nazis.

Fritsch built on this aspect of his business by founding a publishing house. The Dürer Verlag was a contact point for people fresh off the boat, some of whom were even taken on as "editors" until something better turned up. Hans Hefelmann, a doctor of agronomy who was also one of the organizers of child euthanasia, and the head of the committee that classed people as "mentally ill," found work there. When later put on trial, he would claim that he had ended up at Dürer quite by chance and worked on publications that were "the most pernicious and criminal that existed or were rumored to exist anywhere in the world after the war." The fact that Gerhard Bohne knocked purposefully on Dürer's door a short while later and also became an editor there was a similar sort of coincidence. Bohne had been the head of the T4 Central Bureau, which had planned the murder of seventy thousand people in psychiatric hospitals who had been earmarked by the *Reichsausschuß* under Hefelmann.[26]

But Fritsch did more than draw in the criminals who had been forced to leave Germany. He also targeted the camp followers, the far-right authors with infamous names who were allowed to remain in Germany but no longer had any way of getting published. Fritsch's method was simple: he wrote letters. (These letters can now be found in the estates of these outmoded authors, in archives all over Germany.) Fritsch piqued their interest by painting himself as the spokesman for a group with political ambitions. He wanted only the best for his publishing house, with the aim of preserving "German culture." "The good old names," he said sycophantically, "are hardly to be heard today. And it is so important to get them back on the agenda."[27] He enclosed recommendations from other authors to whom he had already written,[28] making Hitler's flagship writers curious about this new offer. Werner Beumelburg asked his colleague Hans Grimm (notorious author of *Volk ohne Raum*—A People Without Space) about Fritsch. Grimm replied: "The people out there, including him, seem not just to be old party members but German expats with some backbone."[29] Fritsch became a promising contact for these writers, and above all, he began to collect addresses. He had something special to offer: the magazine *El Sendero—Der Weg* (The Path). By the end of the 1940s, the publication had begun to fuel concern in the West German press about an approaching "Fourth Reich" and powerful Nazi circles in Argentina. This pulpy magazine had an irresistible pull for dedicated National Socialists, with its Nazi ideology (including nightmarish racial theory) and fascist nostalgia—a combination of Alpine kitsch, sentimentality, and Teutonic romanticism, like a lace doily with a swastika pattern.[30]

Far-right authors were desperate to write for *Der Weg*. Wilfred von Oven, who was taken on as a Dürer author but never made it into *Der Weg*, spoke wistfully about the "world-renowned quality of this neo-Nazi magazine. Who wouldn't want to be listed alongside such admired writers as Werner Beumelburg, Hans Friedrich Blunck, Herbert Böhne, Hans Grimm, Sven Hedin, Mirko Jelusich, Hanna Reitsch, Will Vesper, Anton Zischka, to mention ... only the most important names. But I was never taken up into this Parnassus of the Third Reich."[31] Eichmann was to be more successful in this regard.

Aside from their fascination with his right-wing nationalist tone, these authors were attracted to Eberhard Fritsch for a far more tangible reason: he offered to pay them. Even his letters to potential authors usually came with a little Knorr packet, as a "small gift." Dürer's overseas authors actually welcomed the fact that they were mostly paid in grocery parcels rather than money: these people didn't know how to write anything other than "blood and soil" literature, and when faced with a ban on teaching and publishing, they had no idea what they were going to live on. For all their uplifting dreams of an all-powerful ODESSA, it was the food parcels from the EROS Liebesgaben-Dienst that actually delivered the goods.[32]

At first, Fritsch sent parcels via Caritas, Pax (a charity in Basel), and Christian Aid, but then EROS established an office at 680 Reconquista, Buenos Aires. It was no coincidence that the EROS travel service was situated in the same part of town as the offices of CAPRI and Horst Carlos Fuldner's bank. It had good reason to be there, as it was known as a "Nazi agency."[33] EROS was managed by Heiner Korn, who also headed the Argentine branch of the NSDAP and was the successor to its first leader, Heinrich Volberg, the head of the overseas arm of IG Farben.[34] They advertised in *Der Weg*. Fritsch and Korn knew each other from their Nazi Party work, and they were alternately named as silent partners. Korn, who looked after his business well into his old age,[35] built up a firm that was partly a bank and partly a money transfer business, aid organization, travel agency, and courier service. It was improvised and flexible. Its central warehouse for "charitable" aid supplies was in Düsseldorf, but it also had outposts in Switzerland, used for sending manuscripts and complementary copies back and forth.[36] Fritsch was able to offer his authors a variety of things: as well as scarce and highly prized goods like coffee, cocoa, canned meat, fat, and chocolate (which were also a black-market currency), he could provide leather shoes and tailored suits. He had contacts for money transfers, and subscribers could pay their bills directly into the authors' accounts. The letters of thanks from Dürer's freelancers were suitably effusive, though there was also the occasional complaint when unexpected fees were levied at the transport stations. Even in the best Nazi circles, it would seem, people still liked to turn a profit from others' desperate situations.

Eichmann's new home country was a land of opportunity. *Der Weg* provided pragmatic route maps for people who had been forced to flee Germany, in the form of ads for travel agencies and Kameradenwerk, along with legal aid and people-tracing services. It also printed contact addresses in Buenos Aires, from the ABC Café to the store that specialized in quality German products—and was naturally staffed by "honest German servers."

Fritsch's greatest stroke of luck came in 1948, when he met the Dutch war correspondent and SS man Willem "Wim" Sassen. Fritsch not only rented a house to Sassen and his wife and children;[37] he immediately signed him up to his publishing house. Sassen, a charismatic man with a remarkable talent for self-promotion, had a skill that the old overseas authors did not: he wrote in a fresh, inspiring, modern style of German. Writing under a number of pseudonyms, and ghostwriting for former Nazi bigwigs, he almost single-handedly raised Dürer's circulation figures to previously undreamed-of levels. Sassen was also working as a chauffeur for Hans-Ulrich Rudel when Fritsch commissioned him to write Rudel's first book, *Trotzdem* (In Spite of Everything). With his addition, the young, ambitious trio was complete.[38] Rudel, Fritsch, and Sassen, with their diverse contacts, became sworn companions. They were bound by personal sympathy, a shared National Socialist worldview, and, not least, a common eye for profit. The existence of the trio far outlasted Dürer, and their joint projects would even include the defense of Adolf Eichmann.

Rudel, the flying ace, opened doors to vital contacts all over the world and kept up the connection with Germany through the legal aid he provided to comrades in need. Fritsch's publishing house offered a refuge and a contact database. Sassen's seductive language gave voice to Nazi nostalgia and kept the hope of a National Socialist renaissance alive. Backed by the highest Argentine circles, from Horst Carlos Fuldner all the way up to Perón himself, the far-right German immigrants had a powerful organization on their side. It's no wonder that over the following years, they came to vastly overestimate their political influence.

By 1950 *Der Weg*'s circulation in West Germany had reached five figures. Distribution had largely been banned the previous year, and Fritsch tasked one of his authors with restructuring the distribution network, using intelligence service methods. The author, Juan (Hans) Maler, was a National Socialist who had been born in Harburg, near Hamburg; his real name was Reinhard Kopps. His methods didn't rely on the official mail service, meaning that distribution could be neither prevented nor checked—and they were also fast. The two German distribution centers that have come to light also have strangely familiar names: Lüneberg and Berchtesgaden.[39] The fact that the magazine was circulated regularly to 16,000 illegal subscribers in Germany, and to a further 2,500 in South Africa, tells us just how efficiently this network must have functioned. Unfortunately, in the 1960s Eberhard Fritsch instructed his wife to use the handwritten card index file of subscribers as fire lighters.[40]

Rudel hints at a crucial element of what Eichmann called the "ring circle" in his book *Zwischen Deutschland und Argentinien.* "Contact with the old homeland," it claims, was "frequent and active" in Argentina, because "almost every week one acquaintance or another takes a trip to Europe, and every week there is someone who has 'just got back from Germany.'"[41] Fritsch and Rudel were adept at making people dependent on them, and they easily convinced travelers to carry more than just their own luggage. For men like Eichmann, whose CV prohibited any return to Germany, Nazi-run organizations like EROS, and Fritsch and Rudel's willing mailmen, were the only sure way of sending letters and money home. Eichmann used this network because it was by far the most established. He worked for CAPRI and Horst Carlos Fuldner, for whom Willem Sassen also did the odd bit of work.[42] Over the years that Eichmann spent in Argentina, the circle of people around Eberhard Fritsch would play an important role.[43] The mutual trust was so great that in 1952, Eichmann charged Fritsch with taking care of the most valuable thing he had: his family. He didn't have to improvise a method of making contact with his wife and children—plenty of organizational structures were on hand, and he was clearly aware of how to use them.

Over Christmas 1950, news reached Vera Eichmann in Altaussee that "the uncle of your children, whom everyone presumed dead, is alive and well."[44] From then on, she began telling her sons her very own Christmas story, about a far-off uncle they were going to visit, who had a horse named El Bravo. The letters were presumably sent via Vera's father-in-law in Linz, for as Adolf Eichmann rightly suspected, various people were still keeping a close eye on his wife and children. Ever since Dieter Wisliceny and Wilhelm Höttl, under interrogation at the end of 1945, had told the CIC that Eichmann's family was in Altaussee, Vera Eichmann had grown accustomed to house searches and constant surveillance. At first it was just the Allies' representatives, but other hunters were soon sniffing around. Henryk "Manus" Diamant, the Romeo agent dispatched by Asher Ben Natan, had not only managed to find the first photo of the wanted man in the house of one of Eichmann's lovers; he was also getting closer to Eichmann's wife and children in his search for clues. Surveillance recommenced in 1947 at the latest, after Simon Wiesenthal prevented Vera Eichmann from having her husband declared dead. In July 1948 the family moved to an even smaller fishing village in the Altaussee commune, which did nothing to make discreet observation easier.[45] The Christmas attempts to capture Eichmann in the late 1940s had not gone unnoticed; this little community was clearly too tight-knit for anything to remain a secret.[46] Sending letters direct to the little village from Argentina would have been careless, particularly since the criminal investigator Valentin Tarra regularly questioned the mailman.[47] And in Altaussee any visit from a stranger would be spotted. Linz, however, was an ideal place for a covert exchange of information, particularly as the Eichmanns still had an electronics store on one of the main shopping streets. Eichmann's father relayed the happy news of his son's safe arrival in Argentina to his brother in the Rhineland, making it all the more certain that the Christmas greeting had originally arrived in Linz.[48]

Once again Vera Eichmann was extremely circumspect. She took care not to tell the children the whole truth, so they would be in no danger of accidentally letting it slip. They had already mentioned "nice men" to her on several occasions. "They gave us chocolate and chewing gum," Klaus Eichmann remembered many years later. "They wanted to know where Father was."[49] When Valentin Tarra questioned nine-year-old Dieter, the boy unwittingly gave out a cunning piece of disinformation:

"He told me they were going to a big house in northern Germany, and he would have a father again. His uncle in northern Germany was going to give each of the boys a riding crop, and they would be very rich."[50] Vera Eichmann had to make preparations for their trip, and her husband made sure she received the necessary money and support for their travel documents. She was able to count on the support of her husband's family. Tarra observed: "Eichmann's brother who had the electrical store in Linz began to visit more often."[51]

On February 12, 1952, the German embassy in Vienna issued Vera Eichmann temporary passports for herself and her sons. She had been able to show them a *Heimatschein* (certificate of family origin). This document had been used in Germany and Austria up to the mid-1930s as proof of nationality, giving people citizen's rights in a particular commune; *Heimatscheine* are still recognized today as proof of German citizenship.[52] Through her marriage in 1935, Vera Eichmann had *Heimat* rights to her husband's place of birth, in Solingen, and the children of that marriage inherited the same rights. The *Heimatscheine* she showed the German embassy were produced on January 2, 1952, by the regional authority in Cologne. She hadn't been to Cologne herself, so this must have been one of the services provided by the "organization." The family disappeared in summer 1952, as inconspicuously as they could. "Frau Eichmann did not register her departure with the police, hand in her ration books, or request a leaving certificate for Klaus Eichmann from the school in Bad Aussee, not wanting to advise anyone of her new address. The rent continued to be paid," as the observant Valentin Tarra later reported. By January 1, 1953, Tarra had more detailed information. "As I learned an hour ago," he wrote to Simon Wiesenthal, "Veronika Liebl-Eichmann seems to have emigrated to South America in July 1952."[53] Disappearing from Altaussee was no easy matter. Still, the family accomplished their escape just as Adolf Eichmann had done two years previously, with flying colors. Vera Liebl and her sons, Klaus, Horst, and Dieter Eichmann, traveled from Vienna to Genoa and on to Argentina, with a visa from the Argentine embassy in Rome issued in their real names.[54]

We have known since the start of 2011 that the Eichmann family's travel preparations did not go entirely unnoticed. On July 24, 1952, shortly before they boarded a ship in Italy, someone informed the

Gehlen Organization (the precursor of the BND) that "*Standarten-führer* EICHMANN is not in Egypt, but is using the alias CLEMENS in Argentina. E's address is known to the editor-in-chief of the German newspaper *Der Weg* in Argentina."[55] In contrast to intelligence that claimed Eichmann was in Damascus or Egypt, the Argentine information is incredibly precise. Even with the knowledge we have today, it still provides a couple of remarkable insights. The news clearly didn't come from an informant in Argentina, as we can deduce from the incorrect rank it attributes to Eichmann. Eichmann had been promised a promotion to *Standartenführer* at the end of 1944—a fact that had been celebrated by his department—but he had not actually received it. The judgments from the trials of leading Nazis were the only places where he was referred to as *Standartenführer,* although the judgment from the Nuremberg Trials was so well known that this information had spread throughout Europe.[56] But in Argentina, Eichmann introduced himself using the rank under which he had become notorious: he was SS *Obersturmbannführer* Eichmann from the Jewish Department, and this was how he signed dedications to comrades old and new. He chose to stick with the rank he had made into a symbol of terror for four years. In Argentina, at least, this wasn't an attempt to make himself seem less important; as we will see, he used it ostentatiously, like a trademark. In Argentina, no one would have thought to pass on information about a *Standartenführer*. The misheard name *Clemens* also suggests this is secondhand intelligence. But the card from the intelligence service file reveals much more.

With help from his Argentine contacts, Eichmann had ensured that his wife received money and information for her escape, but Vera Eichmann also needed an address in Buenos Aires that she would be able to find in case of emergency. During the four-week trip, something unforeseen might happen, and a shack in a distant province would have been a tricky place for her to locate on her own, with no knowledge of the local language. A smarter idea was to give her Eichmann's alias and the name of that reliable Buenos Aires host for German refugees, Eberhard Fritsch. It was this message that an informant, someone close to the "ring circle," conveyed to the Gehlen Organization.[57]

There could hardly have been a more precise clue as to where Eichmann was. The name of the editor-in-chief of the German newspaper in Argentina could be found in every issue of 1952: "Editor-in-chief: Eberhard Fritsch" was plainly printed in the masthead, together with his address and telephone number.[58] We could give the Gehlen Organization the benefit of the doubt here and accept that the misheard name and the incorrect rank made the information too vague for a successful search, so that "in 1952, even a thorough check would not have turned up a match," especially as Eichmann didn't even live in Buenos Aires.[59] But this assumption is an insult to the German intelligence service, whose employees should at least have been able to manage a job one might assign to a newspaper intern. The rank was no reason to be "skeptical"; this was how Eichmann was described at the Nuremberg Trials. And a "double misspelling" of the name is also nonsense: anyone operating in the Spanish-speaking world knows that C and K can be interchangeable, meaning the residents' register should be searched for both variations.[60] But most important, Gehlen now had a contact address. No special training was necessary to read Der Weg's masthead: if someone had made a call to colleagues in the BfV, which collected issues of Der Weg, they wouldn't even have needed to purchase a copy.

The only hurdle then would be getting Fritsch to talk. But that would not have required extreme measures, as the behavior of the expats around Eichmann demonstrated—just a little cunning and a good story, the tools of the intelligence service trade. The Dürer office was like Grand Central Station; it was not a secret organization carefully concealed down a back alley. The publishing house was the place to go to find old friends in Argentina, no matter where they had moved, and the names Clemens and Eichmann would have meant something to people there, even if an erroneous "s" had crept into the alias. Misheard names were a common phenomenon in Argentina, as people so rarely used their aliases in their own circles. It may be an uncomfortable insight for the German authorities, but a single check carried out in Buenos Aires would have sufficed to find Eichmann in 1952. We don't know whether it was done, but we know only too well that neither the information nor the intelligence service's response to it had any consequences.

Some might object that other, similar leads pointed to Eichmann being in the Middle East, and with such a confused mass of material, it was difficult to act on any one piece of information. Leaving aside the fact that imprecision was a common basic feature in these tip-offs, not one of the Middle East sources provided anything that was simultaneously as precise and as easy to check out as the Argentine lead, which was given to the Gehlen Organization before Vera Eichmann left Austria. Reports back from Syria and Egypt, where investigators soon reached a dead end, for obvious reasons, prove that in all those years, the German intelligence service assiduously checked out even the most fantastic of rumors. So there is no reason to suspect that the Gehlen Organization was less thorough in the case of the Argentine tip-off. On closer inspection of the index card, one detail jumps out: *Clemens* is not only quoted in the informant's report of June 24, 1952; the name also appears in the card index and the file itself.[61] Until the start of Eichmann's trial, the former *Obersturmbannführer* was suspected of having used a number of other aliases in the Middle East. However, on this index card, Eichmann's "DN" (for *Deckname,* or alias) is not Rudolfo Spee, Eckermann, Hirth, Alfred Eichenwald, Ernst Radinger, Smoel, Veres, Azar, Karl Brinkmann, or Eric.[62] The entry is simple and almost correct: "Eichmann, Adolf DN Clemens."

The tip-off and the alias remained hidden away in the Gehlen Organization's card index. It took until 1957 for the people who were openly searching for Eichmann to piece together this puzzle, using information that had been available to the German intelligence service since 1952. In 1958 the CIA noted that the BND had an old report of Eichmann living in Argentina under the name Clemens. Nonetheless at the end of 1959, when the Rhineland-Pfalz State Office for the Protection of the Constitution put some specific queries to the BND, it replied that unfortunately, nothing more was known on Eichmann's whereabouts than that he had been rumored to be in Egypt in 1952 and later in Argentina.[63]

During the shooting of his film *Eichmanns Ende* in 2009, the director Raymond Ley asked Rafael Eitan, the leader of the Israeli kidnap team, why it had taken Mossad two years to recognize the accuracy of a tip-off and put it to use. Eitan answered, with some embarrassment, that the clue had remained unheeded for two years: "We did nothing! It was only after two years that we started doing anything about it." It is about time the heads of the German authorities summoned up the courage to be this candid about the failures of their long-dead predecessors and opened their archives to the public. Instead, they leave it to a tabloid newspaper to finally make these shaming documents available to all. In the best-case scenario, West Germany simply did nothing for eight years. It was only the Israelis, and a courageous German attorney general, who stopped Germany from being guilty of inaction for even longer.

The *Salta*[64] docked in Buenos Aires on July 28, 1952, when the country was in mourning: Evita Perón, the first lady who had been held up as a saint, had died two days previously. Eichmann's helpers in Argentina took their task seriously, making sure the family wasn't being tailed by someone trying to find Adolf Eichmann. "There were several gentlemen down on the quay," Klaus Eichmann remembered. "They were nice to us. I didn't know any of them. Later in the hotel, there was another man. Mother said: children, this is Uncle Ricardo. He gave us 100 pesos, a lot of money at that time. We bought ice cream, sweets, and I bought my first cigarettes."[65] This allowed the married couple some time alone together. Eichmann had pulled it off: after seven years apart, living in the underground and working to finance their escape, he had a new life, and his family had been returned to him. Years later he would be uncharacteristically reticent about this subject, but his feelings were obvious all the same: "The reunion was indescribable."[66] As a prisoner in Jerusalem, he would be more verbose, explaining that he had been unable to tell his children who he was: "I was not allowed to be the father of my own sons. For Klaus, Horst, and Dieter, I was 'Uncle Ricardo.'" But this was only for a short time, except on paper (as his documents were still in a false name), and in the company of strangers. The legend that no one knew Ricardo Klement's true identity was part of Eichmann's effort to shield his friends and helpers in Argentina. The reunited family ate dinner together and spent the night in the hotel, then took the Pullman Express to Tucumán, and from there they continued to Rio Potrero, where Eichmann had rented a house. When they were settled, he revealed his identity to his children, as Klaus Eichmann remembered: "He just said: 'I am your father.' Nothing more."[67]

For Better, for Worse

After so many years apart, family life may not have been as harmonious as everyone involved later claimed. A house in the wilderness, with no electric lights, was a far cry from the standard of living Vera Eich-

mann had been used to in the early years of her married life. But this
gaucho existence must have been incredibly exciting for the boys, who
were sixteen, twelve, and ten—even if their strict father was also push-
ing them to learn Spanish as quickly as possible. They had to learn one
hundred words a day—exactly one hundred. Eichmann's wife brought
old memories, photo albums,[68] and greetings from the family with her
from Europe, but she carried new information as well. "I brought him
newspaper clippings," Vera Eichmann recalled, "'Murderer, Mass Murderer Eichmann,' and when he saw that, he said: 'They've gone mad, I'm
no murderer, I won't stand for it, I'm going to go back to Germany.'"
But his wife argued convincingly against it: "'That's out of the question,
I'm here with the children now, what will we do. Wait a while until the
children are older,' and he said, 'Very well, I'll wait.'"[69]

Still, the press clippings clearly reawakened the feeling of powerless-
ness that had tormented Eichmann in the northern German underground (though it had not made him any more peaceable). The rumor
quickly spread among Austrian Nazis that Eichmann had sworn to kill
Wilhelm Höttl for his testimony in Nuremberg.[70] His name had been
leading a life of its own for some time. But now Eichmann had to think
up an explanation of these headlines for his wife (and later his children).
Nobody knew better than he that it would be no easy task.

The claim that he wanted to go back to Germany and turn himself
in was not just pathetic posturing to support his "innocence." He had
worked hard to create his dubious fame, but he had not acted alone and
he knew his accomplices had got off relatively lightly in Germany by
exaggerating Eichmann's role. Being happily united with his family in
the mountains of Tucumán was one thing, but knowing that his former
colleagues were able to go on with their lives, drawing their pensions in
Germany as if nothing had happened, dampened his newfound happiness a good deal. His forgetful comrades still had a few years to go before
the thought of Eichmann would start robbing them of their sleep. Eichmann, however, could not shake off the worries about his reputation
and how he would be perceived by history, even in the early 1950s. If he
had been able to forget all about it, he could have lived quite happily as
Ricardo Klement, a harmless German immigrant, and he would probably have died a natural death in Buenos Aires at a ripe old age.

But before he set about defending his "honor," Eichmann used his
time in Tucumán to show his children this newly conquered world. He

impressed them with his new job: not every child had a father who led men through the mountains, was in charge of the dynamite, and built dams for the president.[71] They listened to the stories of his expedition to the tallest mountain in the Andes, where he had made it all the way to the high plateau. (Hans-Ulrich Rudel actually reached the summit of Aconcagua despite his prosthetic leg, as mentioned in his books.)[72] The children also met their father's new friends and colleagues, among them Herbert Kuhlmann, who seemed to lead an exciting life close to the Argentine presidential palace. Berthold Heilig's daughter remembers her whole family "going to the Eichmanns' to make orange marmalade."[73] If people had had any doubt that Klement was Eichmann, the arrival of his wife and children, who lived under their real names, would have quelled it.

"I taught the boys to ride," Eichmann said proudly, "and a few times we went to the magnificent Buenos Aires together, where I made the acquaintance of President Perón, who always had a lot of time for us Germans."[74] Once he had had direct access to the *Reichsführer*-SS, and now he was an acquaintance of the Argentine president. The idea might sound fantastical, but in fact it was not. Perón's support of the German immigrants didn't end with the generous government contracts he awarded to CAPRI. He liked to rally his new citizens around him at official receptions and on occasions when he honored the CAPRI troops with a visit. He had conversations with the concentration camp "doctor" Josef Mengele (though the latter went by his new name, Helmut Gregor), and it is entirely possible that Perón also met Ricardo Klement.

But the idyll of Tucumán didn't last long. In 1953, barely a year after Eichmann's family arrived, CAPRI went bust, and Eichmann and his colleagues lost their secure jobs. But the CAPRI troops didn't disband overnight.[75] The firm remained their point of reference for some time. Berthold Heilig and Hans Fischböck claimed they continued working "for CAPRI" until 1955. In 1960 Horst Carlos Fuldner would tell the police he was the managing director of CAPRI, a firm that was still in bankruptcy discussions and that was now called Fuldner & Hansen.[76] The actual scope of Fuldner's companies and activities is still not known.

Eichmann must have stayed in the CAPRI milieu for a while as well: Berthold Heilig's oldest daughter was in the same school class as Eichmann's son Horst.[77] Heilig's daughters lived in Argentina only from March to December 1953, which roughly corresponded to the Argentine school year. They lived with their father in Tucumán, before moving to Rosario, Argentina's third-largest city, 185 miles northwest of Buenos Aires. Another large group of German immigrants had settled in Rosario, which was known for its educational establishments. According to Heilig, CAPRI also had an office there. But something else also made this area interesting for the men from Tucumán. In 1952 the German firm Siemens had started planning a similar project there: the San Nicolás power plant.[78] The construction phase held the promise of work, especially for men with a CAPRI background. Constantin von Neurath was officially on the Siemens payroll from 1953; one of the founders of Kameradenwerk, he continued to support people in his new role. Josef Schwammberger (a former ghetto commandant who had committed multiple murders) was one of his protégés and worked for Siemens Argentina S.A. for many years. Neurath said he had hired Schwammberger in 1950.[79] Eichmann sent at least one of his children to school in Rosario, which suggests he may have thought about finding work there before he moved the family to Buenos Aires.

Tellingly, once Fuldner's business was gone, Eichmann didn't consider staying on in Tucumán and opening a café or leading some other kind of ordinary life. Even then this northern province was one of the most populous in Argentina, and he could easily have made a living there. But the prospect doesn't seem to have tempted him, which may also have had something to do with the comparatively good salary he had been earning. He spoke of getting a raise after a short time; his son would remember Eichmann's final salary at CAPRI as being 4,000 pesos per month. At around 800 Deutschmarks or US$190, it was far above the gross average income in West Germany.[80] Understandably, Eichmann was keen to continue at this level. In July 1953 he moved the family to Buenos Aires, where Ricardo Klement duly registered as a resident and received a new identity card (no. 1378538).[81] With a guarantee provided by Herbert Kuhlmann, who had quickly found another income and had fewer financial worries, the family was able to rent a little house with a garden in a northern part of the city called Olivos. The house belonged to an Austrian, Francisco Schmitt. Chacabuco 4261, the Eichmanns' new address, was certainly not a step down in the world. Olivos was one of the better quarters of Buenos Aires, and the family could make use of the city's infrastructure and its good schools. The house also had electricity. Nearby were places like the ABC Café-Restaurant and Die Eiche, where Eichmann could meet old comrades and new friends over a glass of wine. He was a sociable man; people would claim he was shy and retiring only later on, when it would seem risky to have been friends with someone kidnapped by Israelis on his way home.[82]

In 1953 the glory years of the Perón era were drawing to a close. Argentina's economy, dependent on the price of raw materials on the world market, suffered from the slump that followed the Korean War. Economic conditions were generally deteriorating. Eichmann attempted to open a laundry with two of his ex-CAPRI colleagues, but the sector was dominated by the Chinese, and the venture soon failed. Attempts to get into the textile business proved to be an equally bad investment.[83] But Eichmann was not alone, and when these projects failed, his comrades stepped in once again. At the start of 1954, he got a job as head of transport for Efeve, a large sanitary products firm with offices in the well-to-do Florida quarter of Buenos Aires. Among its investors was another German refugee, Franz Wilhelm Pfeiffer. He had an entrepreneurial spirit and a reputation for having been involved in the transport of German gold during the last months of the war, but most important, he was a friend of Sassen's and Rudel's.[84]

Eichmann's starting salary, 2,500 pesos, according to his son, was far below what he had been earning, but it was hardly a pittance.[85] He may have had some financial difficulties in the second half of 1953, but they passed before long and certainly weren't typical of his life in Argentina. Eichmann had more opportunities available to him than his modest living conditions suggest. Even as an SS careerist, he had not embraced a lavish lifestyle. He may have made use of the well-stocked pantries and cellars of the confiscated houses that were his official accommodation and accepted invitations to social events or use of an armored service vehicle—but as a private individual, he was never tempted to live the high life. In contrast to others of his ilk, he didn't abuse his position for personal enrichment. He would reproach himself for it later, as he thought out loud about this period: his family would have been much better off if he had filled his pockets. But he was proud that, even at the height of his power, he still made his peppermint tea every morning and cleaned his own boots. He embraced the frugality of a field bed and a locker.[86] Even his colleague Dieter Wisliceny, who in 1946 hadn't missed a single opportunity to place blame on his former boss, reported: "Eichmann's lifestyle was inherently modest. He had few needs." And Wisliceny had even added: "Financially speaking, I am convinced Eichmann was clean."[87]

Adolf Eichmann may have been a mass murderer, but his greed was for death tolls, not for luxury and riches. The widespread cliché of the Nazi criminal, who lost his sense of social norms along with his inhibitions about committing mass murder didn't apply to Eichmann: a life of secure prosperity had never been one of his ambitions. If it had, then it was an ambition he had every opportunity to fulfill. He had had control of bank accounts chock full of extorted money, and repeated opportunities to personally extract money from his victims. After 1945 he lived in austere conditions, to an extent that Mossad agents marveled at his threadbare clothing and baggy underwear.[88] But one fact cannot be ignored: Eichmann succeeded in bringing his family to Argentina and managed to finance food, school, and training for three children. He also took a few trips, enjoyed a vacation in the Plata del Mar, and finally bought a plot of land and built his own house. He was no failure. The myth of "a life of privation and solitude" was a lie he told in Israel to gain sympathy. It was easily spread: it corroborated the stories told by Eichmann's contemporaries who, following his arrest, naturally claimed not to have known him—and certainly not to have been on vacation with him.[89]

Financially speaking, Eichmann never had any difficulty living up to Himmler's expectation of "reputability." He only ever stole, extorted, plundered, and flaunted money on behalf of the Reich. Eichmann-in-Argentina was by no means a rich man, but neither was he badly off. He never had to be self-reliant, either in the provinces or in the capital: he benefited from being part of a community whose members all knew and helped one another. If he lacked one thing, it was the power that had come with his position in the Nazi regime, and the exciting, fast-paced life that had been filled with audiences with Himmler and visits to Auschwitz, traveling in his official car and having jovial conversations with underlings, who knew what the *Obersturmbannführer* was like when he was angry.

"I was an idealist," Eichmann liked to remind people—and an idealist works for honor and the cause, not for money and splendor. At least in theory. In practice, Eichmann could have been a silent, conscientious servant of the German Reich, attracting no attention, but that wouldn't have been enough for him: he wanted to be a man of importance. What he lacked in Argentina was a great task that would make his name in history, and the fact that he had not been entirely successful in the last one made this present lack all the more painful. There were still Jews alive in the world. Ricardo Klement got along just fine in Argentina, but Adolf Eichmann still had an old score to settle. Without that discontent, the events that followed would otherwise be difficult to explain. For when Ricardo Klement returned to Buenos Aires, a rumor spread among the ex-CAPRI workers who had moved there, one that could no longer be kept locked away in the files of Europe's intelligence services: Eichmann was alive and well and living on the Rio de la Plata.

2

Home Front

Therefore one cannot say that in 1953 Israel knew Eichmann was in
Argentina: only the file knew.   —Tom Segev[1]

In 1953, as the oft-repeated story goes, the Nazi hunter Simon Wiesenthal visited an aristocratic gentleman in Innsbruck who wanted to sell
him some interesting stamps for his collection. The conversation happened to turn to Nazis: Wiesenthal had started the collection on the
advice of his doctor, to distract him a little from his fixation on hunting
criminals. At this point, his fellow collector fetched an envelope with
some particularly attractive colored stamps, which had been lent to him
by a friend. Wiesenthal took a moment to realize that this letter from
Argentina contained a remarkable P.S.: "You'll never guess who I saw
here . . . that miserable swine Eichmann, who was in charge of the Jews.
He lives near Buenos Aires and works for a water supply company." This,
of course, quickly put an end to the distraction prescribed by Wiesenthal's doctor. Wiesenthal tried to purchase the letter, but—alas!—the
collector couldn't sell it, as it belonged to his friend. For Wiesenthal (and
here we come to the hard facts), this was final confirmation that the trail
Eichmann had laid in the Middle East was a red herring. The organizational force behind the Holocaust, the man he had been searching for
since the end of the war, was hiding in Argentina. Wiesenthal hurried
home and wrote a letter dated March 24, 1953, to Arie Eschel, the Israeli
consul in Vienna, telling him about this incident.[2]

Wiesenthal gave a more sober description of the episode a few months
later, in a letter to Nahum Goldmann, the president of the World Jewish
Congress in New York—although he claimed there that the incident was
more recent: "In June 1953 I met one Baron Mast, who was an intelligence officer in the Austrian Armed Forces, and afterwards worked
for the American and German intelligence services. Mast, a monarchist
with every fiber of his being, and an anti-Nazi and anti-Communist, . . .
showed me a letter that a former officer from Argentina had written

him. The letter was dated May 1953, and it said that the writer had met Eichmann at this time in Buenos Aires. It also said that Eichmann was employed on a building site for a power station somewhere near Buenos Aires."[3] We now know that Simon Wiesenthal was holding the truth in his hands, seven years before the Mossad team took Eichmann prisoner. The only thing that remains unclear is the extent to which he was aware that it was neither a love of stamps, nor pure chance, that had brought him this information.

Baron Heinrich "Harry" Mast, fifty-six years old in 1953, was not just a man of independent means with a passion for stamps. He was an experienced agent who had worked for the Vienna intelligence service and then for Admiral Wilhelm Canaris, the head of the Abwehr, Germany's military intelligence organization. After the war, he had secured large parts of the Canaris archive and the state secrets it contained. "Count Bobby" was recruited by the American secret service shortly after the war ended. He and a friend invested in a publishing house in Bad Aussee, and in 1951 he started building up the Austrian branch of the Gehlen Organization, the German intelligence service that would become the BND in 1956. Wiesenthal was aware of this fact: contrary to his story of a serendipitous meeting between two stamp collectors, he had met Heinrich Mast before, and Mast had introduced himself as a Gehlen employee.[4]

Heinrich Mast had been brought into the Gehlen Organization by a man with just as much ambition as he had—a man who, during this period, was one of his generation's most successful retailers of Nazi history: Wilhelm Höttl, the same Wilhelm Höttl whom Adolf Eichmann once thought his friend. Mast employed Höttl in his publishing house. Höttl and Mast worked for Gehlen for a short period, and in 1951 they went over to the Heinz-Dienst (FDHD), the competitor organization to Reinhard Gehlen's intelligence service, founded by Friedrich Wilhelm Heinz in 1950 with direct backing from German chancellor Konrad Adenauer.[5] Adenauer wanted his own source of information, independent from the Allied powers, particularly when it came to developments in East Germany, the former Soviet-occupied zone that had become the GDR. Of course, the FDHD was not completely independent of the Allies either. But the real problem in its Linz branch was actually posed by Mast and Höttl themselves, who called their little club "XG" and tended to act on their own authority. Höttl in particular was so adept at juggling his relationships and pulling off confidence tricks that at times he probably forgot exactly who he was working for. He cared more for money than for loyalty, and his ambition knew no bounds. In the year before the Wiesenthal episode, he had tried to establish an intelligence service base right in the middle of Franco's Spain, partly to spy on North Africa but also to spy on political groups in Argentina.[6] Höttl specialized in making big promises, and he considered Josef Adolf Urban one of his main competitors. One reason the CIA and the other services would eventually part company with this oracle was that more than a few pieces of "information" that he gave them turned out, on further investigation, to be entirely made up. This unenviable experience was repeated by numerous historians who approached Höttl in later years, sometimes with disastrous consequences for their work. Peter Black notes with annoyance: "In many cases, the surviving documentation does not support his speculations or reveals some of his anecdotes to be inaccurate."[7]

But too many people didn't notice the problem, and Höttl continued to appear indispensable. Not long after Simon Wiesenthal reported Mast's letter with the colorful stamps, Wilhelm Höttl was arrested[8] on suspicion of being involved in the Ponger-Verber affair, working with two spies from the Soviet Union. The authorities clearly didn't put much past him. During the interrogation, which was carried out in quite a conversational tone by the CIA, among others, Höttl said that Curt Ponger had contacted him on behalf of the American Jewish Joint Distribution Committee or "some other Jewish organization" and offered $100,000 for Eichmann's capture. But Höttl didn't want to work with Israeli secret agents.[9] The CIA assumed that it was not Ponger but Wiesenthal who had offered the money, as it was known that Curt Ponger and Simon Wiesenthal were friends.[10] Ponger was a Jew who had fled Austria and returned to conduct interrogations for the CIC after the war; Wiesenthal had obtained Wisliceny's statement about Eichmann though him.[11] Heinrich Mast, for his part, later wrote to Höttl that he had always thought Ponger was an Israeli spy.[12] The German intelligence service received a warning about Höttl,[13] and Heinz thought him "crude and characterless," though he continued to rely on him at least some of the time. Then Heinz too finally dropped him.[14] A month after Wiesenthal's letter, *Der Spiegel* made an effort to publicly crucify Höttl and his friend Mast for all their intelligence service work, using material from the CIA.[15] There was a general fear that Höttl could ultimately be spying for the Soviets, or for Israeli agents like Wiesenthal.

If by this point you have lost sight of the bigger picture amid all these names and connections, you will have a very good idea of the confusion created by the myriad spies of the postwar years, particularly in Austria, which was now governed by four different powers. Everyone knew and mistrusted everyone else: two men couldn't sit and have a cup of coffee together without a third man watching them and without a fourth having infiltrated all three—the whole thing was like a giant children's party with added surveillance equipment. "Against the background of this fantastic and complex network of relationships," says Tom Segev, "Mast may have had some reason to disclose to Wiesenthal that Eichmann was in Argentina."[16] Another piece of the jigsaw puzzle takes us closer to what this reason might have been: Wilhelm Höttl later claimed that he was the friend from Austria who had given Heinrich Mast the letter for Wiesenthal.[17]

If this is true—and some things certainly speak for this version of events—it means that the crucial information came from a man who purported to have been friends with Eichmann.[18] Eichmann and Höttl's relationship was multifaceted, and an understanding of it is vital if we want to comprehend not just these events but the historiography of the Holocaust. Höttl was one of the principal witnesses who condemned Eichmann in absentia at Nuremberg, and he was therefore also one of the leading witnesses to the scale of the genocide. It was he who had mentioned the notorious conversation with Eichmann in Hungary, in which the latter allegedly cited the figure of six million Jews. This testimony had made Höttl famous overnight. Höttl welcomed his fame, bolstering it at every opportunity, though he always posed as simply the man fate had chosen to bear this knowledge. A short time after Mast handed Wiesenthal his letter denouncing Eichmann, Höttl was arrested by the CIC in Salzburg, and he took the opportunity to point out his special role as witness once again. *Der Spiegel* commented on the interview: "This explanation [Eichmann to Höttl] is still the only authentic source for the figure of six million Jews murdered by the Nazis."[19] That wasn't true, as Eichmann had mentioned the number to more people than just Höttl, but it chimed well with Höttl's grandstanding. In the postwar period, Eichmann and Höttl seemed like inseparable antipodes:

Höttl's unique insider knowledge made Eichmann a wanted criminal; Eichmann's story made Höttl an authority. Their personal relationship, however, had certainly not been formed by opposition.[20]

Eichmann first met Höttl, who was nine years his junior, in Vienna, when he arrived there in 1938 to organize the expulsion of the Jews. The two men worked closely from the beginning, as Höttl headed up the part of the Jewish Office responsible for Vienna. When Eichmann needed the keys to Jewish institutions that had been sealed off, he turned to Höttl, who had custody of them. During this period, they had regular contact both in and out of the office, and Eichmann had fond memories of his conversations with Höttl, whom he admired for his education. Thereafter their contact was limited, as Höttl remained in Vienna, returning to Department IV of the RSHA once a month to give progress reports. After being transferred to the RSHA in 1943, Höttl did not stay long in Berlin and pushed ahead with the relocation of his office back to Vienna. Eichmann and Höttl became close again only in March 1944, when both men were deployed to Hungary, with different assignments: Eichmann was to deport hundreds of thousands of people to their deaths, while Höttl was sent there by the Foreign Secret Service. He acted as an adviser to the Reich plenipotentiary Edmund Veesenmayer, who relayed the murder figures back to Berlin. Both Eichmann and RSHA head Kaltenbrunner later said that no one was better informed on the situation in Hungary than Wilhelm Höttl.[21] At the end of 1944, Eichmann went back to Berlin and met Höttl again in April 1945, in Altaussee. Once the war was over, however, there was only one thing on which the two men were agreed: they really *had* been friends. They even had the same birthday. Höttl's brother-in-law was none other than Josef Weiszl, one of Eichmann's closest colleagues in Austria, otherwise known as the "Jews' emperor of Doppl." He was the whip-wielding commandant of the first camp personally initiated by Eichmann, and he later excelled as a deportation expert in France, though afterward he claimed to have been Eichmann's "driver." Weiszl, who liked to brag, could have informed his brother-in-law about Eichmann's activities at any time. But Höttl managed to make all this disappear from view by promoting himself as the key witness to Eichmann's crimes. The success of his disinformation campaign means it is still almost impossible to get a clear picture of Höttl's own activities in Vienna from 1938 and later in Hungary. He began to style himself as a resistance fighter. Meanwhile he created an image of Eichmann using dates and details that he could not possibly have known and that bore no resemblance to the truth. Using what he already knew about the extermination of the Jews, and what other people had told him about Eichmann's escape, he established his reputation as an authority on both.[22] The year 1953 was not the first time Höttl betrayed Eichmann's escape plans, even if the clues he initially gave about the Middle East proved false.

Höttl was not driven by an unusual love of truth or even a desire for justice. When it came to his close associates, like Walter Schellenberg and Ernst Kaltenbrunner, he could be extremely cagey and tended to tell lies. One of his principal strategies for protecting himself and his friends was to incriminate a small group of former colleagues. Eichmann was at the very top of this list, and with extraordinary dedication, Höttl spent the rest of his life doing all he could to flesh out and publicize his own image of Eichmann. He was deeply cunning in what he told the intelligence services, and his manipulation of historians, journalists, and filmmakers was masterly. Shots of a jovial man in a traditional Austrian jacket against an Alpine backdrop, telling Eichmann anecdotes and revealing indiscretions with a wry smile, have become part of the stock in trade of war documentaries. Tellingly, a wartime friend of his termed the media's fondness for this professional witness *"Höttelhörig"* (under Höttl's spell).[23]

Höttl used his knowledge (both genuine and assumed) to establish his reputation as an important witness to the war years, and he did a brisk trade in this knowledge with various intelligence services. But from the very beginning, he also used it to write books. Under the pen name Walter Hagen, he wrote *The Secret Front: The Inside Story of Nazi Political Espionage,*[24] an imaginative sex-and-crime version of events, told from the viewpoint of the German intelligence services. It was translated into several languages and quickly caused a furor. In Argentina, it gave rise to both criticism and anxiety. The identity of the man behind the pen name was no secret, and Höttl's gossip formed the basis for hours of discussion. There was even a long guest lecture on him in the Sassen circle. After Wiesenthal's pamphlet about the grand mufti of Jerusalem, this was the first book to contain a chapter on Eichmann's superiors Heinrich Himmler, Reinhard Heydrich, Heinrich "Gestapo" Müller, and the "Jewish question." Eichmann read that he had belonged to a tiny group that was secretly guided by "Heydrich's boundless malevolence and misanthropy." Under Heydrich's direction, this group had almost single-handedly carried out "'the Final Solution of the Jewish Problem'—that most devilish masterpiece."[25] Above all, Eichmann discovered that Höttl was peddling insider stories in public: the tittle-tattle that Eichmann had passed on to him in Vienna, Berlin, and Hungary.[26] While Höttl was becoming a best-selling author at others' expense, Eichmann had been fleeing across half of Europe, all the way to Argentina. This was no way to behave toward an old friend and comrade.

The letter to Höttl about Eichmann's location, which Wiesenthal supposedly saw in summer 1953, has never been found.[27] Neither Höttl nor Mast seems to have handed it over, or even given out copies of it, although such a letter would have fetched a considerable price even after 1960. If we choose not to assume that the letter was simply a forgery that they both feared would be discovered, the reason for their secrecy must lie with the parts of the letter that undoubtedly contained other names from Argentina—even if only that of the sender. In contrast to Mast, Höttl was respected and famous enough to have received such a letter. He was constantly swamped with inquiries from people, asking for information on the whereabouts of all manner of old comrades. In 1953 he was planning to start a business that would operate between Switzerland and South America, in partnership with Friedrich Schwend, a counterfeiter and one of his associates from the old days, who had escaped to Peru.[28] Whoever wrote the letter to Höttl in 1953 knew precisely whom he was entrusting with this explosive information: a man who earned his living by selling this sort of intelligence and was therefore unlikely to keep it to himself. Even before his first book appeared, Höttl was seen as a security risk in Nazi circles. Everyone knew he was building his postwar career on betrayal, and his old comrades believed he had sold himself to the Allies. Some people, like Otto Skorzeny, went so far as to attribute the "invention of the six million" to Höttl, who was acting out of pure opportunism.[29] After Höttl's book and newspaper articles came out, people didn't need intelligence service experience to realize that passing secret information to Höttl had a similar effect to putting it on a billboard. Whoever told Höttl where Eichmann was living must have known he was effectively turning him in.

The source of the information could have been any one of a great number of people. But from the start, Adolf Eichmann's family believed one man in particular had betrayed their father (without even knowing

about this letter). This was Herbert Kuhlmann, who had made the journey from Europe with him. "My father paid for his passage," Klaus Eichmann said in 1966. "He betrayed my father. He put it about: 'Be careful
around that Clement. He's really Eichmann. Eichmann is a swine.'"[30]
The similarity of the phrasing here is hard to ignore. Still, Kuhlmann
was not the only person with a penchant for colorful language who
might have given Eichmann away. Even in 1953, there were plenty of
ways a person could have got hold of the information: not only was
Adolf Eichmann becoming increasingly careless, his acquaintances had
started traveling back to Germany for business or pleasure, carrying
their knowledge with them.

German-Argentine Relations

By the early 1950s, the men of the Dürer circle were following events
in West Germany for more than just sentimental reasons. Their overtly
political ambitions were expressed in *Der Weg*, in increasingly direct
comments on the new democracy. The people behind this magazine
didn't hide the fact that they had no interest in any other country, not
even in a special German community in Argentina: they wanted the
return of a different Germany. They started trying to intervene in German politics and increasingly wrote for a German audience. Even if this
idea sounds as naïve today as it did in the early 1950s, Sassen, Rudel,
Fritsch, and the other authors were trying to foment a revolution in
Germany. Their National Socialist stance was primarily defined by what
they opposed: the Western integration of the Federal Republic; rearmament; the United States; and Konrad Adenauer, the man who stood for
it all. They wanted to do more than just produce the *Monatsschrift für
Freiheit und Ordnung* (Monthly Magazine for Freedom and Order—*Der
Weg*'s new subtitle). They wanted a strange kind of freedom and a palpable new order. They wanted the "building of a new Germany." For a
while, there was even talk of forming a German government in exile.[31]

The behavior of these men, who were now nicely established in Argentina, cannot be explained rationally—though closer inspection reveals
the principal motivation for their political ambitions. Anyone who has
labored under the delusion that he belongs to the world's new elite, and
who helped shape the politics of the German Reich that shook the world

for twelve years, would be incapable of resigning himself to a normal life. Hans-Ulrich Rudel phrased it memorably, with help from Sassen:

> We live on, and we certainly live better from a material point of view than many millions of our defeated countrymen. But can one really narrow one's field of vision like this, down to the most limited circle, in the space of a few years? I often . . . think back over this short time, to my last conversation with Hitler, and the idea that always got us back on our feet and kept us doing our duty during those last months of war, the great goal that had ruled my entire life until this point: the prosperity and happiness of the Fatherland. And then my present existence seems so pitiful, so small and meaningless! Is it possible suddenly to change so much, to think only of yourself and the smallest circle of your family and comrades?[32]

The end of the war, and their escape from the Allies, had thrown these men back into an everyday reality that had never really been the norm for them and that must now have seemed trivial. It was difficult to dream of world domination from the sobering context of exile in Buenos Aires. And the change hit them all the harder because they were still relatively young. The end of the war had pulled them up abruptly in the middle of their careers. Rudel was born in 1916, Sassen in 1918, and Fritsch in 1921; Eichmann, in his mid-forties, was among the oldest. But back in West Germany, people were electing a chancellor of over seventy. All this reminded the exiles of the Weimar Republic, where "the youth" had succeeded in seizing power from the old Reich president, Hindenburg, and getting rid of the hated democracy. They wanted to try the same thing again. For them, National Socialism was a mission that had not yet ended.[33]

It was not only in Argentina that people were dreaming of a second coup d'état. In the early 1950s, all the influential far-right groups were attempting to organize themselves in greater numbers. The most famous example is the group led by Werner Naumann, the former state secretary to Joseph Goebbels. He attempted to infiltrate the North Rhine–Westphalia Free Democratic Party, pursuing opaque political ambitions in West Germany—and by 1952 he had also started making contact with fascists from other European countries. The most important names here were also to be found on Eberhard Fritsch's list of authors and correspondents: the Englishman Oswald Mosley, and the Frenchman Maurice Bardèche. At the same time, the Dürer circle was attempting to build its political influence in Germany. The first step was an association with the Sozialistischen Reichspartei (SRP), a National Socialist party led by Otto Ernst Remer and the *völkisch* author Fritz Dorls. Both men were radical anti-Semites, who could potentially be very useful to anyone in the business of falsifying history.[34] The "solution of the Jewish question" was an overt part of their manifesto, though they took pains to be at least a little critical of Hitler's methods. The immediate aim was to win a large number of votes in the upcoming federal election of 1953, preventing Adenauer's victory and thereby becoming an influential voice in the conservative camp. Like Remer and his party, the men of the Dürer circle firmly believed that the majority of the population was secretly right-leaning and on their side. The SRP's first electoral victories at a national level fueled their hopes.[35] In 1951 there was clear cooperation between the far-right *Der Weg* and the equally unambiguous magazine *Nation Europa,* which had been founded that year. Willem Sassen wrote a caustic polemic against the United States and rearmament for *Nation Europa,* raising the circulation figures in Germany so significantly that the rest of the press, including *Der Spiegel,* began to take note of the publication.[36] There is also evidence of contact between Argentina and the Plesse publishing house in Göttingen, in which Werner Naumann was involved.[37] And perhaps Fritsch really did travel to Germany, as he claimed in letters to his authors, for a personal discussion on how similar waves could be made in the future with the newspaper cofounder Karl-Heinz Priester.

In summer 1952 several members of the Argentine camp traveled to West Germany. They formed close working relationships there, with positive outcomes for Fritsch's network in particular. The SRP's established network of members was integrated into *Der Weg*'s card index of subscribers, boosting circulation by three thousand. This also meant three thousand extra contact addresses for the "ring circle." A political career had always been part of the plan. The war hero Hans-Ulrich Rudel was seen as a good potential election candidate, and he traveled to Germany several times, closely observed by the Federal Office for the Protection of the Constitution (BfV).[38] Press reports even claimed that Eberhard Fritsch (who was also on the BfV's watch list) had secretly entered the country.[39] There is evidence that one of Fritsch's closest colleagues, Dieter Vollmer, moved back to Germany permanently, though he stayed in regular contact with the Dürer circle and had an intimate knowledge of their plans and projects.[40] All these travelers knew that Adolf Eichmann was in Argentina, and men looking to impress like-minded friends are not usually reticent about their sensational contacts.

Before the election, the SRP was found to be unconstitutional and was outlawed. Remer was also convicted of slandering the July 20 resistance group. The new Argentines then placed their hopes on the Deutsche Reichspartei (DRP) in Hanover, which was not a great deal more democratic. But this party had the added advantage of not objecting to a market economy—a stance that accommodated the approach of the economically active émigrés. Rudel's new contact was Adolf von Thadden, who was a similar age to Eberhard Fritsch and one of the most active Nazis of the postwar period; he would later make a substantial contribution to the rise of the National Democratic Party of Germany (NPD). By December 1952, Thadden had met Rudel, and he financed Rudel's next trip in 1953, to support the DRP's election campaign.[41] Like Remer, Thadden expected the flying ace to exude the old National Socialist glamour. Rudel appointed Werner Naumann as his political adviser after only one meeting, a man whom the *Frankfurter Rundschau* called the "spider in the web of systematic infiltration."[42] He too joined the DRP. Thadden, however, seemed disillusioned by his Argentine reimport: "Personally he seems to be a very proper man. In terms of German domestic policy, he sometimes has completely incorrect ideas, which are evidently the result of him only associating with a certain type of former comrade." Thadden, who had some fairly peculiar ideas about the future of Germany himself, was irritated by Rudel's suggestion of "getting a real populist movement going." He thought a more realistic option was to infiltrate the new democracy and use a political party to put some National Socialists in government—a goal that seemed "extremely modest" to the impatient Rudel. Thadden did, however, see the "allure of his name" and immediately recognized Rudel's drive: "In any case, he has political ambition, and may play a role in Germany."[43] He was also impressed by the Dürer circle's logistics.

Adolf von Thadden's later notes show that Rudel was anything but reserved in their meetings, chatting openly and without inhibitions. Long before Eichmann's arrest, Thadden knew that the Adviser on Jewish Affairs was living in Argentina and had connections to the Dürer circle.[44] The DRP fielded Rudel as a candidate, though nothing came of it. He didn't even fulfill the formal criteria to become an election candidate, and his National Socialist speeches kept getting him banned from appearing in public. The files that the BfV compiled on Rudel and Eberhard Fritsch in the early 1950s are still under wraps (though parts of them, at least, will apparently be classified "archivable" in the future). The German Foreign Office was also keeping an eye on these new far-right machinations. Rudel and Fritsch had been traveling around South America since 1950, collecting for Kameradenwerk and advertising the coming revolution. The German diplomatic mission in Chile had sent back alarming reports, fearing for Germany's reputation abroad in the face of so much open Nazi nostalgia. The Foreign Office was, however, reassured by the answer to its inquiry from the embassy in Buenos Aires: at the end of 1953, there were apparently only fifty to one hundred German emigrants there, and none of them were of any importance. They were therefore not worthy of being mentioned or properly counted.[45] The CIA clearly thought otherwise. In the same year, its report on the activities of German nationalists and neo-Nazis in Argentina was fifty-eight pages long.[46] We still don't know the length of the report compiled by the West German intelligence services.

In the early 1950s the many activities of National Socialists, and of fascists of whatever stripe, might look like a huge, worldwide conspiracy, but that is the one thing the postwar Nazis never achieved. On the face of it, the conditions for such an undertaking were not unfavorable. A few years after the war, West Germany was a long way from reaching the democratic consensus that the Allies had hoped to achieve with their "re-education" measures. Even so, the old faithful and their dreams of coups did not make it big in the postwar world. Taking a closer look at the pieces in this bizarre game, we can guess at the reasons. Quite apart from the fact that "an international alliance of National Socialists" was always a contradiction in terms, the men involved came from completely different worlds. As much as they wanted a conspiracy, they lacked something unifying to swear allegiance to and common aims that went beyond the purely negative. Their memories of old times were also wildly divergent. Ultimately, their conspiracy was based on an image of the past, and they had no practical ideas on how to bring about a coup in the present. And mourning the past did nothing to inspire faith in their abilities, either within their own ranks or with potential voters.

Still, the connections between the Nazis who had fled to Argentina and those in Germany and Austria were multifaceted and went far beyond sending airmail letters with colorful stamps. Even without a secret-monger like Höttl, with his multiple intelligence service contacts, in 1953 plenty of people knew about Eichmann's hiding place and Perón's power plant project. If the Gehlen Organization had followed up on the clue it received in June 1952, its agents could have discovered where Eichmann was working, a fact not mentioned in the original message. The nervousness with which the West German institutions reacted to Fritsch and Rudel's ambitions shows that they had at least some idea of who else was in Argentina. They would not have needed to pay Mast and Höttl a small fortune to obtain this information.

Eichmann on a Silver Platter

However Höttl and Mast got wind of of Eichmann's whereabouts, their decision to pass this information to Simon Wiesenthal, of all people, is worth examining more closely. At the start of 1953, anyone with a connection to the intelligence services knew what Höttl did with information, but they also knew exactly who the philatelist Simon Wiesenthal was. He had always been a loud and enthusiastic voice in the hunt for Nazis, founding the Jewish Documentation Centre in Linz in 1947 and making his own contacts with the American and Israeli intelligence services. Höttl and Mast must have been well aware of what they were doing: they were turning Adolf Eichmann in. The power plant clue was so precise that a few inquiries in Buenos Aires would have led straight to CAPRI, a company working on one of the Argentine government's largest projects. The only reason they failed to expose Eichmann was because, in classic Nazi fashion, they overestimated Simon Wiesenthal's influence. Their belief in a Jewish world conspiracy made them think of "the Jews" as a single entity.[47] National Socialist thought ascribed more influence to any little Jewish corner-store owner than even large Jewish organizations had in reality. "The Jews" were entirely focused on world domination and revenge. Outwardly, sending this letter looked like handing "the Jews" their enemy Adolf Eichmann on a silver platter. This fact forces us to ask the difficult question: who had a vested interest in this development in 1953?

When one person wants to damage another, he or she may well be acting from a personal motive like fear or revenge or from some other desire to see them suffer. Höttl doubtless knew that Eichmann had sworn to kill him for revealing his confession about the six million. But Eichmann was far away, and Höttl was no stranger to this kind of threat, having made plenty of other enemies through his work for the Allies. Dr. Langer, a member of the Sassen group, told people in Argentina that by May 1945, threats were being made against Höttl all over Vienna: "Everyone had a great hatred for Höttl. So I heard 'if I catch that fellow, I'm going to kill him' etc. not from one person, but from several of these people."[48] Wilhelm Höttl clearly took great pleasure in painting Eichmann in the worst possible light, and he seemed to envy Eichmann's fame even after he had been hanged—but it is difficult to believe that malice alone would have driven him to such lengths. If it had been Höttl's intention (or the intention of whoever made him take this step) simply to reveal where Eichmann was, he could have made copies of the letter and distributed them to the international press. But as far as we know, Höttl and Mast didn't show the letter to anyone apart from Wiesenthal in 1953. As the Germany security services' archives remain firmly closed, we can only speculate on whether Höttl and Mast could have made this move without the Gehlen Organization, the Heinz-Dienst, or the BfV knowing about it, being involved in it, or at least being informed of it after the fact.

For men of boundless ambition, one possible motive could have been the desire to raise their profile in the intelligence business. But if they had wanted to score points by tracking down a war criminal, they would surely have made their own intelligence services the first recipients of the news. But then Höttl's reputation with the American and German services was by then so terrible that an indirect approach might have seemed best. In November 1952 Höttl had become a candidate for blacklisting by the BfV. All the German and American services treated him as unreliable, for having invented one piece of intelligence after another.[49] An indirect approach via a suspected Israeli spy would, however, have been a very complex plan. Greed was not the motive, either: the letter was never sold, and Wiesenthal certainly didn't pay them $100,000, if only because he never had access to that kind of money. Even if another party had paid Mast and Höttl a princely sum for their action, the question remains why anyone would have had an interest in publicizing Eichmann's address.

What might have been accomplished if this action had done something beyond just causing Wiesenthal's heart to skip a beat and had actually succeeded in telling "the Jews" where Eichmann was? What reaction might Mast and Höttl, or their paymaster, have been expecting from Nahum Goldmann, the man whom the crazed Jewish-conspiracy theorists believed to be the supreme head of world Jewry? What could "the Jews" have done? From today's perspective, there are two possible scenarios. One of the vengeance squads that were still active could have quietly murdered Eichmann or he could have been brought to trial (as he was, later on)—provided he didn't hear that his cover had been blown and manage to find another hiding place in time. But apart from his victims, the Jews, who would have had an interest in pursuing either of these possibilities?

Höttl made a very good living from being the only person able to offer a firsthand account of what Eichmann had said. For him, having this man killed on the quiet would have one benefit: Eichmann's knowledge about the Holocaust would vanish along with him. There was one problem with the theory that Höttl and Mast were hoping the Jews would get rid of Eichmann (do the dirty work, so to speak), so that the real key witness would no longer be able to testify to the figures: it would mean they had to accept that the numbers Eichmann had quoted corresponded to the truth. Silencing someone makes sense only if you think they have something unpleasant to reveal. In 1953 few people in Germany and Austria, not even Wilhelm Höttl, believed that of Eichmann.[50]

Today it's difficult to imagine what people in the early 1950s knew or wanted to know about the National Socialists' crimes—namely, almost nothing. Most of the information to be had on the Holocaust in Germany and Austria (for those who weren't too busy making a new start to find out) came from press coverage of the war crimes trials. In a recently defeated country, these trials didn't have a particularly good reputation. Terms like "victors' justice," "propaganda statements," "atrocity stories," "collective guilt," and "vengeance verdicts" were widespread, and the number of six million seemed so extraordinary that people needed more evidence and explanations to make it even remotely comprehensible. These were not yet available in 1953. Although the first books about Hitler and National Socialism had begun to appear, there was as yet no published account of the Holocaust. Eight years after the end of the war, the only way to get an impression of this mass extermination was to study the trial documents, and very few people had access to them. Under the circumstances, the easiest reaction was to disbelieve and repress the facts. Holocaust deniers had an easy ride, when even the perpetrators could reassure themselves that "nobody knows the details."

Today we have the testimonies of the concentration camp commandant Rudolf Höß, the Wannsee Conference transcript, reports from the *Einsatzgruppen* commandos, descriptions of concentration camps, murder statistics, and of course Eichmann's testimonies, not to mention brilliantly edited collections of documents—enough secondary literature to fill a library, and more images than we can bear. In 1953 there was not a single book, aside from the Nuremberg judgment. The perpetrators and the people in the know relativized and denied everything, and the survivors had barely started finding their voices again. Even statements from the representatives of the new West Germany often sounded like stock phrases and political correctness: things people knew they had to say, without really acknowledging what they meant.[51] Aside from the people who knew exactly what had happened because they had been directly involved in the crimes, most of the population couldn't imagine that Eichmann might have anything worse to reveal. It would just be another incomprehensible witness statement that nobody wanted to hear. So why spare a thought as to why someone might want to keep this statement quiet? You would have to have been in the know to want Eichmann silenced before he started naming names. But betraying Eichmann, rather than leaving him to ride through the mountains of Tucumán in peace, was a risky business.

Things looked rather different from the perspective of vehement Holocaust deniers—people who were stubbornly clinging to a different truth. The writers associated with *Der Weg,* ex-general Otto Ernst Remer, and a frightening number of unreformed anti-Semites had such an intense hatred of Jews that they favored the idea of extermination. But they also either believed the millions of murders to be a lie, or tried to relativize those murders as far as possible. From this point of view, the figure of Adolf Eichmann, the man who knew the truth better than anyone, took on a different significance. In the deniers' world, the only truth

Eichmann had to tell was theirs: he would say it wasn't at all like people had claimed in Nuremberg, and that "the Jews" had lied about the scale of the killing. His statement would lift the burden of blame from the Germans and reveal that—as usual—the Jews had abused the truth, to gain the upper hand. One of *Der Weg*'s most successful articles was entitled "The Lie of the Six Million."[52] Written under the pseudonym Guido Heimann, this text claimed that there had only been 365,000 deaths among the National Socialists' opponents, with no systematic mass murder, gas vans, or gas chambers. All claims to the contrary were a gigantic falsification of history. A key witness was needed to refute this "lie," and even in this crude vision of history, that was Adolf Eichmann.

In the middle of the election campaign in West Germany, this alleged "lie" had gained a political dimension that would change the country. Konrad Adenauer finally brought himself to publicly acknowledge the German people's guilt and responsibility for the crimes of National Socialism. He spoke of every German's duty to Israel and to the Jewish people.[53] Pressure from the Western Allies on the issue of reparations had made it impossible to remain silent any longer. West Germany had to acknowledge the past; otherwise it would be impossible to rejoin the international community. There were protracted negotiations between the federal government and the representatives of the Jewish Claims Conference. In 1952 the government signed the Luxembourg reparations agreement, promising Israel payments, goods, and services totaling 3.45 billion Deutschmarks over twelve years, and in many people's eyes, this agreement was a scandal. For the Bundestag to ratify it, Adenauer needed the Social Democrats' (SPD) votes, as too many members of his own coalition had withheld their consent. The debate over the contract with the Jewish Claims Conference led to a huge crisis within the Christian-Liberal coalition government, and Adenauer seemed stricken. Far-right voices were not the only ones arguing against any kind of payments. Opinion polls showed that only 11 percent of Germans were in favor of the Luxembourg Agreement.[54] If the conspiracy theorists' version of Adolf Eichmann could step into this situation—a man who could produce detailed calculations showing that the Nazis' crimes had not been committed, or at least not by Germans—the consequences would be tremendous. Adenauer would be discredited, the rug would be pulled from under the whole agreement, the Jews would lose all respect on the world stage because of their "deception," and—most important—the Germans would be freed from guilt. The truth would finally come out: "the Jews" had staged the whole thing themselves, just so they could get their hands on Palestine and reap the financial rewards.

People really did think like this (and in fact, some still do),[55] as we can see from numerous published treatises featuring an ever-changing array of conspiracies. They range from unsophisticated denial to an elaborate outline of a Jewish-infiltrated Gestapo, working behind Hitler's back to stage a mass murder of Jews *by Jews*. As the deniers rode roughshod over reality, the perpetrator Adolf Eichmann mutated into a figure of hope, the star witness to this peculiar truth. The frightening extent of these paranoid hopes of redemption would be revealed immediately after Eichmann's arrest, in media reactions that did not come exclusively from right-wing publications. The articles were full of warnings to Israel about the unwelcome things Eichmann would supposedly reveal. *The New York Times* prophesied that a public trial would "do Israel more harm than good" and that "reprisals against Israel" would be unavoidable. *Der Spiegel* quoted the "first unexpected reactions" before they had even happened. The far-right monthly *Nation Europa* listed all these warnings with relish. Or almost all—*Stern*'s warning "that the State of Israel is now in danger [of] coming into the Nazis' inheritance" was apparently not worth repeating to *Nation Europa*'s National Socialist readers.[56]

Willem Sassen, the Dutch SS man, would encapsulate the deniers' delusions neatly in an interview at the end of 1960. It was, he explained, quite obvious that the Israeli government could have had nothing to do with Eichmann's capture: the Israelis were the last people who wanted Eichmann to talk, for fear that he would expose the lie upon which their country was founded. A small group of Jews acting independently— *elementos fanáticos*—must have kidnapped him, and now the truth that people had tried to suppress for so long would finally come to light.[57] As late as 1981, Adolf von Thadden, one of the most influential far-right voices in the new Federal Republic, would still hold out hope for the publication of Eichmann's thoughts from Argentina: "The 'six million' would be proved a lie, an untruth consciously disseminated over 35 years."[58] This whole tangled mess, however, had one problem: the mass murder of the Jews was not a Jewish lie but a thoroughly German idea, and Eichmann, as a German, was much too proud of having implemented the murder project to deny it. Any hope that this man could in some way free Germany of its guilt was plainly absurd. In the event, the only thing Eichmann's statements would reveal was the monstrous scale of this German crime and the immeasurable suffering of the people who had fallen victim to the German mania.

Now that we have access not only to those statements, but to more than fifty years of documentation and research, it's hard to imagine that in 1953 many people still believed that Eichmann would bring to light their idea of the truth, or that his very survival could be a threat to Israel's position and to Adenauer's reconciliation policies. The Federal Republic and postwar German society were far from stable, and "revelations," if they had been possible, would have shaken the country. This paranoid belief in Eichmann as a key witness for the far right might have been the hidden motive that made Mast show Wiesenthal the letter from Argentina. It would have allowed people to threaten "the Jews" with Eichmann's testimony, and it could have unleashed explosive political consequences. Where people's reasoning runs so far into madness, their actions are not based on reality.

Wiesenthal was now certain that all the information he had obtained in the hunt for Eichmann would lead to something. The clue to where Eichmann was living, from Wilhelm Höttl and Heinrich Mast, was not the only one he received during this period. A friend of Vera's sister near Linz told him that Vera had emigrated to South America and that "in July 1953 I was in Vienna and . . . had a talk with the Director General for Public Security, Min. Rat Dr. Pammer, and the conversation happened to turn to Eichmann. Pammer also told me he had information that Eichmann . . . was living in Argentina." Wiesenthal had already been given another, equally portentous hint in a letter from none other than Amin al-Husseini.[59] This letter, received by an acquaintance of Wiesenthal's in Munich named Ahmed Bigi,[60] who translated it for him, contained a direct question from the mufti "on Eichmann's whereabouts." Wiesenthal received this news with a degree of mistrust. It could, of course, have been "a cunning move on the mufti's part." The question to Bigi could have been an attempt to deflect suspicion that Eichmann was living in the Middle East. Wiesenthal spoke no Arabic, but his personal connection with Bigi made him believe that the letter genuinely contained what Bigi had translated for him. When it then emerged that the inquiry had come not from al-Husseini but from another Muslim who had worked for Hitler's Foreign Ministry, it changed nothing for

Wiesenthal. He could "of course not guarantee 100% that Eichmann is in Argentina," as he wrote to Nahum Goldmann,[61] but he was certain that the headlines about the "Reappearance of Eichmann in Tel-Aviv," the "Mass Murderer as Military Adviser to the Egyptian Army," the "SS General in the Middle East," or the "German Adviser" to the mufti were simply wrong.[62]

Within a relatively short space of time, Wiesenthal received several hints that Eichmann was to be found in South America and not the Middle East. But surprisingly, although he passed his new information on to all his contacts, from the Israeli consulate in Vienna to Nahum Goldmann—and there is also evidence it also reached the CIA[63]—nobody stepped up the hunt for Adolf Eichmann. The information was practically everywhere, but it was ignored. The non-German intelligence services showed as little enthusiasm for bringing this war criminal to justice as the Gehlen Organization had the previous year.

Anyone who had hoped that divulging information about Eichmann's whereabouts would have an impact was disappointed. Wiesenthal was hardest hit by the lack of interest. In his memoirs, he painted himself as the lone campaigner for a justice in which hardly anyone else was interested: "I feel that, along with a few other like-minded fools, I was quite alone."[64] The politics of the day were more important. A cold war was going on between the world powers, a hot war had broken out in Korea, and "against this background the picture of Adolf Eichmann was fading. If I tried to talk to my American friends about him, they would reply a little wearily: 'We've got other problems.'"[65] Konrad Adenauer had made his declaration of responsibility, but that didn't mean he wanted a thorough search for those responsible. Immediately after the Luxembourg Agreement was finalized, people started asking questions about some surprising people working for the Foreign Office. Adenauer announced to the Bundestag: "In my opinion, we should call a halt to trying to sniff out Nazis."[66] For the next few years, the chancellor's word became law for German institutions.

3

One Good Turn

You must understand that I was reluctant to release a subject expert and specialist like Eichmann from Head Office, and today he seems irreplaceable to me.

—Franz Alfred Six, on his employee, 1938[1]

Although Eichmann could have known nothing of the letter sent to his former friend Wilhelm Höttl, he was not oblivious to the Dürer circle's political ambitions. Rudel was openly making plans to move back to Germany in order to enter politics there, and Sassen had caused such a stir with his open letter to President Eisenhower that nobody who moved in the exiles' circles could fail to notice the new focus on Germany. Fritsch was celebrating the success of *Der Weg* and working with German papers on propaganda to promote an unreconstructed Nazi ideology. They all followed the 1953 Bundestag elections closely: after all, they would shape the future. Germany's "economic miracle" boom must also have been a draw, as Argentina slipped further and further into crisis.

We still don't know when Eichmann first met Fritsch and Sassen, as none of the three gave much reliable information on the matter, for obvious reasons. An independent witness, a Polish man who was in the German Wehrmacht and occasionally worked for the better-off Germans in Argentina, reported that Sassen had met Eichmann in Tucumán, though the pair began to see each other regularly only once Eichmann returned to Buenos Aires in 1953.[2] Eichmann claimed he met Fritsch and Sassen at a large society event in honor of Otto Skorzeny but became friends with Sassen only after Fritsch approached Eichmann as a publisher, asking him to collaborate on a book.[3] Neither of these scenarios is unlikely: Sassen knew Horst Carlos Fuldner and CAPRI and was also a frequent guest at social events. People were interested in him as a National Socialist, and he cultivated relationships with various groups and individuals, all the way up to President Perón. Otto Skorzeny's version, in which he introduced Sassen to Eichmann in 1954, is nonsense: by that point all those involved had known one another for some time. Skorzeny was clearly trying to distract the authorities from his own deep involvement in the German-Argentine community.[4] He probably arrived in Argentina in 1949, long before Eichmann, then spent a few years shuttling between Buenos Aires and Madrid. He bragged about his daring coup in which he had snatched Mussolini from his prison after the Allies invaded Italy. He had been a sabotage specialist under Hitler and enjoyed great respect in far-right circles into his old age. He was thus on familiar terms with all the intelligence services, from the CIC to Mossad. He had met Eichmann at a propaganda event in Berlin and would have been in a position to introduce him to Sassen and Fritsch—but Fritsch and Eichmann already knew each other by June 1952. It's possible that they met through "the organization" that helped reunite the Eichmann family. But however it happened, anyone who knew Fritsch inevitably knew Willem Sassen as well.

The former war correspondent from the Dutch Voluntary SS must have had a particular appeal for Eichmann: he wrote books, which was something Eichmann was keen to do himself. Sassen also published sensational articles under his pseudonym Willem Sluyse (who everyone knew was really Sassen) and bragged about his success as a journalist in international newspapers. But most important, he wrote the biographies of Rudel and Adolf Galland. The years 1953–54 were particularly busy for Sassen. He was working up Rudel's reports on Germany, which had been captured on "magnetophone"[5] right after his return, as well as writing his own novel. Both books appeared in 1954, with the novel being published by the middle of the year.

While Rudel's book *Zwischen Deutschland und Argentinien* (Between Germany and Argentina) was full of exciting details about his (partly illegal) travels through Germany and his political work there, Sassen's novel used metaphor to depict the mentality of the postwar Nazis. It was brought out under his pseudonym, which had been made famous by his open letter. *Die Jünger und die Dirnen* (The Disciples and the Prostitutes) is a composition made up of seven ideal types. When the final victory fails, each of these characters must decide what and who they really are: disciples of the National Socialist idea, or prostitutes for the enemy, the occupying forces whose goal is to torture, humiliate, convert, or expel Hitler's poor idealistic devotees. The Allies' most important aim is "re-education," by which they hope to extinguish the National Socialist spirit that Sassen felt so strongly about.

The novel's elements were bound together into a hymn to perseverance and resistance, which far surpassed the usual Nazi literature in its pathetic eloquence. Sassen had mastered the music of the German language as a virtuoso masters his instrument. The range of voices he had at his command makes it all the more tragic that he chose to waste his talent on this intolerable garbage. It was not literature at all but an orgy of pornographic violence, voyeurism, anti-Semitic conspiracy theories, defamation of all Nazi "opponents," and sentimental, theatrical fascist kitsch. Still, we must thank Sassen for affording us a direct insight into the minds of his generation. These men had had their careers cut short and were left stranded in mental or literal exile, together with their broken ideology. Sassen plundered his own biography[6] and those of his associates for the novel (which was naturally published by Dürer), so it also provides valuable information about his circle. Eichmann recognized himself in a character in the second chapter, and it is hard to believe that the resemblance was mere coincidence.

In chapter 2, Erwin Holz, a former SD *Standartenführer* and concentration camp commandant, explains his thoughts and actions to the psychiatrist Dr. Thomas Bauer. The doctor has been tasked with ascertaining whether his patient is of sound mind, after he has been "tortured to within an inch of his life" in an American prisoner of war camp. The doctor's verdict will determine whether Holz remains in the hospital or is condemned to death. He is at first repelled, then disconcerted by the final-solutionist and eventually falls under his spell. In the end, having been handed the death penalty at Landsberg in West Germany, Holz takes his own life. In this chapter, the doctor's sober voice contrasts with that of the main character, Erwin Holz, to whom Sassen gives a unique speech justifying his actions. His voice is unsettling, "penetrating" like a "scalpel," and it is everywhere: once you have heard it, you can never escape its "arguments and assertions, which were at times so primitive" but which remain the final word.

Fritsch was so keen on this chapter that he published it as a preview of the book in *Der Weg*.[7] Anyone who has heard recordings of Adolf Eichmann's voice and observed the way he argues a point will find similarities between him and this character, right down to individual phrases.[8] The character's physical appearance is more like that of the concentration camp "doctor" Josef Mengele, another of Sassen's friends, but Mengele's tirades of self-justification were of an altogether different sort, as his diaries reveal.[9] In the speeches Sassen puts into Holz's mouth, Eichmann's voice literally forces itself upon the reader: "We were simply the bookkeepers of death," "I have no use for regret," "We wanted to expel the Jews from our midst, and we failed."[10] It is highly implausible that Sassen wrote this book before meeting Eichmann.[11] But if he did, then Erwin Holz is a frighteningly accurate presentiment of the man with whom Sassen was to spend the most intense period of his working life, and whose thought he already understood so well in 1954 that he was able to imitate him.

Another episode, however, clearly shows that a long-standing, close personal relationship existed among Fritsch, Sassen, and Eichmann in mid-1954. Reading the August issue of *Der Weg*, Adolf Eichmann would have learned that he and his wife had been dead since May 1945. The untimely death notice appeared in a long reader's letter from a "well-known American," with the entirely unknown name Warwick Hester, entitled "On the Streets of Truth." This long article is devoted to dismantling all the evidence for the systematic extermination of the Jews, and it is the direct sequel to the successful article by Heimann on "The Lie of the Six Million" from July. The author discredits every possible witness as a liar or a dupe, and on the third page, after "refuting" the existence of gas vans, he mentions almost incidentally that Adolf Eichmann is dead:

> A junior SS officer claimed he was an acquaintance of a more senior officer named Eichmann, under whose command he had been for a time. Shortly before the end of the war, Eichmann, an expert on Jewish affairs, told him in confidence that around two million Jews had been killed by special commandos. When the Germans capitulated, Eichmann and his wife took poison. This information could not be verified, but I could see no motive for this man giving a false statement.[12]

This is the first and only instance of the story of an Eichmann family suicide. The idea that Adolf Eichmann might have taken his own life never seemed particularly likely, although Wilhelm Höttl apparently attempted to spread it at the start of 1947, with some success where the British Nazi hunters were concerned.[13] Dieter Wisliceny thought it inconceivable.[14] The "witness" to this exit à la Goebbels was blatantly invented, along with many of the article's other "facts." The author was clearly aiming to give Eichmann and his family some peace while they were still alive, by stopping the hunt for him. This method was not without its risks, as Eichmann's name had never before appeared in *Der Weg*. The self-evident way the author mentioned his "area of expertise" suddenly made it obvious that his name had been deliberately missing from the magazine's recent reports on the matter, although it would have had a natural place there. Holger Meding, who made a systematic analysis of *Der Weg* and spoke to the former *Weg* employee Dieter Vollmer, concluded that "*Der Weg* had largely avoided mentioning Eichmann up to this point, in order not to give any indirect clues to his whereabouts."[15] Nobody seems to have realized that this suicide announcement would be a clue for people like Wiesenthal or Höttl, who knew it to be a lie, having seen Eichmann or his wife at a later date. The people who worked for Dürer, and the magazine's Argentine readership who knew Ricardo Klement's true identity, must have had a good laugh about this coup over a glass of wine with the dead man in the ABC Café. But the text held much more—it revealed a great deal about the link between its author and Eichmann.

The article in *Der Weg* was an attempt to discredit all the witness statements relating to the extermination of the Jews. The same piece contained a character assassination of "Dr. Höttl." He offered the CIC his services, sold himself to the Jews, spied for the Soviet Union at the same time, extorted "large sums of money," lied systematically, and was now playing all these parties off against one another with his "intelligence service stretching over West Germany, Austria, and the South East." His knowledge of the "lie of the six million" had made him untouchable.[16] Astonishingly, the author had calculated that a mass extermination would have been impossible, due to the demographic of "the Jews," and for good measure, he quoted a confidential conversation with a "North American of Jewish descent whom I greatly respect" and who was evidently also a psychologist. According to Warwick Hester, this man had confessed openly that the figure of six million was a scam: "We thought that six million wasn't too many to seem improbable, but enough to give people the shudders for a century to come. Hitler gave us this opportunity, and we are just making use of it, with great success, as you can see."[17] And because Warwick Hester had nothing but good intentions toward the Jews, he finished by warning them not to take these games too far. It was only a matter of time before the "inner rebellion against the lies" became an outer rebellion, as soon as the lies were exposed. "I fear," he concluded, "they may take retrospective revenge on the people who originated the lies, which will then, in a turn of events both tragic and cynical, [!] become truth." In other words: if millions of Jews are murdered once again, they will only have themselves to blame. Whoever Warwick Hester was in reality, he was a master cynic himself.

Leaving aside the news of Eichmann's death, "On the Streets of Truth" was also a textbook example of the falsification of history known as revisionism. Proponents of Nazi revisionism work with the intention of debunking the whole of written history since 1945 as propaganda and thoroughly revising it. But the article is more than that: it became the principal source text for Holocaust revisionists, a fact that has long been overlooked. In the space of a few months, Hester's report, and the article written by "Guido Heimann," who claimed to be from Salzburg, were woven together and spread right across Germany. In his pamphlet *Volk ohne Führung* (People Without Leadership, which also appeared under a pseudonym), the far-right author Herbert Grabert mentioned the "American journalist Warwick Hester" and introduced the figure of 365,000 victims of the Nazi regime, only some of whom were Jews.[18] An article also appeared in the neo-Nazi sheet *Die Anklage: Organ der entrechteten Kriegsgeschädigten in Bad Wörishofen* (The Indictment: Voice of the Disenfranchised, War-Damaged People of Bad Wörishofen), which attempted to refute what it called "the basest falsification of history." It was able to cite a new expert—a "universally renowned North American"—none other than Warwick Hester.[19] There was also a notoriously fake Red Cross report, stating that the number of regime opponents killed was—coincidentally—365,000. With clever cooperation between far-right books and magazines, and carefully aimed readers' letters in serious journals, these texts created one of the main "sources" for Holocaust denial, which remains the core of revisionist history even today.[20] An invented American expert, an "insider" from Salzburg (both writing for an Argentine Nazi paper), and a fake Red Cross report supposedly emanating from Germany were cleverly linked so that they all cited one another. It was enough to unleash a barrage of press coverage.

The Hester article was reprinted in 1990, with the note that the name Warwick Hester was a cover for the equally famous "American jurist

Stephen F. Pinter." This sorry effort has haunted right-wing publications and the Internet ever since, under the name of "The Dr. Pinter Report."[21] Pinter, it was claimed, had all this information because he had been a prosecutor in the Dachau trial. He was from St. Louis, and for good measure he was sometimes said to be a Jew himself. And no one could doubt a Jewish-American jurist bearing witness against the Holocaust—at least, no one who thought like a Nazi. Would it surprise anyone to learn that there never was an American prosecutor named Stephen F. Pinter? The name first appeared around New Year 1959–60, attached to two readers' letters that reiterated the Hester-Heimann nonsense almost word for word. One of them appeared in the popular U.S. magazine *Our Sunday Visitor* and was then picked up by *Nation Europa*—the monthly that had printed Sluyse's open letter and had a long history of cooperation with *Der Weg*.[22]

An analysis of this concentrated campaign reveals the power that small groups can wield and that gave Fritsch and his circle the self-confidence to dream of seizing political power again. Deniers of the systematic extermination of the Jews have the forgers' workshop in Buenos Aires to thank for their most often-cited sources. Argentina had a freedom of the press that did not exist in other countries, and it was fully utilized. The transatlantic exchange between old comrades' publications was frighteningly effective, and following the "reparations" agreement, it seems these were the depths to which people were prepared to stoop.

The question of who really penned the article by "Warwick Hester" remains unanswered. Its use of metaphor and its theatrical aspect are reminiscent of Sassen, but it could also have been Johann von Leers, who wrote for *Der Weg* under a number of pseudonyms and later reluctantly admitted asking Eichmann about the number of victims when he was in Argentina. We know that Dürer Verlag had no problem publishing made-up letters to the publisher and fantastical-sounding biographies by invented authors. And we know the "renowned American" stemmed from within the Dürer circle—not just because the article is riddled with phrases typical of *Der Weg*'s style, but also because this is the only explanation for the bizarre news of Eichmann's death. In 1954 Adolf Eichmann, who had been trying to have himself declared dead since the end of the war, was finally able to see himself vanish without a trace, in black and white. This was also the proof he needed that Fritsch and Dürer Verlag wielded enough influence to have a political impact.

Once again, or so it must have appeared to him, he was at the center of a new movement.[23] An added bonus was the character assassination of Wilhelm Höttl, the man who had taken such delight in making life difficult for Eichmann. It was one more good turn among comrades of the death's head order.

Another interesting death notice appeared in 1954, this time in Austria. At the start of June, the Linz and Vienna papers printed information that supposedly came from Reuters in London, to the effect that SS *Oberscharführer* Wolfgang Bauer had been shot dead in mid-1946. He had been killed in the Salzkammergut Mountains (at Traunauen, near Linz), by a Jewish vengeance squad that had mistaken him for Eichmann. The corpse had been buried hastily in the woods, and the error was realized only weeks later. Perversely, this report made people suspect it really had been Eichmann who was shot after all. Eichmann received these articles in Argentina (or at least, the one from the *Oberösterreichische Zeitung*), probably from his father. In typical fashion, he promptly wove the story into a legend that he trotted out to Sassen. He started claiming he had heard about the execution when he was still on the Lüneberg Heath, and he proudly quoted the articles, which according to him said that "Eichmann died with remarkable decorum." "That amused me greatly." And Eichmann cheerfully lied: "I kept the cutting for a long time, but then I burned it."[24] He had to forestall anyone who might want to see the article for himself. When Sassen inquired about when exactly he had read it, he responded vaguely: "It must have been four to five years after the war."[25]

Simon Wiesenthal, who was still on the alert for anything to do with Eichmann, made a concerted effort to expose this canard for what it was, before the idea that Eichmann was dead took hold. However, it continued to appear until September, even making it into Israeli newspapers.[26] Wiesenthal sent a press release through Austria's Jewish Religious Community to counter the story, but he couldn't prevent Eichmann's version of this affair from finding its way into the research literature. The story of the chicken farmer in Altensalzkoth reading about his own assassination in an Austrian newspaper was simply too tempting.[27]

Valentin Tarra, the Altaussee criminal investigator, also had his ear to the ground. In 1960 he told Fritz Bauer about the newspaper articles and expressed his suspicion that "Nazi circles in London" had spread the information to end the search for Eichmann. The original source of the news is still unknown.

Undeterred, the Gehlen Organization sent out a completely different message: it had received new details about Eichmann's career in the Middle East. The source was Saida Ortner, the new wife of the former SS man Felix Ortner. She said Eichmann had escaped from an American prisoner of war camp in Italy in 1947 and had traveled to Syria and converted to Islam in 1948. In 1951 he had tried to make contact with the notorious grand mufti al-Husseini in Cairo, who refused to help him, and he was forced to leave Egypt the same year.[28] To give her the benefit of the doubt, this woman, who was used to Arabic names, may have confused Eichmann with Alois Brunner, who was often introduced as "Eichmann's right-hand man." Brunner, who had killed more than 128,000 people, was now representing a number of German interests in Damascus, under the name Dr. Georg Fischer, and he was also an unofficial employee of the West German intelligence service. Despite knowing this fact, Gehlen still passed the news on to its American friends, which suggests some internal communication problems among the BND's data gatherers.

In 1954 a remarkable number of people started speculating about Eichmann's death. Eager to be declared dead, he relayed the news to his family, as Klaus Eichmann remembered vividly in 1966: his father "was constantly being brought newspaper articles" about how he had been shot in Linz.[29] A father who reads descriptions of his own execution, to children who spent seven years of their young lives coming to terms with the fact they might never see him again, is not exactly the image of a sensitive parent. It's no wonder this episode remained in the children's memories.

During the same month that *Der Weg* announced the Eichmann family's suicide, the German embassy in Buenos Aires renewed the passports of two young German nationals. They were accompanied by their mother and provided identity papers from Cologne and Vienna, in the names of Klaus and Horst Eichmann.[30] As the legal guardian of the two boys, the "late" Veronika Katharina Eichmann, née Liebl, signed the documents, giving her address as Chacabuco 4261, Olivos. On being questioned, the boys were able to name their father's SS rank at the time of their births.[31] The record does not state whether anyone told them to wish their daddy all the best as they left. But given the behavior of the German embassy's staff over the years that followed, we can't rule it out.

Even without assuming the worst, the Eichmanns' visit to the German embassy gives rise to the suspicion that its staff had no particular interest in coming to terms with Germany's past. In 1954 Adolf Eichmann came to the welcome realization that he was surrounded by willing helpers who found him important enough to write about. He also became aware that life in Buenos Aires posed as little threat as life in the remote province of Tucumán, even from the legal representatives of West Germany. Only two months previously, they had issued a new passport to an old acquaintance of his, the mass murderer and former ghetto commandant Josef Schwammberger—in his real name.[32]

Different Headlines

While these attempts were being made to create confusion about Eichmann's life after the end of the war, there had been another, less favorable development: Eichmann's deeds were inexorably coming to light. In 1953 Gerald Reitlinger's book *The Final Solution* was published in London, the first attempt at an overview of the German crimes against the Jews. The thick volume contained not only statistics, maps, and a wealth of detail but also a whole chapter on Adolf Eichmann. Initially, it did not find a publisher in Germany. The Institute for Contemporary History in Munich turned down first a translation, then even a review for the journal *Vierteljahrsheft für Zeitgeschichte* (Contemporary History Quarterly).[33] But Reitlinger's book still changed the debate on a fundamental level, even before a German translation was finally published in 1956. His attempt to calculate the scale of the genocide set a benchmark for future research. In 1954 Helmut Krausnick wrote a remarkable article on the likely number of Holocaust victims in a supplement to the magazine *Das Parlament*, edited by the Federal Homeland Service, which of course also gave details about Eichmann.[34]

But from Eichmann's point of view, another event was a more immediate cause for concern: a court case that went down in history under the misleading name of the Kasztner Trial and that began on January 1, 1954, in Jerusalem.[35] It was actually a libel case against the author Malchiel Grünwald, who had described Rudolf "Reszö" Kasztner as a Nazi collaborator in Budapest. The case quickly became a bizarre trial against Kasztner himself, partly due to an error by the judge, Benjamin Halevi, which was later acknowledged. Kasztner found himself having to justify his attempts to save Jews in Hungary by entering into "negotiations" with Eichmann.[36] A lack of knowledge about the circumstances, and the fact that Kasztner's work for the Israeli government made the trial a political issue, turned the proceedings into a global news story focusing on what Kasztner had done. Particular emphasis was placed on the dramatic duel over human lives between Kasztner and Eichmann. Over the following years, the world's major newspapers carried detailed reports on the trial and its consequences.[37] The *Argentinisches Tageblatt,* Buenos Aires's liberal newspaper (or "Jewish" paper, as the Dürer circle would say),[38] also wrote about it. Eichmann, who made a point of reading this paper, would have come across familiar phrases like "blood for goods" and names like Joel Brand, Kasztner, and most frequently, Adolf Eichmann. The rest of the world was struggling to comprehend these new facts: the unequal negotiations between Jews and their murderers; the deportation of more than four hundred thousand people in the space of a few weeks; and the chaos of the war's final years. Eichmann, however, always knew what would be coming. He kept a close eye on the public reaction to each new revelation and recognized early on that his advance knowledge would allow him to turn Kasztner's downfall to his advantage and put his own spin on events. "Eichmann was a master of turning people into traitors," the judge said in the announcement of his verdict. "Kasztner sold his soul to the devil." The press headlines aided Eichmann's line of defense: Kasztner had been Eichmann's partner. When the intensive work in the Sassen circle began three years later, this was the first topic to be addressed. Eichmann was well prepared, explaining to his astonished listeners: "Kasztner and I, we had a sovereign command over the situation in the Hungarian territory—forgive my use of this word, 'sovereign,' but it may serve as clarification."[39]

Nazi Gold

In fall 1954 Eichmann's name was all over the Austrian newspapers again, this time in a very different context. A rumor was going around that he'd had something to do with the disappearance of Nazi treasure—the stolen goods that had been gathered in Berlin and had last been seen in packing crates, on their way to the "Alpine Fortress." People therefore suspected the treasure was now somewhere in Styria. It was probably the speculations about Eichmann's death that sparked investigations in Austria. Journalists soon became convinced that he was alive and living under a false name in Upper Austria. On October 1, 1954, the tabloid paper *Der Abend* published rumors from the Altaussee region about the wanted man hiding in the Austrian mountains, under the headline "Where Is the SS Mass Murderer Eichmann?" It raised the possibility that "former SS General Adolf Eichmann, who slaughtered the Jews of Eastern Europe, is alive, is held to be an established fact in Altausseerland." He was said to have paid several visits to his wife in Altaussee, around the time she was trying to have him declared dead. In summer 1954, the report went on, he had been seen in his wife's apartment, although his wife had vanished in 1953 and her whereabouts were unknown. Yet the rent for the empty property was still being paid. The people the reporter interviewed had probably mistaken Eichmann's half brother for Eichmann himself. After a suitable period of time had elapsed, the brother had quietly cleared out Vera Eichmann's apartment (a fact that had not escaped the observant investigator Valentin Tarra).[40]

The National Criminal Court in Vienna was alerted to this coverage and commissioned a report at the end of the year. A field investigation took place, which also uncovered neighborhood gossip about Eichmann's alleged wealth, and a secret life he was leading now that he had changed his appearance.[41] The rumors were stubbornly persistent. On January 10, 1955, the Austrian edition of *Die Welt am Montag* carried an article entitled "Mysterious Events: A Ghost Is Abroad in Alt Aussee." Adolf Eichmann, it said, had returned to claim his gold.

There are plenty of legends about missing Nazi treasure, with tales of chests sunk in mountain lakes and lavish exports to foreign countries. The stories excited people's greed and fueled the myth of a Nazi conspiracy continuing to operate underground. They fed into the far right's hope that the war had not managed to defeat National Socialism entirely. The speculations of 1954 also sparked an interest in Eichmann from people who otherwise wanted nothing to do with the "slaughter of the Jews." The stories reassured Eichmann that people were looking for him in the wrong place and that he was safe in Perón's country. Even treasure-hunting Nazis, hungry for gold, posed no threat to him: any-one could see from his standard of living that he wasn't a wealthy man. But when people saw him in the ABC Café, or at a gathering of newly Argentine old associates, they could still ask him about it. And the fact that Eichmann sometimes worked for the man who was suspected of being the real guardian of the Nazi gold, Franz Wilhelm Pfeiffer, lent the rumors an extra weight in Argentina.

A Specialist Once More

Throughout his murderous career, Eichmann knew how to use his public profile to further his own interests. In Argentine exile in the mid-1950s, he recognized the prospect that even his postwar image might have its advantages. The more witness statements, newspaper articles, and rumors made the rounds, the more interesting the *Obersturmbann-führer* (retired) became to men like Eberhard Fritsch and Willem Sassen. This was particularly true of the publisher, who had had no experience of Nazi Germany beyond his visit to the Hitler Youth Congress. Fritsch believed every exile had been an insider. But Sassen too had seen a different side of the war, through his role as an SS war correspondent, and he had moved in completely different circles from Eichmann. He had never met Heinrich Himmler, Hermann Göring, or even Reinhard Heydrich. Eichmann, however, had known them all and knew a good deal about the various Nazi offices and institutions. He had been the one coordinating these offices, like a lot of little cogs, to set in motion the extermination machine. In the mid-1950s the exiled Nazis were beginning to put out feelers toward sympathizers in West Germany again. They wanted to know who their contacts really were, and there was no better way to find out than to inquire about who knew whom. Wilhelm Höttl's book made them nervous, and the Dürer circle was on the lookout for people who could tell them more about the author and give them a better idea of the potential danger he represented. Rudel and Sassen, as well as men like Ludolf von Alvensleben, Johann von Leers, and Josef Mengele, had never met him. The changing times demanded a pooling of knowledge—and suddenly the specialists were back in business.

A specialist was even required when it came to the most repressed and feared topic of all: the Jewish question. The media activity, and the demand for articles, show that even the Nazis in exile felt a growing need for information. And they wanted it from sources that these great lovers of conspiracy trusted: other National Socialists. Those who were too deeply mired in stereotypical National Socialist thought to trust "enemy literature," as the Sassen circle called it, needed answers from within their own ranks. Most of them had no trouble dismissing every new revelation about concentration camps and mass murder as atrocity propaganda from their opponents. But over the years, all the little stories and details from their own memories had coalesced to form an unsettling picture. And now their children were asking questions. While these men clearly had no right to claim they "didn't know about any of it," there were also large gaps in their knowledge, because they had only ever wanted to know about "it" to a limited extent. They may have stood by their lies and their own polemic, but eventually even devoted National Socialists had to face the uncomfortable question: between their own suspicions and the stories in the news, what was truth and what lies? What had Hitler really known? Had gas chambers existed? Gas vans? Had partisans really been shot? How many people had actually been killed?

Each of them had a different viewpoint and a different set of questions, but at long last, they all wanted to know the details. The "Final Solution" had become an issue they could no longer avoid, now that it was affecting global politics. Germany's status on the world stage depended on its taking a clear position on the Holocaust, paying "reparations," and committing itself to a pro-Israeli foreign policy. The events in the Middle East were significant, and if you wanted to understand the new alliances, you needed knowledge, or you wouldn't get far without harming your own cause. This was even more the case if you continued to suspect that "the Jews" were behind everything and that they were one of the principal forces in the United States, a country that Der Weg's editorial named as an enemy power.

Eichmann soon had a reputation for being the only surviving Nazi with any reliable information on the scale of the Holocaust, and on how the extermination process had worked, which made him increasingly sought after. He had actually met "the enemy," having spoken to representatives of Jewish organizations and communities. Names like Joel Brand and Rudolf Kasztner were familiar to him, and not only from the newspapers. And his talent for promoting himself as a "respected spe-

cialist" achieved one more thing: after he was abducted, no one voluntarily admitted to so much as having heard his name, yet the number of
people who could be proved to have spoken to him about the extermination of the Jews was remarkably high. In Tucumán, the Schoklitsches
and Herbert Hagel had asked him directly how many Jews had been
murdered, and even if Eichmann's answer was as evasive as their reports
suggest, the fact remains that people knew Ricardo Klement was really
Adolf Eichmann, and that Adolf Eichmann was a specialist on these matters. Nobody who found themselves in a northern province of Argentina would strike up a dinner-table conversation with the first German
immigrant they came across by asking what he had to say about the
Nazis' murder of the Jews.

Another exile known to have approached Eichmann directly was
Johann von Leers. Four years older than Eichmann, he was a legal expert
who had written books with titles like *Blut und Rasse in der Gesetz-
gebung* (Blood and Race in Legislation, 1936), which had earned him a
professorship at the University of Jena. There he had lectured on "Legal,
Economic and Political History on a Racial Basis" and described "The
Criminal Nature of the Jew" (1944), when he wasn't busy advising the
Reich Ministry for Propaganda on racial issues. He fled to Argentina via
Italy in 1950.[42] There he remained what we might most accurately call
a professional anti-Semite, busying himself by writing horrific articles
for *Der Weg*. He left Buenos Aires again, in the mid-1950s, for Cairo.
In Egypt, much to the amazement of his old comrades in Germany,
he made a different name for himself as an advocate of Islam (his new
name being Amin Omar von Leers). But before he left Argentina, he
found the time to have a conversation with Eichmann, asking him about
the exact number of Jewish victims, among other things. This episode,
which Leers described in order to defend himself against the accusation
of having been "Eichmann's best friend in Argentina," speaks for itself:
"I never knew Eichmann, I heard his name for the first time in 1955, in
Buenos Aires, where I had a short conversation with him and tried to get
the historical truth from him about the number of Jews who died in the
concentration camps. But he didn't give me any information."[43]

Despite Leers's claim not to have heard the name before, he knew
exactly who Eichmann was: the expert on victim numbers. And the fact
that he postdated their conversation underlines his intent. Leers left
Argentina in 1954, so he must have already known exactly who he was

questioning by this point and had a strong enough sense of guilt to know what it meant.[44] The incident can be interpreted in two ways: either Leers was lying when he claimed never to have heard the name before, or someone had introduced Eichmann to him using the description that had been linked to Eichmann's name since the Nuremberg Trials. Leers confessed his acquaintance with Eichmann in self-defense, which leads us to conclude that their conversation lasted rather longer than Leers's description suggests. Of course, it could not have escaped a man who had been one of *Der Weg*'s major contributors that his publisher cared so much about Eichmann. When Leers moved to Cairo in 1954, he took the memory of his encounter with him. His obvious postdating of the conversation throws an interesting light on Eichmann's public life in Argentina prior to the start of the project with Willem Sassen.

Admittedly, not all the Nazi exiles needed to question Eichmann in order to learn about the scale of the Holocaust. Men like Erich Müller, Josef Vötterl, and Curt Christmann had their own experience in this field. They had been in the *Einsatzgruppen* that shot people en masse behind the front lines from 1941 and that later murdered them in gas vans. Gerhard Bohne and Hans Hefelmann were specialists in "euthanasia" murders, and former ghetto commandant Josef Schwammberger had a pretty good idea of what extermination through labor meant. Most of them had the opportunity to meet—and not only because the immigrant world is usually a small one. Like Hans-Ulrich Rudel, Dieter Menge was a former Luftwaffe pilot. He had an imposing estate near Buenos Aires and a lucrative scrap metal business. He also had the unpleasant habit of surrounding himself with his ghoulish contemporaries. To this day, people still speak of the social events at his house as cultish gatherings of the dregs from the Nazi regime. At these events, no one held back or used an alias, and men like Eichmann and Josef Schwammberger became attractions. One of the running jokes there was a play on the names of the host and his favorite guest: Menge particularly liked to play host to Mengele.[45]

Later, Sassen claimed he had introduced Eichmann to the concentration camp "doctor," who had his own special interpretation of the Hippocratic oath. Many Jewish survivors were unable to forget him: he was the man who had conducted the "selections" in Auschwitz. And how could you forget a man who decided the fates of hundreds of people with a wave of his hand?[46] The two men did not necessarily get to know each other over the course of their murderous careers, although they may well have met briefly during one of Eichmann's frequent visits to Auschwitz in 1944. However, they took the same route to Argentina, and the false identity papers they both had received from Termeno were produced in fairly quick succession. Mengele arrived in Argentina the year before Eichmann—though unlike Eichmann, he had the advantage of his father's generous financial support. Still, the two men's paths crossed repeatedly in Argentina. Sassen, who was a close friend of Mengele's and still had a high regard for the latter's "experiments" in 1991, was convinced that Eichmann and Mengele had little to say to each other: "They embodied two completely different types."[47] As far as their financial prospects and their educational background went, this was true. Mengele had plenty of money and two doctorates, one in medicine and another in philosophy (the latter with a thesis entitled *Racial-Morphological Investigation of the Lower Jaw Segment in Four Racial Groups*). But Sassen was not entirely correct. When Eichmann was hanged in 1962, of all the acquaintances from his old circle, it was only the "Auschwitz Angel of Death" who acknowledged the organizer of the genocide and dedicated some surprisingly sensitive words to him. They must have found some common ground after all.

Long before the start of Sassen's recording sessions, Eichmann had once again become part of a society that interested him and, more important, that was interested in him. And contrary to later claims, their curiosity was probably not the result merely of horrified fascination. People's general forgetfulness and discreet silence would become a direct consequence of Eichmann's abduction. But in the mid-1950s, Eichmann was recognized as a specialist who was much too interesting to be forgotten, and it is only human nature to talk about unforgettable things. This interest posed a threat to Eichmann, because at this point, ten years after the war's end, many of his fellow Nazis were starting to lose their fear of prosecution and were making contact with West Germany and Austria more frequently. While some were placing advertisements in Germany to find a wife,[48] many even dared to move back there. The father of the "economic miracle," Ludwig Erhard himself, paid a visit to Argentina in December 1954, and Otto Skorzeny, who had been working for the intelligence services for some time, traveled to see Perón as the official representative of Krupp's industrial empire. Mengele even managed to get divorced in Germany in 1954.[49] Former comrades with Nazi pasts were making surprising new careers. Josef Vötterl, who came from Salzburg and was four years younger than Eichmann, had also fled the country on a Red Cross passport. As a member of the criminal and border police with Einsatzkommando 10A of Einsatzgruppe D, his role had involved reconnaissance, and then carrying out "border protection" and "partisan control." Nonetheless, in 1955 he moved back to Germany for three years. He found employment with the BfV; we will meet him again later on.[50]

When he went off to meet his comrades, both old and new, Eichmann left his family at home. He was probably eager to avoid questions from his wife, who was naturally convinced that her husband was an innocent man. Admittedly, he couldn't entirely prevent his wife and children from meeting these people, because the world of Buenos Aires was a small one: "One day, Father said: last week you shook hands with Josef Mengele." But according to Klaus Eichmann, disclosures like this were the exception rather than the rule: "Father was very serious about keeping secrets. If someone came to visit, he would give us boys a clip round the ear to remind us not to blab about it the next day at school." When the journalist asked what sort of visitors these were, Klaus Eichmann answered, "I only remember the slaps." Looking at the interviews and witness statements from later years, Eichmann's abduction must have had a similar effect on the memories of all the people in Argentina who knew who Ricardo Klement really was.

The Triumph of Life

Marriage: A union between two different sexes for the reproduction of their kind.
>   —Eichmann's psychological evaluation, early 1961[51]

The year 1955 opened a period of great unrest. The president of Argentina, who had had so much time for the Germans, was deposed; on June 16, Argentine naval officers began a series of attempted putsches that soon led to Perón's fall. In 1960 *Life* reporters heard rumors that Eichmann had worked as a gaucho under the name Ernst Radinger; spent time in Paraguay, Chile, Uruguay, and Peru; and gone to Bolivia for several months after Perón was ousted.[52] It was clearly a case of mistaken identity, but the legend provides a vivid reflection of the German immigrants' situation. Nobody was sure what the political change would mean for them, particularly as the new regime was taking action against the corruption of the Perón dictatorship and, in the process, closed seven German firms that were under suspicion.

In December 1955 the police called at Hans-Ulrich Rudel's house in Córdoba province, as he had been an intimate friend of Perón's. On searching the house, they discovered numerous documents, three passports in different names, and proof of his political activities and contacts.[53] Although it had been known that Perón's protégé had been attempting to create an international network of fascist movements for years, the extent of his connections still came as a surprise, particularly as Rudel had clearly burned numerous other documents prior to his hasty departure. Unfortunately, the documents confiscated by the police have not resurfaced. However, the investigating commission's report contained some initial findings, including notes on the Red Cross passport that, together with various entry and exit stamps in the false passports, proved that Rudel had been hard at work peddling his far-right dreams. Among his papers were found begging letters to Kameradenwerk, some from eager networkers in West Germany like Hans Rechenberg, who was collecting money for Hitler's sister. Both Rechenberg and Rudel would later work on Adolf Eichmann's defense. The greatest sensation in this affair was understandably caused by the news that Rudel had succeeded in bringing the British fascist Oswald Mosley into the country and arranging a personal audience for him with President Perón. The German embassy was so alarmed that it took the precaution of sending newspaper articles from Buenos Aires to Bonn.[54] But after the initial excitement, it came to the conclusion that "Peronazism" was just a "charade" and that Rudel represented "the typical postwar course taken by so many 'heroes' . . . who refused to surrender even though their roles had long been played out."[55] The media told Rudel's allies that their figurehead was a "fairly laughable and arrogant" character. Their political ambitions and their connections were now out in the open. Rudel took temporary refuge in Paraguay. Argentina obviously no longer held the same attraction it had in Perón's era—especially for those who, unlike Rudel, had no means of escape.

The fear of currency inflation had been in the air for some time in

Argentina, and the putsch against Perón had partly been a reaction to the worsening conditions. The economic situation may also have prompted Eichmann's change of job. In uncertain times, the best policy is to invest in natural resources, and in March Eichmann took over management of the Siete Palmas rabbit farm in Joaquín Gorina, twenty-eight miles from Buenos Aires. The business belonged to Franz Wilhelm Pfeiffer, who wanted to return to Europe and leave a reliable deputy in his place.[56] Klaus Eichmann spoke of "two uncles, who are now [1966] back in Europe," with whom his father ran the farm. "They had around 5,000 hens and 1,000 rabbits." The rabbits were Angora.

The cuddly white animals provided both expensive wool and a coveted fertilizer. Rabbit dung contains high concentrations of nitrogen, phosphate, and potash, a very useful mixture that was highly sought after in Argentina (a country that remains a major exporter of citrus fruits). Day-to-day life on the farm consisted, quite prosaically, of feeding the rabbits, mucking out their cages, and collecting the dung. They were sheared three or four times a year. It was an economically sound route to independence and success. During the war, Eichmann liked to tell his fellow murderers, he had put in a request to the *Reichsführer*-SS for an estate in Bohemia after the final victory so he could become a farmer.[57] The disciples of the Black Sun allegedly revered the simple life, but when they had been in power, none of them would have traded in their careers to work the soil. And so it was no real comfort to Eichmann that he had once been successful with chickens and could now have told *Reichsführer*-SS Heinrich Himmler that he was a rabbit farmer. This also meant a major change for his family. Life "on the ranch," as Eichmann liked to call it, was rural, and although he did occasionally take his family with him, they were still separated for much of the time. His three sons, who were now between thirteen and nineteen, had to carry on going to school. His writing, and his children's recollections, show that he was concerned about their willingness to learn. Eichmann deplored his three sons' "intellectual arrogance" and "ignorance," as they were unable to summon any enthusiasm for identifying the differences between the Nazi *Gottgläubigkeit* and Marxism.[58]

It was like being back in Altensalzkoth. Eichmann didn't have to worry about his family; he could just earn his money and dwell on his thoughts. The only difference was that the rabbit farm was a little more remote than the village on the Lüneburg Heath, meaning that on balmy evenings, Eichmann was unable to make the local women swoon with his Schubert and his gypsy airs. On those long evenings, the former master of deportation now played to thousands of hens and fluffy white rabbits. But the income was pretty good—Eichmann put it at 4,500 pesos a month, which was just over 1,000 Deutschmarks.[59] The family urgently needed the money, as an unexpected event had taken place: Vera Eichmann was pregnant again. Five years later Eichmann would come up with some bizarre words to describe his feelings about it: "Our happiness found its zenith through the birth of our fourth son. This meant more to me than just becoming a proud father. For me this was a symbol of freedom, and life triumphing over the powers that sought to destroy me. Even now, thinking about it in my cell, the birth of my son fills me with triumphant satisfaction."[60]

The birth of a child as a triumphal victory? Considering Eichmann's circumstances in 1955, other concerns must have occupied his mind at first. The pregnancy had numerous risk factors: this was the 1950s, and at forty-six, Vera Eichmann was very old to be having a child. She was also not in the best of health, having suffered from a severe bilious complaint for years. She was in a foreign country, with an unfamiliar health care system and a language she had not mastered. The father-to-be would have had good reason to be worried for his wife, quite apart from the additional expenditure a new baby would involve.

We cannot overlook the fact that Eichmann's wife and children were genuinely important to him. He couldn't imagine escaping to live in exile without his family. He shared this absolute resolve with his wife, who had fought with equal persistence for their life together and had supported his escape from Europe. Admittedly, it was not only outward circumstances that made the marriage difficult. But there is much to suggest that in 1935 they had married for love. Eichmann met Vera Liebl, three years his junior, on a trip to Bohemia, where her mother owned a farm. Dieter Wisliceny, who would later become Eichmann's friend and colleague, described Vera as "small and very fat, with smooth black hair, dark eyes and a round face of the Slavic type." But Wisliceny, next to whom anyone would look svelte, clearly envied Eichmann, and he was generally not a fan of women. A full-length photo of the young Vera shows a decidedly attractive woman with a fashionable pageboy haircut, large, expressive eyes, and full lips. She is elegantly dressed, with a fur stole. In terms of appearance, she was entirely Eichmann's type: he told Sassen he had never warmed to the National Socialist ideal of the tall, slim, blond lady, as embodied by Lina Heydrich and Magda Goebbels, finding it "too cold, too distant as a woman."[61] The stories Wilhelm Höttl told about Eichmann being ashamed of his wife's farming background are nonsense: for one thing, in the Nazi ideology of blood and soil, there was no better heritage, and for another, Eichmann always wrote and spoke of his wife with respect and admiration. She was the "proud farmer's daughter from Mladé." His wedding underlines the fact that his choice of wife was personal, not career-driven: he fiddled the documents required for an SS wedding, as his fiancée could not provide all the necessary papers. He also agreed to go through with a church ceremony at the request of his deeply religious bride, even though the SS frowned upon it.

The Eichmanns lived first in Berlin, then in Vienna, and finally in Prague, where Vera's sisters moved into the same apartment building, thanks to the progress of her husband's career. Eichmann accepted that his wife was not comfortable in Berlin and allowed the family home to remain in Prague. He shuttled between Berlin and Prague at the weekends. Of course, his work also continued to take him through or near Prague, as he often had to visit Vienna and Theresienstadt, and his office soon established its own outpost in Prague, at 25 Belgische Gasse. In spite of the happy start to his marriage, by the time he was posted to Vienna in 1938, Eichmann's staff knew their boss had a lover. The affair caused some gossip when Eichmann hurried through the sale of Maria Mösenbacher's real estate to the Vienna Central Office. Eichmann was suspected of paying too high a price for it, for the sake of his girlfriend.[62] And his staff clearly had a few other things to gossip about: people tended to confuse Maria with Mitzi, the manager of a little guesthouse nearby, with whom Eichmann also allegedly had an affair.[63]

Vera Eichmann must have heard rumors about it, at the very least, but it obviously didn't dent the marriage. On her birthday, over Easter 1939, the couple vacationed in Italy.[64] Weekends, wedding anniversaries, birthdays, and Mother's Day were all important to Eichmann (although the story that he was finally caught out while buying a bunch of flowers for his wedding anniversary in 1960 is untrue).[65] The couple's three children were the center of both their lives. After they were born, Eichmann was said to have had other women in his life, for varying amounts of time. We should not take Wisliceny's reference to Eichmann's "womanizing" too seriously, but there is evidence that he was anything but faithful to his wife. The women who worked in his department, and his lovers, all described him as "attractive," very "charming," an entertaining man who enjoyed parlor games and making music. He was "a lovely man."[66] Men too remember that "Eichie" was "popular and welcomed everywhere," at least if we believe Camp Commandant Höß.[67] One of the tapes from Argentina sheds some light on Eichmann's behavior toward women: it documents an encounter between Eichmann and his "comrade" Sassen's wife. She brings him tobacco, saying apologetically that the store was out of his favorite brand. His sharp, scratchy voice momentarily becomes deep and soft, and his "Thank you for your trouble . . . my dear lady" sounds unmistakably submissive.[68] We know about his relationships with at least three women during the Nazi era. And in Altensalzkoth, there were rumors that in addition to Nelly, the dainty blonde from Prien am Chiemsee, he had relationships with a young widowed mother and with his landlady. Whatever credit we give to this village gossip, it reveals the incredible truth: even in a shabby Wehrmacht coat, without his position of power, Eichmann was seen as sufficiently desirable for people to make these assumptions.

For his part, Eichmann always made an effort to keep his affairs secret: his middle-class facade was important to him. Hungary was the only place he was less discreet about this double life. He had an affair with Margrit Kutschera, from Vienna (who Wisliceny scornfully implied was a professional mistress) and with Ingrid von Ihne, a divorced society lady who was the epitome of National Socialist womanhood: tall, blond, and slim, with a cold beauty. This made her the perfect companion for social occasions. "Eichmann was not the sadistic, lustful beast that the press later made him out to be," David Cesarani summarizes, "but he was certainly not a dull-witted clerk or a robotic bureaucrat, either. Power, the power of life and death, corrupted Eichmann. By 1944 he was rotten from the inside out."[69]

We may doubt whether his sexual escapades were a result of this thorough corruption. They look more like the result of lowered inhibitions, in which alcohol played a decisive role. "During the final years," Wisliceny wrote, "Eichmann was completely unscrupulous when it came to women, for in Budapest, too, he got drunk every night."[70] The intoxication of power alone was not enough to make the son of a good middle-class household into a decadent rake with no sense of "propriety." The striking thing here is that Eichmann had no problem recounting his "dynamic" actions in Hungary (where he was "the master," organizing the most efficient deportations of the Nazi period). He talked about it in his memoirs, and in the discussion sessions in Argentina, proudly telling stories of the horrific transport conditions and terrible death marches. But his affairs made him so uncomfortable that he tried to explain them away. The aristocratic society lady had been merely a "dinner companion"—and that had been only on one occasion, when he gave a dinner party. "I had no hostess," he explained, "and it was necessary to have a hostess, after all. And so I asked Frau von Ihne. . . . That was all." To be on the safe side, Eichmann reiterated, "I had no hostess . . . I had no concubine, like someone says somewhere here [referring to a book], you know? And I'm not going to count a nice little friendship with someone I may have gone out to dinner with, but with whom I never once had intimate relations." And when the need for a lady of the house arose once more: "I asked another lady, with whom I certainly had no intimate relations," namely "Fräulein von Kutschera," who at the time had apparently been engaged. "And so she played hostess for the evening."[71]

Eichmann only ever had *friendships* with women—in Altensalzkoth, as he did elsewhere. He mounted a moralistic defense against any insinuations about affairs and refused to rise to Sassen's teasing. Sassen had a predilection for obvious innuendo and a love of detail that can only be described as pornographic.[72] But Eichmann's success with women was not something he was proud of. When rumors about his love life (most of them complete fabrications) caught the press's attention soon after his arrest, and after he had read Wisliceny's denouncement, he once again began to stress that he had never taken a lover. All relationships with women apart from his wife had been "purely platonic."[73] But he wasn't entirely happy with this image, either, and he added the "assurance" that "nature was kind enough to bestow upon me, too, that resource with which certain bearers of organic life generally seek to be endowed by the aforementioned nature. I was certainly no sexless common horsetail."[74]

This stilted, awkward declaration is not just a confession of male vanity, but the expression of a profoundly National Socialist belief: potency and a "natural" sexuality were part of Nazi race biology's definition of the SS man. The SS, as Himmler understood it, was the nucleus of a new, racially pure elite. This was the sole aim behind the ideal of careful selection.[75] Future SS wives—and the men themselves—had to submit to thorough medical examinations before the Office for Race and Resettlement would allow the marriage. Impotence, or any kind of deviant sexual tendency, barred men from entering the ranks of the SS.

For Adolf Eichmann, taking a relaxed attitude to his own sexuality was more a challenge than an opportunity. When Himmler wanted to give his lover an expensive present on the birth of their baby, Eichmann saw the necklace that had been stolen to order and reacted with horror on two grounds. It wasn't just the corruption that disgusted him but the fact that his *Reichsführer*-SS, Heinrich Himmler, was not even keeping his second family a secret from his underlings. "Such a senior superior officer" could not allow himself to grant others an insight "into the most difficult of matters." People would "see through" him, and he would become "a prisoner" of those who knew his secret.[76] Himmler believed that his SS men were the very people who should overcome "the prevailing moral outlook," because it was founded on "supposedly moral laws built up by Christianity." The "falsehood" of these laws needed to be brought to an end. Eichmann evidently shared neither this opinion[77] nor Sassen's lightheartedness about sexual matters. Even in all-male gatherings like the Sassen circle, he did not approve of ribaldry. Sassen's predilection for very obvious innuendo regularly caused Eichmann to fall silent. Much as he liked to keep pace, and had no difficulty making intolerably cynical remarks about the conditions in concentration camps, he stonewalled Sassen on topics like the camp bordellos, just as he did on his own extramarital affairs. He took no pleasure in this kind of macho talk. During his psychological examination in Israel, prisoner Eichmann, who was usually so cooperative, displayed the same attitude he had in Buenos Aires. "The first and only time that he refused to cooperate during the interviews was when we questioned him regarding his sexual experiences," said the investigating psychologist, Shlomo Kulcsár. "The sexuality in the case of E. is so repressed, concealed and disguised that its reconstruction is . . . difficult."[78] The experienced team of psychologists (which also included Kulcsár's wife) evaluated the various tests they had carried out and came to the conclusion that Eichmann had "very strong inhibitions in sexual subjects." All three psychologists suspected a "sadomasochist complex."[79] They were certain that there was something more to Eichmann than the self-consciousness typical of that generation when it came to intimacy. Unfortunately, the examinations they carried out were not enough to discover any more about his unanimously diagnosed "latent aggression."

The emphasis Eichmann placed on his own potency is particularly striking when seen in this context. He made several such insinuations even to the prison staff. Eichmann, who had been provided with Nabokov's *Lolita* as reading matter for his cell, declined further novels, claiming they were too erotic—a thought bound to strike someone in his position, imprisoned in a brightly lit cell, with guards present at all times. On other occasions, Eichmann emphasized quite pointedly how difficult it was for him to get by without a woman for so long.[80] If we consider these statements, and the fact of his affairs, in isolation, we are in danger of giving in to the comforting notion of the "Holocaust monster," as portrayed in a few novels and even some more recent films. Here Eichmann is cast as the orgiast who, having become intoxicated by murder and lost his moral compass, satisfies his sexual urges over the graves of his victims.[81] But Eichmann's character was far removed from this sort of pornographic Nazi kitsch. His concept of propriety allowed for the murder of Jews but restricted his personal life to strictly bourgeois mores. He could only abandon them where Nazi ideology provided him with the support, the categories, and, above all, the vocabulary. Hypocrisy and embarrassment made him fall silent when it came to his own physical needs, but reproduction was a topic of conversation about which he had no inhibitions. This was the "fight for survival" against the Jewish race, until final victory. Reproduction was crudely politicized, with talk of "the drive to preserve the race."[82] Eichmann was too prudish to admit to even one of his affairs in conversation with a notorious Don Juan like Sassen, but this language made it possible for him to boast about his enduring potency and about becoming a father for a fourth time at an advanced age.

Heinrich Himmler expected his SS men to each have at least four children. Adolf Eichmann may not have succeeded in killing all the Jews, but by November 1955 he had his four children, all of them sons; this was one duty, at least, he had more than fulfilled. It would have been difficult for him not to brag. In this respect, he knew he was united with National Socialists like Willem Sassen, who had also called the birth of a child following his escape from Europe "a challenge to the world of [his] enemies, his fierce assertion of life, of values that had been trampled and spat upon by his enemies."[83] Only committed anti-Semites of a racial-biological disposition could see children as a triumph "over the forces that tried to destroy me." Only where the race war is so total that it must be continued after the military defeat could the birth of a son give one a "triumphal satisfaction." In the war of the races, potency was an unbeatable long-range weapon, and even in retirement the SS *Obersturmbannführer* had shown his commitment and done his duty.

Vera Liebl gave birth to her son in November 1955, in the Pequeña Compañía Maria, a Catholic hospital in Buenos Aires.[84] "I was not officially allowed to claim my son as my own, since I was not officially married to my wife,"[85] Eichmann explained later, as if it were not clear to everyone that the missing marriage certificate could never have been the reason. Astonishingly, the nurses referred to the child quite openly as "Baby Eichmann,"[86] but it would still have been careless to register the birth under this well-known name. Eichmann's son was registered as Vera Liebl's illegitimate child and was given his father's pseudonym, plus a middle name that was a tribute to the priest in Genoa who had made this "triumph" possible: Ricardo Francisco.[87] The enforced discretion threw Eichmann into a quandary. "It pained me to have to do this," he wrote later.[88] And it was perfectly clear to him who was responsible for this personal offense: "Political circumstances are to blame for the complication that our legitimate son, born inside marriage, has been registered as illegitimate."[89]

A Forsaken Bunch in a Forsaken Position

Yes indeed, my dear friend, we are a forsaken bunch in a forsaken position. This is our strength, and this is why we have no worse enemy than our own despair.
　　　　　　　　　　　　　　　　—Willem Sassen, Christmas 1955[90]

Eichmann should have been satisfied with the way things were going. He had a new job, his wife was doing well after the birth, the child was healthy, and he had a round-number birthday coming up. Ordinarily, all this would be cause to celebrate. But for Eichmann, it was a nightmare, and not just because births and fiftieth birthdays have a tendency to precipitate crises in a lot of men. Even men without mass murder on their conscience start to question themselves after the birth of a baby, wondering what their child will think of its father. And Eichmann knew his children could read all about the fact that he was a war criminal and a mass murderer. He had a good, faithful wife, but he had to pass her off as his lover, thereby denying her the respect she deserved. He had a healthy child, but officially the baby was not his. And his fiftieth birthday was approaching in March 1956, but Ricardo Klement's birthday was not until May, and in any case he was seven years younger. And all that was left of his glittering career was a name he could no longer control. Eichmann wanted a change, and both his associates and the world beyond were happy to oblige. "It's my own fault that the Jews were able to catch me," he would say later, and looking at his life after 1955, we must conclude that he was right.[91]

It wasn't just Eichmann's personal circumstances that changed in 1955. Over the course of the year, several pieces of bad news arrived for all those still dreaming of National Socialism, whether in the former Reich or in exile. Austria signed the Independence Treaty; occupation came to an end in the West German Federal Republic; West Germany was allowed to form its own armed services and to join NATO; and the Hallstein Doctrine gave West Germany the sole right to represent German interests abroad. For those who were still of a National Socialist bent, it meant the renunciation of all interests for Germany as a whole and an orientation toward the victor, the detested United States. Their election hopes had also come to nothing: in 1954 Hans-Ulrich Rudel had fantasized about a "small minority of clear-sighted people" convincing the stupid majority over time, but he achieved a meager 3.8 percent of the vote when he stood for the Deutsche Reichspartei in the Lower Saxony state elections, where right-wing parties had previously had most success. The German people had clearly not yet realized there was a "web of lies over Germany" or "what wicked games those circles who seek to rule the world have been playing with us."[92] They were delighted with their prosperity and with Chancellor Konrad Adenauer, who had succeeded in negotiating the release of German prisoners of war in Moscow. The West German president, Theodor Heuss, came straight to the point, addressing the men of the Dürer circle directly in one of his speeches: Der Weg "remains embarrassing reading," but "as voters, the population has shown quite plainly in the elections of recent years that in spite of the great slogans, or perhaps even because of the great slogans, there are some things to which they are immune." The "group . . . warming itself in the sun of Peron" could carry on spreading "its ridiculous polemical notions about a future Germany, using the old vocabulary." The Germans, said Heuss, had chosen a different path.[93]

In summer 1955, an Israeli mission (the forerunner of an embassy) was established in Cologne, while patriotic German comrades in Argentina were still awaiting a general amnesty. At the start of 1955, Willem Sassen optimistically announced that democracy in Germany was a temporary arrangement with no future, an "interregnum."[94] He was proved wrong. Little remained of the "will to the Reich" and the "indefatigable spirit of the perpetual German," and prospects for a return to power and to Germany were worse than ever. The only thing the exiles in Argentina could hope for over the coming year was to inspire the few remaining valiant comrades in their homeland with hope of a sort of transcendent racial victory. "Our struggle is a dream," Sassen wrote, resorting to the slogans of perseverance in which he had become an expert during the previous unsuccessful push for final victory. "And because our blood dreams that dream within us, our physical life is meaningless: our blood will dream on in our children, for centuries to come."[95] Scattered across the globe, all the National Socialists had left was blood. There was no more soil. And if things went on like this, Eichmann's newborn son wouldn't even have the right name to go with his blood.

Things were set to get worse. At the end of 1955, the discussion about crimes against humanity, in which Adolf Eichmann was so substantially involved, shifted. The first books about the National Socialists' persecution of the Jews appeared in quick succession. The French documentary film *Night and Fog* was released, showing the systematic incarceration of regime opponents in concentration camps, and those camps' everyday horrors. It disturbed viewers to the extent that the Federal German government tried to prevent it from being shown—not only in German cinemas but also at the Cannes film festival. While German historians hesitantly began the work into which they should have thrown themselves with full force, public debates about dealing with the past made the headlines for months.[96] Even Willem Sassen sounded upset when he spoke to Eichmann about the film.

The publications on the extermination of the Jews, and the changing discussion in West Germany, also influenced discussions within the Dürer circle. It started at the end of 1955, when Léon Poliakov and Josef

Wulf's *Das Dritte Reich und die Juden* (The Third Reich and the Jews) landed like a thunderbolt. Shortly after it was published, Otto Bräutigam from the Foreign Office was temporarily placed on leave, as the book contained a document on the "Jewish question" that bore his signature.[97] The book was principally a collection of documents, and its ineluctable strength rankled with Sassen and his colleagues. It contained the Führer's orders for theft and persecution; jubilant commentaries and notes from Göring; tallies of robbery and murder from Operation Reinhard; reports about gold teeth, Reichsbank deposits, and forced labor; gas chamber plans; extracts from the *Gerstein Report*; Himmler's order to liquidate the Warsaw ghetto; Stroop's final report; and, most notably, statistics on "special treatments" and "extinction." There was Dieter Wisliceny's report on the Final Solution; the Wannsee protocol; and an incredible number of memos, on Auschwitz, racial fanaticism, human experiments, and forced sterilizations. The reader was given an insight into the National Socialists' anti-Jewish "policy" through a combination of excerpts with commentaries, complete documents, photographs, and facsimiles. This was all much more difficult to deny than the previously published memoirs and newspaper articles. Letterheads and signatures were clearly reproduced for all to see. A whole chapter was devoted to the "Grand Inquisitor without magic," Adolf Eichmann.

This wealth of detail could not easily be dismissed as enemy propaganda. It could not be refuted by fake experts like Hester and Heimann. Most important, doubt was growing within the Dürer circle's own ranks. It was slowly dawning on every last National Socialist that the extermination of the Jews really had taken place. Even people who had grown accustomed to looking the other way when they were in power, relativizing and playing everything down, couldn't get past this evidence. Reviews of the book soon appeared in all the papers, and Eichmann's name cropped up in every article. *Das Dritte Reich und die Juden* was also mentioned in the July edition of *Der Weg*.[98] Even a publication run by the most hard-bitten postwar Nazis was starting to feature terms it had always carefully avoided or used sarcastically: Auschwitz; Majdanek; the Final Solution to the Jewish Question; the Wannsee conference; grave mistreatment of the opponents of the Nazi regime; the deportation of forty thousand French Jews.[99] It talked of "people who were thoughtlessly driven into the concentration camps, to their death," the "concentration camp terror" and the "Jewish atrocity."[100] The top names were mentioned: Reinhard Heydrich, Heinrich Müller, Arthur Nebe, Odilo Globocnik, and Theodor Dannecker,[101] the "adviser on Jewish affairs" from Department IV B 4 in France. The facts were so overwhelming that even in Buenos Aires, people started calling a spade a spade. In this 1956 article, the only name noticeable by its absence was Eichmann's.

But attention and acceptance are very different things. Instead of recognizing that the Nazi extermination of the Jews had been a "dance of death unique in world history,"[102] the postwar Nazis dreamed up a new conspiracy theory. If the facts could not be denied, they could at least be reinterpreted. A series of articles entitled "The Role of the Gestapo" painted a picture of the "conspiracy that has been raging since 1933." Amid all the incomprehensible nonsense of this series, one thing emerges with clarity: the desperation of the men who still dreamed of a National Socialist redemption.[103] Briefly, the soothing story they told themselves went like this: it was not the SS but the Gestapo that was to blame for everything. The Gestapo had "never been the pure National Socialist police organization that it was claimed to be in the posters of that time, and today." From the very beginning, it had practiced "subversion." It was really a cover for a small group "disguised as upright citizens" that tried to "frustrate, corrupt and compromise the policies of the Third Reich." It aimed to topple "Hitler's hated government of the people [!]" and to do permanent damage to Germany's standing in the world, which Hitler had done so much to advance. The man to blame for all this misery, as the article explained in fantastical detail, was the head of the Abwehr (Germany's military intelligence organization), Admiral Wilhelm Canaris, who had enthroned the intriguer Reinhard Heydrich. All the violence was chalked up to the accounts of these two men, and "today we may suspect a very specific system designed to compromise and make enemies for the new government." Apparently, when Heydrich discovered how Canaris was misusing him, Canaris had him summarily killed. Then Heinrich Müller, who in reality was not a National Socialist at all, organized the extermination of the Jews in the east. The "criminal element in the Gestapo leadership" was a group of unscrupulous men "who unthinkingly drove people into concentrations camps, to their deaths, in order finally to strike down a king—Adolf Hitler." And recognizing that people would want to know why no one else had realized it, the author of the article explained: a lie had been constructed instead. "The victors obviously knew all about the real background of the Gestapo campaigns. They had to help suppress the truth, so that the betrayed world would not one day learn that it was Hitler's opponents, not Hitler, who organized this." So it all turns out well in the end, for Hitler and Germany and National Socialism.

The article was attributed to Paul Beneke, allegedly writing from Madrid. The real Paul Beneke lived in the fifteenth century and was, depending on whose side you were on, either the selfless hero who defeated the English fleet in 1468 and restored the trading rights of the Hanseatic League, or a savage pirate who stole every vessel that crossed his path. Gustav Freytag, an author much loved by the National Socialists for his "images from German history" and his clearly anti-Semitic writing, created a literary memorial to the Danzig admiral, which could be purchased in a splendid edition from the German military's publishing house. In Danzig itself, Paul Beneke was a particular hero, with streets and civic buildings named after him. Knowing the special relationship the people of Danzig have with their city,[104] we might conclude that the author of these "Gestapo secrets" articles came from East Prussia. However, we still do not know who he was. The content clearly points to a member of the SS. The working method, the style, and the detailed knowledge behind the article also suggest the usual suspects: Sassen, Leers, or Fritsch.[105] Eichmann also used the catchy phrase "the greatest and most violent dance of death of all time," but who "inspired" whom has so far been impossible to discover, particularly as the articles question everything Eichmann held to be true. He cannot have been hugely pleased with them.[106]

Whoever was making this attempt to release his comrades' souls from the nightmare of acknowledgment, he was neither alone nor without successors. The story of a small criminal clique, cheating Hitler and his people of their life's work and driving the country into war and mass murder, is still being told on websites and in a certain kind of literature today. The perfidious keystone of this story was laid in 1956, when Paul Beneke left the answer to who was behind it all hanging in the air. The transcript of a Deutsche Reichspartei meeting in Berlin on November 30, 1956, records a party member getting worked up over it, claiming that Eichmann, the Gestapo's Adviser on Jewish Affairs, was a "full Jew." With the help of Himmler and foreign Jews, Eichmann had infiltrated the SS and instilled anti-Semitism there. He was now safely back in Tel Aviv.[107] This meeting was the birth of Adolf Eichmann's tenacious counterbiography,[108] and from then on its seemingly unstoppable career saw it providing comfort to anti-Semites in need. Had Eichmann not always said he came from Sarona, and did he not speak fluent Hebrew and Yiddish? No wonder he was able to make a career as a specialist on Jewish affairs, if he was one himself. . . . Even Johann von Leers, who met Eichmann for the last time in 1954 before moving to Cairo, was completely convinced of this idea in hindsight.[109] The classic reality-free story about "Eichmann the Jew" is the final consequence of this falsification of history, which was perpetrated by people who could no longer avoid the fact of the Holocaust but were not prepared to acknowledge it as a "German act." The only things connecting this nonsense to the truth are Eichmann's imagined intellectual intimacy with Judaism, and the newspaper articles post-1945, documenting survivors' fears that Eichmann could be masquerading as a Jew to escape his pursuers. It was no coincidence that the conspiracy theorists liked to quote the old article "The Man We Are Looking For." People intent on falsifying the facts could easily reinterpret this article as an admission by the Jews that Eichmann was one of them. Still, the Holocaust deniers' story, which once again painted the Jews as the puppet masters responsible for their own destruction, continues to have a persistent following, and a frightening level of international fame. In Buenos Aires, meanwhile, people were very receptive to the Canaris theory, according to which the Führer was the innocent gull—but SS *Obersturmbannführer* Adolf Eichmann's Jewish heritage was a little harder to swallow. Nevertheless, Sassen and his fellow believers later made a huge effort to tempt their old comrade into confessing he was "un-German."

Léon Poliakov and Josef Wulf's collection of documents even gave Willem Sassen pause. "In recent days," he told *Der Weg*'s readers, "I have, with painful self-discipline, worked through a thick tome containing essays and documents on the relationship between the Third Reich and the Jews. Sometimes it choked me, and I struggled as if gripped in a stranglehold, before—completely naïve once more—crying out: 'It is not true!' I knew the cry was simplistic; it sprang from my own helplessness. And I believe one should not simply brand everything a lie: neither all that is written in this terrible book, nor every cry of 'It is not true!'"[110] But anyone hoping Sassen's reading might have had a lasting effect on his worldview will be disappointed. The confession of his dismay at the book appears in an accusatory text on nuclear weapons—an invention for which "the Jews" were also to blame. A true Aryan would never split an atom. Sassen applied his rhetorical skill to describing how this "terrible book" had relieved him of a burden: "The truth is probably relative." Ultimately, the "little" assistant operating the death camp gas chambers was "a puny dwarf next to the Nobel Prize winners and giants of this scientific extermination technology, to which mankind has been helplessly delivered up." Alluding to the originator of the theory of relativity, Sassen relativizes into a mere nothing the crimes against humanity he had briefly mentioned, by setting them against this true, Jewish, extermination plan—all in the space of a few lines.

In spite of the way this review was packaged, with the aim of lessening the book's effect, something had clearly happened to *Der Weg*'s editorial policy. Only a few months previously, the likes of Heimann and Hester were telling readers that "there were no gas chambers, gas vans or incinerators for exterminating humans in any of the concentration or internment camps inside or outside Germany."[111] And now here were the names Belzec, Hockenholt, and Wirth—the extermination camp, the gas-van diesel technician, and the man who oversaw operations on the ground. For a moment, reality arrived in Buenos Aires, and in spite of all his reassurances, it refused to leave Sassen in peace. He didn't restrict himself to penning platitudes about blood-soaked dreams; he went to Germany and registered as a resident there. Willem Antonius Maria Sassen van Elsloo, a journalist and author by profession, of German nationality. Official emigration from Argentina to Konstanz am Bodensee: August 25, 1956. Forsaken positions were obviously easier to deal with when you had other temporary quarters available.[112]

Poliakov and Wulf upped the ante with a second volume of documents, *Das Dritte Reich und seine Diener* (The Third Reich and Its Servants), also published in 1956. It focused on the Foreign Office, the Nazi judiciary, and the Wehrmacht. Two more influential books were also published in quick succession. First, Gerald Reitlinger's comprehensive *The Final Solution,* the first ambitious study of all aspects of the Holocaust, had finally found a German publisher. The second book sprang from the extensive discussion of the so-called Kasztner Trial in Jerusalem: *Die Geschichte des Joel Brand aufgeschrieben von Alex Weissberg.* (An English edition, *Advocate for the Dead: The Story of Joel Brand,* appeared in 1958.) Most of the numerous reviews mentioned Eichmann, the Adviser on Jewish Affairs from the RSHA, who had sent Joel Brand abroad to buy trucks to trade for Jewish blood. Reviewers occasionally accused the Jewish authors of a lack of objectivity,[113] but set against the backdrop of Poliakov and Wulf's documents, their books were more than unsettling.

The Dürer circle read them closely, and with every page the question of what had really happened became more insistent. They were desperate to believe that it wasn't true. The last article on the topic in *Der Weg* before the start of the Sassen interviews was headed "The 'Final Solution' to the Jewish Question." It claimed that the real aim behind the extermination of the Jews had been the founding of the State of Israel, and that the blame for this crime had been "laid at Hitler's door using sophisticated means."[114] Adolf Hitler had never ordered a "program of murdering Jews." And thanks to the small group of conspirators who met at Wannsee—and here Eichmann was mentioned for the first and only time[115]—Hitler had never even got word of it. The Führer's headquarters was (and one has to admire the tactful choice of words here) a "concentration cloister," and he was cut off from what was really happening. "The conspiracy group started in the police, betraying the fact that these were the same Jewish secret agents who perverted the formally National Socialist Gestapo." The line was that Zionists had murdered the "assimilators" they hated, in order to force the international community to give them their own state. This made the extermination of the Jews look like an internal Jewish matter, against which the poor Führer in his bunker could do nothing.

This intolerable nonsense appeared under the name Wolf Sievers, a pseudonym that was also used for other articles in *Der Weg*. The name is significant even at face value: Wolfram Sievers was one of the war criminals who had been hanged in Landsberg, and the Dürer circle looked on him as a martyr. When Hans-Ulrich Rudel visited Germany in 1953, he made a special pilgrimage to the gallows in the Landsberg prison and wrote emotionally, "Since my return home, I never felt so close to Germany as I did here."[116] Wolfram Sievers was condemned to death at the Nuremberg Doctors' Trial, for his management of the "research team" known as *Ahnenerbe* (ancestral heritage), which had been responsible for human experiments and murders. He made contact with Adolf Eichmann for projects that showed total contempt for humanity, like the infamous "skeleton collection"—someone had to organize the transportation of the people destined to become exhibits. We still don't know who was behind this pseudonym, though the style, content, and examples given in this article suggest it was one of Sassen's pieces. He proclaimed the basic principles of the argument again in an interview in 1960, when he told a reporter from La Razón that someone else was to blame for the extermination of the Jews. Even "Eichmann was doubtless just an instrument in the hands of the people who initiated this diabolical plan," and it had certainly never been Hitler's idea.[117] The pseudonym also suggests his authorship, as Sassen had already chosen two other aliases with the initials W.S.[118] In any case, the article "The 'Final Solution' to the Jewish Question" dealt with the very same topics and theories that formed the focus of the interviews with Eichmann: the Führer's orders; a "Zionist conspiracy"; the attempt to preserve Hitler's honor; the search for conspirators within the Gestapo; the surviving documents; and the books.

Not even expatriate Nazis equipped with an entire media arsenal could fight this flood of information. Sassen might have heard a few rumors after the Russian campaign, and known much more than he wanted to let on even to himself, but his knowledge of the Nazi leadership was nowhere near adequate for him to mount a credible rejoinder. He had never seen the documents, never heard anything about the conference they named, and was simply overwhelmed by the mass of material. For all their bluster about conspiracies, the postwar Nazis, both in exile and in the former German Reich, were rendered speechless and powerless by the books on the murder of the Jews. But unlike readers in West Germany, the men in Buenos Aires knew where to find someone who would have an answer for their questions. And more important, this man was famous enough that when he exposed what they imagined was another step in the ideological war, it would have some public impact. He would blow the Jewish conspiracy wide open. The witness himself was receptive to this request, unlike more cautious candidates, such as Himmler's former chief adjutant and the "doctor" Josef Mengele. Talking had two great advantages for Eichmann: first, the Dürer circle gave him accesss to the new books, which he could not have afforded himself—books from Germany were expensive in Buenos Aires. And most important, these media-savvy comrades could enable him to regain what he so desperately wanted: control over his place in history. Then his children would be able to say, openly and proudly, that they were Adolf Eichmann's sons.

THE SO-CALLED
SASSEN INTERVIEWS

Herr Sassen—he was the journalist who often visited me at home with the tape, to record the story of my life. I permitted him to publish these reports if I should die, or fall into the hands of the Israelis. As I see, he has now published something people believe is my memoirs.

Everything that has been published in the USA is plain lies. Only a madman could believe I wrote that.

—Eichmann, "Meine Flucht," March 1961, on the articles in *Life*

For many years, Willem Sassen was credited with having tracked down the mass murderer Adolf Eichmann and persuaded him to talk. Journalists' natural sympathy for their colleagues goes some way to explaining the success of this story, as does the fact that this former war correspondent for the Dutch Voluntary SS was a charismatic man. To an outsider, Sassen looked like the kind of star author, adventurer, and bon vivant who could have pulled off such a coup, and he did everything in his power to promote this image. Of course, one didn't have to be particularly charming, sensitive, or convincing to get Adolf Eichmann to talk. The real problem was getting him to stop: once the SS *Obersturmbann-führer* (retired) got started, there was no holding him back. This image still hardly seems credible: we think of a man on the run wanting to stay as unobtrusive as possible, remaining extremely cautious and reticent. But that wasn't how the National Socialists lived in Argentina. The myth of silence and secrecy merely helped them erect a wall of silence, for various reasons, after Eichmann was kidnapped. How much credence should we give to someone claiming not to know a man who was on trial for mass murder? When Israelis had just kidnapped a former colleague on his way home from work, who in their right mind would admit to having a glass of wine and working on a book about National Socialism with this very colleague? Eichmann's associates were eager to avoid anything similar happening to them on their own way home. Their most obvious course of action was to describe Eichmann as a recluse who never spoke to anyone but Sassen—and Sassen was a journalist, who *had* to talk to people "like him." But the numerous bouquets of flowers and good wishes that Eichmann received in Israel, sent from Argentina, would soon correct the impression that he had led a solitary life.[1]

In Argentina, Eichmann's urge to speak had always been greater than his sense of caution. Among men he believed to be trustworthy, as we have seen, he never kept quiet about who he was. But the occasional chat at a social gathering or a conversation in the bar after work was something very different from what Eberhard Fritsch and Willem Sassen were proposing: a systematic discussion of the history books and the current debates. Serious preparations were under way. By the end of

1956, Eichmann was also making plans, for a book he wanted to publish with Dürer Verlag. We may therefore assume that serious discussions had already taken place, to draw up a plan of work and consider who else might participate in the project, for financial reasons. Later, Willem Sassen, Eberhard Fritsch, and Adolf Eichmann all confirmed independently that they had signed a contract with one another at this point, agreeing to divide all proceeds from the work equally among them.[2] The dream of making a fast buck played a significant role for them all, even if the "dream of blood" was what united them. Life in Buenos Aires always had its "soldier of fortune" aspect.

Before the official recordings began, in April 1957 at the earliest, something remarkable happened in the Sassen household. Saskia Sassen,[3] who was around ten years old, saw men drilling holes in the living room ceiling and hiding microphones there. As Sassen's daughter remembered in 2005, there was a palpable tension and a nervous bustle in the house. Eichmann arrived, then disappeared into the living room with her father, and a strange man spent the whole time he was there on the floor above, listening in. Saskia Sassen is certain that the man with her father was Adolf Eichmann, and that this was the only time she saw the man in the attic: it was a one-off occurrence.

Children's memories are known for being a problematic source; at this age they are eager to see "secrets" in what may be a simple case of a cable layer installing a new light fixture. But there is a second source that can be connected to this episode. An old friend of the family, who had come to Argentina from Ireland with them, said that Sassen's wife, Miep, had complained to her that she was all "wired up."[4] Unfortunately, we do not know whether her annoyance at the wires was related to microphones in the ceiling. Miep Sassen watched her husband take over the living room with his equipment every weekend for months on end. He would set up his tape recorder with several microphones positioned around the room, like trip wires, and spend hours conducting interviews with old comrades. Anyone who is prevented from entering their own living room without knocking, and is told to keep the children quiet,[5] has good reason to complain about being "wired up," even if no one has drilled holes in her ceiling. Still, Saskia Sassen's recollection brings into play the possibility that one day before the start of the official recordings, Willem Sassen let an eavesdropper into his attic without Eichmann's knowledge.

Saskia Sassen never forgot the strange surveillance episode, and later she would search for explanations for what she had seen. The most likely scenario she could think of was a connection to one of her father's acquaintances, Phil Payne, the Latin America correspondent for *Life*, one of the magazines for which Sassen worked. "Mr. Payne from Time/Life" was someone even the children knew about. It may not have been Payne himself listening in the attic,[6] but for Sassen's daughter this connection was the only reasonable explanation for what she saw. Her interpretation was that, even before the official recordings began, her father was angling for a contract with Time Inc. and had to provide proof that the man he was interviewing really was the former SS *Obersturmbannführer* Adolf Eichmann. This possibility also fits temptingly well with a report in the French magazine *L'Express* (large parts of which were admittedly rather imaginative).[7] It claimed that Sassen had offered the interviews to Time Inc. "four years" before Eichmann was abducted, without success. The article angered Sassen, who denied having said any such thing.[8] Whatever truth it published, *L'Express* was wrong about the dates: the interviews began considerably later and hadn't been completed, or even started, at the time it claimed. So let us begin cautiously, with what we know to be true.

Phil Payne was the South America correspondent for Time, Inc. He arrived in Buenos Aires shortly after Perón's overthrow and lived there in between his long trips reporting on events elsewhere. He left again in 1958. Willem Sassen provided Time Inc. with research material, acting as a source for a big article on Perón and Pedro Aramburu after the putsch in Argentina, which appeared in *Life* in November 1955.[9] However, he was not credited in the magazine until the Eichmann articles in 1960. This suggests that Payne was Sassen's contact at Time Inc. and a welcome visitor in the Sassen household. Prior to April 1957, if Sassen had wanted to sell the U.S. magazine a story on Eichmann, or a Holocaust exposé, he would certainly have told Phil Payne about it. Payne, in turn, would have had to convince his employer that the investment in Sassen's information would prove worthwhile, and bugging the house as Saskia Sassen remembers would have been a good way to do it. He could check the authenticity of Sassen's contact without scaring Eichmann away. Sassen, for his part, would have wanted to prevent a potential competitor[10] from making contact with his most important source, which is a sensible precaution on such a delicate story. But Payne had little interest in exploring the past, and he may still not have been convinced by the Eichmann story. Phil Payne specialized in high-risk, up-to-the-minute stories: he had reported on the civil war in Colombia and the arms trade in Nicaragua; he had gone in search of guerrillas in Costa Rica and explored almost every trouble spot in Latin America, from Guatemala to Bolivia. He was interested in the grand narratives of revolutionaries, leaders who had gained power and lost it again, like Jacobo Arbenz Guzmán and Juan Domingo Perón. In 1957 he would finish in South America and spend the next few years reporting from Rome. In 1961 he would go to Jerusalem to cover the trial of the man who had organized the Final Solution.[11] In 1956 in Buenos Aires he valued Sassen not for his fanciful ideas or his insufferable friends but for his insider knowledge of the city, and for the close relationship he maintained with Perón, even when the ex-president was living in exile in Spain. In Payne's eyes, old Nazi stories didn't hold the same attraction—even if Eichmann's name had found its way into the pages of *Time* magazine by this point, in an article about Rudolf Kasztner.[12] But if Payne really did reject the Eichmann story in 1956–57, he must have been kicking himself later, as he covered the trial.

However, a few things in this story remain unclear. To begin with, why was it neccessary to go to these lengths for Adolf Eichmann? He had been far from reluctant to take up Fritsch and Sassen's offer and showed no qualms about revealing his identity. In fact, during the first recording, he was asked if he could think of anything "to convince people that the writer of this book is really *the* Eichmann," and he answered: "Yes, there is the following: the material cannot be denied, either one is familiar with the details or not.—If these gentlemen have their doubts, they can compare the pieces of handwriting, which have come out in bursts, in the files, and if necessary—though I would prefer not to do this—I could personally give them a photograph . . . from this period."[13] In light of the lengths to which Eichmann and his family had gone, for so many years, to ensure that not a single photo fell into the hands of his pursuers, his openness toward his new friends is striking. Later, he really did autograph a photo for Willem Sassen: "Adolf Eichmann. SS Obersturmbannführer (retired)." Whatever Fritsch, Sassen, and Eichmann were planning to publish, it was clearly a team effort, and a pseudonym or any sort of cover for Eichmann was not part of the plan. Quite apart from these considerations, we cannot be sure that the microphones were even being set up for Eichmann. Considering who else Sassen invited to join the discussion group, he might well have been testing the listening equipment on Eichmann in case someone refused to be recorded openly.[14]

Children aren't the only people who find the idea of people drilling holes in walls and laying wires irresistibly mysterious. The possibility of men eavesdropping in the attic is clearly much too appealing for a prosaic explanation. Could the bugging operation have been carried out by an intelligence service, rather than having a financial motive? The important question here is whether anyone was actually interested in Adolf Eichmann at this time. The National Socialists who were still at large had dropped off the U.S. priority list—apart from those the CIA had recruited for itself.[15] Israel's newly formed intelligence service had other things on its plate: the Suez crisis began in October 1956, and the Israelis had not followed up on Wiesenthal's clue.

What about Germany? Fritz Bauer, the attorney general of Hesse, was just beginning the difficult and unpopular task of prosecuting Nazi perpetrators. He had requested Adolf Eichmann's "wanted" file from Vienna.[16] On November 24, 1956, the district court in Frankfurt finally issued an arrest warrant for "Adolf Eichmann, whereabouts presently unknown." It issued the warrant in connection with the case against "Krumey and others," and according to its wording, it suspected Eichmann of "killing people in numbers that cannot be precisely established, in a cruel and underhand manner, acting from low motives, during the period 1938–1945, in various countries of Europe. As an SS Obersturmbannführer and head of Dept. IV B 4 of the RSHA, Eichmann was responsible for the 'resettlement of the Jews' in Germany and in the lands occupied by Germany during the war. In the context of the so-called Final Solution of the Jewish question, he ordered the transport of several million members of the Jewish faith, and their extermination by gassing in concentration camps."[17] From 1957, Eichmann's name would appear on the German "wanted" list. But Fritz Bauer's investigations were unwelcome in Germany, and there is no evidence of any other institutions' energetic involvement in the hunt for Eichmann. The Bundeskriminalamt (BKA, Federal Office for Criminal Investigations) even said that fundamental things about the case prevented an

Interpol search for Eichmann.[18] At first, Bauer was kept extremely busy with the cases in which the whereabouts of perpetrators was known—for example, Hermann Krumey, Eichmann's deputy in Hungary. With a judiciary whose ranks had some Nazi history of their own, this work proved extremely difficult. Krumey was arrested on April 1, 1957. As we will see, these events were followed closely in Argentina, but even in this case, criminal proceedings were not brought immediately. Bauer certainly wasn't in a position to take any action in Argentina at this point. But the Bundesamt für Verfassungsschutz (BfV, Federal Office for the Protection of the Constitution) had begun to take an interest in Rudel and Fritsch quite independently of Bauer's investigation; more on this later.[19]

In any case, the possibility that a spy under Sassen's own roof might have prompted the West German investigation is pure speculation. To begin with, it is highly unlikely that a man who had cursed and sought to destroy "Rumpfdeutschland" (the leftover western half of a divided Germany) and its institutions would allow one of these West German institutions into his attic—he also had far too much to lose. If someone from the German intelligence service had wanted to know what these old comrades were up to in Sassen's living room, that person would have had to find a way of placing himself among them. It would not have been a particularly difficult task—and certainly easier than going to the trouble of eavesdropping on Sassen.

So what are we to make of this childhood memory of the Sassen house being bugged? From today's perspective, the likeliest explanation is still that it was a journalistic operation. Phil Payne was often in Argentina between 1955 and 1957, and we have evidence he was in Buenos Aires on May 10, 1957.[20] But until further documents or witnesses emerge, or reports are unearthed in the Time Inc. archive, this explanation too is mere speculation. The only certainty is that preparations for the group discussions with Adolf Eichmann appeared to be exciting and mysterious to the Sassen children. Willem Sassen had never taken on a project of this magnitude, and he was probably just as excited as the other participants. If Sassen's house was bugged, it would have been expressly permitted by Sassen himself. But what purpose it served and who carried it out remains, for the moment at least, a mystery.[21] Eichmann's explanation for how he could be identified shows that, from the beginning, some of the people involved in the project were not part of the core Dürer circle. Eichmann discovered only gradually that Sassen was not always honest with him and was entirely prepared to go over his head—whether there were eavesdroppers in the attic or not. But Eichmann signed up for this new task enthusiastically, throwing all caution to the winds.

1

Eichmann the Author

The binding and dust jacket should be kept to one colour; pearl- or dove-gray perhaps, with clear, linear and attractive lettering. It is clear that I do not want a pseudonym, as it is not in the nature of the thing. —Eichmann, 1961[1]

We cannot know when Adolf Eichmann first hit upon the idea of writing down his thoughts. He later said he made a first attempt (a work combining murder statistics and descriptions of Nazi institutions) directly after the war—meaning in Altensalzkoth. The document, he said, then became too much of a risk, and he burned it. It may sound strange that he could have begun to write so soon after a defeat, and when he was only in partial safety, but at that point he may well have felt the urge to commit himself to paper. It would not have been a bad idea to practice his defense in preparation for a possible trial. In any case, if Eichmann did compose a manuscript in northern Germany, it wouldn't have been his first.

Today, we have thousands of pages of Eichmann's stories, thanks not only to the trial transcripts but to a remarkable tendency he shared with many other National Socialists. Throughout his life, Eichmann was fascinated by writing and fancied himself an author. He was so taken by the idea of publishing a book that in 1961, after the trial had taken its disastrous course and he was awaiting the verdict in Israel, he was enthusiastically talking about jacket colors, potential editors, fonts, and dedicated copies—though it was still unclear whether publication was even a realistic possibility.[2] There have been only a few attempts to engage with Eichmann's texts as such. For one thing, his tireless writing has been seen as a symptom of his drive to justify himself. For another, as authors like Harry Mulisch and Hannah Arendt have emphasized, his prose has affected, posturing qualities. Someone who has thoroughly analyzed their own compulsion to write cannot ignore the provocation of Eichmann's claim to be "one of us." This claim will also be unpleasantly familiar to historians later, when we are confronted with Eichmann posing as a historian. Writers and historians have a strong impulse to make this aspect of Eichmann seem ridiculous, or to discredit his ambitions as a petit-bourgeois fantasy.

The National Socialists' penchant for publicly burning mountains of books has distorted our view: National Socialism had a great—perhaps too great—respect for the power of the written word. People burn books only when they attribute power to them; in other words, because they fear them. This fear was one of the Nazis' fundamental motivations. In the early twentieth century, people had enough experience of the book as a mass medium to know that history didn't just happen; it was an interpretation of events written for the generations to come. This insight was part of Adolf Hitler's aggressive path, along which the "creative" struggle, and the destruction of what had been created before 1933, steadily advanced.

The National Socialists didn't just rewrite history through their actions. From the outset, theirs was also a cultural and literary project: they vilified the culture industry as "Jewish," and discredited whole branches of academia as "too much under foreign influence." This orientation made the book one of their enemies' greatest weapons, particularly in the case of the Jews. Sorting and burning books—as the Nazis went on to do to humans—was just the first step. The second was to care for and cultivate the German race, and to found a Nazi culture and academic tradition. They needed their own books, in both the arts and the sciences, for they believed that in National Socialism, they had finally found the basis on which to build a truly German literary and academic tradition. As a result, the production of books under National Socialism was prodigious—and the reinterpretation of contemporary standards of knowledge was an act of violence.

This new culture was promoted by the self-proclaimed ideological elite, in particular the SD. The SD strove to be "creative": the "creative human" was the opposite of the clerks and pencil pushers of the day, and the Nazis believed this creativity would spell their end. Eichmann's "work" in Berlin was shaped from the very beginning by the production of texts. His first task, he said, was to produce a summary of the Zionist classic *The Jewish State* by Theodor Herzl. This kind of work was new to Eichmann, but not to many of his colleagues, who were university educated. One of his first commanding officers, Leopold von Mildenstein, was a relatively prominent author. Following his travels in the Orient in 1933, he had published "A Nazi Tells of a Journey to Palestine" in the SS magazine *Der Angriff,* to great acclaim. The magazine even had a commemorative coin made to accompany the series, which— incredibly—featured a swastika on the front and a Star of David on the back.[3] Eichmann admired his superior officer and emulated him (or so he remembered it). Mildenstein's successor, Herbert Hagen, with whom Eichmann made his trip to the Middle East in 1937, instituted a book group with a demanding reading list. He also commissioned more book reviews, press reviews with commentaries, and sometimes lengthy *Leithefte,* or "guidance booklets," for professional and training use. Eichmann was so fascinated by these booklets that he always claimed he had written one himself, and that it had been "printed."[4] "In this report I gave a factual account of the establishment of the Zionist world organization, the goals of Zionism, its sources of aid and its difficulties, and also underlined the challenge, because Zionism complied with our own wishes in this respect, because Zionism was also seeking a solution." Strictly speaking, *Leithefte* were not printed but were produced on a typewriter. An SS *Leitheft* was a secret dossier for use within the SD, not to be confused with the SS magazine of the same name, or a published book.[5] The title mentioned by Eichmann has not been found, but his outline sounds suspiciously like the terrible anti-Semitic book *Das Weltjudentum: Organisation, Macht und Politik* (World Jewry: Organization, Power and Politics), published in 1939 under the pseudonym Dieter Schwarz. Wisliceny claimed that Hagen and Franz Alfred Six compiled this volume. The department was proud of it. Its style doesn't suggest Eichmann's authorship, though he obviously would have loved to have been its author. The number of SD *Leithefte* to which he laid claim increased every time he talked about his activities as a writer.[6]

But even during the Nazi period, Eichmann's ambitions went far beyond internal pamphlets. In May 1942, as he told both Sassen and his interrogator in Israel, he wrote a hundred-page work titled "The Final Solution of the Jewish Question." It was to be published "for training purposes" by Nordland Verlag, with a print run of fifty thousand. As well as general explanations of the "Jewish question" and the transportation process, it apparently contained statistical material. He told Sassen he had offered the manuscript to Heydrich for publication under his name—and when Heydrich was assassinated in June, Eichmann decided he would at least dedicate it to him. But nothing came of it, and at the end of the war it had to be burned.

There are numerous inconsistencies in Eichmann's stories about this book, which suggest that he was greatly exaggerating.[7] The SS's Nordland Verlag published two prestigious series for RSHA Department VII from 1939 onward: "Books on the Jewish Question" and "Sources and Accounts on the Jewish Question." A volume of statistics was to be part of it. Franz Alfred Six, the head of Department VII, subsequently discussed the task with Eichmann, in connection with a conference. Six made quite clear, however, that it was to be "a group project, according to our directives" and that, strictly speaking, all he wanted from Eichmann was the raw data.[8]

But Eichmann found the very idea of publishing his own volume in this well-known series so flattering that, even years later, he still remembered the date and the publisher and claimed to be one of the authors chosen for this magnificent series of books.

Eichmann may have said he was never interested in the "limelight," but his behavior clearly shows he was fascinated by publicity. He gave speeches at internal conferences and was a regular lecturer at the SD school in Bernau,[9] to say nothing of his miserable speeches to his victims. His penchant for dramatic public appearances and his desire to leave something for posterity (beyond the history he wrote by committing mass murder) were not just a reaction to exile. But in Argentina, three things happened to increase his motivation even further. First, in 1955 the first books about the extermination of the Jews began to appear. Eichmann viewed them as "enemy literature" and provocation, like the numerous newspaper articles. Second, following the collapse of the Third Reich, the ideological warrior had been left with only one weapon: writing and publicity. And third, this was the first time he had fallen in with people who were actually fighting this battle, pen in hand. They had a publishing house at their disposal and—most important—they seemed to be interested in what he knew. These men were Willem Sassen and Eberhard Fritsch. In reality, the Dürer Verlag was a tiny, makeshift operation with no presence or potential beyond its own readership, but Adolf Eichmann was a newcomer to the book trade, and this fact clearly passed him by. Perhaps he fell into the trap of all inward-looking communities, whose self-referential thinking eventually makes everything outside appear marginal. From his perspective, *Der Weg*'s role in the far-right publishing scene must have looked incredibly impressive: Sassen knew Perón, he had written a novel, and he had published articles in *Nation Europa* and Adolf von Thadden's paper, *Reichsruf*. Hans-Ulrich Rudel had written his memoirs and other short texts, and he was a candidate for a German political party. Leers sent articles from Cairo, and even the mufti sent his regards. German and Austrian publishers like Druffel placed ads in *Der Weg*, and Eberhard Fritsch diligently collected responses to his magazine from the German media, ranging from *Der Spiegel* and *Die Zeit* to radio programs.[10] Even the West German president, Theodor Heuss, had mentioned him. For Eichmann, the idea of becoming part of this feared group must have been irresistible.

The Argentina Papers

Eichmann's productivity is astonishing—even to someone with their own experience of writing, and even just looking at the extant material to which we have access. Today Eichmann's Argentina Papers are distributed across three archive collections. They include not only the famous Sassen transcript and Eichmann's notes on it (which alone comprise around one hundred pages) but also a similar volume of Eichmann's texts, written for his own purposes before 1957. To date, anyone wanting to read Eichmann's stories has had to approach the task with a great deal of patience and an excellent memory, in order to piece together the original from the scattered pages, some of which are barely legible. The transcripts are incomplete and sometimes locked away in cupboards. Between the manuscript's beginning and its end lie the hurdles of Eichmann's difficult handwriting and 150 miles.[11] This may explain why no one has yet made the effort to read it all or even considered the notion that extensive Argentina Papers could exist—let alone that we might be able to completely reconstruct at least one of Eichmann's large manuscripts. But in reassembling the pieces of this puzzle, it quickly becomes clear that we have more than just the thousand pages of the Sassen interviews. There are also 107 pages of a stand-alone manuscript with the programmatic title "Die anderen sprachen, jetzt will ich sprechen!" (The Others Spoke, Now I Want to Speak!), several introductory essays with accompanying notes, and around one hundred more pages of notes and commentaries on books.

Apparently, another of Eichmann's manuscripts has also survived, though it is not available to researchers. The "Roman Tucumán" (Tucumán Novel) is still in the possession of the Eichmann family. It is said to be 260 pages, in which Eichmann attempted to give a detailed account of his life and actions, explaining himself first and foremost to his children, his family, and the "generations to come," on which he placed so much importance. At present, only the Eichmann family has a detailed knowledge of this text.[12] The only other clues to its contents come from conversations between Eichmann and his lawyer, Robert Servatius, and Eichmann's statements during the trial. Servatius announced the submission of this text to the court as the settlement of Eichmann's account with National Socialism and "proof of the accused's real attitude."[13] We might suspect that the "novel" is a variation of an appeal he made to his sons, which Klaus Eichmann remembered well: "I don't want you ever to go into the military, or politics, he said. When I say 'said,' I mean he *ordered* us."[14] But only the release of what is probably Eichmann's last currently unknown text will clarify this question. And as the pages of the Argentina Papers to which we already have access have not yet been subjected to close scrutiny, historians have plenty of work to fill the time until this point: reading Eichmann is anything but simple. For one thing, his handwriting is extremely idiosyncratic; the typists Sassen employed to make fair copies found it so difficult that this material should not be used without checking the originals.[15]

Eichmann may have had an usually pronounced sense of order, but it clearly didn't extend to his writing. His terrible scrawl, and his habit of using every conceivable kind of paper, were anything but orderly. And his expressions and ideas are just as idiosyncratic, revealing a man with no particular feel for words or language. Hannah Arendt, whose linguistic and conceptual sensibilities had been honed on classic German literature, wrote that Eichmann's language was a roller coaster of thoughtless horror, cynicism, whining self-pity, unintentional comedy, and incredible human wretchedness. Shlomo Kulcsár implied that Eichmann's style was not that of the typical Nazi or bureaucrat.[16] His texts demand a twofold feat of concentration: the reader must constantly exercise her judgment, while always keeping in mind who the author is and what he did before he started writing. But as unalterable as our knowledge of the historical facts is, we run the risk of underestimating Adolf Eichmann if we simply present the Argentina Papers as evidence.

Men like Eichmann write for quite different reasons from the rest of us, namely to hinder historical research and steer it toward their own goals.

In order to interpret pieces of self-justification like Eichmann's Argentina Papers, we should not expect them to yield new insights into historical events. A man who writes in order to justify himself is neither a historian nor a chronicler of his age. Furthermore, anyone with such a vested interest behind his public "thought" is not a reliable witness. Every single date and detail could be a lie. These texts bear witness to only one thing with any reliability, and that is the thought process involved in any kind of writing, whether it proclaims truth or lies. A lie still has to be set on a foundation of what the writer believes to be the truth. The new historical fact to be discovered by interpreting Eichmann's writing—his self-representation and his falsification of history—is his thought itself.

Eichmann said he started to write during his time "on the ranch," meaning from March 1955. And in the last part of the 107-page text, he makes a clear reference to the Suez crisis, so we can at least be sure that the final three pages were written in October–November 1956. When the interviews finally began in April 1957,[17] Eichmann brought one of his manuscripts along.[18] The idea of him writing "on the ranch" seems to fit the facts. Separated from his family during the week, he had plenty of time to read the books that made accusations about what he had done and that condemned what he still viewed as his greatest achievement. "Writers began scribbling about me early on, creating the legends," with "their lies about the six or eight million." Even "non-Jews are making me their scapegoat." All this, Eichmann wrote in a separate set of notes under the heading "General," was at best "a mixture of truth and fiction." He had been scapegoated without reason, or as he tactlessly phrased it, he had been "branded as one of these halo-wearers."[19] He wanted to explode this "bomb of lies." Writing seemed like the right way to do it, as he explained to his wife: "This book will be my defense, and I will then go to Germany, and turn myself in in Germany."[20] As absurd as it seems to us today, Adolf Eichmann was aiming to use this book to reclaim not just his name but his life in Germany.

If we consider the reality of criminal prosecutions in West Germany in the early 1950s, we must concede that Eichmann's plan didn't look entirely futile. There was no death penalty, and the prosecution of Nazi criminals tended to result in comparatively lenient sentences. The Nuremberg Trials in the Allied and American courts were over, and prosecution had passed into the hands of the new German institutions, which were frequently headed by old staff. Eichmann knew plenty of former colleagues who were now living unchallenged in Germany. War criminals could bank on receiving short sentences, and a statute of limitations might be on the way even for major Nazi criminals. After all, it had been nearly a decade since the fall of the Third Reich. But Eichmann must have been very naïve if he really thought the rest of the world would permit Hitler's Adviser on Jewish Affairs to spend a few years in jail and then stroll back into Germany a free man. A lot of people had a million reasons to find the thought of a living, breathing Eichmann unbearable. Once he had served his sentence, it would never have been safe for him to live under his own name—at least, not in the democratic Federal Republic. But then, Eichmann was no great defender of democracy: he was among those who could well imagine a return to other political conditions. His attempt to speak out about his past quickly revealed that he was trying to square the circle. On the one hand, he wanted to go back to an ethnic German community, meaning a right-wing community, which had fundamentally changed since May 1945. On the other, he wanted to justify what he had done and was still unable to see there might have been an alternative course of action. It was impossible to achieve both of these aims at once, and this fact seems to have become clear to Eichmann as he was writing.

The "Anonymous Wanderer in a Submarine"

What happens in the perpetrator's mind—even when he does not speak the truth—is essential to an understanding of this chapter of history. —Moshe Zimmermann, 1999[21]

The most frequently quoted phrase from the Argentina Papers, which is often taken to be Eichmann's closing remark, has never been verified.[22] The original handwritten version does not entirely correspond to this memorable quote about the "anonymous wanderer," which can probably be explained by the simple fact that this section is extremely difficult to decipher. Eichmann had neither a bureaucrat's orderly handwriting nor any feeling for literary formulations. What he did possess was an astonishing talent for nonsensical mixed metaphors. "I am beginning to tire of living between worlds, as an anonymous wanderer in a 'submarine,'" he says in the notes headed "Personal," which are one of his attempts to formulate a suitable introduction to his book. "The voice of my heart, which no man can escape, constantly whispered the search for peace to me; it may even find peace with my former enemy. Perhaps this too is part of the German character. And I would be the last person not to be willing to turn myself in to the German authorities, if . . ."[23]

Eichmann's "if" did not relate to the fact that no one could remember him and his colleagues ever behaving in a peaceful way, or the German character showing a particularly peaceful side between 1933 and 1945. Nor did it occur to him that "the enemy" in the singular was part of the Nazi vocabulary, an unmistakable synonym for "the Jews." And anyone still cherishing the hope that Eichmann had realized the insolence of this search for peace in light of his past actions, or that he was about to cast doubt on his own capacity for peace, will be disappointed. Eichmann's "if" placed the blame elsewhere: ". . . if I did not have to consider that the interest in the politics of the case might still be too great to bring about a clear, objective outcome to the ~~affair~~ matter."[24] Eichmann then announced this "clear, objective outcome"—the verdict, in other words—as an incontrovertible fact. His conscience was clear: he was "neither a murderer nor a mass-murderer," and if he could be accused of anything, then it was "abetting the killing during the war" while acting under orders. "I passed on the evacuation and deportation orders I received, and oversaw the compliance with and following of these orders that I received and passed on." He also claimed not to know which of the people who had been deported were subsequently killed.[25]

Of course, this was a catalog of lies from a man who played a large role in the development and implementation of the Nazis' expulsion and extermination policies. Eichmann certainly hadn't just been "passing on orders." But more interesting is the reason he could not force himself to make even the most minimal of confessions: "I said I had to accuse myself of abetting the killing of enemies during the war, if I were to pass a severe and unreserved judgment on myself. I just do not yet see clearly whether I also have the right to judge the people who were my direct subordinates at that time, or to make this judgment before there has been a general consideration of others—because so far I have not heard (forgive me the comparison) that my colleagues on the other side, some of whom have been highly decorated and are in senior official positions or are enjoying their pensions, have been prosecuted for abetting killings, or have accused themselves of this." Eichmann may have sent thousands of Jews on death marches in 1944, and continuted to involve himself in new plans for gassing into 1945, but he had not the slightest pang of conscience in comparing the extermination of the Jews with the expulsion of "many millions" of other people, "the majority of them after the war." He demanded "the same justice for all." "And—this one must understand—as someone who was a mere receiver of orders, I cannot be holier than the Pope," a statement which was not meant "cynically" or "sarcastically." Of course, Eichmann did not suggest how else it should be taken. Someone who had already been compared to czars and other dignitaries clearly didn't have a problem assuming the holy throne. Anyway: everything that he had done, he had done "with a clear conscience and a faithful heart." He had been convinced of "the people's need," and as the "leaders of the former German Reich" "preached" the "necessity of total war," he did his patriotic duty. "The morality of the Fatherland [!] that dwells within me quite simply did not allow me, given these considerations, to declare myself guilty, as I believed I should, of abetting killings during the war. So I may act on the balance of my inner morality, just as the gentlemen receiving the same orders on the other side obviously have."[26]

We may doubt whether Eichmann ever "believed" that he should confess anything. He was clearly someone who was out to "create" a verdict rather than to reach one.[27]

The yardstick against which this "inner morality" was measured was not an idea of justice, a universal moral category, or even a kind of introspection. It was quite clear to Eichmann that any verdict on his actions would always rest on the wrong political mind-set—a measure that lay outside the "morality of the Fatherland" and therefore outside an ethnic German perspective. What sounds on a first reading like an invocation of universal justice, an appeal for all men to be judged by a common human law, is revealed on closer inspection to be an entirely different kind of "equal right." Eichmann was not demanding a common human law, which would also apply to him because he, too, was human. He was actually demanding recognition for a National Socialist dogma, according to which every people has a right to defend itself by any means necessary, the German people most of all. And they had not stopped defending themselves: it had merely been necessary to post-

pone the final victory, when military supplies ran out. The people, however, had not surrendered their ideological weapons. Eichmann was still
convinced that "the people's need" existed, and his ultimate justification
was that one's own people stood above all other interests. Otherwise,
you became a "filthy swine and a traitor."[28] And conscience? Conscience
was simply the "morality of the Fatherland that dwells within" a person,
which Eichmann also termed the "voice of blood." There is as little universal law within us as there is a right to the starry sky for everyone. For
a German, the law is a German law.

Eichmann didn't see "conscience" as a corrective to all thoughts and
actions, something that even allowed people to question the prevailing
customs. Nor was it the guiding light in the search for what was right
and good. On the contrary, anyone who thought of "conscience" in these
terms would be a traitor to the voice of blood. If Eichmann listened to
the "voice of his heart," he would be showing a sentimental weakness,
which was a fundamental evil for National Socialists. His heart could
whisper the search for peace till it was blue in the face; he would always
remain strong enough to ignore these vestiges of an "un-German" education. Eichmann clearly still believed in "victory in this total war, or the
downfall of the German people." There could be no "search for peace"
that was not preceded by victory—and the victory was that of ethnicity
over a genuine universal right to justice. Without further ado, Eichmann
put off his confession of guilt until after the final victory of German
morality. "The more often and intensively I . . . consider these things,
the more convinced I am that in truth I have not made myself guilty
of any crimes, even according to today's laws."[29] After all, "the enemy"
wasn't confessing his guilt, either. The only universal element here is
"guilt," not justice: guilt, under which heading all actions in war become
equal. The real perpetrators of war crimes and crimes against humanity always welcomed the theory of collective guilt. It allowed them to
disappear into a vast guilty crowd and persuade the rest of the population that they had been their accomplices. The declaration of universal
guilt also became Eichmann's get-out clause. First, everyone else had
to recognize that they were all just as guilty as Eichmann was, and only
then would he do the same—because when everyone is guilty, nobody
is, and confessions can be made without legal, or indeed moral, consequences. These evasive acrobatics might be termed justification by accusation. This was the master race making the rules once again. And the

train of thought in the short handwritten texts of "General/Personal" provided the framework for the larger manuscript they were intended to introduce.

"The Others Spoke, Now I Want to Speak!"

It is now time for me to step out of my anonymity and introduce myself:
Name: Adolf Otto Eichmann, Nationality: German
Position: SS Obersturmbannführer (retired)
—Eichmann, "The Others Spoke," 1956

Only the middle section of the original 107-page manuscript called "The Others Spoke, Now I Want to Speak!"[30] is really well known, as a fragment of it was contained in the pages that found their way to Israel for the trial.[31] The text consists of a ten-page introduction, followed by a segment entitled "Re: My Findings on the Matter of 'Jewish Questions' and Measures by the National Socialist German Government to Solve This Complex During the Years 1933 to 1945," and a twenty-six-page final section containing thoughts on the question of guilt.

Eichmann's planned reentry into public life comes across as self-assured and even forceful. The author presents himself as the victim of malicious defamation and misrepresentation. His patience, which until now has been almost superhuman, is finally at an end: these vicious attacks have become too much for him. Now it's his turn—surely people will understand that. "I want to create clarity. I want to name and shame the lie at its source," the brave hero proclaims.[32] And again, he announces that he is ultimately willing to confess his guilt (under certain conditions), but not straight away: "I don't want to act prematurely," he says mysteriously.

Eichmann had a very clear idea of his text's target audience. These "accounts" are for "my friends and non-friends"—but especially for his friends. To his surprise, he adds, he has discovered that he has "a large circle of friends, many millions of people." However, anyone curious to know who Eichmann is talking about will have to wait another hundred pages to find out. By the second paragraph, he is explaining that his own judgment of himself is a foregone conclusion: "Now I am neither a murderer nor a mass murderer; to prove this, I now intend officially to sit in judgment on myself." Eichmannism, as the psychologists who examined him in Israel explained, is essentially monologism. When Eichmann says he doesn't want "to gloss over anything in this justification" or even "sidestep" what he has done, the words have a hollow, rhetorical ring, even for those who don't know what the following pages contain—as do the references to his own "average character" and his playful allusions to German literature, where he speaks about "human deeds and striving" and his "trials and tribulations."[33]

The arguments Eichmann used as justification are well known: the oh-so-depraved world, and the claim that he "certainly did nothing worse" than the many other people acting under orders. A more interesting aspect of this text is how he dramatizes the return of his real name. Eichmann skillfully builds the tension: "Who am I, in any case," he asks, before presenting himself as the savior of all his fellow men who find themselves in a moral quandary.[34] "You human, who were my superior, you human, who were of equal rank, you human, who were my subordinate, in war you are obviously not guilty, just as I am not."[35] And I shall take away your sins, "just as I" forgive myself. "Evidently," says Raphael Gross, "theological rhetoric works particularly well for reclaiming a universalized understanding for the Germans, without having to look too closely at past events, or even recognize a specific responsibility toward the victims."[36] This clearly applies even to this perpetrator, in conversation with his peers. Eichmann, in any case, writes himself into a state of euphoria, proclaiming the "logic" and "clarity" that will free the oppressed Germans from the incubus of their own victims. Not that a few words of understanding for the victims would have made matters any better, but the fact that there is not a single one here tips Eichmann's words of comfort over into accusation. Regret is something this perpetrator feels only for himself and perhaps for his peers. The victims, meanwhile, implicitly remain the real guilty party, as Eichmann had always believed.

The man whose passport said he was Ricardo Klement must have yearned desperately for his return to the public eye. Hence the well-calculated introduction of his real name, at the height of the suspense he has built during this first section: "It is now time for me to step out of my anonymity and introduce myself: Name: Adolf Otto Eichmann."[37] The specialist had returned, to correct the liars who claimed to be his victims. If we imagine the circumstances in which Eichmann produced this text, the sense of triumph that writing it must have given him is tangible, even now. At the end of his working day, the rabbit farmer returns to a time when he was "famous." Eichmann's handwriting displays his euphoria as he scales this height: on the first page it is tiny and laboriously legible, but by the second page it is already more expansive and idiosyncratic. The ballpoint pen was clearly flying over the paper, and the author formatted his text in exactly the same way that he spoke on the tapes he recorded later: with pauses for effect (paragraphs) and accentuated punctuation—the familiar attributes of an orator's manuscript. Eichmann was aiming to create the same effect here as he did elsewhere: decisive, energetic, professional. These sentences were to be published. Eberhard Fritsch and Willem Sassen had big plans, and Eichmann made every effort to rise to the occasion.

A Rounded History

May current and future historians be objective enough not to stray from the path of the truth set down here.
—Eichmann, "The Others Spoke," 1956[38]

Following his introduction, in which he has steeled himself to tell "the truth" (directing a threatening undertone at all the liars), Eichmann turns his attention to historical events. He calls his "record" "Re: My Findings on the Matter of 'Jewish Questions' and Measures by the National Socialist German Government to Solve this Complex in the Years 1933 to 1945." He wants to depict "the truth" in a "sober and factual" way, "the way things took place," without personal judgments based on his own experience.[39] As he hastens to explain to Sassen, and to the general reader, he is the only true surviving insider; everyone else is already dead. He is the only one who can help "current and future historians" "to get a rounded and truthful picture."[40] As evidence of his preeminent expertise, Eichmann adds that he had had "to steer and lead" "a large part of this complex" during his time in the SD and Department IV B 4. And "where I was not responsible, as for example with the physical extermination of the Jews, I was still obliged to get an overview of the matter."[41] This demonstrates the two-pronged tactic that Eichmann used, both in the Sassen circle and in Israel: he presented himself as an irrefutable key witness, while editing out the final years of the National Socialist regime, when his department was called IV A 4b. Self-promotion and manipulation would return control of written history to him. He alone could establish the path of truth "objectively" and for all time. The presentation of one's own interpretation as objective truth is traditionally known as "preaching."

Giving a "factual account," in this section, means avoiding questions of anyone being "guilty or not guilty." Instead, Eichmann presents such a "rounded" picture of the Nazi period that it is a wonder we have any questions left. If we are to believe him, it was all quite simple, and surprisingly unspectacular. The responsibility for dealing with the "Jewish question" rested solely with the German government, meaning Adolf Hitler "and his ministers, which is to say his Reich leaders." The rest was just a question of oaths and obedience. But then, of course, "the former Führer" was also just doing his duty: there was a war on, and all sides lived by the "slogan" "our enemies will be destroyed." And this meant one enemy in particular: "world Jewry declared open war on the German Reich through its Führers [!], especially Dr. Chaim Waitzmann." And open war was what they got. Eichmann the historian calmly explains that the peaceful emigration of the Jews from the Reich was the initial goal, but this effort failed due to lack of cooperation from other countries. Then there was Theresienstadt, which had made the "Jewish leaders" happy, because here the recalcitrant, egoistic Jew "was committed for the first time to communal life and work." The members of the Red Cross, following their visits, were full of enthusiasm for it, even in 1945. Everything was done in strict accordance with the law, and in mutual agreement with "the Jews," in a controlled, "correct," and nonviolent manner. But then the war arrived, and emigration was banned. At that moment he, Adolf Eichmann, knew that nothing good could come of it—and yet he was the one who, at the first Nuremberg trial, was called "the most sinister figure of this century." (Evidently the actual words of the American prosecutor, Robert Jackson, hadn't reached Eichmann in Buenos Aires—he had simply called Eichmann "the sinister figure who had charge of the extermination program," without the hundred years and the superlative.)[42] Anyway, Eichmann continues, he certainly wasn't responsible for the extermination of the Jews. He had preferred to devote his efforts to the Madegascar Plan, until this "dream" too was struck down by the war with Russia. Unfortunately, the Russian campaign didn't develop "as quickly as people 'at the top' expected"; they found themselves fighting a war on two fronts, and then "world Jewry" declared war on them as well. This was why, "as I suspect," "any last constraints" fell away, and Hitler gave the order for "physical liquidation." "What I felt at this time," says the historian, "is hard to put into words, and I shall not do it." Still, he had sworn an oath to the flag. However, when he saw the air raids, he realized that "my work actually had an uncanny similarity with—indeed, it was the same as the work" of the people transporting the bombs. Sabotage—secretly dispatching trains full of Jews abroad—would have been no use. "Who would have taken them from me?" What else could a person do, Eichmann suggests, but commit murder? He spares himself and his readers the details of the "physical liquidation," as if it were an episode of little importance. Instead, he focuses on the tall story of his "negotiations" with Kasztner, which would have been a complete success, he says, had not the enemy hindered them once again. Nobody wanted to take on "even these million" Jews,[43] and then, of course, the war came to an end. Eichmann spent sixty-five pages mapping out this "path of truth," as if none of it could be doubted.

Naturally, he knew that one thing in particular might bring his creation crashing down about his ears, and that was the number of victims. He therefore rounded off his account with a statistic that counts among the most perfidious lies he ever told. At the end of 1944, he says, a statistician drew up some figures for Himmler and Hitler, and Eichmann is able to draw on them, "particularly as I had to redraft the 'Führer report' twice at that time."[44] Later, he consistently denied having anything to do with this document, which achieved notoriety as the Korherr Report. But the real lie is hidden in the detail: he dates the statistician's report to the end of 1944, when the figures were actually prepared in March 1943. Eichmann was a master of fudging dates and frequently employed the technique to paint himself in a more favorable light. And if somebody were to rumble his numbers game, he could rely on people's willingness to believe that, after so many years, a man might accidentally mix things up from time to time. Eichmann gave a detailed explanation of this method during one of his conversations with Sassen, which was as ill advised as a magician explaining his tricks. By presenting figures from early 1943 as a final balance, Eichmann made almost two years, and over a million murders, vanish from the books—if the earlier figures were even correct in the first place.

But the story of Eichmann and Korherr is more than a cynical redating game played in Argentina. The statistician's name was a synonym for one of the greatest embarrassments of Eichmann's career. On January 18, 1943, Heinrich Himmler wrote an angry letter to Heinrich Müller, officially relieving Eichmann of the responsibility for providing murder statistics, which he had been doing until that point: "The RSHA . . . has no further statistical work to do in this area, as the statistical documents produced thus far lack scientific exactitude." Instead, Himmler appointed Richard Korherr as the sole official statistician, the inspector for statistics in the office of the *Reichsführer*-SS. Korherr was granted direct access to all the data from Department IV B 4, where he was also given an office—right in the middle of Eichmann's empire.[45] In the period that followed, Eichmann had to help Korherr compile the figures. A career-minded man like Eichmann would not simply forget or mix up such an experience.

It is all the more remarkable, then, that in 1956 Eichmann arrived at a completely different body count: fewer than a million victims. His text inflates the emigration quotas and the number of survivors and stresses that a large proportion of Jews must have died during the Allied air raids. This kind of numbers game is hard to stomach when it comes to murder statistics. And in Eichmann's case, it is unbelievably shameless. This was the man who took pride in showing visitors the "card room" in his office, the walls of which were plastered with diagrams representing his own "successes" and those of National Socialism as a whole. This was the man whose deputy pinned deportation charts on the wall behind his desk for all to see, the way a hunter displays antlers.[46] And this was the man trying to tell us that it wasn't worth it for his department to expend effort over the murder quotas? Eichmann, of all people, who was looking at numbers of between five and six million in 1944–45 (which, as we now know, were an exact representation of the facts)? And yet here he manages to play down the perverse pride he took in his "work" to such an extent that the National Socialist extermination program becomes a regrettable footnote to history. This piece of denial is so far-fetched, we can only marvel that Eichmann thought for a second that anyone would believe it. Even among the knowledge dodgers in Argentina, this distortion didn't hold water for long. Eichmann's figures chimed perfectly with the project that Sassen and his colleagues were working on, but unfortunately, the Korherr Report was one of the documents in Léon Poliakov and Josef Wulf's sourcebook, which the Sassen circle had in front of them. Debates about victim numbers consequently occupied a large part of the discussion group's time.[47]

But the greatest barrier to anyone believing Eichmann was actually one he had erected himself, in the image of himself he had presented to his colleagues at the end of the war. He knew that if he wanted to avoid suspicion, he would have to confront this issue, and on the last page of "Re: My Findings" he takes the bull by the horns. "The war was drawing to an end. In that final period—I almost want to say the final hours—I said to a few lower-ranking officers: '. . . and if it must be, I will leap joyfully into the pit, in the knowledge that around[48] five million enemies of the Reich have been killed along with us."[49] He made this statement, Eichmann adds by way of explanation, in a mood shaped by the war's end and the destruction it brought with it. And the "highest number of enemy victims" had been the "standpoint" of the enemy as well. Eichmann firmly denies he said anything about "Jews," a story he ascribes to Wilhelm Höttl and Dieter Wisliceny. To make sure there is no misunderstanding, he then repeats: "It is not true!" For the life of him, he cannot explain how the two of them could have happened upon such an absurd misrepresentation.[50] Although he faced probing questions on this point from the Sassen circle, Eichmann defended his version of events, and it was another five years before he admitted that, of course, he had not said "enemies of the Reich."

Today, it's easy to recognize Eichmann's lies: fifty years of research have given us the arguments we need to resist him, and we can see the facts behind the fiction. We can spot his intentions before his words can have any influence on us. But in 1956 the danger of falling into his traps was incomparably greater. All the more interesting, then, to take a closer look at the methods of obfuscation and manipulation that this man employed. After all, this text is Eichmann's first postwar statement, and his first attempt to claim the sovereign right to interpret history. A few telltale details in this first draft reveal how he developed and refined his methods.

The text of "Re: My Findings" quivers with an inner tension that stems from several dilemmas in his falsification of history. The first relates to Eichmann's image of Hitler. On the one hand, he claims that the Führer expressly ordered the complete extermination of the Jews in the German-occupied territories; on the other, he claims a very low murder rate. In order to do both at once, he has to explain how the head of a totalitarian state could give an order that had so little effect. Either the Führer's word was not as binding as Eichmann suggests (which weakens his "just obeying orders" argument as a justification for his own actions), or his figures are too low (meaning his own crime was greater than he is trying to claim). Eichmann simply says that Himmler was "not in too much of a hurry to carry out the Führer's order," because he still believed in "a halfway favorable outcome for the war."[51] And at least to start with, Germany's reliance on forced labor ("the workforce") was so great that the Economic and Adminstrative Head Office had not complied with the Führer's extermination order. But this explanation reveals a conspicuous weakness in Eichmann's "rounded" picture of history. He would go on to use the Sassen circle discussions, and the books, to come up with a better design.

The second structural flaw in Eichmann's argument had to do with the people he was addressing, and his own self-image. The Dürer circle had sought him out because they wanted a man with as much knowledge as possible and a fundamentally National Socialist outlook. Consequently, the Adolf Eichmann of 1956 had far fewer problems saying "I" than the Eichmann who appeared in Jerusalem. In "The Others Spoke," with a combination of vanity and sporadic bursts of honesty, he provides his readers with evidence of his qualifications as an indispensable witness and a legitimate member of the Sassen group. His text reads a little like a job application. It might overemphasize things he believed would show him in a positive light, but this is still Eichmann presenting himself as the successful and respected National Socialist he had really been. He includes explanatory notes for any negative aspects with which he does not wish to be associated. Eichmann was proud of his "lifetime achievements for Führer and people," but he also knew he had to defend himself, and this tension would make him vulnerable later on.

The third basic problem he faced in giving this version of history was gauging the extent of his potential readers' prior knowledge. Anyone setting out to manipulate and deceive needs not only superior knowledge but also an intimate acquaintance with the actual and hypothetical knowledge of his audience. In a historical context, we would call such knowledge the body of source material. But in 1956 the only thing Eichmann knew about the recently published books was their titles. Unlike Eberhard Fritsch and Willem Sassen, he had to rely on the book reviews in the press to help him parry critical questions. Having "been there," Eichmann's knowledge of events may have been superior, but he also had one worry that the others didn't: in contrast to them, he knew exactly what horrors might come to light. Authors of fantasy literature have free rein when they create their narratives, but a liar does not: he has to make sure people will believe what he says. And this becomes more difficult when his audience's background knowledge might expand at any moment, without warning. Sassen recognized the small advantage this fact gave him and tried to play it out against Eichmann.

The fourth dilemma Eichmann faced in this draft was founded in the fundamental evil behind his crimes: his radical anti-Semitism. In order to exonerate himself, and the Nazi regime as a whole, he stresses that he had an excellent relationship with his Jewish "negotiating partners." Their dealings were harmonious on both sides, as they worked toward a mutually agreeable solution. But this emphasis stands in irreconcilable opposition to Eichmann's belief in the necessity of a "final victory" of one race over another. The goal of National Socialist anti-Jewish policies had ultimately been the "Final Solution of the Jewish question," and Hitler's plans for world domination would not even have allowed space for Jews on the moon. There was no middle ground between the gentlemanly diplomat negotiating with "world Jewry," and the fundamentalist taking on the "enemy race" in the struggle for world domination. This disparity causes Eichmann some difficulties when he attempts to reconcile the two. Not wanting to confess to the criminal extermination plans, he has to talk about his political, nonviolent negotiations with the "Jewish representatives." But this tactic made him an object of suspicion to other, dedicated racial anti-Semites like Sassen and Fritsch.

If Adolf Eichmann really wanted to create a "rounded picture of history," he had to obliterate the tensions contained in his first draft of 1956: they were the weak spots in his ideal vision. By the time he reached Israel in 1960, he would have a wealth of experience to fall back on, gained during intensive discussions over the months following the writing of this draft. The basic problems may have been insurmountable, but by then he would have had a frightening amount of practice in addressing them. With this "clear and factual" account of events, and the hours he then spent in discussions, Adolf Eichmann would be much better prepared for his return to the public eye than the defendants at Nuremberg or any of the other people who were tried for war crimes and crimes against humanity. As always, Eichmann seized the chance to profit from a difficult situation. This time it may also have had something to do with the fact that in Buenos Aires in 1956, the limelight of publicity was becoming an increasingly realistic option for Eichmann once more.

An Open Letter to the Chancellor

*I do not wish to court the limelight of publicity in any way. I have
no ambition.*   —Eichmann, Sassen discussions[52]

The original manuscript of "The Others Spoke" reveals something that the poor-quality copy from File 17 at Eichmann's trial obliterates. Eichmann's "findings" were planned as an open letter to the West German chancellor, Konrad Adenauer. Above the title, Eichmann's handwritten note (which was later crossed out) reads: "The pencil additions apply only to the 'open letter' to the Chancellor."[53]

In the 1950s, open letters were a popular genre among far-right publications. They were usually published under a pseudonym, the content being more "open" than the authors' willingness to be called to account for it. Anyone believing that this sort of self-promotion in the name of free speech is a present-day phenomenon will be set straight by a glance through the publications in question. As with "reader's letters," the advantage of "open letters" was that an editor could publish them in the name of freedom of expression, while at the same time distancing himself from them by declaring that their content was the author's personal opinion and not necessarily endorsed by the magazine. This trick allowed publications like *Der Weg, Nation Europa, Der Standpunkt,* and *Reichsruf*—which for obvious reasons were under constant threat of being banned and having their stock confiscated—to write whatever they wanted without fear of prosecution: officially, these words were someone else's. The inclusion of letters from "Jewish" readers was particularly perfidious, and the most crudely anti-Semitic hate speech was labeled as "readers' opinions." Eichmann had seen Sassen use one of these reader's letters to cause President Eisenhower some considerable trouble. And now Eichmann was writing an open letter himself. This casts the work that the Dürer circle and Adolf Eichmann were planning in an interesting light. On the one hand, Eichmann could never have published such a text by himself without recklessly endangering his cover; he needed middlemen with the right connections. On the other, this plan demonstrates that the project he was undertaking with Willem Sassen was not simply meant for posterity. The first opportunity to have an impact with an open letter to Konrad Adenauer would have been the upcoming elections, in the fall of 1957. It seems particularly likely that the men taking a timeout in Argentina planned to take this opportunity, as they were still dreaming of toppling Adenauer's government. Eichmann clearly wasn't satisfied with the idea of writing a book that would be published after his death—and he was prepared to take a huge risk in order to have his say. Even published anonymously, the content of this letter would inevitably lay a trail to the door of the Adviser on Jewish Affairs, and it was provocative enough that someone might consider calling its author to account. Eichmann was too certain that he had unique insider knowledge to believe that a pseudonym would afford him any kind of protection, and placing this piece in *Der Weg* would have led the Nazi hunters directly to where he was hiding. The only conclusion to be drawn is that Eichmann accepted the risk as part of the deal. It is even conceivable that he had a more or less conscious desire to be discovered.

In 1952 Eichmann had told his wife he wanted to stand trial in Germany, and he repeated this intention to his family over the years that followed. "He considered handing himself over to an international tribunal in Europe," his son remembered later. "He was pretty clear that he wouldn't get off without punishment, but he didn't think he would get a harsh sentence. He thought he might even be released in four to six years."[54] Considering how the law was applied in West Germany in the mid-1950s, Eichmann's expectation wasn't all that far from reality. A man of fifty, he must have told himself, would still be able to spend his twilight years with his family, under his real name, in the country of his birth. But this action would also have brought him closer to another dream: achieving prosperity for his family. The project with Sassen was partly a moneymaking scheme, and he was well aware that the market value of a book by Adolf Eichmann would go up rapidly if there were a trial.[55] Being arrested and going before a court would be a service to his family, whose future he was always trying to safeguard. What would a few years matter? Eichmann's son recalled: "He told Mother: 'you can live without me for that long, it will be ok.'" And afterward everything would be right with the world once more—at least, it would have been, if Eichmann's name had not been too inextricably linked with millions of murders for him to simply return to normality in West Germany.

But however Eichmann managed to shield himself from this reality, his plan to write an "open letter to the Chancellor" shows without doubt that he and his associates weren't just fooling around with these ideas to fill the dull weekends of their Argentine exile. All of them, Eichmann included, had concrete political ambitions. They weren't working quietly for the benefit of the history books, or to have their efforts consigned to the desk drawer; they wanted to make a difference, to get back to Europe and involve themselves in West German politics. From a distance, this plan looks insane, but it was based on Eichmann's empirical experience. Fifteen years previously, his plans and suggestions had been passed on to *Reichsführer*-SS Himmler and, above him, all the way to Hitler. Hermann Göring and Reinhard Heydrich had made speeches and given lectures from Eichmann's drafts,[56] and the things he initiated—the central offices, re-education camps, and death marches—had allowed him to put his stamp on world history. All these murderous projects, beyond anything the civilized world could imagine, were schemes Eichmann pushed through with his superiors. Small wonder then that the *Obersturmbannführer* (retired) had the self-confidence to believe that, using this historical sketch, he could accomplish something similar with Konrad Adenauer's office. His version of events would put an end to these tiresome questions of guilt, which was something a lot of people in Germany desperately wanted. In theory, a simple explanation of the Nazis' anti-Jewish policies, from a professional source, would have been an interesting offer. Argentina wasn't the only country that was home to old comrades with familiar dispositions. Eichmann's pen could well have been driven by a desire to provoke an opportunity for his return to Germany; people of a similar persuasion might even have welcomed him back to his homeland. He knew there were still one or two people in the German government who would have found his ideas just as familiar and seductive as the former Adviser on Jewish Affairs did.

What About Morality?

The drive toward self-preservation is stronger than any so-called
moral requirement.   —Eichmann, "The Others Spoke," 1956[57]

Once Eichmann had laid out his "factual and clear," "rounded" conception of history in the second part of "The Others Spoke, Now I Want to
Speak!" with all its relativization and misdirection, he turned, as promised, to a question pertinent "today" (i.e., post-1945). Apparently, this
was a question nobody had ever asked before: "Guilty or not guilty?"[58]
Anyone familiar with Eichmann's self-portrayal in Jerusalem might
expect this Argentine chapter to display a similar mixture of lachrymose
self-pity and grim disillusionment with his former superiors. In Jerusalem, the defendant's explanation followed an endless loop as he tried to
convince the world (and apparently himself) that although he had been
obliged to witness and involve himself in all this misery, he had been
against it from the start. But in Argentina, surprisingly, Eichmann said
something fundamentally different. Even in this chapter of "The Others
Spoke," he presents us with his irrefutable truth in an accusatory tone,
with the self-assurance of a demagogue.

Adolf Eichmann came from a good middle-class home, and although
National Socialist thought had taken hold even there, he had still
learned enough about traditional bourgeois morality and general moral
concepts to realize that most people would condemn what he had done.
Even he knew that ideas like morality, conscience, justice, and so on
existed, and he didn't want to ignore fundamental questions pertaining
to them. He had lofty aspirations for his worldview, and the set of ideological building blocks of National Socialism were never going to provide everything he needed. The court-appointed psychologist Shlomo
Kulscár later said that Eichmann's personality probably made him incapable of subordinating himself completely to any system he was presented with. Eichmann's texts also demonstrate that he had reflected on
National Socialist concepts and adapted them to his own ideas. In 1956,
as a free man, he was above merely parroting the popular phrase about
the "shame of Versailles." Recently, the far right had begun to claim that
the 1919 peace treaty was to blame for everything: it had been so unfair

that it had driven the masses toward National Socialism. Eichmann's use of the phrase is more differentiated: "Perhaps I was already an adherent of National Socialist thought before I properly grasped and understood the dishonor of Versailles." He had other reasons for choosing his political direction, and in hindsight, National Socialism gave him an understanding of it: "To a certain extent, it molded into super-nationalism."[59] This was not the only way Eichmann remolded the National Socialist worldview to make it his own.

Eichmann presents his answer to the question of his own personal guilt right at the start of this section. "Without making any kind of Pilate-like gesture, I find that I am not guilty before the law, and before my own conscience; and with me the people who were my subordinates during the war. For we were all . . . little cogs in the machine of the Head Office for Reich Security, and thus, during the war, little cogs in the great drivetrain of the murdering motor: war." The oath of allegiance that bound everyone, "friend and foe," was the "highest obligation that a person can enter into," and everyone had to obey it. Across the world, leaders had really only given a single order: "the destruction of the enemy."[60] For Eichmann, the idea that the war had been a total, global one, in which the goal was to eliminate the enemy, was a simple statement of fact. His radical biologism led to the belief that a "final victory" was imperative: the unavoidable war between the races would leave only one remaining.

The question Eichmann puts to himself in this section—"What about morality?"—is one for which he has a surprisingly provocative answer. "There are a number of moralities: a Christian morality, a morality of ethical values, a morality of war, a morality of battle. Which will it be?" Eichmann then applies his rhetorical skills to a complete demolition of the philosophical approach (even though he invokes philosophers to support his argument). What is the relative importance of morality versus power? Did not Socrates himself submit to law and order when he accepted his death sentence? "Socratic wisdom bows down before the law of the state. This is what the humanists teach us." (In National Socialist thought, of course, humanists were effeminate fellows, with whom it would be impossible to win a war, as they refused to recognize that war was inevitable.) The leadership of the nation, Eichmann goes on to explain, has always stood above the thought of individuals. To illustrate, he brings in the Old Testament and also modern science: the church, too, recognizes the power of the state as the highest guiding principle on earth, and hierarchies exist even in an anthill. Eichmann founders only on the question of whether thinkers like Nietzsche and Kant could be useful to his argument. Did these two have "a clear German orientation"? "I doubt it," he concludes, then encapsulates National Socialism's basic mistrust of all scholarship in a single sentence: "I mean that philosophy is international," and as such, he prefers to seek his answers without it.[61] His own "inner morality" is all well and good, but the most important thing is always the will of the nation's leaders—not simply because they have the power to force people to obey, but because they act only on behalf of the people. Therefore a person should not allow his inner morality to conflict with his orders; he should see that these orders are for the good of the people and carry them out with conviction. He, Eichmann, found an easy way to overcome this problem: "I found my parallels quite plainly and simply in nature. For the allegiance to the flag did not forbid self-willed [!] thought, even if the result of my thought and searching was somewhat negative for the will and the goals of the government, to which it was naturally subordinated. But the more I listened to the natural world, whether microcosm or macrocosm, the less injustice I found, not only in the demands made by the government of my people, to which I belong, but . . . also in the goals of our enemies' governments and leaders. Everyone was in the right, when seen from his own standpoint."[62] In other words: everyone wanted total war, and that fact provided the legitimation for everyone to wage it, using every means necessary, both "conventional and unconventional."[63] A universal war of extermination also frees people to use unscrupulous violence. Even the use of death camps suddenly becomes an inventive battle tactic, made necessary by the "eternal fate of all organic beings, for which there is no consolation. It has always existed, and will always exist." Eichmann has no trouble identifying with this notion or seeing the ideal parameters for his behavior within it. Thinking and morality are no longer international—only war. But it is *völkisch* alone that will be victorious, and only those who understand that fact will survive.

In Israel, Eichmann told his astonished listeners that all his life he had oriented himself by Immanuel Kant's categorical imperative. "I believe in Kant," he said earnestly[64]—it was just that his orders had sometimes prevented him from acting according to his own beliefs. On being questioned further, he even managed to provide a passable definition of Kant's categorical imperative, the wisdom of which he attempted to praise wholeheartedly.[65] In 1956, as a free man, things were a little different.[66] "The drive toward self-preservation is stronger than any so-called moral requirement," he wrote.[67] Who would choose to rely on an international approach like Kant's, with his exhortations to individual responsibility and universal human categories, once you had realized it was all sophistry and levity? "From the tellurian worldview of Copernicus and Galileo, to the hyper-galactic worldview of Homo sapiens today: the law creates and expects order. The sick and the degenerate are the only exceptions."[68] This law, which creates order and destroys the sick and the "degenerate," has nothing to do with humanist ideals or other weaknesses. "I must obey it, so that a greater community, and I within it, can live. It was this thought that made me subordinate myself and obey."[69] A few weeks later, in the Sassen circle, Eichmann said that anyone claiming they had suffered a crisis of conscience during the war was lying: telling oneself in hindsight that one had only been acting on orders "is cheap hokum, it's an excuse." And "humanitarian views" only helped people "hide comfortably behind regulations, decrees and laws."[70]

Eichmann completely rejected traditional ideas of morality, in favor of the no-holds-barred struggle for survival that nature demanded. He identified entirely with a way of thinking that said any form of contemplation without clear reference to blood and soil was outdated and, most of all, dangerous. Here, reason, justice, and freedom were not permissable central concepts of human society. The very idea of a common understanding among all people was a betrayal—to the minds of both Eichmann and his Führer. For one thing, the Germans' superior might came from their ethnicity, and for another, the world didn't have room for everyone. The struggle among the races was in essence a struggle for resources—a basic idea familiar to many people concerned about future wars over oil and drinking water today. However, Eichmann refused to countenance the idea that there might be room for a mutually agreeable solution. The only thing that mattered was one's own people. "What is right, is what aids the people,"[71] and no one apart from one's own people had any rights. Philosophy in the classical sense, as the search for transcultural categories and a global orientation, was an error, because it sought universals and did not accept dependence on ethnicity. Its outlook (and here Eichmann is quite correct) was fundamentally "international." As such, philosophy has no homeland, but—and it is crucial to realize this connection—to the purveyors of Nazi ideology, philosophy had a people. According to Nazi ideology and Hitler's tirades, there was one "race" that, having no homeland, had an international bent and revered the unbounded freedom of the mind: the Jews. "The Jewish intellect," says a typical Nazi publication, "breaks away from the soil in which it is rooted and makes a rootless existence for itself." Further-more, the Jewish attitude of mind "breaks apart the German human and undermines the German way of life," because it is not an "ethnically based thought."[72] Only an ethnic thought makes it possible to build a national character, and humanitarian talk only allows this character to become confused and weakened. In an ideology that sees reconnecting with "blood and soil" as the only means of survival, any international outlook mutates into the ultimate threat. This threat must be destroyed before a global morality destroys concepts of the German ethnic moral-ity and undermines German defenses. Or as the head of the NSDAP Head Office for Racial Politics clearly stated in 1939: "There can be no possible agreement with systems of thoughts of an international nature, because at bottom these are not true and not honest, but based on a monstrous lie, namely the lie of the equality of all human beings."[73] In the Argentina Papers, Eichmann leaves us in no doubt about his own orientation toward these categories of thinking.

In Jerusalem, Eichmann spoke rather differently of philosophy and philosophers, in particular Kant, who he said had always provided the guiding principle of his thought. This statement was a bit much to swal-low coming from a mass murderer, and even if Eichmann did manage to demonstrate considerable knowledge of Kant's fundamental moral con-cepts, his views on philosophy and National Socialism drew sneers from the trial observers. Hannah Arendt wrote of Eichmann's "rather modest mental gifts" and his "vague notion" of the philosophical dimension of the obedience issue.[74] The historians followed her lead, dismissing Eich-mann's words as paradoxical drivel and pseudophilosophy, rendering them a mere curiosity for the footnotes. But this was both overly hasty and dangerous. Arendt judged him on the basis of the few statements he made during his interrogation and trial. She was unaware of Eichmann's lengthy essays. She didn't know about the pieces he wrote in Israel, in which he elaborated on his supposed love of Kant, or about his debate on religious philosophy with the radical theologist William L. Hull.

These texts, along with other sources, were withheld from the trial observers, so Arendt couldn't know that Eichmann planned to base his closing statement almost entirely on Immanuel Kant, before his lawyer talked him out of the idea.[75] What Arendt did correctly observe was that Eichmann was deliberately posturing as a student of philosophy. She just drew the wrong conclusion, imagining that the main reason for this pose was foppish vanity and a lack of rhetorical skill and philosophical knowledge. A person who does philosophy herself is often reluctant to accept that someone could be familiar with the basics of philosophy but not willing to embrace its guidance, and this must have played a role in Arendt's assumption that hers was the only possible conclusion. But Eichmann, as the records from Israel reveal, was capable of powerful arguments. Avner W. Less, who spent almost three hundred hours interrogating him, described him as a "self-made man, with good knowledge, very intelligent, very skillful. . . . He tends to listen for the form my question will take, and adjust himself to it accordingly."[76] Eichmann was familiar with philosophical ideas that were by no means part of a general education: in addition to Kant, Nietzsche, and Plato, he also mentioned Schopenhauer and—in all seriousness—Spinoza, the greatest Jewish philosopher. From his cell, he conducted a debate on the principles of religious philosophy with a fundamentalist Christian. He was desperate to win him over to the far-right cause, and some of his arguments were so masterfully constructed that the theologian exclaimed in exasperation: "If you had stuck to your childish beliefs and not gotten involved in the philosophical ideas of Spinoza and Kant, you could now be living a normal, happy life."[77] Religion is seen as a private matter in enlightened nations, so even Eichmann-in-Jerusalem didn't have to hide what he thought—especially as this religious debate began only after the trial was over. In contrast to his writing on the question of guilt, Eichmann didn't have to think tactically to avoid incriminating himself. If he seems far more cautious and wooden in his other texts, that is because everything he said in Israel was an attempt to disguise his own systematic thinking. Such thought obviously existed, as a comparison with the Argentina Papers shows, but in Israel he took pains to paint himself as precisely the type of benevolent humanist and admirer of philosophy that he had sought to destroy while the Nazis were in power. He just hadn't had much of a chance to practice this role.

Of course, the task of listening carefully to a man like Adolf Eichmann as he expounds his philosophical thoughts is far from easy, but the fact that he wrote about them gives us a rare chance to take a peek behind the front he presented in Jerusalem. His real convictions are to be found in the Argentina Papers, which describe a nonvitalist philosophy of inescapable natural laws. Only thinking based on ethnicity offers a chance of final victory in the battle of all living things. But if we call this thought "pseudo-philosophy," we run the risk of underestimating a dangerous dogma of pure natural causality that does not allow for freedom. We are also wasting the opportunity to fight this revocation of the Enlightenment and the proclamation of a science with no moral requirement. Instead of countering this declaration of war on philosophy with something better, we expose ourselves to the suspicion that we are idealizing philosophy in and of itself. But philosophy is not automatically good. There, too, we find dangerous wrong turns, for which dilettantes in SS uniforms like Eichmann are not the only ones to blame. "We have freed ourselves from the idealization of a groundless and powerless thought. We are seeing the end of a philosophy that is subservient to it." These words were spoken in 1933 by a man who not only called for an "ethnic science," but was also convinced that the "mental world of a people" was "the power of preserving the strength that lies in its blood and soil," understood as "the power that excites the deepest feeling and shakes the furthest reaches of existence." This man was Martin Heidegger.[78] His name was also known to Adolf Eichmann. Shortly before his execution, Eichmann asked his brother to find out what this German philosopher thought about the last rites. "Not that I would presume to liken myself to this great thinker in anything, but it would be important to me with regard to my relationship with Christianity."[79] It is not known whether Heidegger replied.

For Eichmann, ideology was not a pastime or a theoretical superfluity but the fundamental authorization for his actions. Explaining, disseminating, and implementing it was therefore also a means of gaining power. Eichmann wanted power but not via capricious acts, ruthless aggression, a uniform, or an order; it had to be legitimated by a system of thought and values that allowed his actions to seem "right." He wanted his authorization to come from within. He was seeking self-authorization, to act according to his own convictions. He didn't make things easy for himself, as his theory of legitimation didn't conform to the usual Nazi slogans. What Eichmann presents in his 1956 draft is a National Socialist worldview that deviates from the worldview of other National Socialists on crucial points. Unlike Alfred Rosenberg and the official propaganda (which attempted to co-opt every famous German for the Nazi cause), he didn't think Kant could simply be incorporated into the new "German thought." Eichmann didn't subscribe to the notion that the categorical imperative actually meant "live according to your nature and defend the values of your race," as the self-appointed mastermind of the Third Reich proclaimed.[80] He obviously realized that neither Kantian teaching nor any other philosophy could be reconciled with the racial-biological struggle. For him, Kant represented the same "so-called" morality that made life difficult when you were trying to implement an extermination policy. Kant's thinking was not "ethnic" but "international." This position is evidence of Eichmann's consistently National Socialist attitude but also the consistency in his desire for total power. The power of fundamentalist thought is much greater than the power of an order given by a superior. That authority would still hold when all his superiors were dead and he was sitting on a rabbit farm in Argentina. With this in mind, Simon Wiesenthal was wrong to suggest that Eichmann would have persecuted red-haired or blue-eyed people with the same commitment if someone had ordered him to. The reason Eichmann was so receptive to the totalitarian system was that he was already in thrall to totalitarian thought. An ideology that scorns human life can be very appealing if you happen to be a member of the master race that proclaims it, and if it legitimates behavior that would be condemned by any traditional concept of justice and morality. Eichmann wanted to do what he did, but above all, he wanted respect for having done the right thing. And he wanted to proselytize. That is what makes his writings so sickening.

Eichmann consistently placed his hope in "generations to come"—a phrase he never tired of repeating. He wanted to change the way they thought, if only so that they would acquit him of this charge of mass murder. That charge could be made only by people who had not yet grasped true National Socialism, and who were still being spoon-fed by foreign powers. If you believed in the final battle of the races, the battle could never be over as long as a single enemy was still alive. On his farm, surrounded by thousands of rabbits and chickens, Eichmann no longer had much chance to exterminate the enemy, so all that remained to him

was to argue against what he saw as the "intellectual schooling" of Judaism. In 1956 he arrived back where he had started in the early 1930s:
waging "ideological warfare." He wanted to win this battle for interpretational sovereignty "using conventional and unconventional means."
The immense quantity of text he produced expresses his need to justify
his actions, but even more his desire to become a demagogue, forcing
his vision upon people with the power of his persuasive rhetoric. This
desire also came from inside the hermetic seal of racial theory: having
a strong argument in a closed system means having power, and power
over people was something Eichmann missed terribly, now that he was
anonymous.

Before 1960, Eichmann viewed "so-called" moral requirements as the
sand the enemy threw in your eyes to undermine your fighting strength.
This sand started to become useful only when Eichmann was sitting
in an Israeli prison cell. In an attempt to avoid being called to account
for the crimes of his people, he was now searching for something to
obscure other people's vision. He didn't hesitate to pose as a devotee
of Kant or to tell other unscrupulous lies. When the court psychologist
mentioned Pontius Pilate, Eichmann (who in 1956 had judged himself
not guilty, "without making any kind of Pilate-like gesture") thanked
him kindly, because he never would have thought to compare himself
to this historical figure. He exclaimed enthusiastically: "That's exactly
my position! When he washed his hands, Pilate was signifying that he
didn't identify himself with that course of action. He was forced to do
it. If I am entitled to compare myself with such a great historical figure,
then his situation was the same as mine."[81] When Eichmann wanted
something from people, he was always very good at telling them what
they wanted to hear, and talking them into submission, until it was too
late. We would do well not to underestimate Eichmann's will to power:
even in his writing, he used all the tools of manipulation at his disposal
to serve it.

In "The Others Spoke," written in 1956, Eichmann is openly proud
of the willpower he showed in enduring the "icy cold legality" of the
struggle: he "resigned [to it], trembling,"[82] and not only accepted it but
also grasped its quite unique "warmth." *Das Atom* by Fritz Kahn contains the same concepts of macrocosm and microcosm that Eichmann
used for the draft of his own book. In his copy of *Das Atom*, Eichmann
wrote: "I have spiritually 'absorbed' this book, like others on the topic,

and found a wonderful confirmation of the National Socialist 'belief in God,' '*Gottgläubigkeit.*'" This is "hearty, natural and always alive."[83] "Hearty *Gottgläubigkeit*" is a doctrine in the inevitable final war of the races. It provides the intellectual basis for genocide and for carrying out "screening" even on ethnic Germans, in the "euthanasia" project to which Eichmann also gave his wholehearted support.[84] Anyone looking to segregate and exterminate people requires thinking that is hostile to life, to prevent himself from becoming conscious of how abysmal his actions are, and this was certainly the case with Eichmann.

Having an ideology wasn't all about power; it was also a religion that brought comfort when even the murderer was horror-struck by his own crimes. According to Eichmann, the only hope lay in "finding the path that may provide comfort in the natural world."[85] A glance at the writings of Rudolf Höß shows that Eichmann was not alone in this belief. "In the spring of 1942," the former commandant of Auschwitz remembered, "hundreds of blossoming people walked beneath the blossoming fruit trees of the farmstead, most of them never guessing they were on their way to the gas chambers, and to death. I can still see this image of growth and decay quite clearly."[86] Thinking about the eternal cycle of growth and decay made the extermination of millions of people into a natural occurrence, and the murderers into a force of nature, the right hand of natural law. According to this principle, the murderers' actions didn't catapult them forever out of a morally upright community; on the contrary, they proved that they were part of the German racial corpus. Any doubts on this score were the hangover from a sentimental concept of morality, which could be overcome by orienting oneself toward natural laws. In later writings, especially "Götzen" (Idols), the longest thing he wrote in Israel, Eichmann gave a specific example of how he comforted himself in this way. Visiting Auschwitz by day was made bearable for him by the orderly's punctual appearance in the evening to collect the brave Adviser on Jewish Affairs. He would drive him straight to his own private religious service, which filled the business of murder with a sense of immutability: "Herr *Obersturmbannführer,* the sun sets in 15 minutes!"[87]

Against all our hopes, Eichmann was perfectly comfortable in his own company. In Altensalzkoth, in Tucumán, and in the pampas of Argentina, he enjoyed the open space, a bottle of wine on the veranda, and solitary rides through the countryside. For him there was no link between the aesthetics of nature and the contemplation—or even-fleeting consideration—of morality. Quite the reverse: although we can only call his actions an affront to all forms of civilization, he saw them reflected and acknowledged in the beauty of nature. This man could have stayed locked away, talking to himself, for decades without experiencing even a hint of the irritation he causes to readers today. It is temptingly easy to dismiss his endless ramblings: like all dogma, his is ultimately just bad philosophy. But it is a disturbing fact: for Eichmann the logic of these terrible constructs provided stability and inner fortitude. To unbalance one of the most effective mass murderers in history, the ability to think in itself was not enough.

Old Culprits and New Soldiers

I will simply not *do penance.*
—Eichmann, 1956[88]

By May 1945, Eichmann was well aware that many people didn't share his way of thinking and would be horrified by the details of the Holocaust. And by then, his name was so closely associated with the subject that even his family demanded an explanation of who was really to blame for everything. In an interview in 1962, Vera Eichmann recalled her husband's parting words before he went underground: "'Vera, I just want to say one thing. My conscience and my hands are clean. I have not killed any Jews, or given a single order to kill. I want to tell you that.' And he swore it on his children's lives, and that was all."[89] He went on to repeat this assurance like an incantation. But for the book he was planning in 1956, it wasn't enough to declare his "clean conscience," and he added two further points: "Secondly, the other sides were not as meek as lambs, and you could not say it was only the Germans who were bad people, and thirdly was I the originator of this very bloody Final Solution?"[90] Eichmann went on to enlighten his readers as to the true originators, the people who were really guilty of this mass murder, and to suggest who might execute these criminals.

The answer to the question of who was guilty will come as no surprise. From the outset, Eichmann explains, one man had been the warmonger behind the invasion of Poland. "The war waged by the German Reich

against Poland would not have been necessary if special people, envy-
ing the economy of the German people, had not set their mind on it."[91]
After all, "Poland certainly did not want the war, and Germany did not
want it either." Both nations had been innocent victims of these jealous
people, who "further prepared for war" and "caused it to break out." And
if anyone is in doubt as to whom we talk about, Eichmann explains: the
"spokesman for the Jews who are scattered across the world, the leader
of the world Zionist organization in London, Dr. Chaim Weizmann"
set himself against any "German-Polish agreement," in order to "declare
war on the German people in the name of Jewry." This was the sole
reason (and here, Eichmann repeats one of the Nazis' greatest propaganda lies) that Hitler then announced that the approaching war would
be the downfall of the Jewish race. "Well," Eichmann continues, "today
we know he was wrong about this."[92] The Jews, the former Adviser on
Jewish Affairs informs us, suffered relatively few losses, which then gave
them "national independence." The Germans were the real victims, with
seven million fallen, and millions of murders committed as Germans
were expelled from their former territories after the war. "The victims
were Germans," Eichmann says three times, and no one was bringing
the people who had murdered the Germans to justice. Eichmann writes
himself into a frenzy: "Yes, where, where in damnation are the gallows
now, for these war criminals and perpetrators of crimes against humanity?"[93] After all, you could see that the Nuremberg Trials had done nothing to promote peace: the old aggressors would just keep starting new
wars.

The dedicated anti-Semite Adolf Eichmann wasn't content with his
theory of international collective guilt. It wasn't enough for him to relativize his own murder statistics and offset deaths in the extermination
camps against fallen soldiers. Once again he had to paint Jewry as the
guiltiest of all guilty parties, the driving force behind everything. With
the obvious triumph of one who sees himself vindicated, he points to
the Suez crisis:

> And while we are considering all this—we, who are still searching
> for clarity on whether (and if yes, how far) we assisted in what
> were in fact damnable events during the war—current events
> knock us down and take our breath away. For Israeli bayonets are
> now overrunning the Egyptian people, who have been startled

from their peaceful sleep. Israeli tanks and armored cars are tearing through Sinai, firing and burning, and Israeli air squadrons
are bombing peaceful Egyptian villages and towns. For the second time since 1945, they are invading. . . . Who are the aggressors here? Who are the war criminals?[94]

With a pathos he never managed to summon up for his victims, the
specialist on Jewish affairs forges a new alliance: "The victims are Egyp-
tians, Arabs, Mohammedans. Amon and Allah, I fear that, following
what was exercised on the Germans in 1945, Your Egyptian people will
have to do penance, to all the people of Israel, to the main aggressor and
main perpetrator of war crimes against Arab peoples, to the main perpetrator against humanity in the Middle East, to those responsible for
the murdered Muslims, as I said, Your Egyptian people will have to do
penance for having the temerity to want to live on their ancestral soil."
The Germans had good reason to see the Jews as their greatest enemy—a
race that had to be annihilated. Germans had always been in the right:
"We all know the reasons why, beginning in the Middle Ages and from
then on in an unbroken sequence, a lasting discord arose between the
Jews and their host nation, Germany."[95] He, Adolf Eichmann, had therefore done nothing wrong. From the very beginning, the Jews had been
to blame, as Adolf Hitler had recognized.

In 1956 the man who would later claim he had acted only reluctantly,
and under orders, authored a text that fulfilled all the criteria for the
most evil sort of rabble-rousing literature. Eleven years after a total
defeat, and despite having experienced the horrific reality of genocide
in all its detail, the same hatred still burned within him, and the same
merciless theory of perpetual war. And because most people still failed
to grasp this theory, he rationalized, men like him were forced to live
under false names on the other side of the world, instead of collecting
their pensions in Germany and being lauded as heroes—to say nothing
of those who had died for their beliefs.

Explaining his decision to "step out from his anonymity," Eichmann
is once more seized by the fervor of the redeemer: "I, who unlike my former comrades can still speak and *must* now speak, cry out to the world:
we Germans were also just doing our duty and are not guilty!"[96] Behind
the cry for justice lies the typical National Socialist interpretation of "to
each his own": the dogma of a Jewish world conspiracy and the only

imaginable final solution to the Jewish question, complete annihilation. Eichmann-in-Argentina wasn't about to do penance, and not because regret was useless ("something for little children," as he claimed under cross-examination), but because he wanted his own children to see something entirely different from their father's guilt.[97]

But his crowing over current events in the Middle East was more than just the affirmation of an old resentment. As always, Eichmann immediately saw a personal advantage in the political events of the day. If he was going to give himself up to be put on trial, it would only be in certain knowledge that the punishment would be lenient. Eichmann believed he would be declared guilty only "for political reasons"; the facts of the case would make a guilty verdict "an impossibility in inter-national law." And for this reason, a guilty verdict, "which I would never accept," would simply be "nonsensical" and "presumptuous." However, Eichmann reveals he is playing a tactical game when he says there is some doubt whether he will obtain justice "in the so-called Western cul-ture. The true reason may be that in the Christian Bible, this time in the New Testament (Joh. . . . .),[98] to which a large part of Western thought clings, it is expressly established that everything sacred came from the Jews." No, it would do no good to give himself up to a German or an international court. The Western world still didn't understand; for Eich-mann, Christianity was corrupted by Jews from the bottom up. And so he looks to the "large circle of friends, many millions of people"[99] to whom his whole manuscript is directed, hoping they will give him justice, at least in a symbolic sense. "But you, you 360 million Moham-medans, to whom I have had a strong inner connection since the days of my association with your Grand Mufti of Jerusalem, you, who have a greater truth in the surahs of your Koran, I call upon you to pass judg-ment on me. You children of Allah have known the Jews longer and bet-ter than the West has. Your noble Muftis and scholars of law may sit in judgment upon me and, at least in a symbolic way, give your verdict."[100] In 1956, the man who many people still thought was in the Middle East was seeking a symbolic salvation in the Arab cultural sphere, which he saw as a monolithic whole, the same way he saw Judaism. He believed that there, at least, he would not have to feign a change of heart, as he later did in Israel. He could be *Obersturmbannführer* Eichmann openly and proudly—and a ruthless anti-Semite to boot. Eichmann must have been quite open about his supposed friendship with the Arabs. After he had been abducted, his family became concerned about his second son. "As Horst was easily excitable," the police report stated, "the Eichmann family was afraid that when he heard about his father's fate, he might volunteer to fight for the Arab countries in campaigns against Israel."[101] Eichmann had obviously told his children where his new troops were to be found.

Eichmann was not the only person in Argentina to place his hopes in the Arabs. The final year of *Der Weg*'s existence saw its focus turning toward the Middle East: in 1956–57, it adopted an overtly pro-Islamic tone and made no secret of its sympathies for Egypt's president, Gamal Abdel Nasser. Admittedly, this looked more like clutching at straws than a deliberate political stance. But concrete connections did exist between Buenos Aires and the Middle East: Johann von Leers had been living in Cairo for a year or more, had converted to Islam, and was writing fiery pro-Islamic texts. These were admittedly starting to alienate West Germany's far-right circles, including the editors of *Nation Europa,* an effect that wasn't confined to Germany. Still, the rumors about the new careers that former SS and SD men were making in Egypt had not escaped the diaspora Nazis in Argentina. Their names had even started to appear in the newspapers: there was Leopold von Mildenstein, for example, who had brought Eichmann into the Jewish Department before becoming an adviser in the Ministry of Propaganda. On one of the Arabic radio stations, Mildenstein was now broadcasting speeches, of a sort that made the CIA finally develop an interest in him.[102] And from time to time, the Argentine Nazis had the opportunity to meet up with former comrades who had been in the Middle East. Walter Rauff, the RSHA specialist who had helped create the notorious gas vans, spent a few months in Buenos Aires in 1950, after making a guest appearance in Syria, then settled down in Chile (as Eichmann seems to have known).[103] And the irrepressible sabotage hero, Otto Skorzeny, may also have bragged about his assignments in the Middle East. Eichmann himself suspected that some of his former associates were there, in particular Alois Brunner, whom Eichmann had liked to call his "best man." In Damascus, Brunner made a name for himself in commerce. What Eichmann said about him implies that he knew Brunner was still alive—though he would have been less overjoyed if he had known that his best man was now working for the West German intelligence service. So was a former colleague of Eichmann's from the Foreign Office, who quite openly fled to the Middle East before the start of his trial in 1952. But Eichmann was anything but well intentioned toward Franz Rademacher, who at Nuremberg had submitted an old telephone note on which was written the incriminating sentence: "Eichmann suggests shooting them!"[104]

In spite of these personal connections, we have no indication that Adolf Eichmann, Eberhard Fritsch, or Willem Sassen ever seriously contemplated moving to the Middle East. At least in Buenos Aires there was a large community of German immigrants, with its own restaurants and stores, and life in Argentina was by no means uncomfortable. Such thoughts were attractive only because political developments in the Federal Republic hadn't turned out as the Dürer circle had hoped—and probably also because crude ideologies require a sounding board, whereas the Dürer circle were sitting on the other side of the world with a doctrine that no one was interested in anymore. Eichmann refused to do penance and longed for applause. But first and foremost, of course, he hoped his "Arab friends" would continue his battle against the Jews, who were always the "principal war criminals" and "principal aggressors." He hadn't managed to complete his task of "total annihilation," but the Muslims could still complete it for him.

The Apologist and the Demagogue

Eichmannism is a monologue.
—Shlomo Kulcsár[105]

When the discussions at Willem Sassen's house began in 1957, Eichmann brought along the finished version of his manuscript, and Sassen at least gave him the feeling that something could be done with it. Sassen had the handwritten version transcribed, as far as this was possible, and the course of the discussion shows that Eichmann's text was repeatedly used and circulated among the other participants in the Sassen circle. Their reactions suggest that everyone was impressed by the flood of thought it contained, and they posed numerous questions to him about it. Eichmann had managed to formulate clear, trenchant, effective points (presumably much to the surprise of anyone who had heard him speak before), which he had successfully incorporated into a grand design. True, submarine dwellers might have wandered the earth and people might have been branded with halos, but metaphor was not one of his strong points. In any case, Eichmann took the reaction to his writing as an encouragement and prepared more, shorter manuscripts, still searching for the right words to form the introduction to his planned book. Vera Eichmann often saw her husband writing, but she later gave an assurance that she never read these texts. Since Eichmann kept most of his writing at Sassen's house, this is perfectly plausible. Anyway, conversations about the head of the family's previous area of work were clearly unwelcome. "He always said: children, there was a war on, and we want to forget all that. War is war," his son recalled. "He often said: we live in peace, and we don't want to worry now about what happened in the war."[106] Eichmann himself forgot nothing; he just changed his version of history depending on whom he was addressing, honing the art of deception. Every book that Sassen made available to him spurred him on to write more, and to his interviewer's displeasure, Eichmann would come to the Sassen circle with lengthy speech texts. As the transcripts reveal, it was even more difficult to stop Eichmann in midflow when he was reading than when he was speaking off the cuff.

Eichmann's preferred form was clearly the monologue, a speech with no interruptions. In a monologue, he could lay out his hermetic interpretation of the world and abandon himself to the pathos of his own language. Avner W. Less observed the effect of a short Eichmann speech during his interrogation: "In the end, the man was literally moved to tears by his own words."[107] The speed at which Eichmann was able to fill hundreds of pages may have its origin in the monologic structure of his thought. Eichmann didn't write in order to develop or refine an intellectual construct, his thoughts taking shape as he went; he was laying out a fully formed, rigid train of thought, and—as his handwriting and the tone of his voice reveal—giving free rein to his aggression toward "the enemy." In his writing, he was permanently covering his back.

When he reached Israel, this training would stand Eichmann in good stead. On the one hand, he could keep the investigating authorities and the state prosecutor busy with all the information he seemed so willing to provide; on the other, his writing gave him stability, especially when he had to pretend to thoughts very different from the ones that really motivated him. In Jerusalem, of course, he wrote nothing about the eternal guilt of the "principal aggressor," the race that had made the Germans into its victims by enticing an unsuspecting Hitler into its trap.

His thoughts on the inherently subversive nature of the Jewish intellect were revealed only in his despicable attempt to ingratiate himself with the court. Eichmann was just filling out another application form, this time for the role of exemplary, voluble prisoner, and although he was not quite as successful as he had been in the Sassen circle, his new texts did more than enough to cause confusion.

Eichmann wrote incessantly in Israel. As soon as he arrived, he began "Meine Memoiren," a 128-page story of his life. Mountains of commentaries followed, regarding papers, books, people, and every question that was put to him. As the precisely documented interrogation shows, Eichmann-in-Jerusalem had no difficulties filling as many as eighty pages between one interrogation session and the next, despite his enforced early bedtime and a day filled with examinations. He produced extensive dossiers on every imaginable topic for his defense, as well as popular texts for the press. When the trial was adjourned between cross-examination and verdict, Eichmann compiled more than one thousand pages for the large book that was designed to defend him once again, though this time aimed at those who had declared they were not his friends. "Götzen" (Idols) reads like a counterargument to "The Others Spoke, Now I Want to Speak!" and he had also considered the philosophers' creed *Gnothi Seauton* (Know Thyself) as a title. Even when the verdict was announced, he didn't remain paralyzed with shock for long. He quickly began to fill more pages: "Mein Sein und Tun" (My Being and Actions); his thoughts "Even here, facing the gallows"; letters; interview answers; and texts on religious philosophy. He wrote and wrote, literally until the end: he was still composing his last lines when they came to take him to the gallows.[108] It is certainly correct to see Eichmann as an apologist, his writing driven by the need for self-justification, but anyone reading this flood of words cannot overlook another motive. Eichmann reveled in the play of arguments, the power of words, and his own power to manipulate. A desire for effect is ever present in his writing, a desire to lead the reader on and force him to accept Eichmann's own thought constructs. There had once been a time when Eichmann's suggestions, input, and plans—which fell outside all the rules of civilized society—were able to influence policy. His thoughts made their impact on the development of anti-Jewish policy as it headed toward the idea of extermination. If ever there was anyone who recognized the power of the written word, it was Eichmann. It could become the power over life and death, and in Israel, he hoped it would give him nothing less than his own life. From Willem Sassen and Eberhard Fritsch, by contrast, he simply wanted a return ticket out of his anonymity. Sassen and Fritsch would come to realize the difficulties of trying to conduct a dialogue with a monologist.

2

Eichmann in Conversation

But that is apparent to you gentlemen, is it not? That must be apparent to everyone.   —Eichmann in the Sassen circle[1]

The Contracted Parties

In Argentina, Adolf Eichmann knew the magnitude of the horror behind the phrase "the Final Solution of the Jewish question" better than anyone. He was also well aware of how much danger lay in historical research and any kind of investigation. Compared to Eichmann, even Josef Mengele and the former camp commandant Josef Schwammberger had only limited insight. This pair, far away from Berlin, the decision-making process, and the decision makers, had experienced only the end result of the extermination plans. Rudolf Höß's memoirs reveal an atmosphere in which contempt for human life, torture, and murder had become the norm, and in this atmosphere, facts, figures, and concepts become hazy. But from where Eichmann was stationed, he had both distance and oversight. He was the appointed coordinator, by the grace of Himmler, and many different strands of the operation came together in his office. Even while Hitler was in power, Eichmann was one of the few people who were able, at least in some measure, to gain a real overview of the National Socialist extermination of the Jews. By 1957 all his superiors were dead, and Eichmann's knowledge was unparalleled. The awareness of his own authority must have allowed him to enter into discussions with the Dürer circle with confidence. Of course he ran the risk that the others' curiosity might touch upon things that could endanger his ideal version of history, but he would always have the upper hand. Understandably, the last thing he wanted was to open people's eyes to reality. He was fifty-one years old and had been living in Argentina for almost seven years—long enough to have asked around and got the measure of Eberhard Fritsch and Willem Sassen. When the recordings began, sometime around the end of April 1957, Eichmann certainly thought he knew enough about his partners to take part in the project.

The Publisher: Eberhard Fritsch

From Eichmann's perspective, the least dangerous of those involved was the man who offered the infrastructure to make his book a success: a publishing house, and a range of relationships with National Socialist circles both old and new. Eberhard Ludwig Cäsar Fritsch was born in Buenos Aires on November 21, 1921,[2] and thus was fifteen years younger than Eichmann. For this reason alone, he had no insider knowledge. The German Reich, its Führer, its debauched everyday life, war, and extermination were all things he had never experienced. Contrary to rumors that he had worked for Goebbels in Berlin, Fritsch had visited the legendary Third Reich only once, for the international congress of the Hitler Youth, which took place near Berlin in 1935.[3] For a Hitler Youth leader who had grown up in Buenos Aires, Hitler's Germany during an accelerated economic recovery must have appeared an intoxicating prospect—even more so than it did to the international and more adult audience who fell for the facade of the Olympics the following year. In Argentina, which was generally friendly toward Germany, nothing prevented the young Fritsch from immersing himself in his Hitler mania and declaring anything that didn't fit this high ideal to be malicious propaganda. The news that emerged after the German defeat did nothing to change this enthusiasm, and in Argentina, radical political views didn't prevent a young man from getting a job teaching German at the Fredericus School. Things were slightly different when it came to his youth work: the camp that Fritsch set up during the school holidays was so overenthusiastically modeled on the Hitler Youth that even the Sassens found it excessive and brought their daughter home after just a short time there. The driving force behind this parental rescue may admittedly have been Sassen's wife, Miep, who was never able to reconcile herself to her husband's extremist friends, but this episode still demonstrates the overzealous nature of Fritsch's work.[4] He was more Nazi than the Nazis, Saskia Sassen remembers, without any distance or humor—but then, it was much easier for Fritsch to be an idealist than it was for the exiles. He had never witnessed the horror. For him, National Socialism remained the unsullied dream that he had dreamed as a boy on the campsite, now enriched by heroic tales from the new-comers in Argentina. His Argentine perspective meant he had both a friendly inclination toward Germany and enough skepticism toward the United States that any Allied explanation of the Hitler regime's crimes sounded untrustworthy to his ears. And Fritsch was surrounded by National Socialists from Germany, who mentioned wartime atrocities and crimes against humanity only when they were trying to incrimi-nate the people who had actually been their victims. He heard about the "victor's justice" of Nuremberg and "torture in the CIC camps," and as his articles in Der Weg show, he dismissed any criticism of the Hitler regime as anti-German propaganda. He dedicated himself to trying to improve the position of his "comrades" who had been incarcerated, got involved in Hans-Ulrich Rudel's Kameradenwerk, and helped spread the National Socialist philosophy. As he wrote to one of his authors in 1948, he wasn't interested in articles "that defame the past, which is close to many Germans' hearts."[5] He wanted a "philosophy to heal our people, and with them Europe and the world," without the "impotence that comes from anti-ethnic perspectives."[6] On his travels through Latin America, he found that these "ethnic perspectives" were essential, espe-cially in the face of "the angry half-negro mob" in Brazil.[7] In order for Fritsch to take an interest in the poor and the persecuted, they did, of course, have to be Nazis in exile. He had no time for stories of the other refugees from Germany—Argentina's Jewish immigrants, for example.

Fritsch's aid was not entirely selfless: offering his many services to Nazi fugitives was how he made his living. He was what we would today call a successful networker. He had no direct connection to the government or (unlike Horst Carlos Fuldner and Rudolfo Freude) any way of rescuing Nazis from Europe and helping them start over in Argentina; but he still managed to offer stranded Nazis a place to start in Buenos Aires, and he obtained support from all sides.[8] The Dürer House was a meeting place where people fresh off the boat could exchange addresses, have innocu-ous reunions, and buy German-language books. Through placing ads, providing courier and travel services, and, not least, furnishing the Ger-man fugitives with fascist kitsch from the Fatherland, Fritsch had estab-lished what you might call a lucrative one-stop store for Nazis in exile. American intelligence service files indicate that Fritsch received support from the highest circles: Horst Carlos Fuldner was named as one of the Dürer House's financiers.[9] In practice, this support may not actually have been financial, but the enterprise would have been untenable without the right political backing. While the *Argentinisches Tageblatt,* the liberal paper read by many Jewish immigrants, repeatedly had to battle publication bans or allocation limits on imported paper, Fritsch carried on publishing, unhindered.[10] We know very little about the business's financial background, but Fritsch must have been a man of some means, at least part of the time. He managed to keep the publishing house above water in difficult circumstances, and he owned real estate: the first house that Willem Sassen rented in Buenos Aires belonged to none other than his publisher.[11]

Eberhard Fritsch had an unconventional combination of characteristics. On the one hand, he was an eccentric Nazi enthusiast, standing at a safe distance in South America, who liked to prattle on about the "Fourth Reich" and whose admiration for National Socialists knew no bounds. On the other, he was a shrewd exploiter of those who still felt a sentimental longing for what they had lost when the Third Reich collapsed. Later events also reveal him as a gullible man who admired Willem Sassen and was almost in thrall to him.[12] Admittedly, Fritsch wasn't alone in this respect: Hans-Ulrich Rudel stuck by Sassen with a faithfulness that his associates didn't always understand.[13]

Two details illustrate Adolf Eichmann's attitude toward Fritsch. Eichmann called him "Comrade Fritsch"—a form of address he usually reserved for people he looked on as fellow soldiers (SS men) and the contacts who had helped him during his escape and in Argentina. These naturally included "my dear Comrade Sassen." If Eichmann didn't regard someone as being of equal rank to him, he simply called them by their last name. During his trial in Israel, Eichmann would make a great effort to downplay Fritsch's role in the Argentine publishing project,[14] although the Dürer circle no longer existed by this point, at least in Buenos Aires. Much suggests that Eichmann even put Fritsch in touch with his family in Linz, when Fritsch emigrated to Austria with his wife and children in 1958.[15]

The "Co-author": Willem Sassen

None of the National Socialists who fled to Argentina fulfilled the cliché of the *vivo* as much as Willem Sassen. He was a multifaceted bon vivant, a man of many talents (which didn't include any form of self-restraint). He liked to party and was always on the lookout for the big coup, the fast buck—but he had no staying power, either in his private or his professional life. If there was one constant in Sassen's life, it was his fascination with National Socialism, which, unlike Fritsch, he had experienced firsthand. Wilhelmus Antonius Maria Sassen[16] was born into a Catholic family on April 16, 1918, in Geertruidenberg (North Brabant, Netherlands). After leaving school, he considered studying theology before deciding on law, and at university he became closely acquainted with National Socialism. As an eighteen-year-old, his trip to the Olympic Games sparked his fascination with Adolf Hitler to such an extent that when he returned home, he made an emphatically pro-German speech that got him thrown out of Ghent and lost him his place at the university. Sassen's first journalistic experience was on newspapers, and he started to write for the military when he was drafted in 1938. He didn't spend long in the Utrecht Artillery: when the Germans marched in, Sassen was briefly taken as a prisoner of war, then demilitarized. He returned to journalism. He also married for the first time in 1940 and became a father, then started to look around for a second wife. During the Russian campaign, Sassen signed up for the Dutch Voluntary SS and joined the "Kurt Eggers" SS squadron. This was a reservoir of propaganda assistants, where writers and broadcasters like Henri Nannen and Vitus de Vries spurred the troops on to final victory. Sassen knew them both. According to Stan Lauryssens, he was also a witness to war crimes: he once watched as the SS forced twenty-seven Jews to beat one another to death.[17] Sassen's path led him across Poland to Russia, into the middle of the Caucasus offensive of 1942. On July 26, Sassen was so severely wounded that he had to spend the next eight months being patched up in military hospitals in Kraków, Munich, and Berlin. This got him a promotion to SS *Unterscharführer* and made him a war hero to his fellow Nazis. Sassen had belonged to the Waffen-SS and had the frontline experience and the scars to show for it, while Eichmann was in the General SS, which the frontline soldiers looked upon with disdain.

His only scar was from a motorcycle accident, and his broken hand had been caused by a slippery parquet floor. This lack of combat experience was still an obvious stigma among ex-SS comrades in exile, and Eichmann was painfully aware of it.[18]

After Sassen's recovery in April 1943, his career really took off. He was allowed to make live broadcasts, in contravention of the censorship laws, which became so successful and popular that even Radio Sender Bremen broadcast his reports. Until mid-1944, Sassen worked for Sender Brüssel, setting a new benchmark for extreme anti-Allied radio with his heavy-handed, hair-raising, tear-jerking style. This same mix of pornographic violence, pathos, and sentimentality would characterize his writing in Argentina. He was skilled in catering to mainstream tastes, producing vast numbers of reports, and earning a commensurate amount of money. The personal high point of his career as a war correspondent was a live frontline broadcast from Normandy on June 6, 1944 (D-day), when at times he found himself behind enemy lines as the Allies landed. When the evacuation order came for troops to return to Germany, Sassen started working for mobile war broadcasters, propaganda sheets, and radio stations. However, he increasingly became a gossip-column character himself, plundering supply depots and disobeying orders. Only his good contacts repeatedly prevented him from suffering serious consequences. In March 1945 Sassen fled to Utrecht and continued to broadcast his miserable slogans about perseverance there until the power failure on April 7. At that point Sassen seems to have realized it was time to look elsewhere. He made contact with his brother, who had also been in the Waffen-SS since 1944 and had built up a network to help Dutch Nazis go underground. It was a systematic counterfeiting operation to support the creation of new identities that used mobile radio broadcasters as contact media. After Hitler's death, the brothers fled to Alkmaar and went underground themselves.

Sassen's CV features some impressive escapes: on June 5, 1945, he was imprisoned and interrogated by British Field Security in Fort Blauwkapel, before managing to escape the camp in December with forged papers, money, and food. Shortly afterward he was arrested and interrogated again in Berlin. His captors then tried to hand him over to the Dutch authorities; Sassen used the transfer to effect his final escape. In May 1947 he made the journey to Ireland, and a few days later his second wife, Miep Sassen (née van der Voort), and their daughter joined him. Sassen's friendship with the daughters of the schooner captain Schneider, one of whom lived with the Sassens for a while,[19] provided him with an opportunity to escape to Argentina. Many years later Inge Schneider said she had never known how Sassen made his living in Ireland, but he had traveled a lot, and during their last year there, he had a very nice apartment. In September 1948, Sassen boarded the schooner *De Adelaar* in Dublin, with his pregnant wife and their daughter Saskia. He set foot on Argentine soil on November 5. He used a false name during his escape, traveling as Jacobus Janssen, in the company of two Belgian war criminals and their families. Sassen was a charmer and a gifted linguist. He learned his fifth language on board and showed an obvious interest in Antje Schneider, the captain's second daughter. This affair didn't stop him from describing the arduous voyage in his novel from the point of view of a devoted husband with an extremely pregnant wife. The level of horrific detail in this section gives the reader a very vivid impression of seasickness.[20] The Argentine immigration authority issued entry permits for the whole group.[21] After they arrived, Sassen, his wife, and their two daughters lived in Pilar with the Schneider sisters for a time: money was tight, and they were eager to help one another out.[22] Shortly after their arrival, as Inge Schneider remembers, Sassen started working for magazines in the Federal Republic. The first commission was apparently a two-page investigation for *Stern,* and Sassen told his family he also worked for *Der Spiegel* and *Life*.[23]

By the time Adolf Eichmann arrived in Buenos Aires in mid-1950, Sassen was already established.[24] He had quickly gone into the fugitive-aid business with Hans-Ulrich Rudel and was now working as his chauffeur and ghostwriter. He was also writing the memoirs of Adolf Galland, the second flying ace to make an emergency landing in Argentina, and he was welcome in all the Nazi-friendly circles within Argentine society. Sassen was a talented actor in Buenos Aires's German Theater—and an irresistible Don Juan, both on and off the stage. He was a politically ambitious friend of the president, a correspondent for European magazines, and a gifted author who enjoyed playing around with names as much as he loved poker: he was Wilhelm, Willem, Wim, Willy, Sassen, and W. S. van Elsloo, to say nothing of his many pseudonyms. This fugitive had made it. He was soon able to afford a small house for himself and his family on the most desirable street in Buenos Aires, at 2755 Liberdad in Florida. He never managed to create a life of ease for them, but that was purely due to his own inability to deal with money. He was a born survivor, and one might almost think fondly of this hard-drinking, sociable man with his education and his gift for languages, were it not for the burning enthusiasm he still harbored for Hitler and for German plans for world domination, and his implacable hatred of the Jews. He was fond of conspiracy theories and had a talent for unscrupulous manipulation, which he employed to lie about everything, to everyone. His behavior toward his wife was decidedly disrespectful: his contemporaries give the impression that no woman could withstand Sassen's charms, even if she was in a relationship with one of his friends.[25] In any case, whatever he was doing, he seemed to give little thought to his wife or children. This was probably not how Miep Sassen imagined her life would turn out, trapped in financially unpredictable circumstances with a notoriously unfaithful husband, particularly as she didn't share his outlandish political views and avoided his SS comrades. This was partly because her brother had been part of the Belgian resistance during the occupation.[26] Still, she tolerated the presence of Adolf Eichmann and the others in her house, despite her annoyance that the visits took place on Sunday, the family day. For several months in 1957, Miep Sassen proved an attentive hostess to at least two mass murderers and thus lent her own support to the Sassen-Fritsch project.

"Comrade Sassen" became one of Eichmann's most important attachment figures within the Dürer circle. Even as the evidence mounted that Sassen had betrayed him and his family, Eichmann still spoke of him with admiration and only reluctantly accepted the unfavorable reports he was given. In Israel, Eichmann named Sassen as his "co-author," adding that a "friendship" had developed between them "over the years."[27] Even Vera Eichmann found "Herr Sassen" to be a helpful man, who seemed to be doing everything he could to aid her and her family.[28] The change that the Sassen discussions wrought in her husband cannot have escaped her notice, even if she was seeing much less of him on the weekends. In her husband's eyes, Sassen was providing a gateway back into political life, back to dynamism and importance.

The Sassen Interviews

Only in the spring of 1957 did the Dürer circle decide to record their conversations about the National Socialists' extermination of the Jews. They had already tested this method with other book projects. Hans-Ulrich Rudel had recorded his recollections onto tape for the book *Zwischen Deutschland und Argentinien,* so that Sassen could then polish them to a pathos-rich shine. Pedro Pobierzym, a former Polish soldier in the Wehrmacht who had a business relationship with the scrap metal magnate Dieter Menge, said that Sassen bought the tape recorder from him especially for this project. Pobierzym had smuggled it into Argentina from the United States.[29] Willem Sassen also used tape for his own texts and was plainly fascinated by its possibilities. At the time, the tape recorder was a very modern piece of technology. He started using it as a matter of course, and played with it in private as well, recording plays, dance music, and his own singing and whistling, which can still be heard on the few surviving tapes.

Together with the transcripts and Eichmann's corrections, the recordings that reemerged in the late 1990s present a very precise picture of Sassen's working methods. The tapes were typed up relatively quickly by various helpers, then recorded over. New tapes were expensive, both in Buenos Aires and elsewhere, and they weren't easy to get hold of. Today we have around one thousand pages of the transcript (including the pages of corrections) and twenty-nine hours of recordings, including doubles of tapes that were copied later. Not only do they prove that the transcripts are an authentic source; they are also a window into the year 1957—and the front room of the Sassen house.[30]

A group of middle-aged men met in the neat living room of a house in Florida, a popular district of Buenos Aires. Their surroundings suited the aspirations of their project: the room was also a kind of study, full of books, records, art, pictures, and European furniture—with an atmosphere that made the conversations seem meaningful. Sassen's was a convivial house, full of "Dutch comforts."[31] He liked to live at the very limits of what he could afford: apart from National Socialism, he valued beautiful objects, education, and expensive whiskey. Games of "guess the composer" and discussions about books were part of the family's dinner table conversation, even when the children were small.[32] Sassen's living conditions were by no means luxurious, but they were still very different from what Eichmann was used to. He spent his weeks "on the ranch," providing loving care for the Angora rabbits, and he didn't inhabit rooms like Sassen's at home, either. But this wasn't the only reason his weekends with Sassen were like taking a trip to another world.

The meetings themselves were what really mattered: being reunited with former fellow travelers, having access to literature, and taking part in discussions that gave his life another dimension once again. The Sassen circle's politics had some obvious far-right features, and Eichmann was made to feel that his knowledge and his judgments were an indispensible part of the new movement. It wasn't mere flattery: they really needed this one surviving insider. When it came to the question of victim numbers, so hotly debated in far-right circles, Eichmann was generally regarded as the only person with an overview of all the mass shootings, death-by-labor operations, starvation, and gassing—a reputation he had cultivated himself. In Argentina this image had always been his entry ticket to postwar Nazi circles.

Four years later, when he was on trial in Israel, Eichmann managed to draw a veil over the true scale of the Sassen conversations. His defense strategy essentially rested on his no longer being a National Socialist and having spent the last fifteen years as a blameless, unremarkable, and above all apolitical citizen. He had left all his old resentments—in particular, his anti-Semitism—behind long ago. If the background to the Sassen circle were ever to come to light, there was no way he could maintain this lie, so Eichmann told his lawyer a story about Sassen being a headline-hungry journalist who had met the harmless Argentine citizen Klement by chance in a café. Sassen then paid him regular visits at home with a tape recorder, convincing him these discussions would help him write his biography. And yes, with the aid of a lot of alcohol, Sassen occasionally tempted Eichmann to lapse into old habits, and then had distorted everything afterward, the way journalists do. According to Eichmann, not a word of the resulting material corresponded to what he had really said. This version of events was in perfect accord with the game of hide-and-seek being played by the other witnesses, none of whom wanted to admit to sitting around a table with Eichmann. Sassen, in particular, made an effort to conceal his National Socialist convictions behind the façade of the professional journalist.

The evidence shows that the discussions were never held at Eichmann's house but at Willem Sassen's, where regular debates about the "Final Solution"[33] were held on Saturdays and Sundays from April 1957.[34] It is entirely possible that other people hosted similar sessions: contemporaries have mentioned discussion groups hosted by the affluent former SS man Dieter Menge, and some at the Dürer Verlag's premises. But these discussions probably weren't recorded. Evidence shows that the recordings were made in Sassen's house. The tapes contain the sounds of Sassen's wife and daughters in the background, noises from the same doors and windows throughout, and most significant, a few private snippets from Sassen's everyday life. Rooms have their own characteristic sounds, and the tapes contain none that suggest a location other than Sassen's house.

Contrary to what Eichmann would later claim, alcohol didn't play an important role at these meetings. The tapes and the transcripts contain references to the noise of bottle corks, but alcohol appears to have had no influence on the course of the conversation. In the 1950s, almost all social gatherings involved alcohol, and these were no exception: spirits were part of a well-laid coffee table, and a "gentlemen's discussion" was unthinkable without them. Tobacco also came with the coffee and alcohol, which must have been extremely welcome to a chain-smoker like Eichmann. But the typical indications of drunkenness are nowhere to be heard: there are no slurred words, and even during the most heated debate, everyone is alert and concentrating. Tempted as we might be by the cliché of drunken Nazis toasting one another with *"Sieg Heil"* until their crystal glasses shatter, the recorded conversations were very disciplined. There were no toasts, no clinking glasses, just the rustle of paper. Everyone remained polite and considerate, even after a verbal duel. These men were deadly serious about their discussions. The characterization of the meetings as "tavern talk" is obviously a defensive move by an accused man, and we should stop helping Eichmann perpetuate it.

With one exception, all the men addressed one another using the formal *Sie* and sometimes as "gentlemen," though with a relaxed and occasionally even friendly undertone. This was expressed in the old familiar titles: Eichmann frequently used "Comrade Sassen," "my dear Comrade Sassen," and also "Comrade Fritsch."[35] Absent members of the group and old associates were simply referred to by their last names.[36] Only Sassen and Ludolf von Alvensleben used the informal *du* with each other. In general, real names were used, rather than pseudonyms or aliases. There was no Ricardo Klement in Sassen's house, only Adolf Eichmann.[37]

The atmosphere and the course of the discussion are most reminiscent of a subject conference: a changing cast of participants spent hours at a time discussing historical theories, interpreting documents together, and arguing—occasionally fiercely—over the evaluation from the perspective of their own individual experiences. They read and discussed exhaustively every book they could get hold of. Sassen often set assigments between meetings and urged the participants to devote some proper attention to them.[38] The men made notes, read out their commentaries on the books, formulated new questions, and even gave lectures. The original recordings show that as a rule, people spoke very slowly, accentuating their words. A lecture by Dr. Langer, preserved both on tape and in transcript form, lasts for twenty minutes but covers only a page and a half of typescript, which conveys an impression of how long these discussions must have lasted.

The stamina of those present sometimes wavered, but the debate was mostly concentrated. The participants made material available to one another for the meetings: Sassen lent Eichmann books and distributed copies of important documents;[39] Eichmann brought newspaper articles he had received from Europe.[40] Sassen once translated an American magazine article for the group. People reported things they had read in the Argentine press and discussed current events in world politics, as well as the increasing juridical effort in West Germany to come to terms with the Nazi past. A few of these discussions lasted well over four hours and certainly do not give the impression of being a relaxed, enjoyable way to spend one's leisure time. The seriousness with which even the most absurd theories were constructed can be seen on every page.

Dating and the Advantage of Dilettantes

In a few cases, references to political events of the day allow us to pinpoint the particular week that a conversation took place. On tape 3, Eichmann mentions the year of the recording (1957), and in tapes 8 and 9, the arrest of Eichmann's colleague Hermann Krumey is still a hot topic. (He was arrested on April 1, 1957.) On the same day Eichmann refers to the assassination of Kasztner (who was attacked on March 3 and died on March 15). This must have been old news by then, as Eichmann ponders aloud: "He died at the start of this year, I believe, not before."[41] The discussion also covers a newspaper article from the *Argentinisches Tageblatt* of April 15, 1957.[42] On tape 37, Sassen translates an English article from the current edition of *Time* (August 1957), and on tape 39, Eichmann mentions the celebrations to mark Ballin's one hundredth birthday, which he has recently read about in the *Argentinisches Tageblatt* (again, August 1957).[43] Finally, tape 72 contains a direct reference to the sentencing of General Ferdinand Schörner in Munich (October 15, 1957).[44] Eichmann also occasionally alludes to times that give us further insights: "yesterday evening"; "for four months now"; "a few weeks ago."[45] Sassen talks about another meeting the following week. All this shows that the recording sessions began in April 1957 at the earliest and lasted until at least mid-October of the same year.

The rather unprofessionally produced transcripts reveal that Sassen and Eichmann were not the only people involved in the discussions. The surviving tapes provide audio evidence not only of other participants but of passive listeners as well. Nobody can listen to a conversation for hours at a time without making some kind of noise: throat clearing, coughing, paper rustling, footsteps, murmured excuses, hurried farewells, banging doors, jammed windows, the noises of drinks and cigarette lighters. In places it is possible to discern six separate people making these noises in the room. Contemporaries in Buenos Aires always implied that a lot of people knew about these sessions with Eichmann, and one took a certain pride in being able to say one had been there. Of course, we can't rule out the possibility that some people who met Eichmann elsewhere confused their experience with the Sassen circle, or that people said they had been at the discussions to make themselves look important. But the documents and tapes prove that they really were a big event.

The transcripts have one foible that greatly increases the difficulty of reading them: the person who typed them up omitted any indication of who was speaking. There are no names or initials, and nothing to show whether something is a question or an answer. Sometimes there are handwritten marks (F for *Frage*, or question; A for *Antwort*, or answer), but sometimes they are simply wrong.[46] The consistency with which names were omitted suggests that it was deliberate. The precaution was undoubtedly sensible: with such an extensive project lasting several months, pages from the transcript could very well end up in the wrong hands, and not everyone was as keen as Eichmann to see their names in print. This way, at first glance the transcript appeared anonymous. Unfortunately a huge amount of concentration is required to read transcribed conversations in which the speakers are not identified, especially if several people are speaking at once. To cap it all, the transcribers occasionally forgot to start new lines, meaning a change of speaker can only be surmised from the content and style. Quotations are also unmarked. When Sassen or his companions read long passages from books, as they often did, this is only apparent to someone who recognizes the quotes and can differentiate between them and the speaker's own words. Over 10 percent of the Sassen transcript is made up of quotations from books.[47] All this makes a perfunctory reading of the transcript impossible. But if you have enough time, it is possible to distinguish between the speakers: Eichmann and Sassen's speech patterns are so individual that they quickly become recognizable when you immerse yourself in the text. The fact that we now have a few of the original tape reels also means we don't have to rely completely on a feeling for language and our own reading experience.[48]

For the most part, the sequence in which the recordings were made corresponds to the numbering of the tapes, as the topics and the transitions show.[49] There is only one weekend (tapes 58–61) that Sassen seems to have accidentally misfiled. The correct chronological order is therefore: 1 to the middle of 54; then 58 to 61; then the middle of 54 to 57; and then 62 to 69 and 72 to 73.[50] (An "unnumbered tape" containing a short recording of a conversation between Sassen and Eichmann, in the middle of a "private tape by W. S. . . . filled with music and a Flemish stage play," appears to belong with tape 61.)[51] In spite of some small aberrations, an attempt was obviously made to work in an orderly and systematic way over the course of many months, and today we are largely able to follow the order of the tape labels. The material, however, demonstrates the fact that no one involved had any experience of a project on this scale or was familiar with the scholarly methods that would have been helpful for conducting it.

As surprising as it may sound, bad transcripts have an undeniable advantage over those that were professionally produced. They reveal a lot about the people who typed them, whose mistakes—repeated typing errors, for example—become identifying marks. The observant reader can decipher each transcriber's idiosyncrasies. The full transcript was typed on three different typewriters, the majority on a single machine. But because each transcriber leaves an individual and easily identifiable set of marks, three different typists can be discerned. The first and last tapes were done by people with some secretarial experience. The paragraphs are clearly separated, the transcript reproduces what was said right down to the grammatical errors, and the mistakes made with names, places, and internal Nazi affairs suggest that the typist had no insider knowledge of German history. Contemporaries recall that Sassen liked to make use of Dürer Verlag's secretaries for various other activities, and it seems likely that he had them make the first transcriptions. By contrast, most of the tapes were typed out by someone we can clearly identify as a man with Nazi experience: the abbreviations he uses for ranks, people, and institutions correspond to Nazi bureaucratic usage. This typist also has a particular quirk—he cuts repetitions as he goes and communicates with Sassen in more than one hundred comments added in brackets. Some raise direct objections, but others have a clearly political tone. The typist addresses Sassen as "Comrade Sassen," which was the norm in the discussion group, and all the parenthetical remarks are clearly addressed to him. They go far beyond comments like "could he have spoken any faster?!," "thoughtlessly unclear," "words unclear, it's enough to drive you mad!," or "thank you for the tape information." There are also sarcastic comments after Eichmann's speeches, like "blah blah blah" or "drivel," and petulant remarks directed against Eichmann, like "pig-headed Austrian" or "peddler" (in reaction to Eichmann using a foreign word that another speaker usually used). The remarks show that the typist was eager to take part in the discussion, at least remotely, as he scatters "humorous" comments through the typescript. Thus Eichmann's statements are sometimes followed by a comment like "aha" or "Buenas Noches" and, after a story that Eichmann tells about Göring, a "poor Heinrich." There is even some friendly ribbing about Sassen's sexual proclivities. The same typist makes a note of noises ("a tomcat yowls in the background, God have mercy"). Obviously a little envious, he remarks that he can hear a "wine bottle," and four pages (around two hours) later, "another bottle of wine already." A professional typist clearly wouldn't permit himself these cheeky or personal comments. But a comparison of the transcript with the original tape shows why Sassen relied on a friend for the most part: this man was sympathetic, able to distinguish between the conversations useful to the project and those that were not, and he was equal to the content. He was obviously aware of the project's aims and so allowed himself to cut conversations, leave out Eichmann's personal anecdotes, and omit repetitions. Nazi history was neither foreign nor, apparently, distant to him. It would otherwise have been an unreasonable demand for him to type out some of these detailed descriptions of war crimes and atrocities. Sassen relied on an "initiate" for most of the transcription, and in return he tolerated his high-handed comments. One of the tapes contains a dictation by Sassen in which he gives express instructions for the transcription. He wants the recorded conversations to be "gone over and edited" and explains that "this means any incorrect sentence constructions, any unfinished sentences, any sentences that are no good, I mean, that are far too long, make them shorter, without losing the natural sense or changing the wording."[52] Sassen's instructions extend to guidelines for spelling and abbreviations, although the transcripts show that the typist often had his own ideas. We do not know this man's identity.

Despite all the cuts and comments, a comparison of the transcripts and the original recordings (where both exist) reveals one thing very clearly: what we have today is a direct transcription of the tapes. Some material may have been cut, but this is in no way an edited version. The transcript is incomplete and contains some intrusions, but there is no evidence of deliberate distortion or falsification. It is a reliable transcription of the project, and although from an academic point of view we might wish it were more complete, we have no reason to doubt the authenticity of this extensive source.

A Social Event

Eichmann read most of the transcript in Argentina and added his corrections and comments right up to the final tape. He knew just how difficult it was to read the text in this format and used this fact in Israel to lessen the threat posed by this paper witness. He promoted the image of secret one-on-one conversations between the drunk, sentimental ex-Nazi Eichmann and the inquisitive journalist Sassen, in Eichmann's kitchen, far from the eyes of the world. This story must have aroused suspicion immediately, as Eichmann's wife categorically denied there were any recording sessions in their house.[53] The transcript also clearly shows that more than two people participated in the discussion. But most of the rumors still circulating about the members of the Sassen circle have their roots in Eichmann's deliberate disinformation. The only person he mentioned who was really present was "the publisher" (Eberhard Fritsch). However, although Fritsch can be easily identified on tape 47, Eichmann claimed he was there only for the first few recordings. All the other names he gave were just shameless false leads.

In Eichmann's version of events, Rudolf Mildner was invited to the meetings as an expert. He had been, among other things, head of the Political Department at Auschwitz and chief of the Gestapo in Katowice from 1941, then commander of the SiPo (Security Police) and the SD in Denmark. Mildner's name often came up in the Sassen discussions, but not because he was present. On the contrary, the participants wondered whether anyone knew where he might be, and the tapes and transcripts suggest that they thought him "missing."[54] In 1960 Eichmann had an obvious motivation for claiming he had "picked apart" Nazi history with Mildner "for the first time, around three years ago, . . . in the presence of a certain Herr Sassen."[55] He still had a score to settle with Rudolf Mildner, whom he held responsible for one of his greatest defeats (and a personal insult): the failed deportations from Denmark.[56] He also resented Mildner's incriminating testimony at Nuremberg. Finally, the Mildner story was a diversion: a senior Nazi had spoken in the Sassen group, in the person of Ludolf von Alvensleben, and Eichmann knew it was only a matter of time before someone came across that fact in the transcript. Eichmann could cover for him effectively only by using another high-ranking name. His main motive in choosing Mildner for this role seems to have been a desire for delayed revenge.[57]

As a rule, Eichmann didn't betray any of his former colleagues during his trial, as long as he didn't feel they had betrayed him. He mentioned names only of people who were long dead, and even then he made an effort to cause confusion wherever possible. During his interrogation, he tried to protect Alois Brunner by failing to correct the authorities' confusion of him with Anton Brunner, who had been executed after the war. He also protected a member of the Sassen circle by leaving his name uncorrected: reading the Sassen transcripts in 1961, Polish journalists had discovered the name Langer. When Eichmann was asked about it in court, he had the presence of mind to shorten the name to

"Dr. Lange, alias Dr. Klan," a man he had happened to meet at the time of the Sassen interviews. This started a wild-goose chase for the notorious "Dr. Rudolf Lange," who had been involved in the *Einsatzgruppen* mass shootings and was present at the Wannsee Conference.[58] The hunt was unsuccessful, as Lange had not survived his encounter with an anti-tank gun in February 1945. If we want to find out about the discussion group, we can expect little help from Eichmann's testimonies. Happily, the documents and tapes are more cooperative.

We are a long way from knowing everything about the members of the Sassen circle, but the transcripts have significantly more to tell us than people have seen to date. In addition to Eichmann, Sassen, and Fritsch, there is clear evidence of at least two others: Dr. Langer and Ludolf von Alvensleben, a guest from Córdoba who seems to have been entirely overlooked until now. Certain clues hidden in the transcript suggest women were present. Word of the meetings at Sassen's house obviously got around quickly, and they became a social event. Much was expected of this project, which was certainly no secret and attracted a great deal of attention. Eichmann, undaunted, spoke quite frankly even when he didn't know some of the guests. He was only occasionally unsettled by their questions. In one case, he notes a complaint on the transcript: "It is too annoying to read further on page three how certain assumptions were made about me here. I am thankful that Dr. Blau edited this collection [referring to a book]. It proves to this peculiar questioner how stupid it is to assume, when you are not much troubled with expertise in the matter."[59] But Eichmann seems not to have asked who the peculiar questioner was. On the tape of another session, he can be heard whispering that he doesn't like a listener who has just departed, whose name he doesn't know. Nobody who was worried about their safety and anonymity would be this relaxed.

Sassen was not always happy with his guests, either. In one case, his irritation shows as he tells the person transcribing the latest recordings about "a Patagonian show-off" he has met "this afternoon." "Between you and me," he remarks, "that was another little kick in the pants." He then gets his revenge by stating for the record that the show-off arrived "in a crappy old car ... that wasn't exactly the image of the fat new cars people drive in Patagonia."[60] It just so happens that at the start of the 1950s an old rival of Sassen's from his early years in Argentina had moved to Bariloche: Hans Juan Maler (real name Reinhard Kopps).

Like Sassen, Maler was a prolific writer. Four years older, he had made himself indispensable to Dürer Verlag in *Der Weg*'s first years. He specialized in finding cunning and illegal methods of circulating the magazine, one of which was the use of a distribution point in Hamburg, Maler's hometown.[61] Some differences of opinion developed with the magazine's editors, as Maler, the anti-Freemason expert, increasingly deviated from the line taken by Fritsch, Leers, and Sassen. Maler developed a crazed theory that could have been put to excellent use in starting a cult, had he not been driven by paranoia. He no longer felt safe in Buenos Aires and thought murderers were pursuing him. He also considered himself a great intellect.[62] In the early 1950s, Maler moved to Bariloche in Patagonia, where he intended to start up a rival to the Dürer House. Despite founding his own hotel and travel agency, things didn't turn out as he had hoped. The business became a self-publishing enterprise for books that were largely unmarketable, though in his memoirs he nevertheless boasted about his great successes. Bariloche was popular with exiled Nazis. Around eight hundred miles from Buenos Aires, it lay at the foot of the Andes and was reminiscent of the Swiss mountains, which made it particularly popular with émigrés from the Alpine regions. Franz Rubatscher, and Gustav and Friedrich Lantschner, former *Gauamtsleiters* in Innsbruck, worked in this popular tourist area as ski instructors, and Erich Priebke ran the successful Wiener Delikatessen butcher. Rudolf Freude also had a house there.[63] Bariloche was a fashionable metropolis, and the "fat cars" that Sassen referred to were part of the cliché. Fritsch had evidently stayed in touch with Maler, so he might have invited him over to get an idea of the project. It's possible that we even have a recording of him: one of the fragments of tape contains a voice with a strong Hamburg accent.[64] In any case, people came from far and wide to see what Sassen was up to in Buenos Aires. And the "show-off with the crappy old car" doesn't seem to have been invited by Sassen himself.

The transcript and tapes also allow us to rule out a few people as possible listeners. Everything speaks against the concentration camp "doctor" Josef Mengele having been present. Eichmann and Sassen knew Mengele personally, and Eichmann would have insisted on drawing him into the conversation, as he did with other participants. When the discussion turns to Höttl, he addresses "Dr. Langer," as "he knows Höttl professionally." Eichmann also likes to take on a familiar tone, in order to avoid having all the questions directed at him. "Well, you know Heydrich," he says. He would have handed responsibility for the discussion to Mengele on certain topics, given the latter's knowledge of Auschwitz and Nazi "medicine"—two issues from which Eichmann tried to distance himself as far as possible. Several times he expresses his regret at having nobody to back him up: "It's a shame I don't have any comrades from this time whom I worked with, as I have come to realize, having abstained from all these thoughts for many years, that there is much I have forgotten."[65] Sassen also gives a lengthy reading from a text about Mengele; surprisingly, the typist doesn't recognize the name and, as he does with other unfamiliar names, simply leaves a space. Josef Mengele, as his diaries show, was mistrustful and exceedingly cautious. For this reason alone he would never have involved himself in an undertaking as open as the Sassen discussions. However, Sassen must have spoken to Mengele about Auschwitz at some other point: he was still justifying Mengele's "experiments" on people in the camp, and talking about how "cultured" he was, in an interview for Argentine television in 1991. Mengele, he said, had always sought to discover "the essence, the philosophy" of human existence, by examining people "under exceptional circumstances." Sassen saw sadistic torment without sense or reason as "a demonstration of humanity."[66] He prudently omitted to tell the interviewer that, after Eichmann had been abducted, he had accepted payment from Mossad to track Mengele down.

Not everyone in 1957 was as publicity shy as Mengele. During his extensive investigations, the Argentine author Uki Goñi met a surprising number of people who claimed to have witnessed the discussions between Eichmann and Sassen. The fact that people with no access to the Dürer circle made such claims is only human nature. Goebbels's acolyte Wilfred von Oven even said he introduced Fritsch and Sassen, despite having only arrived in Argentina in 1951, long after Sassen. All this boasting just shows how attractive these ghoulish gatherings and their protagonists must have been. Anyone who thought they were anyone claimed to have been there. In one of the first recording sessions, Eichmann hints at the reason he allowed himself to become a public attraction in far-right circles: "They stopped looking for me a long time ago, that much is clear."[67]

The Lady Visitors

We have grown so used to the image of a Nazi fugitive's secret life that, when reading difficult source documents, we sometimes overlook something obvious:[68] the Sassen circle was not only large, it was a social event to which even women were admitted. This fact, documented in one of the first transcripts, allows us to dismantle the picture of the Sassen circle Eichmann later painted. The women's visit was a disaster. At the end of the recording, "the ladies" are ushered out courteously, before Eichmann explodes with rage: "It was only because I kept myself under control that I was able to say a conventional farewell to the ladies."[69] What had happened?

We don't know exactly how the discussion began, because the tape was defective and didn't start recording right away. But the transcript shows that the conversation began in a rather clichéd fashion, with the same question Goethe's Gretchen put to Faust: So tell us, Adolf, where do you stand on religion? Eichmann tells them about his wife, who was deeply religious. "My wife even reads the Bible. I let her read it," he says, giving an insight into his marriage. "I once tore up a Bible and threw it away, and afterward my wife was unhappy. And then she took a second Bible—we had another one—and at some point I tore that one as well, but only into two parts. . . . And now my wife reads the two parts, and I have sworn to let her read them, so she is happy." He just wants his family to have a better life than he had, and before anyone can start thinking he has lost sight of the political hoizon, he adds: "I do everything I can for my wife, as I did for Germany, and my family is only a little piece of Germany."[70]

In spite of the Bible incident, Eichmann was largely accepting of his wife's religious nature, even though the SS regarded it with disdain. His own family's religious background might have played a role here. Eichmann's father was a Protestant, and when the family moved to Linz, he found himself in the minority. Still, he played an active part in the community and was even a presbyter. When his first wife died, Karl Adolf Eichmann consciously chose a woman from his own church to join his large family. Maria Eichmann, whom Adolf Eichmann still called "my new mother" in 1957, was a religious woman who often read the Bible. When her stepson acceded to his father's wishes and went to work in the mine for a while, she gave him his own Bible. He "was very pious at that time," as Eichmann later told Sassen in confidence. Whether as a result of his upbringing or the traditional piety of mountain dwellers, the sixteen-year-old Eichmann read the book—though in his typical manner. "I read my Bible every evening, underlining the passages that particularly interested me, with red and blue pens. The battles of the Old Testament."[71] These color-coded meditations were soon followed by a special religious conversion: Eichmann became *gottgläubig,* an adherent of the racially based religion advocated by National Socialism. However, he left the church for good only at the start of 1938, three years after his wedding.[72] When Eichmann married Vera Liebl, he agreed to a church ceremony against the wishes of the SS and repeatedly defended his wife's decision not to give up her faith. But he probably didn't tell her that in November 1943 he officially reported to his masters that his wife was "now *gottgläubig.*"[73] The documentary evidence of this deception that he was shown during his interrogation in Israel clearly made him uncomfortable. Eichmann's concept of religion was one of the few topics on which he remained frank and consistent for the rest of his life. He even went against the advice to profess Christian beliefs that he was given in his final months. But however true he remained to his decision, he was aware his wife had other needs. He acquiesced to her wish for their youngest child to attend a Catholic school. And when the Reverend Hull, the theologian who visited him in Israel, suggested sending Vera his prison Bible, he did that too.[74] We can therefore assume that he really was as sorry about the torn book as he claimed to have been to the inquisitive ladies in 1957.

On the tape, Eichmann also gives a vivid account of his "professional" life. He chats about the room in the office for Jewish affairs where he and his colleagues played music at the end of the murderous working day: "My assessor played the piano, I was the second violin, the noncommissioned officer played first violin, he was a much better musician than me." He also recounts his heroic deeds at the war's end, when all his colleagues crowded around the men who were producing forged identity papers: Eichmann didn't want any, preferring to kill himself in the event of a final defeat. The fact that the man with the death wish is alive to tell this tale in Buenos Aires doesn't knock Eichmann off his stride. He boasts of the recognition he got from his superiors: "Müller said to me once, if we'd had fifty Eichmanns, we'd have won the war for sure. And

I was proud." This chatter then apparently starts to irritate him: "That should have given you an insight into my interior—since you don't know me, not from within, and that is important."[75]

The inner life of a mass murderer seems to arouse the ladies' curiosity, and they want to know more about Eichmann. "And if you are such a fanatical Nationalist [meaning National Socialist],"[76] someone asks, is there perhaps also a "mysticism, a doctrine, a worldview of *völkisch* life that plays into this for you?" At this point the tape cuts out, but the transcript shows how enthusiastically Eichmann answered this question. Yes, his first commanding officer, Gregor Schwartz-Bostunitsch, was a mystic. Schwartz-Bostunitsch stood five foot eleven, with flat feet and a goatee, and he had actually been a kind of comical curiosity, a carnival demagogue with a fake professorship. Once he had launched into one of his endless monologues about the danger of Freemasons, it was difficult to stop him, as his deafness shielded him from objections. He had been an object of suspicion even in Himmler's circles—and *Reichsführer*-SS Himmler was someone who had charts drawn up by witches, thought the Externsteine rock formation in northern Germany was "ur-Germanic," and believed all sorts of other nonsense about grails and fraternities that could only very generously be described as "mysticism."[77] Eichmann had little interest in it. "I don't see anything in mysticism . . . we have to ensure that our offspring live a proper life, and that's that. I have to forge my weapons according to the strength of the resistance." But he was also no stranger to the tempting idea of a grand mission, which is obvious even in the fragmentory transcripts. "The integration into the whole, because in the whole lies the *völkisch*, one blood."

Eichmann wasn't lying: he had always believed the ritual-murder horror stories about Jews were propaganda and had recognized the *Protocols of the Elders of Zion* as a forgery from the beginning—much to Sassen's surprise. Eichmann used this stuff when it came to manipulating foreign representatives, but he didn't need it to persuade himself to commit murder.

At this point, the person typing up the tape inserts five dashes and picks up again only with what Eichmann says once the ladies have left. Still, it is clear what has happened. "And for this we gave everything," Eichmann splutters, losing his composure. "Everything, youth, everything, and freedom, and others gave still more, even their lives. And so I can't stomach somebody saying to me, what could have been worse,

worse [than] National Socialism taking the reins on January 30, '33? I'm going to lose it!"[78] One of the "ladies" had dared to touch on something that nobody would follow up in the discussions over the months to come: she had asked about the inherently criminal nature of the totalitarian state, which was revealed when the Nazis "seized power" in Germany in 1933. It doesn't require a great deal of imagination to work out that the ladies must have been ushered out politely but hurriedly, before Eichmann's patience wore out. "It was only because I kept myself under control that I was able to say a conventional farewell to the ladies."[79]

The episode is remarkable because it shows how little consideration was given from the very start to who witnessed the discussion and whether the guests held similar beliefs to the principal protagonists. We don't know who the women with the reasonable views were. One may have been a secretary from Dürer Verlag, who came from Belgium and had a relationship with Sassen.[80] Inge Schneider, the schooner captain's daughter from the Lüneberg Heath, who had crossed the Atlantic with Sassen, remembers her sister Antje telling her she had been present at these recording sessions. Antje Schneider, whose married name was Löns (and whose husband was Bayer's South American representative), still carried a torch for Sassen and collected his photos and theater reviews. Inge Schneider later married the submarine captain Heinrich Lehmann-Willenbrock (played by Jürgen Prochnow in the 1981 film *Das Boot*). She was much more distanced from the Dürer group and insisted she had never attended the meetings herself, meeting Eichmann only at other social events.[81] Unlike the man they met, the women who made Eichmann boil with rage were clearly not "fanatical National Socialists." He was a fanatic, who didn't hide what he believed and gave them an unsolicited insight into his "attitude of mind" (an important concept in the philosophy of Kant). Eichmann, Sassen, and Fritsch were certainly not afraid of people who thought differently. And who would the women have told about Eichmann's views, in Buenos Aires? It was no secret that there were unreconstructed Nazis in Argentina, and their names were no secret either. Nobody would have been interested in hearing that "if we'd had fifty Klements, we'd have won the war for sure."

The Unknown Helper: Dr. Langer

Keep drilling!
—Sassen whispering to Dr. Langer[82]

These occasional visitors were not the only guests: Sassen made very few recordings of himself and Eichmann alone. In most cases, a man whom everyone called "Dr. Langer" was also present.[83] This man played a large part in shaping the Sassen interviews, and it is a mystery why his role has been overlooked. We have not only a wealth of his questions and opinions but also a long lecture, which has been preserved both on tape and in the transcripts. With palpable excitement in his slightly hesitant voice, Dr. Langer describes the character of Wilhelm Höttl, whom he knew very well from his work in Vienna. He also gets into some heated exchanges with Eichmann. And to forestall any questions: we don't know who this man was, though he obviously had a remarkable Nazi career behind him.

Langer, as Eichmann often remarked smugly, had been with the SD in Vienna and had done no military service. During a heated discussion, Eichmann asks him why he is getting involved in things he clearly has no idea about; or as he phrases it: "You ridiculous pipsqueak! Did *you* fight at the front?"[84] But Langer knew about law, and when Eichmann speaks about his time in Austria following the annexation, he emphasizes his experience: "At this time I worked in another part of the SD in Austria, and within the framework of this law we had the task of assessing civil servants, i.e., determining whether or not they were Jews."[85] In other words, Langer was one of the men who implemented the Civil Service Restoration Act of 1933 in Austria. He had decided who was allowed to remain a civil servant and who was not.

This Dr. Langer from the Vienna SD was clearly a man of no small importance, having held at least one position that still made Eichmann envious in 1957. When Eichmann explains that his commanding officer, Heydrich, was so busy in Prague that he had little time for RSHA problems in Berlin, Langer firmly contradicts him: "I don't believe that, he at least took time to sign things." Eichmann bristles and replies: "You don't believe that, then I must say, then you were lucky you were in the SD, . . . everything else, in Department IV, was signed by Müller at that time."

But Langer doesn't give up easily. "In Department IV—but I remember very well, we got a lot of things with his signature on them." He then adds, rubbing salt into the wound, "and he certainly took the time for it when I was with him in Prague." This leads Eichmann to say, awkwardly: "I was with him in Prague as well"[86]—as if anyone in the group would have doubted that. This silly game of My-Heydrich-Your-Heydrich reveals Eichmann's attacks as an attempt to downplay Langer's obvious importance. Heydrich was one of the most ambitious men in the Reich, and he didn't grant an audience to just anybody. Langer emerges as an expert on the percentage of Jews in the SS: "It was small, though there were a few more after the Aryan Certificate, it wasn't possible to establish a percentage, there were probably more in Austria than in the Old Reich."[87] He is able to give personal impressions of prominent Nazis like Hans Rauter and Arthur Seyss-Inquart,[88] and even Eichmann occasionally defers to his superior knowledge, when it serves his purposes. "We'd have to make specific inquiries to Dr. Langer on whether H[eydrich] was also the president of the International Criminal Police Commission in 1939."[89]

We may not know who Dr. Langer was, but his position cannot have been lowly. "I had an *Ustf.* [*Untersturmführer*] in my office, who found out he was a quarter Jew, he wanted to kill himself, I stopped him, then he went into the Luftwaffe, and was a great hit there . . . and I was told he played a large role in Austria again after the war, in the new national movement."[90] His obvious pride in his men also has another significance. In reply to a question about his staff, Langer complains to Eichmann that he kept losing his best men: "I was disadvantaged by the RSHA department heads always taking the good people away from me [!]."[91]

In spite of their rivalry, Dr. Langer had information that Eichmann was keen to hear. In one session, Eichmann presses Sassen to question Dr. Langer on a topic that had caused him particular headaches: the witnesses to his boastful speech at the end of the war. Eichmann points out that "Dr. Langer . . . knows Höttl professionally."[92] He should therefore be asked to talk about it. For around twenty minutes, Langer gives a sort of lecture on Wilhelm Höttl: he can be heard using prepared notes, which include interpretations of the Höttl book. Despite his aloof, fussy style, over time Langer loosens up and speaks with a degree of humor about Höttl's terrible reputation and scheming ways. But now too much attention is being given to Eichmann's rival, and he gets impatient and interrupts. With an irritable interjection ("Is that everything, then?") he embarks on a long-winded explanation of his own, which is so lacking in content that you cannot help but get the impression that he was just making sure the other man didn't take up any more of the session.

Langer puts some critical questions to Eichmann, which at times suggest he may have a sense of guilt. Still, it would be wrong for us to imagine that the former SD man from Vienna represented the last vestiges of morality within the Sassen group. The original tapes betray something the transcriber in Argentina chose to leave out: Dr. Langer had access to the Mauthausen concentration camp. "During one of my frequent visits there, the Dutch Jews were paraded in front of me."[93] Through his close relationship with Commandant Franz Ziereis, Langer also heard about an order to exterminate the Dutch Jews through labor. He recalls "a personal experience, when the camp commandant explained to me: this group of Jews, they were assigned to this work that, in practice, was work that a person could only manage for a few days."[94] The Sassen circle discusses the horrific methods of extermination through labor openly and with interest.

Nor is Langer out of place in the Sassen circle in other regards. He shares their belief in the Jewish world conspiracy and, like Sassen, keeps a keen eye out for stray facts that might serve the "Jewish" academic community. When Eichmann talks with comparative candor about his superior officer's capricious tendencies, Langer points out the danger: "You are, of course, giving the enemy even more arguments that will allow him to claim capriciousness ruled."[95]

Hardly any of the stories about Langer's own involvement in the Holocaust were reproduced in the transcript, suggesting that Sassen had guaranteed him a level of discretion. Sassen certainly doesn't seem to have brought him into the circle because he was interested in hearing specifics from him. Langer had something very different to offer. Unlike Sassen and Fritsch, he was in a position to be able to evaluate at least some of what Eichmann said. It is inconceivable that Langer and Eichmann didn't have at least a fleeting acquaintance from their time in power. If nothing else, then in the final months of 1944, Eichmann's appalling death marches would surely have brought his name to the attention of an SD man of Langer's rank. Langer was able to judge and to ask questions where Sassen foundered. He was there to run Eichmann through the mill on Sassen's behalf. A former employee of *Der Weg* stressed that Eichmann was literally interrogated in the Sassen circle.[96] During a concentrated discussion between Eichmann and Langer, Sassen can be heard on the recording whispering "keep drilling!" But Eichmann quickly discovered how to handle Langer—by turning his own weapons against him: laws and regulations. He liked to cite one of the books that the Sassen circle discussed page by page and put his superior knowledge to good use, backing up his partly dishonest theories by saying: "Lange[r] also saw it for the first time when he saw Dr. Blau's collection of statutes."[97]

Eichmann also relied on a skill he had used to promote his interests during interministerial negotiations in Berlin: playing the petty-minded bureaucrat. For example, on one tape, a text is put before him where his department is referred to as "IV A 4." Eichmann at first becomes nervous, and then nitpicking: "IV A 4—just a moment. What?? Can I see that please? Look at this, you can see this jackass of an author, you know. These authors believe they sucked wisdom at the teat. And if you ever see a collection of Roman numerals and upper and lower case letters, these morons will have mixed them up. That's IV A. IV A is a completely different group!" And then Eichmann gives a long-winded, self-assured, overbearing, and ultimately convincing explanation of why this departmental designation could not have existed.[98] But the fact of the matter is that from March 1944, Eichmann's department really was IV A 4. His office had four different designations over the years: IV R; IV D 4; IV B 4; and finally IV A 4.[99] He knew very well that these numbers were all that linked a file to a particular department, and that if you removed the labels, you could deny those dossiers had anything to do with you, and make whole mountains of documents vanish. The Israeli interrogating officer Avner W. Less was almost amused at "the incredible doggedness and vehemence" with which Eichmann denied every department name except IV B 4. Eichmann carried on batting official terms and internal designations back and forth until documents were submitted to remind him that all his attempts to baffle the authorities were in vain.[100] Things had been very different when the Nazis were in power. When your job is murder, you don't have to win anyone over, you just have to play for time. Numerous documents prove that Eichmann used tricks to create precedents for things he wanted to do. Bureaucratic chicanery is different from bureaucracy itself, and no one knew this better than Eichmann, who found all bureaucracy by definition tiresome. This was what staff were for. "These matters to do with bureaucracy," he explained to Sassen, "I just relied on my civil servants for them." He deployed these "living articles," like Ernst Moes and Fritz Wöhrn, as "bureaucratic brakes."[101] With Langer, he took up the position of "living article" himself, for as long as it served his needs. And if a question still made him too uncomfortable, he quickly changed tack: "You can't put [yourself] in my shoes, you can never do that, because you were in the SD until the very end."[102]

Who was Dr. Langer? Whose was the voice with the slight Viennese accent, who said a polite "God bless you" when someone handed him a drink, but whose reminiscences about the horrors of Mauthausen never stuck in his throat? Once again Eichmann-in-Jerusalem is no help to us. There he claimed he had briefly met a man named "Lange," the former head of an *Oberabschnitt* division in Austria, around the time of his conversations with Sassen in his kitchen. He said this man's real name was "Dr. Klan."[103] Significantly, there was only one person Eichmann knew with this exotic-sounding name: the doctor in the Mossad team who cared for Eichmann immediately after he was abducted. None of these names have yet been discovered in Argentina. In contrast to the way the SS was divided, there were no SD *Oberabschnitte* in Austria, since the whole of Austria came under a single division, SD Oberabschnitt Donau.

Langer's identity remains a puzzle. All we have are his stories, his voice, and his name: no aliases were used in Sassen's house, and as Eichmann and Langer could easily have met through their work, it would have made no sense for Langer to conceal his identity from Eichmann.[104] SS lists,[105] the records of doctorates awarded in law or politics from the University of Vienna,[106] and the expertise of many colleagues[107] have thus far yielded no further insights, apart from a long list of people to rule out. The example of "Dr. Langer" shows how much remains to be discovered in the Sassen interview material, and ultimately how little we know about the Nazis in exile.

The Weapon: Violence by Words

SASSEN: "Can you just hit the fly with that?"
VOICE: "Yes!"
 Sounds of slapping and laughter
SASSEN: "A Jewish-minded fly . . ."
 A slap
SASSEN: "A corpse fly."

—Sassen discussions[108]

What makes the Sassen documents such a powerful source in the first instance is the men's language, which the text and the recordings bring to us in an unmediated form. Anyone who has heard Adolf Eichmann's interrogation by Avner W. Less, or listened to the trial recordings, will be familiar with his idiosyncratic speech, by turns whining, cold, and occasionally petulant, as he speaks about himself and his crimes against humanity. His endless sentences are full of twists, turns, and circular thinking as he exhausts listeners with descriptions of opaque hierarchies and responsibilities, and with excuses about a sense of duty and being under orders. The experience of listening to Eichmann-in-Argentina, in a circle of sympathizers, is clearly different (and still more intolerable). It is impossible to hear the material on the tapes without getting at least some impression of how he must have appeared to people in Argentina. If we want to analyze what the Sassen circle produced over those months in 1957, we must take a moment to expose not only their thought but their language. Apart from anything else, this is one of very few sources that give us access to the jargon of these self-proclaimed sages.[109]

At first glance, the discussions are dominated by Eichmann's perfidious phrases. This man had his own way of categorizing his victims. His sole concern had been "Jews of a level that made them important to the Reich"; "a common or garden Jew was of no interest."[110] To his mind, there were "valuable Jews," and then "old and assimilated" Jews who were no use to anyone. The fanatical racist explained this as if it were the most self-evident thing in the world. The Jews, he argued, also wanted to preserve "biologically valuable Jewish blood."[111] "It is exactly the same as when I have a chicken farm today, and I need one hundred or ten thousand egg-laying hens, in truth I have to let two hundred thousand chickens hatch in the incubators, because half will be cocks and half hens."[112]

Naturally, care was taken with the deportations, "since it wasn't in our interests for the material to be used for labor in the concentration camps to arrive completely useless and needing repair."[113] Eichmann was proud of the fact that he had frequently been successful: "Look, how can you make 25,000 Jews, or people, or let's say 25,000 cows, how can you simply let 25,000 animals just disappear en route. . . . Have you ever seen 25,000 people in a pile? . . . Have you ever seen 10,000 people in a pile? That's five transport trains, and if you pack them in the way the Hungarian police planned, then at best you'll get no more than 3,000 people in one transport train."[114] The people to whom Eichmann is speaking have no idea of the problems faced by someone trying to organize an extermination operation: "Loading a train is a tricky business anyway, whether it's with cattle or flour sacks . . . and so much more difficult to load it with people, especially when you have problems to reckon with."[115] It was always the same. To start with, things looked "very hopeful," the transports "rolled in the beginning, you could say it was glorious."[116] Deportations progressed "splendidly and without any difficulty."[117] Some operations were "particularly nice and neat, with all the bells and whistles,"[118] but then the "damned problems" arose.[119]

Eichmann's brainchild was to send people hundreds of miles on foot, in the middle of winter, during the last months of the war. But he didn't call them "death marches." "These Jew-treks, as I called them," were carried out "in the most elegant way."[120] And without hesitation, he adds: "I can tell you today that I saw two bodies on the whole route, they were old Jews—it's clear, you can't make an omelette without breaking eggs. And were no eggs broken when much larger contingents of Germans marched from the East after 1945?" Eichmann thought it absolutely fair to deport hundreds of thousands of Hungarian Jews to their deaths: the transports were "to everyone's advantage, including the Jews themselves."[121] Men like Kurt Becher wanted to let the Jews live just so they could rob them—but not Eichmann. "While we were working with the Jews to solve the Jewish question, the others used the Jews as a means to an end, to milk them for their own ends."[122] Better a respectable Final Solution than underhanded extortion—Eichmann naturally never stooped to that himself, even though it meant not squirreling anything away for his family: "Thank God I did not become a swine."[123] Regrettably, however, not everyone realized this fact: "And this is why there are still a whole lot of Jews enjoying life today who ought to have been gassed."[124]

Naturally, these things were considered only on a large scale. There was no interest in individual cases: "Whether one bellyacher or another . . . somehow played a role" carried no weight.[125] It wasn't worth making a fuss over "a few little remainders or groups"—the Jews who couldn't be murdered. Still, you always had to take care not to make any exceptions: "The single individual no longer plays a role in such a crowd, but I couldn't do it in front of my lawyers, who had to keep a close watch on these regulations."[126] In a systematic extermination, people who have been overlooked are called "folks," who "have been kept alive and did not suffer typhus or a physical extermination."[127] But his colleagues occasionally "took care of these left-overs."[128] Wisliceny, for example, "then also finished off the Jews in Slovakia."[129]

If the Jewish representatives entertained hopes of being able to achieve something through discussion with Eichmann, it meant they had already lost: he saw these encounters as nothing more than an intellectual challenge: "I loved playing an open hand against all the Jewish political functionaries."[130] "For me, 'open hand' is a winged word."[131] As he freely admitted, this "game," which he played in Hungary with Rudolf Kasztner, was really just about "him continuing to play his role as appeasement councilor [!] with his Jewish community."[132] Eichmann was clearly proud of the tricks and lies he used to achieve his aims: "Over the years I learned which hooks to use to catch which fish."[133] Unscrupulous blackmail was part of the "game": "Naturally I used the Brandt family to pressurize Kasztner, well, that's a game the Abwehr played, it's understandable"[134]—or at least, Sassen and the others understood it.

In Eichmann's world, people who risked their lives for the sake of humanity were worthy only of verbal assaults. Raoul Wallenberg did everything in his power to provide refuge and Swedish papers for people who were being persecuted in Hungary. To Eichmann, he was just a "pseudo-diplomat" who "made himself at home" there.[135] Anyone acting for the Jews and holding up the "extermination machine"[136] was an "interventionist," who didn't understand what was at stake. Many of them "had very limited horizons, from going to church every Sunday."[137] Anyone who spoke to the enemy about the extermination program, like Kurt Gerstein, "is an a . . . with ears."[138] The transcriber makes a polite omission here as he felt the expletive was improper (unlike detailed descriptions of torture and murder). Talking about a subordinate who did not meet the deportation quotas, Eichmann insinuates that "it is humanitarian intentions here, allowing him to hide comfortably behind decrees, acts and laws"—for what was human fellow-feeling if not an "excuse"?[139]

The language becomes entirely perverted where Eichmann turns metaphors on their heads, talking about expulsion and murder using gentle images of life. An institution for forced emigration was his "first child,"[140] where he was able to "be creative in my work."[141] All the individual acts of robbery and expulsion that took place in Austria were committed to "provide [the country] with injections of Jewish solutions."[142] Even exterminations and deportations were "born."[143] This was why he felt so superfluous in Budapest, when he was forced to stop deporting people to Auschwitz: "As far as I know, I couldn't have done anything fruitful anymore."[144] When the fruits of your labor lie in the rising columns of murder charts, you need a rather different understanding of growth and life. In Eichmann's language, he didn't send people to the death camps; the camps were "fed with material."[145]

Resistance was not anticipated in this "business of the Final Solution," and when it happened, Eichmann found it completely incomprehensible—for example, when concentration camp officials were "beaten to death by some Jew who had gone crazy."[146] Anyone who survived the inferno had "absconded."[147]

Neither Eichmann nor his interlocutors had a problem calling things by their names: Jews were "gassed"; "idiots sent to the slaughter"; those who were deported were "killed nonstop in concentration camps like on a conveyor belt."[148] As Himmler had hoped, people seemed to feel more strongly when they didn't beat about the bush. "It made no difference to me," Eichmann casually declares on one recording, "where the Jews went, as far as I was concerned they could have marched to Madegascar, or gone to Globocnik to be gassed, as far as I was concerned they could have gone to Auschwitz, or to Riga."[149] But even tastelessness is individual, and all the particpants have their own particular preferences: Sassen favors sexual innuendos about the "technical implementation of the reproductive urge" and "men's desires," when faced with the atrocities in the camps.[150] Anyone who seems suspect is a "jackass" or a "chump." Alvensleben likes to bluster about "the way crowds of Jews can be incredibly rowdy"[151] and a "responsibility" that "is in the blood."[152] Dr. Langer, meanwhile, enjoys giving detailed accounts of the torture methods used in Mauthausen.[153]

But let no one say that these men didn't also have delicate feelings. Eichmann, as he tells his comrades here, feels "genuinely heartsore for the Reich." "I trembled for the Reich,"[154] he says, from which people could see "how fully I was committed to this struggle, with my whole being."[155] He was shocked to hear about the extermination plans for the first time and comforted himself using Himmler's words: "The word is easy to say, but it is monstrously difficult."[156] "The whole business of the Final Solution"[157] was a "killer of a job"—words Eichmann spoke without any sense of irony.[158] Only Himmler's calls not to murder with "unnecessary cruelty" were "music to my ears."[159] This was the reason some Jews were allowed into the "Theresienstadt old people's home,"[160] because "there they received the lightest work, work for the elderly who through some oversight were not yet dead."[161]

Eichmann still had plenty to be proud of in Argentina in 1957. Deaths had been necessary: "The only good enemy of the Reich is a dead one. In particular I have to add, when I received an order, I always carried out this order with the executioner, and I am proud of that to this day."[162] "If I had not done this, they would not have gone to the butcher."[163] Hungary, and the mass deportation of more than four hundred thousand people in a few weeks, had been his masterwork: "It was actually an achievement that was never matched before or since."[164] If only there had not been all those problems before that point! The thing that pained Eichmann most was when the trains weren't full. It was "a very poor business in Belgium."[165] And it was even worse in Denmark, when he wasn't allowed to transport people to their deaths as he wished. "I had to recall my transports, for me it was a deadly disgrace."[166]

Cynical, pitiless, misanthropic, morally corrupt, with no understanding of tact or limits—these are all inadequate descriptors for the words Eichmann, Sassen, and their group came out with in 1957. There is nothing here to remind us of the future prisoner in Jerusalem, about whom Shlomo Kulcsár noted: "The examiner is well acquainted with the style of Nazi literature. E.'s style was quite different, more dry, lacking the *Kraftausdrücke* [strong words]. It was not made to provoke emotions."[167] And although Hannah Arendt may have been right to point out the "macabre humor" with which horror sometimes tips over into comedy, in light of the Argentine documents, her characterization of Eichmann's "inability to speak" and "inability to *think*" seems insupportable.[168] Eichmann's words in Argentina, like those of the other participants, weren't thoughtless drivel but consistent speech based on a complete system of thought. They were, we might say, judgments in excess. It isn't the foundations of the argument that are missing here, but the group's willingness to criticize the structures of totalitarian thought and to change their dogmatic approach. These men valued consistency for the violence that it allowed them to wield over themselves and others. It became an end in itself. Twelve years after the war, they still hadn't obtained any degree of distance from it: Fritsch, Sassen, and Eichmann were still ideological warriors, in the midst of the battle, who had lost all weapons but language and magniloquence. For this reason, confronting their language can open up these documents in ways that knowledge of historical facts and the power of imagination alone cannot. This language reflects the disconnection from civilized society that allowed the National Socialists to commit monstrous crimes against their fellow man. Systematic mass murder is not just the sum of isolated instances of sadism but the result of a political thinking that is perverted from the ground up. In the same way, the discussions in Sassen's living room were radically alienated from any measure of morality. If the term *worthless* is ever justified, then it is in relation to the system of thought upon which these men's speech was based. This is what makes reading the Sassen transcript so taxing in comparison to Eichmann's words in Jerusalem. In his interrogation and trial, we see an Eichmann who is clearly more withdrawn. The voices of those addressing him in Jerusalem are oriented toward reason and justice: the interrogating officer, the judge, and the prosecutors—and not least, the press, commenting on it all. They allow us to retain a sense of moral values and to feel that we and they are in the majority. In the Argentine discussions, however, we are on our own.

At no point in the material from the Sassen circle does anyone object to the tone of the discussion. For these gentlemen, the language is evidently suited to the topic, and no one thinks to call for respect for human rights and humanity, or to bring things to an end, or at least to leave in protest. Nobody is sickened; no one is horrified. The only arguments are over exactly what it means to be German, and anyone leaving the circle expresses his regret at having to go.[169] Arrangements for other projects and day-to-day business follow on effortlessly from confessions of murder.[170] When Sassen leaves the tape running as he tidies up after a meeting, in order to dictate a few instructions for the transcript or to make scurrilous remarks about the recently departed guests, he can be heard whistling cheerful tunes and talking to his family, like anyone else returning home, satisfied with a good day's work.[171] The "business of the Final Solution" is as routine here as it was when murder was more than just a discussion topic. Examining the language used by the group gives us an idea of the violence that met people whom the National Socialists declared to be non-German: they could then be denied all rights, ultimately including the right to exist. Our norms have no voice within the Sassen group, whose speech comes from a spiritual abyss—though that doesn't seem to worry anyone. There is no better argument for the need to listen to language: there the possibility of a moral universe finally dies. Once thought has arrived at categories of this sort, no argument will prevent it giving rise to murderous deeds.

The Enemy: Books

Authors lie left and right, left and right, I say. Whether it's Poliakov or this clown, what's he called? Reitlinger! Well, he lies even more than Poliakov. Or Kogon—or whatever they're called, the brothers.
—Eichmann, Sassen discussions[172]

Reading and evaluating books together played a crucial role in the Sassen circle from the outset. In 1957 the secondary literature on the National Socialists' extermination of the Jews was still negligible, so it is striking that the group in Buenos Aires managed to obtain a copy of every German-language book on the subject—particularly as some of them had been brought out by small publishers. Sassen and his colleagues had done their research thoroughly, and at some expense, since German books didn't come cheap in Buenos Aires. *Der Weg* had its own reviews section, but Dürer Verlag wasn't able to rely on being given review copies. Banned from distributing so many of its products in West Germany, the publishing house had a terrible reputation, and it was unlikely anyone would value a review from that corner of the world or send a book on a costly journey there at their own expense. For this reason, Eberhard Fritsch repeatedly used his editorials in *Der Weg* to implore his faithful readers for help, asking them to send in books or newspaper articles on relevant themes. Of course, for individual requests, Fritsch also had recourse to his authors and his former colleague Dieter Vollmer. In any case, the group made an effort to hunt down every available publication. The list of books they discussed at Sassen's is a further indication of the systematic approach he and his associates took to the emerging historical research.

Eichmann and Sassen quote from texts on the very first recording. Eichmann reads from the transcript of the Nuremberg Trials;[173] Sassen asks about key phrases in Alex Weissberg's *Advocate for the Dead: The Story of Joel Brand*[174] and Gerald Reitlinger's *The Final Solution*.[175] They discuss these two books over the course of almost thirty tapes, and the discussion of Léon Poliakov and Josef Wulf's document collection *Das Dritte Reich und die Juden* (The Third Reich and the Jews) lasts just as long. From tape 39, the conversation also covers Nazi lawmaking, following the first attempt that had been made to summarize it: *Das Ausnahmerecht für Juden in Deutschland 1933–1945* (1954) by Bruno Blau.[176] Blau was someone Eichmann might have remembered: he had been an involuntary inmate of the Jewish Hospital in Berlin, where Jews who could not immediately be deported were interned. There is evidence that Eichmann visited the hospital, which fell under his department's jurisdiction. Wilhelm Höttl's *The Secret Front* took on a special significance, though this was largely to do with Höttl himself and his role as chief witness to the mass murder, as well as the fact that Langer and Eichmann knew the author personally. But the group devoted the most attention to the German translation of Reitlinger's *Final Solution,* returning to it again and again. Even the final recordings were spent arguing with this mammoth work.[177] Sometimes parts of the books were copied so that participants could read them at home, but Langer, at least, also had his own books, as we can see from the preparations he made for his Höttl lecture.

In addition to the volumes discussed as a group, there were books and articles that Eichmann and the others read independently. Eichmann mentioned *Der SS-Staat* (The SS State) by Eugen Kogon, and *Das Urteil von Nürnberg* (The Nuremberg Judgment), an edition with a foreword by the American prosecutor Robert Kempner. We know Eichmann read almost everything there was on the topic.[178] He also contributed information on newspaper articles: he received cuttings from the German and Austrian press from his family, and unlike Sassen, he also read the *Argentinisches Tageblatt,* a traditional German-language newspaper in Buenos Aires, which was considered liberal and, more important, Jewish. Perusing the "enemy press" was evidently one of the professional duties he continued in Argentina—and it was also useful for finding out whether anyone was on his tail. The articles Eichmann chose to bring Sassen show that he was still monitoring "the enemy." And the book-lined front room of Sassen's house offered the luxury of current European newspapers and magazines. These periodicals didn't come just from the right-leaning corner of the market, like Thadden's *Reichsruf* (for which Sassen had also written) or the *Wiking-Ruf;* there was also *Stern, Der Spiegel,* and the Dutch paper *De Volkskrant.* The head of the household occasionally translated articles for the others from the current issue of *Time.*[179] By the end of the 1950s, probably no one had made such a detailed study of the literature on the Final Solution, in such a well-informed group, as the men in Buenos Aires—although they understood hardly any of it, as the principal aim of their reading was not to broaden their horizons.

Three years later in Israel, Adolf Eichmann must have been grateful, on many occasions, for this period of study. One of the most famous photos of him shows him sitting at the table in his cell, before the start of the trial, books piled high in front on him. They are all books he knew well, and the numerous slips of paper marking particular pages show that he knew exactly how to make use of them.[180] Avner W. Less, the captain of the Israeli police who interrogated Eichmann, noted it with concern: "As it emerged, the man was so well-versed in this area, it was incredible!"[181] Less said how difficult it was for him and his colleagues to get a handle on the literature in such a short space of time, and he neatly summarized: "Reitlinger was our Bible." Their prisoner knew this Bible backward before the investigating officer had even purchased a copy. Eichmann showed his awareness of the advantage that Sassen had given him by the fact that he tried to hide it. He pretended to be thankful that he was finally allowed to read books again and, in an exceptional display of deceit, expressed his regret that he hadn't had the opportunity before. Of course, he had not only read the books in Argentina, he had practiced his rejoinders to them. You might say that in battling with the secondary literature, Eichmann had preempted the interrogation that awaited him. Sedate reading had never been how Eichmann engaged with books.

The Sassen circle agreed on one point: this literature came "from the enemy,"[182] "from the opposing side";[183] it was "enemy propaganda,"[184] "enemy literature"[185] by an "enemy author,"[186] "enemy press,"[187] and above all, "enemy reasoning."[188] In short, it had all been written by the "Jewish enemy."[189] They reproached the victims' side for writing on the topic, while on the perpetrators' side, nobody had yet been interested enough to write their own book. In labeling the books "Jewish," they were also making the supposition that they were dealing with propaganda, not proper research. "It's very simple for these Jews," Eichmann explained, "to scribble away after the event, writing whatever they like, as it suits them."[190] If he didn't like the content, Eichmann attested that the author was either "ignorant or malevolent."[191] "Hacks,"[192] "bunglers,"[193] "jackass,"[194] and "swine"[195] are Eichmann's customary titles for authors who we recognize today as pioneers of historical research on the Holocaust, though he and his associates refused to see them as such. The Sassen circle all shared his reservations that the whole body of research was "so-called scientific effusions."[196]

But this lack of respect for the research was more than just an attempt to defend themselves against accusations by striking out at anything within range. As a result of its crude racial theories, National Socialism rejected any "international" or nonracial system of thought. Ultimately, this meant that nonracial sciences could not exist either. There was a "German physics" and a "Jewish physics"—indeed, even the science commonly accepted as the epitome of universality was not spared this division: for National Socialists, there was also a Jewish mathematics.[197] Even science was a racial battle for final victory, bringing all scientific and scholarly endeavor down to the level of simple tactics. In other words, the search for truth had to weaken the "enemy's ideological struggle." Naturally, they assumed their "enemies" were also behaving in this way. Ultimately, everyone was playing a tactical game, the Jews most of all: "As the author of his book, why should the Jew Brandt lie any less than accords to the Jewish mentality?" After all, proclaims the specialist Eichmann, Joel Brand is "the son of a half rabbi."[198]

Really, who had written the books was irrelevant: Eichmann discredited the volume by Wilhelm Höttl with the same consistency. Höttl's text "is ridiculous, is stupid claptrap, is fibs from people taking any opportunity to try and make themselves interesting, or even wanting to carve out personal advantages after '45."[199]

The Sassen circle read these books principally in order to discover how the authors manipulated the facts to bring out their truth. They wanted to learn how to blow open these alleged tactics and, where necessary, put them to better use themselves. They were convinced that everyone in this war for interpretational sovereignty was manipulating the truth. At least, they did everything they could to convince themselves. They weren't always successful: even the readers in Buenos Aires weren't immune to the persuasive power of this wealth of information.

The more Sassen and Langer immersed themselves in this literature, the more frequently they found themselves worrying that what they read might actually be true. So many of the details were impossible to doubt. Even the things Eichmann actually admitted to were more than the men wanted to hear. Eichmann, who could see that this was problematic, borrowed the most Germanic of phrases from Goethe to describe the books: "It's like I said already, the whole library that has appeared from the calamitous days of '45 to the present is a hodgepodge of *Dichtung und Wahrheit* [truth and fiction]."[200] It didn't occur to him that some people found days other than those at the end of the war "calamitous." Anyone who talks as much as Eichmann did will occasionally give the game away: in a fit of exuberance, he revealed the criteria by which he separated "truth" from "fiction": "Everything . . . in the book that speaks against me leaves a bad taste in the mouth—I take it to be lies."[201]

His self-declared war on enemy literature saw Eichmann fighting on two fronts. While the others concentrated on defending their fantasy version of history against the research, Eichmann was also attempting to tell the Sassen circle what they wanted to hear. He knew his interlocutors would not be fellow soldiers but enemies. He had to put a slant on his interpretations, diverting the group away from facts that he knew only too well. Sassen and Fritsch may have been refusing to acknowledge historical facts, but Eichmann had to conceal knowledge that went far beyond the literature. This must have cost him a huge effort: knowing the magnitude of the crime, he first had to find out what was written about it, then consider how to distract the others from the books' threatening content, while simultaneously appearing to share their perspective, which was one of denial. And then the specialist consultant had

to add "new" information to the discussion—though without exposing himself too much. Most important, he had to avoid getting caught
doing any of it. It's no wonder Eichmann was in peak condition for his
police interrogation in 1960.

The additional difficulty in this already complex situation was that,
when the Sassen conversations began, most of the books were new to
Eichmann. Generally speaking, he was familiar only with the reviews,
not with the books themselves. Sassen frequently used this advantage to
try to offset Eichmann's huge head start on the information. He would
confront Eichmann with historical details without revealing his source.
Of course, Sassen's alliance with the books didn't go unnoticed by Eichmann, and he kept asking specific questions about the books' contents.
But above all, Sassen aroused Eichmann's curiosity about what might
actually have been written about him and his crimes. The process was
always the same, starting with the first book that Sassen lent him, *Advocate for the Dead: The Story of Joel Brand*. In one of the early discussions
(tapes 6, 8, 9, and 10), Eichmann mentions that he isn't familiar with
it: "I have not read the book either, unfortunately I have not had access
to it, it was published only a few months ago, but I have read several
reviews in various newspapers."[202] Sassen deliberately ignores his hints,
reassuring Eichmann that *he* knows the book well. Eichmann doesn't
dare ask straight out to borrow the book. But he does make frequent,
pointed remarks about how reading it would be sure to jog his memory,
if he were able to "study" it at some point:[203] "I might be able to say more
if I had the stimulus, through one of the explanations in his book, or if
some other tome makes reference to something he says."[204] But Sassen
held out for weeks, and the books were read only communally, during
the discussion sessions. Only on tape 24 is Eichmann allowed to look
at the book for himself and read out his own notes on it without inter-
ruption from the others.[205] Sassen, as Eichmann quickly realized, wasn't
naïve, and at bottom, he wasn't really a friend.

But then, the books were not just the enemy, either. One of Eichmann's most dangerous talents was for making effective use of all kinds
of interpretations, even if that meant misusing them. As a trained ideological warrior, he naturally feared an attack from the "enemy" on every
page. He saw the manipulation of history as the political aim of "the
Jews." But perhaps more surprisingly, he also sought help from these
same volumes. Even the review of Weissberg and Brand's publication

fueled Eichmann's hope that the books could support his claims, as he explained to Sassen: "If I now speak of a discussion with Dr. K[asztner], I can do this because today, after Joel Brand brought out his book, people will believe me, I doubt that they would ever have believed me before the book by the Jew JB came out."[206] At first glance, this hope may seem reckless, but it isn't as crazily naïve as it appears: Eichmann had had years of practice in using books to support his theories, counter to the authors' intentions. In 1938 he had exploited a seminal work on the history of Zionism to such an extent that the author never wrote another word. Eichmann learned early on that books could be his allies, provided that the focus of his interpretive technique was not to learn anything. Even Sassen thoroughly underestimated this ability of Eichmann's; time after time he failed to put him off his stride by quoting from books. Sassen did not realize—nor would anyone who reads books in order to learn from them—that he would never catch up with Eichmann by using books or producing documents. For someone who has been "there," books are an aide-mémoire, whereas for someone with no firsthand experience, they only tell him things he doesn't already know. While Sassen was trying to formulate a rough idea of Eichmann's activities from the books, Eichmann was reading them from a different perspective: knowing more than the authors, seeing their misunderstandings and the gaps in their knowledge, and making unfair use of their scholarly fairness. But this is how war works: you use your enemy's weaknesses to every possible advantage. Consequently, Eichmann often referenced books that were actually denouncing him, as part of his strategy of lies and self-justification. "I believe one of the authors said that in a book,"[207] he liked to say. When someone raised grave doubts about some of his observations, he replied with the advice: "I would ask you to look it up in the relevant literature that has been published since the war."[208] It is possible to make anything set out in black and white look as if it supports quite different theories from the author's own.

If Eichmann genuinely wanted to learn one thing from these books, it was battle tactics. He seemed to be constantly on the lookout for tricks to use in constructing his own version of events. The introduction to *Advocate for the Dead* advises the reader, in a spirit of honesty, that the dialogues it contains have been reconstructed by Weissberg and Brand, and while they are an approximation of the truth, they are not reliable sources. Eichmann sees "Jewish artfulness" here rather than the desire for transparency. And he was obviously very impressed by this "artistic license," as he started to explore its possibilities for himself. "It is clearly very difficult," he noted for Sassen on the transcript of this tape, "to work up the memories of a lot of things after so much time has passed. And if we are sticking to the truth, this has to be expressed in the book as well. Joel Brand and his author did something similar, of course."[209] Four years later, when drafting "Götzen," his last great piece of self-justification, Eichmann would use this argument as if it were self-evident, to render himself immune to attacks at the outset: "This writerly endeavour cannot be weighed in the scales of the articles of law."[210]

As Sigmund Freud says, you can judge an author by the way he treats his readers. Eichmann shows that this maxim also works the other way around. He treated books the way he treated the people he made into his victims: violently, without respect or scruples, and with the end result of annihilation. His reading habits may teach us something about his great success as the "Adviser on Jewish Affairs." The agility with which Eichmann—who hadn't finished school and was certainly no intellectual—made use of texts is every bit as surprising as the career that saw this former salesman become a master of unprecedented and terrible improvisation, in the business of exterminating human beings. At least one cause of this deadly effectiveness is plain: Eichmann had determined his own course of action long before involving himself in books or discussions, and this course was war and annihilation. The fatal mistake the Jewish representatives made in dealing with him was to believe they could still exert an influence on his decisions. He, meanwhile, had already set his sights on murder and was unreceptive to any doubt. He did the same with texts, which was what made his use of them so fast and effective. He went through a book the way a burglar goes through an apartment: he took whatever he could use, judging everything purely on its functional interest. He cared little for what was broken in the process, or for what he left behind. What Eichmann looked for between the covers of a book was not confirmation of his thinking but material to back up his lies. This difference is crucial, because the latter excludes the possibility of doubt. A real reader remains open to doubt, even if it means questioning himself. This openness to doubt, this distance from one's own thought, takes time, if the author's interests and the text's inner coherence are to come into their own. To put it simply: a reader is usually looking for a conversation with an author. But

Eichmann was interested only in neutralizing this enemy, disguising his intent under an apparent interest in the literature, and feigning openness to other theories and respect for the people proposing them. This made him a faster reader than anyone who was interested in a serious discussion. In particular, it makes him a threat to historians: academic study is oriented toward integrity and solidity, and it is vulnerable to no enemy more than one who views scholarship as just another tactic. In turning to books, Eichmann once again revealed his desire to destroy anything that upset his conception of reality and threatened his self-image. Whether in his office at 116 Kurfürstenstraße or in Sassen's living room, anyone believing he could influence Eichmann using fact or argument had lost before he even began. For someone waging a total war, discussion is a weapon just like any other. Eichmann's problem in Argentina was that he couldn't decide whether to use this weapon against Sassen or explain it to him.

The Realization: Extermination

I am by nature a very sensitive person, it's not easy for me to just see something like that, it gives me the shudders.
—Eichmann, Sassen discussions[211]

For men like Sassen and Fritsch, the Eichmann experience must have been a radical one. They had hoped to learn from the discussions, but they hadn't reckoned with anything like the major insight they received into the National Socialists' extermination operation. Adolf Eichmann confronted them with the magnitude and, above all, the face of the horror. Just as he would do at his trial in 1961, he spoke about the inhuman murder campaigns he had seen with his own eyes: the mass shooting of men, women, and children; people being rounded up and deported; murder by gas vans; extermination camps; selections; the burning of corpses. His words confirmed and gave substance to everything that *Der Weg* had dismissed as enemy propaganda. He knew enough about it, even though—as at Auschwitz—he hadn't wanted to see this industrial mass murder close up and had kept his distance, preferring to let the commandant describe it to him "in the most colorful way." "But I never saw the whole extermination process right from the beginning, I was not the man for that."[212] The open incinerations at the end of the process had been enough for him. Eichmann thought it had been right to exterminate the Jews, but he had taken no delight in confronting the victims' fears, torment, and death in person. "When I went to the camp, it was for matters that did not stem from my personal curiosity," he asserts in the transcript, and we can believe him. He tells how the camp commandant "took pleasure in showing a pencil-pusher the situations here that he was burdened with day after day."[213] A few of Eichmann's descriptions convey the impression that as he told his listeners what he had seen and experienced, he was doing to the Sassen circle something like what Höß had done to him. His reports are frank and detailed, and they don't sugarcoat. There is no talk of smoothly functioning killing machines, quick deaths, or German efficiency when it came to murder. Instead, Eichmann describes how awful mass murder was—awful for *him*, naturally: he was ordered to observe, he felt sick, and his "kneecaps trembled." The problem wasn't that children had been put to death; it was that he had been forced to watch—when, at that time, he had two children of his own. "I am one of those people who can't stand to see corpses," he confessed to the Sassen circle.[214] His stories are full of horrendous self-pity, for the burden of having to watch other people suffer fates that he had set in motion. But Eichmann manages to play the witness in these accounts, a mere historian of the horror, persuading himself and the others that he had nothing to do with the extermination. He couldn't have changed anything, and these "business trips" made him "an unhappy man."[215]

But something else is at work in these descriptions. Heinrich Himmler had told the Auschwitz commandant that he must carry out the slaughter so that the generations to come wouldn't have to. This imperative turned the extermination of the Jews into something that men like Höß and Eichmann had missed out on: fighting on the front lines. Not that any of Eichmann's staff, or men with comparable positions in "reserved occupations," would have traded places with soldiers in Stalingrad. We have no evidence that anyone from Eichmann's department actually requested a transfer to the front lines. But they still felt they were missing out on the much-lauded experience of camaraderie, proving oneself in battle, gallantry, and heroic deeds, and the frontline troops never really acknowledged the office staff as comrades. The Waffen-SS disliked and mocked the Allgemeine-SS (the "general" SS).

Understandably, anyone who had been promoted while surviving the conditions at the front didn't take kindly to someone earning the same reward behind a desk in Berlin. This distinction was still being brought home to Eichmann in Argentina.[216] And so it pleased him not only to recall this recognition that Himmler had given them but to demonstrate to the others that during his visits to the extermination camp, he had proved himself. Fountains of blood and splintering bones, willpower and acts of violence: Eichmann had come through it all as well. He too had known comradeship and supported his fellow soldiers. On the tape, he leaps to the defense of Höß, the commandant of Auschwitz, saying he was so very different from how you might imagine a man in his position. "And if I had had to take up the post of commandant of a concentration camp," he says in defense of his dead comrade, "I would not have acted any differently. And if I had received the order to gas Jews or to shoot Jews, I would have carried out that order. And I have already said I am neither grateful nor ungrateful to fate that I did not receive that order. Because, you know, there's no point peeing against the wind."[217] But by the time he screams at someone in Sassen's living room, "You ridiculous pipsqueak! Did *you* fight at the front?,"[218] he has obviously come to believe in his own frontline experience. "Just take a moment to think," he continues, "about how I told you that we had a total war, and the front and the hinterland had become completely blurred, and today I have to expressly oppose and fight against obstinate intellects, including Germans, who are of the opinion that the last war was fought only on the front lines. . . . There is no difference between the annihilation of enemy powers when a total war has been declared."[219] Eichmann really had seen some terrible things, but he had clearly forgotten that his "enemy powers" had been defenseless, frightened humans, and that he had been chauffeur-driven to their annihilation in a warm winter coat. He wanted to prove that he too had suffered for Germany. This desire goes a long way to explaining why Eichmann describes the horror so frankly.

His listeners react in different ways. Dr. Langer starts talking about the torture and extermination he heard about in Mauthausen, but the confrontation with reality renders Sassen and Fritsch speechless. They make no queries, in the main: they have already heard more than enough. Sassen instructs the transcriber to leave out repeated accounts of extermination campaigns. The listeners' horror and revulsion are

obvious: Sassen the novelist might have indulged in excesses of violence when it came to the torture allegedly inflicted on Germans by the
"victorious powers," but the suffering of the Jews silenced him. And not
because he didn't believe Eichmann and Langer. While these two had
both been involved in concentration camps and were able to share their
experiences and their self-pity with each other, Sassen was quite clearly
horrified. But he granted Eichmann's wish for recognition, as he then
dictated a trenchant sentence with which Eichmann could doubtless identify: "The battlefields of this war were called death camps."[220]
Here was the respect that Eichmann was demanding for his "frontline
experience." However, the long dictation in which Sassen recorded his
thoughts also includes the assertion that the crimes against humanity
in which Eichmann, Höß, and Odilo Globocnik were involved could
"not be forgiven."[221] Sassen then hurriedly says their actions could be
"understood": Eichmann, and other people all the way up to Hitler, had
simply been manipulated. Still, Sassen never revised his opinion that
these crimes were unforgivable. And in the transcript, when the group
reaches the reports of the children's transports—which Eichmann refers
to in all seriousness as the "children story"—even Sassen's "understanding" deserts him temporarily.[222] Eichmann clearly notices Sassen's horror and shamelessly denies that any such thing had happened: "But you
have found so many documents and papers, and now I am wondering
where the documents on the matter of the children are, I mean documents that can be believed. And so I have nothing further to say on this
matter for the moment."[223] We cannot know if Sassen was reassured.
He couldn't prove Eichmann wrong, and he didn't want to. Eichmann
would finally get to see the documents on these crimes in Israel. But he
obviously always knew they existed and that he had been the one who
set the "children's transports rolling."[224]

What separated Sassen and Fritsch, as well as Alvensleben, from
Langer and Eichmann, was the latter's personal experience of the camps'
reality. Langer, so the transcripts suggest, had admittedly witnessed only
a fraction of the crimes Eichmann had, learning most of what he knew
from conversations with the commandant of Mauthausen. However,
Langer and Eichmann were noticeably united in their conviction that
they had been the victims here. Langer, who had seen such abomina-
tions as the "stairs of death" with his own eyes, bemoaned the fact that
he had been shown this sort of thing, displaying a sensitivity that neither

he nor Eichmann had been able to muster for the real victims. Both gave the impression that they had looked on powerlessly—as things were enacted that they had helped bring about. The same self-centered attitude can be found in the accounts of many other perpetrators, all the way up to Himmler, whose Posen speech was full of sympathetic words for the poor, suffering murderers.

This reversal of perpetrator and victim is a psychodynamic shift that does more than just ease the perpetrator's burdensome memory of what he has done; it is more than an act of retrospective repression. It is the suppression of the very consciousness that allowed these perpetrators to commit their deeds in the first place. Eichmann was clearly aware of the need to shield himself as much as possible. "But there is one good thing nature gave me," he explains. "I can switch off and forget very quickly, without trying to."[225] He had some effective methods for helping this process along, the primary strategy being the consumption of alcohol. His knowledge of the mechanisms of repression, however, like his self-awareness, went far beyond the use of this simple drug.[226] The conscious mind can be deliberately distracted, and not only by escaping into nature, as he described in "The Others Spoke." "I still have a very devout saying from my youth," Eichmann explains to the Sassen circle, "and I always do it when I find something horribly unpleasant and I can't stop thinking about it. And in order to forcibly distract myself, do you know what I say? You'll laugh! I believe in God the Father, and the Holy Spirit, born of the Virgin Mary, died under Pontius Pilate, suffered and so on and so on, was raised from the dead, and so on."[227]

Father Anton Weber, one of the people who helped Nazi fugitives obtain new identities in Rome, said there was a trick he used to check that they had really found their way back to the Faith. "I made them say the Our Father. Then it quickly emerged who was genuine and who wasn't."[228] Eichmann would certainly have impressed him with the pace of his creed, managing it in five seconds: "I somehow realized early on, as a child—still a devout believer at that time, of course—that once I'd said that, I didn't think about anything else."[229]

Breaches of Trust

I can read only one single motive in this report, a single impetus: he hates you like sin.

—Sassen on Wisliceny, Sassen discussions[230]

Over time Sassen must have come to recognize that these discussions weren't bringing him close enough to Eichmann. His interlocutor was always a little faster, always a little more agile in his engagement with documents and information, and it seemed impossible to catch up with his head start on the facts. Neither the additional listeners, nor Dr. Langer's critically framed legal questions, managed to unsettle him. However, Sassen's growing frustration was also due in part to his reluctance to hear the truth about the Nazis' crimes against humanity; he therefore assumed that this truth had to be a lie. He wrongly imagined that the truth was hidden, and he wanted to get at it. By tape 41, Eichmann had become so self-assured that he gave a short address to the group, and at the end of August Sassen decided to change tack: he laid a trap for Eichmann.[231]

The conversation began as it usually did. Sassen picked up the book by Poliakov and Wulf, but he didn't tell Eichmann that the document they were about to discuss was not written by an "enemy"; nor was it "Jewish scribblings." Rather, these were the words of a man Eichmann believed to be one of his best friends: Dieter Wisliceny.[232]

Eichmann had first met Wisliceny, who was five years younger, in the fall of 1934, though it isn't clear from Eichmann's statements whether it was in Munich or Berlin. At first their contact was rather infrequent, but once Wisliceny was transferred to Department II 112 in February 1937, they worked more closely and saw each other on a daily basis. For a short while, Wisliceny was Eichmann's superior officer, but when Wisliceny failed to get a promotion, he left Berlin and worked in the SD in Danzig until August 1940. When he returned to work for Eichmann in his department, their contact again became more regular, but then Wisliceny was deployed as an "adviser on Jewish affairs" in the Balkans, and they had few opportunities to meet in person. Only in March 1944, when Wisliceny joined Eichmann's special operations commando in Hungary, did the two form a close relationship once again. This connection allegedly suffered at the end of 1944, as a result of Wisliceny's futile attempts to create a better image of himself for the postwar world. Eichmann later refuted the claim that they had fallen out, and he may have been telling the truth: Wisliceny stayed with Eichmann until April 1945, though he did his best to deny it afterward.[233]

Eichmann and Wisliceny had a complex personal relationship. Eichmann clearly felt that he and Wisliceny, after whom he named his third son, were true friends. He openly admired the younger man's education and intelligence. (Wisliceny had studied theology but had broken off his study because his family was in need of money.) Decades later Eichmann would still remember their discussions. But for Wisliceny, the relationship had another dimension. In 1946, when he was in jail in Bratislava and the authorities asked him to write about Eichmann, Wisliceny came up with a dossier containing twenty-two densely written pages about this one man. Reports on "The Final Solution," the "Grand Mufti," "The Fiala Affair," and numerous other topics fill more than one hundred additional pages, in which ever more details about Eichmann emerge.[234] For all his attempts to degrade Eichmann, Wisliceny's texts still show signs of admiration and attachment: over the years, he seems to have observed everything and everyone around Eichmann, and he continued to proclaim his intimate knowledge of his boss even where it harmed his own line of defense. He also knew what had happened during the period when he and Eichmann had worked in different places—he had kept himself well informed while he was away. This attentiveness has all the hallmarks of obsession. Wisliceny knew the color of Eichmann's eyes, his scars, the sound of his breathing, and the way he moved; he even remembered his teeth. He would recognize Eichmann's "gold crowns even on his corpse."[235]

Wisliceny made several offers to track Eichmann down, so he could be brought before a court. The authorities refused to release him for this purpose, but he still took pains to list everywhere he could think of that Eichmann might be hiding, which also demonstrates how well Wisliceny knew him. All his suggestions turned out to be wrong, but only because Eichmann wasn't as predictable as everyone thought. Wisliceny's testimonies were obviously shaped by two motives: self-defense and a strong emotional connection to Eichmann. This attachment was sometimes expressed positively through idealization, and sometimes negatively, in a sort of impulse for revenge. In Bratislava, as Wisliceny attempted to distance himself, his strong emotional connection became a blind hatred. It unleashed a huge number of lies and attempts to libel Eichmann, which went far beyond what others had done, and for which there seems to have been no rational cause. His behavior cannot be explained purely as an attempt at self-defense.

By 1957 Eichmann knew that Wisliceny had testified against him in Nuremberg—it had been in all the papers—and that he had been executed in Bratislava.[236] Eichmann may have told Sassen the testimony was an exaggeration, but he knew Wisliceny had been telling the truth. It wasn't pleasant, but it was understandable. However, Eichmann hadn't reckoned on what Wisliceny wrote afterward. He thought of his friend as a victim of the Allies' "victor's justice" and maybe even of "torture" at their hands—and Eichmann knew very well what you could achieve by that means, having made frequent use of it himself.[237] In Argentina, Eichmann enjoyed talking about Wisliceny and did so at length. Wisliceny had specifically applied to be part of the Hungary commando and had always been one of his most dependable men. Eichmann would dearly have liked to promote him, but unfortunately there was one SS norm that Wisliceny didn't conform to: he refused point-blank to get married. Eichmann had tried and failed to talk him into it in Hungary. He could never figure out why.

In the transcript, Sassen begins to read from Wisliceny's text on "The Final Solution" (which had been published as part of Das Dritte Reich und die Juden). Eichmann does not know who the author is. As usual, he tries to contradict this so-called "author," exposing his lies and "childish inexperience"[238] to protect himself and his colleagues. He even ends up defending Wisliceny against what was, unknown to him, Wisliceny's own testimony. Sassen plays this bizarre game over two tapes on this particular day,[239] watching for hours as Eichmann gets his teeth into the text and works himself into a rage, using flimsy arguments to attack every sentence this author has written. The author seems to pose a real threat, and, continually spurred on by Sassen, Eichmann finally claims that "there is a lot of truth in this, but the author has also not gone into the matter thoroughly." Sassen then reveals just how thoroughly the author was acquainted with the facts: "This report is by Wisliceny." Eichmann is shaken by this news, as the transcript shows: "What is truth? Do you know what truth is? I know it, you don't. How was he interrogated?" Sassen listens to this stammering for a while, then ups the ante:

"I can only tell you my personal feeling, that in my opinion this report was absolutely not obtained under any direct, immediate force, torture or similar, and I can read only one single motive in this report, a single impetus—not redemption in general, this doesn't play too large a role with intellectual people, which I am starting to realize that W[isliceny] is—he has a basic motive and it is a very primitive motive: he hates you like sin." "Envy[. . .] became a pure hatred, particularly as he had been caught, and Eichmann hadn't." To cap it all, Sassen then gives a detailed account of how eager Wisliceny was to help the Allies find Eichmann. Eichmann, apparently exhausted, replies: "That is groveling." Perhaps he is referring in part to himself. The day's discussion ends with one of the very few moments that give us a glimpse of Eichmann without his mask—tired, disappointed, perturbed, and wounded: "I don't understand all this . . . I don't understand it all."[240]

Sassen had deliberately put Eichmann in an awkward situation, which obviously overwhelmed him. But Sassen didn't know enough about interrogation techniques to realize that this method leads to success only when there is enough time to carry on the discussion afterward. It works in lengthy interrogations, when someone is under arrest. But when the person you have just shaken to his core then has the option of going home, he'll realize what has taken place, and the result will be reversed. This is exactly what happened in Argentina: Eichmann recognized that Sassen had been playing on his emotions and had entrapped him. In the discussions that followed, his contributions became more halting, filled with latent or open aggression. The convivial tone of the previous sessions vanished at a stroke.[241]

Sassen, the keen poker player, had overplayed his hand. His notes give us a clue as to why he took such a great risk: he was convinced that Wisliceny was still alive. "Personally, I want to assert once more," he dictates for the tape, "that I do not believe Wisliceny is dead. Wisliceny is being held in reserve as long as they remain unsure about Eichmann."[242] Who "they" were was self-evident to Sassen—they were the Jews again, with their secret machinations, pretending to the world that Wisliceny had been executed in Bratislava. In reality, "international Jewry" needed someone who could repeat on demand that millions of Jews had been murdered. Then—as Sassen's fairy tale continues—Israel could extort payments from Germany. But because the millions were only a "legend," "international Jewry" couldn't be sure that Eichmann would confirm it. Significantly, Sassen told Eichmann nothing of this crazy theory, because in reality it was Sassen himself who was "unsure about Eichmann." He was plowing all his resources into the effort to find out which "side" Eichmann was really on, and he did everything he could to isolate him, attempting to discredit every one of his superiors and colleagues: Heydrich had been a mere policeman working for clandestine forces; Müller wasn't really a National Socialist at all. Eichmann's subordinates had been renegade liars or incapable underlings, none of which Eichmann had noticed. Sassen was trying to shore up his conspiracy theory, according to which Eichmann was a puppet in the hands of the international conspirators, and that meant he first had to make Eichmann see that everything he believed was wrong. There was no greater threat to Sassen's version of history than the existence of a group of devoted National Socialists who had committed genocide against the Jews, consciously and by consensus. In order to co-opt Eichmann as the chief witness to his story, Sassen had to unsettle him to such a degree that he would lose all certainty, until he acknowledged and supported Sassen's "truth." This process, also known as brainwashing, didn't succeed with Eichmann. He immediately realized that a very dangerous document existed, about which he had known nothing—and it had already been published. He realized that the former colleague he had thought of as his best friend had done everything he could to turn him over to the enemy. And he realized that the man he thought of as his new friend in Argentina wasn't afraid to manipulate him. Eichmann learned that he had been betrayed by two so-called friends, one old and one new. It was Langer, not Sassen, who led the next discussion, and the topic was relatively innocuous: they continued reading through the collection of National Socialist "Jewish legislation." But this deescalation strategy did no good—quite the opposite. Over the sessions that followed, the discussion lurched from one dispute to the next. Eichmann put his own opinions across quite forcefully, even when Sassen didn't want to hear them. No, of course he been acting on Hitler's orders, and no, the extermination of the Jews had not been "un-Germanic": it had been a fundamentally German operation, which they had to keep on justifying, and he was the German officer who had carried it out. Eichmann, the specialist on Jewish questions, had implemented exactly what Hitler wanted. "Read through the speeches, ask a psychiatrist, and you'll see I'm right."[243] The tapes reveal the keen, implacable, and consistent

Eichmann whose vague presence would still be felt in Israel. This man didn't need a uniform to spread fear and terror among old comrades. Sassen, Fritsch, and Langer could do little in retaliation; the discussion sometimes veered off course, and the project threatened to collapse. "My thoughts are of no concern to you, at least not today, because I'm annoyed," Eichmann complains in the transcript, "because there has been an attempt to derail the whole matter. . . . Yes, gentlemen, if people are not remaining objective, I may remain objective, but then I will not say anything."[244]

The Arbitrator: Ludolf von Alvensleben[245]
(For Uki Goñi, to whom a part of this chapter belongs in any case)

In the last third of the Sassen transcript, we suddenly encounter an entirely new interviewer. In a discussion conducted with gentle insistence, someone tries to get through to Eichmann. "Of course, I'm not claiming I know you through and through," the new man begins unctuously, then goes on to make tentative, thoughtful inquiries about the feelings of the mass murderer, who "must have had his concerns."[246] Again and again the group tries to lead Eichmann into confessing that he was an instrument manipulated by foreign powers. The identity of this new influence is revealed by the long interview that Sassen conducts with him on tape 56.[247] It is Ludolf von Alvensleben.[248]

The discovery that the highest-ranking Nazi in Argentina had found his way into the Sassen circle is as irritating as the fact that his presence could easily have remained undiscovered, although most of Sassen's in-depth interview with him was available for all to see. In 1957 Ludolf von Alvensleben had been living in Córdoba, another hub for immigrants with a certain kind of past, which over many years became notorious for its Midsummer Night celebrations. Hans-Ulrich Rudel also had a house there. But Alvensleben was still, without doubt, a frequent participant in the debates at Sassen's house in Buenos Aires and helped him get Eichmann to talk. The theory that there was little or no contact between the Nazi fugitives, because "only a few of them knew each other before, or met after their escape," is insupportable, particularly when it comes to Alvensleben. Even his escape route went by the same points of contact as Adolf Eichmann's and Josef Mengele's.[249]

"So, you'd like to know what I think of Heydrich? I'll try and say it in a few words." So begins the conversation between Willem Sassen and Ludolf von Alvensleben: two friends chatting. They are familiar and comfortable with each other, using the informal *du*, joking and talking about the past. But they also look to the future and to an idea that still enthralled everyone present: that "crystal clear" worldview called National Socialism. The section of the conversation available to us begins (cryptically, for anyone unpracticed in deciphering the Sassen transcript), with exasperated remarks from the man typing it up, explaining that the tape was faulty. The result is a stuttering text that gives a good impression of the mangled tape. Anyone who doesn't give up at this point (and who is also familiar with the books being read in the group) will quickly realize what these men are talking about. They are reading from Wilhelm Höttl's *The Secret Front: The Story of Nazi Political Espionage*. For the conversation with Alvensleben, Sassen has selected the chapter about Reinhard Heydrich, to discover what Alvensleben thinks of him. Fortunately, the tape then starts working again, and we are able to follow the discussion as it covers Heydrich, Himmler, Nazi plots, Nazi ideology, the murder of the Jews and the reasons behind it, SS morality, and the Führer's dreams.

Sassen could not have found a better interviewee on the subject anywhere in Argentina. The man from Saxony had been big in more senses than just his mighty six-foot frame. Alvensleben had been a member of the "movement" from the outset, meeting Goebbels in the early 1930s and spending years working as *Reichsführer*-SS Heinrich Himmler's chief adjutant. He then went to Poland and the Crimea, to implement Nazi policies and all their iniquities there. He ended his career as a *Höherer-SS und Polizeiführer* (higher SS and police leader), the personal representative of the *Reichsführer*-SS in Dresden, before sneaking away from the scene of the crime. Alvensleben, as he phrased it, knew "most of the gentlemen who played in this orchestra well." They called one another by their nicknames in official letters, and everyone in Nazi circles knew (and still knows to this day) who "Bubi" was. His victims didn't forget his arrogance and high-handedness either, let alone his cataclysmic impact in Poland and the Crimea. He led the "Ethnic Germans' Self-Defense" initiative, to which an estimated twenty to thirty thousand people fell victim in the space of four months, and that even hard-bitten SS henchmen found overly savage. It targeted Polish intellectuals, priests, Jews, and anyone else Alvensleben regarded as a "partisan." His direct participation in 4,247 murders in Poland sufficed for him to be sentenced to death in absentia, and an arrest warrant would be issued for him in West Germany in 1964. But Alvensleben and his family had escaped to Buenos Aires after the war, which was a stroke of luck for Sassen and his friends. Alvensleben, who used to send his "dear *Reichsführer*" sycophantic letters and photos of his children, had not even been tarnished by insulting the Goebbels family and making some extremely critical remarks about Hitler. Among the surviving Nazis worldwide, he was one of those with the most insider knowledge, and he was the highest-ranking Nazi functionary in Argentina: an SS and Police lieutenant general, who by 1944 had become number 147 in the SS[250] (with Himmler being number 1), and number 90 in the Waffen-SS[251]—numbers, it should be noted, that pertained to the whole Third Reich.

As Himmler's adjutant, his sphere of influence and his fame were tremendous. The adjutant's job was to coordinate the *Reichsführer-SS's* daily activities, including all visits and trips. As a result, the lanky Alvensleben can be seen in many of the films that show Himmler on his travels. He had been at the center of power from the word go, and as his evaluation of 1938 says, he knew "how to place himself and his work firmly in the foreground."[252]

Alvensleben can be clearly identified from just three of the many pieces of information he gives about himself in the transcript: he was born in Halle an der Saale, had been a Reichstag deputy, and was a lieutenant general in the Waffen-SS. Further details merely serve as confirmation: his proximity to and acqaintance with Himmler; where he was deployed in Russia in 1942; the respect and authority he commands in his stories about the Nazi era; an obvious class-consciousness; and not least, the friendships he mentions with big names in the music scene, like Paul van Kempen and Herbert von Karajan. "In Dachau," Alvensleben recounts with some pride, "the Americans picked up a photo of me when they couldn't find anything else, and hung it on a tree and shot at it." It would not have been difficult for them to find the photo, which had been in every Reichstag handbook since 1933.

Several people put questions to Alvensleben during the interview, but Adolf Eichmann could not have been present. For one thing, Eichmann had a tendency to interrupt someone when he felt they were taking up too much of the discussion time,[253] and for another, he couldn't help interjecting when his own role in a story ran counter to his self-image. The participants in the session with Alvensleben make plenty of state-ments that would have directly offended Eichmann. Alvensleben gives free rein to his arrogance as he rails against social climbers and careerists, which, measured on his scale, Eichmann had been. Alvensleben speaks of Eichmann's "heroes" Heydrich and Müller in a way that Eichmann did not usually tolerate, and what he says about anti-Jewish policy is so controversial that even Sassen feels moved to contradict him. And Eich-mann would have made a violent objection to the way the participants evaluated the "successes" of forced Jewish emigration. Eichmann's work on "Jewish emigration," which he claimed had been so "constructive," was one of the main pillars of his grandstanding.

No evidence has yet emerged to show when and under what cir-cumstances Alvensleben and Eichmann first met, but it was very likely while the Nazis were in power: Alvensleben was Himmler's adjutant in 1938–39, at a time when Eichmann was beginning to establish his reputation as a "specialist," through his "Vienna model" and his "suc-cesses" in the forced emigration of Jews from Austria. Alvensleben had a placement at the RSHA in April–May 1941, learning how it was orga-nized and about the work it did, just when Eichmann's department was becoming increasingly important. Alvensleben and Eichmann were also some of the last people Himmler summoned to the Ziethen-Schloss at Hohenlychen at the end of the war—a fact to which Alvensleben explicitly referred.[254] The two men had plenty of opportunities to meet, and as Alvensleben belonged to Himmler's retinue and Eichmann was the adviser on Himmler's favorite project, we can assume that in Buenos Aires they both knew exactly who they were dealing with.

Ludolf von Alvensleben was a prize catch for Sassen in several respects. He was able to clarify connections that no one else could have explained, since he had been closer to people in power than any of the other exiled Nazis. To Alvensleben, most of the key historical figures were not just names but people he had known. This gave him a different, elevated perspective, where the others had only a view from below. He saw things differently from an *Obersturmbannführer* (even an exceptional one) with his own department, or a Dutch war correspondent who had occa-sionally seen Goebbels from a distance, or an SD lawyer from Vienna with access to the Mauthausen concentration camp. Alvensleben was a prominent Nazi with the corresponding level of insider knowledge, which was more important for Sassen and his circle than the possibility that his lofty position had made him out of touch. Sassen and Alvensleben were clearly bound by friendship, and Sassen was sure that he and Alvensleben shared "high" National Socialist ideals,[255] which made him a reliable ally.

But the debate between Sassen and Alvensleben was by no means unproblematic. Alvenleben's continued admiration for Heinrich Himmler, whom Argentina's far-right circles saw as an irredeemable figure, was an unbridgeable divide.[256] But more problematic still was that Alvensleben acknowledged the Holocaust as a historical fact and as a crime. The Alvensleben of 1957 saw Nazi anti-Jewish policy not only as a mistake but as inhuman. Despite the fact that he was openly racist and anti-Semitic, he described the Holocaust as "distinctly savage," "un-Germanic," and "ignoble." It didn't occur to him that his own position as accomplice to and defender of a murderous "war on partisans" might also be described in these words. He managed to tell anecdotes about Herbert von Karajan and talk about racist persecution in the same breath. "I am personally resistant to the idea," he explained to Sassen, "of taking defenseless people, even if it's my greatest enemy, defenseless people who have done nothing whatever against me personally, only through their birth—and simply hounding them into a gas oven."[257]

This stance created difficulties for Eichmann, who was forced to hear that his lifetime achievement, namely having killed millions of "enemies of the Reich," had suddenly become "un-Germanic" in the eyes of other National Socialists. It brought Eichmann to the limits of his self-control, and unexpectedly, Sassen was also riled by Alvensleben's views on National Socialist anti-Jewish policy. Alvensleben, as all his statements show, was not an anti-Semite of a specifically Nazi stripe; he represented a rather old-fashioned, nineteenth-century anti-Semitism based on envy. He made no secret of the fact that he—a man whose hatred of the Poles meant he had no problem ordering thousands of people to be shot and enriching himself at every opportunity—thought the attempt to exterminate the Jews was a lunatic project.

This vestige of humanity, expressed in a circle of racial anti-Semites, moved Sassen, who usually kept his own views under wraps, to make a radically anti-Semitic confession. He, Willem Sassen, saw the very existence of the Jews as a threat. National Socialist anti-Jewish policy had been no mistake, from where Sassen was sitting, but the order of the day.

His conversation with Alvensleben reveals something we can only guess at from the rest of the transcript, namely the connection between Sassen and Eichmann. They shared the insane idea that a war of the races really existed and that it would still come down to the "final battle," which only one race would survive. This was where Sassen's motives lay, and this was the reason for his encounters with Eichmann. As much enthusiasm as Alvensleben had for the "crystal-clear National Socialist worldview" and the "SS idea," on this point he couldn't agree with Sassen's vision. From Sassen and Eichmann's perspective, Alvensleben, who was anything but the noble member of the Nazi aristocracy he made himself out to be, must have looked like he hadn't grasped the "real danger." He could imagine sharing the world with Jews; Eichmann and Sassen couldn't.

In Argentina in 1957, Eichmann and Alvensleben were bound by more than just a shared admiration for Heinrich Himmler. As they fled Germany, they had both used identity papers produced in the same South Tyrol commune. Three prominent Nazis had traveled on papers issued in Termeno: Josef Mengele, with papers from April 1948; Alvensleben (May 1948); and Eichmann (June 1948). We are a long way from knowing everything about Alvensleben's escape, but what we do know is surprising and reveals a great deal about the way this route was organized. I am able to tell at least a small part of this complex story following a lunch I had with the Argentine journalist and historian Uki Goñi. I told him about the Alvensleben discussion, and he confided to me his suspicion that Alvensleben had used a Red Cross passport in the name of "Kremhart." The Austrian historian Gerald Steinacher had searched in vain for Kremhart's true identity.[258] Over the following weeks, meticulous comparisons of handwriting and photographs proved Goñi's suspicion to be correct.

Alvensleben's escape began with a letter sent from Lübeck, in northern Germany. On November 30, 1946, a "Lona Kremhart" wrote to the police in Bozen, asking about her husband, "Theodor Kremhart," whose name might also be written "Kreinhart."[259] He had been born in Posen (Poznań) on September 18, 1905. The last information she had received about him came from Innsbruck. And they had three children. The answer to this slightly odd letter came promptly: Kremhart had been in Bozen since September 1946, in the Zwölfmalgreien guesthouse. A closer look at Frau Kremhart's handwriting reveals something astonishing: it belonged, without a shadow of a doubt, to Ludolf von Alvensleben.[260] Following a spell in a prisoner of war camp in Neuengamme, he had managed to escape on September 11, 1946 (according to Karl Wolff). Early on, he was suspected to be hiding in the north. Alvensleben had family in Lübeck, so it's no surprise that he wrote from there to Bozen, the town in South Tyrol where Eichmann would collect his new papers. But why was he posing as a woman, asking about two spellings of a name, and saying he had three children? The answer seems to be that this man was looking for a new identity and wanted to leave Europe with three children.[261] The fact that a letter to a South Tyrolean authority helped him achieve this identity still comes as a surprise, even to people who have spent years researching National Socialist escape routes. But the application form for Theodor Kremhart's Red Cross passport still has a photo of Ludolf von Alvensleben attached to it. And to cap it all, the applicant's signature is incredibly similar to that of Lona from Lübeck.[262] The Red Cross records show that he presented an identity card issued in Termeno in May 1948 and that his application was supported, like Eichmann's, by the Catholic priest Edoardo Dömöter, proving that this would-be escapee received preferential treatment.[263] "Kremhart" was planning to travel on the *Cabo Buena Esperanza,* the very same ship that Melitta von Alvensleben would name on her application for an Argentine passport a few years later. It docked in Buenos Aires in December 1949. Uki Goñi found both names on the passenger list—and this was how the escape route of the highest-ranking Nazi in Argentina was discovered.

We can only guess at what lay behind the fateful letter. Did Alvensleben initiate the route in this way? Did Eichmann and Mengele do the same thing to organize their own escapes, or was Alvensleben looking for a separate route? The answers may be revealed by searching the Bozen city archive for more letters written by concerned wives with masculine handwriting, looking for their husbands with a number of spellings. But it is now certain that Alvensleben used the same papers as Josef Mengele and Adolf Eichmann for his escape, all of them produced in three consecutive months. In the face of this information, it would take some nerve to continue talking about improvised escapes by a variety of routes. In fact, it suggests there was an even greater degree of organization than previously thought.

When Ludolf von Alvensleben stumbled across the Sassen circle, he was reunited with at least one man who had not only idolized the same superior officer but had the same people to thank for his new life. This must have been more than just coincidence, even if he subsequently decided that Eichmann was far too common for him. Alvensleben applied for and was granted Argentine citizenship for himself and his family in 1952, which effectively protected him from being prosecuted by the Federal Republic. He made a good life for himself in Argentina, becoming the manager of a fish farm in Santa Rosa de Calamuchita, Córdoba. He was the head of the Argentine office for fishing, hunting, and sailing in his district and posed for photos as president of the soccer club Clubo Atletico Union. Juan Maler even said that for a few years, Alvensleben had been mayor of the nearby Nazi enclave of Villa General Belgrano.[264] Despite the death sentence the Polish authorities passed on him in absentia for thousands of murders, and attempts by the Federal Republic to prosecute him in 1964, he would die peacefully in Argentina in 1970. In a television interview, a family member from a younger generation defended the possibility that Alvensleben had reformed during his Argentine exile, abandoning his National Socialist convictions as quickly as he had his homeland.[265] Obviously in 1957, when Alvensleben sought out Sassen, Fritsch, Langer, and Eichmann and spent days deep in conversation with them about the Nazi era, the extermination of the Jews, and the pure ideas of National Socialism, this conversion had not yet taken place.

Sassen's deployment of Alvensleben was effective only for a short time. Eichmann adjusted to this new interviewer very quickly and defended the "sanctity of his struggle," complete with death camps, against the conspiracy theorists. He refused to be intimidated—once again—even by men of the highest ranks, when he believed he had been fulfilling an order from the Führer. Alvensleben's entry into the Sassen circle reveals the scale of the group's ambition for this project. They weren't just producing the memoirs of an adviser on Jewish affairs (Eichmann wasn't even the subject of the Alvensleben interview) or hosting a reading group; they were undertaking a wholesale revision of history, targeted at redeeming Hitler and National Socialism. Even Alvensleben wanted to be part of it, despite his genteel reserve and sense of caution. Later, when Sassen dug out the transcripts to sell them, he removed almost the entire transcript of the tape with the Alvensleben interview on it. This suggests that we have the second part of the interview only because Sassen forgot about it. He may well have assured Alvensleben of his discretion, as he did Langer. In any case, he never put the interview up for sale, although the confessions of the man who had been Himmler's chief adjutant would have been easy to sell. He didn't even try after Alvensleben's death. Sassen's greed reached its limit at personal alliances. Eichmann never betrayed Alvensleben either, inventing the presence of Rudolf Mildner to cover him, though he may well have had Alvensleben's patronizing Nazi-aristocrat manner in mind when he complained in Israel about the "salon officers in white gloves"—the men who hadn't understood the core of the National Socialist movement.

"The Lie of the Six Million"

I did speak to Höttl very often, that's true, and probably about the extermination of the Jews, what else would we have been talking about.   —Eichmann, Sassen discussions[266]

No topic provoked the Dürer circle more than the number of Jewish victims. By 1957, no one in Buenos Aires still believed that articles like "The Lie of the Six Million" and the Hester Report could throw the genocide into doubt—mainly because the Dürer circle had been largely responsible for manufacturing these revisionist denials. Once the new body of source material became available, all they could do was try to make the scale of the genocide appear as small as possible. It is difficult to understand why the question of victim numbers continues to occupy old and neo-Nazis, and the New Right, like no other, considering that the legal and moral problem of the Nazis' persecution of the Jews does not depend on an absolute number. The "reparations" negotiations would hardly have had a different outcome if four or eight million, rather than six, had been the figure under discussion. It is as if these men, who had mastered the power of symbols with their cult of the Führer, were always more afraid of their "enemy's" powerful symbol—the six million—than anything else. But another question has a simpler answer: who was the source named by all the post-1945 witnesses, and who was the first person to mention this unimaginable figure? *Der Weg* itself heralded the appearance of this witness in 1957. In the July issue, another "reader's letter" said it was "particularly regrettable that it has not been possible to track down the person who, according to all the Jewish publications and witness statements in the Nuremberg IMT trial, is regarded as the only person qualified to speak on this entire complex: SS *Obersturmbannführer* Adolf Eichmann. After the deaths of Adolf Hitler, Himmler, Heydrich, and Kaltenbrunner, he may be the only credible inside witness to what really took place."[267] The vigilant "reader" then asks whether anyone has any information on this key witness, who has thus far been "impossible to find."

Published at the end of 1955, the collection of documents edited by Léon Poliakov and Josef Wulf gave readers access to Wilhelm Höttl's full three-page declaration under oath, in which he set out his conversation with Eichmann. Document PS-2738 had been one of the most important documents in the Nuremberg Trials.[268] Here Höttl says that Eichmann had come to his Budapest apartment at the end of August 1944, as usual wanting information on the military situation. Höttl took this opportunity to ask him about the exact number of Jews murdered, and Eichmann answered: "Around four million Jews have been killed in the various extermination camps, while a further two million met their end in other ways, the majority being shot by the Security Police's *Einsatzkommandos* during the Russian campaign." Höttl emphasized Eichmann's credibility as a source in some detail: "I have to assume that this information I had from Eichmann was correct: of all the relevant people, he was definitely the one with the best overview of the number of Jews murdered. Firstly, he 'provided' the Jews to the extermination camps, so to speak, using his special commandos, so he knew this number precisely. Secondly, as departmental head in Office IV of the RSHA, which was also responsible for Jewish affairs, he definitely had the best knowledge of how many Jews had died in other ways." Eichmann had even written a report for Himmler, who thought his figures too low.

Naturally, everyone in the Dürer circle was familiar with Höttl's statement. *Der Weg* had polemicized against it, but reading the occasional newspaper article was a very different matter from undertaking a close reading of the text itself. Sassen recognized immediately that Höttl's declaration had to be discredited if his group were to have any possibility of denying the Germans' systematic extermination of the Jews. He questioned Eichmann directly, at the very start of the discussion, about "the theory of the six million" and his conversation with Höttl, then returned to it again and again.[269] The group tried to find out as much as they could about this witness, and to discover his every personal weakness, by asking Dr. Langer to give a lecture on him. The crucial question for Sassen was "how to make a mockery . . . of this explanation?"[270]

The problem was compounded by the fact that Dieter Wisliceny had quoted numbers of a similar magnitude from his former superior. In Nuremberg he reported several conversations with Eichmann on the topic, in which the figure had always been at least four million. And he repeated Eichmann's notorious farewell speech in Berlin, with the words: "He would leap laughing into the grave, because the feeling that he had five million people on his conscience gave him an extraordinary sense of satisfaction."[271] Unlike Eichmann, who knew exactly who had been present when he made these claims, Sassen had no idea how many other witnesses might remember this sort of statement. During Eichmann's trial, Theodor Grell, adviser on Jewish affairs at the mission in Budapest and Eichmann's ally, would testify that in late fall 1944, Eichmann had proudly told him he was responsible for the deaths of "six million people."[272] Sassen became aware of the greatest hindrance to his efforts much too late—namely, the fact that a high body count really did give Eichmann an extraordinary sense of satisfaction. Still, Eichmann took great pains to tell Sassen and his associates what they wanted to hear. No, of course he had never talked about millions of murdered Jews, only "enemies of the Reich." No, he had not said "people," either: he had definitely said "enemies of the Reich." Only during his trial in Israel would Eichmann be forced to admit that he had said "Jews" after all. In a momentary lapse, he had actually written it down himself.[273]

In Argentina, Eichmann said it was inexplicable that he, of all people, should have "this explanation falsely attributed" to him.[274] Höttl had just "happened upon the same lie as Wisliceny."[275] Eichmann even said the statistics he had prepared for Heydrich before the Wannsee Conference were a forgery, made at a later date.[276] He "did not know [the] extermination figure at all,"[277] as he had never prepared any statistics—and here his vanity proved treacherous, as he added that in any case, Himmler would never have been dissatisfied with his statistics.[278] Eichmann sometimes overdid his reticence to the extent that Sassen had to remind him why he was there in the first place, namely as a guarantor for the figures. "We have to throw all our weight against the theory that Eichmann's office had no overview of the numbers," he complains to

Eichmann on one tape, "all our weight!" Eichmann can only answer: "Of course, if it helps."[279] If it all weren't so cynical, it might be comical: Eichmann denied what he knew to please Sassen's circle, while they were consulting him precisely because he was the only one with that knowledge—except that they imagined what he knew was something very different. In this charade, Sassen is the impatient beau, using honeyed words to convince the beauty he adores to remove her mask at long last, not imagining in his wildest dreams that behind it lurks a snake-headed Medusa.

In this complex constellation, the attempt to refute the Jewish "lie of the six million" became a farce in two senses. The group read one murder statistic after another—tellingly, leaving out those they themselves had falsified over the preceding years.[280] In 1953 Gerald Reitlinger arrived at 4.2 to 4.7 million; the report to the World Jewish Congress from June 1946 put it at six million; Léon Poliakov thought eight million was possible. The Sassen circle tried to analyze each figure in the Wannsee transcript and in Korherr's report to Hitler from 1943. They read the statement by Camp Commandant Höß about the extermination capacity of Auschwitz. Sassen rounded the numbers down; Eichmann rounded them up. Eichmann exaggerated the number of survivors; Sassen cast doubt on this, and together they tried to extrapolate a figure. Reading this discussion sometimes feels like being in a bazaar: once again only numbers, not people, exist for Eichmann: "So, he [Reitlinger] says 65,000, I say 40,000, so let's call it around 50,000."[281] Another instance: "381,000 is a little high, but it may have been around 300,000."[282] And whenever Sassen starts to be even slightly optimistic, Eichmann's words invariably throw everything into confusion again. "Half of them always lived," Eichmann claims on the selections in Auschwitz, and although this is an incredible underestimation of the murder rate for the transports from Hungary, Sassen's reaction is almost panicked: "No, no, we worked out that the absorption capacity was around 250,000, but if two million went there in total . . . ," then a million Jews would have been gassed in Auschwitz alone.[283] As we now know, this is close to the truth, but it certainly wasn't what Sassen wanted to hear in 1957.

The Sassen circle's grotesque tug-of-war over the numbers reveals a cynical misanthropy that is almost as unbearable as the thought of the National Socialist genocide itself. The only emotions displayed during this discussion are impatience or annoyance at the slow progress being made. The participants make hardly a single allusion to the victims, let alone express sympathy, shame, or guilt. And still, the researcher who is listening to these men conduct their investigations in Sassen's living room, and struggling through the transcript, notices that despite their will to deceive and to deny everything, they were unable to make any headway against the might of the facts. However hard they tried, they still heaped up number after number, even without meaning to. As the total grew under their sharpened pencils, the magnitude of this crime against humanity started to look like the writing on the wall. All the participants, apart from Eichmann, had clearly been so convinced that the systematic mass murder of the Jews was a propaganda lie that they really expected that a closer inspection would only confirm their view. Sassen figured that if "the Jews" were forced to provide lists of names, to prove exactly who had been killed, then it would emerge that the dead would be only a tiny proportion.[284] The fact that this very method would prove the opposite over the following decades was something he began to sense only gradually. Ultimately, no one can examine something this closely without also reexamining their own views. For his part, Eichmann learned that the first "final balance" he had given in "The Others Spoke" was indefensible, and he grasped the fundamental problem of using statistics to back his lies. In Israel he would be more cautious, implying that the number of Jews murdered would never be known for certain.

Paradoxically, the men in Argentina were moving closer to reality, precisely because they had imagined a very different reality. They delved into an area of research that had only just begun, with all its beginners' mistakes. In the first decade after the war, all the historians who tried to work to high academic standards, using only figures that could be proved, arrived at totals that we can now see were much too low. But the beginnings of this research were incredibly difficult: contrary to the idea of a systematic murder operation carried out with Germanic efficiency, the extermination of the Jews was an improvised and sometimes chaotic crime. The Germans then tried to burn their records—but even they had no real overview of what they had done. What went on in the death camps bore no resemblance to the clinical, "humane" killing of Himmler's plans for extinction, which were modeled on pest control. In the camps, where the sole aim was to produce mountains of corpses, it was probably inevitable that all sense of structure and procedure would collapse over time. To imagine that historical research could ever yield an exact number of victims is to idealize the circumstances of this gigantic crime. And anyone trying to gain an accurate picture of these processes would require access to many more documents than were available in the mid-1950s. At that point, only the perpetrators had any real details, even if some of the survivors had some idea of the scale of what had happened. Raul Hilberg estimated 5.1 million in 1961. Martin Gilbert's estimate of 5.7 million in 1982 was not sufficiently backed by evidence. Only since the 1990s, and the opening of the Russian archives, have we understood that the true magnitude of the crime is close to the figure that Theodor Grell heard (and that Höttl claimed to have heard) from Eichmann in 1944.

Ironically, Höttl's statement is still regarded as unreliable. Much of what he told American investigators after the German defeat in 1945 was not information he had heard himself: he "borrowed" it from other people's reports and added the occasional exaggeration of his own. It was a perverse attempt to make himself indispensable as a witness and to show his worth as a potential spy for the U.S. intelligence service. At that point, he was in contact with Theodor Grell and Dieter Wisliceny and would have been able to avail himself of their recollections as well. Höttl's biggest problem was distracting people from his own role in the Nazi regime. His meeting with Eichmann in Hungary clearly had had nothing to do with historical research; he was sounding out his own position as the regime collapsed. Eichmann was in touch with Heinrich Himmler, who was one of the greatest unknown quantities in the plans that Höttl and his superiors were making to save themselves. Through Eichmann, he could also discover what the head of the Gestapo, Heinrich Müller, was planning. Höttl was no small cog in the machine either, but being a man of importance would do him no favors with the Allies. Instead, he managed to dodge any probing questions, loudly proclaiming a different story to distract people from his own. This is exactly what he did with his conversation with Eichmann in Budapest in August 1944. And we can't rule out the possibility that this detailed story was a macabre attempt by Höttl to outdo his competition.

Later, Höttl would unintentionally strengthen people's doubts about his credibility. In his autobiography, he claimed to have been aware that this statement would make him a sought-after (and well-paid) witness to the Nazi period. In his final years he managed to start a television career based solely on this statement, then hinted several times that he had never really believed the scale of the Holocaust was so vast. This suggestion, like many things in his last book, proves how easy Höttl found it to spend a lifetime saying things he didn't believe. In one of his last interviews, he said: "As is so often the case, something I lied about came true."[285]

It is remarkable that Eichmann should have named such a large figure at this point in time, prior to the notorious death marches from Budapest and prior to the gassing operation in Ravensbrück, with which he can also be linked. From his visits to Theresienstadt and the remaining concentration camps (Bergen-Belsen, Buchenwald, Mauthausen, and Dachau) during the final months of the war, he obviously knew people were dying en masse in the abysmal conditions there. But Theodor Grell was not the only one who thought Eichmann was just boasting in 1944. Eichmann had had nothing to do with the *Einsatzgruppen* mass murders that started behind the eastern front in 1941, though he had heard reports about their scale. Still, he clearly wanted to take responsibility for the total. He therefore impressed upon everyone that the various extermination campaigns perpetrated against the Jews were all part of a single large project. Viewed from the periphery, much of it might have appeared improvised, actionistic, and arbitrary, but viewed from Berlin, every anti-Semitic attack was a realization of what the Nazis were striving for. Eichmann identified himself with "Project Genocide" the way a director sometimes does with his production, seeing his will enacted even when the actors are improvising or interacting with the set. The atmosphere of possibility created an effect that makes Eichmann's identification with everything that happened in the German Reich understandable. He and others constantly fed the atmosphere of violence that led to innumerable atrocities. He was aware of it and voluntarily added all the murders to his own conscience.

Even so, the fact remains that Eichmann gave a very close approximation of the number of people who we can now prove fell victim to the Nazis' murder operation. Whether he said five or six million (or perhaps both, depending on the point in time and who he was speaking to), he came close to the correct figure decades before historians managed to gather enough material to prove it. This striking accuracy shows how well informed Eichmann was about the scale of the genocide and how deceitful were his later attempts, in both Argentina and Israel, to feign ignorance. Sassen and his associates turned to Eichmann because they were certain Höttl was lying, and only the man whom Höttl had claimed to be quoting could prove it. Eichmann had to make a public declaration that he had never mentioned that kind of figure. And so he spent months assuring Sassen that he too wanted to travel "the streets of truth" and disprove "the lie of the six million," by giving another Eichmann quote—a real one, this time. But each document the Dürer circle read became a paving stone on an entirely different road. By the time Sassen noticed, it was too late to turn back: his own key witness had unexpectedly overtaken him in the inside lane and made the Argentine discussion group witnesses to a new confession that could not be refuted.

An Untimely Peroration

This is just by way of a conclusion . . . which I also feel compelled to
tell you.   —Eichmann, Sassen discussions[286]

The version of the transcripts that Sassen sold in 1960 ended with the notorious tape 67. Its last two pages, "Eichmann's Concluding Remarks," immediately became the section of the transcripts most quoted by journalists and historians. But the little speech Eichmann gave in 1957 was by no means the end of the Sassen interviews. It was, admittedly, an unusual meeting for the Sassen circle, the mere announcement of which had been enough to give Eichmann the mistaken impression that it was going to be a celebratory finale to the project. He therefore prepared an explicit "conclusion." The background noises on the tape reveal the presence of a relatively large group. Eichmann refers to his audience as a *Tischrunde,* a round-table group. He must have assumed that this session, which took place in September or October 1957, would be the ideal setting for another of those parting speeches that had become notorious among his colleagues—and in the history books. Using skill and intuition, he found the right moment to launch into his address, during a discussion of the final documents in *Das Deutsche Reich und die Juden.* He gave this speech in the same tone he struck elsewhere when speaking from notes rather than off the cuff: accentuated and strident, but also slow and solemn, with frequent pauses for effect. We have the whole of this speech, along with the preceding discussion and the reactions to it, on one of the original tapes.[287] The significance of this speech for an understanding of the Sassen discussions and, above all, as proof of how valuable Eichmann's statements in Argentina are as a source, make it worthy of a full word-for-word transcription.[288] Explanations of various words and phrases are given in the endnotes.

> EICHMANN: ... and please don't try and confuse me on this after twelve years, whether it was called Kaufmann[289] or Eichmann or Sassen, or Morgenthau,[290] I don't care. Something happened, where I said to myself: fine, then I must drop all my misgivings. Before my people bite the dust, the whole world should bite the dust, and then my people. But only then!
>
> I said this. I—and I tell you this as a conclusion to our matters—I, "the cautious bureaucrat,"[291] that was me, yes indeed. But I would like to expand on the issue of the "cautious bureaucrat," somewhat to my own detriment. This cautious bureaucrat was attended by a ... a fanatical warrior, fighting for the freedom of my blood, which is my birthright, and I say here, just as I have said to you before: your louse that nips you, Comrade Sassen, does not interest me.[292] My louse under my collar interests me. I will squash it. This is the same when it comes to my people. And the cautious bureaucrat, which of course I was, that is what I had been, also guided and inspired me: what benefits my people is a sacred order and a sacred law for me. Yes indeed.
>
> And now I want to tell you, as a conclusion to all these records,[293] for we will soon be finished, I must first tell you: I have no regrets! I am certainly not going to bow down to that cross! The four months[294] during which we have gone over the matter here, during the four months in which you have taken pains to refresh my memory, a great deal of it has been refreshed, it would be too easy, and I could do it cheaply for the sake of current opinion ... for me to deeply regret it, for me to pretend that a Saul has become a Paul.
>
> I tell you, Comrade Sassen, I cannot do that. That I cannot do, because I am not willing to do it, because I balk inwardly at saying that we did anything wrong. No. I have to tell you

quite honestly that if of the 10.3 million Jews that Korherr[295] identified, as we now know, we had killed 10.3 million, I would be satisfied, and would say, good, we have destroyed an enemy. Now through the vagaries of fortune, most of these 10.3 million Jews remained alive, so I say to myself: fate wished it so. I have to subordinate myself to fate and destiny. I am just a little man and don't have to fight against this, and I couldn't, and I don't want to. We would have fulfulled our duty to our blood and our people and to the freedom of the peoples, if we had exterminated the most cunning intellect of all the human intellects[296] alive today. For that is what I said to Streicher,[297] what I have always preached: we are fighting an enemy who, through many many thousands of years of schooling,[298] is intellectually superior to us. Was it yesterday or the day before, or a year ago, I don't know, I heard or read: even before the Romans had their state, before Rome had even been founded, the Jews there were able to write. This is an understatement. They should have said, aeons before the Romans erected their state, aeons before the very founding of Rome itself, they were able to write. Look at the tablets of the Ten Commandments. Look at a race that today has recourse to, may I just say, six thousand years of written history, a race that has been making laws for let us say five thousand years or six thousand years— and I am not wrong, I believe, when I estimate a seventh millennium. The fact that the Christian church today makes use of this law making[299] is very depressing for me. But it tells me that this must be a race of the first order of magnitude, since lawmakers have always been great. And because of these realizations I fought against this enemy.

And you must understand that this is my motivation when I say, if 10.3 million of these enemies had been killed, then we would have fulfilled our duty. (Pause for effect.) And because this did not happen, I will say to you that those who have not yet been born will have to undergo that suffering and adversity. Perhaps they will curse us. (Pause for effect.) Alone, we few people cannot fight the Zeitgeist. We have done what we could.

Of course, I must say to you, human emotion also plays a

role here. I too am not free of this, I too was defeated by the same weakness. I know this! I too am partly to blame for the fact that the real, complete elimination, perhaps foreseen by some authority, or the conception that I had in mind, could not be carried out. I gave you some small examples of this. I was an inadequate intellect and was placed in an office where in truth I could have done more, and should have done more.

What I told you must serve as an apology: one, that I lacked a profound intellect. Second, that I lacked the necessary physical toughness. And third, that even against my will there were a legion of people who fought this will, so that while I myself already felt handicapped, I was then also curtailed in carrying out the other things that would have helped me to a breakthrough, because for many years I was bogged down in a struggle against the so-called Interventionists.[300] I want to close by telling you this.

Whether you will put this in the book, I do not know, perhaps it is not a good idea at all. And perhaps it should not go in. This is just by way of a conclusion, to what I have taken on in all these months of refreshing my memory, and which I also feel compelled to tell you.

SASSEN: Yes.

A long, tense silence; fidgeting around the table.

EICHMANN: We're done with the whole recording now, yes?

SASSEN: Excuse me?

EICHMANN: We're finished now, yes? Aren't we?

SASSEN: Actually, no. I still have a few pages to discuss. But I'm sure we can manage that.

EICHMANN: Oh, we're really not done with the book?

Sassen laughs (half sympathetic, half indulgently).

EICHMANN (anxious and confused): I think we're done with . . . that's why I . . . I gave a little conclusion . . . er . . . address to . . . to . . . er, the group.

SASSEN: Doesn't matter.

It is only at this "Doesn't matter" that Eichmann seems to realize how out of place his "little address to the group" was. When there is no immediate reaction, he asks Sassen directly what he thinks of the speech and, not getting a reply, the no-regrets orator finally acknowledges that he is aware of the monstrosity of his words: "It is hard, what I have told you, I know, and I will be condemned for being so hard in my phrasing, but I cannot tell you anything else, for it is the truth! Why should I deny it?" It came "in the moment, from my heart," which is why he wanted to say it, for the future and for posterity, "for study of some kind." Anyone who can bear to listen to the complete version on tape will not fail to notice that during the "address," the style and content of this pathetic performance makes the audience increasingly uneasy and alarmed. It's no surprise that Sassen then attempts to gloss over this grotesque scene, as Eichmann has done nothing less than caricature the whole Sassen project and make fools of its initiators. They had spent months try-ing to distance National Socialism from "the one thing of which we are always accused"—namely the Holocaust—finding reasons to discredit each statistic as "enemy propaganda," and trying to minimize the figures as far as possible, in order to be rid of the problem that they believed had been created by Eichmann and his speeches during the final days of the war. And now the man they hoped would be their chief witness had laid a few million more lives on the table. Everyone present must have realized that the attempt to correct Eichmann with Eichmann had failed. Furthermore, this incomprehensibly cynical speech made it quite plain that when Wisliceny and all the others quoted Eichmann's con-fession about millions of deaths, it hadn't been because the straitened circumstances of Allied occupation had made them lie. And perhaps the detested Wilhelm Höttl had been exaggerating to make himself look important, but he still fell short of the reality that emerged at Sassen's table in 1957. The group had not exposed the "six million" speech, that most hated of quotations, as a desperate lie told under torture, or as an enterprising invention by Wilhelm Höttl. Instead, they had made them-selves witnesses to this monstrous confession, confirming it once and for all. Eichmann had really said it in 1945. And twelve years after the war's end, in a discussion group with a tape recorder in the room, the mass murderer gave an unsolicited repeat performance of his confession. The extermination of Jews had taken place; he had helped to plan millions of murders—a total genocide, in fact; he still believed this aim to be right; he was satisfied with his part in it; and his only criticism of this lunatic National Socialist project was that "we could and should have done more." Instead of shaming the "enemy" in Israel and every Jew the world over, by proving "the lie of the six million" to be a Jewish battle tactic, Sassen and Fritsch had inadvertently proved that the real enemy of their own fanciful idea of "pure National Socialism" lay in the midst of Nazi ideology itself, personified in one of its most successful functionaries, one of the last devoted National Socialists still chasing Hitler's ideal: Otto Adolf Eichmann, SS *Obersturmbannführer* (still retired). As much as Sassen tried to play it down, his project ended here, in failure. Anything else—victims' testimonies, rediscovered statistical documents, telegrams about murder rates and books of the dead, films and photos and studies of every kind—the group could have cast doubt on, describing it as "anti-German," "propagandist," "exaggerated," or "counterfeit." But they couldn't doubt Eichmann, when he had confirmed the whole thing so convincingly. Eichmann was a National Socialist and *for that reason* a dedicated mass murderer—nothing, nothing at all, could have "mattered" more.

An End Without a Conclusion

It boils down to Eichmann only believing in his own word.
—Harry Mulisch[301]

We can only guess how that evening must have continued, as the tape recorder was then switched off, despite Sassen's announcement that he still had a few pages left to discuss. Nobody seems to have had much enthusiasm for working on the literature anymore: the advertised discussion didn't take place until the following week, starting on tape 68. What happened next suggests that Eichmann had received a clear impression of the group's general lack of understanding. Immediately afterward, he wrote Sassen a riposte to his unsuccessful "conclusion," sheepishly requesting more material to support his crude understanding of the "Kaufman Plan" and the "Jews' impulse" toward their own destruction. He was attempting a redraft in accordance with Sassen's interpretation of history.[302] He clearly thought it necessary to tell Sassen what he wanted to hear, both in his letter and in the words he composed for the discussion following this incident, with which tape 68 begins.[303] "Yes, I want to register one point," he stutters. "During or in the course of the last records that were recorded . . . I gave a kind of concluding

statement. . . . Now I have read this book by Poliakov and found . . .
er . . . things there that were done . . . I no longer feel this conclusion
was correct in the form in which I gave it."[304] Eichmann is obviously
aiming to please, like a schoolboy with a guilty conscience. But he is not
entirely successful in playing the contrite orator: he can't help but add
that he will relent only if "the documents are genuine, and not bogus
documents." However, he immediately backpedals: "which admittedly,
given the whole situation etc., I almost doubt, and I believe that a few
things have to be accepted as genuine. . . . What do you think?" On the
tapes that follow, Sassen is obviously too irritated to think anything anymore and is also seriously lacking in motivation. He continues to read
from books, slowly and with less concentration than usual, then stops,
starts again from another point, and breaks off again, for minutes at a
time. He seems to ask questions more out of habit than of interest. Only
Eichmann retains his usual level of engagement, though he is increasingly mistrustful of Sassen. He begins to answer much more evasively:
"I am hearing that for the first time, . . . but I have to tell you I cannot
say anything about it, since I had nothing to do with it"; "I don't know";
"I've forgotten."[305]

Sassen barely follows up on Eichmann's remarks, putting very few
queries, not wanting to probe further, and simply checking off each
subject on his agenda. The transcripts are also incomplete, and in the
text, the ordering of the tapes becomes uncertain.[306] The final tapes and
transcripts give the impression that Sassen had simply lost interest. It
was impossible for him to re-create the excitement of the earlier tapes.
Eichmann had become a disappointment for his circle. He was forced to
recognize that he had failed to take Eichmann in hand, though he had
employed plenty of tactics, books, and helpers in the attempt. In the end,
Eichmann remained Eichmann. His meetings with Sassen had been just
another opportunity for him to put across his version of history, and his
plans: "Your louse that nips you, Comrade Sassen, does not interest me."
And as cunning as Sassen had proved himself to be when he interviewed
South American politicians, he was no match for Eichmann's love of
hearing his own voice. Like everyone who has come into contact with
Eichmann and his texts, Sassen simply became irritated—not only by
his regular guest's terrible sentence structures and neologisms but also
by the realization that the idea of Germany under National Socialism

that Sassen had been nurturing was so flawed as to be untenable. Sassen's daughter stressed several times that her father could not and would not deal with the subject of the Holocaust, because it didn't accord with his dream of the "pure idea of National Socialism." But through Eichmann, Sassen had come to understand that ignoring the Holocaust was the same as denying it. Mass murder and gas chambers had happened, they were part of German history, and National Socialists like Eichmann had played a decisive role in creating them, out of their dedication to the cause. Sassen may have been a dedicated National Socialist and a racial anti-Semite, but he viewed this kind of murder project as a crime, and he was too self-aware to see denial as a solution. He failed in his attempt to write a book based on these discussions that would please him as well as Eichmann. The project had only served to make him realize that if he wanted to remain a National Socialist, he had to stop working with Eichmann. It would be possible to falsify history, and dissociate Hitler and "Germanness" from the murder of the Jews, only by going against Eichmann.

The fall of 1957 brought with it a significant change for postwar Nazis the world over. Konrad Adenauer won the election in West Germany with an absolute majority. The far-right movement in both Germany and Buenos Aires had dreamed of preventing this election victory and of effecting a turning point in German postwar politics—a dream that was far removed from reality even in the 1950s. It had come to nothing, along with the prospect of using this route back to a seat at Germany's top table. The German population, as Adenauer had realized, was no longer keen on experiments.[307] Everyone had now come to appreciate that there was no way back, and they would have to adapt to the new world as it was. Eberhard Fritsch, Ludolf von Alvensleben, Willem Sassen, and Hans-Ulrich Rudel, as their biographies show, were slowly beginning to grasp that Hitler had been dead a long time: the Third Reich was past and would never return. Even the most sentimental of dreams, in the isolation of exile, had a limit, when the rest of the world was moving on—and the world had moved on significantly, even in Argentina. In 1957 the country was a long way from the vibrant boom years it had enjoyed a decade previously, under Perón. The "movement" had become outmoded, and those who didn't want to be stuck in the past had to start keeping pace with the new world and its possibilities.

Even *Der Weg* ceased publication. And so the Sassen project didn't go out with a well-orchestrated bang or a dramatic bombshell; it simply died of boredom and disappointment.

But Eichmann's confession had changed not only the eyewitnesses in Argentina. It was spreading inexorably among the other people who were still dreaming of the Führer-state's return. The first role that the Sassen interviews played in Eichmann's downfall was to help destroy the virulent sympathy for the National Socialist worldview that had protected the perpetrators of crimes against humanity for so long.

A FALSE SENSE OF SECURITY

Eichmann was pretty stupid. Everyone knew where he was.
                    —Inge Schneider, an acquaintance of Sassen's

The chief prosecutor of Frankfurt, Arnold Buchthal, held a press conference at the start of April 1957. On April 1 he had ordered the arrest of Hermann Krumey, the man who had spent many years working for Eichmann and had been his representative in Hungary in 1944. Buchthal had been tasked with the central handling of all investigations into the historical murder of more than four hundred thousand Hungarian Jews, and over the next few days, his words were published in all the Federal Republic's large daily newspapers, and even in the *Argentinisches Tageblatt*. Naturally, the article said, the hunt was still on for Krumey's superior Adolf Eichmann, a warrant for whose arrest had been ordered on November 24, 1956: "He is said to be living in an unknown location in South America."[1] We know that Eichmann read this article, as he talked about it in the Sassen circle. And there is much to suggest that someone else also heard about it: Lothar Hermann, a blind man whose family had been killed by the National Socialists and who had escaped this fate himself only by fleeing the country.

People have always delighted in the story of the former inmate of Dachau whose daughter met Eichmann's eldest son at school. The thought that it was his son's love life, and not the intelligence services, that proved to be Eichmann's undoing is so satisfying that it seems to have brushed all questions aside. But as neat as this story of sex and secrets might be, historians must not succumb uncritically to its pulp-fiction charms. We must point out the things that don't add up and, most important, look at the sources. As is so often the case, the story is much more complex than it appears.[2] The information about the German jurist Fritz Bauer, Lothar Hermann, his daughter, and Klaus Eichmann became public only many years later. It first appeared in *The Avengers* (1967) by Michael Bar-Zohar, a close friend of David Ben-Gurion's. He was the first person to mention Fritz Bauer in connection with the hunt for Eichmann, though initially he did so by implication. Only in interviews, and in the Hebrew edition of the book that appeared after Bauer's death, did Bar-Zohar talk openly about Bauer's secret collaboration with the Israeli authorities.[3] His book may have been a popular paperback, but Bar-Zohar still had a good reputation as an historian.

He wrote well-respected biographies of Ben-Gurion and Israeli defense minister Moshe Dayan and had access to the head of Mossad, Isser Harel. He was without question very well connected, so we must take seriously his claim to have spoken to Fritz Bauer in person in March 1967.

Encouraged by the Bar-Zohar book's success, Isser Harel also went public about the events leading up to Eichmann's capture, telling his story in interviews, newspaper articles, and finally a book.[4] By this point, Harel assumed that Hermann was long dead, and he wanted to create a memorial to Mossad's work (and to himself), for the tenth anniversary of the trial. He quite rightly saw abducting Eichmann as the greatest achievement of his career. His book was published in numerous editions worldwide, on the strength of the love story between the son of a Nazi and the daughter of a Jewish survivor. Sex and Nazis always sell.

When Lothar Hermann heard about Harel's story, he was aghast: most of it was "completely wrong"; the facts had been twisted "deliberately and publicly." "I never imagined that men of the Jewish faith could be so bad and treacherous," he said. Harel had "misused my name and the name of my daughter."[5] Hermann rejected the public accolade for his role in Eichmann's abduction and an invitation to Israel. Given the background to the story and his living conditions at the time, the fact that he still accepted the $10,000 reward from the State of Israel is perfectly understandable, even though by so doing he added the possibility of another anti-Semitic cliché to the story. A glance at the correspondence between Hans Dietrich Sander and Carl Schmitt shows the extent to which Harel's story played to the public taste. "I recently read a story in the Süddeutsche Zeitung about Eichmann's arrest," Sander writes. "According to this, E was not discovered through the resourcefulness of the Isr. secret service, but through a bounty that the secret service put on him. An old blind Jew from Argentina then got in touch, who knew where E was because his daughter was friends with E's son. E was gotten out of the country as we know, but the bounty was not paid. The old Jew started a legal dispute that went on for years," Sander continues, adding with regret: "The daughter doesn't appear in the article again."[6] His sense of voyeurism obviously wanted more salacious details.

There are no independent sources for Isser Harel's version of the Silvia Hermann story, as the events to which he referred took place before the official Mossad operation. All the agents who later gave details about what happened prior to 1960 got them from their superior, Harel.

None of them knew anything about the search for Eichmann before the formation of the abduction team. Ephraim Hofstaedter, who had visited Lothar Hermann at the start of 1958, subsequently fell victim to a terrorist attack in Istanbul. Zvi Aharoni, the first Mossad agent to see Eichmann's address and conduct any real fieldwork, did not stint in his criticism of Harel's book, accusing him of courting publicity at the expense of the truth, just as Hermann had done.[7] In his biography of Simon Wiesenthal, Tom Segev also shows how jealously Harel tried to raise his profile as he got older, attempting to efface Wiesenthal's part in the hunt—which had been officially recognized with an award from the State of Israel. Fairness wasn't part of Harel's PR campaign. And there is one more fact we should not ignore: in this version of events, Klaus Eichmann's behavior played a significant part in his father being discovered, but he never gave any indication that he blamed himself for the events that led to his father's death, which he saw in a very different light.[8] We should therefore be a little more cautious than to use Harel as our only source: for one thing, a tactical understanding of truth comes with the job for intelligence service chiefs, and for another, there are alternative routes by which to access the events in Argentina.

The Informant Lothar Hermann

This way I am probably forgoing historical fame.
—Lothar Hermann to Fritz Bauer, June 25, 1960

When Klaus Eichmann[9] met Silvia Hermann, they were both at school and were at most nineteen and fourteen, respectively. By January 1956, the Hermanns had moved from Buenos Aires to Coronel Suárez, 310 miles away.[10] Lothar Hermann and his first wife had moved to Argentina after he was forced to leave Germany because he was a Jew—a "full Jew," as he stressed to Harel, who had described him, using Nazi terminology, as a "half-Jew."[11] Hermann, who had been born in Quirnbach in Germany in 1901, was a lawyer. He said he had spent the period between September 14, 1935, and May 7, 1936, in "protective custody" in Dachau, probably because of his interest in socialism.[12] He was then expelled from Germany as a "politicizing Jew" and emigrated to Argentina via Holland, where in 1938 he was finally able to marry his "Aryan" wife. His parents and siblings didn't survive the National Socialists. In Argentina, Hermann went completely blind, but he continued to work as a legal adviser, specializing in pension claims. He moved to Coronel Suárez, where there was a large German-Jewish community, because his services would be much sought after there. There is nothing to suggest Hermann was ever rich, or even well off.

Silvia Hermann, born in Buenos Aires in 1941, was a gifted child. A friend of the family and Lothar Hermann's secretary both recall the Hermanns deciding to send their daughter back to Buenos Aires to attend high school. That would enable her to go to college in North America, where the Hermanns had some distant relatives. From Lothar Hermann's letters, we know that by the fall of 1959, when she was eighteen, Silvia left Argentina for the United States. This makes it impossible that her departure was directly connected to Eichmann's abduction, but it does tell us when Silvia Hermann and Klaus Eichmann could have met.

The fact that their paths crossed was certainly no bizarre coincidence. In German immigrant life in Argentina, former victims and perpetrators lived quite literally next door to each other, and their children attended the same schools. To be sure, there was a cultural divide—a German-Jewish newspaper, theater, and cinema on the one hand, and German-national and/or National Socialist institutions on the other—but young people seldom adhere to such divisions, having little concern for their parents' mental barriers. Lothar Hermann never said when and where his daughter met Eichmann's son; in 1959 he simply indicated that his daughter could confirm everything he had said about Eichmann's identity and where he was living. But a friend remembers that Silvia met Klaus, who was five years older than she, at school. She fell in love with him and kept a photo of him. It may have been a school photo, a snapshot taken at a party, or something else, but it has never been found. However, numerous people claim to have seen it, and it was even said to have hung on a wall in the Hermanns' house.[13]

Lothar Hermann had always taken an interest in the Nazis in Argentina, wanting to see the people who had murdered his family brought before a court. It wasn't surprising, therefore, that the name Eichmann immediately rang a bell with him. By the fall of 1957, when Hermann and his family had been in Coronel Suárez just over a year, Fritz Bauer had in his hands the information that Eichmann was in Argentina. Bauer may even have received Hermann's letter by June 1957.

How Hermann hit upon the idea of sending the information on Eichmann's exact whereabouts to Fritz Bauer, the attorney general in Frankfurt, is unclear. Hermann mentioned only the time of their correspondence, "the years 1957/58."[14] His first letter has disappeared, and its date is uncertain,[15] but it could have been addressed to the man named in the *Argentinisches Tageblatt* as having said Eichmann was in South America: Arnold Buchthal. He may have passed the letter on to Fritz Bauer, about whom nothing had yet been written in Argentina in connection with Eichmann. Bauer and Buchthal not only knew each other, they were both backed by the prime minister of Hesse, Georg August Zinn, a great advocate of coming to terms with the past who placed a lot of hope in these two Jewish jurists. By the time Arnold Buchthal had to vacate the post of chief prosecutor because of a political affair, in favor of a man with a Nazi history, he would certainly have started passing his search results on to Bauer rather than leave them lying on his desk.[16] We know that Bauer took the first real steps in the hunt for Eichmann when he had Vera Eichmann's mother questioned on June 9, 1957. She said her daughter had been living abroad since 1953, having married an unknown man and gone to America with him.[17] At the start of July, Bauer experienced a significant setback. The Bundeskriminalamt (BKA, the Federal Office for Criminal Investigations) informed the Hesse State Office for Criminal Investigations that it would not initiate an Interpol search for Eichmann. He was wanted for crimes of a "political and racial character," and Interpol's statutes prevented its involvement in this kind of prosecution. "I therefore have no way of conducting the international hunt for Eichmann via the BKA as a German central office," Bauer said.[18] The BKA allowed the former SS officer Paul Dickopf (among other old comrades it employed) to make a good career for himself: he eventually became its president and was even president of Interpol. In general, the BKA cannot be accused of showing any real enthusiasm for hunting Nazi criminals. Eichmann would later claim that he had always been reassured by Interpol's refusal to search for him, but how he could have heard about that remains unclear.[19]

At exactly this point in summer 1957, the old rumors about Eichmann in the Middle East were resurrected. For more than a month, stories about Nazis in Cairo haunted the pages of German newspapers.[20] They were even discussed and refuted (without mentioning Eichmann's name) in *Der Weg*—possibly because in Cairo, Johann von Leers was starting to feel threatened by the articles.[21] And once again, these clues also turn up in the intelligence service files.[22] By this time, Fritz Bauer had to acknowledge that circulating his information within Germany wasn't going to achieve anything; on the contrary, appealing to the German authorities had actually endangered any chance of success. At the start of November, Bauer had his first meeting with Israeli representatives, to whom he gave the information from Argentina. He also told them he had not just taken it upon himself to cooperate with the State of Israel—he had discussed it with Georg August Zinn, the prime minister of Hesse and a personal friend.[23] In January 1958 Mossad sent a spy, Emanuel Talmor, to check out the address in Buenos Aires, but the house on Chacabuco Street didn't fit the cliché of influential Nazis in exile. Fritz Bauer, informed of this conclusion, nevertheless pressed for futher investigation. As a result, Ephraim Hofstaedter, a senior officer in the Israeli police, was given the task of visiting Lothar Hermann at home in March 1958; it was no coincidence that he later led the police investigative bureau during the trial. In any case, Hofstaedter was already going to Buenos Aires, for an Interpol conference.[24] Unfortunately, it is not known which BKA representatives he met there. But we do know that the deputy head of the BKA, Paul Dickopf, who liked to call himself its "architect," was also the head of the "Foreign Division" at this point. He frequently represented the organization at international meetings, and the Interpol General Assembly appointed him as its correspondent for these events between 1955 and 1961. Possibly he could have paid a visit to the country that had become a refuge for his old comrades. A glance at the delegation's report would certainly be worthwhile, if it could be found.[25]

Hofstaedter used an alias with Lothar Hermann, producing a letter from Bauer to identify himself as an employee of the Frankfurt attorney general's office. It's easy to imagine how disappointed everyone must have been to discover that the man claiming to have recognized Eichmann was blind. Hofstaedter prohibited Hermann from making any further contact with Fritz Bauer and gave him an address in the United States to which Hermann was to direct any more mail. Years later Hermann complained that he had never received a reply to the letters he sent there, in which he had enclosed "a photo of Klaus Eichmann" that had fallen into his hands "by chance." (So far none of the letters Hermann sent to New York have come to light. It would be a fitting

recognition of Hermann's achievement to make the documents public.)[26] Hermann later explained that it was "only with great difficulty
and effort" that he had "received the sum of 15,000 Argentine pesos in
two instalments" from "Karl Hubert" (Hofstaedter's cover name). But in
1958, when Hermann stopped getting replies to his letters, he sent the
whole dossier back to Frankfurt and, as he said later, gave up any further
investigations, having received the impression that his work was pointless.[27] The Hermanns then sent their daughter away to college, and Hermann thereby lost his point of contact with the Eichmanns. He now had
no one to carry out investigations on his behalf. However, his contemporaries recall that later on, there was talk of Silvia's departure having
been for her own safety. The investigations had placed her in a dangerous position, and Lothar Hermann, who in any case was understandably paranoid, had therefore pushed for her to move away, although her
enrollment at a foreign university placed a financial strain on the family.
As Silvia Hermann decided not to say anything about these events, we
can only speculate about the real reasons for her departure.

The reaction of the people to whom Hermann gave his information,
however, is quite clear: after Hofstaedter's visit, the informant Lothar
Hermann was no longer taken seriously. He really *had* found Adolf
Eichmann—it was just that he didn't seem all that convincing: a blind
man, living in remote Coronel Suárez, claiming to have tracked down the
"number-one enemy of the Jews" in Buenos Aires, at an address that was
just a modest apartment with no signs of security or luxury. Moreover,
in pursuing his investigations, he had mistaken Eichmann's landlord,
Francisco Schmitt, for Eichmann himself, destroying his credibility once
and for all. The idea that a Nazi might be living in a rented apartment,
in a building like that, was too much for Isser Harel and his colleagues
to swallow. But Fritz Bauer didn't want to give up. Hermann's letters
convinced him, and he was also coming across more and more evidence
to substantiate what his informant in Argentina was telling him.

Back to Germany?

It was pure coincidence that at this time, the German Office for the
Protection of the Constitution was also looking at Eichmann.

          —Irmtrud Wojak[28]

Contrary to the cliché of the rich Nazi, toward the end of 1957 Adolf
Eichmann started to have business problems. The rabbit farm failed,
allegedly because of a crossbreeding error (racial intermingling, of all
things).[29] Pipe dreams about the Jewish race had always been more his
field. But once again all was not lost for Eichmann. At the turn of the
year, helped by yet another old associate, he found a job in a company
owned by Roberto Mertig.[30] Mertig, who was a business partner of Josef
Mengele's father, owned a gas oven factory, and Mengele himself is said
to have been on the payroll. Mengele Sr., who manufactured farm vehicles, had always supported his son, repeatedly finding ways to generate
an income for him. Eichmann's work in a gas oven factory must have
provided a source of macabre jokes among his old comrades, but there
were also signs of a change in him, if we believe what he would write in
Israel to friends and family about his final two years in Argentina. Even
Eichmann, it seems, was starting to pay more attention to the here and
now—though we may doubt that this change was entirely voluntary.

    With the failure of the Dürer project, Eichmann and Sassen's planned
publication also fell through, which had consequences for both men.
The German-Argentine community started to change. Many of the "less
compromised" exiles, from lower down the Nazi hierarchy, felt the need
to return to the place they grew up and went back to Europe. Statutes
of limitation and other rehabilitative legislation in West Germany and
Austria allowed anyone who had not committed capital offenses or
war crimes (or at least none that anyone was trying to prove) to return
and start afresh. And in early March 1958 even Eberhard Fritsch, born
in Buenos Aires, broke down his tents, publishing house and all, and
moved to a house near Salzburg.[31] The German nationalist community
in Argentina lost an important point of reference, and Sassen lost his
job. More important, he lost the person who had published his texts and
allowed him to be an author, thereby guaranteeing him a position in
German-Argentine society as a journalist and writer. The final issue of

Der Weg, which appeared shortly before Fritsch's departure, ended with a piece by Willem Sassen, once again bemoaning the fate of contemporary Germany.[32] Sassen and Eichmann were both hoping that Fritsch's plan to establish a publishing operation in Europe would bear fruit, but Eichmann's dream of having his book published had passed out of his reach. Still, they stayed in touch, just in case. Later events show that Fritsch must have made contact with Eichmann's family in Austria: in 1960, when Eichmann's capture was announced, he promptly met up with Eichmann's brother to organize his defense.[33] Fritsch's move to Salzburg also provided Eichmann with a good way of communicating news about his new life to his father.

But Eberhard Fritsch was not the only one who moved back to Germany. Sassen spent the New Year's holiday in 1958–59 in Europe—partly to gather sworn statements from his old associates attesting that he had a right to German citizenship. (Sassen might have claimed to be a German when he registered in Konstanz in October 1956, but the matter has never been fully clarified.) Within a relatively short space of time, he was not only able to prove that he had successfully applied for citizenship in 1943—an easy undertaking for a member of the Dutch Voluntary SS—he could also provide sworn statements confirming it, including one from his former commander, Günter d'Alquen. Together with his old paybook and his war reporter's ID, this was enough for the Konstanz legal and regulatory authority to issue a certficate of citizenship on January 26, 1959. By Febuary 4, he had registered as a resident in Munich.[34] To the horror of his wife, who was adamant that she didn't want German citizenship,[35] Sassen started telling people he wanted to move to Germany and work as a journalist there. With his typical mix of imposture and the air of the adventurer, he boasted to his family and others that several German newspapers had taken him on as a correspondent. In 1959 he did actually appear on the masthead of a few issues of *Stern,* as Wilhelm S. von Elsloo. Years later, on reaching the bottom of the first bottle of whiskey, he would still mutter conspiratorially that he had had a specific reason to move to Munich: he was planning a secret service career with "General Gehlen." Although this plan would come to nothing, the gossip would create substantial difficulties for Sassen after Eichmann had been abducted, when he would suddenly be suspected of being a traitor.[36] He had rhapsodized about his travels in Germany a little too much. His visit in summer 1959 in particular must have kept the

BfV on its toes: Sassen not only called on his old friend Rudel, he some-how managed to travel to cities in East Germany. At this point in his-tory, the very announcement of such a travel plan would have sufficed to implicate him as a spy for the East.[37] Sassen still met Eichmann from time to time, but he had more exciting plans now. And understandably, Eichmann didn't want to be the only one left behind in the pampas.

Klaus Eichmann remembered that in the late 1950s, his father often talked about handing himself over to a German court. Eichmann's "let-ter to the Chancellor" shows that this was more than just idle talk—unlike his halfhearted assurances that he didn't want the "limelight of publicity."[38] But the other SS leaders and National Socialists, as his son recalled, talked him out of it: "They checked out the possibility of him turning himself in in Europe. An influential man was sent to Europe. After much discussion, the result was communicated to my father. The time, they said, was not right yet. Europe was still too risky. He should wait in Argentina for another five years, at least. They were certain noth-ing would happen to him in South America during this time."[39] Any of several people could have been the helpful Europe expert. Sassen is the most likely candidate: he had been to Germany a number of times since the end of 1958 and could also draw on the experience of his friend Hans-Ulrich Rudel. But others were more knowledgeable on legal mat-ters. Fritz Otto Ehlert, the *Frankfurter Allgemeine Zeitung* correspon-dent, was acquainted with Horst Carlos Fuldner and was also a source for the Foreign Office. Of course, the German embassy in Argentina also had strong enough connections with the Nazis there to have provided information on the current legal situation directly. We now know that the ambassador himself, Werner Junker, maintained contact with Wil-lem Sassen, whom he thought an "unusually capable journalist." Junker even had some sympathy for Sassen's political orientation.[40]

But Eberhard Fritsch's experience in Europe must have been discour-aging for Eichmann. Fritsch told his fellow Nazi sympathizers that, as a child of German parents, he had actually wanted to move to West Ger-many, but his Argentine citizenship meant he had been denied entry.[41] The truth was less heroic: the West German police had an arrest warrant out for Fritsch, for distributing far-right, anticonstitutional literature. The Fourth Chamber of the Lüneberg District Court had also gone against Dürer Verlag's main distributor in northern Germany and had seized the warehouse containing the last issues of *Der Weg*. Fritsch did have Argentine citizenship, and the correct visa and entry permits from the German embassy in Argentina, but he was safe from prosecution only until he entered Germany. He was not denied entry; he was just on a wanted list.[42] His lofty ambitions to continue his publishing activities in Salzburg also came to nothing, as he was issued with a publishing ban and had to take a job as a hotel porter. The hotel was a top one, on the main square, but still, it was not the life that the man from Buenos Aires had imagined for his wife and five children.

If someone like Fritsch, with no criminal Nazi career behind him, was encountering such problems, then Eichmann's chances looked significantly worse. We may also suspect that Eichmann's family in Linz were doing just fine without their notorious brother in Buenos Aires and would not have encouraged him to come back. And Eichmann's family wouldn't have been the only ones advising him to stay put. The men in Argentina who had met Eichmann, or had heard of him, had much to fear from him being put on trial. They knew what he thought—and, more important, Eichmann knew who had listened to what he had to say. His knowledge of the Nazi networks, the escape and aid organizations, and the communication routes could make life very unpleasant for people, and no one wanted to think about the ramifications if Eichmann told the German authorities about them. So Eichmann's friends in Argentina made sure the *Obersturmbannführer* (retired) felt at ease there in an almost touching way, ensuring that he always had an income and could even afford a vacation at the chic resort of Plata del Mar.[43]

The exiles in Argentina were not the only ones worrying about the possibility of Eichmann coming to trial. His reappearance would create serious problems for a lot of people in Germany and Austria. The pertinent question is not why friends advised him for or against a return to Europe, but which of the former Nazi functionaries had nothing to fear from an Eichmann trial in West Germany. Given Eichmann's position within the Nazi regime, we cannot underestimate whom he knew and above all whom he would have recognized. People often mistakenly believe that if they know someone's name, that person must know theirs, which could only have heightened their fears. Looking at the upheaval that Eichmann's arrest would cause in 1960 gives us an idea of what people in the Federal Republic associated with his name and what they were afraid of. Too many former Nazis had managed to make new careers by smoothing over one another's biographies to make them seem harmless. It is difficult to imagine that the BKA's cohort of former SS men, of whom Paul Dickopf is only the best known, would have given their full support to a trial if they had learned of Eichmann's intent. The Foreign Office staff who, thanks to the reinstatement article, were now working as diplomats again, and some employees of the BND, would have felt the same. Eichmann's knowledge of names alone would have threatened to topple his old comrades' carefully erected facade. Even as late as 2010 the publication of the book *Das Amt* (The Office) caused turmoil among members of the Foreign Office, and their sometimes less-than-helpful friends; we can imagine the effect it would have had more than fifty years ago. Back then, it wasn't the more or less posthumous reputation of retired diplomats that was at stake but people's clean slates, elevated positions, and high salaries.

Eichmann, meanwhile, was surprisingly well informed about the prosecution of Nazi criminals that was starting to take place in the Federal Republic. He knew about the arrest of his colleague Hermann Krumey, and trials against people like Ferdinand Schörner. He also heard about the founding of the Central Office for the Prosecution of Nazi Crimes in Ludwigsburg. It had been planned in October 1958, to coordinate all investigations across West Germany. Even news of the Institute of Contemporary History in Munich had reached him in Buenos Aires. At the start of his interrogation in Israel, in June 1960, Eichmann said: "I read that somewhere in West Germany, I don't recall exactly where, there is a kind of central archive concerned with the collection of documentary material."[44] Eichmann's open letter to Adenauer was supposed to be a "report," given in his real name, with a carefully worked out line of defense. All this speaks for the likelihood that Eichmann had given serious consideration to the route he would take to surrender himself to the Federal Republic. He was probably banking on his status as a star witness, and a sensational trial that would work in his favor, and unfortunately we cannot simply claim that this strategy was ludicrous.

Within his family, Eichmann mentioned another reason for not returning to Germany to testify, in addition to the advice from his friends. "As long as Müller was alive, he didn't want to reveal all," Klaus Eichmann said. We still know very little about the life of "Gestapo Müller" after May 1945, although some evidence points to his death.[45] Eichmann, at least, was working on the assumption that Heinrich Müller, whom he admired unreservedly, was still alive and on the run in the

East. "But he never said he was living in Eastern Europe," Klaus Eichmann added nebulously. It is unlikely that Eichmann really knew anything about Müller's life after the war. We cannot rule out the possibility that this explanation for Eichmann's reluctance to give himself up was partly an idle wish and partly a symptom of his indecision. Ultimately, life in Argentina was a life of freedom with his family, and things were going increasingly well for him. He had bought a plot of land, planned and built a house, and watched his sons grow up. Under these circumstances, it was easy to heed his former comrades' advice against returning to Europe.

Whether it was because of Fritz Bauer's initial investigations, or something Eberhard Fritsch said in Austria, or the increasing number of people returning to Germany, or incautious inquiries by Eichmann's friends—by early 1958, the evidence of Eichmann's whereabouts was mounting. In March a CIA agent in Munich saw a BND file that said Eichmann was in Argentina, living under the name Clemens (though of course with the caveat that he might also be in the Middle East).[46] The addition "since 1952" and the spelling error in the name tells us which file the CIA employee had seen: it was the index-card information on Eichmann from the West German intelligence service, based on the informant's report from June 24, 1952. According to that report, Eichmann's address in Argentina could be obtained from the "editor-in-chief" of *Der Weg*. By 1958, the BND should have had more precise information than that; their colleagues at the BfV in Cologne were already much better informed.[47] The BfV was even making a serious effort to discover more details. "According to unconfirmed information we have here," they told the Foreign Office on April 11, 1958, "a Karl Eichmann (further personal details unknown), who organized the deportation of Jews during the 'Third Reich,' fled to Argentina during the years after the collapse, traveling via Rome under the name CLEMENT. In Argentina he is connected to Eberhard Fritsch, co-owner of the 'Dürer Verlag' and editor of the magazine 'Der Weg,' Buenos Aires, and moves in the circles of former NSDAP members." It would be helpful, the BfV explained, to alert the German embassy in Buenos Aires to this man, who might in fact be *Obersturmbannführer* Adolf Eichmann, whose birth date and former departmental designation were given below. In particular, the office in Cologne wanted to know where Eichmann was living. The embassy should also be instructed "to confirm his personal details and report on his political activities."[48] Whoever the source of this unconfirmed intelligence was, he was certainly reliable and well informed. The small spelling error in the surname (Clement instead of Klement) is both understandable and unimportant: the letter K is less common outside Germany and is frequently altered in the Spanish-speaking world. Even in Lothar Hermann's letters, "Klement" is sometimes spelled with a C: Hermann was able only to hear the name, not see it written, and he chose the most likely spelling. However, Hermann was not the source in this instance: the BfV's source knew more than anyone would have been able to discover from remote Coronel Suárez. Like the BND, he knew about Eichmann's associates in Argentina, and he also knew the Catholic Church had aided his escape and that "Clement" was a name Eichmann had used during his escape, rather than an alias adopted in Argentina. Of course, we now know that the Red Cross passport and all his other documents had been issued in this name in 1948. But at the start of 1958, only someone in Eichmann's circle, or who had helped him escape, would have known these details. This person could have had several reasons for wrongly thinking Eberhard Fritsch was still in Argentina: the information could have been given in the period before Fritsch left, at the end of February, or the informant might have thought he returned to Argentina following his unsuccessful attempt to enter West Germany. Neither Dürer Verlag nor the magazine officially existed anymore at this point, and Fritsch had sold all his real estate.[49] This information allows us to rule out one possible informant, namely Fritsch. Unfortunately, the BfV has not yet made Fritsch's file public, so we must continue to wait in eager anticipation of what else we might learn from its reports on the enterprising publisher.[50] But the BfV's letter contains another revealing clue. It was openly working on the assumption that Eichmann might be politically active again, in a way that could affect the West German constitution. We now know this suspicion was well founded.

The reply from the German embassy, just over two months later, is surprising in several respects: "Inquiries about the wanted man, under the name Clement or other names, have so far yielded no results." A naïve researcher might assume that the embassy would begin its hunt for this name in its own archive, where it would, of course, have found it. As you will remember, Vera Eichmann had appeared at the embassy in person with her sons in 1954, when the Eichmann boys needed passports. The person who got the children to name SS ranks could hardly claim that their name meant nothing to him. But "inquiries" would have been a good idea, too, particularly as the embassy had no shortage of contacts in the Nazi scene. The ambassador, Werner Junker, knew and admired Willem Sassen and had a few other connections to the far right as well. When his stepdaughter wanted to do an internship with a magazine, Junker had no problem with the young lady applying to the *Freie Presse;* its editor-in-chief was Wilfred von Oven, Goebbels's former press adviser.[51] Given that the ambassador himself wasn't exactly taking a "hands-off" approach to the right-leaning elements of the German community, we may wonder whether the inquiries had really been all that fruitless—to say nothing of why such a negligible response required over two months.

After Eichmann was abducted and the passport affair came to light, questions were raised about this remarkable failure. The Foreign Office's legal department announced that the embassy could not have known at that time "that conclusions about the whereabouts of the wanted man Adolf Eichmann could be drawn from these applications."[52] Internal investigations revealed the main reason: prior to Eichmann's abduction, "according to a survey in the embassy, with one exception none of the staff, including the ambassador, had ever heard anything about Adolf Eichmann and his crimes." Heinz Schneppen, who was an ambassador for West Germany himself before becoming an author of academic history books, generously calls this rationale "insufficient vigilance by the consular officers responsible."[53] But a closer look at German relations in Buenos Aires at that time quickly leads one to the conclusion that embassy staff must have been lacking in more qualities than "vigilance": for example, money to buy local newspapers. Otherwise they could have read frequent, detailed articles on exactly who Adolf Eichmann was, and what crimes he had committed, in Argentina's biggest-selling German-language paper. The ladies and gentlemen of the embassy had clearly never read any books on German history, or press coverage from their homeland, either. But they must have been gifted with second sight: the name that, with one exception, they claimed never to have heard in 1960 was one they had given a tip-off for in 1958: Eichmann was "suspected to be in the Middle East." Every little bit helps.

The German embassy's employees seem to have rather exaggerated their willingness to assist: "The embassy will, however, continue to investigate Eichmann's whereabouts, and will report in due course. To this end, we would be grateful for notification of any former members of the NSDAP who at one time were resident here—for example, the editor or employees of the magazine *Der Weg*—who have now been identified in Egypt or the Middle East."[54] Even the BfV was irritated by this disingenuous request. Quite apart from the irrelevance of this information to the search for Eichmann in Argentina, the Foreign Office had forgotten one thing: on August 11, 1954, its own employees had told the BfV that Johann von Leers, who was sometimes mistaken for *Der Weg*'s editor rather than a contributor, had left for Cairo.[55] From today's perspective, it looks like someone was taking the opportunity to find out exactly what the BfV knew. In any case, the BfV in Cologne chose to remind the Foreign Office about its own file in minute detail and to dispense with any further questions about Eichmann.[56] Its correspondence with the Foreign Office would return to the subject only after Eichmann's abduction. In 1958, the BfV must have come to the conclusion that it was pointless asking the Foreign Office and its embassy in Argentina about him.

Unfortunately, we don't know what else the BfV did to find Eichmann in 1958. Apart from the files already mentioned, no further documents have been made public. This also means we are unable to clarify whether Josef Vötterl's position played a role here. Vötterl, who came from Salzburg, had made a career in the criminal and border police, including an assignment with Einsatzgruppe D "in the East," conducting "border security" and "partisan control." Like Eichmann, he had escaped to Argentina, but in 1955 he moved back to Germany for three years. He found work with the BfV. In September 1958, a few days after the BfV's depressing correspondence with the Foreign Office, Vötterl returned to Buenos Aires. He had, as Heinz Schneppen phrases it, "received an offer from an Argentine firm"—and in any case, his salary at the BfV had been so very low.[57] We have no further information about this new, more lucrative offer, but it could hardly have been made on the strength of his experience in "partisan control."

In spite of the behavior of West Germany's offices abroad, and the people there who were authorized to issue directives, the fact remains that in early 1958 the West German authorities once again had enough information to find Eichmann. However, very little is known about it even now: all the files that have been accessed so far have been incidental discoveries. Neither the BND nor the BKA has made its documents available to researchers, even after more than fifty years. And as nice as it would be to reference editions of primary sources like the *Akten zur Auswärtigen Politik der Bundesrepublik Deutschland,* the collections of files commissioned by the Foreign Office, the volumes produced so far reveal the problem: they cover 1949–53 and 1963–79. The 1962 volume was published only in 2010.[58] If one thinks how many classified documents must still be sitting in various archives, and how little enthusiasm there is for transparency, the facts become both obvious and embarrassing: before Eichmann was abducted, people didn't want him to be brought to trial in West Germany—and there are still people who don't want transparency on who, and why this was.

In 1963 the Foreign Office did at least take steps to counter its leading diplomats' dreadful ignorance of German history, by appointing Ernst-Günther Mohr as the new ambassador to Argentina.[59] At least they could be sure he knew who Eichmann was: at the embassy in The Hague in 1941, Mohr had prepared detailed progress reports on the deportation of Dutch Jews for Eichmann's office. Eichmann certainly remembered this episode, mentioning Mohr's energetic support in "Götzen" in 1961.[60] This concern for continuity was not confined to Argentina. Hubert Krier became the ambassador to Paraguay at the end of 1965. In an interview he gave in retirement, he was still visibly perturbed as he recalled: "At that time, before my departure, I received the instruction from the Foreign Office to leave the matter of Mengele alone."[61] If Eichmann had been as cautious as Mengele and confined himself to weeping silently over his deep hatred of Jews and writing paeans to National Socialism in his diaries, then he too would have had a good chance of dying at leisure. Mengele would drown in 1979 while swimming in the sea.

Bormann in Argentina

They had radically changed names, histories and much else. This is
the only way for one man or another to live when the world is hunt-
ing them, or believes them dead.

—Eichmann on Nazis in South America, 1962[62]

Eichmann was hardly unobtrusive during his final year in Argentina.
Since he had gone out on a limb in 1957, making no secret of his presence or his worldview, it would have been impossible for him to retreat
into anonymity once more. He would have had to vanish from Buenos
Aires and start over somewhere else. Instead, he bought a plot of land
on the edge of the city. Klaus Eichmann remembered his father paying
56,000 pesos for 755 square feet of land. Eichmann himself spoke of a
lease with a ten-year duration.[63] A person with so many good friends
could bank on having a steady income. The receipt for building materials was in the name of Señora Liebl de Eichmann. Eichmann threw himself wholeheartedly into the plans for constructing his house, though he
also continued to move in Willem Sassen's circles.

Eichmann's corrections on the transcripts of the Sassen interviews
appear right up to the final tape. He even reviewed the texts Sassen had
written, though he couldn't give them his blessing as they had very little
to do with what he had actually said. Eichmann's wife said more than
once that her husband finished his work with Sassen at the end of 1959.[64]
There is even hard evidence that Eichmann's political activities didn't
stop when the Sassen conversations came to an end. He started writing
a new manuscript for his children, the "Roman Tucumán" (Tucumán
Novel), and took part in a surprising project that historians have never
really been able to evaluate: the collection of documents from the Nazi
period. In 1966 Eichmann's son Klaus would speak of the National
Socialists' attempt to create a tighter international network. "There are
connections among the National Socialists in South America, the Middle East, North America and Europe," he explained. The far-reaching
cooperation of right-wing publishers at the time gives us an impression
of what that might mean. In the last issues of *Der Weg*, these contacts
were obvious even to the outside world. In Cairo, Johann von Leers was
writing a large number of articles from the Middle East, under various

names, and the section of news from around the world expanded significantly. But Klaus Eichmann also spoke of another network: "The thing is [!] organized in such a way that every former department head living somewhere abroad edits and collects the material from his former field. My brother Horst says that departments whose original bosses are dead were allocated other specialists, but under the name of their dead boss. So there was a 'Göring' for the Luftwaffe, a 'Goebbels' for propaganda and so on." And Eichmann's son specifically said: "Our father helped gather this material."[65] Eichmann had one thing in particular to offer in this regard: his second son, who was in the merchant marine. He traveled "between Canada, USA, Africa, South America and Europe from 1959 to 1961," transporting "thick bundles of files." Despite all his later assertions that he wanted his children to stay out of politics and the military, Eichmann clearly involved at least one of his sons in his political activities. And dispatching an international courier with the name Horst Eichmann was anything but a good cover for a perpetrator of crimes against humanity living in Buenos Aires.

The structure of this document-gathering operation throws some light on a frequent question about senior Nazi functionaries in Argentina. Apart from the ridiculous legend about Adolf Hitler in Antarctica, awaiting his return like a deep-frozen version of Napoleon on Elba,[66] one of the most stubbornly persistent rumors about postwar Nazis has been that Martin Bormann was in South America. If Klaus Eichmann's story about how the collection was divided is correct, then "Martin Bormann" really was in South America, as the name for the person collecting files from the Party Chancellery. This would at least explain why credulous journalists like Ladislas Farago and Gerd Heidemann kept protesting they had seen pieces of writing and other information from the postwar period that were signed by "Bormann."

"Avoid Eichmann!"

He was quick to learn the ropes and was greatly valued by his manager. —Unidentified Daimler-Benz staff member[67]

It is always claimed that Eichmann was a pariah in National Socialist society, with whom nobody wanted to be associated. Up until the end of the 1950s, this claim is insupportable, but Eichmann's son had the impression that in the last year his father spent in Argentina, people started to avoid him. For Klaus, the reason was clear: "Dr. Mengele had spread the word: avoid Eichmann. Getting close to him could be dangerous." However, this version of events doesn't add up. It's doubtful that Josef Mengele would have initiated this practice, as he was by no means the less dangerous of the two. The idea that he, of all people, had enough influence in the backward-looking German community to warn people off the organizer of the Final Solution is not particularly plausible. Still, the fact that Eichmann's son believed it points to events that really did take place.

Mengele was worried that he was being pursued, and with good reason. In February 1959 the Frankfurt District Court had issued an arrest warrant for him, and unlike Eichmann, he was living quite openly in Buenos Aires under his own name. By the time the warrant was issued, Mengele had given up his house, which was on the same street as Sassen's, and had fled Argentina to go underground in Paraguay. His diaries show that friends in Argentina thought this response was over the top.[68] In any case, Mengele was no longer in Buenos Aires and could not have called on people to avoid Eichmann. But Eichmann did leave Roberto Mertig's company at this point, which was partly owned by Mengele's father. So we can say that Mengele distanced himself from Eichmann, but not because he was avoiding him. He simply disappeared, and his old-boy network with him. What Klaus Eichmann observed was a general change in mood among the Nazi sympathizers in Buenos Aires. Word of Mengele's frantic flight must have gotten around, as well as news of the changing legal situation in the Federal Republic. The arrest warrants and actual arrests were heaping up, and the trial of the *Einsatzgruppen* in Ulm in 1958 had finally given rise to a public debate on the handling of war crimes. Max Merten, the former head of administration for the Wehrmacht, stood trial in Athens in early 1959 for his involvement in the deportation of Jews from Salonika, having been so astonishingly brazen as to take a vacation in Greece, of all places. In September 1959 a warrant was issued for the arrest of Gerhard Bohne, who had returned home from Argentina and was to be tried for the ten thousand insidious murders committed in the name of euthanasia. The press in Argentina reported on all of it.

As interest in prosecuting Nazi criminals increased, so did people's knowledge about the mass murders, and the number of questions being asked about their organizer. Eichmann's name now reliably turned up in newspapers and books wherever there was mention of Nazi crimes. Even the fact that he always appeared as "Adolf Eichmann," and that nobody was confused about his forenames any longer, shows that something had changed. Other legends about him also started to crumble rapidly. "Not a Templar After All" was the title of an article in the weekly magazine *Die Zeit*.[69]

Eichmann's son would later say that people started bringing his father more and more newspaper articles from their travels. And of course, the fact that the men Eichmann used to spend a lot of time with were traveling abroad was another reason for him to feel abandoned.

But the distance between Eichmann and his old associates can't have been all that great, because they were the people who got him his next job. Horst Carlos Fuldner found him a position at Mercedes-Benz Argentina in Gonzáles Catán, an industrial area two hours' drive to the north. Eichmann started work there on March 20, 1959, as a warehouseman for replacement parts.[70] His references were provided by Horst Carlos Fuldner, a Dr. Dr. Ing. Krass, and Francisco José Viegener. As the deputy director, Hanns Martin Schleyer, learned after Eichmann had been abducted, the applicant "had good references and also made a good impression."[71] Ricardo Klement was properly registered for the statutory pension scheme (no. 1785425). He put his salary expectations at 5,500 pesos per month, around 1,100 Deutschmarks—which at this time was more than the average wage in West Germany.[72] The payroll from the second quarter of 1959 shows that this is what he actually earned.[73] Mercedes-Benz employed a lot of Germans during this period, and several members of the SS. One employee stated that "practically the whole management team [was made up of] immigrants from postwar Germany." Some of them would have known who "Klement" was, but the subject would have been taboo.[74] The sociable Eichmann quickly made new friends at Mercedes-Benz. He introduced them to his family, and after he was abducted, Klaus Eichmann and Willem Sassen asked them to help hide incriminating papers.

Eichmann's new job meant commuting for four hours on the bus every day. He spent his weekends working on the house with his sons, on the plot of land he had bought. It demanded all his attention, as Klaus Eichmann remembered. It also reduced his chances of cultivating other contacts. Eichmann spent his remaining free time at home and seemed calm and secure, reading a lot and playing his violin often. He "particularly loved cśardas and other gypsy airs." In 1939 Eichmann had wanted to put the Austrian Romanies on the first transport to Nisko, but that didn't seem to pose a contradiction for him.[75] Not even his son believed Eichmann was as innocent as he appeared in 1959. Still, Klaus did him the favor of getting married the day before his parents' wedding anniversary and bringing a granddaughter into the family shortly afterward. But another family event was to have greater consequences for Eichmann: in April 1959 his stepmother, Maria Eichmann, died in Linz, and the family carelessly named her daughter-in-law as well as her sons among the mourners. They had evidently forgotten that Vera was officially divorced: the death notice gave her name as "Vera Eichmann."

Fritz Bauer's Sources

> *I had no enemies among the Jews.*
> —Eichmann, Sassen discussions[76]

Simon Wiesenthal read the death notice for Eichmann's stepmother in the *Oberösterreichische Nachrichten*—and later wrote, "But to whom should I have given the news?"[77] Although he had people to talk to in Austria—the Israeli ambassador, for example—previous experience may have made him hesitate. Elsewhere, events were gaining momentum in the hunt for Eichmann—ever more people from various corners of the globe were becoming involved. It is no wonder, then, that the threads of this story sometimes become entangled.

In Austria criminal charges were formally brought against Eichmann on March 25, 1959, in the name of Hermann Langbein's International Auschwitz Committee. Langbein had agreed on this course of action with the Frankfurt lawyer Henry Ormond, who specialized in representing the Nazis' victims. An arrest warrant for Eichmann had been out since the end of the 1940s, and he had been on the wanted list since 1955, but these charges sent a definite signal. On his travels through Poland, Langbein managed to get hold of another photo of Eichmann. He was constantly on the lookout for information or evidence that could be useful in the pursuit of war criminals. Ormond and Langbein were both in touch with Fritz Bauer, although no proof has yet been found that Bauer had taken either of them into his confidence at this point. Still, Langbein's efforts in particular raised the pressure.[78] Hence the following message from the authorities appears all the more confusing: the BfV had obtained "unconfirmed information" in spring 1959 that "Eichmann's wife and his four children have been living in South America, while Eichmann himself is said to have been living somewhere in Europe."[79] It's unclear whether this rumor was due to someone confusing Eichmann with, for example, Sassen on his travels, or whether it originated in a diversionary tactic in Argentina. The remarkable thing about it is that by this point, people clearly knew how many children *Adolf Eichmann,* and not Ricardo Klement, had.

In 1959 a voice from Israel caused further concern in the Eichmann case. Tuviah Friedman, who had started hunting Nazi murderers shortly after the war ended, was in touch with Wiesenthal, and since emigrating to Israel, his idealism had led him to start a document collection in Haifa. Now he was asking questions everywhere. On July 13, 1959, he wrote to Erwin Schüle, the head of the Central Office for the Prosecution of Nazi Criminals in Ludwigsburg, accusing the West German government of doing nothing to catch Adolf Eichmann, because it didn't want to deal with what he had done. Schüle replied within a week, informing Friedman of the existing arrest warrant from 1956 and of the rumors that Eichmann was probably either in Argentina or in one of Israel's neighboring countries. A short time later Schüle wrote again, requesting documents and information on Eichmann, since Friedman had written to him on Haifa Institute for the Documentation of Nazi War Crimes letterhead. Friedman threw himself into the work with gusto, but he wanted to go further than discreetly providing documents. What he didn't know was that huge advances had by now been made in the hunt for Adolf Eichmann, and that his actionism actually threatened its success.

Unlike Isser Harel, Fritz Bauer had not been so quick to give up on the Argentine lead. He had heard nothing more from Lothar Hermann, who had dutifully been sending his letters to the address in North America, but Bauer received other clues that he was on the right track. His colleagues remember their boss getting a visit from Paul Dickopf at the BKA, who had an SS past of his own and was still in touch with people on the extreme right of the political spectrum.[80] Dickopf allegedly suggested to Bauer that he give up his pursuit of Eichmann—and that in any case, it was incorrect to suppose he was in Argentina. This "wish" seems to have been the confirmation Bauer needed that he was getting close.[81]

There was another reason that the public, or at least a section of the public, was getting anxious about this perpetrator having gone unpunished. East Germany had begun to use West Germany's failure to come to terms with its past as a weapon in the Cold War and kept threatening the Federal Republic with unpleasant revelations about its leading figures. With the help of documents originally seized by the Soviets, new details were emerging from East Berlin on a weekly basis. The authorities had no idea what to do against this dangerous weapon, since the revelations were, for the most part, entirely true.[82] In this context, Eichmann's prospective reappearance must have looked like the worst possible catastrophe. According to Irmtrud Wojak's reconstruction of events, which uses accounts by Isser Harel, Fritz Bauer met with the Israeli representatives in summer 1959 and pressed for quick action. Harel claimed that Bauer mentioned a second informant who could attest to Eichmann's whereabouts in Argentina, an SS man whom he couldn't name as it would have put him in danger.

Rumors about this SS informant have abounded. From what we know today about the close relationships that dedicated National Socialists maintained after the war, in particular the ties between Argentina and West Germany—and if we consider how many people knew where Eichmann was—then the question is not who this informant could have been but whom we can rule out. In 1961 an article in the far-right magazine *Nation Europa* accidentally revealed how many of the beans had been spilled on Eichmann in right-wing circles: "Let us first note," wrote F. J. P. Veale (who also contributed to *Der Weg*), "that Eichmann's escape to Argentina had been common knowledge for a long time."[83]

We still don't know who Fritz Bauer's second informant was, as Bauer didn't want to reveal the name. When Isser Harel's book proclaimed to the world that Bauer was using his discretion to shield an SS man, some suspected a "traitor" from within Eichmann's own camps. This suspicion supported the speculation that Willem Sassen had betrayed Eichmann to maximize his profits from the sale of the interview—or conversely, that his attempts to sell the interview had laid a trail to Eichmann's door. But later correspondence between Bauer and Sassen proves that Sassen wasn't his contact in this case.[84] There must have been plenty of possible informants who had served in the SS and now knew exactly where and how Eichmann was living. One former SS man accidentally confirmed Bauer's suspicion that he was on the right track in Argentina: Paul Dickopf, with his cautionary visit to Bauer's office. This qualified Dickopf as a first-rate informant with an SS background, and it would be understandable if Bauer was reluctant to point out this embarrassment to the Federal Republic.

Among friends, however, Fritz Bauer did name someone: he had heard about Ricardo Klement's employment with Mercedes-Benz from a man named "Schneider" (though other spellings are possible), as Thomas Harlan revealed toward the end of his life.[85] This Schneider had something of a past himself, in the *Einsatzgruppen*, but in the late 1950s he had been the head of the "trainee department" at Mercedes in Stuttgart. In this position, he was able to assist in the hunt for Eichmann by giving Bauer access to personnel files and other information. Unfortunately, I have not been able to convince Daimler that the possibility their staff may have included not only a notorious mass murderer but also someone who aided a famous German attorney general makes cooperating with a researcher a worthwhile exercise. They didn't even take up my offer of a list of possible Schneiders, with their dates of birth.[86] On making inquiries, I was merely told that in 1959 no one in the company could have known who Ricardo Klement was.[87] I am obviously not the right person to tell them that his identity has now been known for fifty years, and that the knowledge brings its own responsibility. But there are some things it takes time to realize. Perhaps someone else will succeed in convincing a globally respected company that having once employed a man who helped in the search for Adolf Eichmann would not cast a shadow over its history or even dent its image. Even if this Mercedes employee helped Fritz Bauer only because Bauer knew about his (possible) past with the *Einsatzgruppen*, he still showed more courage in doing the right thing than most people could take credit for.

But when it comes to Fritz Bauer's informants, another clue points in a different direction entirely. In private, Bauer once referred to a second Jewish informant in addition to Lothar Hermann. Bauer told a close friend about this source, who had informed him of Eichmann's living situation in Argentina. This was, as Thomas Harlan remembered, a "Brazilian Jew, formerly Polish, a survivor of the Sobibór uprising, but he never told me the name."[88] Shortly after Ben-Gurion announced to the Knesset that Eichmann was a prisoner in Israel, for a brief period claims were made in Tel Aviv that a Jewish refugee from Poland had provided the clue to where Eichmann was living.[89] There was also much talk about Brazil, as Josef Mengele was suspected to be there. Only the key word *Sobibór* is missing from this connection. But in 1960 that name meant very little to most people. Detailed studies of this site of atrocities, and of its survivors, have begun to appear only in recent years.

Sobibór was one of the death camps of Operation Reinhard, and the National Socialists planned to leave no survivors there.[90] Largely thanks to an inmates' uprising, at least forty-seven people managed to escape. In total, only sixty-two people survived the inferno. And only two of those Polish-born men emigrated to Brazil in the late 1940s: Chaim Korenfeld, who was born in 1923 in Izbica, and Stanislav "Shlomo" Szmajzner, born in 1927 in Puławy. Szmajzner was one of the masterminds of the Sobibór uprising. We know little about Korenfeld's life in Brazil, except that he traveled there via Italy in 1949. Szmajzner, however, originally wanted to emigrate to Israel and was just visiting relatives in Rio de Janeiro. He arrived in Brazil in 1947 and stayed there for the rest of his life. He opened a jeweler's, built it into a successful business within ten years, and sold it in 1958, buying an island in the rain forest with the profit. He then went into cattle farming.[91] In 1968 he published his story under the title *Sobibór—The Tragedy of an Adolescent Jew*,[92] which sounds like an understatement in the face of what he had experienced. Szmajzner had arrived in the Sobibór camp in May 1942, with his jeweler's toolkit. He was not yet fifteen and had been naïve enough to believe the lies about "relocation." What saved this goldsmith's apprentice from immediate death was that the SS men in Sobibór were keen on gold rings with SS runes and classy monograms for their whip handles.[93] Gustav Wagner, the deputy commandant, recognized the boy's talent, and fortunately, gold coins and teeth were readily available. Szmajzner always knew where the material came from for the jewelry he had to make. He also knew his parents and siblings had been killed in Sobibór. His forced labor brought him into contact with Wagner and the camp commandant, Franz Stangl, whose faces were indelibly imprinted on the young man's mind. Many years later Szmajzner would meet the pair for a second time. In 1968 he saw Stangl on a street in Brazil, and following effective pressure from Simon Wiesenthal, Stangl was brought to trial.[94] Gustav Wagner's former prisoner also identified him in 1978, and although Wagner escaped prosecution, he committed suicide—at least, according to the official police report. "Szmajzner let it be known," another Sobibór survivor said, "that he was entirely uninvolved in Wagner's death."[95]

Stanislav Szmajzner was a Polish Jew and a businessman in Brazil, and if he had heard about Eichmann's life in Argentina, he might well have put this information to use in the late 1950s. It's certainly possible that he knew where Eichmann was. Business trips between Brazil and Argentina were frequent occurrences. Hans-Ulrich Rudel had been to Brazil early on, and even Eberhard Fritsch had visited the country. Pedro Pobierzym, the former Wehrmacht soldier from Poland who did business with the Nazis in Argentina, and procured the tape recorder for Sassen, also traveled to Brazil on business. A resourceful man could easily have made inquiries in the Nazi community of Buenos Aires, especially if he already knew what he was looking for. If you needed a man to make discreet inquiries in Argentina in 1959, Szmajzner would have been the ideal person to approach. Since we have no reason to doubt what Fritz Bauer said, we have every reason to believe that two Jewish informants in Latin America, as well as former SS men, provided the crucial clues that allowed Eichmann to be brought to trial in Jerusalem.

Eichmann in Kuwait

At the start of 1960, Attorney General Bauer will make a request to the Emirate in Kuwait, via the responsible ministries in Bonn, for Eichmann to be extradited. Bauer sees no impediment to the extradition in international law.

—Press release, December 23, 1959[96]

From mid-1959 the rumors that Eichmann was in the Middle East started to be aired more frequently, with a new variation. Hans Weibel-Altmeyer, a journalist with a vivid imagination, acting on a suggestion from Simon Wiesenthal, traveled to the Middle East to search for Nazis there.[97] During an interview, the ex-mufti Amin al-Husseini apparently handed him an anti-Semitic brochure by Johann von Leers and even confirmed: "Yes indeed, I know Eichmann well and I can assure you that he is still alive." Weibel-Altmeyer was also offered Eichmann "for sale" in Damascus at a price of $50,000.[98] If a reporter was able to find out that "certain Arab circles have been discussing the 'Eichmann deal' for days," then this information must also have come to the attention of one of the intelligence services. The BND in particular had informants in the field, in the shape of Alois Brunner and Franz Rademacher. In any case, in late September 1959, the BfV received information to the effect that Eichmann was in Damascus or Qatar.[99] The informant even claimed he had met Brunner and Eichmann personally. Tom Segev suggests that this source may have been Weibel-Altmeyer himself: the reporter wrote a story for the Cologne tabloid *Neue Illustrierte* in summer 1960, about visiting a bar where Eichmann and Brunner were sitting at the next table.

The BfV, however, had clues of a very different sort as well—clues that pointed to friends in the Middle East trying to create a new life for Eichmann in 1959. The source here was Ernst Wilhelm Springer, an arms dealer from Bad Segeberg who had set himself up in the Middle East. According to the BfV report, Springer "said, regarding the articles in the press in October 1959, that Eichmann is currently in a Middle Eastern country friendly with the FLN, and from time to time meets his associate Fischer [Alois Brunner]. The intention is for Eichmann to be found a management position with an oil company in Kuwait, however this plan is said to have been dropped following the press campaign."[100]

These fresh headlines about the Middle East caused a commotion, and the Federation of German Industry immediately denied the rumors. At least, this is what they said when a query arrived from Hermann Langbein, on Comité International d'Auschwitz–headed paper.[101] But they "took your letter as an opportunity to conduct thorough inquiries into the matter of whether any large German industrial firms are employing a certain Adolf Eichmann in Kuwait." They searched for two months. Even the group representing the interests of German firms in Kuwait had been tasked with this investigation. "The result is completely negative," and no one in the Middle East even knew who this Eichmann was. But anyone who *did* know now also knew how much effort was being put into the hunt for Eichmann in the Middle East. And if anyone had been thinking of employing Adolf Eichmann, Hermann Langbein's inquiry (which had been approved by a confidant of Fritz Bauer's) would certainly have put him off.[102] The BfV's report contains a further remarkable detail: according to Springer, "The Head of the United Arab Republic Medani apparently knew that Eichmann was in Bad Godesberg."[103]

It's impossible to establish whether this story was fantasy, a case of mistaken identity, or a deliberate rumor, but the increasing interest in Eichmann is obvious. Still, it is certain that until his abduction, Eichmann never left Argentina and his family. Whether he might somehow have managed to get to the Middle East and live there incognito in 1959, had he chosen to, is another question. He was already sitting in a trap of his own making; relocating to North Africa would only have made it easier for those hunting him to capture him. In any case, the rumors provided an effective cover for Fritz Bauer's hunt for the mass murderer. All the little pieces of misinformation that emerged in summer 1959 were probably more than just coincidence.

On August 20, 1959, Erwin Schüle sent new, confidential information from Ludwigsburg to Tuviah Friedman: Eichmann was in Kuwait, working for an oil firm.[104] We don't know if Schüle was aware that his information was incorrect or if he was being used to lay a false trail. The evidence suggests that Fritz Bauer, in cooperation with the Israeli police, was using Schüle to spread this new version of the Middle East story. Experience in hunting Nazi criminals in Argentina had shown that the German embassy there was not entirely reliable. Bauer may also not have trusted the head of the Central Office in Ludwigsburg, although nothing suggests that he knew about Schüle's own SS history. In any case, the danger that Eichmann would find out how close they had already come to him was growing with every month, so disinformation was an obvious strategy.

Tuviah Friedman was so delighted with this progress that in October he took it upon himself to give the Kuwait news to the press. An October 12 article in the *Argentinisches Tageblatt* was headlined "Claims Adolf Eichmann Has Been in Kuwait Since 1945." Among other things, it reported that "the leader of the Israeli institute in Haifa, . . . Tuviah Friedman, said this institute had earlier put out a reward of $10,000 for finding and capturing Eichmann." Friedman apologized to Schüle for this obvious indiscretion, though Schüle was angered by it—but that didn't stop Friedman from taking further action. His desire to see Eichmann in court was irrepressible. Fritz Bauer and the Israeli intelligence service made cunning use of the Kuwait feint, acting as if it were a clue

to be taken seriously. On October 13 the *Süddeutsche Zeitung* considered the possibility of having Eichmann extradited, and over the next
few days, the press reported on the official inquiry, apparently made
by the Israeli foreign minister to the West German and British authorities, as to whether Eichmann really was in Kuwait. The spokesman for
the Israeli government said that "Israel is addressing the case of Eichmann, who is on the list of wanted persons from the Attorney General's office in Frankfurt am Main." The *Argentinisches Tageblatt,* among
others, reported this announcement as well.[105] Not knowing anything
about the disinformation, Tuviah Friedman used an election event for
Ben-Gurion to call for a reward to be offered for Eichmann's capture in
Kuwait, which the press also encouraged.[106]

Over the following months, the Nazi hunters did all they could to
keep this erroneous information in the media. Bauer kept holding press
conferences and giving interviews, and more press releases emerged
from Israel, achieving the regular coverage Bauer had hoped for. At
the start of January 1960, there was talk of an extradition agreement,
though the British authorities denied it and the British Foreign Office
refused to help. Bauer fed the press details about the "sheikh" for whom
Eichmann was supposed to be "working as an agent for German companies," although "discretion" prevented him from naming these companies. Bauer even announced he would prepare this information for the
Foreign Office, now that all the obstacles of international law had been
overcome.[107] Journalists were left wondering why the Foreign Office
had stayed so quiet on the matter: "So the question is now," said the
Deutsche Woche in Munich, "why the Foreign Office has neither denied
the rumor, nor officially confirmed whether it is correct."[108] The story
was so convincing that the German authorities started to doubt their
own information. The Foreign Office asked the Federal Ministry for
Justice whether it had any information on Eichmann's whereabouts in
Kuwait or Egypt and received an irritated reply: "It cannot even be said
with any degree of certainty that Eichmann is still alive."[109]

Only a single newspaper firmly refuted the story: *Der Reichsruf,* the
propaganda sheet of the Deutsche Reichspartei (DRP). On October 24,
Adolf von Thadden, the man who was so concerned with Hans-Ulrich
Rudel's political career in Germany, published an article headlined "So
Where Is Eichmann?" "Eichmann was hidden in Italy by a Catholic

monastery," Thadden said, "and, with the help of senior Catholic con-nections, was then taken from Italy to Argentina." It was simple, pub-lic betrayal. "Herr Schüle and Israel's search in Kuwait will be in vain," Thadden scoffed. And he added threateningly, "It is very regrettable, because if Eichmann really were the notorious murderer of the Jews, greater clarity about this horrific event could be gained through his con-viction." The dream of the six million being exposed as a lie oozes from between the lines. And whether *Der Reichsruf* was determined to pro-voke a testimony from Eichmann that would redeem National Social-ism, or the garrulous editor had simply been unable to keep his mouth shut,[110] something very strange had happened. Thadden later expressed contempt for his former contributor Willem Sassen, accusing him of being a faithless traitor to Eichmann—and yet here Thadden himself was, thumbing his nose at the Nazi hunters and trumpeting Eichmann's hiding place when there was no need to. It was the first time Argentina had been mentioned in the press. And the extremist from Lower Saxony made no secret of his source: he openly referred to "German emigrant circles," although he did stress that they "avoided" Eichmann. The clue was given more weight by the fact that everyone—or at least the reader-ship of *Der Reichsruf*—knew that a member of these circles had been on the DRP candidate list since 1953. So did anyone spot Thadden's piece? Yes: the observant staff of the BfV.[111] There, the article from the anticon-stitutional publication was thought "noteworthy" and dutifully pasted into the Eichmann file. This actually causes one to wonder whether even releasing all the government files would suffice for us to grasp what must have gone on among the German authorities during these months.

Der Reichsruf's distribution had dwindled to almost nothing, and the article provoked no real reaction. Thadden, who would later become chair of the National Democratic Party and worked for the British intel-ligence service, MI6, was never accused of having betrayed his com-rade.[112] Fritz Bauer's disinformation strategy, however, was working splendidly. It was a necessary diversion, as Eichmann's reaction to the news demonstrates. Klaus Eichmann remembered the evening his wife heard on the radio that Adolf Eichmann, who was suspected of being in Kuwait, was wanted by Interpol. "I raced out to San Fernando and shook Father awake: 'Interpol is hunting you.' It left him cold. He just said: 'Damn it, you're waking me in the middle of the night for this? You

could have waited 'til morning with it. Go home and get some sleep.'"
His father consulted friends over the following days, and none of them
found the news disconcerting or even took it seriously.[113]

In the meantime, Lothar Hermann had read the article in the *Argentinisches Tageblatt* in which Tuviah Friedman spoke of a reward of
$10,000. He had lost all contact with Bauer and had not received an
answer from anyone else either, so he immediately wrote to Friedman
in Israel offering information. The article gave him the impression that
at last someone was taking the matter seriously. At first Hermann said
nothing about his daughter, who was now living in the United States.[114]
He had no idea that the "documentation center" was the private collection of a dedicated Nazi hunter with no financial resources at his
disposal. He believed it was a national office, which also led to the misunderstanding that a reward really existed. Hermann made it clear that
this time he wouldn't reveal any information without being paid in
advance. Friedman conveyed this information to Schüle on November
8, without mentioning Hermann's name. By this point, Schüle seems to
have heard about the real status of the manhunt and urged Friedman
in the strongest terms to hold back. He had been "disappointed to learn
that there has still been no let-up in the Eichmann affair. Please support me in keeping the 'Eichmann case' absolutely taboo for the immediate future, . . . no publications, no speeches, no other actions of any
sort," because it all "disrupts our efforts to clear up the Eichmann case."
To emphasize this point, Schüle hinted at definite success in the manhunt.[115] Still, he would have to repeat this exhortation before Friedman
actually backed off. Friedman let Hermann know that he had passed on
his information to the World Jewish Congress representative in Jerusalem, and that someone was certain to be in touch.[116]

From Lothar Hermann's perspective, the course of events became
even more tortuous than for Tuviah Friedman. On December 26, 1959,
a representative of the Jewish Community of Argentina, one "Herr G.
Schurmann," visited him, and he couldn't figure out who had actually
sent him. He assumed it was Friedman, but Friedman later claimed not
to have done anything further.[117] Now that he had heard the Middle
East news, Friedman didn't believe Hermann anymore.[118] Hermann's
subsequent letters show that for him, Fritz Bauer, Tuviah Friedman, and
Mossad formed a single entity, conspiring with one another to extract
information from him without providing appropriate compensation.

But only a handful of people knew what had really taken place, in absolute secrecy. Hermann was not one of them. For by this point, the abduction of Adolf Eichmann by Mossad was a done deal.[119]

The hunt for Eichmann is the best example of a success achieved via a complex nexus. Human activity is rarely monocausal; it is usually the cumulative effect of various strands of activity with many people involved, all doing what they do for different reasons. Of course Paul Dickopf had not intended to encourage Bauer with his behavior, and obviously Tuviah Friedman had never wanted to endanger the success of the hunt. Simon Wiesenthal simply refused to give up, and was determined to see Eichmann stand trial. Isser Harel was looking for a sensational operation for his intelligence service, and naturally, he was also searching for the "number-one enemy of the Jews," as was David Ben-Gurion. Ben-Gurion also had to keep in mind the German-Israeli dialogue, on which their trade agreement and Israel's supply of armaments depended. And finally Fritz Bauer wanted to prosecute Eichmann in Germany. Eichmann's capture was the result not of a chain of events but of a series of threads that gradually wove themselves into a net. But then in hindsight, as I said, this is a much more common pattern for human activity than we would like to think.

In contrast to the hunt for Eichmann, his final arrest almost seems a simple matter. On December 6, 1959, Ben-Gurion confided to his diary that he had asked Isser Harel to prepare a Mossad team to identify and abduct Adolf Eichmann.[120] Fritz Bauer had been to Israel again, stressing the need for quick action. In November the Israeli ambassador to Vienna, Ezechiel Sahar, had told Simon Wisenthal about the renewed interest in Eichmann. Wiesenthal put together a comprehensive dossier, using all the information in his possession. This time Sahar was able to tell him that Israel was very impressed with his work. He even gave Wiesenthal a list of further questions. When Eichmann's father, "Adolf Eichmann, retired company director," died on February 5, the death notice,[121] like the one for Eichmann's stepmother, named Vera Eichmann among the mourners. When Wiesenthal saw it, he reacted quickly. On the slim chance that Eichmann or his wife would turn up at the funeral, he had someone take photographs of all the mourners. Neither of them was there, but Wiesenthal now had photos of Eichmann's brothers, who had always looked similar to him.[122] Isser Harel later claimed that Wiesenthal had had no part in the Mossad operation, but his own agent Zvi Aharoni confirmed that these photos had allowed him to identify the fifty-four-year-old Eichmann more easily than the photos from the Nazi period alone would have done.[123] Harel sent Aharoni to Argentina in February 1960. It was not his first time in Buenos Aires: Aharoni had stayed there in March 1959 for another assignment.[124] His knowledge and contacts allowed him to track Eichmann down, even though he had just moved from Chacabuco Street to his new house. The Mossad team followed at the end of April. Helped by useful contacts in Buenos Aires, they achieved the success that would make Mossad famous: the "number-one enemy of the Jews" was abducted on May 11, 1960, outside his house, as he was returning home.

Eichmann blamed himself for his capture. He had "felt so safe in Argentina, where I lived for 11 years in freedom and safety," that he had overlooked all the signs of danger.[125] He had been a "fool" not to go to Tucumán, Chile, or Asia—tellingly, he didn't mention the Middle East. In Israel, Eichmann set down a detailed description of the abduction from his own perspective.[126] These accounts confirmed that it happened the way the Mossad agents claimed, even if their descriptions differ on various details.[127] Eichmann said he realized he had been under surveillance for months, which was more than a refusal to admit he had been outsmarted. In his notes, he describes incidents that had actually happened as the team was searching for him, though he couldn't have read the Mossad agents' report. Aharoni's attempt to question his daughter-in-law had been suspicious. And he had noticed the series of cars parked near his house. The danger had been so palpable that his son had offered to lend him a gun. His wife suffered nightmares commensurate with her Catholic upbringing: she saw her husband in a white, blood-soaked hair shirt.[128] But the man who had felt so welcome in Argentina made one fatal error. "However, I didn't think," Eichmann wrote in 1961, "that this could lead to an abduction, but believed it was an operation by the Argentine police, and that maybe there was an investigation going on here, as had happened with other people."[129] For a National Socialist, the Argentine police force was a true friend in need, upon whose protection one could always rely.

I Had No Comrades

I am especially delighted that my many Argentine friends remembered me with their gifts of flowers on my birthday.
                                    —Eichmann to his family, April 17, 1961

When her husband didn't arrive home that night as expected, Vera Eichmann raised the alarm with her son. Eichmann's disappearance unleashed a flurry of activity that shows how much a part of Argentina's shady German community the Eichmanns had become. Adolf Eichmann was abducted on May 11, 1960. He was hidden in a house in Buenos Aires and put on a plane to Israel ten days later.[130] Until David Ben-Gurion's announcement on May 23, no one in Argentina knew where Eichmann was, though this information was very important to a great many people. Saskia Sassen remembers a crowd, including the Eichmann boys, suddenly turning up at the house, and the days of upheaval that followed, with more and more people wanting information or offering help. It was disconcerting for the children: they were used to social gatherings in the house, but now people had stopped caring what they did or didn't hear. Saskia Sassen's mother was on the verge of a nervous breakdown, and when Eichmann's abduction became known, she left the family for a few weeks, unable to stand the tension or her husband's entanglement in the whole affair.[131] Vera Eichmann claimed she never knew what her husband had done, though she also said her first thought was that he had been kidnapped by Jews. Only Willem Sassen and her husband's other friends prevented her from going to the police. Horst Carlos Fuldner was among those friends. He felt a responsibility toward the family and responded to the call for help right away.[132] "Father's best friend," Klaus Eichmann said later, "forced us to think calmly." Perhaps their father had stayed out after one too many glasses of wine, or maybe he had had an accident and had been taken to the hospital—two possibilities that the Eichmann family had not thought of at first, out of sheer terror of Jewish retribution. "We spent two days searching the police stations, the hospitals and the morgues. In vain. What remained was the realization: they had got him." Klaus Eichmann traveled to Mercedes-Benz with Sassen, to meet his father's friend and to hide manuscripts there.[133] The most trusted of Eichmann's associates spread out across the city and kept watch on the transport hubs: the harbors and railroad stations. Sassen, as Klaus Eichmann recalled in 1966 without a trace of suspicion, took the airport. They also organized a guard for the family. Up to three hundred members of a "Peronist youth group" kept watch over the house, said Eichmann's son with some pride. Some even talked of violent retaliation, like kidnapping the Israeli ambassador or mounting an attack on the embassy. But instead Fuldner found the family alternative accommodations, and for the time being they waited to see what would happen.[134]

In spite of the fevered search that followed the abduction on May 11, 1960, Ben-Gurion's speech almost two weeks later took the rest of the world by surprise. The CIA files show that the agency too had had to ask other "friendly intelligence services" what had actually happened, perhaps because the sympathizers in Argentina behaved with particular discretion in this volatile situation,[135] or because the clues were wrongly evaluated. In any case, the files that have since been released by the U.S. intelligence services, the BfV, and the German Foreign Office contain no evidence to show that anyone had the slightest awareness of the Mossad operation. However, one of the German ambassador's close contacts in the Buenos Aires Nazi scene may not have been completely unsuspecting.

José Moskovits, the chair of the Jewish Association of Survivors of Nazi Persecution in Buenos Aires, remembers a surprising incident in the German embassy. He is entirely certain that it took place "two, maximum three months" before Eichmann's abduction. "Two gentlemen arrived from Bonn, one of them from the German intelligence service, and demanded Eichmann's file." An altercation took place, as a helpful member of the embassy staff had lent Moskovits this file shortly before, together with Josef Mengele's, and so it wasn't at hand in the embassy. The person responsible, according to Moskovits, was fired immediately.[136]

We can prove that José Moskovits was indeed gathering information on Eichmann and Mengele at that precise point, since he was Simon Wiesenthal's point of contact in Argentina, and his correspondence with Wiesenthal documents their exchange of information.[137] He also remained active in the search for Mengele for many years. Moskovits, who was born in Hungary, had excellent contacts in the Argentine security services and was active in many other areas as well. Having made numerous compensation claims that resulted in the return of Jewish property stolen during the Nazi period, he had turned the Association of Survivors into an institution that was taken seriously. And he had another reason to remember the time of Eichmann's abduction. Zvi Aharoni and the Mossad team turned to him for assistance, and he used his connections to help them rent the apartment and obtain the vehicles for the planned abduction.[138]

Moskovits's contacts with the German embassy even enabled him to take Zvi Aharoni into the building to do research. On his first trip, between March 1 and April 7, 1960, Aharoni traveled under a false name on a diplomatic passport, posing as a representative from the finance department of the Israeli Foreign Ministry.[139] There is little reason to doubt Moskovits's recollections and the dates he provided. The only troubling thing in this story is the idea that an ambassador might come down so heavily on an employee, for giving archive access to the recognized representative of a survivors' organization. We will leave aside for the moment the point that the embassy had a file on Eichmann, even though it claimed not to have any kind of information about him in 1958 and, a few months after the abduction, declared that only one person there had known who Eichmann was. Still more irritating is the question of what made representatives of the Federal Republic travel all the way to Buenos Aires in spring 1960 to ask about Eichmann. If they had been looking into the current state of the investigation or the arrest warrant, a glance at the files in West Germany would have sufficed. The timing of the visit is significant, in any case.

At the end of February 1960, as Zvi Aharoni was setting off for Argentina to prepare for the abduction, preparations for another delicate mission were being made in West Germany. The first meeting between Konrad Adenauer and David Ben-Gurion was to be a crucial step for future German-Israeli relations. A wave of anti-Semitism had swept through the Federal Republic just after Christmas 1959; it started with swastikas appearing on synagogues and ended with the destruction of Jewish cemeteries. The BfV counted "470 incidents" up to January 28, 1960, "and an additional 215 instances of childish graffiti." The effect abroad was devastating, and the federal government fell over itself to take action, rushing through changes to the school history curriculum.[140] Its eagerness to avoid any embarrassment in the run-up to the highly sensitive meeting could have led it to conduct investigations in Argentina.

Information had been stacking up on Eichmann's whereabouts, and an "open letter to the chancellor" from *Obersturmbannführer* (retired) Adolf Eichmann at the time of a German-Israeli meeting could have had serious repercussions.

Fritz Bauer's increasing devotion to the hunt for those responsible for exterminating the Jews was also becoming impossible to ignore. As excessively cautious as Hesse's attorney general was, his efforts to take the search to Buenos Aires via Brazil seem not to have gone entirely unnoticed. A short time after Ben-Gurion's declaration that Eichmann was in Israel, *Der Spiegel* published exclusive clues about Fritz Bauer's second informant. It said the initial tip-off on Eichmann's whereabouts had come from a "Brazilian Jew."[141] The article also speculated on whether the Israelis had abducted Eichmann at this specific time to "keep up the moral pressure on the Federal Republic, thereby ensuring further economic aid." The Hamburg magazine was brimming with information from well-informed sources. Bauer was extremely concerned that his progress would be discovered, as shown by more than simply his exasperation as he pressed for action in Israel in late 1959. The wealth of ideas that the attorney general fed to federal German agencies like the Foreign Office, making misleading requests in an apparent effort to force the extradition of Eichmann from Kuwait, reveals Bauer's mistrust of the German authorities. In spring 1960, if the Foreign Office, the BKA, or even the BND had asked Bauer where Eichmann was, it would have received the same answer they had all been giving out for years: Eichmann was in the Middle East.

Some people clearly feared that the Adviser on Jewish Affairs might turn up during this phase of the delicate German-Israeli discussions, as we can see from later insinuations that the Israelis abducted him only to influence these negotiations in their favor. But what must Ben-Gurion have been feeling as he met Konrad Adenauer, knowing that an Eichmann trial was finally within striking distance? The German chancellor had no idea that, three days before the meeting in New York's Waldorf Astoria, Zvi Aharoni had reported from Buenos Aires that he had found Eichmann's new address.

Even for a resourceful agent, it had been no easy task. Investigations in Buenos Aires became more difficult in February–March 1960, despite ample help from the embassy staff. Eichmann had just moved and left no forwarding address: the plot that he had bought was in a kind of no-man's-land on the outskirts of Buenos Aires. Aharoni managed to discover the new address only after making thorough investigations and using some very clever tricks. The man whom people called "Mossad's Grand Inquisitor" laid a trap for one of the Eichmann sons by claiming he had a present for him. Rafael Eitan is still full of praise for Aharoni, without whom, he is certain, the trail would have gone cold. The operation certainly wouldn't have succeeded without luck and a great deal of skill. Still, Zvi Aharoni proved that even an Israeli, who had no relationship to the right-wing German community, could find Eichmann—provided, of course, one really wanted to find him.

Unfortunately, a visit to the embassy would have yielded only the information that Vera Eichmann and the children were known (and on record) there. No current address was given for them. The Federal Republic representatives whom José Moskovits remembered would not likely have been able to discover where Eichmann was living in the short time they were on hand. And what would they have done with this information? Still, following their visit to the embassy, they did not step up their search. People tend not to think others are more resourceful than themselves, and as the events that followed show, the German representatives didn't attribute this quality to the Israeli intelligence service. One of the German Chancellery's reasons for keeping the Eichmann files closed to researchers is the danger that some ambiguous remark made by staff at that time might "substantially compromise or even endanger friendly relations with foreign public offices."[142] Given the events at the start of 1960, we can at least guess what this rationale could mean. But it makes full disclosure of the BND's Eichmann files all the more important. It's bad enough that the service did very little to find Eichmann, and that BND workers didn't think their Israeli colleagues or an attorney general in Hesse capable of it. But unless the files are released, the terrible suspicion also remains that the BND might even have tried to prevent the capture.

Mossad's triumph obviously came as a surprise to everyone. On May 23, 1960, the news of Eichmann's reappearance spread quickly, along with a frenzy of activity. The daily papers were suddenly full of photos of Eichmann and details of his crimes. Based on the wealth of information that had long been held in libraries and archives, people all over the world managed to write pages and pages of articles. The announcement also caused turmoil in West German politics. The news was sprung on the former federal president, Theodor Heuss, during his first visit to Israel. His reaction was remarkably collected, as he explained to the press that Eichmann would, without question, receive a fair trial in Israel. Reactions in Bonn were more horrified: Konrad Adenauer wanted to have Eichmann retrospectively declared to be Austrian, so Germany wouldn't be responsible for him. Defense commissions were hastily convened, and an attempt was made to coordinate all the institutions involved in the case, from the Federal Press Office to the BfV and intelligence service. They formed "Eichmann working groups"— but not, of course, with the aim of discovering who this unknown man in an Israeli jail was. The Federal Press Office mounted an elaborate media campaign in a very short space of time. Raphael Gross has found evidence of a planned film project, designed to paint the Federal Republic in a positive light, titled *Paradise and Fiery Furnace*.[143] The fear and helplessness in the face of the approaching trial could not have been described more clearly.

Only a small percentage of the material that West German institutions prepared at this point is currently accessible, but even that shows that people feared the worst. Eichmann was back and had brought with him more than a shadow of the past. The people who feared the trial most included all those former Nazis who had found their footing in the Federal Republic, with no real repercussions for their own involvement in mass murder. They were all afraid for their jobs. Former employees of the RSHA now had careers in the police, the BKA, and the BND. The staff of the Foreign Office also had cause for concern. The fact that the embassy in Argentina had issued passports to Eichmann's sons in their real names several years previously did not bode well. And the embassy's "inability" to find Eichmann in 1958, following a very specific request, looked embarrassingly like aiding and abetting a wanted criminal. The comprehensive dossiers on Eichmann's life in Argentina, which the embassy personnel were suddenly able to send to Bonn upon request, revealed just how much they could have found out (or had found out) by conducting an investigation there. Their awkward assurance that before the abduction no one in the embassy knew who Eichmann was simply seemed impertinent. And the contact between the embassy staff and Eichmann's circle of friends could no longer be concealed. The German ambassador was able to provide a detailed report on Willem Sassen, which reveals that he not only knew Sassen well but also shared many of his political views. This level of involvement nearly made his boss, Foreign Minister Heinrich von Brentano, lose his composure. It seemed, he said, "that some of our missions are not giving sufficient reports of these remnants [!] of National Socialism, and are not taking adequate precautions to distance themselves from them in an unambiguous way."[144]

Brentano didn't seem worried that some of his colleagues in Bonn were among these remnants. And his instructions were wasted on Ambassador Werner Junker. At the end of 1962, Junker would still do everything in his power to prevent the extradition of the mass murderer Josef Schwammberger. He would be strongly supported by Constantin von Neurath, the director of Siemens Argentina S.A. Neurath would explain at length that he had employed this expert in ghetto management "at the company for 12 years." The idea of handing men like him over to the West German judicial system made both the ambassador and the Siemens director "objectively very concerned." They anticipated that Schwammberger would be "urgently needed" in the following years, "and his absence [would] create huge problems for the firm."[145] And the inventive ambassador added suggestions for how Argentine law could be cleverly deployed against the interests of German courts. So the hope that the Eichmann trial might have changed things was not fulfilled—on the contrary, the affair taught people a few tricks. In the fall of 1960, the embassy's errors were effectively dismissed as a communication issue resulting from a lack of expertise, and a public scandal was avoided. The only fear was that Adolf Eichmann probably remembered his Foreign Office colleagues only too well. Nobody could say whether he would mention them during the trial. So taking care of their charges in Argentina became even more important.

Eichmann's knowledge also posed a problem for institutions that had "denazified" a large number of former comrades by employing them in public services. They included the BKA, where a former SS man served as the president's permanent representative; at least forty-seven gentlemen from the death's head order served alongside him.[146] The intelligence services had also been storing up this kind of trouble for themselves. Out of a fear of Bolshevism, they had taken into their ranks men with a past whom Eichmann knew very well, among them Wilhelm Höttl, Otto von Bolschwing, Franz Rademacher, and Alois Brunner.[147] The BND had succeeded in removing Brunner's name from the wanted

list in Greece only a few months previously, with the help of the German
embassy in Athens. It didn't want to risk losing one of its most important connections in the Middle East.[148]

Compared with such revelations, the case of Adenauer's (far-)right-
hand man Hans Globke looked comparatively harmless. People had
grown used to East Germany's attacks on prominent people like Globke
and routinely discredited them as Eastern propaganda. But these nerves
were particularly raw, as evidenced by the federal government's firm
refusal to provide legal aid for Eichmann—although as a German citizen, he had every right to it.[149] The government preferred to tolerate
National Socialists financing Eichmann's defense in secret, with the
knowledge of the BND. His lawyer, however, would have his "costs" paid
by the State of Israel.[150] As a precaution against too many damaging
revelations during the course of the trial, the deals agreed to in advance
with Israel were frozen "until the end of the Eichmann trial."[151] Only
on January 22, 1962, did Adenauer let Ben-Gurion know the promised
accommodations could now be granted.[152]

Other people had more specific concerns. Luis Schintlholzer had
always taken a great deal of pleasure in telling people he had helped
Eichmann escape Germany and had even chauffeured him personally
to the Austrian border. He was now confronted with a summons to
provide a witness statement.[153] As the holder of a fake West German
passport, he appears to have thought complying too risky a prospect;
he absconded and went into hiding in Munich. An acquaintance of his
told the BND that Schintlholzer had made some inquiries in Innsbruck,
wanting to turn himself in, but had been advised to wait until September 1960 at the earliest. Schintlholzer told this acquaintance, with some
relief, that if he waited, he would apparently face a prison term of just
five to seven years, of which he would have to serve two or three. His
concern about being incriminated by Eichmann's testimony proved
unfounded. Schintlholzer did, in fact, turn himself in at the start of the
trial in April 1961. He was placed in custody and investigated for a year
but was then released and remained a free man until his death in 1989.
He held back a little on the stories about how he had been the notorious
prisoner's chauffeur, but he never hid his political views. His wife headed
his death notice with the SS motto "His honor was called loyalty," and
the notice next to it, placed by his mourning SS comrades, showed that
Frau Schintlholzer had not chosen this phrase unwittingly.[154]

Eichmann's abduction caused alarm outside Germany as well. At the start of June 1960, turmoil broke out in Rome.[155] Umberto Mozzoni, the apostolic nuncio in Buenos Aires, went to see the Argentine foreign minister—and their discussion didn't just cover the president's upcoming audience with the pope. According to a surprisingly well-informed journalist on the Austrian paper *Volkswille,* Vatican diplomats had called on several United Nations member states to demand Eichmann's return to Argentina: "Via semi-official channels, the papal officials expressed their opinion that the Second World War's leading Nazis should no longer be prosecuted. They should be playing an active role in the defense of Western society against Communism: today, it is more necessary than ever to gather together all anti-Communist forces." This view, which had been heard during the Nuremberg Trials, served as a rationale for people helping National Socialists evade justice. If the Church was now invoking international law and the struggle against the "barbarism of the East," it was because everyone would shortly be hearing about Eichmann's Red Cross passport and the character references that Catholic priests had provided for a perpetrator of crimes against humanity. The first detailed newspaper article disseminated details about Bishop Hudal and others, explained their cooperation with the International Red Cross, and described the dubious role of the Yugoslav priest Krunoslav Draganovic. People started talking about "Vatican passports," and no one could predict how many "Vatican documents" Eichmann would know about.

Eichmann's best friends in Argentina, who had earlier done so much to try to find him, now distanced themselves as quickly as possible. When the police went to interrogate his traveling companion "Pedro Geller" (Herbert Kuhlmann), who had been the guarantor for Eichmann's apartment in Chacabuco Street, they met Horst Carlos Fuldner. To their surprise, he opened the door to them and chattered away cheerfully. He said he was still the head of CAPRI, as the insolvency process was a long one, and had known both Geller and Eichmann. The police noted: "Fuldner explained that until May 26, he had not known Ricardo Klement's true name. Klement had given up his post with CAPRI in 1953. . . . On the day in question, at ten in the morning, a distraught young man had come to his house at 2929 Ombú Street. Fuldner had never met him before, but he introduced himself as Klaus Eichmann, the son of the man Fuldner had known as Ricardo Klement." Off the top of his head, the extremely helpful Fuldner managed to tell the police the exact date Kuhlmann and Eichmann had arrived in Argentina and even to name the *Giovanna C* as the ship on which they crossed the Atlantic. Nobody seems to have noticed that he was admitting to assisting Nazi fugitives.[156] A few people made public denials: when the press described Otto Skorzeny as Eichmann's friend, Skorzeny, who now had a mailbox south of Hamburg, published a denial and threatened to take legal action against anyone trying to insinuate this sort of thing.[157] Like Fuldner, Johann von Leers told the police and the press that he had known Eichmann only fleetingly. Eichmann's employer, colleagues, and friends (most of whom were lying) said they had never known who this Ricardo Klement really was.

The seeds of insecurity planted by the impending trial yielded some bizarre fruit. Two weeks after the forthcoming Eichmann trial was announced, a man turned up at the CIA's office in Frankfurt, claiming he had always worked for the CIA and therefore had a right to immunity. He was Leopold von Mildenstein, whom Eichmann had so admired in Jewish Office II 112 of the SD. He was obviously afraid of revelations from the man whose interest in the "Jewish question" he had sparked. But the CIA classified him as uninteresting and denied him any special protection. An inquiry revealed that the agency's last contact with him had been in 1956, when he settled in the Middle East and tried to support Gamal Abdel Nasser against Israel.[158] Some of Eichmann's other fellow soldiers were also spurred into action. At the start of 1961, the CIA received rumors about Otto Skorzeny, who was so admired by his former Nazi comrades for liberating Mussolini. Some of those comrades had been making plans to free Eichmann, but that turned out to be too difficult, so they now wanted to kill the prisoner in Israel.[159] Looking at the files, one wonders which the Americans found more confusing—the fact that such absurd plans allegedly existed, or that their German colleagues in the BND seemed to believe in them. In any case, they give us a good impression of what old Nazi heroes were discussing late into the night.[160]

Eichmann's abduction altered the lives of the SS men and other perpetrators of the genocide more radically than any event since the defeat in May 1945. It changed the way they interacted with one another for good; the years of comfortable exile and the natural trust between old comrades were suddenly over. For those who hadn't known much about the extermination of the Jews, their new knowledge dispelled any sense of nostalgia, and the others were suddenly fugitives once more. They realized there would be no return to normality. "Now they see that I was right," an agitated Josef Mengele noted in his diary, before moving even farther away, to Brazil, in October 1960.[161] Fifteen years after the end of the war, the expatriates suddenly remembered that they had to be careful not to draw attention to themelves. And they only had a short time to consider their strategy.

Israel was eager to put off the inevitable debate about its violation of international law for as long as possible, and it resurrected the old Middle East story, spreading the news that Eichmann had been taken prisoner in a neighboring country.

But the real location of Eichmann's capture soon came to light, and from that moment on, Argentina was full of journalists trying to find out more about Eichmann's life. Wilfred von Oven finally got an opportunity to display his considerable knowledge of the Dürer circle; Fuldner gave interviews to his friend Fritz Otto Ehlert, a correspondent from the *Frankfurter Allgemeine Zeitung;* the Mercedes director William A. Mosetti took pains to convince Ehlert not to publish the company's name, at least. But for the people who had known Eichmann too well, all that remained was to lie low.[162] The Sassen circle disintegrated. Any further involvement in wide-ranging discussions about old times was now impossible, as were prominent positions in society and conspicuous celebrations of Hitler's birthday. In 1965 the Latvian Herbert Cukurs, who had murdered Jews in Riga, was shot dead in Montevideo, reminding the old comrades in South America of their fear.[163]

But one Argentine friend took his Eichmann connection and went on the offensive with it: Willem Sassen. On June 6, according to an Argentine police report, two men in civilian clothing broke into Eichmann's house and took photographs of everything.[164] That was the same day that Sassen persuaded Vera Eichmann to sign the contract with *Life,* which required photos; the police seem to have observed a secret visit rather than a break-in. A short while later pictures from the hastily abandoned house appeared alongside articles in the German magazine *Stern* and the Dutch newspaper *Volkskrant,* to which Sassen apparently also sold material from the Argentina Papers.[165] From then on the former SS war correspondent presented himself as an investigative journalist selling the story of a lifetime. He brazenly claimed that his true friends had always called him (Sassen, the great anti-American) "Willy." To his family, he carefully explained that he had actually never liked the man who had been his guest every weekend for almost a year.[166]

As the trial in Israel approached, accompanied by a media storm, nobody in the world wanted to be connected with Adolf Eichmann. Facts were coming to light, and for the first time people discussed them instead of dismissing them. But Eichmann's appearance before the court also offered an opportunity for one of the most astonishingly success-ful acts of suppression in European history. This nervous shadow of a man in a glass box, who gradually disappeared behind his little desk, the stacks of files, his unintelligible German—how could this man ever have been someone? Eichmann described himself as the man behind the desk, allowing former colleagues who had never actually entered his office to claim they had never met him. Nobody knows a little cog in the machine—especially people who don't know anything else, either. The success of this strategy in the 1960s, and the fact that it still appears today in almost every book about the Holocaust, is frightening. But a glance at the daily papers from May 24, 1960, shows the level of knowledge that journalists assumed of their readers when they wrote articles with headlines like "The Manager of the 'Final Solution.'"[167] Long before the trial began, Eichmann's name had become a symbol that required no further explanation. And yet here we are, still explaining to the world why no one knew this man before 1960—a man whose arrest unleashed an outpouring of emotions from New York to Warsaw, from Bonn to Tel Aviv. This was a moment when world history was suddenly brought into focus, and no further explanation was required.

The saying goes that in a crisis, you find out who your real friends are. But Adolf Eichmann didn't find the friends he expected. Those who still cleaved undeterred to National Socialist ideals wanted noth-ing to do with their comrade. Nor did the far-right press step into the breach: unusually, it stood shoulder to shoulder with public opinion in Germany. It wasn't the Germans—no, it was the *Eichmanns* who had secretly murdered six million Jews, and it was a terrible business. Ever since then the neo-Nazi movement has run roughshod over reality in the way Willem Sassen and Ludolf von Alvensleben planned to in 1957. Their attempts to redeem Hitler and the Reich are based on claims that Adolf Eichmann and his colleagues had not belonged there. *"Das Ver-brechen hat kein Vaterland"* was the new slogan: the crime has no fatherland; the fatherland recognizes only its heroes.[168] The extermination of the Jews in Europe is seldom called that in the country that perpetrated it; Germans prefer the terms *Holocaust* or *Shoah*. In Argentina the crime was dismissed as an imported item that someone must have foisted upon the unsuspecting Germans. Like Hitler, the Buenos Aires Nazis had known nothing, and so ultimately the crime had nothing to do with them. With obvious relief, an anonymous writer for the monthly *Nation Europa* quoted the words Eichmann uttered at the start of his trial: "I never met him [Hitler] personally." That cleared everything up: Eichmann had never seen the Führer in person, and neither the Jews nor the Germans recognized Eichmann's name. The statement cast doubt on the "Führer's order" that he claimed to have been following, and "even Herr Eichmann would never dare appeal to the German people."[169] The writer was wrong about that, too, but the Germans who wrote for far-right magazines took the precaution of not listening to any more of the trial. Still, the number of pseudonyms used increased noticeably: the authors were more frightened than they wanted to admit.

"Nobody shed a tear for him then," said the former Wehrmacht soldier Pedro Pobierzym—but that was not entirely true. After Adolf Eichmann's execution, in far-off Brazil, Josef Mengele wrote a "very heavy-hearted" farewell to his comrade. It wasn't just an expression of gratitude to Eichmann for not betraying him or any of the other people he had met in Argentina. Eichmann's execution had a personal as well as a historic dimension for Mengele: "The event of 1 June [Eichmann's execution], which I only heard about days afterward, did not surprise me, but it made a deep impression. Was there any sense in this killing? One is tempted to draw parallels, but then abandons the idea, horrified by the reality of the course history has taken over the last 2000 years. His people betrayed him despicably. This was probably the heaviest human burden for him. And that is probably the core of the problem in this case! One day the German people will be ashamed of this! Or else they will not be ashamed of anything!"[170]

Eichmann as a German Jesus in Jerusalem? Mengele's Catholic upbringing isn't an adequate explanation for this monstrous idea. But two things are obvious: Mengele understood Eichmann better than any of the other National Socialists in Argentina, and he also knew that something united the two of them. The Germans wanted nothing to do with Eichmann, and since an arrest warrant had also been issued for

Mengele in 1959, they wanted nothing to do with him either. A quarter of a century earlier, the people of Germany had succumbed to the fever of National Socialism just as Eichmann and Mengele had. Without the German people, neither of these men could have become what they became, but now these people refused to extend them the respect that both were certain they deserved. They had considered themselves the executors of the Führer's orders and the executive of the entire German population. And now this population no longer wanted to know them. Eichmann's fears went even further. He advised his family: "Don't go to Germany too much for the time being. I think it's better for you to be careful."[171]

In his concluding statement in Israel, Eichmann said he had the feeling he was being tried as a proxy for others. He was unquestionably an ideal proxy, having heaped a degree of guilt upon himself for which no earthly punishment would suffice—but that didn't change the fact that his feeling was correct. The German people were only too happy to pretend that Eichmann had murdered six million Jews by himself. His offer to hang himself in public, to take the guilt from "German youth," was grotesque, but it revealed the fundamental problem with the trial. Israel was hoping for catharsis, a collective reflection on collective guilt, and even Eichmann grasped the fact that his warped martyrdom might endow his pitiful situation with pathos and heroism. But the perpetrators, collaborators, and willing sympathizers just wanted to be rid of their scapegoat. "You make things so difficult for so many of your sons, sacred Fatherland! But we will not leave you, and we will always, always love you!" wrote Mengele, attempting to comfort himself.[172] "Leave history to create a judgment," Eichmann wrote in his farewell letter to his family.[173] Neither man could expect anything more from the present.

A CHANGE OF ROLE

Eichmann in Jerusalem

*He was pleased he was able to make a statement at the trial,
and said: "Now the murderer and mass murderer has completely
vanished."*   —Vera Eichmann, following a visit to
Eichmann in jail, April 22, 1962

As soon as Eichmann realized he had fallen into the hands of kidnappers
rather than a murder squad, he made a revealing request: "Since I can
no longer remember all the details, and mistake or confuse some things,
I ask to be helped in this by having documents and statements made
available to me."[1] Eichmann wanted the books he had studied so thoroughly, because he knew exactly how to use them to his own advantage.
When the captain of the Israeli police, Avner W. Less, began to interrogate him, he soon got an inkling: "After the end of the first hearing, I was
convinced that Eichmann wasn't telling this story for the first time."[2]
He went on: "I had the feeling the man had been rehearsing it somewhere."[3] The prisoner was no intellectual, but he was incredibly well
read, "very intelligent, very cunning, and there was the way he behaved
during the interrogation." The two men were playing "a sort of chess
game," as they both knew how an interrogation worked.[4] Less quickly
realized that Eichmann was acquainted with all the books, even when
he claimed the opposite, remarking with a sigh how greatly he regretted
being able to read these volumes only now, in Israel. It didn't escape the
interrogating officer's notice that his prisoner was able to find "the passages that appeared favorable to him" with frightening speed. Not for
months would Less learn where Eichmann had practiced, and why he
was so extremely well prepared for the interrogation.

By the time Eichmann unexpectedly found himself imprisoned by
his archenemy, he had already decided which of the images of himself
that were in circulation would be the most useful for his defense. He
gave them the Cautious Bureaucrat—without the incriminating elabo-
rations he had added in Argentina. In this role, he was able to unite two

things that he hoped might save him from the gallows: exclusive knowledge about the murder of the Jews, and his own innocence. He might even gain some room for putting across his personal insights. "I knew it, and yet I could not change anything."[5]

The renowned specialist on "Jewish questions," the interministerial coordinator of the extermination project, the man who celebrated its implementation with his superiors over a glass of cognac by the fire, transformed himself into a helpless minute taker with no power of his own. Even at the Wannsee Conference, he claimed to have been "sharpening pencils at the side table."[6] In Argentina, Eichmann had explained with pride and pedantry exactly why his name had become a symbol even before the war. He knew his collection of press cuttings like the back of his hand, but he now claimed that "until 1946, I had next to no public profile."[7] The approaching trial was really just a misunderstanding, arising from the fact that he had been "accused, slandered and pursued by the whole world for 15 years."[8] "I too," he would say reproachfully, in his concluding statement before the court, "I too am a victim."

As part of this masquerade, Eichmann described himself in terms that would previously have sent him into a screaming rage. He was now "small-minded," a "pencil-pusher," and a "pedant," someone who "did not overstep his responsibilities"[9]—and the last of these lies may even have amused him a little. His former colleagues in the Foreign Office would have to listen to all this without being able to object, though they could have told a very different story about how Eichmann had overstepped his responsibilities. He had always been very proud of his trickery, and his observant interrogator noted that the prisoner grew particularly lively when he was making tactical maneuvers.

All these labels he applied to himself in Israel actually fit National Socialist conceptions of the enemy, and "the bureaucrat" was almost the antithesis of the SS man.[10] Of course, one could use bureaucracy as a weapon, particularly against those who believed in it. During his time in power, Eichmann had used perverse bureaucratic chicaneries to slow down other Reich institutions, as well as his victims, and he was well acquainted with this subtle form of power. But now, in his cell in Israel, *a bureaucrat* sounded far more harmless than *an SS man*. This cautious bureaucrat had not been a fanatical National Socialist; he was an ordinary, nature-loving man with an academic bent and a hankering for enlightenment and cosmopolitanism. In the last fifteen years, he had finally managed to leave behind the onerous orders of a criminal government and return to his roots. This was the image of Eichmann that the prisoner in Jerusalem chose to enact for the last year of his life. His ability to inhabit and perfect a role allowed him to keep up this pretense with surprising consistency. He even built on it: the voluble prisoner and the diligent historian were joined by the pacifist, who venerated international law, and finally the philosopher, who grappled with the ultimate questions of morality and existence with the aid of Kant and Spinoza—only this time, without the "voice of blood."

A study of the racial anti-Semitism of the Nazi period, however, reveals the anti-Semitic clichés that were involved in these roles, too—Eichmann was still thinking like a dedicated anti-Semite. Jews, as he had preached since the 1930s, were universalists. Their weakness lay in placing universal ideas like knowledge above the language of blood. It was an innate "instinct" of theirs, he believed, and he must have hoped that appealing to it would create a loophole for him. Racial anti-Semites were convinced that Jews, and everyone who had been "infected" by them, couldn't help but place their weakness for intellectualism and science above the "sacred egoism of blood." As long as he was satisfying their need to understand the past, they wouldn't kill him.

Even in Israel, surrounded by people who knew exactly who he was, Eichmann managed to do what he had done so many times before as a Nazi functionary: arouse the sympathy of his opponents. Everyone who dealt with Eichmann in Israel said they were sure they had been an important attachment figure for him. Interrogator, prison director, doctor, psychologist, theologian, deputy attorney general—they all praised his willingness to cooperate, remarked on how happy he was to talk, and believed he was particularly grateful to them for their conversations. As much as they fought it and condemned him for what he was, all were touched by the impression of the grateful prisoner.[11] Even Avner W. Less occasionally struggled with Eichmann's surprisingly winning ways, despite being an experienced interrogator and possessing the tools to deal with charm offensives.

Again and again—even with experienced interpreters—Eichmann and his texts led people to false conclusions. A person who takes luggage with them "to the East," and who is asked to take note of where they put their clothes before the "delousing," naturally expects there must be a reason. Anyone who receives a postcard from a relative in the Black

Forest naturally assumes that their relative is in the Black Forest and has not already been gassed in Auschwitz. In the same way, we always search texts and testimonies for their relation to our own knowledge and experience. In other words: we reason. We want to understand. The National Socialist "ideological elite" grasped our susceptibility to this desire to understand. They used it to confuse people and render them incapable of making judgments or taking action. People who want to understand will never give up their search for understanding, even where others have burned all the bridges out of a belief that not everyone has the right to exist. Eichmann's "Götzen" is a paean to philosophy and moral values, to ideals of peace and international law. It expresses disillusionment with Nazism and a supposed change of heart. It is Eichmann's attempt to build a bridge for someone who is desperate to understand but cannot understand a crime like the extermination of the Jews.

Eichmann, by talking like the people who condemned his deeds, in progressive terms of morality and justice, was implying the possibility of a connection, a chance to find out what he meant. Ultimately, whether Eichmann managed to sell himself as a bureaucrat, a schizophrenic, or an amnesiac didn't matter, as long as no one sniffed out his convictions, asked questions, or, above all, listened to him closely enough to see him as he was. Even in excellent publications and documentaries, photos of Eichmann are often laterally reversed.[12] It's no coincidence: our desire to get a picture of him, without looking at him too closely, was one of the fundamental reasons for Eichmann's power. He did a good job of letting people see what they wanted to see. Eichmann-in-Jerusalem made a huge effort to lead the people who wanted to understand over the bridges into his worldview. We can avoid falling into Eichmann's "Götzen" trap only by keeping a wary eye fixed on the perfidious philosophical swamp of the Argentina Papers.

Interrogation officer Avner W. Less and Judge Yitzhak Raveh showed how to get beneath Eichmann's surface, by taking him at his word and observing his role-playing in order to learn about it. You learn nothing about a mirror by gazing in fascination at your own reflection; the trick is to concentrate on the reflective surface itself.

Eichmann's writings in Israel offer insight into injustice, express disappointment in his superiors, and appeal to reason and world peace, but the writings and discussions from Argentina are conclusive proof of their insincerity. These earlier texts allow us to analyze the mechanics of

Eichmann's manipulation and the extent to which he had reflected on the methods of lying and disinformation. Thousands of pages of self-stylizing and historical revisionism don't just happen—they are no mere accident or memory lapse, especially not two such different accounts from the same person. The Argentina Papers allow us to see behind the mirror. They reveal a man who was practiced in the art of manufacturing and conveying stories with an inner coherence, solely to distract people from their fundamental weakness: the fact they had little to do with reality. In power, Eichmann played treacherous games with his victims' hopes of finding a way out of their situation, in order to drive them to their deaths without resistance. In Argentina, in order to gain the respect and assistance of his old comrades, he confirmed their expectations that National Socialism could be separated from the imperative to exterminate. In Israel, he tried to serve what he saw as a "Jewish instinct," the desire to understand and gather knowledge. Like a mirror, he reflected people's fears and expectations, whether they were fearing for their own lives or hoping he would confirm a theory of evil. Behind all the mirror images lay Eichmann's will to power and desire to control people's thoughts, disguised as diligence. One thing unfailingly made Eichmann incautious and therefore vulnerable: his pronounced need for recognition. A man who wears so many masks is always tempted to reveal who he really is. But the desire to control and manipulate ultimately requires what Eichmann thought of as his greatest mental burden: "personal anonymity."

In Israel, Eichmann was trying to "howl with the wolves" once again, trying to draw the gaze of powerful people and make the world see him as an indispensible specialist, a historian, a philosopher, and finally a prophet, preaching peace and international understanding. He was playing for the highest stakes. But this time he lost. Otto Adolf Eichmann was hanged on the night between May and June 1962, and his ashes were scattered in the Mediterranean. The traces of his diversionary tactics, however, are still in evidence today.

AFTERMATH

Silence is less obvious. One must be aware of it before it yields its information.
                                                                —Raul Hilberg[1]

While the man who had been a Nazi in Argentina was busy becoming Eichmann-in-Jerusalem, producing new piles of texts with a new target audience in mind, his comrades in Buenos Aires turned their attention to the paper trail he had left there: one thousand pages of transcribed conversations with commentaries, a few surviving tapes, and five hundred pages of handwritten texts and notes, sometimes with copies. The path these papers took into the public eye would be complex. The story is still not finished and contains enough material for a novel. Although the so-called Sassen interviews have become one of the most quoted postwar sources on the Holocaust, knowledge of the scope and content of these important documents is surprisingly patchy, and researchers have shown surprisingly little curiosity about what the Argentina Papers actually say. The reasons are partly psychological: the fear of opening Pandora's box; Golo Mann's warning that dealing with filthy ideas can leave you with more than just dirty hands. But an overview of what Eichmann left behind from his time in South America is also incredibly difficult to obtain. The papers are strewn across several archives like a giant, cryptic jigsaw puzzle, and missing references and overly hasty ordering make the task even harder. In the Bundesarchiv Koblenz, the greatest find of the last decade boasts the description, "The texts have been available to researchers for years." The additional note that their ordering is only "provisional," due to lack of time, doesn't make this blatant error any less devastating. The crucial clue to the reassembly of a historical puzzle often comes from the story of how it was broken apart in the first place. Solving the puzzle will involve taking the path back to the beginning, before it became a puzzle. So let us start at the point when the Argentina Papers were still as extensive as we know they once were: May 1960.

The Sassen Material

When Eichmann was abducted, what he left behind in Argentina was principally distributed between two addresses: his own and Willem Sas-

sen's. While his notes, private writings, annotated books, a few drafts of
Sassen's texts, and the "Tucumán Novel" were at the Eichmann house,
Sassen had most of the material. Rumors still circulate in Buenos Aires
today about who may or may not have hidden Eichmann's papers, but
as is usually the case, the truth may be simpler. After the far right's election failure in the Federal Republic, the abortive book project, and the
departure of his publisher to Austria, Sassen had grown bored with
the material and set it all aside, turning his attention to new projects.
Only when Eichmann was abducted did it suddenly regain its currency
and explosive power. But most important, the material in his possession posed an immediate risk to him. Twelve days passed between
Eichmann's abduction and Ben-Gurion's official announcement that
Eichmann was a prisoner in Israel. During that time Eichmann's family, friends, and acquaintances had no idea what had happened, or what
might happen next, fearing that this operation might be the start of
something bigger. Sassen's immediate reaction was to get the material
out of his house. Depositing it all in one place would not have been
a smart move. Eichmann's colleague at Mercedes-Benz said that Sassen and Klaus Eichmann left manuscripts with him for a week;[2] others
reported that a collection of tapes and transcripts was buried in a garden somewhere, possibly on the extensive grounds of Sassen's patron
Dieter Menge.[3] The Eichmann family, meanwhile, understandably no
longer felt safe in the house on the edge of the suburbs. Friends like
Sassen and Fuldner helped them once again, taking some private things
to safety. But no further attacks came, and the public announcement of
Eichmann's abduction dramatically altered Sassen's situation: finally, he
had a chance to exploit the old material.

Adolf Eichmann had agreed that Sassen could publish the interviews
"if I should die, or fall into the hands of the Israelis."[4] Sassen stuck to
this agreement and acted fast. Typescripts of the tape recordings already
existed, but as the Sassen circle's project had finally died of boredom, a
few of Eichmann's handwritten texts were still lying around. If they were
going to be usable, they had to be transcribed: Eichmann's handwriting was idiosyncratic and sometimes difficult to read even for people
used to German script.[5] Sassen had some experience with *Life* and was
thinking about the American market, so he employed a secretary to type
up the rest right away.[6] Sassen also took another, very farsighted step:
he had the documents photographed. This was the simplest option, as

today's Xerox machines were not yet in use, and permanent copies could be produced only using photography.[7] By June 1960, Sassen had negatives of all the documents he wanted to sell on 35mm film, the format that was used in analog photography for many years. This was a clever move, not just because Sassen was eager to prevent access to the originals. He was planning to travel, and fifteen hundred pages would have made for heavy luggage. (This bundle of typescript was around eight inches thick and weighed over 15.5 pounds.)

Sassen decided not to sell the whole transcript and only a few copies of the handwritten pages. He removed more than one hundred pages from the interviews and left them at home, where most of them remained until 1979. This hasty clean-up operation was, however, anything but thorough: he forgot about the tape with the Alvensleben interview (probably the second tape from that session). After two years, anyone would find it difficult to remember exactly what was in a suitcase full of haphazardly compiled texts.

The Sale

According to the story that is frequently told, Willem Sassen seized his chance and rushed to sell the manuscript to the press, hoping to make the greatest possible profit from the affair. But it wasn't that simple. Sassen was acting on the agreement he had made with Eichmann, but he was also using the material to pursue the interest that had bound him to Eichmann from the outset. He may have had a good nose for a fast buck, but he was also still a dedicated National Socialist and anti-Semite. Improbable as it may sound to us today, Sassen wanted more than just money: he wanted to use his relationship with *Life* to publish his interview with the world's most notorious prisoner. And later events show that he actually believed the publication would benefit Eichmann. Anyone familiar with the Sassen-Fritsch circle's fanciful conceptions of history will hardly be surprised by this degree of naïveté. Sassen also believed that the Israeli government could not have sanctioned Eichmann's abduction, and that a few rogue fanatics had done something that would now create huge difficulties for Israel. Sassen was convinced that Eichmann talking was exactly what "the Jews" were afraid of. He wrote to Eichmann's defense lawyer that the trial would be decided "like the Dreyfuss Affair back in the day, on the level of public opinion."[8] Sassen, who had once been so successful as a war correspondent, believed he was well versed in the use of this weapon. What Eichmann had said in Argentina would create difficulties for "the Jews." His words would expose "Eretz Israel"; the world would recognize that Eichmann—like all Germans—was the real victim of the Jewish world conspiracy, and "the Jews" would finally be seen for what they were. If one thing could save Eichmann, it was that "the Jews" were afraid of this "truth" being "exposed." There was no doubt about it in Sassen's mind. If he was smart about how he used what Eichmann had said in the freedom of the pampas, it was bound to accomplish more than the Israelis' prisoner could on his own. He believed that in Jerusalem, Eichmann would produce a confession only under torture. Sassen (and a few German journalists, including those on *Der Spiegel*)[9] believed without question that the trial would be unfair. If the Sassen circle's conception of history had not been insane, the strategy should have worked. But as it was, it turned out to be the worst thing that could have happened for Eichmann's defense. He was, in any case, a man for whom there really could be no defense: he had demolished the whole scale of criminality.

Naturally, performing this "favor" would also yield Sassen a profit, and the Eichmann family were sorely in need of money, having lost their breadwinner overnight. Sassen went about the task with a combination of business sense, political ambition, and personal sympathy. It was to be his greatest success, though it also spelled the end of his career as a journalist. He had managed to sell the first interviews with Perón in 1955, and he knew that in journalism, speed was of the essence. He invited a representative from *Life* to Buenos Aires and pressured Vera Eichmann into signing a contract with the U.S. magazine on June 5.[10] Eichmann's wife signed as her husband's legal representative, and Sassen signed as her adviser and the "compiler" of the manuscripts. Publication was to take place only after the trial, and *Life* was given the right to sell the material—although not, under any circumstances, to Israel. Sassen would hand over "150 handwritten pages and 600 pages of typescript," in return for $15,000 and a $5,000 fee for Sassen. Sassen may have received a larger sum of money on the side, without Vera Eichmann's knowledge.[11]

To prove the material was genuine, Sassen allowed the *Life* representative to see a few pages of the original, and he played him part of the tapes. The page numbers, and what was eventually published in the magazine, show that this copy was merely a selection, comprising 60 percent of the interviews and 40 percent of the handwritten pages. It included Eichmann's notorious "conclusion" from tape 67 and the handwritten text about the "anonymous wanderer in a submarine," which vanished for a long time and is difficult to decipher. As Eichmann's lawyer later explained, Vera Eichmann actually had no right to conduct these negotiations. The original rights holder was still alive, even if he was sitting in an Israeli prison cell.[12] Sassen, however, had found a legal loophole with the term *compiler*. In journalism it isn't the interviewee, but the person who conducts and compiles the interview, who gets the fee and the copyright. In this way, Sassen was clearly hoping to retain control over what was published and, most important, to be named as the author. This part of his plan did not work out.

It was still June when Sassen traveled to Europe and Germany again. Servatius later heard that Sassen had flown across the Atlantic in the company of the Argentine president, Arturo Frondizi. It wasn't true, but it shows how well connected people considered Sassen to be.[13] He started negotiations with the German magazine *Stern*, with which Sassen had a special relationship. He and *Stern*'s founder, Henri Nannen, had met during their time in the "Kurt Eggers" SS propaganda unit. Nannen's success rested in part on the courage to employ unusual correspondents, without too much consideration for ethical issues. In 1959 he even included Sassen ("Wilhelm S. von Elsloo") in *Stern*'s masthead, with his actual address in Argentina.[14] Sassen was just as fond of telling his family this story as he was of telling them about his work for *Der Spiegel*.[15] We can only surmise what he must have sold to *Stern*: although the publisher was kind enough to give me access to their archive, the dedicated archive staff couldn't find a single page of Sassen's material. There are two possible explanations for this regrettable loss. Either the archive was cleaned up at some point, or the *Stern* reporter responsible for the Eichmann coverage sent the originals to Israel, as a CIA agent reported.[16] But we have several clues to what was in the *Stern* copy. The CIA report mentions eighty handwritten pages, and Robert Pendorf used extracts from Eichmann's handwritten texts in his book, which was based on his articles in *Stern* (namely the "wanderer in a submarine" and part of the larger manuscript, as well as part of the transcript). A rumor slowly spread among German newspaper editors that someone in Hamburg had an extensive interview with Eichmann. *Stern*'s bundle was probably the same as the *Life* material, and the reticence from *Stern*'s editors, who mentioned only the handwritten pages, was an attempt to avoid a legal argument over the exploitation rights.[17] As well as the documents, Sassen gave the *Stern* reporter an insight into Eichmann's life in Argentina—though he carefully avoided any reference to the Sassen circle. He painted a picture of Eichmann the pariah, whom Sassen had cajoled into sentimental discussions about his obedience to the Reich. There are many indications that Sassen also offered these eighty pages of the Argentina Papers, and parts of the transcript, to *Der Spiegel*, but the magazine made no discernible use of them. A CIA source suspected that its founder, Rudolf Augstein, was waiting for the right time.[18] Sassen also signed contracts with two Dutch companies: *De Sparnetstad*, in Haarlem, and *De Volkskrant* (for photographic material).[19]

Airing Eichmann's Dirty Laundry

At around the same time in Israel, Eichmann began talking about his encounter with Sassen, having been confronted with the name of a former colleague: Rudolf Mildner.[20] During the Sassen discussions, Eichmann had been convinced that Rudolf Mildner was "missing," but now he denounced him as a dedicated participant in the Sassen circle. He quoted Mildner's Nuremberg statement, which in Buenos Aires he had claimed never existed. "This was the first time I spoke to Mildner again, about three years ago, I think it was, and I picked this issue apart in the presence of a certain Herr Sassen, who was the accredited, as you say here, 'journalist,' in the government over there. . . . Mildner stuck by the position he had taken in his witness statement in Nuremberg, and it is de facto the position that the Gestapo had nothing at all to do with the killing process," Eichmann admitted to the Argentine recording sessions and the transcripts.[21] This was a practiced tactic: he would anticipate any difficulty that might arise and mention it, to test how much evidence the Israelis actually had in their hands. At this point, however, the prosecuting authorities had no access to the Sassen interviews, or any more detailed information about them.

In connection with his negotiations with *Stern*, Sassen visited Eberhard Fritsch in Salzburg, who organized a meeting with the brothers

Otto and Robert Eichmann.[22] Sassen was conscious that in the long term, he would need the blessing of both Fritsch and the Eichmann family. Fritsch, after all, had been the intended publisher for the Eichmann project, and according to their agreement, all three of them should profit equally from any publication. Neither the Eichmann brothers nor Fritsch, whom Sassen still trusted and admired, objected to what Sassen told them he was planning. He had, as he repeatedly explained, sold only the U.S. rights. This was a lie, but Fritsch must have welcomed the news: despite the ban that had been placed on him, he would have liked to be a publisher again. Sassen even got away with saying he had mislaid the *Life* contract and so couldn't produce it as evidence. Nor did Sassen allow anyone to see the transcript, so the Eichmann brothers still had no idea of the threat these documents could pose to Eichmann's defense. Sassen's suggestion of writing a book on Eichmann met with agreement, in particular from Fritsch, who was eager to take care of the publishing contacts himself. For this purpose, Fritsch was given a few pages that Sassen had removed from the *Stern* copy. This too would prove to be an error.[23]

Henri Nannen made good use of this opportunity for *Stern,* and on June 25, 1960, he printed the first of a four-part series of articles entitled "Last Trace of Eichmann Discovered." And even without the level of interest with which I was greeted by *Stern*'s current employees, the series can only be described as a journalistic tour de force. A month after Ben-Gurion's declaration to the Knesset, *Stern* published more photos and insider information about Eichmann's life in the underground than any other magazine did or has to this day. The reporter made good use of every clue Eichmann gave about his biography (which Sassen had found entirely uninteresting in 1957). Interviews were conducted in Altensalz-koth; a reporter spoke to Eichmann's helper and lover Nelly Krawietz in the United States; there were pictures taken in Eichmann's house; and quotes from his annotations in books. This headline-grabbing material went far beyond what *Life* had. While the U.S. magazine's editors were still despairing over the mass of almost untranslatable, unstructured transcript pages, *Stern*'s pieces combined north German local color with an Argentine celebrity profile. The articles were full of family photos, ranging from charming children to the violin case beneath the kitschy Alpine panoramas, alongside startling facts about the horrors of Nazi history. From the mass murderer who lived next door to the story of an intelligence service abduction, the series had everything an editor could dream of. Furthermore, the fact that historians still use these pieces today shows that they weren't good just for increasing circulation—they contain more useful information than errors (and a few pieces of disinformation from Sassen). Publishing so early was a high-risk strategy, which in 1983 Nannen and *Stern* would adopt to their cost with the supposed "Hitler Diaries." But in June 1960, it paid off.

Finally, Eichmann's interrogator made use of the *Stern* articles, which signaled to Eichmann that Sassen had begun to sell the Argentina Papers. But as the investigators found no reference to Sassen in the articles, or even to the existence of the interviews, Eichmann had the advantage once again.

The Texts Become a Cash Cow

As the prosecuting authorities in Israel were starting to wonder about the origin of *Stern*'s information, the confessions of a Nazi at liberty began to awaken hopes outside Israel. Like Sassen, other committed National Socialists hoped that the Argentina Papers might help to invalidate, or at least contrast with, the confessions they were expecting to hear from the Israelis' prisoner. Anti-Semites believe Jews are capable of almost anything, and they were sure that Eichmann would end up telling the Israelis everything they wanted to hear. Wider Nazi circles were convinced that Eichmann-in-Argentina would have told *their* truth, denying that the extermination of the Jews had taken place. To start with, then, they were therefore highly motivated to assist their imprisoned SS comrade by making the Argentina Papers public—and in the best-case scenario, also earning some money from them.

The man with the most experience in turning Nazi documents into cash was François Genoud. A shady character, he was a fan of Hitler, comforter of heroes fallen on hard times, aide to the intelligence services, publisher of Goebbels and Bormann, and banker to the Arab world.[24] By 1960 Genoud's contacts had ranged from an early encounter with Hitler to intimate friendships with Arab freedom fighters and the leaders of the BKA. He and his close friend Hans Rechenberg, who at this point was living in Bad Tölz in Bavaria, immediately got in touch with the Eichmann brothers to organize Eichmann's defense. The brothers had already decided on a lawyer: Robert Servatius, whom Rechenberg may have known from the Nuremberg Trials.[25] It was clear that the costs for the defense would be more than covered by the sale of Eichmann's papers—leaving aside the money that the State of Israel put at Servatius's disposal, believing he had no other source of income.[26] A "Linz common interest group" met for this purpose several times, starting in fall 1960. Hans-Ulrich Rudel was even seen at one of these meetings in a Salzburg hotel.[27] The hotel porter Fritsch provided the location, Rechenberg and Genoud the money; and Servatius the contact with the prisoner in his cell in Israel; the brothers functioned as the authorized agents of Adolf Eichmann. The correspondence, and the reports that reached the BND, show that "common interest" was something of a misnomer: the group was anything but united and argued bitterly over the money Adolf Eichmann was helping to generate.

None of the people involved seems to have realized that this undertaking was an attempt to square the circle: they were trying to finance a successful defense by selling documents that, by their very existence, would make an already weak defense impossible. But their first problem was something else entirely: Willem Sassen, the guardian of the Argentina Papers, had no intention of leaving the sale of his documents to other people and refused to hand them over. Eichmann's defense counsel learned of the existence of the Argentina Papers and the *Life* contract from Fritsch and Eichmann's brother—though Servatius, like Eichmann's brother, still didn't know what his future client had said and written in Argentina.[28] When Servatius officially received his brief on July 14, 1960, he had no idea of the danger posed by the Argentine confessions. His client lied to him about them consistently, from their very first meeting in Israel, on October 9, until the end of the trial. Robert Eichmann and Eberhard Fritsch also kept Servatius short of information. Admittedly, Servatius gave the impression that he didn't actually want to know the details, and anyway, he had more than enough on his plate with the flood of documents involved in the Eichmann case.

Meanwhile, Sassen was traveling tirelessly around Europe. Journalists in Bonn reported that he had played them one of the original tapes in July. The "Linz common interest group" noted it all with some anxiety.[29] At the same time, Sassen was trying to prepare a draft of his own Eichmann texts, in the belief that he was going to write the *Life* article himself. Eberhard Fritsch and Hans Rechenberg were less discreet than

Sassen. Fritsch, in his efforts to find a publisher quickly, acted carelessly and information on the Argentina Papers was given to the BND. This was another incalculable risk, caused by the general panic over the upcoming trial.[30]

The BND was alarmed by the information, partly because Fritsch refused to hand over the sample pages to publishers and was making exaggerated claims about the length of the papers. He said there were three thousand pages. The BND in Munich called on Washington for help: friends of Eichmann, they said, were attempting to sell "Eichmann memoirs" for the family's financial support, and a copy could end up in East Germany.[31] The Eichmann case had become dynamite in the war of words between East and West Germany. Fritsch's chatter about the *Life* contract motivated the BND and the CIA to make hurried inquiries to *Life* regarding the documents. They also checked up on Fritsch, whom they took to be an Eastern Bloc spy. Bonn was particularly concerned that Eichmann might have named Globke. The CIA leaped to the BND's aid, putting pressure on *Life* to keep Globke out of its article at all costs. Allen W. Dulles, the head of the CIA, was soon able to reassure Munich that the name Globke appeared only once in Eichmann's statements, and that *Life* had been persuaded not to print it.[32] It hadn't required too much pressure: Globke didn't appear in the Argentina Papers at all.[33] The occasional reference to "Glo . . ." in the transcripts clearly referred to Odilo Globocnik, the leader of the deadly Operation Reinhard. In the end, *Life* printed snippets of Eichmann's texts along with its own short introductions mainly without commentary, but that doesn't mean it had planned an allusion to Globke. Whoever was conning whom here, *Life* was doing nothing that Dulles had to stop. The BND and the Federal Chancellery must have been grateful all the same.

The CIA found out a little about *Life*'s copy of the papers: it consisted of six hundred pages of transcript and forty pages of handwritten text. *Life* told Sassen about the intelligence service inquiries, and he remonstrated with Fritsch: as a consequence, Sassen had been barred from entering the United States. Fritsch's misstep gave Sassen a reason not to send any more documents to Austria.[34] Genoud and Rechenberg can only have welcomed this development, as it meant they could safely cut Sassen out of the profits. And as long as they still had Eberhard Fritsch, the publisher Eichmann admired, then even without Sassen they were assured of the storyteller's trust.

In the meantime, François Genoud and the "Linz common interest group" had found an uncomplicated source for Eichmann's confessions: the prisoner in Israel himself. Immediately after his arrival, Eichmann had begun to compose new texts in response to inquiries by the investigating authorities.[35] To the attorney general's surprise, Eichmann voluntarily produced a wealth of accounts, covering his life ("Meine Memoiren," May 1961); his escape after the war ("Meine Flucht," March 1961); and any other topic they put to him. In these texts he presented himself as the unpracticed author who was, "for the first time in 15 years," making an attempt to write down his thoughts and experiences. He greeted every book supplied to him for this purpose with a show of delight and curiosity, although they were the very same works that he and his friends in Argentina had taken apart sentence by sentence, dismissing them as "Jewish waffle" and a "hodgepodge of lies."[36]

Eichmann assumed that the interrogation would be published in the near future and diligently applied himself to correcting the 3,564 pages of the final text. Much too late he reported to his horrified lawyer that he was "dictating reports daily."[37] Eichmann-in-Jerusalem hid the fact that he was drawing on years of practice in writing, speaking onto tape, and working through literature and was now simply adapting his excuses for a new target audience. From the start, his writing in Israel more or less subtly contradicted his own Argentina Papers.

In the end, Eichmann left behind around eight thousand pages from his time in Jerusalem: manuscripts, transcribed statements, letters, personal dossiers, ideological tracts, individual jottings, and thousands of marginal notes on documents. Servatius (without any real hindrance from the Israeli authorities, and under the BND's observation),[38] Genoud, and Rechenberg helped themselves liberally to this flood of papers. They sold a few of the texts, plus some private photos of Eichmann from Argentina and even an exclusive interview with Eichmann's wife.[39] They showed little deference in their enterprise, and they even allowed a photo shoot in which Vera Eichmann held a bunch of flowers in front of a Dachau street sign. These men quite obviously thought Eichmann's life was forfeit—but this too could be sold at a profit. Their final piece of exploitation was an exclusive interview with the prisoner himself, conducted via questionnaire. It appeared in *Paris Match* a week after his execution, with the charming title: "Eichmann parle d'outre-tombe" (Eichmann Speaks from Beyond the Grave).[40]

Genoud lost interest in Eichmann's defense when he realized that the accused was hopeless either as a witness for the collective innocence of the German people or as the savior of Adolf Hitler's honor.[41] Whether he was in the Third Reich, Argentina, or Israel, Eichmann gave detailed and well-informed accounts of the murder of millions. He simply adjusted the account of his own role, and his attitude toward the murders, to his changing circumstances.

Life and Its Consequences

On October 19, 1960, the Hamburg newsmagazine *Der Spiegel* reported that in the West German newspaper business, rumor had it that *Life* magazine had bought Eichmann's "confession" and would soon publish it. The news reminded Servatius of the texts from Argentina that he still hadn't seen, which necessitated a further discussion with Fritsch and the Eichmann brothers. They decided to summon Sassen back to Austria. He was thought to have returned to South America, and Fritsch even offered to put up the money for his flight. But Sassen refused to let them see any of the material and put off the trip for a month. He told Eichmann's wife he was planning to publish the material as a book in December.[42] While Sassen was still convinced he would be writing for *Life*, the U.S. magazine was stealing a march on him: the story was announced in mid-November, and the articles appeared in the following two issues.[43] Servatius learned of the publication on November 25 and tried in vain to take action against it. *Life* published a few powerful extracts from the interview transcript, and small parts of the handwritten texts, under the headline: "Eichmann Tells His Own Damning Story." Each issue featured a phrase of Eichmann's to great effect: "I transported them . . . to the butcher" (November 28, 1960) and "To sum it all up, I regret nothing" (December 5, 1960). Everyone connected with the case reacted with shock, albeit in their own ways. Sassen, taken completely by surprise, lamented to Vera Eichmann: "Take a look at what LIFE has done to me." For her part, Vera Eichmann was unable to comprehend the title "I transported them to the butcher," so Sassen explained: "That's what LIFE did. I worked for LIFE for seven years, and this is the thanks I get."[44]

Servatius went into a fairly serious panic and spoke in dramatic terms of "catastrophic consequences" for the defense. At a press conference, he said he would renounce his brief if the texts turned out to be real; he believed they had been counterfeited.[45] When Eichmann was confronted with a translation of the *Life* articles, he had an attack of nerves and suffered a mental breakdown. The doctor whose care he was under quoted him as saying "I am finished. I am broken."[46] Servatius made the fastest recovery and, in the initial aftermath of the *Life* pieces, started taking a systematic approach to the Argentina Papers, determined to discover what danger really lurked within them. He telegraphed Vera Eichmann and asked Fritsch and the Eichmann brothers about the copyright. The answer was unanimous. Vera Eichmann telegraphed back saying the publication had been "at wish and agreement of Sassen Otto Vera." She thought she had acted according to her husband (Otto)'s wishes.[47] Fritsch confirmed to Servatius that Eichmann had expressly granted the right to publish the papers if he was arrested, and he provided what Fritsch claimed was an old copy of their contract from Buenos Aires. One slight problem was that it had been typed on a German typewriter, which no one in Argentina owned.[48]

At Servatius's request, Vera sent her brother-in-law, Robert Eichmann, a copy of her *Life* contract and—though Servatius wasn't aware of it—her copy of the Argentina Papers. The Eichmann family must have decided not to tell the lawyer—or Rechenberg, Genoud, or Fritsch—about the arrival of these papers. Servatius continued to demand that Sassen surrender materials that were, in fact, already in Robert Eichmann's office. Robert Eichmann had probably begun to read the documents and to fear that Servatius really would give up the defense if he got a glimpse of them. As we now know, the Linz copy of the Argentina Papers was more extensive than the *Life* copy and contained a great many texts handwritten by Eichmann. The defense would have no way on earth to refute these documents: they couldn't describe them as *Life* forgeries, or the results of Sassen's editorial intervention, because they were written in Eichmann's own hand. While Servatius was making a concerted effort to summon Sassen to Germany and discredit the *Life* articles, Fritsch, Sassen, and Robert Eichmann now all knew what was really in the Argentina Papers. And of the three, Eichmann's brother seems to have been the only one to realize that any further publication of them could only be damaging. Still, as it turned out, leaving the papers in his office did his brother more harm than good.

Meanwhile Sassen found himself at the center of international interest again, just as he had hoped. *Life* had, at least, credited him as the
interviewer (although the reference was to a "German journalist").
Now everyone was wondering who had landed the coup of interviewing Eichmann in Argentina. The sudden interest in this hitherto largely
unknown journalist led to the publication of a rather imaginative "interview with Sassen," which further strained Sassen's relationship with
Servatius. Each blamed the other for passing false information to the
press for this article.[49] Thereafter Sassen gave a real interview in Argentina, where he appeared self-assured and openly anti-Israeli.[50] And once
again he provided words that would come to shape the trial: he called
Eichmann "a cog in the diabolical Nazi machine." Later Sassen would
make an effort to offer Servatius his assistance in the form of insider
knowledge, but Servatius saw his offer as a threat and disregarded it.[51]
Months later Eichmann was still talking to his lawyer about a possible
book by Sassen and the division of any profit from it,[52] but Sassen never
managed to find the time to put together an Eichmann book of his own.
He was also starting to feel hunted, as the man who had sold Eichmann
to the Israelis.

The Hunt for the Confessions

The articles in *Life* had proved so useful to the prosecuting authorities
in Israel that they now had a growing desire to get hold of the complete
Sassen interviews. But the Israeli authorities weren't the only ones with
a burning interest in the material. To the disappointment of many, no
one managed to obtain the *Life* copy. However, on December 21, 1960,
a CIA informant in Germany sent pages of the transcript and sections
of the handwritten texts to Washington, under the heading: "Subject
Eichmann Memoires."[53] He (or she) apologized for the poor quality of
the "thermofax reproduction of the E memoires Photostat," which was
a result of the originals also being of poor quality and even illegible in
places. The copies of the handwritten pages, however, were clearly legible, to one able to decipher German script. The informant also said
that he had not yet compared the copies with the *Life* articles. At this
point, he said, there were numerous copies in Germany, but he made
an urgent plea for confidentiality on the handover of the materials. In

particular, any mention of the sender was to be avoided, as otherwise the source would be revealed: Hamburg. Officially, the only copy in Hamburg was *Stern*'s, so someone must have gone poaching in Nannen's office. It wouldn't have been the first time. If the CIA had been correctly informed, the journalist Zwy Aldouby, Ephraim Katz, and the specially engaged speedwriter Quentin Reynolds had also used material from the *Stern*'s editorial office. They had allegedly obtained it directly from a secretary there.[54] They used it for the book *Minister of Death*, which was on the market by the end of September 1960. The clue from the CIA files also tells us more about the Hamburg version of the Argentina Papers (and therefore also about the copies of it that were in circulation): it contained bad copies of the transcripts and legible copies of the handwritten pages. When the attorney general in the Eichmann trial finally submitted the Israel copy of the Argentina Papers in May 1961, it looked very different, consisting of clearly legible copies of the transcript, and less legible handwritten pages. So the CIA report tells us where the Israeli authorities *didn't* get their copy: Hamburg. It is impossible to copy a poor-quality version into legibility.

In February 1961 Robert Pendorf, the Hamburg reporter who had written on Eichmann for *Stern,* published his book *Mörder und Ermordete: Eichmann und die Judenpolitik des Dritten Reichs* (The Murderer and the Murdered: Eichmann and the Third Reich's Anti-Jewish Policy). In this book, Pendorf describes his source (and thus what *Stern* received from Sassen) as a handwritten document on squared paper, "a manuscript of around 80 pages, reporting on Eichmann's activities in the German Reich in very general terms, without details."[55] He also had access to numerous "books which Eichmann furnished with marginal notes" and "pages of commentary, prepared on loose sheets, on all the publications of note concerning the Third Reich's anti-Jewish policy." However, Pendorf had *not*—and he may have overemphasized this— used the Sassen interviews, the "'memoirs' [note the quotation marks!] that Eichmann later spoke onto tape, assisted by the former Dutch SS officer Willem Sassen van Elsloo, and which, after Eichmann was captured, were printed in a heavily abridged [!] form by the American illustrated paper *Life*." Pendorf was clearly aware of the interviews' scope, and traces of the transcript appear in his book. In all probability, his disclaimer was intended to avoid a conflict over the rights with *Life*. Pendorf's description, however, shows how much material Sassen had shown (if not given) to *Stern*'s reporter in Argentina. It also tells us what was known about the scope of the Argentina Papers in February 1961. In any case, Pendorf had seen material that was not available to the public (or even to researchers) until a few years ago.

At the start of 1961, the *Life* extracts, sections of the transcript, and around eighty pages of handwritten text were circulating around the offices of newspaper editors and at least two intelligence services. But nothing suggests that the Israeli prosecutors—or the Hesse attorney general Fritz Bauer—had copies of the Argentina Papers available to them at this point. That changed in March 1961, though not through the efforts of helpful journalists or, apparently, the German or American intelligence services.

The Security Breach

At the start of March 1961, a notable but little-known meeting took place, in a Frankfurt hotel, between Hermann Langbein from Vienna, Thomas Harlan from Warsaw, and Henry Ormond from Frankfurt. Each of these three men had an unusual biography and a desire to come to terms with Nazi history and see justice done. Had they not, they would surely never have met.

Hermann Langbein, born in 1912, was active in the Austrian Communist Party as a young man. He survived several concentration camps and became the first general secretary of the International Auschwitz Committee in Vienna. He later became secretary of the Comité International de Camps and was awarded the honorary title "Righteous Among the Nations."[56] After 1945 he devoted his life to the exposure and punishment of Nazi crimes, publicizing the survivors' misery and demanding systematic prosecution. He also compiled a substantial press archive on the hunt for Nazi fugitives, did educational work, and organized fact-finding trips to Poland. His excellent contacts put him in a position to find witnesses on the other side of the Iron Curtain. He facilitated Fritz Bauer's contact with Polish jurists, as West Germany and Poland had no diplomatic relations. Eichmann was right at the top of his list: Langbein had conducted a search for photos in Poland at the start of 1959, and in the same year—by agreement with Henry Ormond—he brought official criminal charges against Adolf Eichmann in Austria.[57]

Henry Ormond, born Hans Ludwig Jacobsohn, in Kassel, was a German jurist whose Jewish heritage lost him his position as a judge in the Mannheim District Court in 1933. In 1938 he was arrested during the November pogroms. Three months later he was allowed to leave Dachau concentration camp, after providing evidence that he was able to emigrate. Following his internment, he was almost unable to move one of his hands, which served as a reminder of this period for the rest of his life. He fled to Switzerland, then to Britain and Canada, and finally returned to Europe as a soldier in the British Army. During the occupation, he remained in Hanover and Hamburg as an officer and was responsible for building up a new press sector. Henri Nannen and Rudolf Augstein got their licenses through Henry Ormond, who would cast a critical eye on *Stern* and *Der Spiegel* for the rest of his life.[58] In April 1950 he started work as a lawyer in Frankfurt, where he conducted the first forced-labor trial against IG Farben and championed the recognition of Nazi victims' rights. In the Auschwitz trial alone, he represented fifteen joint plaintiffs.[59] He was also one of the first to recognize and denounce the Foreign Office's revisionist version of history.[60]

Thomas Harlan, born in 1929, was the son of the director Veit Harlan, who became notorious for the anti-Semitic 1940 film *Jud Süß*. In 1959 he moved to Warsaw, turning his disappointment in his father (and the memory of Goebbels giving him a train set for Christmas) into creativity and historical journalism. He took an unusual path, conducting most of his research in Poland and breaching the general East-West divide in other ways as well. Harlan's mission was to uncover Nazi criminals and call out perpetrators by name. With this in mind, he was planning a huge publication, to be called *Das Vierte Reich* (The Fourth Reich), on the postwar lives of influential Nazis. In May 1960 he published one of the first articles about Eichmann in the respected Polish weekly paper *Polityka*.[61]

Ormond and Langbein had known each other since at least 1955 and quickly developed a mutual respect. They issued press releases together; Langbein helped Ormond find documents and witnesses for his trials; and Ormond helped Langbein navigate the German legal system. In 1959 the Hesse attorney general, Fritz Bauer, made contact with Langbein via Henry Ormond, as Langbein had offered to arrange a site visit to Auschwitz for Bauer and his colleagues. Unfortunately, this trip foundered in bureaucracy at the last minute.[62] Langbein and Harlan

knew each other through Harlan's Polish girlfriend, who had survived
Auschwitz, and also because Harlan was active in journalism and the
media in Poland. Finally, Ormond and Harlan met in 1960 at the latest,
through either Langbein or Fritz Bauer.

On March 3–6, 1961, these men met at a hotel in Frankfurt to work
through the most comprehensive copy of the Argentina Papers in existence.[63] Langbein had brought it with him from Vienna, directly from
the desk of Eichmann's stepbrother Robert in Linz. A "locksmith," as
Langbein told Thomas Harlan, had gained access to the office at 3
Bischofstraße and had given Langbein the nine-hundred-page copy
that Vera Eichmann had sent her brother-in-law. We cannot know for
sure, but a locksmith may not have been necessary. At the start of 1960,
Simon Wiesenthal made contact with Robert Eichmann's secretary, who
was in her early twenties, via the Austrian secret police. She may have
been the person who opened the door to the "locksmith."[64]

The spoils were, in any case, passed on to Hermann Langbein.[65] He
quickly contacted the people he thought could put the papers to good
use. Irmtrud Wojak has found evidence that Fritz Bauer reserved the
copying facilities in his office on March 7. All other copying work for
his colleagues in Hesse's Justice Ministry had to be postponed because,
as an office memo said, the "Frankfurt copying facilities are not sufficient." Attorney General Bauer required facilities for copying the
transcript of a tape "allegedly dictated by Eichmann himself, when he
was still at liberty."[66] The documents to be copied, as Harlan's Polish
girlfriend, Krystyna Zywulska, recalled, came directly from Hermann
Langbein. This means Bauer also profited substantially from the meeting in Frankfurt. Meanwhile in Linz, Eichmann's stepbrother evidently
kept quiet about the theft from his office. Eichmann's lawyer was still
waiting to get a copy from Willem Sassen, and Hans Rechenberg's letters
show he was still convinced that only Sassen had the transcripts. Robert
Eichmann must have been so embarrassed about his lack of security for
such sensitive material as the Argentina Papers that he didn't even tell
his stepbrother's family about it. And so far no evidence has emerged
that the theft was reported to the Linz police.[67] The whole operation
went so smoothly that it didn't even reach the intelligence service files.

The meeting between Ormond, Harlan, and Langbein served another
purpose. Langbein needed money to have Robert Eichmann's copy of
the Argentina Papers transferred to microfilm, and to allow Harlan to

undertake a detailed analysis of this extensive source. Above all, Lang-bein wanted this material to be published as quickly as possible. As a financial statement from the end of March reveals, Henry Ormond did in fact manage to finance the microfilm copy. At the same time, the left-wing Italian publisher Giangiacomo Feltrinelli promised to finance Harlan's work.[68] It seems likely that Fritz Bauer played some kind of role here, but we have no evidence: all the correspondence went through Henry Ormond. Thomas Harlan took the film to Warsaw, started read-ing immediately, and contacted his friend Daniel Passent, the editor of the weekly newspaper *Polityka*.[69] Passent suggested to his editor-in-chief that the material should be used for a series of articles. Mieczysław F. Rakowski must have been a cautious man, as he enlisted the expertise of the criminal investigator Milicja Obywatelska. On May 6 *Polityka*'s editor-in-chief was presented with the evaluation: the material was genuine, and the handwriting was that of Adolf Eichmann.[70] Rakowski, Harlan, and Passent agreed on a different course of action from the one taken by *Life:* starting on May 20, *Polityka* published a five-part series, which presented the unedited texts for the first time and also provided its readers with images, facsimiles, and a handwriting analysis. The series included historical criticism and potted biographies of the men Eichmann had named as his collaborators. In only this short time, Har-lan and Passent had written 350 pages of commentary on the papers.[71] To date, it remains far and away the most thorough attempt to docu-ment the Argentina Papers for the general public.

Polityka was therefore disappointed by the series' impact—or rather, the lack thereof. Even in the Eastern Bloc, it generated no reactions worth mentioning. After the series concluded, Rakowski noted with resignation that neither Soviet Russian nor other Eastern Bloc media had shown an interest in the pieces. Radio Berlin in East Germany had been the only organization to ask for a copy of the first issue.[72] In the West, the *Allgemeine Wochenzeitung der Juden* and *Die Welt* mentioned the series in side columns, but *Polityka* didn't hear about it.[73] Everyone seemed to think the series was just a reprint of the *Life* articles: a few other magazines had reprinted them, including the French illustrated paper *Paris Match* (at the start of May).[74] But Rakowski also couldn't understand why Gideon Hausner, the Israeli attorney general, claimed he had received a copy of the Argentina Papers only after *Polityka* got its copy—and why Hausner didn't present all the documents. Hausner was talking about sixty-seven tape transcripts and eighty-three hand-written pages. What Rakowski (and Gideon Hausner) could not have known was that the copy in Poland was more complete, with more than one hundred additional pages. Rakowski simply couldn't imagine that a newspaper editor in Warsaw could be using documents that the prosecution in Israel had no idea existed—Eichmann's trial was, after all, one of the most important of the twentieth century. And Rakowski was in good company—not only with the Israeli prosecutors but also with people researching Eichmann.

The Israel Copy

Where Gideon Hausner obtained his copy of the Argentina Papers, and when it became available to his team, has always been a puzzle. But having traced the story of how the papers were divided up to this point, we have at least taken a few more steps. Hermann Langbein could have offered his great find to Gideon Hausner (or at least ensured that Fritz Bauer did so on his behalf). And we can safely assume that Fritz Bauer would have helped his colleagues in Israel in this regard: it would make no sense for him to assist in the hunt for Adolf Eichmann, only to then hold back important documents that had been put into his hands through a useful relationship. But the material that the Israeli prosecutors submitted as evidence didn't come from Bauer. The Israel copy is not only less extensive but of a much lesser quality: the handwritten fragments are difficult (and in some places impossible) to read, and the copy of the transcript comes from a version that was dirty and damaged in places. Robert Eichmann's copy is occasionally a little blurred, and in places the text veers very close to the edges, but there is no evidence of dirt on the transcript or the handwritten passages. This suggests that Bauer (and perhaps Langbein) offered Hausner the documents but Bureau 06, the special unit set up to interrogate Eichmann and collect evidence against him, politely declined them, assuming that it already had everything Fritz Bauer had. It certainly couldn't have been a lack of interest: handwritten texts cannot be surpassed as evidence. Not even Eichmann would have been able to claim they were a misrepresentation of his true thoughts in Argentina.

By the time Fritz Bauer obtained his copy, at the start of March, then,

the Israelis seem already to have had their own—though it was unconnected to the burglary in Linz. Eichmann's interrogator, Avner W. Less,
remembered discussing whether the prosecution should confront Eichmann with the Sassen transcript it had just received, but Servatius had
prohibited any further questioning.[75] Less was confident he could still
get Eichmann to cooperate and could persuade him to authorize the
documents before the start of the trial. He feared Eichmann would be
less responsive in the courtroom. This narrows down the time frame for
the papers' arrival to February or early March 1961. But whenever the
copy arrived, Henry Ormond and Hermann Langbein both agreed that
it must have come from a risky and illegal operation.[76] When Gideon
Hausner told the court on April 26 that he did not yet have access to the
documents on which the *Life* articles were based, that certainly wasn't
the truth—unlike the same declaration by Eichmann's lawyer Servatius,
who by this point had set eyes on only a fragment of the Argentina
Papers.[77] The people involved in the acquisition of the copies remained
silent for many years. Only in 2007 did Gabriel Bach, who had been
Hausner's deputy, make a vague statement about the Sassen transcript.
After Eichmann had been abducted, he said, "this journalist gave it to
Life magazine, and we got it from there."[78] However, judging from the
appearance of the Israel copy, this explanation seems unlikely. One
thing is obvious: these pages were not copied carefully and methodi-
cally, as you might expect if their source were the magazine to which
Sassen gave his first copy. Gabriel Bach, like most other people, seems to
have assumed that the "*Life* material" and the "Sassen document" were
the same thing. The truth is a little more complicated.

During his extensive exploration of Simon Wiesenthal's papers, Tom
Segev found a letter to Attorney General Hausner, written decades later,
reminding him that it had been he—Wiesenthal—who had given him
access to the Sassen transcripts.[79] We should exercise due caution when
dealing with quotes from Wiesenthal, but in this case it's hardly likely
that he would lie to the one person who definitely knew the truth. It
must therefore have been the enterprising man from Linz who tracked
the papers down. The help that Wiesenthal provided during preparations for the trial was not generally known until very recently. Emphasizing the role he played was not in the interests of those involved, and
so no one remembered it. Isser Harel in particular twisted the truth and
told tall stories to diminish Wiesenthal's part in his prestigious Eich-

mann case. It is thanks to Tom Segev that we now have a more bal-
anced view. Wiesenthal's letter does, however, show that he had found
only a part of the transcript: "As You will remember, I brought for the
Eichmann trial 28 transcripts from tapes with Eichmann's handwritten
notes."[80] The letter also reveals that Wiesenthal had no official source.

A page-by page comparison shows that the Israeli prosecutors had to
do some work in piecing together their Sassen copy. It is fundamentally
different from Hermann Langbein's excellent version, which points to it
being a copy made from what Sassen originally sold to the press.[81] The
question of whether Wiesenthal got the papers from a journalist or an
intelligence service colleague will be answered only when the archives
are opened, and we can discover when the BND actually got hold of
them. One BND worker claimed that they first received "the diary of the
Jew-murderer" from Mossad, but this is clearly nonsense. The pertinent
question is why the BND office didn't send the Israeli prosecutors the
papers they already had at the end of 1960.[82]

Hausner kept the existence of the material a secret from the court
for as long as he possibly could. The attorney general was probably trying not only to lull Eichmann into a sense of security but also to buy
time. Even without the Sassen transcripts, the prosecution had to wade
through mountains of documents, and this new material was difficult to
decipher. In April 1961, it therefore announced that it was asking *Life* to
hand over its material (which the Israelis, of course, already had). Even
Gideon Hausner wanted an evaluation of the papers before they were
used, and he gave his copy to the Israeli police's handwriting expert,
Avraham Hagag.[83]

We have Avraham Hagag to thank for the first ordering and complete
description of a copy of the Sassen transcript. He sorted the pages and
put the mountain of paper into manageable folders, with several tape
transcripts in each, ordered according to their numbers. This is how the
famous "two binders with 17 files" came into being: sixteen for the transcripts, and "File 17" for the eighty-three pages of handwritten text.[84]
The ordering wasn't completely accurate—Hagag allowed a few pages
of Sassen's own dictations and a fragment of a separate text by Eichmann to slip in unnoticed among the transcripts—but given the time
pressure, it was an impressive achievement.[85] Officially, Inspector Hagag
counted 716 pages of transcription and 83 pages of handwriting. If we
discount three accidental double paginations,[86] the Israel copy contains

713 typed and 83 handwritten pages or partial pages. Transcripts of some tapes were obviously missing, as a gap yawned between tapes 5 and 11; the third page of tape 41 was missing;[87] and tape 55 consisted of only two pages. The transcript in Israel ended—to great effect—with Eichmann's "little address to the group" from tape 67. Nobody in Israel had any idea that there might be more recordings, or that there had originally been more than seventy tapes. Mieczysław F. Rakowski (of *Polityka*) immediately noted that he, at least, knew there was a tape 68, though he didn't draw the right conclusions from that fact. But the gap between tapes 5 and 11, and the missing pages from tape 55, were the same in Robert Eichmann's copy and all the other copies in circulation. Sassen had removed these sections in 1960, as well as the first part of the Alvensleben interview, before distributing the copies across the world. Even he realized that a trial would be the wrong moment for the sort of rampant anti-Semitism regarding the "Jewish world conspiracy" and the "robber-state of Israel" that appeared in the first conversations.[88]

Dismantling the Evidence

When new evidence comes to light at short notice during a trial, time is always the crucial problem. Even the Israel copy, at a mere 796 pages, was more than enough of a challenge for Hausner's colleagues to process. But when *Polityka* started publishing extracts and facsimiles of sample pages on May 20, and even made a public offer to send the material to Israel for the prosecution, Gideon Hausner couldn't wait any longer without looking foolish. On May 22, 1961, he announced that he now had photostats of the manuscript. He responded to the judge's inquiry about them with a half-truth, saying that he and his team had had access to these documents for three weeks and had not received them directly from *Life*.

From then on, the papers were referred to as the "Sassen Document." The defense was given a copy, which—complete with the annotations made by Eichmann in his cell—is now held in the Bundesarchiv Koblenz (Servatius Estate). German jurists were granted access to it on request. Dietrich Zeug, the trial observer from Ludwigsburg, sent a copy to Fritz Bauer, saying he could compare it with his own.[89] But what had started out as a success for Hausner ended with unexpected misery:

when he tried to submit the papers as evidence in court, the attorney general was faced with the problem Avner W. Less had foreseen: Robert Servatius raised an objection. Even though Hagag's evaluation proved that the handwriting was Eichmann's (also submitted on June 9), Eichmann vehemently denied the material was authentic. And how does one prove that a typed transcript actually corresponds to what was said, when there are no tapes to prove it? Hausner was forced to fight over every page, and on June 12 it was agreed that only the pages Eichmann had corrected by hand, or had written by hand himself, could be used. The prosecutors watched helplessly as the most powerfully revealing postwar source on Eichmann and the Holocaust shrank from 796 pages down to the marginal notes on 83 pages, and another 83 pages of barely legible handwriting.[90] Powerful texts like the "little address to the group" couldn't be quoted. Over the days that followed, Eichmann worked tirelessly to disqualify as evidence what little of the text remained. He disputed "the famous Sassen Document" by stressing the influence of alcohol, claiming that most of his corrections had been lost, and lying that he had given up on correcting the transcripts because they were so bad. Unlike the handwriting expert (and anyone who had eyes), Eichmann couldn't recognize a few of the handwritten comments as his own. The handwritten pages were pretty much unusable, he said, as they were incomplete, which was bound to create a false impression. He also claimed there had been an agreement with Sassen that every page should be authorized by hand before being released for publication—a process he had become familiar with in Israel, where his interrogator had him sign off on each individual page of the interrogation.[91] But the most incredible of his lies was that Sassen had spoken very bad German (July 13). The man whose melodious, assured language had warmed the fascist hearts of nostalgic German Nazis; the man whom Eichmann had idolized for this very reason—this man was suddenly supposed to have blundered along, hardly understanding a word! Recklessly, Eichmann kept demanding the submission of the original tapes, though he also took the precaution of saying that Sassen had goaded him into making false statements to produce good headlines (July 19). He painted the discussions as "tavern conversations." Hours of studying historical theories and Nazi history suddenly became a lot of casual boasting and booze-fueled sentimentality (July 20). Sassen, he said, had occasionally tempted him to "relapse" into National Socialist ways of thinking. Naturally, he didn't mention that the entire Sassen circle was one big relapse. Eichmann also told his lawyer that what he had really written in Argentina was something very different. As Servatius then explained to the court, Eichmann would present these writings "as evidence of the real attitude of the accused."[92] Eichmann cleverly defused and dodged any question about why these discussions had taken place, by adopting the rumor that Sassen and *Life* had brought into the world: the legend of the "Eichmann memoirs."

This was the title Sassen had given the Argentina Papers when he sold them to *Life*. Eichmann's abduction had created a demand for details of the life and thought of the mass murderer in exile, and the "memoirs" label gave Sassen an exclusive on it. He achieved three goals at the same time: protecting the participants in the Sassen circle, presenting himself as a journalist without any National Socialist inclinations, and raising the value of his material.[93] He didn't mention the fact that a few years previously, he had instructed the transcriber to leave out all the anecdotes about Eichmann's life. Still, no one questioned the story that Sassen had been planning a book about Eichmann.

This piece of disinformation was a great help to Eichmann-in-Jerusalem, despite the fundamental problem of the Argentina Papers' existence. He was trying to convince people he was a reformed Nazi, who—without Hitler and his orders—could go back to being the completely harmless and entirely apolitical man he had always been. He had been an upright citizen in Argentina, delighted that he no longer had to carry out such terrible orders. In view of this effort, he was hardly about to correct the "memoir" headlines. His participation in a National Socialist political project—the continuation of an anti-Semitic war by other means—didn't fit the image of the harmless Argentine national. Without any prior agreement, Sassen and Eichmann both told the same lie. They let the world believe that an exile down on his luck had met a journalist greedy for money and had talked about old times over a bottle of whiskey or two. And the world willingly believed the cliché of the drunk, boasting Nazi—not least because everyone else involved stayed silent.

Only one man from the Dürer circle spoke out in public about the background of the Sassen transcripts. Dieter Vollmer, Eberhard Fritsch's deputy, had returned to Germany in 1954; he had kept writing for *Der Weg* until the very end and was apparently involved in the difficult distribution of Dürer publications. In 1961 Vollmer wrote a rather far-fetched article entitled "On the Professional Ethics of Journalists," for the tendentious West German monthly *Nation Europa,* in which he cleverly dismantled the embarrassingly clear evidence of the Sassen transcripts.[94] Sassen, he said respectfully, had questioned Eichmann "systematically about his past for several months." "Now, tapes were very difficult to procure in Buenos Aires at that time. So when a tape was full, the contents were briefly [!] jotted down in pencil [!], and the tape was wiped for the next recording. From these brief pencil notes, our diligent journalist compiled a manuscript." Eichmann gave an "impressive" refutation of the authenticity of this document in Jerusalem, and Vollmer assured his readers with surprising certainty that "the truth about what Eichmann said during these months can certainly no longer be investigated." Not even, he added as a precaution, "from the pencil notes, photocopies of which two acquaintances of mine have seen." Vollmer's story, with its brevity and its thrice-emphasized pencil, was obviously concocted to keep at bay the danger that the transcripts represented to everyone who had been involved in their creation, but also the danger they posed to revisionist history and the Nazi network outside Argentina. He was also feeding the doubt in the minds of people who hadn't been involved, and who didn't believe that Eichmann could have provided the material for such a significant piece of documentary evidence.[95] And the people who knew better, even those in Germany, didn't contradict him.[96]

The situation of Israeli attorney general Gideon Hausner had a tragic aspect: he had seen what Eichmann said in Argentina but was unable to use most of it. Fritz Bauer tried to help his colleague in Israel, attempting—apparently without success—to have Eberhard Fritsch questioned in Vienna, so he could authenticate the transcript.[97] Later, he even wrote to Sassen.[98] Hausner had hopes of obtaining at least one original recording, but the earth seemed to have swallowed up all traces of them.[99] Later, witnesses in Argentina reported that that was exactly what had happened: Willem Sassen had buried them in the garden.[100] These few yards of tape could have earned him a lot of money, so this story quashes the theory that he was a profit-hungry journalist, with no sense of responsibility toward Eichmann. Hausner later implied that he had put some considerable effort and expense into the search for the tapes. Because of the trial's length, he hoped he would eventually be able to refute Eichmann-in-Jerusalem using the recordings of Eichmann-in-Argentina.[101] As it was, the evidence against Eichmann was still overwhelming, and even reading the transcripts kept the prosecution from falling for his stories of reformation.[102] But still it was a defeat, and we will never know how the public impact of the trial might have been altered if Eichmann's unpleasantly penetrating voice could have been heard on the news all over the world, giving his "little address to the group." When Eichmann said, "No, I did not say that," there was simply no way to argue against him.[103] So the Sassen transcript acquired the reputation of being an unreliable source, and anyone who wanted to write about Eichmann, including Hannah Arendt, had to content themselves with the few pages admitted as evidence and the articles in *Life*—although no one really knew whether the latter were genuine texts or exaggerated tabloid journalism.[104] The articles in the Polish paper *Polityka*, which were a more reliable source, remained unused. The Israeli attorney general was never granted the opportunity to listen to the tapes and to confirm that he had been right about the evidence of the transcripts from the start. Gideon Hausner died in Jerusalem in 1990.

Evaluations and Old Resources

The Argentina Papers continued to be labeled "Eichmann's memoirs." They had not been admitted as evidence, and Eichmann's attacks on their authenticity were impossible to refute, so in the context of the trial, a more thorough evaluation wasn't necessary. This, and the Sassen transcripts' various foibles, also explains why little attention was given to the Alvensleben interview, the pieces of writing by Eichmann and Sassen, and the Langer lecture. The difficulty of spotting these "foreign bodies" in the papers can be gauged from the fact that the prosecutors weren't the only people who failed to notice them. Fritz Bauer was also eager to use this source in his investigations. In 1961 the Eichmann trial created more interest in hunting down hidden war criminals. Bauer commissioned a detailed "evaluation of the Sassen interview" from the Baden-Württemberg Landeskriminalamt (LKA), the federal state's office for criminal investigations. On December 4, 1961, the results were given to the Ludwigsburg Central Office, the office of the attorney general, and the Essen District Court (in connection with a trial that was taking place there). The evaluation was more than seven hundred pages long and included a comprehensive index of names and contents, paragraph by paragraph. I found the first reference to this mammoth work in a covering letter from the LKA,[105] and the index of names was also listed in the collection in the Bundesarchiv.[106] It comprised 467 entries over five hundred pages, with summaries of where and how each name was mentioned in the transcript—although such an index could never be complete, due to the transcript's numerous spelling errors and misheard names. Interestingly, the LKA officials had used two Sassen copies for this index: one on photographic paper, which was still the standard way of making copies, and one on microfilm. The paper copy was also indexed in the Bundesarchiv, but there was no sign of a film, and the list of contents seemed also to have vanished. The fact that it has all become accessible again is partly thanks to a handwritten pencil note discovered in the Central Office. But the documents wouldn't have been found without a curious official from the LKA, and equally curious staff at the Bundesarchiv Ludwigsburg, who were spurred on by my persistent inquiries. Norbert Kiessling (of the Baden-Württemburg LKA) helped with the reading of his predecessor's letterhead, which was difficult even for him to decipher, and explained to me the problems of special commissions.[107] Tobias Hermann got his Bundesarchiv colleagues interested in searching for the Central Office cabinet mentioned in the old handwritten note. The two binders came to light—and with them an envelope full of films, which turned out to be another copy of the Argentina Papers. There was also another binder that none of us had expected to find, with the promising title "Sassen Interview Miscellaneous." At this point, none of us knew that we had found the first extant copy of the handwritten texts stolen from the office in Linz and given to Hermann Langbein half a century ago.

The LKA's list of contents runs to just over 250 pages and contains information on every single paragraph of tapes 1–5 and 10–67, including page 3 of tape 41, which is missing from Hagag's Israel copy. The list was made not by historians but by civil servants working to bring criminal charges. Such works are produced under time pressure, in this case within the space of a few months. And anyone who has seen a few pages of the Sassen transcript will understand the difficulties of reading it. However, this synopsis is still the only one we have, and it allows the reader to gain a quick overview, although in the details there are numerous incorrect interpretations and abbreviations. Citations in later court transcripts show that this list of contents was put to use. But what the LKA staff failed to notice was the presence of several speakers in the transcript. They read Langer's lecture as a statement by Eichmann, and they counted the Alvensleben interview as another interview with Eichmann. The latter in particular had strange and frustrating consequences. When the Munich District Court II brought charges against Karl Wolff in 1963, Alvensleben would have made an excellent witness. Instead, tape 56 from the Sassen transcript bore witness against Wolff. The indictment included two lengthy quotes about Wolff from "Eichmann's" statement.[108] If the authorities had known who was really speaking on tape 56, the prosecutor would have been able to use Alvensleben as a witness in absentia. Given Alvensleben and Wolff's long, close working and personal relationship, it would have been hard to find more credible evidence. Pitting Eichmann against Wolff, however, meant pitting an RSHA head of department against the chief of *Reichsführer*-SS Heinrich Himmler's personal staff. Ludolf von Alvensleben had an office right next door to Himmler's for years—just as Wolff did. A word from him about the accused would have carried a great deal more weight.

After Eichmann

On May 31, 1962, after the failed appeal, Eichmann was also denied a stay of execution. The hanging brought to an end Eichmann's ability to influence his public image. He was no longer able to make people forget his confessions in Argentina—or his attitude toward his own crimes. The Sassen transcripts remained veiled in mystery: thanks to Eichmann's baseless lies, the people who had them didn't quite trust them as a source, and hardly anyone else had an opportunity to study them. One exception was Gideon Hausner, who published his account of the Eichmann trial in 1963–64 under the title *Justice in Jerusalem*. He quoted the Sassen transcripts—though confusingly, he gave the number of pages as 659 rather than the 713 of the Israel copy. Thomas Harlan, meanwhile, faced increasing problems in Poland in the early 1960s and was not allowed to return to Warsaw. His intention of publishing the Argentina Papers ran aground, first in Poland and then in Italy, where the publisher Giangiacomo Feltrinelli feared there would be rights issues. Eichmann and his heirs were probably the copyright holders, or possibly Sassen—and then there was Time Inc. and all the other people to whom Sassen had sold exploitation rights. Feltrinelli had likely at least heard of François Genoud, who was in Rome in 1961–62. He confidently claimed to be the owner of the exploitation rights to Eichmann's writing and had gotten himself a reputation across half of Europe for being an unpleasant opponent in copyright matters.[109] Henry Ormond and Hermann Langbein searched for arguments to reassure Feltrinelli. "In my opinion," Langbein wrote to Ormond, "Eichmann is not the legal owner of these tape transcriptions. Sassen sold them . . . to LIFE. So Sassen is no longer the owner either. Copyright could possibly be claimed by LIFE, if anyone. But since we obtained the text of the recording neither from LIFE nor from Sassen, but in the same [!] way as the court in Jerusalem, this also seems problematic to me." Langbein even wondered whether they should officially reverse the route the papers had taken and claim that their copy had come from Israel or Poland, to reassure Feltrinelli.[110]

But the main problem lay with Thomas Harlan, or rather with the job as a whole. Reading the 3,564 pages of the interrogation transcript was a monstrous task, and even the people who had done it thoroughly, like Hannah Arendt,[111] had to admit that the interrogation alone—or indeed the trial transcripts—were not reliable enough to function as the basis of an incontrovertible historical text. The detailed examination of the Nazi period really only started with the Eichmann trial. Today we have recourse to decades of research, excellent document collections, and statistical data, but the authors of 1961 were practically alone, gazing at the mountains of Eichmann's Jerusalem stories.

Compared with other authors, Thomas Harlan was facing a whole mountain range: Fritz Bauer had given him all the trial documents and, most important, exclusive access to the Argentina Papers. He still wanted to write his book about the "Fourth Reich," the unpunished war criminals still living in Germany. And he also intended to support Fritz Bauer, Hermann Langbein, and Henry Ormond in their preparations for the Auschwitz trial. Such a task might overwhelm even someone with no additional personal problems. Harlan struggled with a terrible guilt about disappointing his friends and supporters.[112] In later years he would find other, more artistic ways of dealing with the recent past, and a few years ago he gave his remaining Eichmann papers to Irmtrud

Wojak for further research; she still has them.[113] Unfortunately, so far I have been able to see only the small remnant of this collection still held in Harlan's archive.[114] So all I can do is refer to the promise Frau Wojak made me some time ago that we would definitely get a viewing of these papers organized, maybe, at some point. We therefore still have no real appreciation of what Thomas Harlan achieved—a man who was prepared to offer me crucial advice in spite of his illness, which eventually killed him in 2011.

The Missing Tapes

In the years after the trial, research on Eichmann and National Socialist anti-Jewish policy increased dramatically, largely based on the transcripts of the interrogation and trial in Jerursalem and the growing collections of historical documents. But curiosity remained about Eichmann in Argentina: nothing piques the imagination like inaccessible or missing documents. Nobody had any idea how extensive the Argentina Papers were (and no one read old Polish magazines), so researchers' curiosity concentrated on the missing tapes, numbered 5 to 10.[115] What could have been so secret that Sassen removed them before selling the transcript?

Academics often refrain from even touching questions of this sort, preferring to let journalists lead the way. They want to avoid getting a reputation for courting popularity with sensational research topics (or to call it by its real name: they don't want to stick their necks out and risk making fools of themselves). The disastrous thing about this division of labor is that both parties are then blinded: one to the old world, and the other to the newly discovered country, so that in the worst-case scenario, one is paralyzed with shock, while the other sinks helplessly in the morass.

Ladislas Farago has become one of the most successful distributors of dubious secrets about the Sassen interviews, which he trenchantly dubs "horror stories." His book about the war criminals who fled to South America is a sad combination of journalistic flair and historical naïveté: very few authors have managed to present highly explosive information and complete nonsense so close together.[116] Farago, who was born in the same year as Eichmann, was a screenwriter by trade and also wrote a wealth of popular books about espionage and the Second World War. This sort of book is meant to entertain (and his books serve that purpose extremely well). We shouldn't have to judge them by the standards of academic research—except that their content has entered academic literature by the back door. Other authors copied from them, forgetting—a simple oversight, naturally!—to use quotation marks and cite their source. Occasionally there is even an "I" where it should say "Farago."[117] Farago's wonderfully entertaining stories were thus transformed into actual witness statements, which have now been quoted in some otherwise very serious works. This makes it difficult to get away from the Farago story without closer consideration.

Farago's *Aftermath: Martin Bormann and the Fourth Reich,* published in 1974, was one of the first books about the escape routes that took Nazis overseas. Two chapters are devoted to Eichmann.[118] Farago did at least stumble over some of the names of Sassen's associates, like Hans-Ulrich Rudel and the Dürer circle around Eberhard Fritsch,[119] although his story suffers from claims that he also spoke to people who never existed, characters dreamed up from the pseudonyms used in *Der Weg.* He paints Sassen as a politically neutral and historically rather underexposed writer. Sassen didn't let himself "be confused by the Rudel-Fritsche crowd's spurious propaganda. . . . This was to be no whitewash, no apologia."[120] Farago reported his visit to Sassen in detail, claiming he saw the Sassen transcripts and even read them, the "sixty-seven tapes with that many transcripts neatly kept in seventeen 'Leitz' document binders," together with "marginal notes" and "extra pages" that Eichmann (!) had produced on a typewriter.[121] In total, Farago said, there were 695 (!) pages. This number tells us what Farago really saw: books about the Eichmann trial, in particular Hausner's *Justice in Jerusalem,* from which he skillfully lifted descriptions of the Israel copy, including an incorrect number of pages. In Argentina, there were neither seventeen binders nor only 695 pages.[122] The "summary" of "the sixty-two tapes," in which Farago says Eichmann principally spoke "about the escaped Nazis who had gone underground," shows he had never read the transcripts. Sassen would certainly not have had to ask Eichmann for this information, since he and Horst Carlos Fuldner knew far more about the escape routes Nazis had taken to Argentina than Eichmann did. The crowning moment of this imaginative eyewitness report comes with the "exclusive information" that Farago shares from his own interview with Sassen: "Today we know that Willem Sassen was holding back . . . five additional tapes the very existence of which was kept a secret. He also suppressed fifty-one pages. . . . On those five tapes which Sassen was withholding, Eichmann had recorded the sordid story of his own escape and presented his knowing account of Bormann's journey to Argentina." Farago goes on: "[Sassen] readily conceded that Bormann figured prominently both on the tapes and in his decision to withhold them, but refused categorically to surrender any of them or to let me as much as listen to the five mysterious tapes. 'I know,' he said ruefully, 'how far I can stretch my luck.' He was, he told me quite bluntly, 'afraid of the long arms of certain people.'" Apparently, Sassen would publish "the Eichmann book as a whole . . . 'only after the death of either of us, Bormann's or mine.'"[123] Let us generously assume that Sassen really was afraid, because other Nazis saw him as a traitor following the Eichmann episode; and let us also assume (with extreme generosity) that Sassen might have repeated rumors about Bormann to a sensation-hungry journalist, as such rumors have always changed hands for a fair amount of money. The fact still remains that there were never "five tapes and fifty-one pages" missing, on which Eichmann recounted the story of Bormann's part in his escape. Martin Bormann, the man who was head of the party chancellery and Adolf Hitler's private secretary, didn't survive beyond May 1945. He had neither the opportunity nor the will to get himself to safety, let alone show one of his comrades the way to Argentina. Tapes 6 to 10 (which are only four tapes, and sixty-two pages) contain not a word of any postwar encounter between Eichmann and Bormann. Nor are there any Bormann references on tapes 68 to 73, or in the discussion fragment on Sassen's private tape—which, tellingly, none of the people who claimed to have visited Sassen's house and looked at his original papers said they had seen.

We have no reason to suppose that Sassen tried to sell a fellow writer a pack of lies. He didn't share stories of this kind in any properly documented interview but rather provided extremely reliable information.[124] Farago's "Sassen interview" can safely be dismissed as artistic license, part of the dramatic structure of literature written for entertainment— and with it, all the reports that followed about visits to this fictive Sassen with his sixty-seven tapes and seventeen binders. The path that this legend took into the secondary literature does, however, reveal the possible repercussions of citations taken on trust, of which there are many examples in Eichmann research.

Farago was by no means the only person to place his longings in the missing parts of the Argentina Papers. Like anyone clinging to a shred of hope, he believed he would find his answers in the place to which he had been denied access. Similar expectations arose in a very different context: the anti-Zionist discourse in the Arab cultural world. In the Middle East, people had always assumed that Israel would suppress evidence, both at the Eichmann trial and in historical research in general. At first glance, this discourse looks a lot like the historical phantasms created in (neo-)Nazi circles. Its conspiracy theories said that Eichmann would eventually be revealed as a Jew, who had sacrificed millions of people in order to found the State of Israel. In the Arab world, doubts were also raised about the reasons for and the scale of the Holocaust. But the motives here were quite different. The Arabs weren't trying to rehabilitate Hitler or the National Socialists; they were trying to undermine Israel's Holocaust history and challenge the state's legitimacy. This effort gave rise to a host of different arguments.[125] One was based on Eichmann's tactic of seeking out German Zionists as his points of contact, to let them know that his sole aim was the emigration of the Jews to Palestine. In a culture that felt itself to be the real victim of the Second World War, this piece of information gave rise to a conspiracy theory that said that Zionists and National Socialists had had a contract from the outset, a secret alliance against the Arabs. The Nazis' extermination of non-Zionist Jews had been a necessary part of it. "As a central figure in some of the most important deals of cooperation between the Zionists and the Nazis," Faris Yahya explains in *Zionist Relations with Nazi Germany,* "Eichmann, while not the most senior surviving Nazi war criminal, was probably the Nazi with the most detailed knowledge of the Zionist movement's relationship with the Nazi regime." The Jews executed him too quickly and questioned him too little: "All that knowledge died with him." Unless, of course, he had already committed it to tape in Argentina.[126]

Anyone hoping that the undiscovered Eichmann texts will reveal him as the key witness to a Nazi-Zionist conspiracy will be bitterly disappointed. The Argentina Papers express a different kind of hope: there

Eichmann announces his dream of the great National Socialist–Arab alliance. He had seen it foreshadowed in the presence of the grand mufti, Amin al-Husseini, in Berlin, and in the RSHA's cooperation with his liaison officers. Then after National Socialist plans to wipe out the Jews failed, Eichmann's hopes rested on the Arab world eventually recognizing his "lifetime achievement" and celebrating—or even completing— his extermination work. *Ex oriente lux* stood for the insane nightmare of a Final Solution aided by "Arab friends." Other National Socialists had dreamed the same dream, even drawing up implementation plans for special gas-van commandos in Palestine.[127] Eichmann was still speculating about "the desert" as a "Final Solution idea" in Argentina.[128] He wanted to be an ally to the Arabs, not a witness to an anti-Arab plot, and certainly not an ally to Israel. The "missing" tapes and handwritten texts make this fact abundantly clear. Even in Israel, Eichmann kept telling his brother and his lawyer that he was happy for the Argentina Papers to be reedited, as long as his *Ex oriente lux* position remained.[129] This caused Western intelligence services to fear the worst. And as if on cue, Eichmann also rose to meet this expectation: in a letter to his brother, the prisoner in Israel excitedly announced his recent conversion to Communism. Communism was the only doctrine against "the root of evil: racial hatred, racial murder, and"—he actually wrote this— "anti-Semitism."[130] Anyone hoping to find his own fears confirmed in Eichmann's words will not be disappointed.

Rediscoveries

No fundamental change in the research landscape occurred until 1979. Up until that time, only those who had access to the collection in the Central Office in Ludwigsburg were able to read the Sassen transcripts. Now another find emerged, when the Bundesarchiv (at the time, a single archive in Koblenz) bought Robert Servatius's estate. The trial documents and correspondence, financial statements, collections of notes, and other materials left by Servatius were all deposited there for researchers to access, under the heading Alliierte Prozesse, or All. Proz., 6. These documents include the Israel copy of the Sassen transcript, which now became accessible to people outside legal circles—albeit in the version annotated by Eichmann in Israel.[131] We cannot say today that this collection has been sufficiently researched, but it still made a considerable difference to the material available for historians.

At the same time, Willem Sassen decided to hand all his papers over to Adolf Eichmann's family. We have two clues to Sassen's possible motives: first, he and his new, young wife were expecting a baby,[132] and such an event often sparks a desire to clean up the past. And in 1979 the Sassen house became a meeting place once again. Karl Wolff, the former chief of Heinrich Himmler's personal staff and one of the highest-ranking Nazis still alive, came to visit old "comrades" in South America, along with a reporter from *Stern*. Sassen was therefore expecting two "colleagues" and, as Gerd Heidemann remembers, was feeling nervous: he was still being accused of having betrayed Eichmann to the Israelis. A National Socialist in Peru even claimed that Sassen had never been in the SS and had deceived and used Eichmann from the beginning: he "betrayed Eichmann's hiding place."[133] Sassen never managed to shake off this suspicion, and it lost him his position as an important contact point for the South American Nazi network, which he had taken up when Fritsch moved to Austria. "When he was supposed to pass on important information, he sold it to two sides," Friedrich Schwend claimed. "Letters were opened as they passed through his hands." Sassen was "a traitor."[134] Forced to flee Buenos Aires for a while, he was for many years disadvantaged by people's lack of faith in him. In the meantime, Sassen really had done some work for Mossad: over a discussion lasting several hours, Zvi Aharoni had persuaded him that that would be a smart decision. This fact can't have improved Sassen's self-confidence.[135] No wonder Gerd Heidemann, who also thought Sassen a traitor, got the impression that he was making a special effort to be helpful to his guests.[136] Sassen probably wouldn't have wanted the notorious papers in his house, if there was a chance the *Stern* reporter and the former SS *Obergruppenführer* could start asking about them.

Eichmann's heirs made what turned out to be a less-than-shrewd decision, signing a contract with a publisher that had knowingly fostered a reputation for its right-wing bias. The publisher commissioned an editor, Rudolf Aschenauer, who had a similar reputation. In 1980 Druffel Verlag published *Ich, Adolf Eichmann*. It was a collage of Willem Sassen's Argentina Papers, some of which had been compiled incorrectly, with a revisionist commentary. Even right-wing circles had their doubts about the book's shoddy editing. Adolf von Thadden was one of the most active postwar right-wingers in West Germany: a friend to Hans-Ulrich Rudel, a member of the Deutsche Reichspartei (DRP), and a founder of the NPD—and even he criticized the volume, in the monthly magazine that was now called *Nation und Europa*. Against the intentions of the Aschenauer edition, Thadden read Eichmann's recollections as clear proof of the extermination of the Jews, even if he did stick to the "lie of the six million." In letters to the publisher, Thadden also stressed that this edition did not completely correspond to the real collection of texts.[137]

Right-wing extremists like David Irving, however, still praise Aschenauer today for "pointing out that a number of Eichmann's statements were incorrect." These "errors" correspond surprisingly often to the historical denials with which Irving created a reputation for himself.[138] However, the biggest problem with the Druffel edition was not Aschenauer's overpowering commentary but the decision to change the order of the texts, and to make the dialogic structure of the interview unrecognizable. The result is that, even with the best will in the world, it is impossible to tell who is really speaking. The editor obviously didn't know and attributed everything—Sassen's dictations, Langer's remarks and lecture, Alvensleben's answers, and so on—to Eichmann. "Unfortunately," as Dr. Sudholt from Druffel Verlag helpfully told me, the publisher got rid of the manuscript in 2000 during an office move. Nor could Dr. Sudholt find Vera Eichmann's sworn statement, published as part of the introduction. Fortunately, this doesn't mean that the Aschenauer edition can only be analyzed through a meticulous, sentence-by-sentence comparison. The Aschenauer manuscript, together with all the Argentina Papers and the tapes, has now reappeared. And since for several years now researchers have had access to all the papers in the original, they no longer have any reason to draw on such a problematic edition.[139]

In October 1991 David Irving managed to get hold of the remaining papers in Argentina, which Vera Eichmann had deposited with her husband's best friend. Irving claims that Hugo Byttebier, a compatriot of Sassen's who had taken over the documents from the "industrialist friend," gave Irving the "426 type-written pages" in a garden in Buenos Aires. Irving's evaluation of the material, and the sample pages he released, reveal to anyone familiar with the Argentina Papers what these

documents were. Irving had received typed versions of a few pieces originally handwritten by Eichmann, and a few pages of the Sassen transcript, all of which were also held in the Bundesarchiv.[140] There was also
at least one chapter of Sassen's draft for the planned book.[141] All that had
previously been seen of it was Eichmann's disparaging remarks about it.
He had told the Sassen circle he refused to authorize this compilation, in
which his words had been heavily edited and sometimes misinterpreted.
David Irving, who incidentally received only sixty-two tape transcripts,
announced he was going to publish all the papers he had been given on
his website. The "Chapter IV" already released gives a good impression
of Sassen's idea of the project, which even Eichmann was justified in
arguing against.[142] Eichmann's statements were moderated and embed-
ded into Sassen's conspiracy theory. These rediscovered papers would
be especially useful for an exploration of Willem Sassen's thought and
work.

In 1992 ABC Verlag in Switzerland bought the Sassen material from
the Eichmann family, together with a few tapes, the microfilm negatives,
and the Aschenauer manuscript. They prepared an overview, and new
prints of some of the transcript pages from the film, but failed to agree
on how to use the material. What happened over the years that followed
was essentially determined by changing economic circumstances. The
publishing house changed hands, and word slowly got around that after
more than forty years, the original tapes had been rediscovered. Guido
Knopp was the first to use well-judged snippets of them, in his 1998
documentary *Hitler's Henchmen II: Adolf Eichmann, the Exterminator*.
This film allowed an audience of millions, including astonished modern
historians, to hear for themselves parts of Eichmann's "little address to
the group" and the story of his grotesque "credo" ritual during mass
shootings. Shortly afterward, cultural broadcasters spread the news that
an editor from the publishing house (which in future does not want to
be named) had given the Sassen material to the Bundesarchiv Koblenz,
to be made available to researchers. Irmtrud Wojak was the first to pluck
up the courage to gain an initial impression of the tape collection, and
her 2001 book *Eichmanns Memoiren* conveys an idea of the task posed
for researchers by the audio material alone. It has admittedly taken
some time for the true significance of the Swiss owner's generous and
farsighted decision to be recognized, which is due in part to a critical
error made in cataloging the documents. The introductory text for the

collection reads: "The documents in the 'Adolf Eichmann Estate' collection are Adolf Eichmann's drafts for his autobiography, which offer no fundamentally new information beyond what is already known. Copies of the texts are already held in the collection Allied Trials (All. Proz.) 6: Eichmann Trial, in the Bundesarchiv, and have been available to researchers for many years." The last statement, at the very least, is simply incorrect. More than a third of the papers taken into the Eichmann Estate collection had never been available to researchers before. By comparison, the fact that the Argentina Papers can be viewed as an Eichmann "autobiography" only to a limited extent is a harmless misunderstanding. A shortage of time and manpower has made the job of Bundesarchiv staff difficult for many years, which was doubtless also to blame for the false evaluation. The consequences, however, were far-reaching, and researchers have continued to rely on the documents in the Servatius Estate, even in recent years—a collection containing only 60 percent of the full Argentina Papers. The highly problematic Druffel edition has also been quoted frequently, resulting in the misunderstandings of Eichmann's life and thought in Argentina that such a fragmentary and inexpertly edited source is bound to yield.[143]

My mistrust of the label "no new information" was aroused by the discovery of the index of names and paragraphs in the Budesarchiv Ludwigsburg. It referenced a page I had searched for in vain in the Servatius Estate: the infamous third page of tape 41, which mentions Eichmann's deputy, Rolf Günther. This clue made me take another look at the Ludwigsburg copies of the Sassen transcripts, which until then I had thought were identical to the copies from Israel. But even at first glance, it is obvious that the Ludwigsburg paper copy[144] is fundamentally different from the Israel version. Having realized that several copies from different sources existed in 1961, I saw that it was worth looking at a further copy—even if it had the same label—to find out if there was a third version. At this point, I couldn't even have hoped to discover that the Bundesarchiv Koblenz's Eichmann collection was, for the most part, the long-vanished original transcripts and handwritten texts.

The generous Swiss publisher's donation to the Bundesarchiv Koblenz contains the tapes—the conclusive proof of the transcripts' authenticity—and all the original transcripts, handwritten texts, and films that Willem Sassen still possessed in 1979. Sassen was anything but meticulous, and he was certainly no archivist. Even this original Argentina version is still not quite complete. The transcript of tape 29 is missing (the tape that Eichmann designated as "for your information only"), as are the page on Rolf Günther and the transcripts of tapes 70 and 71, if these tapes ever in fact existed. But the original material does contain the "missing" transcripts between tapes 5 and 11, namely 6, 8, 9, and 10.[145] There are also two further pages for tape 67, tapes 68–69, 72–73, and another, unnumbered, with the descriptive label: "On a private tape by W.S. filled with music and Flemish drama, there is a section of conversation between E. and W.S."[146] The handwritten texts and typed copies of handwritten texts are incomplete and are divided confusingly, as the structure of the complete draft has been ignored. There is also a typed copy of some notes made by Sassen during one of the discussions.[147] The film, which ABC Verlag had sight of in 1992, has yet to be compared with the prints. But the handwritten text and typed copies comprise more than two hundred pages, although a large number of the handwritten pages from the Israeli "File 17" are missing. In contrast to the handwritten papers in the Eichmann Estate in Koblenz, the papers in the Ludwigsburg binder labeled "Miscellaneous" are good, clean copies of pages that allow the "File 17" texts to be reordered into the large manuscript "Die anderen sprachen, jetzt will ich sprechen!" (The Others Spoke, Now I Want to Speak!), to which they originally belonged.

To simplify this confusing picture: anyone wishing to study the Argentina Papers today first has to reassemble Eichmann's texts and the Sassen interviews from three separate archive collections, sometimes page by page. That is what I did for this book (and my other work), and I can therefore report that the effort is worthwhile. But it's quite enough for *one* person to squander a lifetime on such a puzzle, and as such I am happy to provide a page concordance to people undertaking further research in the Bundesarchiv, with references to where each paper can be found. The same goes for an overview of the tape contents. Not all the tapes are the originals from Argentina, and the contents don't span the full twenty-nine hours of playing time: some parts are repeated several times. A few of the tapes have been transferred to different tape speeds, evidently to make the speech more comprehensible. But even where the recordings are original, the same cannot be said of the tapes. At least one of the copies has been made only in recent years, although the tape looks old. As is often the case with old tapes that have been recorded over several times, it is possible to hear remnants of what the tape previously contained: a children's radio play with multifrequency push-button tones and polyphonic sounds, suggesting 1990s technology. But there are also tapes recorded in 1957 on which you can still hear (or guess at) previous Sassen discussions. Analyzing these in a recording studio might offer up a few more surprises.

Excursus: The BND files; or, Eichmann's Fourth Career

The Mossad agents were the first people to publish an account of the events surrounding Eichmann's abduction. Zvi Aharoni, Peter Z. Malkin, and Isser Harel all wrote detailed books, allowing us an insight into the Mossad operation. Asher Ben Natan's memoirs and the estate of David Ben-Gurion, meanwhile, help us to better understand the decision-making process that led to the abduction and trial. Disagreements and dislikes also developed among the people involved, so the reports provide a multifaceted and occasionally inconsistent picture. And a trend of increasing transparency is obvious: when Isser Harel, the former head of Mossad, updated his book *The House on Garibaldi Street* for the 1997 edition, he decided to drop most of the aliases he had used in the early years and replace them with people's real names.[148] Many of the Israeli team also gave interviews, explained their motives and thoughts, and answered questions. Not all the documents connected to the abduction and trial are accessible to researchers, but there has been a substantial step in the right direction.

When the U.S. National Archives started releasing intelligence service files on National Socialists in 1998, expectations among researchers ran high. Although many of the pages that emerged were banal, and others were censored to an absurd extent, the CIA "Name File Adolf Eichmann" yielded a considerable amount of information. Without these files, it would have been impossible to reconstruct some of the events around the Sassen transcripts. The people who compile intelligence service files are not historians; nor are they concerned with assembling archives for future research. They are carrying out their mission to protect the interests and security of a country. It is thus all the more important to realize that at some point the damage caused by revealing your predecessors' disinformation strategies, errors, and shortcomings cannot be greater than the damage caused by wild speculations and the suspicion that you have something to hide.

Intelligence service documents always contain reports from other countries and information from "friendly" intelligence services. In spite of great care taken in this regard, the CIA files that have been declassified still contain some intelligence that obviously comes from the West German BND. No international outcry was heard about the release of the files (at least, none that reached the ears of the public). But anyone with an interest in the matter was reminded that the BND had compiled its own Eichmann file, as had the German Foreign Office and the BfV. And access to the BND files is still restricted. Only a few sections of files, regarding incidents with a marginal bearing on the Eichmann case, have been handed over to the Bundesarchiv (in November 2010).[149]

It is only thanks to the journalist Gaby Weber that a wholesale extension of the declassification deadline has been prevented. In 2010 she managed to have a block on the files' release declared unacceptable by the Federal Administrative Court. Weber was the first to successfully petition for a limited view of the files, and she was able to study at least part of the collection, though in places the pages were heavily censored. Unfortunately, this incident has not led to a general release of these selected files. In other words: anyone wishing to get a glimpse of them can do so only by bringing their own lawsuit. The German tabloid *Bild* made one of the documents available to the general public in January 2011, after one of the Springer Verlag reporters, Hans-Wilhelm Saure, petitioned for access to the files.[150] In February 2013 the Federal Administrative Court dismissed the case for further files to be released. The plaintiff still has the option to take the case before the Federal Constitutional Court and the European Court of Justice. Other journalists have announced their intention to follow Mr. Saure's example and bring their own lawsuits for complete declassification of the Eichmann files. It looks as though the German courts will be dealing with the "Eichmann case" for a long time yet.

This bizarre state of affairs ultimately makes research and public-interest disclosure dependent on having the money for court costs and lawyers. It raises the question of what could be so explosive about these BND files that releasing them after more than fifty years is still not a political option. The most substantial explanation lies in the eleven-page justification of the declassification ban, issued to Gaby Weber by the Federal Chancellery on September 10, 2009, before her challenge was successful. She has generously made it available to the public on her website. The attempt to withhold all files on the Eichmann case, which was declared invalid by the Federal Administrative Court, deserves closer consideration. It gives us an insight into the fears that are still associated with the idea of transparency—and the BND's refusal reveals more than the files alone ever could. Anyone who denies something is always talking about themselves, in the first instance. And the more we know about Adolf Eichmann as the subject of research, and the extent of the documents available today, the clearer this effect becomes.

The official statement from the Federal Chancellery, given on September 10, 2009, says that the relevant collection of files comprises around 3,400 pages in five storage units. This is the result of a broad search, it says, including files "with only isolated references to Eichmann in Argentina"—though they were contained in the same five storage units, so another staff member must also have thought they were connected.[151] The reason for not releasing the BND files tagged with the search term *Eichmann* essentially boiled down to three points that had to take priority over the "rather abstract . . . interest in finding the truth" (p. 9). They were: the common good, the protection of informants, and the general right to privacy of affected third parties.

The term *common good* suggests that releasing these files would have a negative impact on the country's security interests. The collection also contains copies of documents given to the BND by foreign agencies, which apparently are not theirs to release. This argument is immediately illuminating: intelligence services that rely on international cooperation also rely on all parties to treat anything that they are given responsibly. Of course, foreign agencies are also aware that a service in a constitutional state is subject to that state's law, and that declassification deadlines will also apply to foreign material. But it is entirely inconsistent to uphold one's government's discretion regarding "foreign agencies," yet then point a finger at the State of Israel, saying that "not all the official [!] papers relating to the Eichmann trial have been made public." Be that as it may, someone requesting access to BND files from the BND wants just that and nothing more: BND files. Which made it all the more surprising that the files handed over to the Federal Administrative Court contained material from Israel.[152]

The argument goes a crucial step further: "Evaluation documents produced by the BND [could be] wrongly seen as attempts to discredit specific persons from foreign public agencies. In the case at hand [the files relating to Eichmann] and in general, this could substantially compromise or even endanger friendly relations with foreign public offices" (p. 3). This hint raises fears about what the BND appraisals might contain, if they could potentially threaten current international relations. It is, after all, a perfectly normal procedure to evaluate all information from third parties, whether they are intelligence documents or historical sources. But the thought that appraisals by 1950s BND staff—Federal Republic officials—of "persons from foreign public agencies" (Israel, for example) might still be seen as derogatory is frightening.

The second point relates to the protection of informants: the duty not to endanger, through indiscretion, a person who has given information in the course of an intelligence service operation. The protection of informants is connected to the security interest: if word were to get around that an intelligence service wasn't protecting the providers of its intelligence, it would soon have none left. In this light, the fact that the BND's statement provides details about a specific informant is quite surprising. This helpful person, we learn, is "comparatively easy" to discover, as he had exclusive "access to the relevant information." "The content and scope of the information . . . allow conclusions to be drawn about the source of the information, as well as the identity of the informant" (p. 5). He has also "asked for . . . special source protection." The informant in question was still alive in 2009 and "still active in his [!] professional field." The "revelation of his identity would threaten the private and professional spheres not only of the informant" but also of "several of his current business associates." Speculations about his "cooperation with the BND . . . would probably mean economic disadvantages for his business as well as disadvantages in terms of his reputation" (p. 5). The informant was not only "still active in professional life" but was "mentioned by name and searchable on the Internet" (p. 9). He had also been "reactivated . . . for another BND operation" in the early 1980s, and any public association with this operation would also pose a threat (p. 5). With all due respect for the willingness of the people making this statement to explain their reasoning in detail, the question must be asked: why would intelligence service personnel give such a detailed description of someone who could be damaged by speculations about his pivotal role in the Eichmann case? Someone who had been of service in that case might not be given a medal in every part of the world (only in most): there are still some cultural spheres that wouldn't recognize that as an honorable achievement.[153] But the danger of Nazi sympathizers attacking the person in question is surely an excellent reason for not "protecting" him through this explanation. The BND gives us a person who is at least in his late sixties and has been "particularly present" as a businessman in these parts of the world for the last fifty years. In half a day, a resourceful researcher[154] could narrow down the list of possible informants (using the Internet, as helpfully recommended) to such a dangerously small circle of people that a dozen men are now the subject of these threatening speculations. "Protection of informants" at the cost of endangering people unconnected to the case seems untrustworthy to me and anything but reassuring to present and potential BND informants.

The privacy rights of third parties, according to the statement, concerns around fifty people named in the files, since a large number of files are involved, although they have only a "marginal" relation to the subject (p. 9). It would be necessary to censor these names, but this would mean a "disproportionate administrative effort," weighed against the likely gain for research. Of course, any academic would dispute the claim that one or more BND employees could be in a position to judge what might or might not serve research in this field. The usefulness of even a single index card depends so fundamentally on an academic's education and close reading skills that anyone speculating about it from the outside can only ever be wide of the mark. All academics necessarily overestimate the importance of their own area of research, to give them the stamina for work that takes years to complete—but the significance of Adolf Eichmann, for scholarship and the wider world, cannot be doubted in the slightest. Whether you are arguing against a declassification ban or not, Eichmann is much more than a popular subject for backroom scholars, and Germany's engagement with it is valued all over the world in anything but an "abstract" way (p. 8). It is one of the criteria by which the Federal Republic is judged internationally. Respect for Germany is rightly coupled to our willingness to learn from the past. If anything is going to damage the "common good," it is an opinion expressed on Chancellery letterhead that the administrative effort of opening the BND files on Eichmann "for the purposes of finding the truth" (p. 8) is "disproportionate" (p. 11).

In addition to these three points, the statement warns against the publication of research findings from the files in question. "The documents," it says, "contain political (and diplomatic) implications for other countries in addition to the Federal Republic of Germany, which, freed from the historical content of the archive documents, have current significance, and could be exploited in the context of foreign policy aims and interests (Middle East policy)" (p. 8). The statement vindicates everyone who has long claimed that studying documents from contemporary history is always about more than reading historical tea leaves. The people who live and breathe this research are convinced that it has an impact in the here and now, and they do it for that reason. The fact that misinterpretations or overinterpretations can crop up in academic writing, as they can in any form of publication, is as clear to any enlightened person as the fact that there are people who can and will use any information for their own ends. Intelligence service dossiers serve this purpose exclusively: the exploitation of knowledge in order to set political goals, particularly in an international context. A glance at the BND files relating to Eichmann is also a glance at the work of the intelligence service and the position of German society in the 1950s and 1960s in relation to the world—but this is not an unfortunate disadvantage of source research, but its declared intention. The exploitation of documents in some kind of political context is nothing new, after all. The history of the twentieth century has, however, also shown that propagandists can misuse any information at all, yet the attempt to keep material from them would resemble total censorship.

The BND's effort to explain its handling of the Eichmann files has made the release of this statement a public event with an international impact. You only have to speak to scholars from other countries to see how disconcertingly dishonest it appears to the outside world. The withholding of files is a normal process, for which constitutional states have clear rules, but in Germany we are also committed to the principle of transparency. This is why, before a declassification deadline has been reached, there are rules for the partial release of files, with words blacked out where necessary. And when, despite these regulations, people still have to litigate for the right to see files, it damages a country's image, making any citizen who also happens to be an academic feel uncomfortable in the international research community. In one respect in particular, this behavior has now caused irreparable damage. It has created the impression that the government has a pronounced interest in witholding information on Eichmann. Because the release of the files has been contested, people now suspect that any future release will never really include all the documents in the BND's possession. One reason for creating laws around the handling of classified documents was to guard against such conspiracy theories.

Unfortunately, you don't have to be a fan of conspiracy theories to suspect that the collection of files now presented to litigants is incomplete. You don't even need to see the files yourself to spot it: for anyone who has studied Eichmann before Jerusalem, a single piece of information is sufficient. The files contain fewer than thirty pages covering the period before Eichmann's arrest in May 1960, and four of them relate to Willem Sassen's travels and his passport applications. They were probably added to the Eichmann files only after the Sassen interviews had come to light. Neither Simon Wiesenthal's information nor the arrest warrants from Austria and Germany are there. There are no notes on the information exchanged with the CIA in 1958, or on Fritz Bauer's large-scale diversionary strategy from summer 1959, to name just a few key points. Apart from the index card with Eichmann's cover name and contact address from 1952, nothing suggests even those events and pieces of information with which we are now very familiar from other sources. If we compare the available pages with the five documents that the BfV released several years ago, it becomes clear how glaring this gap is, even against a backdrop of general reticence. A single index card may reveal a great deal to someone who has done their homework and is able to interpret it, but the real problem cannot be overlooked: whatever the reason for the current slender size of the Eichmann file, it was certainly not always the case. We have no reason to suppose that the way the BND carried out its duties was as inadequate and unsystematic as these papers suggest. Unfortunately, this observation holds true for more files than those up to May 1960.

Where does the fear of transparency come from in the Eichmann case? If we don't want to assume that that is a general principle when it comes to the release of intelligence service files, we should perhaps

consider further. What differentiates the Eichmann case from other
Nazi legacies is everything that became connected with his name. Even
before his abduction in 1960 people were gripped by a fear of what he
might say. And the coordinator of the National Socialists' persecution
of the Jews had touched so many areas of political and economic life
that the abduction unsettled not only Nazi fugitives but also economic
and industrial representatives, and people working in justice, medicine, government, and the diplomatic services. From the outset, Eichmann's name had an impact in places that Adolf Eichmann himself had
never been. This was part of the mechanism of power that governed
the National Socialist system to perfection. In the network of the criminal state from which so many had profited, a lot of people must have
felt they had been accomplices, even if the period after 1945 had not
been a time of embarrassing questions for them. The reappearance of a
name that had become a symbol disrupted their collective silence. And
after Ben-Gurion announced the Eichmann trial, a tremendous unrest
spread to all the corners of the world where people knew this name. In
1960 no one knew that Eichmann would take the old loyalty among
comrades seriously, or that he would refuse to betray them despite his
garrulous nature.[155] In summer 1960, as he had in the Third Reich, Eichmann was once again making an impact in places he had never been.
Anyone observing the global reactions to Eichmann's capture, as an
intelligence service was bound to do, would also have been confronted
with reactions even from regions Eichmann had had nothing to do
with. For years, people had suspected that he was in Syria or Egypt, so
investigations also had to consider the largely unexamined network of
Nazis in the Middle East. This network, as we know from individual
cases, quickly built important economic relationships, some of which
are still revelant today. They are, of course, also relevant to the Israel-
Palestine conflict ("Middle East policy"). Individuals may have thought
they saw Eichmann in the Middle East, or as Erich Schmidt-Eenboom
suggested, someone there may have been cavalier enough to give himself
the alias "Eichmann"[156]—in any case, these rumors provide a key to a
piece of very current postwar history. No thorough investigation by the
intelligence service at the start of the 1960s could have been carried out
without hearing stories of this sort. Whether in Argentina, Germany,
Austria, Spain, or the Middle East, the general unrest was a reaction less
to Eichmann than to the memories of people's own involvement in the

Third Reich, which were not so easily done away with. Just as a book that looks at Eichmann before 1945 is necessarily also a book about the Nazi period, the intelligence service files cannot avoid painting a picture of the postwar period, in the attempt to find Eichmann after 1945. The publication of the Eichmann files would unveil this picture. It might well also provide some uncomfortable insights.

But it would be a mistake to hold the actions of one institution and its inadequate handling of fifty-year-old files against this institution alone. The BND wasn't a small-scale, secret unit, pursuing dubious aims behind the backs of the new Federal Republic and its representatives. If our engagement with National Socialist crimes has taught us anything, it is that small groups are able to act only when society and its representatives instruct and allow them to. One-sided accusations of guilt, as when people style the organization as a "state within a state," cloud our judgment as much as the assumption of broad responsibility. The intelligence service was unable to operate outside Germany's political interests in the 1950s, and its staff cannot be blamed today if the Federal Chancellery wants to block access to historical files or delay declassification by setting up commissions with working plans that stretch over years—especially when there has been no public outcry to speak of.

There is something grotesque about the attempt to keep files secret by hinting at their explosive content: we are once more allowing a lack of resolve, and the desire to avoid necessary decisions, to become inescapably linked with the name Adolf Eichmann. Half a century after his execution, the danger is very real that his name could become a symbol once more, this time for the temptation to look the other way, when we should be looking straight at this issue. This is the only way to avoid future mistakes. And it really has nothing to do with what might be contained in the historical files, or what a federal German institution neglected to do or prevented from happening in the 1950s. In the German Bundestag's 2011 debate on the BND Eichmann files, Jerzy Montag urged a radical rethink of how we handle these unpleasant legacies: "We have to change direction. . . . If we discover something through the executive supplying us with new material three or four times, rather than hearing it from investigative journalists, or by chance, then something will have changed."[157]

I had already finished writing this book when, unexpectedly, a journalist allowed me to get a look at the BND files. As much as it pleases

an author not to have to completely rewrite her book, as a German academic I must confess that this experience left behind a lasting unease.
I would have preferred to learn more than would fit into a few pages
of additional comments. Among the 2,425 pages of File 121 099 in the
BND archive, there is one that provides grounds for hope. It contains a
single instruction, in capital letters: "Please collect everything on Eichmann carefully—we still need it."[158]

Not the Last Word

Anyone wishing to study the thinking of Adolf Eichmann in Argentina now has more material at their disposal than ever before: most of
the original transcripts; several different copies of them; a number of
handwritten texts and typed copies; and Eichmann's notes and commentaries on the most important publications of the day. We also have
an advantage over the people who witnessed the trial, in the form of a
body of research on contemporary history, and an excellent edition of
the interrogation and trial transcripts.

But the task is still huge: Eichmann has always managed to brow-
beat and transfix people. Willem Sassen, even after the Eichmann trial
and his failure with *Life,* continued to tell people he was going to write
about Eichmann. Even when he decided to hand over the papers and the
tapes to the Eichmann family in 1979, he was eager to retain the right
to quote the Argentina Papers in an essay of his own. He never revealed
details about the Sassen circle, keeping the knowledge to himself even
after most of the people involved, like Ludolf von Alvensleben, were
dead. But his encounter with Eichmann would not let him be. In his last
interview, which shows him to be a broken alcoholic, barely able to utter
a coherent sentence, his thoughts still circle around the Eichmann book
that he would never write.[159] In the end, he seems to have suffered a fate
similar to a character he created for the novel *Die Jünger und die Dirnen,*
just when he was starting his discussions with Eichmann.[160]

> When he came home, he did not enjoy his dinner. He went into his
> study, where the walls were lined to the ceiling with books, took a
> bottle and a glass out of the small mobile bar, and settled back in
> the armchair. He took up a newspaper, then a book, and finally a

specialist journal with a glowing review of his latest publication, but he could not concentrate his mind for a single moment. He drank quickly and without much enjoyment; intoxication came just as quickly, and brought no comfort. It started up again—this hammering in his temples, the unease in his heart—and again he heard the penetrating voice of Erwin Holz, in snatches from the many conversations he had conducted with him in recent days. For Erwin Holz, these were the scalpel with which he had ruthlessly gone to work on himself and his generation. The doctor had tried to defend himself against Holz's arguments and assertions, which were at times so primitive—to dismantle them with analysis or sarcasm. And afterward, he had always been dissatisfied with his destructive effort. It had been an exciting adventure for his calm, methodical mind, letting Holz light his way into the labyrinth of the modern world's spiritual privations, and the catacombs of the self-sacrificing idealists. It had been an exciting adventure, but it had also become a burden. For now Holz's voice was everywhere, round about him, inside him, and it even spoke in places where Dr. Dr. Thomas Bauer believed he himself had the last word. He pulled up his outstretched legs, folded his arms across his knees, and drew in his head as if to protect himself. He closed his eyes and let the voice attack him.

Sassen really did lose his own voice. The encounter with a mass murderer and his thinking paralyzed forever his most impressive talent—his skill with language, his writing. Sassen died in 2001, without ever being published again.[161]

When Eichmann found himself in Jerusalem in 1960, it was his Argentine past as well as his crimes that caught up with him. He couldn't have been surprised—unlike the people around him, including his lawyer. He had told Sassen and Fritsch several times to publish the material as soon as he was dead or had been taken prisoner. And once again Eichmann had a distinct advantage over everyone else: he knew exactly what he had left behind in Argentina. He was well prepared to give his supposedly spontaneous reaction. Denying the authenticity of the papers was as risky as it was effective. In so doing, he not only managed to protect everyone involved in the Argentine interlude, and to make the Sassen circle largely invisible; he also ensured that the worth of the invaluable

Argentina Papers was questioned for decades afterward. What he hoped to gain by playing this risky hand was the ability to determine his own place in history once more, in this final battle of the ideological war. But this strategy also caught him in the snare of a National Socialist error: his place in history was never a matter of his free choice, let alone a diktat to posterity. Now the age of his ability to manipulate and distract people with his lies is over. Now it is our job to create transparency and put Eichmann where he belongs, rather than be struck dumb by his torrent of words. Nearly thirteen hundred pages of the Argentina Papers, and over twenty-five hours of tape, have survived many years and numerous games of hide-and-seek. The curse of a man who was desperate to write and to explain himself is that this urge has put others in a position to read his every word, more thoroughly than he could ever have imagined.

Acknowledgments

I would like to thank a great many people at the archives for their willing assistance and interest, for fetching materials, for countless letters, telephone conversations, and e-mails, and especially for all their ideas on possible shortcuts through the depths of the archives, which I would never have found without them. Particular acknowledgment is due for their courage in opening cabinets for which the contents had no index book. You can imagine how much I owe to their curiosity, enthusiasm, and personal encouragement.

For their personal assistance and information, individual corrections, and in some cases extensive correspondence and access to private archives, my thanks to: Hildegard Becher-Toussaint (Oberstaatsanw. FFM), Sonja v. Behrens, Barbara Bieringer (Vienna University archive), Wolfgang Birkholz (*Kölnische Rundschau*), Reinhard Brandt (Marburg), Detlef Busse (Lower Saxony State Archive), Michel Davis (*Parade,* United States), Nicolette A. Dobrowolski (Syracuse University, New York), Helmut Eichmann, Dr. Franke (Pattensen), Daniel Fritsch, Christian Ganzer (Kiev), Uriel Gast (ETH Zürich), Christian Gerlach (Washington), Uki Goñi, Peter beim Graben, Jasmin Gravenhorst, Georg-Michael Hafner, Martin Haidinger (ORF Vienna), Thomas Harlan (†), Gerd Heidemann, Helmut Heinen (*Kölnische Rundschau*), Tobias Herrmann (BA Ludwigsburg), Raul Hilberg (†), Birgit Kienow (DLA Marbach), Norbert Kiessling (LKA BW), Andy King (*Telegraph*), Elisabeth Klamper (DÖW), Lotte Köhler (†), Michael Köhler (Hamburg), Peter F. Kramml (Salzburg City Archive), Annette Krieger (*Kölnische Rundschau*), Manuela Lange (BA Koblenz), Raymond Ley, Deborah Lipstadt, Walter Lorenschitz (ÖStA), Marcel Marcus (Ludwig Mayer Bookstore, Jerusalem), Holger Meding (Cologne), Paul Mevissen, Beate Meyer (IGDJ), Lutz Möser (BA Berlin), Harry Mulisch (†), Annegret Neupert (BA Koblenz), Christoph Partsch, Daniel Passent, Anton Pelinka (Innsbruck), Timorah Perel (Yad Vashem), Bertrand Perz (Vienna), Manfred Pult (HHStA Wiesbaden), Doron Rabinovici, Oliver Rathkolb (Vienna University), Werner Renz (Fritz Bauer Institut), Dirk Riedel (Dachau Memorial Site), Francisca Sassen, Saskia Sassen, Hans-Wilhelm Saure (*Bild*), Esther Schapira, Patricia Schlesinger (NDR), Stefan Schmitz (*Stern*), Werner Schroeder, Carlo Schütt (FZH), Kurt-Werner Seebo (Bergen City Archive), Katrin Seybold-Harlan, Christoph Stamm (AdsD), Alexander Stühmer, Roelf van Til, Sidar Toptanci (BA Ludwigsburg), Michaela Vocelka (Simon Wiesenthal Archive), Angelika Voß (Archiv FZH), Klaus Wiegrefe (*Spiegel*), Michael Wildt, Irmtrud Wojak, Natasja de Winter (Buenos Aires), Frank Wittendorfer (Siemens AG), and the people who only helped me on the condition that they would remain nameless.

A few inquiries remain unanswered. I would still be delighted to hear from: David Cesarani, Liane Dirks (on *Polityka*), Guido Knopp (on sources), Jörg Müllner (on the sound editing of the tapes), and Time, Inc.

I would also like to thank all the people who have made this English edition possible. First and foremost, my publisher, Carol Janeway, who from the start gave me the feeling she really wanted my book, and who put an excellent team in place to work on it. Joshua LaMorey was responsive and good humored in his management of the strict publication schedule. Kathleen Fridella, a brave production editor. Oliver Munday, who designed the striking book jacket. My sensitive translator, Ruth Martin, gave me an English voice, and her clever work on my text brought it to an international audience that I could not have imagined while writing it. And last but not least, my thanks go to my dear friend Willi Winkler, who was not only the editor of the original German edition, but also for the English version my wise and true guard against all losses and sorrows.

For those conducting it, research is always also a piece of your own life. I had the good fortune to meet people along my path who reminded me of this fact when the garbage threatened to poison me. I have these encounters to thank for the strength to see this project through to the end. And above all, they are the only reason I can see for traveling such a road again: Eckhard Haspel, Peter Müller, and Willi Winkler.

Abbreviations

BA   Bundesarchiv (German Federal Archives, documenting modern and contemporary history)

BDC   Berlin Document Center, now at BA Berlin Lichterfelde

BfV   Bundesamt für Verfassungsschutz (Federal Office for the Protection of the Consitution)

BKA   Bundeskriminalamt (Federal Office for Criminal Investigations)

BND   Bundesnachrichtendienst (the federal intelligence service; replaced the Gehlen Organization in 1956)

BVerwG   Bundesverwaltungsgericht (Federal Administrative Court), Leipzig

CIC   U.S. Army Counter Intelligence Corps

DÖW   Dokumentationszentrum Österreichischer Widerstand (Documentation Center of Austrian Resistance), Vienna

ETH   Eidgenössische Technische Hochschule, home of the Archiv für Zeitgeschichte (Archives for Contemporary History), Zurich

HHStA   Hessisches Hauptstaatsarchiv (Hesse Main State Archives), Wiesbaden

HIS   Hamburger Institut für Sozialforschung (Hamburg Institute for Social Research)

IMT   International Military Tribunal; IMT numbers refer to published protocols from the Nuremberg Trials (Blue Series)

Interrogation refers to the police interrogation of Eichmann in Israel.

NA   U.S. National Archives, College Park, Md.

ÖStA   Österreichisches Staatsarchiv (Austrian State Archives), Vienna

PA AA   Politisches Archiv des Auswärtigen Amtes (German Federal Foreign Office Political Archive), Berlin

RSHA   Reichssicherheitshauptamt (Main Office for Reich Security), under National Socialism

RuSHA   Rasse- und Siedlungshauptamt (Main Office for Race and Resettlement), under National Socialism

Sassen transcript refers to transcripts of the 1957 Sassen discussions, numbered according to (tape):(original pagination)

Session refers to the sessions of the Eichmann trial. Quotations have been translated from the German transcript.

SÚA   Státní ússtreédní archive (National Central Archive), Prague

T/xx refers to the numbering of prosecution documents in the Eichmann trial

Notes

Introduction

1. Hannah Arendt to Karl Jaspers, February 5, 1961, in *Hannah Arendt and Karl Jaspers: Correspondence: 1926–1969*, ed. Lotte Kohler and Hans Saner, trans. Robert and Rita Kimber (San Diego, Calif., 1992), p. 423.

2. Answers to questionnaire for *Paris Match,* May 1962, BA Koblenz, All. Proz. 6/252, p. 38.

3. I know of no publication about Eichmann in which this sentence does not appear in one form or another. Seven years ago I was fully convinced of its truth myself. One current example is the extensive study on the German Foreign Office by Eckart Conze, Norbert Frei, Peter Hayes, and Moshe Zimmermann, *Das Amt und die Vergangenheit: Deutsche Diplomaten im Dritten Reich und in der Bundesrepublik* (Munich, 2010), p. 604.

4. Jean-Jacques Rousseau, *Discours sur l'origine et les fondements de l'inégalité parmi les hommes* (Amsterdam, 1755), the first few sentences of part two.

5. After the end of the war in 1945, some confusion arose about Eichmann's forenames, and it has stubbornly persisted over the years. His name is, however, clearly verifiable. It appears not only on his birth certificate (BA Koblenz, All. Proz. 6/236) but also in official documents from the Nazi era—for example, in the records of the Central Office for Race and Settlement (BA Berlin-Lichterfelde, BDC, RuSH record Adolf Eichmann). The name *Karl* was the result of a conflation of his name with his father's. Eichmann's father, who was in the Linz telephone directory, was also a card-carrying member of the National Socialist German Workers' Party (NSDAP). Eichmann's name was also mentioned in Israel in the same breath as his father's (Adolf, son of Karl Adolf Eichmann), and so the misunderstanding persisted. Not unusually for an eldest son, Eichmann was named after his paternal grandfather.

6. "Meine Flucht," p. 22, written in March 1961 in Israel. The text, which Eichmann wanted to call "On a May Night in 1945," is quoted from the typescript according to the handwritten pagination. BA Koblenz, All. Proz. 6/247.

7. Anyone supposing these details to be literary embellishment can find the proof of their existence in photos taken in Eichmann's house on June 6, 1960, after he was kidnapped, and published in a number of contemporary magazines (in particular *Stern,* June 26–July 16, 1960). Other details are taken from the let-

ters written by Eichmann in Israel to his family. Copies in the Israeli National Archive and in BA Koblenz, All. Proz. 6/165 and 248.

8. *Eichmann in Jerusalem* was first published in New York and London in 1963 (Viking Press). The later, enlarged edition (Penguin, 1994) will be quoted here. German readers initially only had around twenty pages available to them, a shortened version of chapters 2 and 3, published in the journal *Merkur*. The first German edition of the book appeared in 1964 as Piper Paperback no. 35.

9. Hannah Arendt to Mary McCarthy, June 20, 1960, in Arendt and McCarthy, *Between Friends: The Correspondence of Hannah Arendt and Mary McCarthy, 1949–1975*, ed. Carol Brightman (San Diego, Calif., 1996), pp. 81–82.

10. Ibid., p. 82.

"My Name Became a Symbol"

1. "Meine Flucht," p. 22, BA Koblenz, All. Proz. 6/247.

2. The most recent and striking example is Klaus W. Tolfahrn, *Das Dritte Reich und der Holocaust* (Frankfurt am Main, 2008). His chap. 4.22, "'Notes on the Trial Against Eichmann,'" which is problematic in many respects, states: "The impression Eichmann made on the world's public rested not least on his unremarkable character and invisibility. Before the war, Eichmann was an invisible SD official, during the war he was an invisible SS officer, after the war a Nazi in hiding and, until the start of the trial, an invisible prisoner in Israel" (p. 359).

1 The Path into the Public Eye

1. Here Eichmann was able to use his first-hand knowledge to his advantage: in 1960–61 very little was yet known about the SD. But by the time he applied to the SD in 1934, the organization was already past its start-up phase and listed eighty-six officers besides Heydrich (according to the SS's organizational chart from October 1, 1934).

2. Franz Mayer, witness statement at Eichmann trial, session 17.

3. Sassen transcript 24:2 (cited according to the 1957 Sassen discussion, as tape: original pagination).

4. In the heads of departments' meeting of December 18, 1937, Hagen detailed various failings in discipline and organization and set strict deadlines for improvement. Prosecution document T/108.

5. Ernst Marcus dates his first encounter with Eichmann at November 1936. The incident he describes, however, must have taken place in November 1937, at the same time as the description of Eichmann's behavior that follows. So Marcus is incorrect either on the occasion of their first meeting or on the year. Probably he met Eichmann before November 1937, so his date is correct and he has merely confused the occasion. Ernst Marcus, *Das deutsche Auswärtige*

Amt und die Palästinafrage in den Jahren 1933–1939 (Yad Vashem Archive O-1/11, 1946); English translation in *Yad Washem Studies* 2 (1958).

6. The surveillance photo was made available for the Eichmann trial, but the file is still classified.

7. Joachim Prinz was given a huge send-off on June 26, 1937, when he emigrated to America. Benno Cohn, *Frankfurter Rundschau,* June 1, 1960; Eichmann trial, session 15. Eichmann described the event in his lecture on November 1, 1937 (published as document 16 in Michael Wildt, *Die Judenpolitik des SD 1935–1938: Eine Dokumentation* [Munich, 1995], p. 123) and justified his behavior again in Argentina; see "The Others Spoke," Argentina Papers.

8. Otto von Bolschwing denounced Ernst Marcus and Ernst Gottlieb to Eichmann, having eavesdropped on their conversation about him. Eichmann's reaction can be found in handwritten comments on the letter. Documented and with a commentary by Günter Schubert, "Post für Eichmann," in *Jahrbuch für Antisemitismusforschung* 15 (2006), pp. 383–93, facsimile pp. 392–93.

9. For the development of the SD and the self-image of those who worked for the Jewish Department, see the introduction from Wildt to, *Judenpolitik des SD.*

10. Eichmann's handwritten commentary on Bolschwing's letter: see the facsimile in Schubert, "Post für Eichmann."

11. Progress reports from II 112, in particular that of February 17, 1937; prosecution document T/107.

12. Minority status for Jews was repealed on May 15, 1937. Thereafter, on May 22, Eichmann traveled to Breslau to oversee the province's implementation of anti-Jewish measures and legislation. There he had his first independent experience of registering and creating card indexes for Jews. See progress report July 6–October 5, 1937, BA Koblenz, R58/991, SD Central Office collection, II 112. See also Wildt's introduction to *Judenpolitik des SD,* pp. 13–64, esp. p. 34; and David Cesarani, *Eichmann: His Life and Crimes* (London, 2005), p. 52.

13. Eichmann's contact was Paul Wurm, the editor of *Der Stürmer* in Berlin. Eichmann accepted Wurm's invitation (September 2, 1937) after discussion with his superiors (August 3). They hoped that this was the way to gain access to *Der Stürmer*'s archive "without Gauleiter Streicher's knowledge." BA Koblenz, R58/565, note II-1 Six. Eichmann attended the party congress from September 5 to 9, 1937, also meeting Julius Streicher and a group of American anti-Semites who frightened even him. SS *Hauptscharführer* Eichmann's duty report, II 112 v. 9/11, 1937, prosecution document T/121; identical with BA Koblenz R58/623; discussed in Magnus Brechtken, *"Madagaskar für die Juden": Antisemitische Idee und politische Praxis 1885–1945* (Munich, 1997), pp. 72ff.

14. Sassen transcript 62:1.

15. This encounter happened between March 15 and 25, 1938; it has not been possible to date it more accurately. There are several descriptions of the incident. Afterward Adolf Böhm had a nervous breakdown and was admitted to the closed ward of a psychiatric hospital. See Doron Rabinovici, *Instanzen*

der Ohnmacht: Wien 1938–1945: Der Weg zum Judenrat (Frankfurt am Main, 2000), pp. 70ff.

16. Dr. Jehuda Brott, interview by Herbert Rosenkranz, "Advice Center of the Vienna Youth Alijah," Jerusalem, March 22, 1977, Yad Vashem Archive O-3/3912; quoted in Herbert Rosenkranz, *Verfolgung und Selbstbehauptung: Die Juden in Österreich, 1938–1945* (Vienna and Munich, 1978), p. 109.

17. On December 14, 1939, Eichmann became special plenipotentiary for the assets of the Jewish Religious Community in the Eastern March. "The Reichskommissar's Directive for the Reunification of Austria with the German Reich," signed by Bürkel, December 14, 1939, ÖStA, AdR Bürkel-Material, 1762/1,31; quoted in Rosenkranz, *Verfolgung und Selbstbehauptung*, pp. 221 and 334.

18. See the somewhat one-sided but impressive contrary view, focusing on the role of the Gestapo: Thomas Mang, *"Gestapo-Leitstelle Wien—Mein Name ist Huber": Wer trug die lokale Verantwortung für den Mord an den Juden Wiens?* (Münster, 2004).

19. Eichmann to Herbert Hagen, May 8, 1938, prosecution document T/130; identical with BA Koblenz, R58/982, folio, pp. 19ff. Twenty-five issues of the newspaper (editor-in-chief Emil Reich) appeared, between May 20 and November 9, 1938. The censor's direct influence is discernible.

20. Dr. Martin Rosenbluth to Dr. Georg Landauer, May 17, 1938, in *Deutsches Judentum unter dem Nationalsozialismus*, ed. Otto Dov Kulka (Tübingen, 1997), p. 1:381. See also Leo Lauterbach, "The Jewish Situation in Austria. Report Submitted to the Zionist Organization," strictly confidential, April 19, 1938, quoted in Rosenkranz, *Verfolgung und Selbstbehauptung*, pp. 275ff; and Israel Cohen, "Report on Vienna," Prague, March 28, 1938, ibid., pp. 51ff.

21. Israel Cohen in "Report on Vienna."

22. Tom Segev, *Simon Wiesenthal: The Life and Legends* (New York, 2010), p. 12.

23. Ben-Gurion diary, entry for November 30, 1939, Ben-Gurion Archive, cited ibid., p. 13.

24. Short-term requirement of November 11, 1938; conference on November 12, 1938; prosecution documents T/114; identical with IMT 1816-PS (compare with IMT vol. 28, p. 499).

25. Bernhard Lösener (Reich Ministry of the Interior and contributor to the "Nuremberg Laws") agreed to visit, even if his subsequent report misrepresents his own role. Manuscript June 26, 1950, reprinted as "Als Rassereferent im Reichsministerium des Innern," *Vierteljahrshefte für Zeitgeschichte* 9, no. 3 (July 1961), pp. 264–313. There is also evidence of visits by Heydrich and by representatives from the Reich Ministries of Finance and Propaganda.

26. Sassen transcript 32:8.

27. Sassen transcript 4:3, 60:2, and elsewhere.

28. Sassen transcript 32:8.

29. SS *Gruppenführer* Hinkel gave Eichmann a dedicated copy of his book *Einer*

unter 100 000 (One in 100,000) on this occasion, which Eichmann mentioned proudly both to Sassen and in "Meine Memoiren."

30. The work camps at Gut Sandhof (near Waidhofen on the Ybbs) and Doppl (in the Mühltal near Linz) were active from May 1939 to December 1941 and were called "camps for the compulsory re-training of Jews in technical and agricultural jobs." They were run by staff from the Vienna Central Office. For more on this long-overlooked step in anti-Jewish policy, see Gabriele Anderl's groundbreaking study "Die 'Umschulungslager' Doppl und Sandhof der Wiener Zentralstelle für jüdische Auswanderung," at www.david.juden.at/kulturzeitschrift/57-60/58-Anderl.htm (2003 and 2004).

31. Eichmann was suspected of paying too high a price when he bought his lover's real estate; see Anderl, "Die 'Umschulungslager.'"

32. Sassen transcript, unnumbered tape, sheet 2. Also 54:12.

33. Minutely detailed in Gabriele Anderl and Dirk Rupnow, *Die Zentralstelle für jüdische Auswanderung als Beraubungsinstitution* (Vienna, 2004); and Theodor Venus and Alexandra-Eileen Wenck, *Die Entziehung jüdischen Vermögens im Rahmen der Aktion Gildemeester* (Vienna and Munich, 2004).

34. *Wiener Völkische Beobachter,* November 20, 1938 (illustrated Sunday edition).

35. Ladislaus Benes, in *Pester Loyd,* February 11, 1939.

36. Benno Cohn, subpoena of representatives of the German Jews in spring 1939 to appear before the Gestapo (Eichmann). Reported to the meeting of the "Circle of German Zionists," report recorded by Dr. Ball-Kaduri, April 2, 1958, Yad Vashem Archive O-1/215. Transcript of the 1958 meeting published in Kurt Ball-Kaduri, *Vor der Katastrophe: Juden in Deutschland 1934–1939* (Tel Aviv, 1967), pp. 235–39. See Rabinovici, *Instanzen der Ohnmacht,* p. 151, though it incorrectly cites Yad Vashem no. 227 (containing the transcript for the 1940 meeting with Erich Frank). Benno Cohn emigrated at the end of March 1939, as stated in session 14f.

37. Many times, according to the Sassen transcript 2:4 and 6:1.

38. The *Pariser Tageszeitung* was the successor to the *Pariser Tageblatt,* which explains the confusion about this title in the memories of the people involved. The paper was published in German from the start and not, as is occasionally reported, in Yiddish.

39. BA Berlin Lichterfelde, ZA I, 7358, A.1, 1 (former NS-archive of the MFS, ministery for state security of the GDR, German Democratic Republic: 15.5(6!), 1937. This relates to a discussion between SS *Hauptscharführer* Eichmann and SS *Oberscharführer* Hagen; quoted in Venus and Wenck, *Entziehung jüdischen Vermögens,* pp. 48ff. Report from Heinrich Schlie to Eichmann and Lischka, March 5, 1939, Yad Vashem Archive O-51/0S0-41; quoted in Avraham Altman and Irene Eber, "Flight to Shanghai, 1938–1940: The Larger Setting," *Yad Vashem Studies* 28 (2000), pp. 58–86, esp. p. 59.

40. At the first meeting with the Jewish Council in Budapest. Eichmann admitted to Sassen that he had said this "out of a mixture of humor and sarcasm." Sassen

transcript 72:6. The Sassen transcripts are cited according to the original 1957 pagination: (tape number): (page).

41. Anton Brunner, statement, October 3, 1945. Anton Brunner was a civilian colleague in the Central Office, unrelated to Alois Brunner; Anton Brunner was executed in Vienna in 1946. DÖW, Document 19 061/2. See Hans Safrian, *Eichmann und seine Gehilfen* (Frankfurt am Main, 1995).

42. Josef Weiszl to his wife Pauline, no date, no place given (Doppl), trial of Josef Weiszl at the District Criminal Court in Vienna, Vg 7c Vr 658/46, File no. 56, from sheet 2567; quoted in Anderl, "Die 'Umschulungslager.'"

43. Witness statement from *Inheritance,* a documentary by James Moll (USA, 2006).

44. Sassen transcript 40:1 and 32:8.

45. "As I sometimes said to the important Jews, when I had them, something like: 'Well then, do you know where you are? You're with the Czar of the Jews. Don't you know that, didn't you see the *Pariser Tageblatt*?!'" Sassen transcript 72:16.

46. During the Eichmann trial, Benno Cohn recollected the incident for a second time: "He was very upset that we had published something about him in that paper ... that he was 'der Bluthund Eichmann' (bloodhound Eichmann)—I am using the language used at that time—'Der Bluthund Eichmann,' 'blut-unterlaufene Augen' (blood-shot eyes), 'ein neuer Feind,' 'Judenfeind' (a new enemy, an enemy of the Jews). I don't remember all the expressions, but they were very trenchant" (session 15).

47. Benno Cohn, witness statement at Eichmann trial, session 14–15.

48. Sassen transcript 13:5 and 6:1.

49. Contact with the editor of *Der Stürmer* was motivated by business consid-erations. It was so uninteresting for II 112 that Eichmann evidently let the contact drop, particularly as he increasingly disagreed with *Der Stürmer* on the basic tactics for anti-Semitic "reconnaissance." As a result, Wurm made con-tact with Franz Rademacher at the Foreign Office and had substantial involve-ment in the Foreign Office's Madagascar Plan. See Brechtken, "*Madagaskar für die Juden,*" p. 72.

50. Sassen transcript 6:1.

51. Franz Novak, witness testimony for Eichmann trial, April 3–5, 1961. Eich-mann had "made a certain name for himself among the Jews." Novak blamed Eichmann's contact with functionaries from Jewish organizations for it.

52. No one has reconstructed this collection, for any of several possible reasons: the attractive image of the "man in the dark"; the necessary doubts cast on Eichmann's boasts (if they were noticed in this case); and the fundamental problems of newspaper research. For this section I searched through the fol-lowing German-language exile papers, from 1938 until they folded: *Aufbau* (New York), *Pariser Tageszeitung* (Paris), and *Die Zeitung* (London). A card index of names and keywords exists for *Aufbau,* though it is neither complete nor free from errors and requires a creative research approach. For all other newspapers, one has no choice but to read through them. To date, apart from

professional information in the official publications, I have found Eichmann's name in none of the Nazi regime's newspapers, including *Völkischer Beobachter* (Berlin and Vienna editions), *Das Reich, Der Angriff,* and *Das Schwarze Korps.*

53. Sassen transcript 6:1.

54. General Alois Eliáš charged Ministerial Adviser Dr. Fahoún with negotiating the "question of the establishment of a Central Office for Jewish Emigration . . . which Herr *Oberfü.* Stahlecker and his representative *Hstuf.* Eichmann had personally communicated to him." Inventory of the Chair of the Council (PMR), SÚA, box 4018; quoted in Jaroslava Milotová, "Die Zentralstelle für jüdische Auswanderung in Prag: Genesis und Tätigkeit bis zum Anfang des Jahres 1940," *Theresienstädter Studien und Dokumente,* no. 4 (1997), pp. 7–30, 2.

55. Information for the Minister. Memorandum from the conference in Petschek Palais, July 19, 1939, SÚA, PMR, box 4018. Memorandum on the negotiations of the Occupation and Protectorate government regarding the Central Office for Jewish Emigration from July 19, 1939, SÚA, Prague Police Authority collection (PP), shelf mark 7/33/39, box 1903; quoted in Milotová, "Die Zentralstelle."

56. František Weidmann, secretary of the Jewish Community of Prague, was ordered to visit Vienna on July 20, 1939, before the government delegation, "on the instructions of Herr *Hauptsturmführer* Eichmann." At the same time, a representative of the Vienna Religious Community was sent to Prague for "training." Weekly report from the Jewish Community of Prague, covering July 23–29, 1939, prosecution document T/162.

57. Stanislav Kokoska, "Zwei unbekannte Berichte aus dem besetzten Prag über die Lage der jüdischen Bevölkerung im Protektorat," *Theresienstädter Studien und Dokumente,* no. 4 (1997), pp. 31–49.

58. Ibid.

59. Stiller to the Reichskommissar of the Netherlands, The Hague September 19, 1941, prosecution document T/526. This "achievement" had a lasting reputation: by 1941, two years into the war, the "Central Emigration Offices" were of little importance. Eichmann no longer led them, even if his Jewish Office in Berlin continued to issue directives regarding them.

60. Sassen transcript 51:7.

61. Such an article appeared on the front page of the *Pariser Tageszeitung* on October 26, 1939: "The immediate thought, according to a report in 'Lietuvas Aidas' [the official news publication of the government of Lithuania], was of establishing a 'Jewish state' in the Lublin Voivodeship. But this plan was not the complete 'solution' of the Jewish question that Hitler has in mind. His 'peace program,' as he announced it in his last speech to the Reichstag, includes a ruling on the Jewish question, and he is thinking of a complete evacuation of the Jews from the whole of Europe, and their resettlement in closed territories overseas."—*Lietuvas Aidas* appeals to government circles in Berlin.

62. "Transportation to Lublin," *Pariser Tageszeitung,* November 18, 1939, p. 2. The

article reflects the uncertainty over how to classify the situation and the Nazis' aims.

63. On October 10, 1939, Josef Löwenherz of the Vienna Jewish Religious Community received the instruction from Eichmann's representative Rolf Günther that Viennese Jews had to report to Eichmann in Ostrava and should prepare for a stay of three or four weeks. Josef Löwenherz, file memorandum on the audience with Herr *Obersturmführer* Günther at the Central Office for Jewish Emigration on October 10, 1939, prosecution document T/148 (identical copy under T/153).

64. The mistake is understandable. When handwritten in capitals, the names EICHMANN and EHRMANN are difficult to tell apart. *Pariser Tageszeitung,* November 25, 1939.

65. On October 19, 1939, Hans Günther noted the "rumors flying around in Ostrava" and the demonstrations. He emphasized they were taking great pains to avoid a riot by holding events to reassure people. Günther's memorandum, "Rumors in Ostrava," October 23, 1939, SÚA, 100-653-1; quoted in Miroslav Kárný, "Nisko in der Geschichte der 'Endlösung,'" *Judaica Bohemiae* 23, no. 2 1987), pp. 69–84, esp. p. 81.

66. Prague Jewish Religious Community, weekly report covering November 10–16, 1939, prosecution document T/162.

67. Sassen transcript 68:6.

68. In order to protect the informant Edelstein, who eventually had to travel back to Prague, no names were mentioned. The article claimed that someone who had escaped from the group of deportees crossing the border into Russia had given them the information. This shows just how precise Edelstein's knowledge and that of the other observers was: when Nisko failed, the Nazis hounded whole groups of deportees over the nearby Russian border, firing shots after them. The correspondent—also unnamed—was Lewis B. Namier (Bernstein-Namierowski). Compare the complete text of the article, documented by Livia Rothkirchen, "Zur ersten authentischen Nachricht über den Beginn der Vernichtung der europäischen Juden," *Theresienstädter Studien und Dokumente,* no. 9 (2002), pp. 338–40. This issue also contains a facsimile excerpt from the original article. See also Margalit Shlaim, "Jakob Edelsteins Bemühungen um die Rettung der Juden aus dem Protektorat Böhmen und Mähren von Mai 1939 bis Dezember 1939: Eine Korrespondenzanalyse," *Theresienstädter Studien und Dokumente,* no. 10 (2003), pp. 71–94.

69. Sassen transcript 57:4.

70. Eichmann trial, session 27.

71. Christoph Hoffmann founded this colony in 1871, after his outlandish settlement plans failed in Turkey. It was not the only Templar settlement in Palestine, but it was particularly tenacious. The British instructed all the German Templars to leave Palestine in 1943. Mildenstein describes his romantically idealized impression in two travel reports: LIM (Mildenstein's pseudonym), "A

Nazi Goes to Palestine," series of articles in *Der Angriff*, September 26–October 9, 1934 (book edition: *Rings um das brennende Land am Jordan* [Berlin, 1938]); and Leopold von Mildenstein, *Naher Osten—vom Straßenrand erlebt* (Stuttgart, 1941), p. 114.

72. There are hints about Sarona in the August 1934 issue of the German journal *Palästina: Zeitschrift für den Aufbau Palästinas* (edited by Adolf Böhm) and again in December 1937. Kaiser Wilhelm II also visited the colony on his trip to Palestine in 1898, thus assuring it a place in colonial literature.

73. Heinrich Grüber, witness statement at Eichmann trial, session 41. For his impression of Eichmann, see also Heinrich Grüber, *Zeuge pro Israel* (Berlin, 1963).

74. Adolf/Dolfi (Daniel) Brunner, 1938 leader of the Maccabees youth organization, remembers many of these conversations. Dr. Daniel Adolf Brunner, taped statement on the "Vienna Maccabi Hatzair," 1977, Yad Vashem Archive O-3/3914; quoted in Rosenkranz, *Verfolgung und Selbstbehauptung*, p. 111

75. Murmelstein told Simon Wiesenthal about it. See Wiesenthal to Nahum Goldmann, March 30, 1954, NA, RG 263, CIA Name File Adolf Eichmann.

76. "In the year 1938/39, when Eichmann came into contact with Jewish personalities in Vienna, he wanted to impress them with his knowledge of Palestine and Jewish problems, and his language abilities. He implied he came from Sarona near Haifa, from a German family in the 'Templar sect,' and so nobody could 'pull the wool over his eyes.' Since then, the rumor has spread through Jewish circles, and Eichmann is always amused by this." Dieter Wisliceny, "Report on former SS-*Obersturmbannführer* Adolf Eichmann," twenty-two-page handwritten paper, Bratislava, October 27, 1946, known as the Cell 133 Document (prosecution document T/84), p. 5. It must be pointed out that Wisliceny is reporting this version from what Eichmann said, since at this time he was not in close contact with him. They began to work together again in late summer 1940. Wisliceny did not have a marked tendency to tell the truth, and when it came to Eichmann, this tendency was hardly discernible.

77. Charlotte Salzberger, witness statement at Eichmann trial, session 42.

78. "The Man We Are Looking For," *Jüdisches Gemeindeblatt für die Britische Zone*, January 6, 1947; Simon Wiesenthal, *Großmufti—Großagent der Achse* (Salzburg and Vienna, 1947), p. 46. The rumor was still being circulated in Tel Aviv even in 1952.

79. Wisliceny dates Eichmann's interest in the Hebrew language to 1935 and appears to give Eichmann's self-description verbatim: "Since he had a lot of free time, he started to occupy himself with old languages, particularly Hebrew, spurred on by a collection of Jewish cult objects and coins that was in his custody. He acquired this knowledge through independent study. He could read Hebrew well and make reasonable translations. He read and translated Yiddish fluently. He could not, however, speak fluent Hebrew." Wisliceny, Cell 133 Document (prosecution document T/84), p. 3. Wisliceny also reported

that Mildenstein had spent "many years" in Palestine, which underlines both his penchant for grandiloquent exaggerations and his distance from Mildenstein (and thus Eichmann).

80. The date that Eichmann gave both in Argentina and in Israel throws up a few problems because of his earlier deployment in the SD and could also be a lie.

81. The first application is mentioned in the second. The teacher who recommended himself for the job was Fritz Arlt. See reference to the SD Oberabschnitt Southeast's initial conversation on July 3, 1936. BA Koblenz, R58/991. See Götz Aly and Karl Heinz Roth, *Die restlose Erfassung: Volkszählen, Identifizieren, Aussondern im Nationalsozialismus* (Frankfurt am Main, 2000); and Hans Christian Harten, Uwe Neirich, and Mattias Schwerendt, *Rassehygiene als Erziehungsideologie des Dritten Reichs: Bio-Bibliographisches Handbuch* (Berlin, 2006), pp. 238–42.

82. Application no. 2, June 18, 1937, prosecution document T/55(11); a better copy under T/55(14), document 13, marked "Betrifft: Übersetzungen neuhebräisch-deutsch." See also R. M. W. Kempner, *Eichmann und Komplizen* (Zurich, Stuttgart, and Vienna, 1961), p. 39. The first application in June–July 1936 is mentioned in the second.

83. *Hebräisch für Jedermann von Dr. S. Kaléko, Buchausgabe des Hebräischen Fern-Unterrichtes der Jüdischen Rundschau: Mit einem Vokabular der 1500 wichtigsten Wörter, Grammatik-Index und Anhang* (Berlin, 1936). Published by Verlag Jüdische Rundschau GmbH, the volume is available in a few German libraries, including the National and University Libraries in Hamburg, A1949/7278 (5th ed., 1936). Eichmann was still able to recall the author's name and the rather odd title during the Sassen interviews. A possible reason is that Saul Kaléko taught Hebrew in Berlin until 1938: Saul Kaléko (Barkali Shaul), *Teaching Hebrew in Berlin, 1933–1938* (1957), Yad Vashem Archive O-1/132; another possible reason is that his book was advertised in the *Jüdische Rundschau,* which also published selected lessons.

84. Simon Wiesenthal to Nahum Goldmann, March 30, 1954, NA, RG 263, CIA Name File Adolf Eichmann. Wiesenthal's source is Benjamin Murmelstein.

85. Dolfi Brunner (leader of the Maccabi Hazair, who encountered Eichmann several times in Vienna) and Ernö Munkácsi (of the Budapest Jewish Council) were convinced that Eichmann was just using set phrases to show off. Dr. Daniel Adolf Brunner, "Vienna Maccabi Hazair," audio recording, Jaffa, 1977, Yad Vashem Archive O-3/3914, quoted in Rosenkranz, *Verfolgung und Selbstbehauptung;* and Dr. Ernö Munkácsis, statement, in *Eichmann in Ungarn: Dokumente,* ed. Jenö Levai (Budapest, 1961), p. 211.

86. Sassen transcript 2:4.

87. Otto Bokisch and Gustav Zirbs, *Der Österreichische Legionär: Aus Erinnerungen und Archiv, aus Tagebüchern und Blättern* (Vienna, 1940), p. 37.

88. Sassen transcript 22:14.

89. Werner Best uses the phrase "Dienststelle Eichmann" (Eichmann's office) in his sworn statement of June 28, 1946: "Himmler [had] his own leader from

Eichmann's office—Günther—come out from Berlin." Documents from the Nuremberg Trials IMT vol. 41, p. 166 (Ribbentrop-320). See also Thadden (Foreign Office) in IMT 2605-PS.

90. Rudolf Mildner, affidavit, read out on April 11, 1946, IMT vol. 11, p. 284.

91. Sassen transcript 14:2.

92. Prof. Dr. August Hirt, Strasbourg University, wanted the collection and persuaded Eichmann to organize this project with the WVHA (the Main Economic and Administrative Office of the SS), via Wolfram Sievers of the Ahnenerbe think tank, whom Eichmann had helped with "Aryanization" measures in 1941. Prosecution document T/1363-1370. The idea for the collection came in February 1942. Eichmann petitioned for an official assignment from Himmler in November 1942, and received it.

93. The old Madagascar idea was taken up again by Franz Rademacher in the Foreign Office, working with Paul Wurm. Eichmann's office became involved only when Heydrich began to fear for his own influence in Jewish policy, and the work was then delegated to Theodor Dannecker and Erich Rajakowitsch. The fact that everyone involved afterward gave a different version of events is one of the most compelling examples of witness statements not necessarily being truthful just because they corroborate one another.

94. Stiller to the Reichskommissar of the Netherlands, The Hague, September 19, 1941, prosecution document T/526. In the letter he discusses his conversation with Lösener from the Reich Home Office on that day.

95. The Germans tried in vain to keep the deportation of thousands of Jews to the General Government of occupied Poland confidential; information still reached the rest of the world. Internal information on the February 15, 1940, press conference for German representatives: the news of thousands of Jews transported to the General Government is correct "but is to be treated as confidential." Prosecution document T/667; identical with IMT NG-4698. On February 15, 1940, the *Neue Zürcher Zeitung*'s Berlin correspondent reported on what was happening, and on February 17 the Danish newspaper *Politiken* published an alarming article on the inhuman deportations from Szczecin: "Germany deports nationals. Old people and toddlers are being deported—to nowhere. As are frontline soldiers from the World War." There were numerous deaths, and even President Roosevelt requested a report. The Germans closely monitored the subsequent press, and translations were prepared. German Translation of the Danish Report for use in the RSHA, IMT NG-1530: Bern German News agency to the Foreign Office with the Swiss Press, February 16, 1940, prosecution document T/666.

96. Ephraim (Erich) Frank, report on the "Representatives of the Jewish Umbrella Organizations in Berlin, Vienna and Prague, Before the Gestapo in Berlin (Eichmann), March 1940," given in the meeting of the circle of German Zionists on June 23, 1958, transcribed by Dr. Ball-Kaduri, Yad Vashem Archive O-1/227; published as document 2 (though under the wrong heading and thus the wrong date for the transcript) in Kurt Jacob Ball-Kaduri, "Illegale

Judenauswanderung aus Deutschland nach Palästina 1939/40: Planung, Durchführung und internationale Zusammenhange," *Jahrbuch des Instituts für deutsche Geschichte* 4 (1975), pp. 387–421. There are several reports from attendees at the discussions on March 27 and 30, 1940, as well as the (also incorrectly dated) Löwenherz-Bienenfeld Report, prosecution document T/154.

97. Sassen transcript 2:4 and 6:1.

98. Correspondence on the exhibition: Archiwum Głównej Komisji Badania, Zbrodni Hitlerowskich w Polsce (AGK, Archive of the Main Committee for the Study of Nazi Crimes in Poland), EWZ/L/838/1/2. BA Koblenz 69/554. See also Götz Aly, *"Endlösung": Völkerverschiebung und der Mord an den europäischen Juden* (Frankfurt am Main, 1995), p. 250. Photos of many of the displays are still extant.

99. On October 28 *Die Zeitung* referred to the same source, reporting that "on October 21 the third transport of around 800 Jews left Grunewald Freight Railroad Terminal for the east. On the same day, the Jewish Emigration Office in Kurfürstenstraße was closed, with no reason given for the closure."

100. In conversation with Sassen, Eichmann made a joke of the fact that someone had taken him for a general. In Israel, he called it a malicious exaggeration.

101. Quoted in Peter Longerich, *Politik der Vernichtung: Eine Gesamtdarstellung der nationalsozialistischen Judenvernichtung* (Zurich and Munich, 1998), p. 282.

102. Minutes of the meeting on March 20, 1941, prepared on March 21, Reichsring Main Office for National Socialist Propaganda, published in H. G. Adler, *Der verwaltete Mensch: Studien zur Deportation der Juden aus Deutschland* (Tübingen, 1974), pp. 152–53.

103. "Expulsions in the Reich," *Aufbau*, October 24, 1941. Zvi Rosen found the article in the Horkheimer Archive. See Zvi Rosen, *Max Horkheimer* (Munich, 1995), p. 40.

104. *The Diaries of Joseph Goebbels,* ed. Elke Fröhlich, commissioned by the Institute of Contemporary History, with support from the Russian National Archive Service (Munich, 1996), pt. 2, vol. 2, p. 194.

105. There were documented deportations from Berlin in 1941 on October 18 and 24, November 1, 14, 17, and 27.

106. "I can't recall exactly now: either I coined it, or it came from Müller." Sassen transcript 1:4.

107. Göring's edict of July 31, 1941, tasked Heydrich with developing the "complete solution to the Jewish question," which Heydrich then used to legitimate decisions such as those taken at the Wannsee Conference. "After this [edict] Eichmann's power in this area [Jews] grew exponentially. He was able to use this edict to brush aside all objections and influences from other ministries and officials." Wisliceny, Cell 133 Document (prosecution document T/84). This is Wisliceny's version of events, in a statement made in his own defense, but Eichmann's typical tone can be heard clearly in his words. It sounds very much like Eichmann explaining to Sassen why the Wannsee Conference was

such a turning point for him personally. The same tone can even be heard in Israel, where he tries to relate the relief the conference brought to his newly discovered conscience.

108. Sassen transcript 17:8.

109. Lead story in *Die Zeitung* (London), March 6, 1942.

110. *New York Times* and *Daily Telegraph* (June 25, 1942), and BBC (June 30, 1942). Mass murder by gas, and the first suggestion of collecting the perpetrators' names, were reported in the *Times* (London), (March 10, 1942).

111. *Die Zeitung* (London), June 19, 1942. After the Baum group's attack on the propaganda exhibition *The Soviet Paradise* in Berlin, there were mass arrests and shootings of the attackers. Eichmann informed the representatives of Jewish organizations about the Nazis' retaliation and organized the transports to Sachsenhausen. Documents corroborate Eichmann's admission in Argentina. Sassen transcript 69:1f. Josef Löwenherz, memo on the hearing with the RSHA, IV B 4, May 19, 1942, prosecution document T/899. See Wolfgang Scheffler, "Der Brandanschlag im Berliner Lustgarten im Mai 1942 und seine Folgen: Eine quellenkritische Betrachtung," in *Berlin in Geschichte und Gegenwart: Jahrbuch des Landesarchivs Berlin* (1984), pp. 91–118.

112. *Newsweek*, August 10, 1942.

113. Eichmann decided that "Kindertransports can roll": Dannecker's note on July 21, 1942, about a phone call with Eichmann and Novak on July 20, prosecution document T/439; identical with IMT RF-1233. Published in Serge Klarsfeld, *Vichy–Auschwitz: Die Zusammenarbeit der deutschen und französischen Behörden bei der "Endlösung der Judenfrage" in Frankreich,* new ed. (Darmstadt, 2007), p. 441. Facsimile in Kempner, *Eichmann*, p. 212. Press reports: *Paris Soir,* August 19–20, 1942; and "Children's Fates," *Die Zeitung* (London), September 4, 1942.

114. *Jewish Frontier*, November 1, 1942.

115. *New York Herald Tribune,* November 25, 1942; and *New York Times,* November 26, 1942, where Rabbi Stephen S. Wise warns of the possibility of four million deaths. See also *New York Times,* December 2 and 4, 1942.

116. Survivors' reports bear nightmarish witness to these moments of recognition. This image of Eichmann emerges in particular from the moving recollections of Leo Baeck, Benjamin Murmelstein, Joel Brand, and Rudolf Kasztner, who all wrestle with their own feelings of guilt and their entanglement in the catastrophe.

117. After Himmler's visit to Auschwitz, Special Unit 1005, under Paul Blobel, was tasked with searching for suitable methods. The special unit was housed in Eichmann's building and remunerated through Eichmann's office payroll, about which Eichmann complained several times in Argentina.

118. Dieter Wisliceny, "Re: Editor in Chief of the 'Grenzbote,' Fritz Fialla [*sic*]," handwritten note, July 26, 1946, Bratislava; prosecution document T/1107. Wisliceny's version seems credible, though not because it corroborates Eichmann's. It is impossible to verify statements by comparing them with Eich-

mann's: he simply corroborated other people's lies if he thought they might exonerate him. The Madagascar case is one example of a tangle of lies and false corroborations that resulted in the falsification of the whole history of the affair. The tangle is masterfully unraveled in Brechtken, *"Madagaskar für die Juden."* Rademacher claimed it was Eichmann, not he, who came up with the idea, although the work on the Madagascar Plan can be clearly traced back to Rademacher. Eichmann agreed with the lie, because the legend that he came up with a plan for a Jewish state, rather than just deporting Poles and Jews to Eastern Europe, was significantly better than the truth for his self-image. The stories are a perfect match but are some considerable distance from the truth. There are many documented examples of Eichmann's use of the lies other people told in their defense.

119. Eichmann is proved to have been with Himmler on August 11, 1942, but it is not known whether they spoke about the Fiala reports on this occasion. *Heinrich Himmler's Appointment Diary*, entry for August 11, 1942.

120. Himmler visited Prague on July 6–7, 1942. *Heinrich Himmler's Appointment Diary*, p. 606. The first article appeared on July 7, 1942.

121. *Der Grenzbote—deutsches Tagblatt für die Karpatenländer,* nos. 301, 302, and 304, Bratislava, November 7, 8, and 10, 1942.

122. Eichmann to Thadden, June 2, 1943, prosecution document T/1108. Eichmann mentions *Slovak, Sklovenská politika: Gardiete, Magyar Hirlap,* and *Pariser Zeitung,* as confirmed by all witnesses (including those for the prosecution).

123. The first reports were broadcast on the radio news from London on March 3, 1942. Print media followed, with the usual delay. See, for example, the front-page story "New Ghetto Policy: Theresienstadt in Place of Lublin—The Martyrdom of Jews in the Protectorate" in *Die Zeitung* (London), March 6, 1942:

> Neutral correspondents in Berlin bring news of Himmler and Heydrich's new plan, to send all the Jews still living in the Protectorate of Bohemia and Moravia to the fortress town of Theresienstadt, whose population is to be evacuated. The town will be turned into a large ghetto. This plan signals a change in the original Jewish policy of the "Third Reich," resulting from the new situation. The vision of the original plan was to transport all Jews from Germany and German-occupied areas to Eastern Poland, where they would live in large concentration-camp ghettoes as slave laborers.—The Jewish center of Lublin was one of the first results of this diabolical plan. The Nazis banked on the unaccustomed hard work and insufficient food supplies decimating Europe's uprooted Jewish population in short order. The remainder—if indeed there was a remainder after the end of the war—would be taken to a Jewish reservation overseas, along with the Jews from the rest of the German-enslaved world. The island of Madagascar was provisionally earmarked for this.

124. Walter George Hartmann from the German Red Cross wrote a fundamentally positive report after the visit on June 28, 1943. Memo on the organizational course of the visit to Theresienstadt, June 30, 1943, Hartmann, Deutsches Rotes Kreuz Archiv, 176/I. See Birgitt Morgenbrod and Stephanie Merkenich, *Das Deutsche Rote Kreuz unter der NS-Diktatur 1933–1945* (Paderborn, Munich, Vienna, and Zurich, 2008), pp. 386ff. In the days following, however, he gave a different opinion of this visit to André de Pilar: "The situation in the ghetto is appalling. There is a shortage of everything. The people are terribly malnourished," and the medical supplies were "entirely insufficient." But Hartmann still fell for the event's most important propaganda lie and referred to Theresienstadt even to Pilar as a "terminus camp," which was reassuring. Gerhart Riegner, World Jewish Congress, notes on his conversation with André de Pilar, July 7, 1943, prosecution document T/853.

125. "Theresienstadt: A 'Model Ghetto,'" *Aufbau*, August 27, 1943, based on an article by Alfred Joachim Fischer in *Free Europe* (London), June 1943.

126. *Aufbau*, September 3, 1943, p. 21.

127. Hannah Arendt, "The True Reasons for Theresienstadt," *Aufbau*, September 3, 1943, p. 21.

128. "Heydekampf Report" on the visit on June 23, 1944; held with the written correspondence on the organization in the Deutsches Rotes Kreuz Archiv, 176/I. See Morgenbrod and Merkenich, *Deutsche Rote Kreuz*, pp. 390ff. Maurice Rossel, the International Red Cross delegate, wrote a blindly naïve report that fulfilled the organizer's wishes. Eichmann's colleagues had managed to get a look at this report by September 22, 1944.

129. In her impressive book, Leni Yahil sees a connection between the rumors of mass murders and the attempt to hide evidence. *Die Shoah: Überlebenskampf und Vernichtung der europäischen Juden* (Munich, 1998), pp. 610ff.

130. Sassen transcript 32:8.

131. See Bettina Stangneth, "Dienstliche Aufenthaltsorte Adolf Eichmanns, 12.3.1938 bis Mai 1945," annotated list for the special exhibition *Facing Justice: Adolf Eichmann on Trial*, Topography of Terror and Memorial Foundation, Berlin, July 2010 (unpublished).

132. Sassen transcript 3:5.

133. Sassen transcript 11:13.

134. Sassen transcript 22:14.

135. Eichmann's extreme reaction to the failed deportations in Denmark has still not been adequately explained. He was with Himmler on September 24, 1943, shortly before the campaign was due to begin, so the possibility that he might have supported it himself cannot be ruled out. Tatiana Brustin-Berenstein, "The Attempt to Deport the Danish Jews," *Yad Vashem Studies* 17 (1986), p. 191, quotes the microfilm of pages from Himmler's diary (Washington; originals in BA Koblenz, September 24, 1943, MF 84/25). According to Thadden's statement (April 16, 1948), Rolf Günther had told him in confidence

that the campaign was "being sabotaged by German offices, presumably the embassy." "Eichmann had already reported to the Reichsführer and wanted the head of the saboteur." Eberhard von Thadden, affidavit, Nuremberg, April 16, 1948, prosecution document T/584.

136. Wilhelm Höttl and Dieter Wisliceny—evidently having colluded while they were in jail in Nuremberg—claimed that Eichmann reacted aggressively toward photographers, even smashing their cameras in the heat of the moment, though he paid for the damage afterward. The collection of photos of Eichmann from earlier years is, for the period, very extensive.

137. Klaus Eichmann, "My Father Adolf Eichmann," *Parade*, March 19, 1961.

138. Bernard Lösener referred in detail to these bully-boy tactics. See Lösener, "Als Rassereferent im Reichsministerium des Innern," *Vierteljahrshefte für Zeitgeschichte* 9, no. 3 (July 1961), pp. 264–313.

139. There is no independent source for Eichmann's claim. He told Sassen that Wolff had tried to push through an exception to the deportations, but he had vehemently refused, citing some basic considerations: "So in this case I had to countermand him, and when he said that I was SS *Obstubaf.* and he was SS *Ogrf.* [a more senior rank], I said yes indeed, I know that *Ogrf.*, but may I remind you that you are attached to the Gestapo and you are speaking to an adviser to the Secret Police, *Ostf.* Eichmann." Eichmann then challenged Wolff to a duel, but Himmler did not allow it. Sassen transcript 14:8–9. The fact that Ludolf von Alvensleben, long a close friend of Wolff's, also belonged to the Sassen group increases the story's plausibility.

140. Wisliceny reports by turns that either he or Eichmann was Himmler's brother-in-law, or that Eichmann claimed either he or Wisliceny was connected to power in this way. *Der Kasztner-Bericht über Eichmanns Menschenhandel in Ungarn* (Munich, 1961) (in fact, the report of the Jewish Rescue Committee from Budapest, 1942–45), hereafter cited as the Kasztner Report; and Wisliceny, Cell 133 Document, prosecution document T/84.

141. The few existing accounts of this affair follow either Wisliceny's contradictory version or the statement Eichmann gave in his interrogation, sometimes without mentioning these highly dubious sources. For example, Klaus Gensicke, *Der Mufti von Jerusalem, Amin el-Husseini und die Nationalsozialisten* (Frankfurt am Main, 1988), esp. pp. 164–67, which relies entirely on the interrogation. Martin Cüppers and Klaus-Michael Mallmann, "'Elimination of the Jewish National Home in Palestine': The Einsatzkommando of the Panzer Army Africa, 1942," *Yad Vashem Studies* 35 (2007), pp. 111–41, base their account uncritically on Wisliceny's, which is a surprising feature of their otherwise impressive work. See also Zvi Elpeleg, *The Grand Mufti: Haj Amin al-Husseini, Founder of the Palestinian National Movement* (London, 1993). Even Wiesenthal, *Großmufti—Großagent der Achse*, remarkable in many other aspects, largely follows Wisliceny, again without revealing this source (pp. 37ff). He also conducted a conversation with Kasztner, from whom he heard Eichmann's Hungarian story.

142. Adolf Eichmann on II-1, Re: Foreign travels, September 1, 1939, BA Koblenz, R58/523, folio 23; identical with Yad Vashem Archive, M-38/194.

143. The meetings were the subject of colorful press coverage, starting with the *Wochenschau* and the *Völkische Beobachter.*

144. Jeffrey Herf, "Hitlers Dschihad," *Vierteljahrshefte für Zeitgeschichte* 58 (April 2010), pp. 258–86.

145. Kurt Fischer-Werth, *Amin Al-Husseini: Großmufti von Palästina* (Berlin-Friedenau, 1943), with a color cover image featuring an unmistakable portrait of al-Husseini.

146. Fritz Grobba (Foreign Office), annotation, July 17, 1942, PA AA, R100 702 C/M, p. 153.

147. Suhr's secretary witnessed this meeting. Margarethe Reichert, hearing, October 17, 1967, BA Ludwigsburg, B 162/4172, sheet 296.

148. Four-page handwritten report "Re: Grand Mufti of Jerusalem," Bratislava, July 26, 1946 (prosecution document T/89) and Wisliceny, Cell 133 Document (prosecution document T/84).

149. Moshe Pearlman, *The Capture of Adolf Eichmann* (London, 1961), p. 98.

150. Andrej Steiner, statement, corroborated by his colleagues Oskar Neumann and Tibor Kovac, Bratislava, February 6, 1946. Wisliceny's commentary of March 5, 1946, quoted next, is handwritten on the transcript of the statement; prosecution document T/1117.

151. Al-Husseini protested to Ribbentrop on May 13, 1943, and wrote to the Hungarian and Romanian foreign ministers. Documented in Gerhard Hoepp, *Mufti-Papiere: Briefe, Memoranden, Reden und Aufsätze Amin al Husseinis aus dem Exil 1940–1945* (Berlin, 2004), documents 78, 82, 83.

152. We now know that al-Husseini's source of information was not Eichmann but a contact in London.

153. One route these lies took was from Eichmann to Wisliceny to Kasztner (passing into the history books via Kasztner's postwar conversations with Simon Wiesenthal). This is evident from the word-for-word agreement between Wisliceny's unpublished reports and Wiesenthal's early texts. Another route went via the Foreign Office. Kasztner Report, p. 115.

154. The contact he claimed to have with Chief of the Abwehr (German military intelligence service) Wilhelm Canaris is one example.

155. "Meine Memoiren," p. 119.

156. Interrogation, pp. 564ff.

157. On March 25, 1944, al-Husseini noted in his diary, in Arabic, that he wanted to meet the "expert in Jewish matters." On September 29, 1944, there is another Arabic entry: "Topic: the Jews of Italy, France and Hungary. And who is the expert on Jewish matters?" The entry containing Eichmann's name, on November 9, 1944, is noted in painstakingly produced Latin characters. We can assume from this that someone had answered al-Husseini's question. The interpretation of this entry is still suspect, but it does allow us to tentatively conclude that Eichmann had not made enough of an impression on

al-Husseini in January 1942 for the grand mufti to remember his name. Facsimiles of all the relevant pages can be found in the trial papers. Prosecution document T/1267-69; enlarged, T/1394.

158. Gerhard Lehfeldt, "Bericht über die Lage von 'Mischlingen'" (Berlin, mid-March 1943), in *Berlin, Rosenstraße 2-4: Protest in der NS-Diktatur: Neue Forschungen zum Frauenprotest in der Rosenstraße 1943*, ed. Antonia Leugers (Annweiler, 2005), as document 6, pp. 233–38; here p. 235. On the background, see Nathan Stoltzfus, "Heikle Enthüllungen. Gerhard Lehfeldts Bericht an Kirchenfürsten beider Konfessionen über den Massenmord an den Juden Europas," ibid., pp. 145–80.

159. Eichmann spoke about Günther at length in Argentina, explaining that Günther had used his absence to push through death sentences against Eichmann's Jewish contacts whom Eichmann had wanted to spare for tactical reasons. But since Eichmann assumed Günther was still alive, he asked Sassen to remove this transcript. It is missing from the Hagag version and from the original transcript (Eichmann Estate). The page is now in BA Ludwigsburg, "Miscellaneous" folder. See "Aftermath" in this book.

160. The fact that the witnesses had the opportunity to discuss their statements with one another in Nuremberg, and to get their stories straight, explains some of the extraordinary parallels in what they said later. There was contact between Höttl, Kaltenbrunner, Wisliceny, Wilhelm Bruno Waneck, and later Rudolf Jänisch, as reciprocally evidenced by their statements. There was a similar connection between Hans Jüttner, Otto Winkelmann, and Kurt Becher.

161. For Eichmann's first appearance in Hungary, see the stenographic transcript of his speech to the Jewish representatives on March 31, 1944, prosecution document T/1156.

162. Sassen transcript 9:10. Eichmann liked this phrase and used it often. See 10:6 and 33:8.

163. Sassen transcript 9:4.

164. Kasztner Report, p. 110. Joel Brand gives a similar quote, but this one is taken from Kasztner.

165. Ibid., p. 244.

166. Eichmann made such dire threats to Raoul Wallenberg that there was a diplomatic protest in Berlin, which the Foreign Office smoothed over for Eichmann. Shortly afterward one of Wallenberg's employees died in an attack on his official car, and the Hungarians saw a probable connection between the attack and Eichmann's threats. Foreign Office to Edmund Veesenmayer, December 17, 1944, prosecution document T/1232. BA Koblenz, *Blue volumes, Dokumente des UD zu Wallenberg von 1944–1965*, 49 vols., no. 800-2: telegram no. 438 of October 22, 1944. See Christoph Gann, *Raoul Wallenberg: So viele Menschen retten wie möglich* (Munich, 1999), p. 126. Based on the memories of Elisabeth Szel, who was married to one of Wallenberg's chauffeurs. From a report by Eric Sjöquist. See Bernt Schiller, *Raoul Wallenberg: Das Ende einer Legende* (Berlin, 1993), pp. 97ff.

167. Kasztner Report, pp. 135ff.

168. Wisliceny reported to Kasztner, "Eichmann is afraid of a new scandal," ibid., p. 295.

169. "As Eichmann confessed to me himself in Hungary, this plan came from him and Globicnig . . . and was suggested to Himmler by him. Hitler then gave the order personally." Wisliceny, Cell 133 Document (prosecution document T/84), p. 8.

170. Sassen transcript 34:6.

171. *Der Weg: Zeitschrift für Fragen des Judentums* (Berlin) 1, no. 26 (August 16, 1946).

172. Kasztner Report, p. 139.

173. Ibid., p. 178, and later in the prison notes.

174. At the end of 1944, Wisliceny even claimed that Eichmann had been dismissed and that he, Wisliceny, had been made the inspector of Theresienstadt, to protect the Jews—two lies he tried unsuccessfully to deny in Bratislava. Kasztner Report, Wisliceny commentary, March 25, 1947, prosecution document T/1116.

175. As early as May 3, 1944, Wisliceny claimed that Eichmann had "cut him off" because of his overly close personal contacts with Jews, but this was a lie. Kasztner Report, p. 85. In the fall of that year, he claimed: "I tried to intervene to help stop the unhappy foot-march out of Budapest. But it was unbelievably difficult to do even the smallest thing against Eichmann." Ibid., p. 274.

176. Sassen transcript 12:6–7.

177. Kurt Becher avoided punishment thanks to an affidavit from Rudolf (Rezsö) Kasztner, having managed to play the role of helper convincingly. Kasztner's support of him was taken badly, but in 1947 he was clearly still not in a position to recognize how Becher had entrapped him. And he was by no means alone in this regard: in 1955, Andreas Biss, Alex Weissberg, and Joel Brand were still trying to secure Becher's cooperation on a book. Kurt Becher, statement for Eichmann's trial, Bremen, June 20, 1961. Becher's image cultivation clearly functioned better than Eichmann's.

178. For instance, Laszlo Ferenczy, who as head of the Hungarian police force was substantially involved in all anti-Jewish measures, He explained to Kasztner that he was terribly afraid of Eichmann. Kasztner Report, p. 155.

179. Ibid., p. 62.

180. Brand was held in Cairo from June 12, 1943, to January 5, 1944. The interrogation of Bandi Grosz, who traveled with him, was submitted to London on July 13, 1944.

181. The cover was blown on Joel Brand's mission after only a short time. On July 18, 1944, a flood of radio reports and newspaper articles appeared. Translations were published in Hungary by July 19. Public opinion was disastrous (prosecution document T/1190). The *New York Times* headline on the same day was "A Monstrous 'Offer': German Blackmail. Bartering Jews for Munitions." See also *New York Herald Tribune,* July 19.

182. Shlomo Aronson, "Preparations for the Nuremberg Trial: The O.S.S., Charles Dwork, and the Holocaust," *Holocaust and Genocide Studies* 12, no. 2 (1998), pp. 257–81.

183. Sassen transcript 73:8.

184. Wilhelm Höttl, statement for Eichmann's trial, Altaussee, May 26, 1961.

185. Sassen transcript 49:8.

186. Horst Theodor Grell, statements for Eichmann's trial, Berchtesgaden, May 23, 1961. See also IMT NG-2190.

187. Presenting the list, Ben-Gurion called Eichmann the "worst and most dangerous of all war criminals," and Wiesenthal used the phrase "number-one enemy of the Jews." Wiesenthal, *Großmufti—Großagent der Achse*, p. 46.

188. Sassen transcript 25:5.

189. Stefan Hördler, "Die Schlussphase des Konzentrationslagers Ravensbrück. Personalpolitik und Vernichtung," *Zeitschrift für Geschichtswissenschaft* 56, no. 3 (2008), pp. 222–48, especially p. 244. Hördler corrects the assumption that the final mass murder using gas was committed on March 30–31, 1945, after which the gas chambers were dismantled. According to his investigation, the mass killings ended between April 15 and April 24, 1945, since Moll's mobile Sonderkommando was also being used in Ravensbrück.

190. Charlotte Salzberger, witness statement at Eichmann trial, session 42. Frau Salzberger dated this interrogation as March 3, 1945. She quoted Eichmann in German at his trial, eliciting one of the few visible reactions from him.

191. Rumors about the building of gas chambers in Theresienstadt led back to Eichmann (not least due to Wisliceny's statement about him to Kasztner). Afterward Eichmann referred to Majdanek, which he had been accused of maintaining, and said this would not happen to him again. Kasztner Report. H. G. Adler assumes that these plans did exist but that Eichmann was forced to withdraw them: *Theresienstadt, 1941–1945: Das Antlitz einer Zwangsgemeinschaft* (Tübingen, 1960), p. 201. At the start of March, Eichmann called a halt to the preparations for extermination and led a second round of "beautification." Adler, *Der verwaltete Mensch*, p. 354. Moritz Henschel also mentioned these plans in "Die letzten Jahre der Jüdischen Gemeinde Berlin," lecture in Tel Aviv, September 13, 1946, extract in prosecution document T/649.

192. "L'activité des CICR dans les Camps de Concentration en Allemagne," prosecution document T/865. A heavily abridged version was published in Jean-Claude Favez, *The Red Cross and the Holocaust* (Cambridge, 1999), pp. 305–6. See also attendee list for the event, prosecution document T/866. The visit was supervised by Ernst von Thadden (of the Foreign Office), Erich von Luckwald, and Erwin Weinmann (head of the SD in Bohemia and Moravia). The evening reception took place in the Hradčany castle district at the house of *Reichsprotektor* Karl-Hermann Frank.

193. Wisliceny and Eichmann both spoke about the promotion to SS *Standartenführer* that Eichmann had been offered. Wisliceny, Cell 133 Document, prosecution document T/84, p. 8; Sassen transcript 4:5.

194. Sassen transcript 11:11. In an earlier transcript, Eichmann spoke of "30 Eich-manns," Sassen transcript 3:1.
195. Wisliceny, Cell 133 Document, prosecution document T/84, p. 14. Wisliceny spoke in detail about the story Eichmann told, and about comparable infor-mation given to him by Höttl in Nuremberg, regarding a conversation he had had with Eichmann.
196. Eichmann gave this version of events several times, and it was corroborated at least on this point by the testimonies of Zeischka, Goettsch, and Waneck. June 17, 1946, information date April 1945, NA, RG 263, CIA Name File Adolf Eichmann.

2 The Postwar Career of a Name

1. CIC Report, June 17, 1946, NA, RG 263, CIA Name File Adolf Eichmann.
2. Facsimile in Manus Diamant, *Geheimauftrag: Mission Eichmann* (Vienna, 1995), p. 224. Also in Simon Wiesenthal, *Ich jagte Eichmann: Tatsachenbericht* (Gütersloh, 1961), p. 25.
3. Robinson to Jackson, July 27, 1945, World Jewish Congress Collection (MS-361), American Jewish Archives, box C106, file 16; cited in Tom Segev, *Simon Wiesenthal: The Life and Legends* (New York, 2010), p. 13.
4. Arrest Report Wisliceny, Dieter, August 25 and 27, 1945, NA, RG 263, CIA Name File Adolf Eichmann.
5. Arrest warrant in Staatspolizei Fahndungsblatt, under the terms of article 1654/46 (1946), paragraphs 3 and 4, KVG (Kriegsverbrechergesetz Öster-reich).The proceedings were unsuccessful, but the file was made available to Fritz Bauer in Frankfurt ten years later.
6. One part was made available according to the Nazi War Crimes Disclosure Act 1998, NA, RG 263, CIA Name File Adolf Eichmann, box 14–15.
7. In the Paris 1945 edition (unpaginated), Kiel University Library. The Berlin, March 1947, edition, mentioned Eichmann seven times (once as Eickmann) and said he was wanted in the United States and France for war crimes, mur-der, and torture.
8. Sassen transcript 10:17.
9. Adolf Karl Barth had been the name of a colonial goods merchant in Berlin, Eichmann later said. In Ulm, Eichmann claimed to be a Luftwaffe *Obergefreiter,* and when he was transferred to the collecting camp at Weiden, Oberpfalz (Sta-lag Xiii B), he said he was an SS *Oberscharführer* in the Waffen-SS. See "The Others Spoke," in the Argentina Papers. The transfer to Oberdachstetten in Bavaria followed, in August 1945. The first reference to the name Eckmann comes from a witness statement from June 1945: interrogation of Rudolf Schneide by L. Ponger, Yad Vashem Archive, M-9, file 584a. The statement is also in the relevant CIC report from December 3, 1946, NA, RG 319, Investiga-tive Records Repository, Adolf Eichmann.

10. Sassen interview, BA tape 10B, starting at 1:14. Word-for-word transcription, abbreviations marked.

11. Shlomo Aronson, "Preparations for the Nuremberg Trial: The O.S.S., Charles Dwork, and the Holocaust," *Holocaust and Genocide Studies* 12, no. 2 (1998), pp. 257–81.

12. One example is David Cesarani, who summarizes: "Eichmann was not mentioned sufficiently often or prominently enough to penetrate the consciousness of those who heard every word of the proceedings at Nuremberg, let alone those who received infrequent and drastically abbreviated reports from the press" (p. 1). German newspaper readers weren't interested in names, either, using their focus on day-to-day survival as justification for their lack of interest. There is also the question of which of the trial observers Cesarani is talking about. Those who knew Eichmann's name from before, like the wide circles of his victims and his fellow perpetrators, had various reasons for either noticing or ignoring things.

13. The English transcripts and documents from the first Nuremberg trial have been made available as part of Yale Law School's Avalon Project: http://avalon.law.yale.edu/subject_menus/imt.asp. In these endnotes, transcript quotations are given by the session date, and documents are cited according to the numbers used in the trial. IMT vols. refers to the printed edition (the so-called Blue Series).

14. Prosecution document T/585, identical with IMT 2376-PS, Gestapo-62 (June 22, 1945).

15. Dieter Wisliceny, witness statement, IMT, January 3, 1946.

16. Gustave M. Gilbert, *Nürnberger Tagebuch* (Frankfurt am Main, 1962), p. 109.

17. This announcement was quickly spread via Eichmann's adjutant Rudolf Jänisch and appears in the CIC files. It was frequently documented. Eichmann confirmed this trick in detail in Argentina: Sassen transcript 10:17.

18. The name frequently given in the secondary literature is Feiersleben, which stems from the incorrect entry in the residents' register from Eversen, and interviews in Altensalzkoth in summer 1960. The additional "von" was crossed out in the registry book (Bergen City Archive, shelf 585 no. 2). Later documents give the correct name. Thanks to Kurt Werner Seebo at the Bergen City Archive for his expert help.

19. Eichmann mentions this stopping point, which has not been closely researched, twice: in conversation with Sassen in 1957 (only on the original tape, BA tape 10B, 1:22:15) and in the manuscript "Meine Flucht," p. 21 (March 1961), BA Koblenz, All. Proz. 6/247. The latter implies that Eichmann obtained new papers in the Rhineland.

20. Sassen transcript 11:2.

21. The brother's housekeeper gave an interview in 1960 that has previously been overlooked, in which she mentioned the letters between the brothers about Eichmann's escape. She knew numerous details that we have only recently been able to verify, lending credibility to her statement. "Adolf Eichmann Dug

His Own Grave: The Family Housekeeper's Story," *Neues Österreich,* June 2, 1960.

22. Much later Robert Eichmann admitted that his stepfather had stayed in constant contact with his stepbrother Adolf—though the family discovered this only after his death. Robert Eichmann to Leo Maier-Frank, police captain (retired), March 8, 1990, in *Die Rattenlinie: Fluchtwege der Nazis: Eine Dokumentation,* edited by Rena Giefer and Thomas Giefer (Frankfurt am Main, 1991), pp. 71–73. (The letter also contains other, more dubious information.)

23. "Henninger" is a mishearing. The entry in the residents' registry book from Eversen is clear. Eversen arrival and departure registry, Bergen City Archive, shelf 585, no. 2. Thanks to Kurt-Werner Seebo.

24. Eversen registry book, ibid.

25. Wisliceny, Cell 133 Document, prosecution document T/84, p. 22.

26. CIC Report, NA, RG 319, Investigative Records Repository, Adolf Eichmann; and NA, RG 263, CIA Name File Adolf Eichmann, SS *Obersturmbannführer* A.E. 1946.

27. Declaration under oath, read out on April 11, 1946.

28. Ibid.

29. Ibid.

30. Eichmann's misremembering of this speech is telling. In Argentina, he quoted Jackson: "He [Jackson] felt he had to attest on the occasion of this trial, that I . . . was 'In truth the most sinister figure of this century'" ("Re: My Findings," part 2 of "The Others Spoke"), which included two separate elevations of what Jackson actually said.

31. IMT, Gest-39, Huppenkothen's declaration under oath.

32. Otto Winkelmann, SS *Obergruppenführer* and senior SS and police leader in Hungary, and Hans Jüttner, SS *Obergruppenführer* and general of the Waffen-SS, told an outrageous story (corroborated by Kurt Becher) absolving each other of responsibility for the death marches, although Winkelmann was responsible for the deportations and Jüttner wanted the forced labor. Jüttner stated: "At that time [November 1944] Winkelmann said he was completely powerless in the matter, and would be very grateful if I could raise an objection." Jüttner attempted it, although "I was well aware of the fact that this intervention could have very unpleasant consequences for me personally." Eichmann, however, claimed both of them had congratulated him on the idea for the foot marches, which is not unlikely. The only thing that may have disturbed Jüttner was the demographic of the foot marches—there were too few men capable of work. Jüttner's statement, Nuremberg, May 3, 1948. All three repeated their performance for the Eichmann trial: Winkelmann at Bordesholm, May 29, 1961; Jüttner at Bad Toelz, May 31, 1961; Kurt Becher at Bremen, June 20, 1961.

33. Kasztner Report, p. 194. For Kasztner, the term stood for the unassailable position of power that Eichmann's system established for anti-Jewish policy in all occupied countries, against which no one could say anything.

34. Judgment read out on September 30, 1946. IMT vol. 1,298.
35. Ibid. IMT vol. 1,283.
36. The handwritten note appears on an internal document called "Suggested Frame of the Judgment, in bare outline (for consideration and criticism only)," which was strictly classified because the news that the judges were already preparing notes for a judgment could itself have disastrous consequences. This suggests it was a very early document. Syracuse University, Syracuse, N.Y., Francis Biddle Papers, box 14. Thanks to Nicolette A. Dobrowolski for her expert help in finding the note and for her information on the document. The description in Bradley F. Smith, *Reaching Judgment at Nuremberg* (New York, 1977), p. 115, is problematic.
37. The final version of the indictment was submitted in the opening session, on October 18, 1945.
38. The apt phrase comes from Moshe Pearlman.
39. Sassen transcript 3:3.
40. Sassen transcript 6:1.
41. The formulation comes from Dieter Wisliceny, who claimed his boss had operated in secret in order to protect himself. Wisliceny, Cell 133 Document, prosecution document T/84.
42. Israeli government, note to the U.S., British, French, and Russian governments, published in full in *Jüdische Allgemeine,* July 27, 1951. The other names are Heydrich, Höß, Frank, and Hitler. Eichmann is named twice in this relatively short text.

3 Detested Anonymity

1. Contemporaries unanimously report that hunger was not a problem in the region.
2. "The Others Spoke," handwritten text, marginal note, p. 57, BA Ludwigsburg, "Miscellaneous" folder.
3. Eichmann claimed Rudolf Höß had told him about this saying of Himmler's. "Meine Memoiren," p. 110, and the interrogation and trial.
4. Sassen transcript 11:2. Eichmann corrected this section in his own hand, excising any mention of helpers. What remained read "there I found a whole pile of old newspapers, with articles about me among other things."
5. Eichmann quoted the book in detail even in the Sassen interviews, although it was not one the group was reading. He also had a copy in Israel (in its fifth edition) and used the volume for his last attempt to justify himself, "Götzen" (1961).
6. The volume was among Eichmann's books in Buenos Aires. His handwritten notes on it have also been preserved. Eichmann Estate, BA Koblenz, N/1497-89.
7. "Meine Flucht," p. 11, BA Koblenz, All. Proz. 6/247.

8. Sassen interview, original tape 10B, 1:22. Word-for-word transcription, grammar errors uncorrected.

9. "Meine Flucht," p. 22.

10. "The Others Spoke," handwritten text, marginal note, p. 57, BA Ludwigsburg, "Miscellaneous" folder.

11. Ruth Tramer, interviews by Robert Pendorf (*Stern*) and Richard Kilian (*Daily Telegraph*), June 1960, used in *Stern* articles (June 16–25, 1960) and in Quentin Reynolds, Ephraim Katz, and Zwy Aldouby, *Minister of Death: The Adolf Eichmann Story* (New York, 1960). Also confirmed in the documentary *I Met Eichmann (Adolf Eichmann—Begegnung mit einem Mörder)* (BBC/NDR, 2002), and in interviews by Raymond Ley in 2009 and on July 24, 2010, in *Menschen und Schlagzeilen* (NDR, broadcast July 28, 2010). The witnesses' names are omitted here at their request.

12. Children's memories are drawn from interviews in Altensalzkoth, July 24, 2010, in *Menschen und Schlagzeilen* (NDR, broadcast July 28, 2010).

13. Journalists (e.g., Robert Pendorf of *Stern*) conducted the first interviews in and around Altensalzkoth in summer 1960. Many people, like Woldemar Freiesleben, claimed to have had "no idea" (*Spiegel*, June 15, 1960). Witness statements still concur on Eichmann's behavior and on his role in the sparsely populated area. When it became clear who had been living in their midst, the general horror was entirely credible. It was also clear that maintaining a fearful silence about one's own past had become a general strategy for survival. Extensive research was done there by Karsten Krüger (2002), partly printed in *Frankfurter Rundschau*, May 30, 2002. See *Neue Presse*, July 23, 2009. See also interviews for the production *I Met Eichmann (Adolf Eichmann—Begegnungen mit einem Mörder)* (NDR/BBC, 2002) and interviews for the docudrama *Eichmanns Ende* (ARD, 2009). The 1960 *Stern* and *Life* interviews with Nelly Kühn (née Krawietz) complete the picture: Reynolds et al., *Minister of Death*, p. 185; *Stern*, June 16–25, 1960.

14. "Meine Flucht," p. 12.

15. Hannah Arendt, *Eichmann in Jerusalem: A Report on the Banality of Evil* (1963; reprint New York, 1994), p. 236.

16. If this "Uncle Willi" who paid Eichmann regular visits really was an SS man himself, then Koch and Eichmann must have known each other. Willi Koch was born on September 22, 1910, and worked at the Central Emigration Office in Posen in October 1940, then headed the Gnesen field office. The emigration office in Posen was under Eichmann's jurisdiction at this point. SS rankings list December 1, 1938, and June 15, 1939, no. 4813, SD main office.

17. See "I Had No Comrades," in this book.

18. Luis (occasionally Alois) Schintlholzer, born December 16, 1914, in Innsbruck, SS no. 308210, no. 2076 in the Waffen-SS rankings list (on July 1, 1944) as *Hauptsturmführer* in the reserves. BA Berlin-Lichterfelde, BDC files. See Gerald Steinacher, *Nazis on the Run: How Hitler's Henchmen Fled Justice* (Oxford,

2011), pp. 50–52. This work also uses the Schintlholzer files in BA Ludwigsburg, Central Office collection.

19. See Philipp Trafojer, "Die Spuren eines Mörders. Alois Schintlholzer (1914–1989)," editorial in the Austrian journal *Vinschgerwind* (September 8, 2005).

20. Schintlholzer said this to an acquaintance who he didn't realize was an informant for the West German secret service. Found in the supplementary file to BVerwG 7A 15.10, *Saure vs. BND*, BND files 121 099, 1664: writings from June 3, 1960, "On Foreign Office Questionnaire"; 1784: August 11, 1960. Thanks to Christoph Partsch for permission to use the quote.

21. Passage found only on original tape and left out by the transcriber in Argentina. BA tape 10B, 1:22:30.

22. A piece of film shot in the living room of these aging women gives us a glimpse, as they were still able to argue vociferously about whether the eyes of that unassuming Herr Heninger from the south who loved sweet things were blue or brown. *I Met Eichmann (Adolf Eichmann—Begegnungen mit einem Mörder)* (NDR/BBC, 2002). Eichmann's eyes were blue-gray.

23. "Liebl, Vera, Ex-Wife of Eichmann, Otto Adolf," November 26, 1946, and "Interrogation of Parents and Brother of SS-Obersturmbannführer Otto Adolf Eichmann," mid-October 1946, NA, RG 263, CIA Name File Adolf Eichmann.

24. Eichmann later said that his wife had spent the whole time living at his uncle's property. According to a report by Valentin Tarra, a policeman in Ausseerland, to Fritz Bauer, January 6, 1960, it was a hunting lodge. On July 30, 1948, Vera Eichmann and the children moved to a farmhouse in Fischerndorf. Valentin Tarra to Fritz Bauer, January 1, 1960, in *Mahnruf* (Austria), June 1960.

25. David Cesarani, *Eichmann: His Life and Crimes* (London, 2005), p. 27; Vera Eichmann, interview in *Daily Express*, December 12, 1961.

26. According to Valentin Tarra's notes, Vera's sister married Leopold Kals in Altaussee after the war. Vera's other sister lived with her mother and husband on the Hörsching airbase near Linz.

27. Wiesenthal dates this attempt at April 30, 1947, in *Ich jagte Eichmann: Tatsachenbericht* (Gütersloh, 1961), p. 85. The date in the corresponding CIA Name File is unclear: "SS Obersturmbannführer Adolf Eichmann, Report from Berlin," June 17/?? (illegible). Wiesenthal gave more frequent reports and described his intervention against Vera Eichmann's application as his most important contribution to Eichmann's capture. For the Altaussee police perspective, see Valentin Tarra, report to Bauer, January 6, 1960.

28. For the house searches, see CIC report on Adolf Eichmann, June 7, 1947, NA, RG 319, Investigative Records Repository, Adolf Eichmann. Ingrid von Ihne's house in Bad Gastein was also searched. For the discovery of the first photo, see Manus Diamant, *Geheimauftrag: Mission Eichmann* (Vienna, 1995), p. 223. The 1945 date was a mistake made by the German press. The photo is often mistaken—the correct one is reproduced in the cited volume.

29. Josef Weiszl was turned over to France in 1947 and sentenced to life impris-

onment for his part in the deportations to Auschwitz. In 1955 he returned to Austria a free man, where he was not brought to justice for his other crimes. See Hans Safrian, *Eichmann und seine Gehilfen* (Frankfurt am Main, 1995), p. 328.

30. Sassen transcript 3:3. Eichmann appeared in the Austrian "wanted" book from March 1955.

31. "Meine Flucht," p. 12.

32. There were only two gauleiters of Carinthia: Hubert Klausner (d. 1939) and Friedrich Rainer (hanged in Yugoslavia in 1947). Uki Göni believes a CAPRI employee called Armin Dardieux was in fact Uiberreither, meaning Eichmann and Uiberreither met in Argentina. See also Holger Meding, *Flucht vor Nürnberg? Deutsche und österreichische Einwanderung in Argentinien 1945–1955* (Cologne, 1992), pp. 150 and 217, and CEANA, *Third Progress Report* (Buenos Aires, 1998). The claim that Uiberreither lived in Argentina was disputed by journalists from KORSO and subsequently by Heinz Schneppen, who suspected Uiberreither was in Sindelfingen under the name Friedrich Schönharting. Eichmann himself made no further mention of Uiberreither's actual location, as far as we know. Eichmann knew about the speculations in 1947, he remembered them in 1960 when he wrote this remark, and he never contradicted them. He had been personally acquainted with Uiberreither since the 1930s.

33. *Neue Zeitung* (Munich), September 23, 1949. See also "The *Weg* That Leads into the Abyss," *Neue Zeitung*, June 7, 1949; "Imported Wehrwolf," *Lübecker Nachrichten*, June 11, 1949; "The Masters of the 'Descamisados,'" *Tagesspiegel*, September 28, 1949; and "The Hitlers in South America," *Gronauer Nachrichten und Volkszeitung*, November 5, 1949.

34. *Spiegel*, June 2, 1949. See also *Lübecker Nachrichten*, June 11, 1949. Rudel, Galland, Baumbach, and Lietzmann are all named.

35. Wilfred von Oven, *Mit Goebbels bis zum Ende* (Buenos Aires, 1949). See Oven's description of his years in Schleswig-Holstein in his *Ein "Nazi" in Argentinien* (Gladbeck, 1993).

36. Neither the identity paper nor the short-term visa has been found, but there are detailed records of them in the application for the Red Cross refugee passport and in the passport itself, also documented in the Argentine Immigration Office records (file no. 231489/48, cited in Uki Goñi, *The Real Odessa: How Perón Brought the Nazi War Criminals to Argentina*, rev. ed. [London, 2003], p. 298n506). June 2, 1948, is theoretically also a possible date, as the Red Cross records switch from Roman to Arabic numerals at random. The extant Termeno papers of Josef Mengele, Ernst Müller, and "Kremhart" (Ludolf von Alvensleben), however, were all filled out between Friday and Sunday. If these were the usual hours when these papers were issued, then the date was probably June 11, 1948.

37. Eichmann knew the name *Hudal* during the Nazi period: the rector of the German Seminary of the Santa Maria dell'Anima German National Church in

Rome often informed the Foreign Office about the mood in Rome. On October 23, 1943, Eichmann received a report in which Hudal warned him not to have Jews arrested in public in Rome, so as not to provoke the pope into taking an official stand against it. Prosecution document T/620.

38. Wisliceny, Cell 133 Document. prosecution document T/84, p. 18.

39. There were high hopes for an east-west conflict within the prisoners' wing at Nuremberg, and it was a frequent topic of conversation outside the courtroom. See also Gustave M. Gilbert, *Nürnberger Tagebuch* (Frankfurt am Main, 1962).

40. Frau Lindhorst, statement in *I Met Eichmann (Adolf Eichmann—Begegnungen mit einem Mörder* (NDR/BBC, 2002).

41. Press conference, October 24, 1960, quoted in "How Eichmann Was Hunted," *Allgemeine Wochenzeitung der Juden,* October 28, 1960.

42. Tom Segev has achieved an impressively delicate juxtaposition of all the available accounts, allowing us to see the discrepancies among them. Where no other sources are mentioned, the following summary rests on the corresponding chapters. Segev, *Simon Wiesenthal: The Life and Legends* (New York, 2010), pp. 19–28.

43. Leo Frank-Maier, *Geständnis—Das Leben eines Polizisten: Vom Agentenjäger zum Kripochef Oberst Leo Maier* (Linz, 1993), pp. 25ff.

44. Bloch's report on the operation, January 3, 1949, cited in Segev, *Simon Wiesenthal.*

45. Eichmann said he had considered this possibility in mid-1950. "Meine Flucht," p. 17.

46. The majority of articles appeared at the end of October 1948 and are for the most part verbatim repetitions of the report in *Welt am Abend.* Quotations here are taken from *Südkurier* and *Oberösterreichische Zeitung* of October 2 and 3, 1948, and *Neue Woche,* November 13, 1948.

47. The BND gave the relevant files to the Bundesarchiv/Federal Archives in November 2010. "Case of Adolf Eichmann. Failed capture by Israel, and Urban's claims about possible help with his escape," BA Koblenz, B206/1986. *Der Spiegel* used this collection of files for its online article "Israelis Tried to Abduct Eichmann from Austria," January 15, 2011, though without reference to current research.

48. Frank-Maier, *Geständnis,* p. 21; photo of Urban for identification purposes, p. 24.

49. Peter F. Müller and Michael Mueller, *Gegen Freund und Feind: Der BND: Geheime Politik und schmutzige Geschäfte* (Hamburg, 2002), p. 226.

50. See also the CIC/CIA file, NA, RG 263, Name File Josef Adolf Urban (born June 14, 1920).

51. Müller and Mueller, *Gegen Freund und Feind,* p. 226.

52. Bruno Kauschen came from Office VI (SD-Ausland), Department C2 of the RSHA.

53. BA Koblenz, B206/1986.

54. For Urban's Nazi career, see Hermann Zolling and Heinz Höhne, *Pullach Intern: General Gehlen und die Geschichte des Bundesnachrichtendienstes* (Hamburg, 1971), p. 217. See also his CIA file.

55. Wiesenthal wrote to Kasztner after the trial, on December 5, 1948, to ask if what was heard there was correct. Cited in Segev, *Simon Wiesenthal*, p. 103.

56. "Causes and Background to the Attack Against Dr. H.," report dated July 16, 1952, quoted in Müller and Mueller, *Gegen Freund und Feind*, p. 227. The report was compiled by someone close to Wilhelm Höttl, who will be spoken of again here. Urban was his direct competitor in the business of selling false news, but Urban's sympathies lay elsewhere.

57. Segev, *Simon Wiesenthal*, p. 14.

58. NA, RG 263, CIA Name File Adolf Eichmann. There are several references to Wiesenthal.

59. Zvi Aharoni said he had asked Eichmann about his children.

60. Otto Lindhorst, the son of Eichmann's landlady, statement in *I Met Eichmann (Adolf Eichmann—Begegnungen mit einem Mörder* (NDR/BBC, 2002). See also Karsten Krüger's interviews. *Life* reporters interviewed Nelly Krawietz in 1960. According to Nelly, Eichmann wrote to her: "'If you don't hear a sign of life from me in four weeks, you can write the sign of the cross over my name," a phrase that sounds very like Eichmann's language. Quentin Reynolds, Ephraim Katz, and Zwy Aldouby, *Minister of Death: The Adolf Eichmann Story* (New York, 1960), p. 188.

61. Eichmann told this story to the Israeli agent Zvi Aharoni after his capture in 1960. Zvi Aharoni and Wilhelm Dietl, *Operation Eichmann: The Truth About the Pursuit, Capture, and Trial,* trans. Helmut Bögler (New York, 1997), p. 147.

62. "Meine Flucht," p. 13.

63. For example, in Sassen transcript 21:10.

64. For unimportant dates, we can give Eichmann the benefit of the doubt: he may just have been mistaken about one or two of them. But we can prove that he also consciously changed dates, claiming things happened later than they did to make himself look better (and later, to aid his defense). The process helped him succeed in the Nazi period as well. This method of outwitting bureaucracy was probably one of the tools the men of the SD learned to use in the early 1930s.

65. Klaus Eichmann, interview for the German magazine *Quick,* January 2, 1966.

66. Even the early CIC reports contain clues that SS men used the innocuous-sounding city name to make themselves known to one another as discreetly as possible. It had the very practical advantage of occasionally getting them larger rations. CIC file Organisation Odessa, first document, October 25, 1946. Heinz Schneppen describes how the myth was created in *Odessa und das Vierte Reich: Mythen der Zeitgeschichte* (Berlin, 2007), although he sometimes focuses too strictly on the word *Odessa* and doesn't look at the organizational structures that were actually present. Unfortunately, Schneppen uses only a few Eichmann statements and ignores notable networks and contacts among

the people who escaped to Argentina. The following text shed more light on these networks.

67. Eichmann didn't mention the names of sympathizers to Sassen: "I was smuggled through Germany," etc. Throughout "Meine Flucht" he refers to "the organization." Schneppen is quite right: Eichmann never once mentioned "Odessa" (*Odessa,* p. 27). However, the absence of a name does not mean that the thing did not exist. Eichmann clearly referred to an organization that was supported by former SS members. He kept quiet about it in Israel, as "the organization" was still in existence, its structures still in place, and it still offered support, not least to Eichmann's family in his absence. Counter to Schneppen's claim, even in 1960 speaking about it would have meant posing a "danger to his own person or to third parties" (p. 23).

68. Moshe Pearlman, *The Capture of Adolf Eichmann* (London, 1961).

69. Supplemental file to case BVerwG 7A 15.10, *Saure vs. BND,* BND files 121 099, 1664: letter of June 3, 1960 "auf AA Anfrage" (on Foreign Office query), 1784: August 11, 1960. See "I Had No Comrades" in this book.

70. Surveillance of the Eichmann family revealed that their financial circumstances visibly improved at this point; Simon Wiesenthal to Nahum Goldmann, March 30, 1954, NA, RG 263, CIA Name File Adolf Eichmann. Eichmann also hinted at this contact in "Meine Flucht," p. 16.

71. Gerald Steinacher assumes Eichmann was baptized by the priest in Sterzing, as the baptism register there shows the rebaptism of Erich Priebke. But there is no evidence of a baptismal certificate for Eichmann. Steinacher, *Nazis auf der Flucht,* p. 167.

72. "Meine Flucht," p. 18.

73. Ibid., p. 24.

74. *Giovanni C* is a frequent misspelling, going back to Eichmann himself. The documents in Argentina are clear, however (and ships usually have female names).

75. "Meine Flucht," p. 17.

76. Ibid., p. 22.

Interlude   A False Trail in the Middle East

1. "Meine Flucht," p. 18, BA Koblenz, All. Proz. 6/247.

2. Two representative examples of the judgment passed on Wiesenthal's error are Heinz Schneppen, *Odessa und das Vierte Reich: Mythen der Zeitgeschichte* (Berlin, 2007), p. 12; and Guy Walters, *Hunting Evil* (London and Toronto, 2009), p. 207.

3. Wiesenthal, who cited the reports from Linz, remained convinced of this hiding place and the Austrian connection long after Eichmann was captured. The theory can be found in all his books and many notes. Simon Wiesenthal, *Justice Not Vengeance: Recollections* (New York, 1990), p. 74. His most detailed

account is quoted here—namely Wiesenthal's letter to Nahum Goldmann, March 30, 1954, NA, RG 263, CIA Name File Adolf Eichmann.

4. One source of information on the Nazi organization suspected to exist in Austria was none other than the disinformation specialist Wilhelm Höttl. NA, RG 263, CIA Name File Wilhelm Höttl.

5. The reports from Linz on the stories told by the imaginative informant Mitterhuber have been publicly available since November 2010, in the BND files held at BA Koblenz, B206/1986. Mitterhuber even claimed that Eichmann was leading a resistance cell to combat any potential Communist overthrow—financed by the United States.

6. NA, RG 263, CIA Name File Adolf Eichmann. "Spinne" also appears in CIC Name File Otto Skorzeny. The United States speculated about these secret organizations' gold reserves and routinely implicated the USSR. Walters, *Hunting Evil*, p. 207.

7. Alfred Fischer, "No Trace of Karl Eichmann," *Der Weg*, August 16, 1946. See Alfred Fischer, "Karl Eichmann—Head of Gestapo's Jewish Section," *Zionist Review*, October 4, 1946.

8. R. B. Haebler, "The Man We Are Looking For," *Jüdisches Gemeindeblatt für die britische Zone*, June 1, 1947. This text was quoted repeatedly over the following years by National Socialist authors, who tried to use it as proof that Eichmann was Jewish.

9. Simon Wiesenthal, *Großmufti—Großagent der Achse* (Salzburg and Vienna, 1947), p. 46.

10. Leon Poliakov, "Adolf Eichmann ou le rêve de Caligula," *Le Monde Juif* (Paris), June 4, 1949. This photo from the early 1930s is reprinted in David Cesarani, *Eichmann: His Life and Crimes* (London, 2005), the first image in the middle photo section.

11. Sassen transcript 22:1. The photo in Poliakov's piece has been clumsily reprinted but not retouched.

12. *Jüdisches Gemeindeblatt für die britische Zone* (the predecessor of the *Allgemeine Wochenzeitung der Juden in Deutschland*), June 23, 1948. More coverage appeared in late 1948, following an article in the Vienna *Welt am Abend*, with headlines like "A Member of the Arab Legion." *Südkurier*, October 2–3, 1948.

13. Tom Segev describes this episode in his biography of Wiesenthal and points to a letter from Wiesenthal to Avraham Silberschein on June 22, 1948. Tom Segev, *Simon Wiesenthal: The Life and Legends* (New York, 2010), p. 121.

14. For example: "Mass Murderer as Military Adviser," *Frankfurter Rundschau*, March 22, 1952; "SS Generals in the Middle East," *Die Gegenwart*, April 1952, and *Allgemeine Wochenzeitung der Juden*, April 18, 1952; "The German Soldier in the Middle East," *Allgemeine Wochenzeitung der Juden*, April 25, 1952; "German 'Advisers' in Cairo Plotting Against Bonn. Former SS and SD Leaders in League with Nagib and Mufti," *Welt am Sonntag*, November 23, 1952.

15. Incorrect information was given by the BND, on the basis of a statement by Saida Ortner, who spoke of Eichmann arriving in Syria in 1947. NA, RG 263,

CIA Name File Adolf Eichmann. See also "New Eastern Connections," BND report to the CIA, March 19, 1958, so far accessible only in the NA, RG 263, CIA Name File Adolf Eichmann. Johann von Leers, who still had contact with Eichmann in Argentina, was one of the most famous Nazis to have converted to Islam. Alois Brunner is also known to have taken the route to Syria.

16. See note 98 to "Eichmann in Kuwait" in this book (page 515), for the article series and the background details. See also Segev, *Simon Wiesenthal,* pp. 140–41.

17. Quentin Reynolds, Ephraim Katz, and Zwy Aldouby, *Minister of Death: The Adolf Eichmann Story* (New York, 1960), p. 189.

18. Reynolds's error could also have been due to Otto Skorzeny being mistaken for Walter Rauff, who really did take this escape route. Reynolds's source is an interview bought from Heinz Weibel-Altmeyer, with a man he claimed to be the third business partner, "Fuad Nahdif."

19. Tom Segev, *The Seventh Million: The Israelis and the Holocaust,* trans. Haim Watzman (New York, 1993), p. 149.

20. Michael Bar-Zohar, *The Avengers* (New York, 1970), p. 65. Bar-Zohar was the first to recognize the true role of Fritz Bauer and is tremendously well informed in other ways as well. His book appeared in many languages but never in German.

21. Segev, *Seventh Million,* p. 148. Segev interviewed Abba Kovner, who survived the Warsaw uprising and founded an avenging force even before the war was over, as was first brought to light in Bar-Zohar, *Avengers.* Both conducted interviews with men from the murder squads.

22. Alfred Fischer, "No Trace of Karl Eichmann," *Der Weg,* August 16, 1946.

23. Eichmann's accident in 1932 resulted in a fractured skull, a broken collarbone, and the scar above his eye. These traces would later give Mossad conclusive proof of their prisoner's identity in 1960. The noticeable asymmetry of his face was not the result of this accident, however: it can be seen in Eichmann's childhood photos, and his siblings have similarly lopsided features.

24. The rumor that Eichmann had had facial surgery surfaced at the end of the 1940s and can be found in various popular articles over the next few years. Wiesenthal reported it in his letter to Nahum Goldmann of March 30, 1954; NA, RG 263, CIA Name File Adolf Eichmann. Benjamin Epstein, who knew Eichmann, spread the rumor in an interview at the time of his arrest. "Mass Murderer Eichmann Had an Operation on His Face," *Neues Österreich,* May 26, 1960. The rumor ceased only after Eichmann's arrest, when subsequent photos proved it to be untrue. Eichmann hinted that he had met Nazis in South America who had changed more than just their names, but this could have been just his usual self-importance talking. Interview for *Paris Match,* June 2, 1952, BA Koblenz, All. Proz. 6/252.

25. "Götzen," p. 589.

1 Life in the "Promised Land"

1. "Meine Flucht," p. 22, BA Koblenz, All. Proz. 6/247.
2. Eichmann mentioned this connection, but in typical fashion, he omitted the name of the person involved. Ibid., p. 23. Evidently people in these circles introduced themselves by their real names and not their new, fake identities.
3. Ibid.
4. Uki Goñi, *The Real Odessa: How Perón Brought the Nazi War Criminals to Argentina* (London and New York, 2002), p. 301.
5. It appears that only forty of the three hundred employees were engineers by trade. See Ernst Klee, *Persilscheine und Falsche Pässe: Wie die Kirchen den Nazis halfen* (Frankfurt am Main, 1992); and Goñi, *Odessa*.
6. Eichmann wrote of this several times in Israel, in "Meine Flucht" and elsewhere.
7. Eichmann mentioned Fischböck during the Sassen interviews: "He's still alive!!!" is his handwritten annotation on the Sassen transcript, 59:9. After Eichmann was arrested, Fischböck's wife said she had been one of the last people to speak to him. She also mentioned that she knew him well from his time at CAPRI, where her husband also worked.
8. Eckhard Schimpf, *Heilig: Die Flucht des Braunschweiger Naziführers auf der Vatikan-Route nach Südamerika* (Brunswick, 2005), p. 110.
9. BA tape 10C, 1:28:00.
10. There is still clear evidence of around twenty contacts, from letters or notes on conversations, including a phone call.
11. Rajakowitsch joined the SS in 1940. See Eichmann's staff report on Rajakowitsch, July 19, 1940, prosecution document T/55(6). Between February and August 1952, there is evidence that Eichmann occasionally went to Buenos Aires during his Tucumán period.
12. Pathetic tales of Germans' fear of being unmasked, which can be found in Juan (Hans) Maler's late texts, belong to the realm of fiction. Buenos Aires had a German infrastructure, with its own restaurants, a cinema, a theater, and many shops, forming a natural part of the city. Argentina was particularly welcoming to Germans.
13. Goñi found proof of Armin Dadieu, Berthold Heilig, Erwin Fleiss, and Franz Sterzinger (*Odessa*, p. 301). The presence of Siegfried Uiberreither, former gauleiter and *Reichsstatthalter* of Styria, also mentioned by Goñi and Holger Meding, is still disputed. Eichmann explicitly mentions Uiberreither as a direct influence on his own escape to Argentina, in "Meine Flucht," p. 12
14. According to his daughter Karin (née Heilig). See Schimpf, *Heilig*, p. 111. Heilig arrived in Buenos Aires on January 17, 1951; his children followed in 1953. He told them he had met Eichmann in Rome, which kept him from having to explain to his family where he had really met the Adviser on Jewish Affairs— Rome didn't sound suspicious.

15. Herbert Hagel, interview by Joshua Goltz and Abel Basti, 1998 and 1999, cited in Goñi, *Odessa*, p. 282n494. Habel (SS no. 112171) was secretary to SS *Obergruppenführer* August Eigruber, the gauleiter of Linz.

16. Heinz Lühr, interview in *I Met Eichmann (Adolf Eichmann—Begegnungen mit einem Mörder)* (NDR/BBC, 2002). Lühr dated the conversation to shortly after Vera Eichmann's arrival, which was in July 1952.

17. "Meine Flucht," p. 24.

18. Occasionally incorrectly written "Davmanin."

19. In Israel, Eichmann was shown to be unable to read French texts. The tapes made in Argentina reveal him as anything but a talented linguist, as he spoke Spanish with a heavy German accent.

20. Identity card no. 1378538, produced by the Buenos Aires district police. The Tucumán district produced two further identity papers for Eichmann in short order: on February 8, 1952, one numbered 341952, and on April 3, 1952, a CdI (identification key) numbered 212430, a facsimile of which is in Gideon Hausner, *Justice in Jerusalem* (New York, 1966).

21. "Meine Flucht," p. 25.

22. Constantin von Neurath (1902–81) was said to have been president of Kameradenwerk for a time. Neurath, interview by Wilfred von Oven (Gaby Weber in "hr2 Kultur," *Wissenswert,* broadcast on May 8, 2008); interviews by Ludwig Lienhardt and Josef Janko. Holger Meding, *Flucht vor Nürnberg? Deutsche und österreichische Einwanderung in Argentinien 1945–1955* (Cologne, 1992), p. 176. Neurath officially worked for Siemens from 1953, becoming director of Siemens Argentina S.A. in 1958. He then worked in Munich (where he gained joint procurement responsibility for the company headquarters by 1965) and retired in 1966. Thanks to Frank Wittendorfer of the Siemens Archive in Munich, where surprisingly little was known about this employee. See "For Better, for Worse" and "I Had No Comrades" in this book, for the help Neurath provided to wanted war criminals.

23. Rudel (with help from his ghostwriter Sassen) talks about Fritsch's life in *Zwischen Deutschland und Argentinien* (Buenos Aires, 1954), p. 220. Also published by Dürer, this book contained a right-wing paean to the publisher. Fritsch's short visit is the only grain of truth to the rumors of his involvement in war crimes and high offices in Germany. He was far too young to have made a career under Hitler. There was only one of these "world congresses," which allows us to pinpoint its date.

24. Holger Meding's first-rate study *"Der Weg": Eine deutsche Emigrantenzeitschrift in Buenos Aires 1947–1957* (Berlin, 1997) has uses far beyond what the title suggests. It is essential reading for anyone wanting to understand these groups of German nationals in Argentina and beyond. And it opens up exciting fields for further research, as we are still a long way from knowing about everyone who worked for *Der Weg.* For in-depth study, there is no substitute for reading the Dürer publications and *Der Weg* itself. The following description is based

on these sources. I thank Eberhard Fritsch's grandson for his willingness to provide me with as much information as he could.

25. "Dry goods store" is a translation error. The descriptions in Fritsch's letters are clear, however.

26. Hans Hefelmann, statement, December 28, 1960, Js148/60 Generalstaatsan- waltschaft, Frankfurt am Main, against Prof. Werner Heyde, Hefelmann, et al. For the particulars, see Klee, *Persilscheine*.

27. Fritsch to Werner Beumelburg, August 19, 1948, Werner Beumelburg Estate, Rheinische Landesbibliothek Koblenz; quoted in Stefan Busch, *Und gestern, da hörte uns Deutschland: NS-Autoren in der Bundesrepublik: Kontinuität und Diskontinuität bei Friedrich Griese, Werner Beumelburg, Eberhard Wolfgang Müller und Kurt Ziesel* (Würzburg, 1998). Thanks to Barbara Koelges of the Landesbibliothek Koblenz for her thorough insight into the correspondence.

28. We can now be certain that Werner Beumelburg, Hans Grimm, Kurt Ziesel, Eberhard Wolfgang Möller, Friedrich Griese, Erhard Wittek, Paul Alverdes, and Heinrich Zillich were among them, and they all went on to write for Dürer. See *Der Weg—El Sendero* but also indirect letters from Fritsch to Beu- melburg of February 10, 1948, and February 9, 1949, in which he brags about his correspondents. Werner Beumelburg Estate, Rheinische Landesbibliothek Koblenz,.

29. Fritsch to Beumelburg, February 10, 1948; Grimm to Beumelburg, March 5, 1948; both in Werner Beumelburg Estate. Rheinische Landesbibliothek Koblenz. Thanks to Birgit Kienow of the German Literature Archive in Mar- bach for access to Hans Grimm's correspondence.

30. This is no literary invention, either: Dürer sold the crochet instructions for it. A contemporary claims she still owns one, which we can believe, as she declined to have her name printed in connection with it.

31. Wilfred von Oven, *Ein "Nazi" in Argentinien* (Gladbeck, 1993), p. 19.

32. For the way the EROS travel service was used in practice, see the corre- spondence between Fritsch and Werner Beumelburg, where it emerges that Beumelburg was also paid in kind. Beumelburg Estate, Rheinische Landesbib- liothek Koblenz.

33. The following information is drawn not only from my own archive research and interviews but also from the excellent fieldwork done by Natasja de Winter.

34. Volberg gave a rather implausible denial of his leading role in his memoirs. See Heinrich Volberg, *Auslandsdeutschtum und drittes Reich: Der Fall Argenti- nien* (Cologne and Vienna, 1981). For background on the office in Argentina, and the extant staff lists, see Frank-Rutger Hausmann, *Ernst Wilhelm Bohle, Gauleiter im Dienst von Partei und Staat* (Berlin, 2009).

35. Heiner Korn's successor, Heriberto Korch, did not want to be interviewed. The company was apparently bought by Kühne and Nagel just a few years ago.

36. Names and addresses mentioned in Fritsch's correspondence.

37. Inge Schneider, interview by Roelf van Til (1999).
38. Ibid.; Saskia Sassen, interview by Raymond Ley (2009); Saskia and Francisca Sassen, correspondence with the author.
39. On February 4, 1959, Gustav Flor was tried before the fourth chamber of the Lüneberg District Court for distributing National Socialist writings. Large stocks of Dürer publications and a list of subscribers had been seized from him; the publisher had recruited him a year before. Fritsch, who was also summoned, did not appear. See the articles in the *Stuttgarter Zeitung* and *Die Welt*, February 4, 1959, and the coverage in the local Hamburg papers. Unfortunately the evidence is no longer available: it was probably destroyed after the retention period elapsed. Berchtesgaden is mentioned in Fritsch's correspondence.
40. Thanks to Daniel Fritsch for his information.
41. Rudel, *Zwischen Deutschland und Argentinien*, p. 206.
42. Sassen is named as an employee of CAPRI in a CIA report from 1953. As the informant was also from Argentina, we can at least be sure that the foreigner Sassen was on the CAPRI staff. *German Nationalist and Neo-Nazi Activities in Argentina*, July 8, 1953, declassified on April 11, 2000 (CIA-RDP620–00 856 R000 3000 30004–4). Pedro Pobierzym, interview by Raymond Ley (2009), also claims Sassen was often in Tucumán for this reason.
43. Eckhard Schimpf describes the distribution channel used by Berthold Heilig, through his old contacts in Rome, whom he also used to obtain passports for his family, and through the SS organization Stille Hilfe (Silent Aid). With Heilig too, letters were sent via a variety of cover addresses. Schimpf, *Heilig*, p. 111. Helene Elisabeth, Princess of Isenburg, who ran Stille Hilfe, also had contacts with Rudel's Kameradenwerk.
44. Eichmann told this version for the first time to the Mossad team's interrogation specialist. Quoted in Zvi Aharoni and Wilhelm Dietl, *Operation Eichmann: The Truth About the Pursuit, Capture and Trial* (New York, 1997), p. 67.
45. According to the commune's records, Vera Eichmann moved to Fischerndorf on July 30, 1948. See also Valentin Tarra to Fritz Bauer, January 1, 1960, in *Mahnruf* (Austria), June 1960.
46. Wiesenthal's press conference in Jerusalem, October 24, 1960, quoted in *Allgemeine Wochenzeitung der Juden*, October 28, 1960.
47. See Tom Segev, *Simon Wiesenthal: The Life and Legends* (New York, 2010). Segev was able to look over Tarra's papers and analyzed his letters to Wiesenthal (p. 99).
48. We know about this letter thanks to Eichmann's uncle's housekeeper in the Rhineland, who was interviewed in "Adolf Eichmann Dug His Own Grave: The Family Housekeeper Speaks Out," *Neues Österreich*, June 2, 1960. When Eberhard Fritsch left Argentina for Austria in 1958, Eichmann had told him his family's address in Linz. See "Aftermath" in this book.
49. Klaus Eichmann, interview in *Quick*, January 2, 1966.

50. Valentin Tarra to Fritz Bauer, January 1, 1960, in *Mahnruf* (Austria), June 1960.

51. This refers to Fritz Eichmann, Eichmann's half brother from his father's second marriage.

52. Current Federal German residency applications confirm this point.

53. Tarra to Wiesenthal, January 19, 1953, Wiesenthal Private Papers, quoted in Segev, *Simon Wiesenthal*, p. 100.

54. Klaus Eichmann, interview in *Quick*.

55. The *Bild* published a facsimile of the first page of the index card from the Eichmann BND file, labeled "Eichmann/Aichmann, Adolf DN Clemens," on January 8, 2011. From supplementary file to case BVerwG 7A 15.10, *Saure vs. BND*, BND files 100 470, p. 1.

56. In Wilhelm Fuchs's trial in Yugoslavia, the accused referred to him as "*Standartenführer*," which suggests that Eichmann had been giving himself airs in advance of this promotion.

57. This message suggests the possibility that the informant was Josef Adolf Urban. But there are too many people it might have been for us to speculate in any meaningful way. The informant could have been any one of the links in the information chain or an employee of the Eichmann family in Linz.

58. Only in the very first issues in 1947 did Fritsch hide behind his printer Gustav Friedl. After that he not only regularly wrote the foreword but gave his details clearly in the masthead. It is sometimes claimed, incorrectly, that Johann von Leers was the editor-in-chief. This error can be traced back to a report from the German embassy in Buenos Aires to the German Foreign Office in 1954, as Leers was leaving Argentina. The embassy was obviously aware of the influence Leers exerted in editorial meetings. West German embassy in Buenos Aires to Foreign Office, June 11, 1954, "Politische Beziehungen zu Argentinien" Aktenzeichen 81.33/3, PA AA, dept. 3, vol. 74, cited in Meding, *Der Weg*, p. 125.

59. This interpretation was given by *Die Welt* (online edition) as a reaction to the publication of the index card from the BND file on January 8, 2011.

60. Jorge Camarasa even found the name *Ricardo Klement* in the Buenos Aires telephone book, as Eichmann seems to have had an entry there in 1952. Jorge Camarasa, *Odessa al Sur: La Argentina Como Refugio de Nazis y Criminales de Guerra* (Buenos Aires, 1995), p. 157; Goñi, *Odessa*, p. 385. This clue can unfortunately not be verified. In 1951–52, the name was neither in the regional edition nor in the full directory for Buenos Aires. This doesn't necessarily mean anything, as the edition containing new entries for 1952 is 1953–54, which is nowhere to be found (either in the official edition or in *Edition Guia de Abonos*). Thanks to Natasja de Winter, who searched for it with admirable patience in various libraries and archives in Buenos Aires.

61. The cover name is not only to be found on the index card; it also features in the mere twenty-two pages on 1960 contained in the file. See the supplementary file to case BVerwG 7A 15.10, *Saure vs. BND*, BND files 100 470, pp. 1–18.

62. The number of aliases appearing in the rumors about Eichmann's disappearance is impressive. If you take into account the CIA reports, newspaper articles, and books prior to the start of the trial, there are around twenty different names, including the false name that Eichmann had actually chosen.

63. Questionnaire, September 1, 1959, and answer, September 8, 1959, in supplementary file to case BVerwG 7A 15.10, *Saure vs. BND,* BND files 100 470, pp. 17–18. Thanks to Christoph Partsch.

64. *Salto* is a misprint.

65. Under the official exchange rate of the time, 100 pesos was a little over 5 U.S. dollars or 20 Deutschmarks—it really was a lot of money. For more on exchange rates, see note 80 for this chapter. Klaus Eichmann, interview in *Quick,* January 2, 1966.

66. "Meine Flucht," p. 25.

67. Ibid.

68. Vera Eichmann had kept the photos of her husband well hidden, as evidenced by the substantial collection she sold to *Life* and *Stern* in 1960 alone, via Willem Sassen.

69. Vera Eichmann, interview for *Paris Match,* April 29, 1962; original transcript in BA Koblenz, All. Proz. 6/252, p. 23.

70. The notorious Nazi Erich Kernmayr (alias Kern) said this in the presence of a CIA informant in March 1952. CIA report, NA, RG 263, CIA Name File Wilhelm Höttl.

71. In 1966, Klaus Eichmann was still full of admiration for his father, whom he said was "able to do a whole lot of things." Klaus Eichmann, interview in *Quick.*

72. Adolf Eichmann was still talking about his trip to Aconcagua in letters he wrote in Israel. Conquering that mountain was clearly an ambition among German immigrants, and Hans-Ulrich Rudel proudly published photos of his climb.

73. Schimpf, *Heilig,* p. 111.

74. "Meine Flucht," p. 25.

75. When he applied to Mercedes-Benz Argentina in 1959, Eichmann said his employment relations with CAPRI ended on April 30, 1953. Facsimiles in Heinz Schneppen, *Odessa und das Vierte Reich: Mythen der Zeitgeschichte* (Berlin, 2007), pp. 160–61.

76. Argentina Federal Police, report on Eichmann's kidnapping, June 9, 1960, Archivo General de la Nacíon (AGN), DAE, Bormann file, pp. 77–79; cited in Goñi, *Odessa,* p. 316.

77. Berthold Heilig's family—Annegret, Karin, and Hannelore "Richwitz"—arrived in Argentina on March 25, 1953, but left on December 21, 1953, as Berthold Heilig (alias Hans Richwitz) was unable to decide between his old family and his new partner. Annegret was the same age as Eichmann's second son. According to him, Heilig worked for Fuldner and CAPRI until 1955. See Schimpf, *Heilig,* pp. 110 and 129. After Eichmann was kidnapped, Hans Fisch-

böck's wife said that he and her husband had been employed by CAPRI until 1955.

78. Siemens Argentina S.A. was officially founded in 1954. The engagement in Rosario predates the founding. Neurath was on the payroll from December 1, 1953. Thanks to Frank Wittendorfer from the Siemens Archive.

79. Neurath lobbied the German embassy in Buenos Aires not to extradite Schwammburger in spite of an extradition order from the Federal Republic.

80. In 1950 the average income in the Federal Republic was 500 Deutschmarks. I am grateful to the employees of the German Bundesbank for helpful information regarding historical exchange rates. The basis for calculation in this case is the Frankfurt am Main stock prices. The information on Eichmann's income comes from the interview with Klaus Eichmann in *Quick* on January 2, 1966. Eichmann's son has a tendency toward understatement when it comes to financial questions, and we can assume that the figures here are the ones his father gave him. In his application to Mercedes-Benz Argentina in 1959, Eichmann said he had earned 3,500 pesos at CAPRI, and 4,500 pesos at Efeve, Buenos Aires. Schneppen (*Odessa,* p. 159) seems to confuse Deutschmarks and U.S. dollars. These exchange rates correspond to what was actually paid, as we can see from the record of fees paid to German authors by Dürer. See Fritsch correspondence.

81. Cited in CEANA's final report, Carlota Jackisch, *Cuantificacion de Criminales de Guerra Según Fuentes Argentinas* (Informe Final, 1998), p. 9.

82. Still, a remarkable number of witnesses claim to have met Eichmann personally, even if they emphasize that he was unremarkable. See the current head of ABC, interview by Raymond Ley (2009), and Pedro Pobierzym, interview by Raymond Ley (BBC, 2002).

83. The Argentine newspaper *La Razón* published the first information on Eichmann's life in Argentina at the end of May 1960. In Germany, the *Frankfurter Allgemeine* used this as the basis for its report from an unnamed "correspondent in Buenos Aires": "Proof of Eichmann's Life in Argentina," *Frankfurter Allgemeine Zeitung,* June 2, 1960.

84. Fabrica Metalúrgica Efeve in Sta. Rosa/Buenos Aires; see Goñi, *Odessa,* p. 385n525. Eichmann mentioned the firm in his application to Mercedes-Benz Argentina in 1959.

85. Eichmann himself gave a higher salary of 4,500 pesos in his application to Mercedes-Benz Argentina. But this was the basis for his salary expectations with Mercedes, so Klaus Eichmann's memory seems the more credible source.

86. This can be seen most clearly in the fifteen-page document he wrote in Israel before the start of the trial: "Mein Sein und Tun," All. Proz. 6/253, p. 12.

87. Wislicency, Cell 133 Document, prosecution document T/84, pp. 12 and 16. None of the witness statements about Eichmann contradicted him.

88. Aharoni and Dietl, *Operation Eichmann,* p. 140.

89. But at the end of May 1960, *La Razón* managed to find people who admitted that Ricardo Klement's true identity was known by 1952 at the latest, when

his wife and children arrived. Quoted in "Proof That Eichmann Was Living in Argentina. Under the Name Ricardo Klement Since 1950. Inquiries Made with His Employer and Family," *Frankfurter Allgemeine Zeitung*, June 2, 1960. Details of the statements show that one of the witnesses was Horst Carlos Fuldner.

2 Home Front

1. Tom Segev, *Simon Wiesenthal: The Life and Legends* (New York, 2010), p. 106.
2. Variations of this story can be found in Simon Wiesenthal's *Ich jagte Eichmann* (Gütersloh, 1961), p. 224, and *Justice Not Vengeance: Recollections* (New York, 1990), p. 76. The letter to Arie Eschel is contained in Wiesenthal's private papers, which Tom Segev has thoroughly analyzed. We therefore know that Wiesenthal did not invent the core of the story, as Isser Harel, the head of Mossad, later claimed he had done. See Segev, *Simon Wiesenthal*, p. 102.
3. Simon Wiesenthal to Nahum Goldmann, March 30, 1954, NA, RG 263, CIA Name File Adolf Eichmann.
4. Simon Wiesenthal to Juniczman, April 18, 1952, Wiesenthal private papers, cited in Segev, *Simon Wiesenthal*, p. 103.
5. For the Heinz-Dienst, see the groundbreaking study by Susanne Meinl and Dieter Krüger, "Der politische Weg von Friedrich Wilhelm Heinz," *Vierteljahrsheft für Zeitgeschichte* 42, no. 1 (1994), and Susanne Meinl, "Im Mahlstrom des Kalten Krieges," in *Spionage für den Frieden?*, ed. Wolfgang Krieger and Jürgen Weber (Munich, 1997). For the connections among the German secret services, see Peter F. Müller and Michael Mueller, *Gegen Freund und Feind: Der BND: Geheime Politik und schmutzige Geschäfte* (Hamburg, 2002), p. 226, particularly the chapter "Parallelaktion in Österreich," p. 166. On Gehlen hearing at the start of 1952 that Höttl was working for Heinz, see CIA Pullach Operations Branch to Special Operations, January 9, 1952, NA, RG 263, CIA Name File Wilhelm Höttl.
6. "Re: establishment of an ND [intelligence service] line for Spain—L909," report from "XG," the group formed by Heinrich Mast and Wilhelm Höttl, March 1, 1952; quoted in Müller and Mueller, *Gegen Freund und Feind*, p. 195n653.
7. Peter Black, *Ernst Kaltenbrunner: Ideological Soldier of the Third Reich* (Princeton, 1984), p. xiii.
8. Höttl tried to play down the incident as an "invitation." Interrogation of Dr. Wilhelm Hoettl, transcripts and notes from February 26–27, 1953 (first interrogation), April 3, 1953, April 9, 1953, NA, RG 263, CIA Name File Wilhelm Höttl. See also Norman J. W. Goda, "The Nazi Peddler: Wilhelm Höttl and Allied Intelligence," in *U.S. Intelligence and the Nazis*, ed. Richard Breitman (Washington, D.C., 2004), pp. 265–92.

9. CIA Report, April 3, 1953, NA, RG 263, CIA Name File Wilhelm Höttl.

10. Segev, *Simon Wiesenthal*, p. 104.

11. Ibid.

12. A CIA report from January 16, 1950, contains a collection of rumors that arose after Wiesenthal was supposed to have recruited Höttl. The source is classified as unreliable, being based on hearsay. This does not mean that Wiesenthal didn't recruit Höttl for the CIC—it just means the report should not be taken as hard evidence that he did. NA, RG 263, CIA Name File Wilhem Höttl. Thanks to Martin Haidinger for bringing me a copy.

13. "The elimination of HOETTL . . . would be to the general good of intelligence in Austria." August 11, 1952, NA, RG 263, CIA Name File Wilhelm Höttl.

14. April 9, 1952, NA, RG 263, CIA Name File Wilhelm Höttl.

15. "Intermezzo in Salzburg," *Spiegel,* April 22, 1953, p. 17.

16. Segev, *Simon Wiesenthal,* p. 105

17. Wilhelm Höttl, interviews (Bad Aussee, 1996, 1998), and Stan Lauryssens, interview, with the usual caveats. The mythical letter has never been unearthed. Thanks to Martin Haidinger, Vienna, for letting me see his interview with Höttl, and for directing me to Höttl's estate, ÖStA, B1226.

18. Höttl never even hinted that Mast had acted against his wishes. Such an act would have been very unlikely, given the bond of trust between Mast and Höttl.

19. *Spiegel,* April 22, 1953.

20. Given in detail in Bettina Stangneth, *Quellen- und Datenhandbuch Adolf Eichmann 1906–1962* (unpublished), in the chapter on Wilhelm Höttl (with suggestions for evaluating witness statements). The literature on Höttl remains unsatisfactory, particularly regarding the Nazi period. The most comprehensive publication, though it is too uncritical in places, is Thorsten J. Querg, "Wilhem Höttl—vom Informanten zum Sturmbannführer im Sicherheitsdienst der SS," in *Historische Rassismusforschung: Ideologie—Täter—Opfer,* ed. Barbara Dankwortt, Thorsten Querg, and Claudia Schönigh (Hamburg, 1995), pp. 208–30. For his postwar activity with an emphasis on his work for the CIC/CIA, see Goda, "Nazi Peddler." The most comprehensive attempt to address the subject of Höttl, using the most source material, is Martin Haidinger's unpublished thesis, *Wilhelm Höttl, Agent zwischen Spionage und Selbstdarstellung* (Vienna). Thanks to the author for sending it to me.

21. Goda, "Nazi Peddler."

22. The complex web of Eichmann stories that Höttl peddled can now be deciphered and traced back to its sources in minute detail. His knowledge of Eichmann's behavior in the prison camp came from his co-worker Rudolf Jänisch, though he didn't reveal that source. Other set-pieces came from Kurt Becher and Dieter Wisliceny. Höttl used his talent for telling stories to make himself more interesting than the original sources. The details are too numerous to list here, but anyone taking the trouble to lay out the original texts side by side and

take note of the dates will find that a comparison reveals exactly who was really borrowing from whom in this case.

23. Friedrich Schwend, one of the organizers of the money-counterfeiting project "Operation Bernhard," helped Höttl with his second book, by writing letters from exile in Peru, where he also pursued a few (sometimes criminal) financial projects. Schwend to Mader, July 15, 1964, HIS, Schwend Collection, Loose folder I 2.

24. Originally published in German as *Die geheime Front* (Linz and Vienna, 1950); English edition *The Secret Front: The Inside Story of Nazi Political Espionage*, trans. R. H. Stevens (London, 1953). The volume is filled with indiscreet pieces of gossip, which are sometimes so far from the truth you have to marvel at them. In this book, Admiral Canaris blackmails Heydrich using his Jewish grandmother (his grandmother was definitely not Jewish), while Heydrich inveigles Hitler into the extermination of the Jews, and Himmler doesn't know what hit him. And in case readers get bored, Höttl scatters bordello stories through the book and hints about the sexual proclivities of men he didn't like. His judgment of the criminals who were close to him is similarly exuberant.

25. Höttl, *Secret Front*, p. 41.

26. The parallels are clear, when you compare Eichmann's stories in Argentina about Hitler's "diet cook" Lina Heydrich, Heinrich Müller, and Heinrich Himmler, with Höttl's book. As we know precisely when Eichmann read Höttl's book for the first time, the influence cannot possibly have worked the other way around.

27. A really thorough investigation of Höttl's estate has yet to take place. Höttl Estate, ÖStA, B1226.

28. HIS, Schwend collection, in particular loose file I 2. Schwend had relationships with Buenos Aires at the start of the 1950s but no contact with CAPRI or the Dürer circle, apart from Hans-Ulrich Rudel. His documents make it unlikely that Schwend himself was the informant, as he knew nothing about Adolf Eichmann or Alvensleben.

29. Otto Skorzeny, *Meine Kommandounternehmen* (Wiesbaden and Munich, 1976), p. 405. According to a letter of December 14, 1956 [!], Höttl let himself be enticed into giving this statement at Nuremberg by "CIC Jews."

30. Klaus Eichmann, interview in *Quick,* January 2, 1966.

31. *Der Weg* (1954), no. 1, p. 28. In *Der Weg* (1952), no. 1, p. 51, there is a reader survey on the acceptance of an exile government.

32. Hans-Ulrich Rudel, *Zwischen Deutschland und Argentinien* (Buenos Aires, 1954), p. 34.

33. Rudel speaks of the "strongest ally we could have, namely our young age, while on the opposing side various gentlemen are gripped by an eleventh-hour panic, as the upcoming election will be their last or their second-last." Ibid., pp. 246–47.

34. On the far-right party landscape in West Germany at this time, see Kurt P. Tauber, *Beyond the Eagle and Swastika: German Nationalism Since 1945,* 2 vols.

(Middletown, Conn., 1967), which remains excellent to this day; Peter Dudek and Hans-Gerd Jaschke, *Entstehung und Entwicklung des Rechtsextremismus in der Bundesrepublik* (Opladen, 1984); Henning Hansen, *Die Sozialistische Reichspartei (SRP): Aufstieg und Scheitern einer rechtsextremen Partei* (Düsseldorf, 2007); and Oliver Sowinski, *Die Deutsche Reichspartei 1950–1965: Organisation und Ideologie einer rechtsradikalen Partei* (Frankfurt am Main, 1998). Details of the contacts described in the following section, where not otherwise indicated, are taken from Adolf von Thadden's extensive estate. Thanks to Messrs. Krake and Frank and to Sonja von Behrens for their support during the intensive study of the largely unexplored yards of shelves in the Magazin Pattensen of the Niedersächsisches Landesarchiv.

35. In May 1951 the SRP achieved 11 percent of the vote in the Lower Saxony state elections, but then quickly lost votes as the burgeoning economy started to make the idea of a "people's socialism" seem less attractive. By the time the SRP was banned in October 1952, it had long been finished.

36. Sassen published this text using the same pseudonym he used for *Der Weg*, Willem Sluyse, along with a collection of academic titles: "Open letter to the European Commander-in-Chief General Dwight D. Eisenhower, from Dr. Dr. Willem Sluyse, Private First Class (retired)," *Der Weg* (1951), no. 7, pp. 46–56. The piece also appeared as a separate supplement with illustrations.

37. Hans-Ulrich Rudel published his books there as well as in German license editions.

38. The BfV was so alarmed that, in the following year, it was seriously concerned about Fritsch and Rudel's contacts in Brazil. BfV (i.A. Nollau) to the Foreign Office, December 8, 1953, PA AA. Thanks to Holger Meding.

39. Fritsch's presence is the subject of a news article, "Der Weg des Obersten a.D. Rudel," in *Hessische Nachrichten*, July 3, 1952. I have, however, found no concrete proof of this trip, even if Fritsch himself announced his first trip to Germany in a letter to Werner Beumelburg. But the cooperation with Karl-Heinz Priester and *Nation Europa* could have come about by other means than a visit to Germany. Thanks to Frau Klein from the *Hessische/Niedersächsische Allgemeine* archive for her help in researching this article.

40. Holger Meding interviewed Dieter Vollmer for *"Der Weg": Eine deutsche Emigrantenzeitschrift in Buenos Aires 1947–1957* (Berlin, 1997). Vollmer also provided an insight into his contacts in later articles and books. See for example *Nation Europa* 11, no. 11 (1961), pp. 37–42. Also see "Aftermath" in this book.

41. Documents including a telegram to Córdoba, dated August 4, 1953, about the financing that had been secured, Adolf von Thadden Estate, Niedersächsisches Landesarchiv, VVP 39 no. 45 II, sheet 508.

42. *Frankfurter Rundschau*, June 9, 1953.

43. "On a conversation with Oberst Rudel in Düsseldorf on December 6 (1952)," file note, Adolf von Thadden Estate, Niedersächsisches Landesarchiv, VVP 39, no. 45 II, sheets 505–7. The New Right's meetings are documented in several places.

44. Thadden also clearly knew much more about the recordings than Sassen's prominent clients like *Life* and *Stern*.

45. German embassy in Chile to Foreign Office, April 18, 1953, PA AA, section III b 212-02, vol. 3; German embassy in Buenos Aires to Foreign Office, December 28, 1953, PA AA, section 3, vol. 74; quoted in Holger Meding, *Flucht vor Nürnberg? Deutsche und österreichische Einwanderung in Argentinien 1945–1955* (Cologne, 1992), p. 177.

46. "German Nationalist and Neo-Nazi Activities in Argentina," July 8, 1953, declassified on April 11, 2000 (CIA-RDP620-00856 R000 3000 30004-4).

47. For anyone who doubts that Höttl was a National Socialist anti-Semite who believed in the Jewish world conspiracy until his dying day, his last autobiography is recommended reading. Here you will find almost all the usual theories, including the claim that the Wannsee Conference transcript is a forgery. Wilhelm Höttl, *Einsatz für das Reich: Im Auslandsgeheimdienst des Dritten Reiches* (Koblenz, 1997).

48. This oath is on record in the CIA files from March 1952 (source: Erich Kernmayr). Report 1952, NA, RG 263, CIA Name File Wilhelm Höttl. For the Langer text: BA tape 03A, 10:00 (corresponding to Sassen transcript 64, though the recording goes into more detail).

49. A CIA report from September 29, 1952, also says Heinz and Achim Oster denounced their contact Höttl as a con man and fabricator of facts. Höttl's reputation was certainly terrible by the summer of 1952. He was officially forbidden to claim to be a representative of the Heinz-Dienst in Vienna but was seen not to be observing this ban, which caused the service some concern. CIA report from Frankfurt, NA, RG 263, CIA Name File Wilhelm Höttl, declassified on March 20, 2009.

50. Anti-Semitic clichés can be found in Höttl's output up to the end of his life, although in a less crude form, as he made a good living from officially recognizing the genocide. He may not have been a Holocaust denier, but he used his final book to cast subtle doubt on the scale of the murder of the Jews. He aimed to represent the Holocaust as the actions of a tiny group, to bring its magnitude into doubt, and to expose documents as forgeries made to benefit Israel—and he was writing in 1997! Höttl, *Einsatz für das Reich,* esp. p. 410.

51. Konrad Adenauer himself was one of these representatives. His few pronouncements on the extermination of the Jews were so wooden that, even taking his usual delivery into account, they stand out as formulaic. So do his memoirs, his speeches, and his (relatively few) edited letters.

52. Guido Heimann (pseud.), "The Lie of the Six Million," *Der Weg* (1954), no. 7, pp. 479–87. The volume is still highly sought after on the antiques market and is sadly unavailable in most libraries. Thanks to Carlo Schütt from the Research Centre for Contemporary History in Hamburg for conjuring forth the article from the Cologne University library.

53. Bundestag reports on the first parliamentary term, 165th sitting, Bonn, September 27, 1951, p. 6697.

54. Survey by the Institut für Demoskopie, Allensbach, August 1952. Forty-four percent of Germans thought the agreement was "unnecessary," 24 percent thought it was correct in principle, though the amount was too large, and only 11 percent were clearly in favor. Elisabeth Noelle and Erich Peter Neumann, eds., *Jahrbuch der öffentlichen Meinung 1947–1955* (Allensbach, 1956), p. 130.

55. Myriad far-right websites—untroubled by expert knowledge of Eichmann's one thousand pages of comments—still hold firm to the belief that "the truth" would have come out if the Israelis hadn't been in such a hurry to kill Eichmann. This theory is also widespread in the Arab reception of the events. On the latter, see "Old Guilt and New Soldiers" and "Aftermath" in this book.

56. *New York Times*, May 29, 1960; *Spiegel*, June 15, 1960; and *Stern*, June 25, 1960. For the press roundup in *Nation Europa*, see *Suchlicht*, 1960, I no. 7ff.

57. "Eichmann Fue un Engranaje de la Diabólica Maquinaria Nazi, Dice el Hombre que Escribió sus Memorias en Buenos Aires," *La Razón*, December 12, 1960.

58. Adolf von Thadden, "Eichmann's Memoirs," *Nation Europa* 31, no. 2 (1981), pp. 60–61.

59. Wiesenthal mentioned this source in his letter to Nahum Goldmann, March 30, 1954, NA, RG 263, CIA Name File Adolf Eichmann. Tom Segev managed to throw some light on this still largely unknown figure in Wiesenthal's life and documented the letter from Ahmed Bigi to Wiesenthal on September 28, 1952. Segev, *Simon Wiesenthal*, pp. 88–90.

60. Bigi, the son of a well-known Islamic intellectual, became a close friend of Wiesenthal's. Segev, *Simon Wiesenthal*, pp. 88–90.

61. Wiesenthal to Goldmann, March 30, 1954, NA, RG 263, CIA Name File Adolf Eichmann.

62. *Illus*, the Berlin *Telegraf*'s Sunday supplement, reported on the reappearance of Eichmann in Tel Aviv on February 24, 1952. The *Frankfurter Rundschau*'s headline on March 22, 1952, was "Mass Murderer Is Military Adviser. Dirlewanger and Eichmann Serving in the Egyptian Army." And the *Allgemeine Wochenzeitung der Juden* reported on April 18 and 25 on an "SS General in the Middle East," who was suspected to be "Karl Eichmann," among others. In "German 'Advisers' in Cairo Plotting Against Bonn: Former SS and SD Leaders in League with Nagib and Mufti," *Die Welt am Sonntag*, on November 23, 1952, Eichmann was said to be one of the grand mufti's direct associates.

63. Nahum Goldmann later admitted that he had immediately forwarded the letter to the CIA. The CIA dossier on Adolf Eichmann shows that Goldmann gave the document to Rabbi Kalmanowitz in New York, who used it to try to convince the CIA and even the U.S. president to search for Eichmann. Appeal to DCI by Mr. Adolph Berle and Rabbi Kalmanowitz, NA, RG 263, CIA Name File Adolf Eichmann,. On the correspondence with Wiesenthal and his reaction, see Segev, *Simon Wiesenthal*, pp. 113–16.

64. Simon Wiesenthal, *Justice Not Vengeance: Recollections* (New York, 1990), p. 77

65. Ibid., p. 74

66. Bundestag report on the first term, 234. Meeting, Bonn, October 22, 1952, p. 10736.

3 One Good Turn

1. Franz Alfred Six to Werner Naumann, "Re: SS *UStf* Eichmann," May 16, 1938, prosecution document T/133. See also the notorious staff report from July 19, 1938, in which Eichmann is referred to a little less quotably as a "special-ist recognized in his field"; prosecution document T/55-3. Six may have been employed, immediately after the war, in recruiting spies for the Gehlen Orga-nization. See Peter F. Müller and Michael Mueller, *Gegen Freund und Feind: Der BND: Geheime Politik und schmutzige Geschäfte* (Hamburg, 2002).
2. Pedro Pobierzym, interview in Neal Bascomb, *Hunting Eichmann: How a Band of Survivors and a Young Spy Agency Chased Down the World's Most Notorious Nazi* (Boston and New York, 2009).
3. Eichmann trial, session 105, July 20, 1960. German transcript, Y1.
4. Skorzeny told this story to the U.S. intelligence service after Eichmann had been abducted. NA, RG 263, CIA Name File Otto Skorzeny; also held in the Eichmann file.
5. Rudel proudly mentions the use of this technology, which was still very new in 1953, in Hans-Ulrich Rudel, *Zwischen Deutschland und Argentinien* (Buenos Aires, 1954), p. 224.
6. The sixth chapter is a reworking of his own escape from Ireland to Argentina, with his very pregnant wife and their child.
7. *Der Weg* (1954), no. 10, pp. 679–85. The chapter was abridged for the maga-zine and made a little "milder."
8. Willem Sluyse, *Die Jünger und die Dirnen* (Buenos Aires, 1954). A few exam-ples of these formulations are the repeated use of the phrases "It doesn't inter-est me" (e.g., p. 55); "If you ask me, . . . so I will answer to you that" (p. 56); "It is not for my own sake that I now say to you" (p. 66); "I—I who am . . ." (p. 68). Like Eichmann, Holz mixes up the Morgenthau Plan and the supposed Kaufmann Plan. See also "An Untimely Peroration" in this book.
9. On Mengele, see "I Had No Comrades" in this book.
10. Sluyse, *Die Jünger und die Dirnen,* pp. 55, 63, 64.
11. Stan Lauryssens has claimed that Eichmann approached Sassen because he felt this fictional character represented him so well, he wanted to meet the author. This claim cannot be true, however, even without taking into account Laurys-sens's rather free interpretation of sources, as Sassen and Eichmann already knew each other by the time the book was published.
12. Warwick Hester, "On the Streets of Truth," *Der Weg* (1954), no. 8, p. 574.
13. A UN wanted list for the key figures in the Nazi hierarchy from February 1947 contained the note on Eichmann: "believed to have committed suicide US CIC source." Archives of the UN War Crimes Commission, UN Archives, New York,

quoted in Guy Walters, *Hunting Evil* (London and Toronto, 2009), pp. 115 and 598. From a document by the British War Crimes Group, also dated February 1947. Walters suspects that this story was believed in England and that this was why the British never made an effort to assist in the hunt for Eichmann.

14. Wisliceny, Cell 133 Document, prosecution document T/84.

15. Holger Meding, *"Der Weg": Eine deutsche Emigrantenzeitschrift in Buenos Aires 1947–1957* (Berlin, 1997), p. 131.

16. *Der Weg* (1954), no. 8, p. 575.

17. Ibid., p. 578.

18. Hugo C. Backhaus (Herbert Grabert), *Volk ohne Führung* (Göttingen, 1955). A second edition appeared in 1956; quotes here are taken from the 1955 edition, p. 233. Grabert was the founder of the "Group of Noncurrent (Displaced) University Lecturers" (from 1950), publisher of the *Deutschen Hochschullehrer-Zeitung* (from 1953), and a conscientious networker in the far-right milieu. See Martin Finkenberger and Horst Junginger, eds., *Im Dienste der Lügen: Herbert Grabert (1901–1978) und seine Verlage* (Aschaffenburg, 2004).

19. Two articles that clearly draw on *Der Weg* (without naming their source) claim that only 300,000 opponents of the Nazi regime were killed, some of them Jews. This is a further reduction of the figure of 353,000 claimed by Guido Heimann, "The Lie of the Six Million," *Der Weg* (1954), no. 7, p. 485. The *Die Anklage* articles are "The Basest Falsification of History" (January 1955) and "Proof from Switzerland. What Now, Prosecutor?," (April 1, 1955). Both are quoted in Wolfgang Benz, who admittedly was not aware of the connection to Dürer's magazine and was therefore unable to pin down the name Warwick Hester. Wolfgang Benz, "Realitätsverweigerung als antisemitisches Prinzip: Die Leugnung des Völkermords," in *Antisemitismus in Deutschland: Zur Aktualität eines Vorurteils* (Munich, 1995), pp. 121–39, esp. p. 130.

20. For the anatomy of this forgery and how it was spread from a European perspective, see Benz, "Realitätsverweigerung."

21. Udo Walendy reproduced this nonsense under the title "The Dr. Pinter Report" in *Historische Tatsachen*, no. 43 (1990), pp. 20–23. He manufactured the reference to Stephen F. Pinter there.

22. Holger Meding searched in vain for a U.S. jurist by the name of Pinter, though he wasn't aware of the connection between Warwick Hester and *Die Anklage*. Meding, *Der Weg*, p. 64. On Pinter, see *Nation Europa* 10, no. 4 (1960), p. 68. This issue contains a reference to a statement by Pinter in the Catholic weekly *Our Sunday Visitor* (Indiana), June 14, 1959. There he (allegedly) bears witness against the gas chambers, in particular Dachau. In reality the item was a reader's letter, which has since been cited as an article. Thanks to John Norton, the current editor-in-chief of *Our Sunday Visitor,* for letting me know that no one in his publishing house knew about the far-right popularity of this letter. Unfortunately, the original letter does not seem to be extant.

23. Eichmann claimed to have seen it this way, in his very restrained remarks in Israel. He praised Sassen as a journalist "accredited" by the Argentine govern-

ment and described Fritsch as a respected publisher. Interrogation, p. 397; Eichmann trial, session 105, and elsewhere.

24. Sassen transcript 3:4.

25. Sassen transcript 6:2. I was unable to find what Eichmann claimed to have read in any of the articles, but if anyone is more successful, I would appreciate references.

26. *Ha'aretz*, September 17, 1954.

27. Reynolds et al. draw on Eichmann's dating of the article to the 1940s and also claim Bauer served in Gustav Noske's Einsatzkommando 12 and in the SS *Einsatzgruppe* under Otto Ohlendorf. Reynolds quotes a newspaper article that states "at the end, he was a man again," which goes back to the Sassen transcripts. These had already formed the basis of the *Life* collage. See Quentin Reynolds, Ephraim Katz, and Zwy Aldouby, *Minister of Death: The Adolf Eichmann Story* (New York, 1960), p. 30. Pendorf, who says he researched the case, also fell for Eichmann's story, as he clearly couldn't find any newspaper articles. Since then, the story has cropped up repeatedly in the literature on Eichmann. It is correctly dated only by Wiesenthal.

28. BND report, "Near Eastern Connections," March 19, 1958, NA, RG 263, CIA Name File Adolf Eichmann.

29. Klaus Eichmann, interview in *Quick*, January 2, 1966.

30. The issue date for each passport is August 20, 1954. The details came to light in 1960. Note by Raab to State Secretary and Minister, July 27, 1960, PA AA, vol. 55; cited in Eckart Conze, Norbert Frei, Peter Hayes, and Moshe Zimmermann, *Das Amt und die Vergangenheit: Deutsche Diplomaten im Dritten Reich und in der Bundesrepublik* (Munich, 2010), pp. 603 and 792.

31. Horst Eichmann, transcript of a hearing with Fritz Bauer. Bauer then passed the information on to the West German foreign minister, via Hesse's minister of justice, on March 10, 1961. PA AA B82/432.

32. The passport was issued on June 23, 1954. It would not be the last: Josef Schwammberger would receive another from the embassy in 1962, according to investigations by the Stuttgart public prosecutor's office. See the letter from Werner Junker (ambassador) to the German Foreign Office, December 13, 1962, published as document 483 in *Akten zur Auswärtigen Politik des Bundesrepublik Deutschland, 1962* (Munich, 2010), pp. 2060–61. Schwammberger and Eichmann had known each other a long time, having qualified in military drill from the same training camp.

33. See also Nikolas Berg, *Der Holocaust und die westdeutschen Historiker: Erforschung und Erinnerung* (Göttingen, 2003), pp. 284–89. The board meeting took place on June 25, 1954.

34. Helmut Krausnick, "Zur Zahl der jüdischen Opfer des Nationalsozialismus," in *Aus Politik und Zeitgeschichte*, supplement to *Das Parlament*, August 11, 1954.

35. *The Attorney General of the Government of Israel vs. Malchiel Grünwald*, Case

124/53. For a detailed account, see Anna Porter, *Kasztner's Train: The True Story of an Unknown Hero of the Holocaust* (New York, 2007), pp. 324ff. Porter relies largely on the Hebrew typescript by Yechiam Weitz, which has been translated only unofficially (as *The Man Who Was Murdered Twice*), and on the documentary film *Mishpat Kastner* (Israel Broadcasting Authority, 1994). See also Ladislaus Löb, *Rezsö Kasztner, The Daring Rescue of Hungarian Jews: A Survivor's Account* (London, 2008), and Tom Segev, *The Seventh Million: The Israelis and the Holocaust*, trans. Haim Watzman (New York, 1993), pp. 255–320.

36. This episode also cost Halevi the leading role in the Eichmann trial in 1961, which he had to concede to Moshe Landau.

37. For example, "On Trial," *Time,* July 11, 1955; "Zionist Ex-Leader Accused of Perjury," *New York Times,* July 8, 1955; and "Israeli Case Revived," *New York Times,* August 1, 1955. An even greater wave of publicity followed after Kasztner was assassinated on March 3, 1957, which was another topic for the Sassen circle.

38. Even in 1993 Wilfred von Oven referred to it as a paper "principally read by Jews and leftist intellectuals." Wilfred von Oven, *Ein "Nazi" in Argentinien* (Gladbeck, 1993), p. 9.

39. Sassen transcript 12:4.

40. Valentin Tarra to Fritz Bauer, January 1, 1960, in *Mahnruf* (Austria), June 1960.

41. The investigations and the newspaper cuttings were included in Eichmann's wanted file, which was sent to Fritz Bauer in Frankfurt am Main in 1956. Unfortunately, in spite of reports to the contrary, this file has now vanished. All that remains are a few pages of notes on the events and collected excerpts. These pages can be found in Vienna National Criminal Court to the investigating judge, November 18, 1954, HHStA Wiesbaden, Section 461, no. 33,531, pp. 118ff. Thanks to Herr Pult from the HHStA Wiesbaden for his kind help in searching for the pages in question and the commitment to finding a few more. Irmtrud Wojak, contains misprints in the footnotes on this source in both of her books. (*Eichmanns Memoiren. Ein kritischer Essay,* Frankfurt a.M., 2001; *Fritz Bauer 1903–1968. Eine Biographie.* Munich, 2009.)

42. Entry on "Johannes von Leers" in *Die deutschsprachige Presse: Ein biographisch-bibliographisches Handbuch,* comp. Bruno Jahn (Munich, 2005), vol. 1, p. 617.

43. Reader's letter, "Johann von Leers: A Correction" in *Nation Europa* 11, no. 4 (1961), p. 68.

44. His departure from Argentina was reported to Germany. See West German embassy in Buenos Aires to German Foreign Office, August 11, 1954, under 212, no. 2116/54. The Foreign Office passed the information on to the BfV (306212-02/5.20973/54). Thanks to the BfV for copies.

45. Pedro Pobierzym, interviews by Uki Goñi (1997) and Roelf van Til (2000) and in the documentary *I Met Eichmann (Adolf Eichmann: Begegnungen mit einem*

Mörder) (BBC/NDR, 2003). Pobierzym occasionally worked for Dieter Menge and evidently observed his guests with surprise and displeasure. Rumors about Menge's memorabilia collection and subscriptions to all the far-right publications still circulate in Buenos Aires to this day. Thanks to Uki Goñi and Natasja de Winter for their help and information.

46. "All the Jews talked about in Argentina was Mengele." José Moskovits, leader of the Jewish Religious Community of Buenos Aires, interview by Raymond Ley and Natasja de Winter (2009), extract in *Eichmanns Ende* (NDR/SWR, 2010).

47. Willem Sassen, interview in *The Hunt for Dr. Mengele* (Granada Television, 1978). For Sassen's statements about Mengele's "research," see the interview fragments in *Edicion Plus* (Telefe Buenos Aires, 1991).

48. Heinz Schneppen, *Odessa und das Vierte Reich: Mythen der Zeitgeschichte* (Berlin, 2007), p. 139.

49. Ibid., p. 153.

50. Ibid., p. 136.

51. Documented in I. S. Kulcsár, Shoshanna Kulcsár, and Lipot Szondi, "Adolf Eichmann and the Third Reich," in *Crime, Law and Corrections,* ed. Ralph Slovenko (Springfield, Ill., 1966), pp. 16–32, esp. p. 28.

52. Quentin Reynolds, Ephraim Katz, and Zwy Aldouby, *Minister of Death: The Adolf Eichmann Story* (New York, 1960), p. 201.

53. "Peron as Protector of Rudel and the Fascist International," *Argentinisches Tageblatt,* December 17, 1955.

54. The research group headed by Norbert Frei quickly discovered a reference to the article from the *Argentinisches Tageblatt* (December 17, 1955) in the Foreign Office archive. Eckart Conze, Norbert Frei, Peter Hayes, and Moshe Zimmermann, *Das Amt und die Vergangenheit: Deutsche Diplomaten im Dritten Reich und in der Bundesrepublik* (Munich, 2010), p. 596.

55. The *Argentinisches Tageblatt* gave a commentary by *Korvettenkommandant* (retired) Hermann Brunswig under the title "Peronazism," the main aim of which was to protect the German immigrants from a collective accusation. For this reason, within its sober realism, it also tended to downplay the issue.

56. Zvi Aharoni and Wilhelm Dietl, *Operation Eichmann: The Truth About the Pursuit, Capture, and Trial,* trans. Helmut Bögler (New York, 1997), p. 70. Eichmann said he started work at the farm on March 1, 1955, but since he wrote it on a job application form, its accuracy is not entirely certain. Personnel form for Mercedes-Benz Argentina, March 20, 1959; facsimile in Schneppen, *Odessa,* p. 160.

57. Wisliceny, Cell 133 Document, prosecution document T/84, p. 16.

58. Eichmann's annotation on the title page of Fritz Kahn, *Das Atom* (Zurich, 1948), quoted in *Stern,* July 9, 1960. Eichmann confirmed the quote was correct in interrogation, September 15, 1960.

59. Application to Mercedes-Benz Argentina; facsimile in Schneppen, *Odessa.*

60. "Meine Flucht," p. 25.

61. BA tape 29:05ff. (corresponds to tape 64, but the remarks have been left out of the transcript).

62. The property-owning arm of the Vienna Central Office, the "Vienna Emigration Fund," acquired a paper factory in Doppl (Mühltal) / Altenfeld near Linz, in Upper Austria, on May 8, 1939. Among the documents there is the note: "a valuation of the property [is] not necessary." AdR, Ministry for Interior and Cultural Affairs, Dept. II, Gr. 4, Office: Foundations and Funds, Emergency Matters, Vienna 1, Ballhausplatz 2, Zi. II / 4-127.517, 1939. Object Emigration Fund (AWF), Acquisition of Property, May 11, 1939; attachments: purchase contract between M. Mösenbacher and the AWF, May 8, 1939: Gudrun Rohrbach, file no. R76/39. Quoted in Gabriel Anderl, "Die 'Umschulungslager' Doppl und Sandhof der Wiener Zentralstelle für jüdische Auswanderung," article at www.david.juden.at/kulturzeitschrift/57-60/58-Anderl.htm (2003 and 2004).

63. An Israeli spy heard this rumor after the war, and as late as the 1990s, journalists conducting investigations in Lemburg heard it there. It concerned Maria "Mitzi" Bauer, the manager of the Pension Weiss, which functioned as the secret meeting place for Eichmann's men and later played a significant role in their escape. Manus Diamant, *Geheimauftrag: Mission Eichmann* (Vienna, 1995), p. 209, and Georg M. Hafner and Esther Shapira, *Die Akte Alois Brunner: Warum einer der größten Naziverbrecher noch immer auf freiem Fuß ist* (Hamburg, 2002), p. 73.

64. Sassen transcript 59:3. Eichmann mentions it only as an Easter trip, but Vera Eichmann's birthday also fell on the holiday that year.

65. Zvi Aharoni convincingly contradicted this with reference to his operation book. Eichmann was not at home on this day: according to his son's statement, he was visiting Tucumán.

66. The description comes from Rosemarie Godlewski and Emilie Finnegan, two department secretaries, interviewed for *I Met Eichmann (Adolf Eichmann— Begegnungen mit einem Mörder)* (NDR/BBC, 2002); from Maria Mösenbacher, Mitzi Bauer, and Margrit Kutschera, Eichmann's lovers (Diamant, *Geheimauftrag*, pp. 210–28); and from Eichmann's female contacts in Altensalzkoth (interviews for *Stern*, June–July 1960, and for *I Met Eichmann*).

67. Eichmann's nickname appears in the first CIC reports and, as the context shows, this information comes from Wisliceny and Höttl. Arrest Report Interrogation Wisliceny and CIC Report Eichmann, NA, RG 263, CIA Name File Adolf Eichmann; Rudolf Höß, *Kommandant in Auschwitz: Autobiographische Aufzeichnungen* (1958; reprinted Munich, 2000), p. 336.

68. BA tape 02 A, from 8:25 (Argentine tape no. 68).

69. David Cesarani, *Eichmann: His Life and Crimes* (London, 2005), p. 188.

70. Wisliceny, Cell 133 Document, prosecution document T/84, p. 13.

71. BA tape 9C, 27:30–29:30. Cuts were made in the transcript because of frequent stuttering in this sequence.

72. Examples can be found in Sassen transcript tapes 17 (concentration camp bordellos) and 67 (BA tape 05B, starting at 20:00) and elsewhere.

73. In Israel, Eichmann even announced his plan for world peace: women should be in power. "Götzen," p. 199. He didn't mention that he thought world peace was "un-Aryan."

74. "Mein Sein und Tun," fifteen-page paper written in Israel, All. Proz. 6/253, here p. 10.

75. Peter Longerich convincingly proved that what was done in practice bore little resemblance to Himmler's theory. Longerich, *Heinrich Himmler: A Life* (Oxford, 2011), p. 370.

76. Sassen transcript 10:7. Kurt Becher showed Eichmann an expensive jeweled necklace that he had obtained by extortion in Hungary on Himmler's orders. Eichmann was also a witness to Becher handing the stolen goods over to Himmler.

77. Himmler's memos from April 1936 and June 1937, quoted in Longerich, *Heinrich Himmler*, p. 370.

78. Kulcsár, Kulcsár, and Szondi, "Adolf Eichmann and the Third Reich," pp. 30–32.

79. Ibid., p. 17. Three people were involved in the psychological examinations. Kulcsár himself conducted the interviews and tests, and his wife and (in one case) Lipot Szondi evaluated them. Many years later a further evaluation of individual test results, partly using blind trials, did not differ greatly from the Kulcsárs' results. They have not been seen outside the profession until now.

80. Hannah Arendt, *Eichmann in Jerusalem: A Report on the Banality of Evil* (1963; reprint New York, 1994), p. 77, and notes by Avner W. Less on February 7, 1961, Avner Less Estate, Archiv für Zeitgeschichte, ETH Zurich, NL Less, 4.2.3.2.

81. Examples are early pamphlet-style publications, like Dewey W. Linze, *The Trial of Adolf Eichmann* (Los Angeles, Calif., 1961); Comer Clarke, *The Savage Truth: Eichmann, the Brutal Story of Hitler's Beast* (London, 1960); and John Donovan, *Eichmann: Man of Slaughter* (New York, 1960). The most extreme example in film is *Eichmann*, dir. Robert W. Young (UK/Hungary, 2007).

82. Sassen transcript 39:3.

83. Chapter 6 of his novel *Die Jünger und die Dirnen* gives an account of Sassen's escape that is only superficially fictionalized; here p. 168.

84. The date 1953, given by David Cesarani and others, is a misprint, which is made clear by Eichmann's paternity declaration of May 29, 1962, and other documents. BA Koblenz, All. Proz. 6/237.

85. "Meine Flucht," p. 26.

86. Eichmann inadvertently gave this away himself, in his written answer to a question on worries about his family, shortly before his execution in 1962. Answers to questionnaire for *Paris Match*, May 1962, BA Koblenz, All. Proz. 6/252, p. 20. The magazine printed parts of the interview immediately after Eichmann was executed.

87. The account occasionally given, of the baby being registered in the name of Eichmann, is incorrect.

88. "Meine Flucht," p. 26.
89. Answers to *Paris Match* questionnaire.
90. Willem Sluyse (Sassen), "Letter to a Despairing Friend, Christmas 1955," in *Der Weg* (1956), no. 1, p. 12.
91. "Meine Flucht," p. 26.
92. Hans-Ulrich Rudel, *Zwischen Deutschland und Argentinien* (Buenos Aires, 1954), pp. 259 and 157.
93. Theodor Heuss, "Der deutsche Weg—Rückfall und Fortschritt," address on the jubilee celebrations of the Evangelical Academy, Bad Boll, published in *Das Parlament* 42 (October 19, 1955), pp. 9–10, here p. 9.
94. Sassen entitled his summary of the years 1945–55 "Interregnum Furiosum" in *Der Weg* (1955), pp. 295–99, here p. 299.
95. Sluyse (Sassen), "Letter to a Despairing Friend," p. 14.
96. Ewout van der Knaap and Nitzan Lebovic, *"Nacht und Nebel": Gedächtnis des Holocaust und internationale Wirkungsgeschichte* (Göttingen, 2008).
97. The first case against Otto Bräutigam was abandoned in 1950. The suspension ended in 1958 with his reemployment, although documents showed that Bräutigam not only had detailed knowledge of the murder plans but was also involved in making them. During the first Nuremberg trial, a paper was produced referring to a meeting with Eichmann. IMT 3319-PS, Ribbentrop material collection, identical with prosecution document T/1003. It was even suspected that he personally led a Wannsee follow-up conference. In August 1959 Bräutigam received the Grand Cross of the Order of Merit of the Federal Republic of Germany. See Michael Schwab-Trapp, *Konflikt, Kultur und Interpretation: Eine Diskursanalyse des öffentlichen Umgangs mit dem Nationalsozialismus* (Opladen, 1996).
98. *Der Weg* (1956), no. 7–8, p. 240.
99. Quotes in order of appearance, all from *Der Weg* (1956): pp. 480, 480, 240, 242, 357, 610.
100. Ibid., pp. 477, 610.
101. Ibid., p. 608.
102. Ibid., p. 477.
103. Paul Beneke (pseudonym), "The Role of the 'Gestapo,'" *Der Weg* (1956), no. 7–8, pp. 353–58; and no. 9, pp. 476–80.
104. The author of these lines is a child of someone born in Danzig herself.
105. I would not completely rule out Reinhard Kopps, who wrote under the pseudonym Juan Maler, among others, and was born near Hamburg. As somebody who was born near Hamburg, he grew up in a city with a special connection to Paul Beneke. But overall the article is presented too academically for Maler. It has footnotes, which were a rarity in *Der Weg*.
106. "Meine Memoiren" (1960), p. 108. The article in *Der Weg* is such a fundamental attack on everything Eichmann held to be true as to rule out the possibility that it was written in collaboration with him. However, it could have been based on conversations with him, as well as other insider knowledge.

107. Report, November 30, 1956, Deutsche Reichspartei Collection, Archiv des Bundes der Verfolgten des Naziregimes, Berlin. Thanks to Ms. Rehfeld for her help researching this report, which is not contained in the estate of Adolf von Thadden, Niedersächsisches Landesarchiv, VVP 39.

108. The most detailed story of this sort can be found in Werner Brockdorff (an alias for Alfred Jarschel, a former Nazi youth leader), *Flucht vor Nürnberg: Pläne und Organisation der Fluchtwege der NS-Prominenz im "Römischen Weg"* (Munich-Wels, 1969), esp. chap. 17. On the history of these fantasies, see the rest of this chapter.

109. Johann von Leers, reader's letter in *Nation Europa*.

110. Willem Sluyse, "Garbage Men! A Balance Sheet for Our Atomic Age," *Der Weg* (1956), nos. 11–12, pp. 673–76.

111. *Der Weg* (1954), no. 7, p. 487.

112. Thanks to the Konstanz City Archive. Sassen remained in Konstanz until February 4, 1959, at 61 Schottenstraße, then moved to Munich and officially registered his address there as 12 Hohenstaufenstraße. It isn't clear why Sassen chose Konstanz, although during this year the census system was changed there, and such fundamental changes always provide loopholes for people with something to hide. This was why Eichmann chose Breslau as his birthplace during his escape.

113. Anti-Semitism does not always forge ahead as it did in Argentina, but presumptions of this sort clearly informed the reception of the first publications on the persecution of the Jews. Hardly a single reviewer omitted a clear labeling of the authors' names as Jewish.

114. Wolf Sievers (pseud.), "The 'Final Solution' of the Jewish Question," *Der Weg* (1957), no. 3, pp. 235–42. All the following quotes are taken from this article.

115. Ibid., p. 239: "The participants (of the Wannsee Conference): as well as Heydrich, Gestapo-Müller, Eichmann, Schöngarth and Lange from the Gestapo, Luther from the Foreign Office, and representatives of a very specific and highly suspicious category of the Reich Ministry bureaucracy." In total, Adolf Eichmann was mentioned only twice in all the articles appearing in *Der Weg* up to 1957, the first being the news of his "suicide." His name appeared once more after this, in a "reader's letter".

116. Rudel, *Zwischen Deutschland und Argentinien,* p. 260.

117. "Eichmann Fue un Engranaje de la Diabolica Maquinaria Nazi . . ." *La Razón,* December 12, 1960.

118. Only some of Sassen's pseudonyms have been pinpointed. We know the names Willem Sluyse, Steven Wiel, and the old family name Sassen chose for respected publications like *Stern,* Wilhelm S. van Elsloo. Other names, like Andre Desmedt and Juan del Rio, are also mentioned occasionally, but it is to be feared that Sassen wrote under a great many more names for *Der Weg* and other magazines in Germany. On his suspected authorship of various articles, see the account of the Sassen interviews that follows.

The So-Called Sassen Interviews

1. Gabriel Bach reported this frequently (and admiringly) in his interviews. Eichmann himself gave thanks in his letter to his family, April 17, 1961, BA Koblenz, All. Proz. 6/165.
2. Sassen contract with Time, Inc.; Fritsch to Eichmann's family and Hans Rechenberg; Eichmann several times in Israel. BA Koblenz, All. Proz. 6/253. See also "Aftermath" in this book.
3. Thanks to Saskia Sassen for providing a great deal of information about this event, and for her generosity in engaging in an exchange of thoughts in 2009. See also Saskia Sassen, interviews by Roelf van Til (March 21 and 27, 2005) and Raymond Ley (June 7, 2000), whom I also thank for our discussions.
4. Inge Schneider, interview by Roelf van Til (2005). More detail on her follows.
5. Both can be heard several times on the surviving tapes.
6. In 2005 Saskia Sassen was still saying that Payne was probably the man in the attic, though she corrected herself in 2009 and is now sure he was a man she did not know.
7. *L'Express,* no. 494, December 1, 1960.
8. Sassen, and Eichmann's defense counsel Robert Servatius, accused each other in 1960 of having given this article to the magazine with malicious intent. This suggests that neither of them was the originator of the article. See "Aftermath" in this book. So many of the claims made in the article are incorrect that Sassen's denial seems plausible.
9. "Coups in South America's Biggest Countries and Forces Behind Them," *Life,* November 28, 1955, pp. 44–47. The article is unattributed.
10. Thanks to Uki Goñi for these thoughts from the point of view of an experienced journalist. Goñi, correspondence with the author (2009).
11. These dates and this information are based on Payne's reportage (*Time,* March 17, 1952; *Life,* January 31, 1955) and on Payne's available dispatches to *Time,* including a report from Buenos Aires dated May 10, 1957, and a report on the Eichmann trial dated April 12, 1961. Estate of Roy E. Larsen, former president of Time, Inc., Harvard University Library, Harvard (Dispatches from *Time* Magazine Correspondents: First Series, 1942–55, MA 02138; Second Series, 1956–1968, MS AM 2090.1).
12. "Israel: On Trial," *Time,* July 11, 1955.
13. Sassen transcript 6:3.
14. Saskia Sassen has patchy memories of the time of the interviews, which is not unusual for children of that age. The children were also not always at home when the guests arrived. In any case, it would have been highly unusual for someone to explain such a large and delicate book project to a child.
15. Stan Lauryssens—an expert weaver of fact and fiction, which unfortunately cannot always be disentangled from his texts—even claims that Payne himself was involved in the intelligence services. Payne, according to Lauryssens, told

no less a person than Isser Harel, the head of Mossad, about the conversations between Eichmann and Sassen, after Harel had received a tip-off about the exclusive offer from Time, Inc. He supposedly traveled to meet Payne in Argentina, who was then able to show him pages of the transcript. Stan Lauryssens, *De fatale vriendschappen van Adolf Eichmann* (Leuven, 1998), p. 179.

16. HHStA Wiesbaden, Section 461, No. 33 531, T 20/1. Bundesministerium der Justiz to chief public prosecutor at the Federal Court of Justice in Karlsruhe, Bonn, October 6, 1956. Thanks to Herr Pult of the HHStA Wiesbaden for his kind help in finding the relevant pages. The complete wanted file, contrary to claims made elsewhere, is unfortunately not held in the HHStA Wiesbaden.

17. Crime according to §§ 211, 74 StGB. A facsimile of the arrest warrant can be found in Heinz Schneppen, *Odessa und das Vierte Reich: Mythen der Zeitgeschichte* (Berlin, 2007), p. 158.

18. Document quoted ibid., p. 162. Unfortunately the author seldom cites sources to academic standards.

19. BfV (i.A. Nollau) to the Foreign Office, December 8, 1953, PA AA, Section 3, vol. 87, 81.11/2. Thanks to Holger Meding.

20. Payne to Time, Inc. on Arbenz, dispatch no. 317, Estate of Roy E. Lasen, former president of Time, Inc., Harvard University Library, Harvard (Dispatches from *Time* Magazine Correspondents: Second Series, 1956–1968, MS AM 2090.1).

21. Thanks to Saskia Sassen for the openness with which she has exposed herself to a complex mixture of memory, emotion, and projection.

1 Eichmann the Author

1. "Götzen," p. 8/AE: 3.

2. Ibid.

3. In 1933 Mildenstein spent six months in Palestine with Kurt Tuchler, writing under his pseudonym Lim. The pro-Zionist article series, which appeared between September 26 and October 9, 1934, had a clear anti-Semitic tone. A blaze of publicity accompanied its publication, which even the *Jüdische Rundschau* (September 28, 1934) commented upon. In 1938 the series was published as a book. For a discussion on the first article series, see Axel Meier, "'Ein Nazi fährt nach Palästina': Der Bericht eines SS Offiziers als Beitrag zur Lösung der Judenfrage," in *Jahrbuch für Antisemitismusforschung*, no. 11 (2002), pp. 76–90. Unfortunately, the biographical information given on Mildenstein's SD career follows Eichmann's (incorrect) account.

4. Interrogation, p. 66.

5. The internal SD *Leithefte* (guidance booklets) were manuscripts for official use only, classified top secret. For example, a text available in BA Koblenz, from March 1937, titled "Verlagswesen" (Publishers) comprises thirty-five pages of A4, is numbered, and bears the header "The *Reichsführer*-SS, Head of the Security Service Head Office." It is a dense account of the topic, clearly meant

only for insiders. BA Koblenz, R58/1107. The *SS-Leithefte,* by contrast, was a popular monthly tabloid magazine, with illustrations and articles by various authors. It was initially edited for the *Reichsführer*-SS by the RuSHA and later by SS head office.

6. Interrogation, p. 66.

7. In Israel (Eichmann trial, session 102), Eichmann claimed he had written the book in May 1942, though he also said he had wanted to dedicate it to Heydrich after his death (which would have been after June 4). To Sassen, he said he had written it "after the trip to Bialystok and Minsk" and that he had suggested to Heydrich that it should be published under his name (so, before June 4).

8. April 20, 1942: U.S. Holocaust Museum, Washington, RG15 007M reel 23: HK Warsaw 362/298 folio 1.5: report on the work conference with Prof. Franz (Günther Franz, professor at the "Reich University" of Strasbourg) with VII C on September 10 and 11, 1942, published as document 6 in Jürgen Matthäus, "'Weltanschauliche Forschung und Auswertung': Aus den Akten des Amtes VII im Reichssicherheitshauptamt," in *Jahrbuch für Antisemitismusforschung,* no. 4 (1996), pp. 287–330, here pp. 309–12. Also folio 6, the remark by Dittel on the position taken by the department head (Six) on April 20, 1942, on the transcript of the conference with the work plan, published as document 7, ibid., pp. 312–14. The plan was apparently then abandoned. See transcript of the follow-up conference on July 1, 1942, folio 12, 15.18–19, published as document 10 in Matthäus, "'Weltanschauliche Forschung,'" pp. 314–20, and the transcript of the conference of January 16, 1943, folio 21, 25, 27, published as document 12, pp. 321–24.

9. For example, "Ziel und Methodik in der Lösung der Judenfrage," February 23, 1938, BA Koblenz, R58/911, p. 144.

10. Rudolf Peckel of the Süddeutsche Rundfunk regularly dissected *Der Weg* in the series *Für und Wider* (For and Against) (June 8, 1954; November 23, 1954; January 4, 1955). Holger Meding also points to programs on the Bavarian radio station Bayerische Rundfunk; Meding, *"Der Weg": Eine deutsche Emigrantenzeitschrift in Buenos Aires 1947–1957* (Berlin, 1997), p. 133.

11. For the discovery of a few documents previously believed to have disappeared, see "Aftermath" in this book.

12. Thanks to Helmut Eichmann (one of Eichmann's grandchildren) for his willingness to talk to me about the manuscript in his family's possession, and for asking his father, Dieter Eichmann, about the possibility of granting access to this document. The family is seriously considering publishing the manuscript but only with an appropriate level of remuneration. Even a critical comparison of the document with accessible material is to be undertaken only in the context of a concrete offer.

13. Servatius, "Einlassungen zu den 'Sassen-Memoiren,'" six pages, Jerusalem, June 9, 1961, BA Koblenz, All. Proz. 6/254.

14. Klaus Eichmann, interview in *Quick,* January 2, 1966.

15. This also goes for many quotations in the so-called subject literature.

16. This distinction is not always seen, but there is plenty of evidence for it. Eichmann wrote and spoke an idiosyncratic language, the main marker of which was its combination of snatches of Nazi and bureaucratic jargon with other styles.

17. The first time in tape 8:1, a conversation that can be dated to mid-April 1957, as it took place after the murder of Rudolf Kasztner (who was attacked on March 3 and died on March 15), and a newspaper article relating to it in the *Argentinisches Tageblatt* (April 15, 1957). Krumey's arrest is also mentioned (8:9.2; April 1, 1957).

18. Sassen dictated a part of the Eichmann manuscript onto tape for typing up. This indicates when it must have been completed, i.e., before tape 15, which contains this dictation. Sassen transcript 15:5–9, corresponding to "The Others Spoke," pp. 54–65.

19. "Allgemein" (General), two-page handwritten text on blank paper, Eichmann Estate, BA Koblenz, N/1497-92. Clearly composed at the same time as "Persönliches" (Personal), ibid. Both texts are attempts to formulate an introduction to the picture of himself he wished to present.

20. Vera Eichmann, interview in *Paris Match*, April 29, 1962; original transcript in BA Koblenz, All. Proz. 6/252.

21. *Die Welt*, August 17, 1999.

22. Irmtrud Wojak, *Eichmanns Memoiren: Ein kritischer Essay* (Frankfurt am Main, 2001), p. 68. Wojak explains that "the manuscript cannot be verified." Most authors quote Robert Pendorf or the highly problematic edition *Ich, Adolf Eichmann*. Eichmann's handwritten text "Persönliches" is in Eichmann Estate, BA Koblenz, N/1497-92. Contrary to what Pendorf claims, it is a manuscript on lined paper of varying sizes, or rather an exercise book with larger pages inserted: nine pages, with two double-sided pages. The manuscript entitled "Allgemein" (General) is on squared paper. As Pendorf evidently knows both parts, he has probably simply confused the two. "Allgemein," handwritten fragment, Eichmann Estate, BA Koblenz, N/1497-92. An unreliable contemporary transcript can also be found in N/1497-73.

23. All quotes in the following paragraphs are taken from the handwritten text "Persönliches" (Personal), Eichmann Estate, BA Koblenz, N/1497-92, unless stated otherwise. Here, p. 4.

24. Ibid., p. 5.

25. Ibid., p. 7.

26. Ibid., pp. 6, 7, 9.

27. In his farewell letter to his family before his execution, Eichmann wrote: "Let history create [!] the verdict." BA Koblenz, All. Proz. 6/248.

28. "Persönliches" (Personal), handwritten text, p. 4, Eichmann Estate, BA Koblenz, N/1497-92, p. 6.

29. Ibid., p. 9.

30. One hundred seven pages, handwritten on squared Din (close to A4-size)

paper. Parts of the manuscript and various fragments are scattered over several archive collections, and sometimes over several files, in BA Ludwigsburg, BA Koblenz, All. Proz. 6 (Servatius collection), and BA Koblenz, Eichmann Estate. See also "Aftermath" in this book. One should not expect an ordered or professional script. We have several disordered collections of handwritten pages and typed copies that have been divided up. None of these is complete. There is neither a consistently logical pagination nor reliable chapter headings. Anyone wishing to read Eichmann's texts must first assemble them—though here they may ask for the instructions I put together, which can be found in BA Koblenz and Ludwigsburg: "Adolf Eichmanns Aufzeichnungen und die sogenannten Sassen-Interviews 1956 bis Frühjar 1960. Annotiertes Findbuch zu den Beständen in den Bundesarchiven Koblenz und Ludwigsburg." Hamburg 2011. The inventory also contains a guide (for use in the Bundesarchive only) to reading Eichmann's handwriting, which is difficult to decipher. In the following text, page numbers are cited as comprehensively as possible. It is, however, impossible to avoid citations that at first glance appear contradictory.

31. For the publication history of the Argentina Papers, see "Aftermath" in this book.
32. "The Others Spoke," introduction (pt. 1), p. 1.
33. Ibid., p. 2.
34. Ibid.
35. Ibid., p. 7.
36. Raphael Gross, *Anständig geblieben: Nationalsozialistische Moral* (Frankfurt am Main, 2010), p. 191.
37. "The Others Spoke," introduction, p. 7. This manuscript page is missing, as Sassen evidently sold the original to *Life*. The reference to it, and to the contemporary copy, can be found in BA Ludwigsburg, "Miscellaneous" folder.
38. "The Others Spoke," pt. 2, p. 1.
39. "The Others Spoke," pt. 2: "Re: My Findings on the Matter of 'Jewish Questions' and Measures by the National Socialist German Government to Solve this Complex in the Years 1933 to 1945." The text is quoted from the handwritten pages. "II: Betrifft: Meine Feststellungen," p. 65; page numbers according to the handwritten original. The manuscript has been reconstructed from the parts contained in the above-named archives, as there was no complete, or completely legible, version in any one collection.
40. Ibid., p. 1.
41. Ibid., p. 2.
42. For the full quotation, see above. Robert H. Jackson's summation, July 26, 1946, IMT vol. 19, p. 397.
43. "Re: My Findings on the Matter," p. 54.
44. Ibid., p. 57.
45. Himmler to Müller, January 18, 1943. See also Peter Witte and Stephan Tyas, "A New Document on the Destruction and Murder of Jews during 'Einsatz Reinhardt,'" *Holocaust and Genocide Studies* 15 (2001), pp. 468–86.

46. Dieter Wisliceny described the "card room" in his handwritten document "Re: Grand Mufti of Jerusalem," Bratislava, July 26, 1946, prosecution document T/89. The descriptions of Rolf Günther's wall charts, and of the map hung behind Franz Novak's desk with flags for the extermination camps, come from testimony of Erika Scholz, former secretary in Eichmann's department, at the Franz Novak trial, March 27, 1972, published as document 46 in Kurt Pätzold and Erika Schwarz, *"Auschwitz war für mich nur ein Bahnhof": Franz Novak, der Transportoffizier Adolf Eichmanns* (Berlin, 1994), p. 171.

47. On the argument about the Korherr Report and other figures, see "The Lie of the Six Million" in this book.

48. The transcriber of this handwritten text, which found its way into the Sassen transcript as part of tape no. 15, misread *rund* (around) as *und* (and). Sassen transcript, Hagag copy, p. 116. The handwriting, however, clarifies the error.

49. "Re: My Findings on the Matter," p. 64.

50. Ibid., p. 65.

51. Ibid., pp. 63–64.

52. Tape 67, BA tape 10B 1:01:00.

53. Eichmann Estate, BA Koblenz, N/1497-90, Bl.1. Sassen probably ensured this note could not be seen on the copies that he prepared to be sold, not wanting to create any difficulties for Eichmann. See "Aftermath" in this book.

54. Klaus Eichmann, interview in *Quick*, January 2, 1966.

55. Eichmann openly calculated, as he was sitting in prison in Israel, that a "monster trial" would turn a simple collection of notes into a best seller. Letter to his family "on the eve of the trial," April 17, 1961, All. Proz. 6/165.

56. Eichmann compiled the source material for Heydrich's lecture at the Wannsee Conference, among others. He explained this to Sassen, as they were discussing the conference transcript. Sassen transcript 47:10 and elsewhere. In Israel, of course, he claimed not to remember this.

57. "The Others Spoke," part 3, p. 10.

58. Ibid., p. 4.

59. Ibid., p. 3.

60. Ibid., pp. 5, 6, 7.

61. Ibid., p. 9.

62. Ibid., p. 10.

63. Ibid., p. 7.

64. Eichmann to Hull, in William L. Hull, *Kampf um eine Seele: Gespräche mit Eichmann in der Todeszelle* (Wuppertal, 1964), p. 75.

65. Bettina Stangneth, "Adolf Eichmann interpretiert Immanuel Kant," lecture at Marburg University, 2002.

66. Lauryssens, *De fatale vriendschappen,* p. 137. Stan Lauryssens "quotes" Eichmann as expressing his admiration for Kant in the Sassen circle, but on closer inspection this text combines his words from Israel with sections taken from the Sassen transcript. Nowhere in the transcript, or on tape, or in Eichmann's

Argentine texts, is there the slightest hint of the devotion to Kant that Eichmann exhibited in Israel.

67. "The Others Spoke," part 3, p. 10.
68. Ibid., p. 11.
69. Ibid.
70. Sassen transcript, 3:3 BA tape 33:10.
71. "The Others Spoke," part 3, p. 3.
72. Karl Beyer, *Jüdischer Intellekt und deutscher Glaube* (Leipzig, 1933), p. 28; and Otto Dietrich, *Die philosophische Grundlage des Nationalsozialismus: Ruf zu den Waffen deutschen Geistes* (Breslau, 1935). There are whole shelves of Nazi literature on the constructs of "Jewish" and "German" philosophy. They can also be found in popular publications, like the later editions of Theodor Fritsch's *Handbuch der Judenfrage* (Leipzig, 1943), especially the chapter "Das Judentum in der deutschen Philosophie," p. 393.
73. Walter Groß, *Der deutsche Rassegedanke und die Welt* (Berlin, 1939) (Texts I, 42), p. 30.
74. Hannah Arendt, *Eichmann in Jerusalem: A Report on the Banality of Evil* (1963; reprint New York, 1994), p. 135.
75. Facsimiles of the redrafting of the closing statement into the form in which it was actually given have been easily accessible since 1996: they can be found in Zvi Aharoni and Wilhelm Dietl, *Operation Eichmann: The Truth About the Pursuit, Capture, and Trial*, trans. Helmut Bögler (New York, 1997). Robert Servatius demanded comprehensive changes. The closing statement was, in Eichmann's mind, part of the "Götzen" (Idols) book he was planning. BA Koblenz, All. Proz. 6/196.
76. Avner W. Less, interview, Avner Less Estate, Archiv für Zeitgeschichte, ETH Zurich, NL Less, tape 7.1.IX.
77. Hull, *Kampf um eine Seele*, p. 131. Hull was a Christian missionary who described himself as an "unofficial observer on Protestant spirituality." He visited Eichmann at his own wish, with the aim of setting a man who had been baptized Protestant back on the right path and saving him from damnation. Hull was a devotee of a fundamentalist, revivalist Christianity, that was shaped by an arrogance toward other forms of belief and displayed clear anti-Semitic characteristics. (In an interview with Canadian journalists, he explained that all Eichmann's Jewish victims would obviously burn in hell anyway, because—in contrast to their murderer—they had not been baptized and had not found Christ.) One of the grotesque consequences of these "conversion conversations" is that Eichmann actually appears in a positive light, having put up a respectable defense against Hull's aggressive attempt to convert him. As a reader, you feel something like genuine sympathy for Eichmann in the face of such an odious fundamentalist visitation—something you then hold against Hull personally. Still, it is a shame his book is almost never used, despite containing three very interesting letters from Eichmann. In contrast to

the back-translated conversation transcripts, made from memory, the letters are undoubtedly reliable sources.

78. Heidegger's infamous address to the campaign rally of German academia in Leipzig, November 11, 1933, document no. 132 in Guido Schneeberger, *Nachlese zu Heidegger* (Bern 1962), and *Die Selbstbehauptung der deutschen Universität* (1934; reprint Frankfurt am Main, 1983), p. 14. Heidegger stands as a representative here for several philosophers who rushed to conform to National Socialist thought.

79. Eichmann mentions this letter to his brother Robert in his answers to the questionnaire for *Paris Match*, May 1962, BA Koblenz, All. Proz. 6/252, p. 27.

80. Rosenberg used these words at the memorial celebration for Copernicus and Kant in Königsberg on February 20, 1939.

81. Shlomo Kulcsár reported that after a brief period of irritation, Eichmann was quite enthusiastic about this new idea and told the psychologist he was correct: "You seem to be right. He was indeed only a *Gauleiter* (Nazi rank of regional officer) in Palestine," and so it was probably appropriate for Eichmann to compare himself to him. I. S. Kulcsár, Shoshanna Kulcsár, and Lipot Szondi, "Adolf Eichmann and the Third Reich," in *Crime, Law and Corrections*, ed. Ralph Slovenko (Springfield, Ill., 1966), p. 33.

82. "The Others Spoke," part 3, p. 13.

83. Quoted in *Stern*, no. 28, November 9, 1960. Eichmann confirmed this was genuine during his interrogation, on September 15, 1960.

84. Eichmann told Sassen that he allowed the killing of a relative during the extermination campaign, and that he had not even stopped it on the express wishes of a family member. Tape 67—in more detail on tape than in the transcript: BA tape 05B, from 21:00.

85. "The Others Spoke," part 3, p. 13.

86. Rudolf Höß, *Kommandant in Auschwitz: Autobiographische Aufzeichnungen* (1958; reprinted Munich, 2000), p. 194.

87. He really did write this: "Götzen," p. 138, A.E. 97.

88. "Allgemein" (General), handwritten text, Eichmann Estate, BA Koblenz, N/1497-92, p. 2.

89. Vera Eichmann, interview in *Paris Match*, April 29, 1962.

90. "Allgemein" (General), handwritten text, Eichmann Estate, BA Koblenz, N/1497-92, p. 2.

91. "The Others Spoke," part 3, p. 14.

92. Ibid., p. 16.

93. Ibid., p. 21.

94. Ibid., p. 23.

95. Ibid., p. 24.

96. Ibid., p. 25.

97. "Regret is something for little children" is much quoted but seldom referenced. Eichmann made this statement in cross-examination, Eichmann trial, session

96, July 13, 1961. He uttered it after denying ever holding the "little closing speech" in Argentina.

98. The reference Eichmann was looking for is John 4:22.

99. "The Others Spoke," introduction, p. 1.

100. "The Others Spoke," part 3, p. 26.

101. Argentine federal police, report on the abduction of Eichmann, June 9, 1960, Archivo General de la Nacíon (AGN), DAE, Bormann files, pp. 77–79; quoted in Uki Goñi, *The Real Odessa: How Perón Brought the Nazi War Criminals to Argentina*, rev. ed. (London, 2003), p. 316n543.

102. On Mildenstein's postwar career, see Timothy Naftali, "The CIA and Eichmann's Associates," in *US Intelligence and the Nazis*, ed. Richard Breitman (Washington, D.C., 2004), pp. 337–74, based on NA, RG 263, CIA Name File Leopold von Mildenstein.

103. In 1960–61 Eichmann wrote about the possibility of hiding in Chile, which he had stupidly not made use of. "Meine Flucht," p. 27, BA Koblenz, All. Proz. 6/247.

104. Franz Rademacher, handwritten note on Felix Benzler's telegram to the Foreign Office, September 12, 1941, prosecution document T/873. Facsimile in R. M. W. Kempner, *Eichmann und Komplizen* (Zurich, Stuttgart, and Vienna, 1961), p. 291. Identical to IMT document NG-3354.

105. Shlomo Kulcsár, "De Sade and Eichmann," *Mental Health and Society* 3 (1976), p. 108.

106. Klaus Eichmann, interview in *Quick,* January 2, 1966.

107. Avner Less, interview, Avner Less Estate, Archiv für Zeitgeschichte, ETH Zurich, NL Less, tape 7.1.IX.

108. The last line in Eichmann's farewell letter to his family reads: "I am now being fetched to be hanged. It is the 5/31/62, 5 minutes before 24:00. Farewell!" (The last words of the letter—"Pfuat Euch!"—were in Austrian dialect.) BA Koblenz, All. Proz. 6/248.

2 Eichmann in Conversation

1. Sassen transcript 18:8.

2. Many thanks to Peter F. Kramml, Salzburg City Archive, who was kind enough to look into the registration cards for me.

3. Rudel (Sassen) mentions Fritsch's visit to Germany in *Zwischen Deutschland und Argentinien* (Buenos Aires, 1954). See also "German Farewells 1974," the obituary in the right-wing publication *Deutsche Annalen, Jahrbuch des Nationalgeschehens*, year 4 (Leoni am Starnberger See, 1975), unpaginated. The rumors about Fritsch's Nazi career were started by Fritsch himself: in his letters to Nazi authors, he claimed to have heard them give a reading in person. See, for example, Fritsch's letter to Werner Beumelburg, February 10, 1948, Werner Beumelburg Estate, Rheinische Landesbibliothek Koblenz.

4. Saskia Sassen, interview and correspondence with the author (2009).

5. Fritsch to Werner Beumelburg, April 23, 1948, Beumelburg Estate.

6. Fritsch to Werner Beumelburg, June 6, 1949, Beumelburg Estate.

7. Fritsch to Werner Beumelburg, August 19, 1948, Beumelburg Estate.

8. "German Nationalist and Neo-Nazi Activities in Argentina," July 8, 1953, declassified April 11, 2000 (CIA-RDP620-00856 R000 3000 30004-4). Uki Goñi also assumes that Rudolfo Freude was a co-owner of Dürer Verlag.

9. Ibid. In the early years, Fritsch also cooperated with Theodor Schmidt, the owner of the El Buen Libro bookstore. However, this partnership seems not to have lasted long due to financial disagreements, if we believe what Fritsch said about it in his correspondence.

10. "Argentinisches Tageblatt," in Asociaciones Argentinas de Lengua Alemana, *Argentinische Vereinigungen deutschsprachigen Ursprungs: Ein Beitrag zur sozialen Verantwortung* (Buenos Aires, 2007), pp. 589–97.

11. Saskia Sassen, interviews and correspondence with the author (2009).

12. Hans Rechenberg, who came into contact with Fritsch after 1960 in connection with the financing of Eichmann's defense, complained about this attachment to Robert Servatius. See "Aftermath" in this book.

13. Adolf von Thadden mentioned in a letter that Rudel was the last person to finally turn away from Sassen. Thadden to Gert Sudholt (Druffel Verlag), September 10, 1981, Adolf von Thadden Estate, Niedersächsisches Landesarchiv, VVP 39, Acc. 1/98 no. 49, correspondence S.

14. In trial session 95, Eichmann claimed that Fritsch listened to the conversations only for a short while, then didn't come anymore. However, the transcripts and tapes show that Fritsch and Eichmann were still in touch during the last recordings.

15. When it became known that Eichmann had been abducted in 1960, Eichmann's brothers Otto and Robert met with Eberhard Fritsch straight away. This suggests that they knew one another before this point. See "Aftermath" in this book.

16. On Sassen's life until he fled Europe, see Gerald Groeneveld, *Kriegsberichter: Nederlandse SS-oorlogsverslaggevers 1941–1945* (Haarlem, 2004), pp. 356–68. See also Sassen's own literary reworking of his escape in his novel *Die Jünger und die Dirnen*, chap. 6. For Sassen's escape and his life in Argentina, see Roelf van Til's documentaries, and interviews with Inge Schneider and Saskia Sassen (as well as those by Raymond Ley in 2009); Saskia Sassen, correspondence (2009); Francisca Sassen, correspondence (2009); Anthony (Hesselbach, December 1960), "He wrote Adolf Eichmann's Memoirs," *Kölnische Rundschau*, December 16, 1960. Huge thanks to Wolfgang Birkholz and Annette Krieger from the *Kölnische Rundschau* for their generous help. Stan Lauryssen's *De fatale vriendschappen van Adolf Eichmann* (Leuven, 1998) has entertainment value more than anything else, and the interviews with Sassen by Stanislav Farago are clearly fiction. See "Aftermath" in this book.

17. The source of this information is problematic. Several of Lauryssens's state-

ments are incorrect, and doubt must be cast on an author who admired the single spire of Cologne's cathedral (which famously has two spires) on a visit to the city, and who claims to have seen document files in Sassen's house that existed only in Israel.

18. Eichmann later emphasized that he had also "fought at the front." For the sharp divide between members of the Waffen-SS and men like Eichmann in Argentina, see Pedro Pobierzym, interview by Raymond Ley (2009): "Eichmann was no SS man . . . he was a filthy swine."

19. The following details come from Inge Schneider's recollections (interview with Roelf van Til) and the documentary *Willem Sassen* (KRO, 2005).

20. Saskia Sassen remembers that the novel *Die Jünger und die Dirnen* led to bad blood between her parents. Even without the abstract level of National Socialist ideals, the chapter that deals with their crossing to Argentina, in which Sassen delighted in describing rapes and dying fetuses, clearly indicates why a woman might object to being immortalized in this way. Pedro Pobierzym heard one of these arguments as a guest of the house; interview by Raymond Ley (2009).

21. Sassen's files: 186 912/48; Uki Goñi, *The Real Odessa: How Perón Brought the Nazi War Criminals to Argentina*, rev. ed. (London, 2003), p. 176. Saskia Sassen, interviews by van Til and Ley (2005, 2009) and correspondence with the author (2009).

22. Inge Schneider, interview by Roelf van Til for *Willem Sassen* (KRO, 2005); Saskia Sassen, interviews and correspondence with the author (2005 and 2009).

23. Saskia Sassen, interview by Raymond Ley (2009).

24. For his life in Argentina, see Inge Schneider, interview by Roelf van Til (2009); Saskia Sassen, correspondence with the author (2009); and Francisca Sassen, correspondence with the author (2009).

25. According to Inge Schneider and Saskia Sassen.

26. Miep Sassen's critical stance on National Socialism was not simply a projection by her daughter, as evidenced by Inge Schneider's memories, and Miep's refusal to take German citizenship, although this would have made it much easier for her to settle down in Europe. There is a reference to Miep Sassen's brother in supplementary file to case BVerwG 7A 15.10, *Saure vs. BND*, BND files 121 099, 1853 (note on the background to the *Life* contract on November 23, 1960).

27. Eichmann trial, sessions 102 and 105; also Eichmann's remarks to his lawyer and to Avner W. Less.

28. Vera Eichmann, interview in *Paris Match*, April 29, 1962.

29. Pedro Pobierzym had bought the tape recorders in New York, to sell on in Argentina, "and one of my customers was Sassen." Interview by Raymond Ley, 2009.

30. Thanks to Saskia and Francisca Sassen for aiding my understanding of the historical documents with their memories of the interior of their parents' house.

31. Saskia Sassen's phrase.

32. Saskia Sassen remembers that both her parents made a concerted effort to pass on their educational ideals to their daughters.

33. All the contemporary witnesses who have spoken about this mention the discussions at Sassen's house (Sassen's daughters, Pedro Pobierzym, Willem Sassen from the 1970s onward, Vera Eichmann, Klaus Eichmann). Not one of them mentions a recording session in Eichmann's house. In particular, the fact that Eichmann's family knew nothing of the content of the tapes speaks conclusively against the story he told in Israel.

34. In Israel, Eichmann talked about Saturday afternoons and evenings, and Sunday mornings (trial session 92). The transcripts and documents allow us to verify this. Details following in this chapter and notes. Saskia Sassen remembers the Sundays in particular, but we can now establish that these were not the only sessions. Of course, Saturday was a normal school day, quite apart from the fact that Miep Sassen liked to take her daughters on outings and little trips.

35. Sassen transcript 10:2.

36. "Comrade Sassen" is used countless times, "my dear Comrade Sassen" (11:13). Elsewhere Eichmann frequently refers to "Langer" and "Fritsch" when they are not present but also to other absent associates like "Rajakowitsch." "Gentlemen" is used in larger groups, for example 18:8: "But that must be apparent to you, gentlemen . . ."

37. Even the transcriber (who was not present at the recordings) occasionally adds "Eichm" in brackets for clarification (13:11).

38. E.g., BA tape 09D 5:59, Sassen to Eichmann: "I would just like to ask you to think about this again this week."

39. E.g., 72:6, Eichmann: "You recently gave me a number of pages on the activities of the Foreign Office."

40. Eichmann: "I believe that these papers that I gave to Comrade Fritsch give a much more exact account of the matter" (meaning newspaper articles on Raoul Wallenberg); 10:2.

41. Sassen transcript 9:17.

42. "The Enthusiasts of Zion"—a long article about radical groups in Israel, in reaction to discussions after the assassination of Rudolf Kasztner, which Eichmann read so closely that he was able to quote it word for word.

43. "Religion: Two Kinds of Jews," *Time,* August 26, 1957 (published August 20). The article refers to a speech made by Ben-Gurion on Zionism at the start of August. Albert Ballin was born on August 15, 1857, and the *Argentinisches Tageblatt* reported on the celebrations on the Thursday ("Albert Ballin's Life's Work," August 15, 1957). This dates the recording sessions 37–39 to the weekend of August 24–25, 1957.

44. Eichmann: "Take the case of Schörner, since it is current right now." Eichmann's thoughts on the verdict follow (72:2). Ferdinand Schörner was sentenced to four and a half years for manslaughter by the Munich I District Court in October 1957.

45. Amendment 3:9 (to vol. 20:2): "Last Sunday we found a dating in the 'thick book.'" BA Ludwigsburg, "Miscellaneous" folder, p. 12.

46. The handwritten attempts to order the transcript were obviously made by Sassen, as they are the same on the originals as on all films and copies. Tape 10, p. 3, is a good example, to gain a quick impression of these markings (including the mistakes).

47. Based on a line-by-line evaluation, the Sassen transcript contains 11 percent quotes from books and 6 percent other material (sections that are not conversations with Eichmann, Sassen's notes and dictations). Eighty-three percent is therefore genuine discussion. The number of quotations on single pages can be well over 90 percent, when Eichmann limits himself to comments like "that's right" and "that's incorrect," as on tapes 63 and 65. In one case, an entire page consists of one such quote, from Poliakov, p. 236, at 63:5. Léon Polikov, *Joseph Wulf: Das Dritte Reich und die Juden* (Berlin-Grunewald, 1955).

48. The putative edition of the transcripts from Druffel Verlag (Aschenauer, *Ich, Adolf Eichmann* [Leoni am Starnberger See, 1980]) is unusable: it smooths out phrases throughout and turns the dialogue structure into a monologue, as the editors failed to recognize the presence of various other speakers and quotations. It puts a jumble of words into Eichmann's mouth that he did not say. Moreover, the Druffel edition effectively blocks any opportunity to recognize that the problem even exists. As a result, things said by Sassen and Alvensleben have slipped into otherwise serious secondary literature as Eichmann's words. On that edition, see "Aftermath" in this book.

49. To mention a few examples: Eichmann's amendments were sometimes written over several tapes at one time and numbered all the way through, showing the order in which the recordings were made. On tape 8, Eichmann has not yet read Brand and Weissberg's book, and his impression of it follows on tape 24. Tapes 11, 12, and 13 feature a discussion that is complete in itself; internal markers like "before" (tape 42), which clearly relates to tape 41, show the order, as do "a few weeks ago" (tape 46, referring to tape 37), "yesterday" (tape 54, referring to tape 51), and planned discussions that subsequently take place (Langer's lecture is announced on tape 50 and follows on tape 64). Discussions of the subject literature was very detailed, following the books' content; it is therefore possible to order the discussions based on quotes from the books. For example: tape 58 ends with a quote from Reitlinger's page 399, and tape 59 starts with Reitlinger's page 399. This also allows us to connect the middle of tape 54 to tape 58. Tape 54 ends with the chapter on France from Reitlinger, and tape 58 starts with the chapter on Belgium that follows it. Such evidence is abundant, allowing for a surprisingly exact reconstruction of the original chronology.

50. Tape 72 has a question mark instead of a number, as it was not clear to the transcriber whether it was tape 72. Tape 7, according to a note from Sassen, never existed. No trace has yet been found of tapes 70 and 71. Tapes 55 and 69 are obviously fragmentary.

51. Tape 61 contains a conversation about the Poliakov book, and then the debate on Reitlinger's pages, 218–20. The unnumbered tape that was made when Sassen picked up the wrong reel contains the previous conversation on Reitlinger, covering pages 212–17.

52. BA tape 8A, 30:10 onward.

53. Vera Eichmann, interview in *Paris Match*, April 29, 1962.

54. Sassen transcript 67:6. The tape goes into more detail: BA tape 10B, 38:50 onward.

55. Eichmann during interrogation by Avner W. Less, June 6, 1960, p. 397: "This was the first time I spoke to Mildner again, about three years ago . . . and I picked this issue apart in the presence of a certain Herr Sassen."

56. The planned large-scale deportations from Denmark could not be implemented as there was too much resistance from the Danes. As Eichmann was directly involved in the plans, he took the failure personally and looked for someone to blame in his own ranks.

57. All the sources that suspect Mildner was in Argentina are based exclusively on Eichmann's incriminating statement in Israel, and appear to be independent only where this basis is not mentioned or not repeated frequently enough, as in Wiesenthal, Goñi, Schneppen, Wojak, and Cesarani. It does not mean that Mildner cannot have been in Argentina. But it does mean that Eichmann should not be called as a witness to it, since to date we have no other evidence. Mildner was certainly never part of the Sassen circle.

58. We can safely dismiss the charitable notion that Eichmann might have misheard Dr. Langer's name in Buenos Aires. Langer was a long-term fixture in the Sassen circle, and Eichmann pronounces the name audibly several times on the tapes and even writes it correctly on one of the transcribed pages. Sassen transcript 59:6.

59. Amendment 4:1 on Sassen transcript tape 37, BA Ludwigsburg, "Miscellaneous" folder, p. 14.

60. BA tape 8A, 27:50 onward. The context suggests that this recording is a relatively early tape, from the first third of the discussion sessions.

61. See also Holger Meding, *"Der Weg": Eine deutsche Emigrantenzeitschrift in Buenos Aires 1947–1957* (Berlin, 1997), p. 117.

62. Juan Maler, *Frieden, Krieg und "Frieden"* (Bariloche, 1987), p. 340.

63. Josef Schwammberger lived there for a while but returned to Buenos Aires by 1954 at the latest.

64. BA tape 03A, from the beginning.

65. Sassen transcript 3:4.

66. From what remains of the Telefe interviews, broadcast in the Argentine *Edition Plus* in 1991. Regrettably the raw material was not archived.

67. Sassen transcript 3:3.

68. I myself noticed the clues to the ladies' visit, and Ludolf von Alvensleben, which were actually obvious, only after several readings—or more precisely, once I had followed the advice of my esteemed teacher in the interpretation

of hermetic texts, Klaus Oehler, and read the material once more from back to front. He had used the method to read Aristotle with us, but it is also an excellent tool for approaching the Eichmann papers.

69. Sassen transcript 3:2.

70. Sassen transcript 3:1.

71. Sassen transcript 29:4. The transcript of tape 29 has Eichmann's handwritten note on it: "This tape 29 is for your information only." The correction sheets also state clearly that this sort of biographical information was "not for the book."

72. Eichmann later told different versions of this story, but his personnel file allows it to be dated to the first half of 1938. SS files, BA Berlin-Lichterfelde, BDC.

73. Document from the SS files; produced at the trial as prosecution document T/37(12).

74. See note 77 to "The So-Called Sassen Interviews" for more information on Hull.

75. Sassen transcript 3:2.

76. The transcriber's habit of shortening "National Socialism" in a way that could easily be misunderstood persists through the first transcripts, until Sassen can be heard on the tape giving clear instructions on these abbreviations. However, the problems with this term continue to crop up.

77. See the SS files, BA Berlin-Lichterfelde, BDC; Karl Schlöger, ed., *Russische Emigranten in Deutschland 1918–1994* (Berlin, 1995).

78. Sassen transcript 3:2.

79. Ibid.

80. Erika Elisabeth Garthe de Galliard, who was married to a Belgian friend of the war criminal Pierre Daye. She didn't conceal the fact that she knew about Sassen's project, as Uki Goñi was kind enough to tell me, or that she had close ties to Wilfred von Oven and Dieter Menge. These close ties don't exactly speak for her being somebody who would have posed a lot of critical questions about the National Socialist mentality.

81. Inge Schneider, interview by Roelf van Til. She explains that she never understood why her sister wanted to listen to this nonsense, or why she didn't end her affair with Sassen, even though Miep Sassen knew about it. Antje Schneider died of cancer in 1990, and Inge Schneider lived in Argentina and Bremen until her death in 2006.

82. BA tape 09D, 29:08

83. The spelling "Dr. Lange" occasionally appears in the transcript, but as Eichmann corrected the name by hand and pronounced it several times on the tapes, there is no doubt that this man was called "Langer."

84. Sassen transcript 47:12.

85. Sassen transcript 44:9.

86. Sassen transcript 46:8.

87. Sassen transcript 44:10.

88. Sassen transcript 59:10.

89. A handwritten amendment on Sassen transcript 16:1.

90. Sassen transcript 44:10, handwritten addition by Eichmann: "This was said by Dr. Langer, not me." Eichmann was evidently keen to avoid any suspicion that he might have helped a Jew.

91. Sassen transcript 47:16.

92. Sassen transcript 50:2.

93. BA tape 09D, 53:45 onward.

94. BA tape 09D, 1:04:30 onward.

95. BA tape 09D, 29:55 onward.

96. Dieter Vollmer, interview by Holger Meding; and Dieter Vollmer, "On the Professional Ethics of Journalists,"*Nation Europa,* no.11, issue 11, 1961, pp. 37–42. Vollmer left Argentina again at the end of 1953 but continued writing for Fritsch until the end, and he apparently looked after the distribution of Dürer Verlag's banned publications in Germany. By 1961 at the latest, he knew so much about the 1957 project that he even made an effort to mitigate the danger that the Sassen transcript represented. See "Dismantling the Evidence" in this book .

97. Sassen transcript 54:14.

98. BA tape 10D, 22:45 onward.

99. See the schedules of responsibilities from the RSHA (IV), all prosecution documents at the Eichmann trial. Prosecution document T/99, BA Koblenz, R58/840. For IV A 4: circular from Kaltenbrunner, February 10, 1944, BStU, RHE 75/70, vol. 3, sheets 12–17; Gestapo schedule of responsibilities in Department IV, dated March 15, 1944, ibid., sheets 2–10. Evidence of department name IMT 42, p. 315, Walter Huppenkothen affidavit (Gestapo-39), and Wisliceny's testimonies.

100. Personal notes, Avner Less Estate, Archiv für Zeitgeschichte, ETH Zurich, NL Less, 4.2.3.2.

101. BA tape 10D, 21:30.

102. Sassen transcript 53:15.

103. Eichmann trial, session 102.

104. I have not come across a single case of anyone trying to hide their identity from anyone else in the group, or not calling someone by their name, either in the transcript or on the tapes. There is not even any evidence of ironic references to aliases. The only "name changes" are the result of typing errors, as names like Globocnik and Wisliceny are not as simple to write as Eichmann or Sassen.

105. The officers lists of the SS (and to be on the safe side, the Waffen-SS) were checked, for Langer or similar names, as were the BDC files in BA Berlin-Lichterfelde. There are only two records that could have come into question here, namely Otto Langer (no SS number given, born March 18, 1899, SS *Scharführer,* with a single entry "Concentration camp Mauthausen") and

Fritz Langer (SS no. 54691, born January 13, 1904, police secretary, possibly Vienna). Fritz Langer's position as "assessment officer" with the *Gauleitung* in Vienna (RS-PK) suggests it might be him, but unlike the Dr. Langer of the tapes, who apparently had no experience of frontline fighting, he received commendations for dedicated fighting against partisans in northern Italy. This "Front deployment" (R70) earned him an entry in the Allies' CROWCASS wanted lists. The files R70 and RS-PK also throw up inconsistencies. I have not been able to find enough documentation on Otto Langer to properly identify him, but his rank is clearly too low for the assignments Dr. Langer describes. Thanks to Lutz Möser from BA Berlin-Lichterfelde for his involvement.

106. Special thanks to Barbara Bieringer, University of Vienna Archive.
107. Thanks to Michael Wildt, Bertrand Perz, and the staff at DÖW, who took the time to consider further possibilities for tracking down Langer. Uki Goñi tried to find traces of Langer in Argentina but found no clues in the records, on Langer or Lange or "Dr. Klan."
108. Tape 73, BA tape 8A, 10:35.
109. I have consciously avoided including speaker names or other reading aids in this chapter. It would not only make the text illegible through all the "sics" and exclamation marks, but would also prevent the reader observing the effect of the language.
110. Sassen transcript 5:6.
111. Sassen transcript 21:10.
112. Sassen transcript 9:3.
113. Sassen transcript 17:1. Eichmann added a handwritten amendment to the phrase to make it read like this!
114. Sassen transcript 18:3.
115. Sassen transcript 21:6.
116. Sassen transcript 34:4.
117. Sassen transcript 5:5.
118. Sassen transcript 68:9.
119. Sassen transcript 34:4.
120. Sassen transcript 11:6 and 11:8.
121. Sassen transcript 23:4.
122. Sassen transcript 13:6.
123. Sassen transcript 13:7.
124. Sassen transcript 17:1.
125. Sassen transcript 12:2.
126. Sassen transcript 14:9.
127. Sassen transcript 14:10.
128. Sassen transcript 41:1.
129. Sassen transcript 22:9.
130. Sassen transcript 8:4.
131. Sassen transcript 13:5.

132. Tape 8 was transcribed onto fanfold paper, which was impractically long. The pagination therefore related to the double pages into which it has now been cut. The reference for this quote, 8:8.2, means "tape 8, page 8, sheet 2."
133. Sassen transcript 9:8.
134. Sassen transcript 10:5.
135. Sassen transcript 10:1.
136. Sassen transcript 13:4.
137. Sassen transcript 64:4.
138. Sassen transcript 50:5.
139. Sassen transcript 33:10.
140. Sassen transcript 72:16.
141. Sassen transcript 68:5.
142. Sassen transcript 26:7.
143. Sassen transcript 73:1.
144. Sassen transcript 21:8.
145. Sassen transcript 19:5.
146. Sassen transcript 61:4.
147. Sassen transcript 52:13.
148. At 42:5 the discussion centered on the so-called euthanasia campaign, in which Sassen had little interest and therefore omitted from the transcript. For most of these quotations, see BA tape 7B, 39:15.
149. Sassen transcript 43:8.
150. Sassen transcript 39:4.
151. Sassen transcript 56:7.
152. Sassen transcript 56:9.
153. Tape 23. For the untranscribed passage, see BA tape 09D, 51:55 onward.
154. Sassen transcript 15:3.
155. Sassen transcript 15:3.
156. Sassen transcript 60:2.
157. Sassen transcript 43:5.
158. Sassen transcript 46:5.
159. Sassen transcript 16:10.
160. Sassen transcript 18:3.
161. Sassen transcript 17:9.
162. Sassen transcript 20:7.
163. Sassen transcript 44:4.
164. Sassen transcript 51:11.
165. Sassen transcript 58:5.
166. Sassen transcript 68:6.
167. Kulcsár, Kulcsár, and Szondi, "Adolf Eichmann and the Third Reich," p. 28.
168. Hannah Arendt, *Eichmann in Jerusalem: A Report on the Banality of Evil* (1963; reprint New York, 1994), pp. 49–50.
169. Some of these departures can be found on the few surviving tapes. E.g., an

unknown voice, clearly audible, on BA tape 06A ,47:55: "Excuse me, but I have to go . . ."

170. See BA tape 09C, 1:51:55. Sassen closes the session, the men fall into a conversation, and a voice discusses with Sassen the submission deadline for another text.

171. Examples: BA tape 8A, 27:50 onward; 10C, 39:46.

172. BA tape 10B, 1:11:00 onward.

173. Sassen transcript 1:1.

174. Sassen transcript 1:2: Eichmann as a "fanatical Zionist."

175. Sassen transcript 1:2, on the claim that a mass shooting was organized in Poland by Eichmann himself. Sassen transcript 1:3, on the Eichmann quote, "I would leap joyfully into the grave . . ."

176. The first edition appeared in 1952, as part of the series *Das Ausnahmerecht für die Juden in den europäischen Ländern*, but the Sassen group used the affordable single edition (Düsseldorf, 1954).

177. A rough overview of the basis for discussion in each case: Weissberg, tapes 6, 8–17, 19–22, 24–26; Poliakov/Wulf, tapes 28, 34, 37–39, 42–44, 49–52, 54–57, 61–67; Blau, tapes 39–40, 44–47; Hagen/Hottl, tapes 10–11, 51, (56), 64; Reitlinger, tapes 1, 18–19, 22–23, 25–27, 33, 49, 52–54, 58–61, 68, 69, 72, 73, and unnumbered tape.

178. For example, Hermann Graml, *Der 9. November 1938, "Reichskristallnacht"* (Bonn, 1955); Gerhardt Boldt, *Die letzten Tage der Reichskanzlei* (Hamburg, 1947); and Charles Callan Tansill, *Die Hintertür zum Kriege* (Düsseldorf, 1956).

179. Tape 37:1 onward. Sassen read that article hot off the press, as we can see from the precise date that can be given to the recording.

180. The photos, which were made public at the start of the trial, were published in various places. Claims that they showed Eichmann working on his "Götzen" manuscript are incorrect—he got the books at the request of his lawyer, who wanted him to take a position on them. In addition to the volumes mentioned, there were a few books that had been published since the Sassen interviews, namely Rudolf Höß, *Kommandant in Auschwitz* (1958); Albert Wucher, *Eichmanns gab es viele* (1961); Joel Brand, *Fakten gegen Fabeln* (1961); Léon Poliakov and Joseph Wulf, *Das Deutsche Reich und seine Diener* (1956); Poliakov and Wulf, *Das Dritte Reich und seine Denker* (1959); and H. G. Adler, *Theresienstadt 1941–1945* (1960). Special thanks to Carlo Schütt, who made the books available at the Forschungsstelle für Zeitgeschichte Hamburg library to reconstruct the pile and, with it, the list of books.

181. Avner W. Less, interview by Rolf Defrank, for *Erscheinungsform Mensch*, at Avner Less Estate, Archiv für Zeitgeschichte, ETH Zurich, NL Less, tape 7.1.IX.

182. Sassen transcript 50:6.

183. Sassen transcript 49:16.

184. Sassen transcript 4:6; 39:8.

185. Sassen transcript 18:1; 33:9; 40:2; 52:1; 52:5; 52:6; 54:4.
186. Sassen transcript 49:14.
187. Sassen transcript 2:7.
188. Sassen transcript 24:1.
189. Sassen transcript 31:10; 61:3.
190. Sassen transcript 17:5.
191. Sassen transcript 21:3.
192. Sassen transcript 62:1; 72:8.
193. Sassen transcript 2:4.
194. Sassen transcript 73:13.
195. Sassen transcript 68:15.
196. Sassen transcript 6:1.
197. The Deutsche Forschergemeinschaft (German Researchers Foundation) published a whole journal series to establish a "German mathematics" (Leipzig, 1936–44).
198. Sassen transcript 20:4.
199. Sassen transcript 11:6.
200. Sassen transcript 11:4.
201. Sassen transcript 25:8.
202. Sassen transcript 8:2.
203. Sassen transcript 10:14.
204. Sassen transcript 10:17.
205. Tape 24 and the start of 25 contain Eichmann's book review. The notes are also extant and are held in Eichmann Estate, BA Koblenz, N/1497-87. They show that Eichmann's lecture was given almost word-for-word from his script.
206. Sassen transcript 8:2.
207. Sassen transcript 12:1.
208. Sassen transcript 14:7.
209. A long handwritten addition by Eichmann on the transcript, 52:16.
210. "Götzen," sheet 19 (Eichmann's numbering: 1) and elsewhere.
211. Sassen transcript 3:6.
212. Sassen transcript 26:4.
213. Sassen transcript 31:9.
214. BA tape 10C, 55:40.
215. Sassen transcript 54:5.
216. Pedro Pobierzym, interviews by Natasja de Winter and Raymond Ley (2009).
217. BA tape 09D, 41:30.
218. Sassen transcript 47:12.
219. Ibid.
220. Sassen transcript 36:2. This sentence clearly comes from Willem Sassen, from a long dictation that he had transcribed in the context of the discussions. It has previously been assumed to be a statement by Eichmann and has always been attributed to Eichmann. This is simply incorrect. There is also no evidence that Sassen took the sentence from Eichmann—quite apart from the

fact that Sassen was much too assured in his own phrasing to help himself to Eichmann's language, of all things.

221. Sassen transcript 36:5.

222. Sassen transcript 52, with handwritten addition by Eichmann.

223. Sassen transcript 54:9.

224. Eichmann, during a telephone call with his subordinate officer Theodor Dannecker, prosecution document T/439; identical with IMT RF-1233. Dannecker's note of July 21, 1942, about telephone calls with Eichmann and Novak on July 20, 1942, is published in Serge Klarsfeld, *Vichy—Auschwitz: Die Zusammenarbeit der deutschen und französischen Behörden bei der "Endlösung der Judenfrage" in Frankreich* (Nördlingen, 1989), p. 416; new edition (Darmstadt, 2007), p. 441. Facsimile in R. M. W. Kempner, *Eichmann und Komplizen* (Zurich, Stuttgart, and Vienna, 1961), p. 212.

225. Sassen transcript 3:6.

226. On one of the untranscribed parts of the tapes, Eichmann demonstrates that he has no idea about other drugs. For example, he doesn't even know how morphine is taken. Sassen interviews, BA tape 10B, 1:14 onward.

227. BA tape 10C, 1:00:00 onward.

228. Ernst Klee, *Persilscheine und Falsche Pässe: Wie die Kirchen den Nazis halfen* (Frankfurt am Main, 1992).

229. BA tape 10C, 1:00:00 onward.

230. Sassen transcript 44:6.

231. Two references date tapes 37 and 39 to the end of August. On tape 37, Sassen translates from a current article in *Time,* issue dated August 26, 1957 (published a few days earlier, on August 20, as is usual for U.S. magazines); and on tape 39, Eichmann refers to an announcement he has read the previous week of the centenary celebrations for Ballin, which can be identified as an article from the *Argentinisches Tageblatt* of August 15, 1957.

232. On his biography, see principally the files on Dieter Wisliceny at BA Berlin-Lichterfelde, BDC. Also the information in the CIC Arrest Report, August 1, 1946, NA, RG 263, CIA Name File Adolf Eichmann.

233. Eichmann always emphasized that Wisliceny had still been with him in Altaussee. Wisliceny disputed this, but there is evidence he was arrested on May 12, 1945, by the lake that gave the little town its name.

234. Wisliceny's essential statements and notes on Eichmann include a discussion with Kasztner, in which Wisliceny tried to promote an image of Eichmann that blamed him as much as possible and exonerated Wisliceny, January–February 1945, *Kasztner Bericht* [Kasztner Report], pp. 273ff; detailed statements after his May 3, 1945, arrest by U.S. authorities, dated August 25 and August 27, 1945 (Arrest Report, and Reports from NA, RG 263, File Name Adolf Eichmann); an affidavit in Nuremberg, November 9, 1945, prosecution document T/57; a witness statement in Nuremberg, January 3, 1946, prosecution document T/58; a statement in Bratislava to Michael Gerd, May 6, 1946, police document B06-899; handwritten notes on the Fiala affair, July 26, 1946,

prosecution document T/1107; handwritten notes on Eichmann's relationship with the mufti, July 26, 1946, prosecution document T/89; a twenty-two-page handwritten report "Re: former SS-*Obersturmbannführer* Adolf Eichmann," aka Cell 133 Document, October 27, 1946, prosecution document T/84; a conversation with Moshe Pearlman about Eichmann, November 14, 1946, Centre de Documentation Juive Contemporaine, Paris, 88-47, published in Pearlman, *The Capture and Trial of Adolf Eichmann* (New York, 1963); and a report on "The Final Solution," aka Cell 106 Document, November 18, 1946, prosecution document T/85, excerpted in Poliakov and Wulf, *Das Deutsche Reich und die Juden* (Berlin, 1955), pp. 87–98.

235. Wisliceny, Cell 133 Document, prosecution document T/84, p. 17.

236. On February 27, 1948.

237. In the early 1930s, Eichmann had been a witness to several Gestapo interrogations, which as an SD man, he could not conduct himself but could initiate. His own interrogation methods can be reconstructed in a few cases and can only be described as perfidious psychological terrorism. In Auschwitz, for example, he tried to break Jacob Edelstein during his interrogation using a letter from his wife, which he had extracted from the unsuspecting woman in the adjoining camp complex. She had written in the belief that her husband was still in (relative) freedom, and that Eichmann would simply be good enough to take the letter to him. Eichmann would leave the room when the physical violence began, but return in order to make use of its consequences. Adler, *Theresienstadt 1941–1945*, pp. 730 and 810.

238. Sassen transcript 44:5.

239. Sassen transcript 42:3–44:6.

240. Sassen transcript 44:5–44:8.

241. We have two recordings from before this turning point, so the change in tone can be observed acoustically. Unfortunately, the crucial session is missing.

242. BA tape 08A, 42:13 onward.

243. Sassen transcript 46:8.

244. Sassen transcript 47:7.

245. This section of the book is a summary of my unpublished manuscript "Noch ein Nazi in Argentinien: Ludolf von Alvensleben im Gespräch mit Willem Sassen," which Raymond Ley and the NDR used as the basis for the docudrama *Eichmanns Ende* (NDR, 2009). The manuscript contains a complete edition of the interviews with a commentary.

246. Sassen transcript 54:5.

247. Tape 56 is not a foreign body in the transcript: it was a component of the discussion project, was numbered and transcribed in the same way, and remains a reference point for further discussions. Sassen did not therefore accidentally put the interview in the wrong pile.

248. The information that follows is primarily based on Alvensleben's SS files, BA Berlin-Lichterfelde, BDC. Also indispensable were Ruth Bettina Birn, *Die höheren SS- und Polizeiführer: Himmlers Vertreter im Reich und in den besetzten*

Gebieten (Düsseldorf, 1986), esp. p. 330, but also pp. 311 and 382ff. (footnote 2); and Christian Jansen and Arno Weckenbecker, *Der "Volksdeutsche Selbstschutz" in Polen 1939/40* (Munich 1992). And of course Stanislaw Mucha's great film *Mit "Bubi" heim ins Reich: Die Spuren eines SS-Generals* (ZDF, 2000).

249. Heinz Schneppen, *Odessa und das Vierte Reich: Mythen der Zeitgeschichte* (Berlin, 2007), p. 125. Schneppen made a concerted effort to dismantle the Odessa myth and trace its origins. Regrettably, some of the research on individual Nazis is not what it might have been, and his depiction of them occasionally tips over into another kind of myth. Even in the source material he cites, significantly more connections can be seen than he actually uses. The idea that one soon hits a brick wall when attempting to research the lives and personalities of these fugitives is unsupportable in the cases of Alvensleben, Eichmann, Mengele, Heilig, Rajakowitsch, and Klingenfuß, although admittedly, the source research is rather taxing. (Rudolf Mildner, incidentally, slips into the list of Nazis in Argentina, because Schneppen did not recognize that Wiesenthal was drawing on Eichmann's testimony in Israel.)

250. In the seniority lists of the Waffen-SS from November 1944, original Berlin 1944.

251. The numbering in the officers lists of the Waffen-SS is confusing at first glance, as the grades were a combination of numbers and letters, but Alvensleben is at place 41f in the SS-*Gruppenführers* and lieutenant generals, after 43 SS *Obergruppenführers* and generals. This puts him at number 90 of all members of the Waffen-SS. *Dienstaltersliste der Waffen-SS. Stand vom 1. Juli, 1944. SS-Obergruppenführer bis SS-Hauptsturmführer* (Osnabrück, 1987), p. 14.

252. Alvensleben's SS file, staff appraisal from June 15, 1938.

253. There are many examples of this, both on the tapes and the transcript. Eichmann had no qualms about shouting over other participants, upstaging them or finding some other way to bring the conversation back to him as quickly as possible. The Alvensleben discussion offered enough inducements for him to butt in and contradict what was being said. And Eichmann didn't tend to suffer in silence.

254. On tape 58, Alvensleben talks about Himmler's reaction to the bombing of Dresden in 1945, which he knows about "from my own experience." Alvensleben reported to Himmler shortly after the event in Dresden, which fell under his jurisdiction as HSSPF. He then gave an account of Himmler's behavior to Goebbels, whom he also visited. The propaganda minister wrote about Alvensleben's visit in his diary on March 6, 1945. None of the other participants in the Sassen circle (apart from Eichmann) had even come close to Himmler or Goebbels.

255. The possibility that Alvensleben was only pretending to be a devoted National Socialist in order to gain access to the Sassen circle, or to "infiltrate" it, is slight. The discussion groups at Sassen's house were no secret, and there is no evidence of any "entry criteria." Anyone wanting to claim that Alvensleben changed his views after 1945 has a heavy burden of proof.

256. See Peter Longerich, *Heinrich Himmler*, p. 3: "In the postwar years no Himmler legend was waiting to be born."

257. Sassen transcript 56:7.

258. Gerald Steinacher, *Nazis on the Run: How Hitler's Henchmen Fled Justice* (Oxford, 2012).

259. The letter and the reply are held in the National Archive in Bozen. Many thanks to Gerald Steinacher for making it available so quickly.

260. The letters from Alvensleben to Himmler in the SS files serve as a comparison. Handwriting is individual in so many respects that very few people succeed in changing theirs. Alvensleben tried to write in a slightly florid, "feminine" way, but the writing samples in the SS files are a clear match. Someone with twenty years' experience in identifying handwriting can show the similarities in detail: the writing angle, the extension of letters above and below the line, the particular capital letters, the way numbers are written, line spacing. But in this case I didn't need my experience—it is obvious at first glance. Anyone wanting to try for themselves could digitally merge the two samples.

261. Alvensleben and his wife Melitta, née Guaita, had four children: two daughters, born in 1925 and 1934, and two sons, born in 1942 and 1944. The elder daughter was an adult by this point (and most probably already married) so didn't count as a child to be registered. Detailed information in SSO File Alvensleben, BA Berlin-Lichterfelde, BDC.

262. There are actually two applications for "Theodor Kremhart" with two different photos of Alvensleben, possibly because an error was made in completing one of the forms. Many thanks once again to Uki Goñi and Gerald Steinacher for their help with these documents.

263. Uki Goñi told me he knew of only two passport applications signed by Dömöter.

264. Juan Maler, *Frieden, Krieg und "Frieden"* (Bariloche, 1987), p. 345.

265. Stanislaw Mucha, *Mit "Bubi" heim ins Reich*, ends with a suspicion of this kind from a member of the Alvensleben family. Mucha had insufficient evidence to argue against it.

266. Sassen transcript 49:15.

267. See *Der Weg* (1957), no. 7, pp. 495–96. The reader's letter is signed "Dr. Ernst Rauhart, Sao Paulo, Brazil." Many of the readers' letters in *Der Weg* were written by the editors themselves, so this name may not be genuine. In any case, Fritsch decided to print this text on this particular date.

268. Published in IMT vol. 31, pp. 85–87; in Poliakov and Wulf, *Das Deutsche Reich und die Juden*, pp. 99–100.

269. Sassen transcript 4:10.

270. Sassen transcript 50:1.

271. Wisliceny, statement at IMT, January 3, 1946, 4, p. 412. On further figures, ibid., p. 411.

272. Grell, statement for Eichmann trial, Berchtesgaden, May 23, 1961.

273. Judge Yitzhak Raveh confronted Eichmann with the sentence in his own handwriting (notes, prosecution document T/43).
274. Sassen transcript 24:1.
275. Sassen transcript 4:2.
276. Sassen transcript 50:10 onward.
277. Sassen transcript 49:9.
278. Sassen transcript 49:8.
279. BA tape 02A, 43:30.
280. If any further proof had been needed that the Heimann and Herster articles were homemade forgeries, this fact would suffice. The Sassen circle read every publication that had anything to do with the topic, even articles from *Time* magazine. Only *Der Weg*'s articles were not discussed. Everyone present knew that it was unnecessary, as they bore little resemblance to reality.
281. Sassen transcript 53:11.
282. Sassen transcript 73:3.
283. Sassen transcript 61:3.
284. Sassen's dictation, accidentally transcribed along with the discussion, and ordered in the Hagag copy as the start and pp. 326–35 of transcript 36. Further details of the dictation can be found on BA tape 08A, 32:37 onward.
285. Thanks to Martin Haidinger for letting me read his interview transcript.
286. Tape 67.
287. The ten tapes held in the Bundesarchiv also contain copies of this speech in various lengths and with cuts made in different places. Unfortunately, for this reason, not every transcription to be found in the literature and media today is complete. The following is the first complete transcript from the uncut BA tape 10B, 52:30 to 1:02:58.
288. Misheard words in other transcriptions have been corrected and are not noted here.
289. "Kaufmann": in the conversations with Sassen, the so-called Kaufmann Plan is repeatedly confused with the Morgenthau Plan. Theodore N. Kaufman self-published a pamphlet with the title *Germany Must Perish,* calling for the extinction of the Germans through sterilization. The Nazi Ministry of Propaganda used the publication to support the thesis of a "monstrous Jewish extermination program"; *Völkische Beobachter,* July 24, 1941. In 1944 Henry Morgenthau, Jr., the U.S. secretary of the treasury, commissioned the development of a plan for the division and deindustrialization of the German Reich. Goebbels used it as a warning in his calls for perseverance. Although both plans remained theoretical, they have always served National Socialists as a justification for German war crimes and crimes against humanity. They also led to the confusion in the Sassen circle. See Wolfgang Benz, ed., *Legenden Lügen Vorurteile: Ein Lexicon zur Zeitgeschichte* (Munich, 1990), pp. 85 and 145.
290. "Morgenthau": see note 289.

291. "The cautious bureaucrat" is a quote from the report by Dieter Wisliceny, who applied the label to Eichmann. For an SS man, it was an unforgivable insult. The Sassen circle read and discussed this report several times.

292. "Your louse" refers to Sassen's effort to distance Hitler and "the essence of the German race" from anti-Jewish policy, to make it impossible to accuse the Führer and National Socialism of historical mass murder. Eichmann, however, wanted to be recognized as typically German, a good officer following the ideas of "the Führer."

293. "Records": Eichmann had no real interest in technical matters. He understood nothing about the recording technology and frequently chose the wrong terms to describe it.

294. "Four months": when it comes to timing, Eichmann is often unreliable. He used such phrases as "decoration" for rhetorical purposes, and liked to cite round or symbolic dates. Even a text that Eichmann wrote, shortly after being incarcerated in Israel, he dated as "15 years and one day" after Germany's capitulation, although everyone present knew that this was a lie, as he had still been at large in Argentina on May 9.

295. "Korherr" and "10.3 million Jews" refer to the Korherr Report, which the Sassen circle had discussed in detail, and to which Eichmann had added his own "disinformation"-style commentary.

296. "Most cunning enemy" corresponds exactly to Hitler's characterization of the Jews as an "enemy race," a single homogenous race that posed a genuine threat to the "Aryan race," whom they must therefore fight for survival. All other races were simply "inferior races" that posed no threat.

297. "Streicher" refers to Julius Streicher, the anti-Semitic and pornographic rabble-rouser and editor of *Der Stürmer* who was executed in Nuremberg and was controversial even among anti-Semites. Streicher and Eichmann are known to have met in 1937, when Eichmann was invited to the Nuremberg Party Congress as Streicher's guest. The direction taken by Heydrich's outfit was influenced by its opposition to *Der Stürmer*'s methods: they didn't want beatings and murder in the streets, but rather a more "respectable" (secret) anti-Jewish policy.

298. "Schooling": the SD saw science and scholarship as a Jewish "weapon" in the struggle for world domination, a view based in the National Socialists' anti-intellectualism.

299. "Law making" refers to the Ten Commandments. In National Socialist criticism of the church, the Bible itself is considered "Jewish"—a reason for Eichmann to tear apart his wife's Bible. See "The Lady Visitors" in this book. Eichmann describes the incident in Sassen transcript 3:1.

300. "Interventionists": during the Sassen conversations, Eichmann repeatedly gives examples of people who got in the way of his extermination plans. They were often senior figures in the regime who were trying to push through exceptions for friends (or hoping to be remunerated for their efforts). By 1944,

Eichmann viewed even Kurt Becher, who was acting on Himmler's orders, as an obstacle of this kind.

301. Harry Mulisch, *Criminal Case 40/61, the Trial of Adolf Eichmann: An Eyewitness Account* (Philadelphia, 2009), p. 114.

302. Sassen transcript 67:11–12. These are two pages that the typist was unable to place, but that Sassen marked as being connected to the "conclusion." However, before the sale of the transcript, he removed them, together with all the pages that followed, allowing the "Sassen transcript" to end with the pithy conclusion, which was not, in fact, the last word. The two pages remained in Sassen's own copy of tape 67 and are there today in Eichmann Estate, BA Koblenz, N/1497-65.

303. The clue to the time of day comes from Sassen transcript 68:15.

304. BA tape 01A, 7:22 onward.

305. Sassen transcript 69:2 and 72:1.

306. The transcript of tape 69 is incomplete, and those of tapes 70 and 71 are missing, making it impossible to tell if they were ever prepared.

307. "No experiments" was the slogan on Adenauer's campaign posters.

A False Sense of Security

1. "Former SS-*Oberstleutnant* Arrested," *Frankfurter Allgemeine Zeitung,* April 4, 1957, but also smaller daily papers like the *Hamburger Abendblatt* and the *Argentinisches Tageblatt*.

2. The following letters from Lothar Hermann have so far emerged: to Fritz Bauer, June 25, 1960, Fritz Bauer Estate, Archiv der sozialen Demokratie, Bonn, with thanks to Christoph Stamm; published in Irmtrud Wojak, *Eichmanns Memoiren: Ein kritischer Essay* (Frankfurt am Main, 2001), p. 27. To Friedman, September 17, 1959; November 5, 1959; March 28, 1960; April 27, 1960; May 26, 1960; May 30, 1960; May 1, 1961; May 26, 1961; May 14, 1971; June 2, 1971. To Ben-Gurion, May 20, 1961. All these letters are in Tuviah Friedman, ed., *Die "Ergreifung Eichmanns": Dokumentarische Sammlung* (Haifa, 1971), along with a few letters between Friedman and Erwin Schüle. In grateful memory of Tuviah Friedman for the documents. Further letters are in BA Ludwigsburg, Central Office Collection, III/24.

3. The text is missing from the French edition, *Les Vengeurs,* which was published in Paris in 1968, before Bauer's death, and from the U.S. edition, *The Avengers*. There was no German translation. For Bar-Zohar's interview with the Associated Press, see "Did Clue from Frankfurt Lead to Finding Eichmann?" *Frankfurter Rundschau,* February 12, 1969. For the reception outside Israel, see the review "New Story About the Hunt for Eichmann," *Neue Zürcher Zeitung,* February 19, 1969.

4. Isser Harel, *The House on Garibaldi Street: The Capture of Adolf Eichmann*

(London, 1975). From the 1997 English edition, the book has (largely) been published with a key to most of the aliases.

5. Lothar Hermann to Tuviah Friedman, June 2, 1971, in Tuviah Friedman, *Die Ergreifung Eichmanns: Dokumentarische Sammlung* (Haifa, 1971).

6. Carl Schmitt and Hans Dietrich Sander, *Werkstatt—Discorsi: Briefwechsel 1967–1981* (Schnellroda, 2008), p. 247.

7. Aharoni analyzes in detail, among other things, the invented dialogues between Malkin and Eichmann that Harel presents as historically verifiable facts, although everyone involved knew that Malkin and Eichmann didn't have a common language. Zvi Aharoni and Wilhelm Dietl, *Operation Eichmann: The Truth About the Pursuit, Capture, and Trial,* trans. Helmut Bögler (New York, 1997), p. 142.

8. At the press conference for his docudrama *Eichmanns Ende* in 2010, Raymond Ley reported that in spite of his illness, Klaus Eichmann had recognized Lothar Hermann's daughter in a photo and reacted positively to the memory of a girlfriend from his youth. Unfortunately, no other statements by the Eichmann family are known. It is difficult to imagine that someone would still think well of a friend if he regarded her as having betrayed his father.

9. Klaus Eichmann was born in Berlin, in 1936; Silvia Hermann in Buenos Aires, in 1941.

10. Thanks to Natasja de Winter, Buenos Aires, for her excellent research on the biographical dates and living conditions of the Hermann family. Particular thanks to Raymond Ley, Jasmin Gravenhorst (docstation, Hamburg), and Patricia Schlesinger (NDR), not only for using an academic adviser on the scripts for the docudrama *Eichmanns Ende,* but also for granting her access to their research findings.

11. Hermann to Friedman, June 2, 1971, which also contains some biographical information.

12. Hermann is in the database of Dachau inmates. Thanks to Dirk Riedel from the memorial site for the detailed information. After this point, Hermann's claims basically tally with information from the available documents.

13. Even people who claim to have owned this photo have not been able to find it.

14. Hermann to Bauer, after Eichmann had been abducted, June 25, 1960.

15. This date is sometimes given as August 27, 1957. Hermann himself only mentioned a letter from the year 1957. The original letter has not been found. According to Wojak, Fritz Bauer gave it to Felix Shinnar. Irmtrud Wojak, *Fritz Bauer: 1903–1968: Eine Biographie* (Munich, 2009), p. 286. This is problematic, as Bauer (also according to Wojak) did not initially reveal the name of his informant, and Hermann used headed writing paper for all the other letters that have been preserved. The "document" in Dan Setton's film "The Hunt for Adolf Eichmann" is certainly not the original, as it contains a factual error: "Hermann" describes himself as a "half Jew" in this letter. But according to Nazi criteria, Hermann was a "full Jew" and was also aware of it, as later letters show.

16. Documents on press affair, Arnold Buchthal Estate, Institut für Stadtgeschichte, Frankfurt am Main, S1/138. See also "The Man Has to Go," *Spiegel*, October 16, 1957.

17. According to Wojak, *Fritz Bauer*: HHStA Wiesbaden 461, 32 440, File 2.

18. July 1, 1957, quoted in Heinz Schneppen, *Odessa und das Vierte Reich: Mythen der Zeitgeschichte* (Berlin, 2007), p. 162. Unfortunately Schneppen does not always cite sources to academic standards, but his access to collections of files is doubtless excellent.

19. As Eichmann reported in "Meine Flucht," p. 28, BA Koblenz, All. Proz. 6/247. He also accuses himself there of having become too careless, on the basis of this kind of information.

20. Based on "Terrorism and Concentration Camps on the Nile," *Allgemeine Wochenzeitung der Juden,* July 12, 1957; see also "Cairo, SS Rendezvous Point," *Frankfurter Illustrierte,* August 17, 1957.

21. Kai Jensen, "Cairo, SS Rendezvous Point—a Canard!" also appeared in *Die Brücke, Auslandsdienst,* no. 18, year 4 (1957), pp. 6–8. The article is a surprisingly pedantic refutation of all possible rumors, using details obviously designed to distract readers from the National Socialists who actually were in the Middle East.

22. NA, RG 263, CIA Name File Adolf Eichmann.

23. Isser Harel dated the meeting as November 6, 1957; Irmtrud Wojak dated it November 7, 1957, in *Fritz Bauer,* p. 295.

24. See Hanna Yablonka, *The State of Israel vs. Adolf Eichmann* (New York, 2004), p. 15.

25. Dieter Schenk, *Auf dem rechten Auge blind: Die braunen Wurzeln des BKA* (Cologne, 2001), p. 302.

26. Lothar Hermann's second wife said in an interview in 2009 that after her husband's death, she had sent all his papers to Germany so they could be kept in an archive. Unfortunately, the old lady didn't remember who the mail sack had been addressed to—just that she never received a reply.

27. Hermann to Bauer, June 25, 1960.

28. Wojak, *Eichmanns Memoiren,* p. 30.

29. At least, this is the story told in the Eichmann family to this day. Thanks to Helmut Eichmann for this detail.

30. Mertig was a former NSDAP member. See Uki Goñi, *The Real Odessa: How Perón Brought the Nazi War Criminals to Argentina,* rev. ed. (London, 2003), p. 289, and Holger Meding, *Flucht vor Nürnberg? Deutsche und österreichische Einwanderung in Argentinien 1945–1955* (Cologne, 1992), p. 162. Eichmann himself dated the start of his work for Mertig to January 31, 1958: application to Mercedes-Benz, facsimile in Schneppen, *Odessa,* pp. 160ff.

31. The records-office card file on Eberhard Fritsch, born on November 21, 1921, in Buenos Aires, begins with his residency application of March 6, 1958. His occupation is given as "publisher, hotel porter." Thanks to Peter F. Kramml from the Salzburg City Archive for his help.

32. The issue is labeled as issue 12, 1957, but it contains a reference to March 1958. The publication of *Der Weg* was not as regular as the issue numbers would have us believe.

33. François Genoud turned to Eichmann's family immediately after his trial was announced, with his typical combination of good business sense and responsibility for comrades in need. He wanted to purchase the rights to Eichmann's story and finance his defense. He found Fritsch with the Linz Eichmanns, when he arrived there a few days after Ben-Gurion's Knesset speech. François Genoud, interviewed in Pierre Péan, *L'extrémiste: François Genoud, de Hitler á Carlos* (Paris, 1996), p. 257.

34. Thanks to Anne-Marie Sana and Jürgen Klöckner from the Konstanz City Archive for the precise information. Unfortunately the copies of the declarations and documents no longer exist. Sassen gave his new address in Munich as Hohenstaufenstraße 12.

35. Inge Schneider said that Miep Sassen's determined stance was to her own disadvantage: without German identity papers she wasn't allowed to work in Germany, although in the summer Inge Schneider had offered her the opportunity to stay with her in Bremen.

36. The history of the Argentina Papers speaks against any contact between Sassen and the BND. The BND evidently didn't obtain its copy of the Sassen transcripts from Sassen himself. See "Aftermath" in this book.

37. Saskia and Francisca Sassen, correspondence with the author (2009); Gerd Heidemann, conversation with the author (2009) about his visit to Sassen in 1979. The BfV files on Sassen and Rudel have not yet been made public. Both of them must contain these notes, as Sassen visited Rudel. Thanks to the BfV for its extremely brief but helpful information. In the case of BVerwG 7A 15.10, *Saure vs. BND,* the files presented don't black out Sassen's reference to the Gehlen Organization and "General G," which suggests that this was just idle talk from Sassen. The question of what documents about Sassen from 1959 are doing in the Eichmann file with documents before 1960 is more difficult to answer. See supplementary file on the above case, BND files 100 470, pp. 9–13.

38. Tape 67, BA tape 10B, 1:03:30.

39. Klaus Eichmann, interview in *Quick,* January 2, 1966.

40. Eckart Conze, Norbert Frei, Peter Hayes, and Moshe Zimmermann, *Das Amt und die Vergangenheit: Deutsche Diplomaten im Dritten Reich und in der Bundesrepublik* (Munich, 2010), p. 608, cited hereafter as *Das Amt.*

41. Fritsch's claims about being denied entry cannot be verified. The Bavarian Ministry of the Interior no longer holds files on these sorts of occurrences, as the file retention period has elapsed for these dates. (The Bavarian border police were responsible for the control of the West German border.) Letter from December 27, 2010. The BfV could confirm only that there was a file on Fritsch. Fritsch's heroic version of the story was given in his obituary in the *Deutsche Annalen,* published by Druffel Verlag. For this right-leaning

publisher, Fritsch counted as one of the "Great Germans." "German Farewells 1974," *Deutsche Annalen, Jahrbuch des Nationalgeschehens*, year 4 (Leoni am Starnberger See, 1975), unpaginated.

42. Eichmann trial, 2JS178/56. According to the letters that Fritsch wrote to Robert Servatius, he had exhausted all the legal means to try and get the Lüneberg District Court's decision reversed, and his appeal against the refusal of his application for a revision finally failed with the Federal Court in Karlsruhe. BA Koblenz, All. Proz. 6. The correspondence is divided between the 253 collections and section 4.

43. When I told Uki Goñi about Eichmann's contacts in Plata del Mar, he was completely taken aback, not having imagined that Eichmann could ever have afforded a trip to this expensive spot. Eichmann mentioned friends and accommodation here gratefully in his letters from prison.

44. Eichmann to Avner W. Less, the interrogating officer, June 1, 1960, Avner Less Estate, Archiv für Zeitgeschichte, ETH Zurich, NL Less, 4.2.3.2.

45. Strictly speaking, we also know little about Müller's biography in the previous period. Most of what has been said rests on claims by Eichmann—unfortunately not always cited as such—which are notoriously unreliable. A glance at the sources for Andreas Seeger, *"Gestapo Müller": Die Karriere eines Schreibtischtäters* (Berlin, 1996), clearly shows how much this biography relied on Eichmann.

46. Report, March 19, 1958, NA, RG 263, CIA Name File Adolf Eichmann: "Adolf Eichmann (201-047132) was born in Israel and became an SS-Obersturmbannfuehrer. He is reported to have lived in Argentina under the alias CLEMENS since 1952. One rumor has it that despite the fact that he was responsible for mass extermination of Jews, he now lives in Jerusalem."

47. Thanks to the BfV for allowing me to read and quote the following pieces of writing from the Eichmann file. For the files submitted in the case BVerwG 7A 15.10, *Saure vs. BND*, see "Aftermath" in this book.

48. BfV to Foreign Office, "Re: Karl Eichmann, Argentina. Connection: none," April 11, 1958, VS-Confidential (downgraded in April 1971 to VS–Official Use Only).

49. In this regard, the rumors are myriad. For example, Ludolf von Alvensleben is supposed to have lived in a house in Córdoba owned by Fritsch. It was not possible to check.

50. At least the files in question from the BfV have been classified "archivable," which gives us the joyous news that they will be given over to the Bundesarchiv over the coming years. It is, however, impossible to know when that will be. Still, I must thank the BfV for taking the trouble to answer my questions. BfV to the author, December 3 and 20, 2010.

51. Michael Frank, *Die letzte Bastion: Nazis in Argentinien* (Hamburg, 1962), p. 108.

52. Foreign Office, July 27, 1960, quoted in Schneppen, *Odessa*, p. 164.

53. Ibid., p. 163.

54. Foreign Office to BfV, July 4, 1958, ibid. Thanks to BfV for a copy.

55. West German embassy in Buenos Aires to the Foreign Office, August 11, 1954, under 212, no. 2116/54. The Foreign Office passed the information on to the BfV on August 25, 1954 (306212-02/5.20973/54). Quoted at length in the draft replies of August 21, 1958; see note 56 below for details of these drafts.

56. The two available drafts of the BfV's reply to the Foreign Office allow us to reconstruct the decision-making process. The first draft contains a request to report any further discoveries in the Eichmann matter to Cologne. This is crossed out by hand. The second draft contains no reference to this apart from the subject heading. BfV to Foreign Office, draft with handwritten corrections and additions, VS-Confidential (downgraded to VS–Official Use Only in April 1974) and draft with censored date, but with a revision date of August 21, 1958 (VS-Confidential). It isn't clear whether the letter, which also contained a few remarks on the case of Franz Rademacher, was sent in this form.

57. Schneppen, *Odessa,* p. 136.

58. The source editions are edited by the Institute for Contemporary History in Munich. We can only hope that the gap in the years 1954–61 will now be immediately closed. The recent volumes on 1962 were taken into account for this book, which, because of the selection of documents they contain, was unfortunately a quick and easy process.

59. Mohr and his predecessor, Werner Junker, who was ambassador in Buenos Aires until 1963, knew each other well. They had met in 1936, when they were working in the embassy in Nanking. For information on their lives, with a few gaps, and certain things downplayed, see *Biographisches Handbuch des deutschen Auswärtigen Dienstes 1871–1945* (Paderborn, 2005), vols. 2 and 3.

60. "Götzen," p. 360; p. 40; the letter from Mohr to the RSHA, February 26, 1941, was a prosecution document.

61. Hubert Krier, interview by Dan Setton in *Josef Mengele: The Final Account* (SET Productions, 2007).

62. Answers to questionnaire for *Paris Match*, May 1962, BA Koblenz, All. Proz. 6/252.

63. Eichmann's note in Israel: "Vorgeschichte der Entführung," BA Koblenz, All. Proz. 6/253.

64. Vera Eichmann, interview in *Paris Match*, April 29, 1962; commentary and explanation to the publisher Dr. Sudholt, according to information given by Dr. Sudholt in 2009, and the sworn statement from Vera Eichmann published in Druffel Verlag's 1980 edition of the Argentina Papers: *Ich, Adolf Eichmann.* See also "Aftermath" in this book.

65. Klaus Eichmann, interview in *Quick*, January 2, 1966.

66. For example, Miguel Serrano, *Das goldene Band* (Wetten, 1987). The legend of Hitler's survival in an eternal block of ice is, as a simple Internet search shows, still around today, although in the age of artificial insemination and cloning, the modern variation is slowly softening to say that Hitler deposited only his "genetic material," so that he could be born again.

67. Unidentifiable staff member to Hanns Martin Schleyer, May 30, 1960, quoted in Gaby Weber, *Daimler-Benz und die Argentinien-Connection* (Berlin and Hamburg, 2004), p. 91.

68. Immediately after the press reported Eichmann's abduction, Mengele noted: "Now you see, I was right."

69. "Not a Templar After All: Eichmann's Birthplace: Solingen, not Sarona," *Die Zeit*, September 11, 1959. The article is a correction to the Israel report by Gerhard F. Kramer, who wrote for the magazine as the former attorney general of Hamburg.

70. Principally Weber, *Daimler-Benz*, pp. 87–95. For a facsimile of the application and the personnel record, see Schneppen, *Odessa*, p. 160. Fuldner made no secret of the favor and mentioned it in his statement to the police following Eichmann's abduction. The information is also in the report from the German embassy, Argentina, to the Foreign Office.

71. Unidentifiable staff member to Hanns Martin Schleyer, May 30, 1960, quoted in Weber, *Daimler-Benz*, p. 91. Weber questions the authenticity of the letter. The content, however, fits perfectly with the other pieces of writing we have from Eichmann's helpers, as they attempted to justify themselves.

72. The contributions to be found in the literature so far rest on incorrect exchange rates and frequently confuse dollars and Deutschmarks. The average gross monthly salary is generally given as around 600 Deutschmarks for men. Thanks to the staff of the German Bundesbank for their help in providing this information. The fact that this exchange rate corresponded to what was actually paid can be traced in Dürer Verlag's statements of fees paid to its German authors. See Fritsch correspondence.

73. Facsimile in Weber, *Daimler-Benz*, unpaginated appendix. For the period April 8 to June 30, 1959, Ricardo Klement received 15,216.60 pesos.

74. David Filc, interview by Gaby Weber (2000), in Weber, *Daimler-Benz*, p. 91.

75. Eichmann to Nebe, October 16, 1939, DÖW. File 17 072/a. Nebe had asked whether they might take the opportunity of the transports to Nisko to also transport "the Berlin gypsies," and Eichmann suggested adding "3 to 4 cars of gypsies" to the trains.

76. Sassen transcripts 13:7.

77. Simon Wiesenthal, *Ich jagte Eichmann* (Gütersloh, 1961), p. 239.

78. Hermann Langbein Estate, ÖStA, E/1797. Evidence, documents, and commentaries on this campaign can be found in several folders and boxes. See, for example, Folder 106, correspondence with Ormond at the start of 1959; the green correspondence folder with Germany (20:21—press; 23:24—justice).

79. BfV to Foreign Office, June 9, 1960 (II/a2-051-P-20364-5a/60). Thanks to the BfV for permission to quote.

80. Paul Dickopf's friends included the famous/infamous Hitler fan François Genoud, with whom he maintained a close relationship after their work for the SS and the Nazi regime. Genoud then helped to finance Eichmann's defense from 1960. See "Aftermath" in this book.

81. Two former colleagues of Fritz Bauer, who prefer not to be named, conversation with the author.

82. Annette Weinke, *Eine deutsch-deutsche Beziehungsgeschichte im Kalten Krieg* (Paderborn, Munich, Zurich, and Vienna, 2002), pp. 151–57.

83. F. J. P. Veale, "Eichmann's Abduction—Coincidence or Staged?" *Nation Europa* 11, no. 1 (1961), pp. 73–78, esp. p. 73.

84. Bauer wrote to Sassen in 1962 with a plea for background information, and nothing in Sassen's reply suggests that they had been in prior contact. Willem Sassen, Comodoro Rivadavia, to Attorney General Bauer, Frankfurt am Main, July 16, 1962, cited in Wojak, *Eichmanns Memoiren,* pp. 48 and 218. Unfortunately the source given there is incorrect (Landesarchiv Berlin, no. 76, BRep 057-01), as the staff there assured me. Nor was it possible to find the letter in any of the other likely archives (Hessisches Hauptstaatsarchiv Wiesbaden, Fritz Bauer Archiv Frankfurt, Archiv der Sozialen Demokratie Bonn).

85. Interview in *Fritz Bauer—Tod auf Raten* (Ilona Ziok, 2010).

86. The search turned up fourteen SS men with this name.

87. Wolfgang Rabus to author, December 7, 2010, which in spite of its banal content was cc'd to four other people in the firm.

88. Thomas Harlan to author, 2010; and the film *Fritz Bauer—Tod auf Raten* (Ilona Ziok, 2010).

89. Also mentioned in Quentin Reynolds, Ephraim Katz, and Zwy Aldouby, *Minister of Death: The Adolf Eichmann Story* (New York, 1960), p. 206.

90. For information on this site of horror, see Jules Schelvis, *Vernichtungslager Sobibór* (Berlin, 1998); Thomas "Tovi" Blatt, *Sobibór—der vergessene Aufstand* (Hamburg and Münster, 2004).

91. In 1967 Szmajzner also sold this business and became the director of a paper-recycling firm in Goiania. He died in 1989. See Schelvis, *Vernichtungslager,* pp. 291, 314, and 220 (photo); Richard Lashke, *Flucht aus Sobibór, Roman* (Gerlingen, 1998), appendix of source material, p. 436.

92. Or rather *Inferno em Sobibór—A tragédia de um adolescente judeu* (Rio de Janeiro, 1968). The work has not yet been translated.

93. Gustav Franz Stangl, the former commandant of Sobibór, confirmed this himself in 1969; quoted in Schelvis, *Vernichtungslager.*

94. Simon Wiesenthal recounted several versions of his search for Stangl, which Tom Segev reconstructed. Segev suspects that Wiesenthal did not give the real information but obviously found no reference to Szmajzner, just a conspicuous hole in the archive. Tom Segev, *Simon Wiesenthal: The Life and Legends* (New York, 2010), pp. 208–9. Szmajzner spoke of his memories of Stangl later, in conversations with other Sobibór survivors. There are photos of the encounter with Wagner where he identified him. See also Simon Wiesenthal, *Justice Not Vengeance: Recollections* (New York, 1990).

95. Jules Schelvis conducted long interviews with Szmajzner for his book on Sobibór; Schelvis, *Vernichtungslager,* p. 314. The journalist Mario Chimanovich,

who acted on Wiesenthal's behalf in Brazil, was convinced that Wagner was murdered. Tom Segev, interview by Mario Chimanovich, October 29, 2008; see also Segev, *Simon Wiesenthal*, p. 209. Even the police photos contradict the story that Wagner hanged himself.

96. This article appeared in almost all the newspapers the following day, including the *Argentinisches Tageblatt*. Quoted here from the *Schwäbische Albzeitung*, December 24, 1959.

97. Segev, *Simon Wiesenthal*, p. 177.

98. Heinz Weibel-Altmeyer, "Hunt for Eichmann," *Neue Illustrierte*, June 11–July 8, 1960, a five-part series.

99. BfV to Foreign Office, June 9, 1960 (II/a2-051-P-20364-5a/60). Thanks to the BfV for permission to quote from this document.

100. BfV to Foreign Office, June 9, 1960 (II/a2-051-P-20364-5a/60).

101. Langbein to the Federation of German Industry, February 12, 1960; the Federation to the Comité International d'Auschwitz, April 26, 1960. Both letters are in Langbein Estate, ÖStA, E/1797-25, green correspondence folder, Germany A-C.

102. As with all operations of this sort, Langbein first asked the Frankfurt prosecutor Henry Ormond whether he would be causing any damage with this letter. Evidence in correspondence folder Ormond, Langbein Estate, ÖStA. For the connections among Ormond, Langbein, and Bauer, see "Aftermath" in this book.

103. BfV to Foreign Office, June 9, 1960 (II/a2-051-P-20364-5a/60).

104. Erwin Schüle to Tuviah Friedman, August 20, 1959, in Tuviah Friedman, ed., *Die "Ergreifung Eichmanns": Dokumentarische Sammlung* (Haifa, 1971).

105. "Israel and the Eichmann Case," *Argentinisches Tageblatt*, October 16, 1959.

106. Some facsimiles of press articles are in Tuviah Friedman, *We Shall Never Forget* (Haifa, undated). Investigating authorities faced an increasing number of issues caused by Friedman acting on his own authority; see the 1970s correspondence between Simon Wiesenthal and the Central Office in BA Ludwigsburg. See also the report by Dietrich Zeug to Ludwigsburg in 1961, both in BA Ludwigsburg, Central Office collection.

107. On Bauer's fabricated statements to the press, and the position taken by the British foreign minister on October 13, 1959. The campaign continued until well into 1960. Evidence appears even in the smaller newspapers; for this account, the *Frankfurter Allgemeine Zeitung*, *Frankfurter Neue Presse*, *The Times*, *Die TAT*, *Schwäbische Albzeitung*, *Weltwoche*, *Deutsche Woche*, and *Neues Österreich* were checked.

108. *Deutsche Woche*, January 27, 1960.

109. Federal Ministry of Justice to the Foreign Office, December 16, 1959, quoted in Schneppen, *Odessa*, p. 163. Schneppen does not give an archive reference but usually consults the Foreign Office's Political Archive.

110. Anyone thinking this is malicious is recommended to spend a few hours with

Adolf von Thadden's estate. The shelves of Thadden's correspondence, comprising thousands of letters, contain reams of genuinely malicious gossip and rumor. Sassen wrote at least one article for Thadden (*Reichsruf*, October 29, 1955). Thadden even denounced Sassen in public. See "Aftermath" in this book for a review of the Druffel publication.

111. BfV to Foreign Office, June 9, 1960 (II/a2-051-P-20364-5a/60).

112. "Neo-Nazi Leader 'Was MI6 Agent,'" *Guardian,* August 13, 2002. Thadden thoroughly cleansed his estate of all evidence that he might have spied for the British.

113. Klaus Eichmann, interview in *Quick,* January 2, 1966.

114. Hermann's correspondence with Tuviah Friedman. Tuviah Friedman, *Die Ergreifung Eichmanns: Dokumentarische Sammlung* (Haifa, 1971).

115. BA Ludwigsburg, Central Office collection, III 24/28.

116. Friedman to Hermann, April 27, 1971, talking about Arie Tartakower. Friedman, *Die Ergreifung Eichmanns.*

117. Hermann to Friedman, March 28, 1960, ibid.

118. Friedman apologized to Hermann in his letters from 1971.

119. For the decision, see Hanna Yablonka's excellent book *The State of Israel vs. Adolf Eichmann* (New York, 2004).

120. Ibid., p. 15; Segev, *Simon Wiesenthal,* p. 141.

121. Interestingly, I also found a copy in Langbein Estate, ÖStA, Eichmann press folder.

122. A photo of them as children shows how similar the brothers were, even then.

123. See also Segev, *Simon Wiesenthal,* p. 143.

124. Aharoni did not say which assignment he had been on in March 1959.

125. "Meine Flucht," p. 26, BA Koblenz, All. Proz. 6/247.

126. "Vorgeschichte der Entführung" (Background to the Abduction), dated November 7, 1961, and the lengthy "Verhaftungsbericht" (Arrest Report), undated but written before the start of the trial, BA Koblenz, All. Proz. 6/253. The content tallies with Eichmann's "Meine Flucht" (March 1961), BA Koblenz, All. Proz. 6/247

127. The theories that Eichmann willingly left Argentina, traveling to Israel via various other places—or that Argentina extradited him—still exist. But the only possible reason for anybody continuing to subscribe to them today would be some evidence that Eichmann was forced to lie in both his written testimonies, and his statements in court. There is no sort of evidence for it. Based on a thorough investigation of the sources, ideas that Eichmann consented to go to Israel, and scenarios other than that of an abduction, simply don't stand up.

128. Klaus Eichmann, interview in *Quick,* January 2, 1966; Vera Eichmann recounted this dream in her interview in *Paris Match,* April 29, 1962.

129. "Vorgeschichte der Entführung," November 7, 1961, BA Koblenz, All. Proz. 6/253; "Meine Flucht," p. 28.

130. Eichmann's own reports also give detailed information, backed up by the other accounts from the people involved.

131. Inge Schneider confirmed this point. She was living in Europe, and Miep Sassen came to stay with her. Inge Schneider, interview by Roelf van Til (2005).

132. Vera Eichmann, interview in *Paris Match*, April 29, 1962; Fuldner's very understated statement to the Argentine police; Klaus Eichmann, interview in *Quick*.

133. Klaus Eichmann, interview in *Quick*; Mohn to Servatius, Servatius Report, BA Koblenz, All. Proz. 6/253.

134. Klaus Eichmann and his family initially stayed in their own apartment, then disappeared from the press's gaze for a while. After May 23, 1960, the press started looking for traces of Eichmann in Buenos Aires. A warning to Israel soon appeared in newspapers from *Nation Europa* to *Der Spiegel*: it would damage the reputation of "the Jews" if they had laid hands on Eichmann's family as well.

135. As it later emerged, Werner Junker, then the ambassador in Buenos Aires, had frequently withheld information from his employer, Heinrich von Brentano.

136. José Moskovits, interview by Raymond Ley (2009). Herr Moskovits speaks a broken but comprehensible German. The content of his words cannot be misunderstood. When probed further, he remained absolutely sure about these dates.

137. Segev, *Simon Wiesenthal*, pp. 333–34.

138. Everyone involved confirms this fact. Moskovits, in his 2009 interview by Raymond Ley, mentions the help he provided: he even made it possible for Aharoni to visit the embassy incognito. Tom Segev found an extensive correspondence between Wiesenthal and Moskovits in Wiesenthal's private papers. Zvi Aharoni mentions Moskovits as a helper from the start, even if he only names him later on. Moskovits helped Aharoni get hold of information and arranged the inconspicuous rental of an apartment and cars for the Mossad team. Even Isser Harel alludes to a Hungarian in Buenos Aires, with good police contacts, who had been Aharoni's point of contact. Isser Harel, *The House on Garibaldi Street* (1997), p. 35. Moskovits's and Aharoni's cover names are not explained.

139. Moskovits's, Aharoni's, and Harel's accounts do not contradict here, either.

140. See the federal government publication *Die antisemitischen und nazistischen Vorfälle: Weißbuch und Erklärung der Bundesregierung* (Bonn, 1960), p. 36.

141. *Spiegel*, June 15, 1960.

142. From the Federal Chancellery Office's explanation of why the BND's Eichmann files cannot be released, even in 2010 (p. 3). See "Aftermath" in this book for more details.

143. Rolf Vogel to Günther Diehl, August 30, 1960, cited in Raphael Gross, *Anständig geblieben: Nationalsozialistische Moral* (Frankfurt am Main, 2010), p. 197. Institute for Contemporary History, Munich, B145, 1132.

144. Werner Junker's report on Sassen, November 29, 1960, PA AA, B83, vol. 55; Brentano to Janz, December 1, 1960, quoted in *Das Amt*, p. 608. There too one can find detailed reactions from the Foreign Office to Eichmann's abduction—although clearly very little was found during the research on the files covering the Nazi community in Argentina in the 1950s.

145. Ambassador Werner Junker to the Foreign Office, December 13, 1962, published as document 483 in *Akten zur Auswärtigen Politik der Bundesrepublik Deutschland: 1962* (Munich, 2010), pp. 2060–61.
146. See Irmtrud Wojak, *Fritz Bauer: 1903–1968: Eine Biographie* (Munich, 2009).
147. For the CIA, see Richard Breitman, ed., *U.S. Intelligence and the Nazis* (Washington, D.C., 2004).
148. *Das Amt*, p. 609.
149. Ibid., pp. 600ff.
150. This double bookkeeping can be clearly seen in Servatius's papers in BA Koblenz, which contain detailed financial statements. For the financing of Eichmann's defense, see "Aftermath" in this book.
151. Quoted from the strictly confidential memo to ministers in *Das Amt*, p. 614.
152. Adenauer to Ben-Gurion, January 22, 1962; published as document 37 in *Akten zur Auswärtigen Politik der Bundesrepublik Deutschland: 1962* (Munich, 2010), pp. 206–7.
153. The events up to the end of 1960 are documented in the supplementary file to case BVerwG 7A 15.10, *Saure vs. BND*, BND files 121 099, 1664: letter of June 3, 1960 "on Foreign Office inquiry" and 1784: August 11, 1960. Thanks to Christoph Partsch for permission to cite these.
154. Members of the family publicly distanced themselves from the notice. See Philipp Trafojer, "Die Spuren eines Mörders. Alois Schintlholzer (1914–1989)," editorial in the Austrian journal *Vinschgerwind* (September 8, 2005).
155. "Eichmann's Route Went via the Vatican," in the Austrian newspaper *Volkswille,* July 23, 1960, which, in comparison to other articles from the time, is extraordinarily well informed.
156. Argentine state police, report on Eichmann's abduction, June 9, 1960, Archivo General de la Nacíon (AGN), DAE, Bormann file, pp. 77–79, quoted in Uki Goñi, *The Real Odessa: How Perón Brought the Nazi War Criminals to Argentina,* rev. ed. (London, 2003), p. 315n543.
157. *Kurier,* May 31, 1960, and others.
158. See Timothy Naftali, "The CIA and Eichmann's Associates," pp. 341–43. On Mildenstein's activities in Egypt, see the CIA report from Cairo, "Combined Allied-Israeli Invasion of Egypt," January 3, 1957, NA, RG 263, CIA Name File Leopold von Mildenstein.
159. A threat to avenge Eichmann and kill Fritz Bauer—the only one that I know of—is in the notorious "ODESSA protocol" from the private archive of Friedrich Schwend. This peculiar piece of work is allegedly the report from a meeting of an SS secret society in Spain in June 1965. (The date was unclear for a long time.) The "protocol" contains a call to murder Fritz Bauer. As Schwend was a professional counterfeiter, it cannot be determined whether this was a counterfeit or the transcript of an overly ambitious men's drinking session. HIS, Archive, Schwend papers.
160. Report from March 3, 1961, NA, RG 263, CIA Name File Adolf Eichmann. Otto Skorzeny himself may have been the source of this report. The story of

the assassination plans probably goes back directly to East German propaganda: on May 29, 1960, the *Berliner Zeitung* reported, under the headline "Eichmann—a Middleman for Bonn Companies in Kuwait," that the BND head Gehlen had personally ordered Eichmann to be liquidated, to protect West German Nazis.

161. Ulrich Völklein, *Josef Mengele: Der Arzt von Auschwitz* (Göttingen, 2003), p. 270.

162. The article in the *Frankfurter Allgemeine Zeitung* by its correspondent "Nikolaus Ehlert" in Argentina clearly rested on information from Wilfred von Oven and Horst Carlos Fuldner.

163. See also Friedrich Paul Heller and Anton Maegerle, *Thule: Vom völkischen Okkultismus bis zur Neuen Rechten* (Stuttgart, 1995), p. 93.

164. Buenos Aires police report, cited in Goñi, *Real Odessa*, p. 315.

165. "Eichmann, alias Klement. Jodenvervolger in zwaar verhoor," *Volkskrant*, June 8, 1960.

166. Saskia Sassen is still convinced that her father couldn't stand Eichmann. But his sympathetic texts on Eichmann, and his later efforts to support his defense, tell a different story. Sassen referred to his Americanized nickname in an interview with *La Razón*.

167. "The Manager of the 'Final Solution,'" *Widerstandskämpfer* (Austria), May–June 1960; "Eichmann: Manager of Mass Murder," *Arbeiterzeitung*, May 25, 1960.

168. "The Crime Has No Fatherland. The Eichmann Trial Throws Its Shadow Ahead," in *Der Heimkehrer,* year 12 (Göppingen, 1961), p. 6:1.

169. "Preview of a Show Trial," *Nation Europa* 11, no. 4 (1961), pp. 37–41, here p. 41.

170. A facsimile of this diary entry from June 7, 1962, is in Schneppen, *Odessa,* p. 155, citing the HHStA as the source. An inquiry, however, revealed that although this archive has a few of Mengele's diaries, it does not have this one. Also cited in Völklein, *Mengele,* p. 270.

171. Eichmann to his family, April 17, 1961, p. 6, BA Koblenz, All. Proz. 6/165.

172. Mengele, diary entry, June 1, 1962, immediately after hearing news of the execution; quoted in Völklein, *Mengele,* p. 270.

173. Eichmann really wrote "create a judgment." He didn't understand that natural rights exist independently of any particular period, because there is a general, human idea of "right," according to which he would never be absolved.

A Change of Role

1. Transfer declaration, prosecution document T/3.

2. Avner W. Less, Avner Less Estate, Archive für Zeitgeschichte, ETH Zurich, NL Less, 4.2.3.2.

3. Avner W. Less, interview with *Gespräch in 3,* Avner Less Estate, Zurich, NL Less, tape 7.1 X.

4. Avner W. Less, interview for the documentary *Erscheinungsform Mensch: Adolf Eichmann* (Hamburg, 1978–79), cassette in Avner Less Estate, 7.1 IX.

5. "Meine Flucht," p. 39, BA Koblenz, All. Proz. 6/247.

6. This tale, which Eichmann polished again in Israel, was one of his most successful fabrications. As he explained several times in Argentina, he had the job of censoring the transcript in accordance with the "language rules," before it was sent to the ministries. Heydrich introduced Eichmann to the conference as the point of contact for everyone involved, and afterward everyone present treated him this way. Why anyone ever believed that Eichmann could have been in charge of transcribing the conference is a mystery, particularly as he lacked the training for it. Eichmann was the one directing the real transcriber. The quote is from "Auch hier im Ansicht des Galgens," BA Koblenz, All. Proz. 6/193, p. 16.

7. Answers to questionnaire for *Paris Match*, May 1962, BA Koblenz, All. Proz. 6/252.

8. "Auch hier im Ansicht des Galgens," BA Koblenz, All. Proz. 6/193, p. 22.

9. Particularly overpowering in his text "Mein Sein und Tun," BA Koblenz, All. Proz. 6/253, p. 8.

10. "The Foundations of Bureaucracy" in *Das Schwarze Korps* (the official SS newspaper), June 12, 1941, develops an impressive image of a new bureaucracy according to SS ideas.

11. See the early documentary *Erscheinungsform Mensch: Adolf Eichmann* (Hamburg, 1978–79), as well as notes and further interviews by all those named.

12. This is also the case with many of the photos in David Cesarani, *Eichmann: His Life and Crimes* (London, 2005). Eichmann's face is so asymmetrical that it is easy to spot a reversal; the uniform also provides a clear orientation.

Aftermath

1. Raul Hilberg, *Sources of Holocaust Research: An Analysis* (Chicago, 2001), p. 160.

2. According to a letter from Mohn, a former Luftwaffe officer, to Eichmann's lawyer, Robert Servatius, who was looking for the Argentina Papers, Sassen and Klaus Eichmann appeared in his office at Mercedes-Benz on May 12. Servatius Report, "Re: copyright ADOLF EICHMANN, publication LIFE, USA," BA Koblenz, All. Proz. 6/253, pp. 10-17 (hereafter cited as Servatius Report).

3. Inge Schneider, interview by Roelf van Til.

4. "Meine Flucht," p. 31, BA Koblenz, All. Proz. 6/247.

5. Quotes from Eichmann's handwritten texts in press and literature can therefore be used only with caution. The hasty transcriptions made from 1960 to 1979 are thoroughly unreliable. Anyone getting horribly tangled up in Eichmann's handwriting is welcome to contact me, however, as transcriptions of

most of the handwritten texts were produced in the course of this research. The tapes, by contrast, were transcribed immediately after the recordings were made in 1957. Eichmann's handwritten corrections can be found even on the last transcript of tape 73 (pp. 2, 3, 6, 7 and 8).

6. Sassen's daughter remembers the long nights during which the texts were typed onto fanfold paper, which had to be neatly cut up by the family. You can still see these cut edges on the originals.

7. Knowledge of the history of copier technology is very important for the evaluation of individual items in the Argentina Papers. During the years of the Eichmann trial, the conversion to Xerox machines was being made. The copier familiar to us today, which allows us to make dry copies on normal paper, came onto the market only at the start of 1960 and gradually took over in private and public offices thereafter. Sassen, and the Hesse attorney general's office, mainly used photostats, a copier based on camera technology, using photosensitive paper. Reflex copies and Thermofax duplicates were also used in the Eichmann trial.

8. The letters from Sassen to Servatius are held in BA Koblenz, All. Proz. 6/253, here January 13, 1961. Sassen said similar things in early interviews.

9. Even *Der Spiegel* imagined in detail the existence of torture chambers directly beneath Eichmann's cell, in which he would be made to change his mind about any statements the Israelis didn't like. *Der Spiegel,* June 15, 1960.

10. Copy in BA Koblenz, All. Proz. 6/253, pp. 18–19, pp. 70–71, copy sent by Vera Eichmann to her brother-in-law in Linz. According to a letter from Mohn to Servatius, Vera Eichmann felt pressured by her "press adviser." Servatius Report.

11. Utopian sums are also sometimes named. Sassen wasn't particularly skilled in business matters, and in his great haste to conclude the sale of the Eichmann papers, alone and without aid, he made crucial mistakes. His lack of experience cost him the copyright to the *Life* articles, which he would have retained if *Life* had actually left the compilation of the texts to him. Servatius was able to find speculations about the sale price between $50,000 and $1.2 million; see Servatius Report, November 26, 1960, BA Koblenz, All. Proz. 6/253, and Servatius to Robert Eichmann, December 5, 1960 BA Koblenz, All. Proz. 6/253.

12. Servatius to Vera Eichmann, November 28, 1960, BA Koblenz, All. Proz. 6/253.

13. Frondizi traveled around Europe from June 14 to July 10, 1960, which was too late for the flight out and too early for the return flight. Sassen did, however, pursue contacts with presidents after Perón. A photo from the national archive shows him with President Arturo Umberto Illia—accompanied by Rudel. Thanks to Uki Goñi.

14. *Stern* published this information itself after a long silence; *Stern,* June 24, 2010.

15. Saskia Sassen has said repeatedly that her father spoke of *Stern, Spiegel,* and *Life.* It has not yet been possible for me to conduct thorough research in this area.

16. Report, December 1, 1960, NA, RG 263, CIA Name File Adolf Eichmann.
17. Robert Pendorf, *Mörder und Ermordete: Eichmann und die Judenpolitik des Dritten Reichs* (Hamburg, 1961), p. 7.
18. According to rumors that I have so far been unable to prove, *Der Spiegel* checked over the material, declined to use it, and sent it "to Munich." Saskia Sassen says that her father claimed he was also a correspondent for *Spiegel*, and a CIA report from a Munich informant on December 1, 1960, talks of Sassen having sold eighty pages to "Spiegel and Stern." NA, RG 263, CIA Name File Adolf Eichmann. Saskia Sassen, interview and correspondence with the author (2009).
19. Servatius researched this contract and spoke of a fee of more than 50,000 Dutch florins (around 50,000 Deutschmarks). This contract could explain why the Dutch filmmaker Roelf van Til found a copy of some Sassen material in Dutch archives. Servatius to Robert Eichmann, BA Koblenz, All. Proz. 6/253, pp. 30–32; Roelf van Til, personal conversation with the author (2004).
20. Interrogation, June 5, 1960, p. 397.
21. Ibid.
22. Servatius Report, November 26, 1960; Servatius to Robert Eichmann, December 5, 1960; both in BA Koblenz, All. Proz. 6/253.
23. Servatius Report and letter both dated November 30, 1960.
24. On François Genoud and Hans Rechenberg, and the details of their involvement with Eichmann, see the impressively well-researched work by Willi Winkler, *Der Schattenmann: Von Goebbels zu Carlos: Das mysteriöse Leben des François Genoud* (Berlin, 2011), esp. chap. 9. A necessarily but less detailed account is Karl Laske, *Ein Leben zwischen Hitler und Carlos: François Genoud* (Zurich, 1996). See also the interview with Genoud in Pierre Péan, *L'Éxtrémiste: François Genoud, de Hitler à Carlos* (Paris, 1996), pp. 257ff. Substantial original interviews appear in the documentary *L'Éxtrémiste de Hitler à Carlos* (Television Suisse Romande, 1996).
25. Servatius was the defense counsel for Fritz Sauckel, and Rechenberg worked on the defense for Walther Funk.
26. Rechenberg and "his friend G." are named as trial financers in the Linz correspondence, and in Servatius's estate there is further clear evidence. BA Koblenz, All. Proz. 6/253, p. 257. Servatius tried in vain to make the German government officially responsible for the trial costs. In the end, the State of Israel paid his fee. The substantial finances raised by Genoud and Rechenberg were never officially declared. The statements in Servatius's estate, however, clearly reveal Rechenberg's role. Rechenberg was also being watched by the CIA; details in NA, RG 263, CIA Name File Hans Rechenberg, but also under Franz Rademacher. The BND file 121 099 also shows that Rechenberg was one of their sources and passed material for the defense on to the BND, who were also kept informed of the activities for financing the trial.
27. Peter Woog, handwritten note, February 24, 1965, ETH Zurich, Archiv für Zeitgeschichte, JUNA archive/567, Peter Woog correspondence.

28. In a meeting on July 25 Eberhard Fritsch promised the defense counsel Servatius his cooperation and provision of all documents, in return for the exploitation rights for Europe. Servatius Report.

29. Servatius Report, November 26, 1960, BA Koblenz, All. Proz. 6/253; correspondence between Robert Servatius and Hans Rechenberg, BA Koblenz, All. Proz. 6/253.

30. Many of the documents so far presented from the Eichmann files are collections of sometimes fantastical fears about what Eichmann might have said. Every page of the Argentina Papers that was released was pored over for names. The work was not so thorough as the evaluation that Fritz Bauer commissioned, but the index of names was entirely usable. Supplementary file, case BVerwG 7A 15.10, *Saure vs. BND,* BND files 121 099, pp. 1–66; 100 470, pp. 181–253.

31. September 13, 1960, NA, RG 263, CIA Name File Adolf Eichmann. Most of this correspondence is missing from the documents so far released from the BND's Eichmann file.

32. CIA report, September 20, 1960.

33. I couldn't find the name while listening to the tapes, or on the pages that *Life* didn't have.

34. The Servatius Report dates the requests from Allen Dulles (CIA) to Henry Luce (*Life*), and the argument with Fritsch, to the end of September or October 1960.

35. On October 11, 1960, a CIA informant reported from Frankfurt (obviously someone close to *Die Welt*) that Eichmann had already written five hundred pages. NA, RG 263, CIA Name File Adolf Eichmann.

36. Sassen transcript 21:2, 12.7.

37. Servatius Report: "While being held in Israel, he has been dictating reports daily." Servatius made an effort to advise Eichmann against it, though without much success.

38. The BND files contain several pieces of writing from Israel and large parts of the Servatius correspondence.

39. Negotiations took place with Patrick O'Connor from Glasgow, who among other things represented the British agency Curtis Brown. There was talk of six-figure sums in pounds sterling. Genoud also negotiated with the Italian *Epoca* and the English magazine *People.* Servatius Report and interview with Genoud, in Péan, *L'Extrémiste.* Eichmann photos from Argentina that had not previously been seen were published in *Epoca,* and selections from "Meine Flucht" appeared in five issues of *People,* April 30–May 28, 1961. Vera Eichmann, interview in *Paris Match,* April 29, 1962; original transcript in BA Koblenz, All. Proz. 6/252; *Paris Match* 683, May 12, 1962.

40. Answers to questionnaire published in *Paris Match* 687, dated June 9, 1962.

41. For Genoud's disappointment, see François Genoud, interview by Péan.

42. Servatius Report. Sassen would only telegraph in December 1960 to say that he was coming.

43. The issues of *Life* went on sale the Tuesday before the printed date, which is normal for U.S. magazines. The advance notice from Harry Golden was published in the November 21, 1960, issue (appearing November 15). The two issues that followed then contained the serial "Eichmann Tells His Own Damning Story." The November 28 issue appeared on November 22, and the December 6 issue on November 29, 1960.

44. Vera Eichmann, interview in *Paris Match*, April 29, 1962.

45. Servatius Report. Reports appeared in almost all the German daily newspapers on December 1, 1960. Another press conference took place on December 9, 1960, and Servatius further qualified his resolution.

46. Zwi Wohlstein was responsible for Eichmann's health and well-being following his imprisonment and kept a diary of what was for him a difficult experience. Extract from Wohlstein's notes, December 4, 1960, published in *Die Welt*, September 1, 1999.

47. Vera Eichmann to Servatius, telegram, November 28, 1960, BA Koblenz, All. Proz. 6/253, p. 59.

48. Servatius Report. A copy also reached the BND files, supplementary file, case BVerwG 7A 15.10, *Saure vs. BND*, BND files 121 099, 1840–43.

49. "Eichmann parle," *L'Express*, no. 494, December 1, 1960; Sassen to Servatius, January 13, 1961, BA Koblenz, All. Proz. 6/253, pp. 113–14. Servatius used this article in the trial to discredit Sassen as a potential witness. Trial transcript, session 105.

50. "Eichmann Fue un Engranaje de la Diabólica Maquinaria Nazi, Dice el Hombre que Escribió sus Memorias en Buenos Aires," *La Razón*, December 12, 1960.

51. Sassen to Servatius, January 13, 1961, BA Koblenz, All. Proz. 6/253, pp. 113–14, and Sassen to Servatius, January 28, 1961, BA Koblenz, All. Proz. 6/253, p. 110. Sassen's advice betrays his intimate knowledge and his anti-Semitic and Nazi attitude, which made some of his offers of help simply naïve, even if we can see they were well intentioned.

52. The letter giving power of attorney to his stepbrother, Robert Eichmann, on February 7, 1961, envisaged 50 percent for his children and 50 percent for Servatius. BA Koblenz, All. Proz. 6/253, p. 6.

53. Report, December 21, 1960, NA, RG 263, CIA Name File Adolf Eichmann. The informant's name is blacked out.

54. NA, RG 263, CIA Name File Léon Degrelle, 023-230/86/22/04. The clue is contained in the Degrelle file because Zwy Aldouby had apparently planned to abduct Léon Degrelle. Heartfelt thanks to Willi Winkler.

55. Robert Pendorf, *Mörder und Ermordete: Eichmann und die Judenpolitik des Dritten Reichs* (Hamburg, 1961), p. 7.

56. The information on Langbein and the following account are supported by Hermann Langbein Estate, ÖStA, E/1797.

57. Langbein, March 12, 1959, reported to Ormond on "a few pictures of SS men"

that he had picked up on his trip to Poland. Ibid., E/1797, binder 106. Correspondence on the criminal charges, ibid.

58. The correspondence with Hermann Langbein includes several commentaries on the magazines. They also consulted one another on their press activity, when they feared a backslide into Nazi hero-worship. Langbein Estate, ÖStA, E/1797, binder 106.

59. Henry Ormond's estate is now held in the Yad Vashem Archive. Unfortunately, I have not yet been able to look into it. Thanks to Werner Renz (of the Fritz Bauer Institut) for sending Walter Witte's Ormond biography (*Alles zu seiner Zeit: Rechtsanwalt Henry Ormond 1901–1973,* undated typescript), which contained no references for this chapter but provided valuable information on his biography. The following reconstruction of Ormond's role rests on his extensive correspondence with Langbein, which is now in the Langbein Estate, ÖStA, E/1797, binder 106. Thanks to Anton Pelinka for the permission to use this incredibly rich source for my Eichmann research.

60. "Too many people are interested in emphasizing the collective innocence of whole departments." Ormond to Lingemann, April 4, 1956, quoted in *Das Amt,* p. 591.

61. Thomas Harlan, "Kto to był Eichmann?," *Polityka,* May 28, 1960.

62. Ormond and Langbein, detailed letters in Hermann Langbein Estate, ÖStA, E/1797, binder 106.

63. The correspondence between Ormond and Langbein from February 1961 contains the meeting arrangements, the questions of finance, the bill for Harlan's travel costs, and the note to Langbein in the hotel about when Harlan would arrive. Langbein Estate, ÖStA, E/1797.

64. Wiesenthal reported this contact to the Israeli ambassador in Austria, Ezechiel Sahar, on February 29, 1960. There is more proof of this event, as Wiesenthal also told his biographer Hella Pick about it, and in February 1960 Isser Harel accused Wiesenthal of endangering the hunt for Eichmann with this action. Hella Pick, *Simon Wiesenthal: A Life in Search of Justice* (London, 1996), p. 147; Isser Harel, *Simon Wiesenthal and the Capture of Eichmann,* unpublished manuscript, quoted in Tom Segev, *Simon Wiesenthal: The Life and Legends* (New York, 2010), p. 144.

65. Thanks to Thomas Harlan for his memories of the events. The extent and the quality of the copy in particular speak for it having come from Robert Eichmann. The handwritten parts also contain the note that these were all the documents, apart from what had been sold to *Life.* See also BA Ludwigsburg, "Miscellaneous" folder.

66. Note dated March 7, 1961, HMJ Wiesbaden, Veesenmayer, Edmund—Novak; now: Adolf Eichmann, vol. 2, sheet 211; documented in Wojak, *Fritz Bauer,* p. 582n93.

67. We can rule out the possibility that Robert Eichmann handed over the Argentina Papers voluntarily, and he surely must have noticed the theft. (If Langbein

had merely instructed somebody to photograph the papers and leave the originals in the office, he would not have needed to get films made afterward, as we know he did.) Robert Eichmann should really have warned his brother via his lawyer. According to helpful information from Helmut Eichmann, Adolf Eichmann's family appeared not to know anything about the purloined documents prior to my inquiry. See also the correspondence from Servatius in March–April 1961, and from Fritsch to Servatius, esp. All. Proz. 6/253, 60–62. A 2009 inquiry with the police and the public prosecutor's office in Linz yielded no results.

68. According to Harlan, in an interview in Jean-Pierre Stephan, *Das Gesicht Deines Feindes: Ein deutsches Leben* (Berlin, 2007), p. 124.

69. Thanks to Daniel Passent for his willingness to share his memories with me. Without his openness, I would never have hit upon the idea of searching for the sources with which these events could be reconstructed. I would never have dreamed that the copies of the Argentina Papers that have been floating around since then might be different bundles, and that it would be worth taking another close look at each pile of papers labeled "Sassen Interview" and counting the pages.

70. Mieczysław F. Rakowski noted in his diary that Daniel Passent had received a copy of the Sassen transcript from Thoman Harlan and that criminologists from the Milicja Obywatelska had found it to be genuine. Mieczysław F. Rakowski, *Dzienniki polityczne 1958–1962* (Warsaw, 1998), p. 286. The written summary of the evaluation from the Central Criminal Police, the KGMO in Warsaw, followed on May 9, proving the authenticity of Eichmann's handwriting on the Sassen transcript presented to *Polityka*. Part of it was printed in the first article. Thanks to Christian Ganzer for his help in translating the Polish documents.

71. The translation of the transcript with the explanations was 1,258 pages long, according to *Polityka*. Unfortunately, the manuscript apparently no longer exists in the newspaper's archive. Krystyna Zywulska, Harlan's girlfriend, claimed that all the copies of it were stolen. However, Zywulska's memories were not always correct, as Liane Dirks (who also wrote a novel about her) recalls. See "Interference at the Highest Level" in *Frankfurter Rundschau*, June 20, 2006, p. 10, and Liane Dirks, *Krystyna* (Cologne, 2006).

72. Mieczysław F. Rakowski, diary entry from June 20, 1961, *Dzienniki polityczne*, p. 293.

73. I am personally grateful to this brief side-column note in the *Allgemeine Jüdische Wochenzeitung* for the first reference to the *Polityka* articles. I must also confess (to my shame) that before this I had not thought to look for any such publications in the former Eastern Bloc. The "wall in our heads" is still frighteningly solid. See also *Die Welt*, May 24, 1961.

74. "Eichmann par Eichmann," *Paris Match*, no. 630 (May 6, 1961); no. 631 (May 13, 1961); and no. 632 (May 20, 1961).

75. Based on his own notes, in December 1960 Avner W. Less was familiar only

with the *Life* articles. On February 2, 1961, Servatius forbade Less from carrying out any further interrogations, so they officially ended in January. But Eichmann himself didn't observe this prohibition. "He was too fond of the sound of his own voice to forgo the 'pleasure,'" and Less wanted to try to get his cooperation. NL Less Notebooks 4.2.3.2, Avner Less Estate, Archiv für Zeitgeschichte, ETH Zurich. But Less's superiors decided against letting Eichmann know that the Sassen transcripts had reached Israel, wanting to save the element of surprise for the trial. Later report by Less, NL Less, 4.2.3.2, personal papers, folder 2, ibid.

76. Ormond-Langbein correspondence, esp. Langbein letter of January 25, 1962, Langbein Estate, ÖStA, E/1797, binder 106. Quotes that follow are also from this source.

77. Eichmann trial, session 16, April 26, 1961.

78. Gabriel Bach, "Conversation with Herr Gabriel Bach, Deputy Prosecutor in the Trial Against Adolf Eichmann, on the Occasion of the 65th Anniversary of the Wannsee Conference of January 20, 1942, on January 18, 2007, in the Haus Der Wannsee-Konferenz," in *Haus der Wannseekonferenz Newsletter* 8 (December 2007), pp. 2–21, here p. 5.

79. Wiesenthal also mentioned this in an early letter to Ben A. Sijes, December 28, 1970. See Segev, *Simon Wiesenthal,* p. 150.

80. Wiesenthal's letter to Hausner, October 5, 1980, Simon Wiesenthal Archiv, Vienna correspondence. Thanks to Michaela Vocelka for sending it so quickly.

81. As a meticulous comparison of the pages shows. Anyone wanting to see for themselves can do so with little effort, by looking at a typical piece of damage that doesn't exist on the Langbein copy (or on Sassen's original). Sassen transcript 18:12 has a large burn mark in the shape of a P on the left-hand side, which has destroyed about 10 percent of the page.

82. This version comes from Heinz Felfe (who was unmasked as a Soviet spy shortly after the Eichmann trial). See Heinz Felfe, *Im Dienst des Gegners: 10 Jahre Moskaus Mann im BND* (Hamburg and Zurich, 1986), p. 248. A glance at BND file 121 099 confirms that they had the Argentina Papers by the end of 1960, from the United States.

83. The Hagag evaluation of May 31, 1961, was submitted to the court on June 9 and is therefore accessible as a trial document (prosecution document T/1392). Hagag clearly marks May 25, 1961, as the date all pages were handed over, but also mentions two previous objective evaluations, from March 17 and April 10, 1961. A mere six days would not have been enough for the evaluation of this mountain of paper. Many thanks to Irina Jabotinsky, Berlin, for the translation from the Hebrew.

84. In the literature, particularly the more popular books, myriad witnesses claim to have seen these two binders with the seventeen files in Sassen's house. We can dismiss their claims immediately, as Sassen owned at least four hundred more pages of material. If he had sorted them the same way Hagag did, he would have ended up with around twenty-eight files.

85. I had the pleasure of ordering the second part of the transcripts together with the BA Ludwigsburg staff. Unlike Inspector Hagag, I had the advantage of being very familiar with most of the pages I had to sort. However, a great deal of humor was still necessary for this undertaking. . . . I would like to take this opportunity to offer my heartfelt thanks once again to Tobias Hermann and Sidar Toptanci for one of the most pleasant archive experiences of my Eichmann research.

86. This is clearly an error, as there is no reference to pages later removed in the double paginations. These doubles are pages 112=113; 224=225; 508=509.

87. This page contains a discussion about Eichmann's former deputy Rolf Günther. On the original tape of this discussion (BA tape 09D), Eichmann asks for these remarks to be left out, because he was convinced that Günther was still alive, and he didn't want to do him any harm.

88. Sassen transcript 6:1.

89. Dietrich Zeug to Fritz Bauer, June 2, 1961, BA Ludwigsburg, Central Office collection, III 44/28.

90. The approved pages, according to Hagag's numbering: 18, 57, 90, 100, 102, 106, 110, 118, 124, 131, 151, 152, 158, 168, 201, 202, 209, 213, 221, 227, 230, 246, 253, 265, 267, 272, 276, 277, 278, 279, 281, 283, 288, 292, 293, 303, 304, 306, 307, 308, 313, 314, 323, 336, 361, 362, 368, 369, 372, 373, 384, 398, 407, 408, 420, 421, 424, 425, 426, 432, 513, 514, 516, 519, 521, 522, 524, 525, 574, 577, 578, 582, 585, 587, 609, 610, 613, 616, 617, 662, 663, 665, 667. A page concordance can be requested from me and viewed in the Bundesarchiv.

91. The initialing was not, as Wojak believes (*Eichmanns Memoiren*, p. 50), an expression of Eichmann's pedantry but a common practice in the hearing of evidence, for continuous authorization of transcripts and corrections. Less described this practice in detail several times. Avner Less Estate, Archiv für Zeitgeschichte, ETH Zurich.

92. "Testimonies on the Sassen Memoirs," six-page typescript, Jerusalem, June 9, 1961, BA Koblenz, All. Proz. 6/254.

93. Only in his last interview did Sassen speak about the autobiography Eichmann wanted to write. Broadcast on *Edicion plus* (Telefe Buenos Aires, 1991).

94. *Nation Europa* 11, no. 11 (1961), pp. 37–42; here p. 41.

95. Vollmer would keep in touch with people in Argentina even after the Eichmann trial. Juan Maler (Reinhard Kopps) said that Vollmer led the "midwinter celebrations" in Punta Chica near Buenos Aires in December 1980. Juan Maler, *Frieden, Krieg und "Frieden"* (Bariloche, 1987), p. 403.

96. Even before reading the *Life* articles, Adolf von Thadden spoke about the extent of the Sassen papers, which he knew quite well—through Rudel, as he later admitted. Thadden to Erich Kernmayr, December 6, 1960, Adolf von Thadden Estate, Niedersächsisches Landesarchiv, VVP 39, Acc. 1/98 no. 49, Sudholt correspondence.

97. On June 23, 1961, Bauer announced to the Hesse Minstry of Justice that Steinbacher (a public prosecutor) would like to question Eberhard Fritsch

in Vienna. Cited in Irmtrud Wojak, memo June 23, 1961, HMJ Wiesbaden, Veesenmayer, Edmund—Novak; now: Adolf Eichmann, vol. 2, sheet 346, in Wojak, *Fritz Bauer,* p. 582.

98. Wojak, *Eichmanns Memoiren.* On the problematic nature of the references, see chapter "One Good Turn," note 41, p. 475.

99. Hausner's reference to Eichmann's note "this no. 29 is for your information only" on one of the tape transcripts refers not to a tape, as Wojak thinks could be the case (*Eichmanns Memoiren,* p. 222n93), but to the transcript on which one can read this inscription. Sassen transcript 29:1. Tape 29 is missing from Eichmann's estate, as his heirs at least heeded this instruction. All references in Hausner's *Justice in Jerusalem* (New York, 1966) clearly relate to the copy ordered by Hagag.

100. Saskia Sassen, interview by Roelf van Til (2005) and Raymond Ley (2009); friend of the family Inge Schneider, interview by van Til (2005).

101. Hausner, *Justice in Jerusalem.*

102. Gabriel Bach, Hausner's deputy, always said how important the knowledge of what had been said in Argentina was for him personally, to prevent him from falling for Eichmann's pretense.

103. Cross-examination, Eichmann trial, session 96, July 13, 1961. The film of the trial shows with frightening clarity how convincingly Eichmann lied.

104. As well as the *Life* articles, Hannah Arendt used the typed copy of Eichmann's handwritten fragment that had been made in Israel ("Re: My Findings") for her book. This fragment was among the prosecution's trial documents and so was available to all journalists attending the trial. She didn't get to read the Sassen transcript. Hannah Arendt, *Eichmann in Jerusalem: A Report on the Banality of Evil* (1963; reprint New York, 1994), p. 27.

105. BA Ludwigsburg, Central Office collection III 44/104.

106. BA Ludwigsburg, B162/428 and 429.

107. The covering letter and the other correspondence from the Baden-Württemberg LKA is on the letterhead of a special commission, about which there are now no records whatsoever to be found in the LKA. As Norbert Kiessling explained to me, this is unusual: the diaries recording outgoing mail are usually kept. The letterhead reads: LKA BW Special Commission Central Office Diary no. SK.ZSt.A/14-111/61.

108. There is a copy in the archive of the Research Centre for Contemporary History, Hamburg.

109. Hans Rechenberg sheds light on the joint public relations activity with Genoud before the start of the trial in his letter of March 31, 1961; since the argument over the Bormann estate and the Goebbels diary, Genoud's litigious nature had become notorious.

110. Langbein to Ormond, January 25, 1962, in Langbein Estate, ÖStA, E/1797, binder 106: correspondence with Henry Ormond.

111. Hannah Arendt, who was accused, among other things, of having attended only a few days of the trial in person, was one of the most thorough readers

of the interrogation and trial transcripts, which she took back to the United States with her.

112. Langbein and Ormond both spoke of Harlan and the book that was never written with respect and understanding, and exchanged views on their regret that Harlan withdrew because he was obviously ashamed. Langbein Estate, ÖStA, E/1797, binder 106.

113. Thomas Harlan described the contents of the box to me as best he could. In 2009 Frau Wojak told me that she had not yet found the time to go through the box and therefore could neither confirm nor correct what Harlan had said. Unfortunately, there has been no further communication from her.

114. Thanks to Katrin Seybold-Harlan for sending me these pages, which not only allowed me to verify Thomas Harlan's information on the document collection but also proved that Harlan's copies came from Henry Ormond's office.

115. The speculations here should not be confused with the so-called "missing pages," documents that are sitting in unused but known archive collections. See Jürgen Bevers, *Der Mann hinter Adenauer* (Berlin, 2009), chapter on "The Eichmann Trial and the Missing 40 Pages."

116. It has since been proved that Farago bought both genuine and false information and invented elaborate stories about Eichmann. However—and this should be emphasized—the book still contains some accurate details about Nazis in South America, which reveal how incredibly good Farago's sources must have been, although they are so tightly interwoven with bad sources that picking them out requires a huge amount of work.

117. Stan Lauryssens, who wrote a linguistically thrilling and imaginative book on Willem Sassen, profited extensively from Farago's work, without always making as clear a division between quotes and his own story as we might wish. *De fatale vriendschappen van Adolf Eichmann* (Leuven, 1998).

118. Ladislas Farago, *Aftermath: Martin Bormann and the Fourth Reich* (New York, 1974), chaps. 15 and 20, starting pp. 283 and 372 respectively.

119. Farago speaks of "Eberhard Fritsche"—the names he gives are imprecise in many cases.

120. Farago, *Aftermath,* p. 373.

121. Ibid., p. 374. Lauryssens also claims to have seen the seventeen files. Contrary to all the stories, Israel is the only place in the world they could have been seen, because they were the work of Avraham Hagag.

122. The numbers 659 and 695 come up only in the context of the Israel copy, in Gideon Hausner's writing. All the other instances come from Farago's typing error, which makes the number a clear indicator of the source that has been used.

123. Farago, *Aftermath,* pp. 376–77.

124. Gerd Heidemann and Karl Wolff stayed with Sassen in 1979. Heidemann said that at this point he (and everyone else) was convinced that Sassen had sold Eichmann, or at least the Argentina Papers, to the Israelis, and Sassen was still anxious about it. Heidemann was also interested in Bormann but told me that

Sassen was no help in this regard—though he did make good on a promise to introduce him to Klaus Barbie, with whom Heidemann then got an exclusive interview. So Sassen didn't need fairy tales about Bormann to impress Farago: he could have introduced him to plenty of other headline-grabbing Nazis, like Josef Mengele, who died only in 1979.

125. For an initial overview, see Meir Litvak and Esther Webman's excellent paper "The Representation of the Holocaust in the Arab World" in the conference volume *After Eichmann: Collective Memory and the Holocaust Since 1961,* ed. David Cesarani (New York, 2005), pp. 100–15.

126. Faris Yahya (pen name Faris Glubb), *Zionist Relations with Nazi Germany* (Beirut, 1978), p. 71. Other examples of this line of argumentation can be found in the reflections of Abu Mazen (Mahmoud Abbas) and Jurji Haddad, who see the commonalities between National Socialists and Zionists in their capitalist aims.

127. Klaus-Michael Mallmann and Martin Cüppers, "'Elimination of the Jewish National Home in Palestine': The Einsatzkommando of the Panzer Army Africa, 1942," *Yad Vashem Studies* 35 (2007), pp. 111–41.

128. Sassen transcript 10:11.

129. Eichmann to Robert Eichmann, February 22, 1961; discussion note about the visit to Eichmann, December 5, 1961, BA Koblenz, All. Proz. 6/238.

130. Eichmann to Robert Eichmann, February 22, 1961, Letters to the Family. A copy entered the BND files by return of mail. See also the CIA report dated October 17, 1961, NA, RG 263, CIA Name File Adolf Eichmann (nonscanned files, declassified May 2009).

131. Some caution is therefore advisable in using this copy, because not all the handwritten notes were made in Argentina. This is true for the large question marks and crossed-out words in particular.

132. Thanks to Francisca Sassen for this idea.

133. Friedrich Schwend, a friend of Klaus Barbie's who lived in Lima, Peru, spread the story that Sassen didn't even know the SS ranks, and because an SS man would never forget something like this, Sassen (whom he called "Sasse") could not be one. HIS, Schwend collection, 18/89, Lima, May 6, 1965.

134. Schwend to Obermüller, Ciudad, January 7, 1966, HIS, Schwend collection, 38/27, 47.

135. Zvi Aharoni, interview by Dan Setton in *Josef Mengele: The Final Account* (SET Productions, 2002), and Zvi Aharoni and Wilhelm Dietl, *Operation Eichmann: The Truth About the Pursuit, Capture, and Trial,* trans. Helmut Bögler (New York, 1997).

136. Thanks to Gerd Heidemann for his willingness to tell me about this stay with Sassen, from which there are also tape recordings and photographs. Unfortunately I have not yet had the opportunity to listen to this material, which is still in Heidemann's possession.

137. *Nation Europa* 31, no. 2 (1981), pp. 60–61. Thanks to Dr. Sudholt for this reference to the review, about which he is still genuinely annoyed today. In

this connection, two letters from Thadden to Sudholt, which can be found in Thadden's estate, are illuminating: they contain even clearer criticism of Aschenauer. Thadden took up a central position, as he recognized the extermination of the Jews as a fact, but tended toward an unrealistically low death toll. Letters of December 10 and 17, 1980, Niedersächsisches Landesarchiv, VVP39, Acc. 1/98, No. 49.

138. David Irving's website, *The Eichmann Papers,* http://www.fpp.co.uk/ Auschwitz/Eichmann/Buenos_Aires_MS.html.

139. Even without access to the Aschenauer manuscript, Leni Yahil managed to write an excellent essay: "'Memoirs' of Adolf Eichmann," *Yad Vashem Studies* 18 (1987), pp. 133–62.

140. Irving's quotes (*Eichmann Papers,* Irving's website) allow a very precise identification of the pages he mentions. There are no references to previously unknown Eichmann texts in the bundle of papers he found. The value of this source lies in the rediscovered missing parts of the Sassen texts it contains.

141. Irving talks about "eight unpaginated chapters of a biographical work, numbered from V to XII," but the chapter that was released had both obvious page numbers and the chapter number IV.

142. In several places, this chapter relativizes, decontextualizes, or twists Eichmann's words to serve Sassen's aims: idealizing Hitler and presenting the extermination of the Jews as the result of Jewish manipulation. Anyone wishing to see this for themselves can find very obvious misrepresentations of what Eichmann said in IV, pp. 15 and 19.

143. The reference even stopped researchers like David Cesarani and Irmtrud Wojak from looking at the Eichmann Estate, BA Koblenz, N/1497, which they both noted. Use of the Druffel edition unfortunately means that Cesarani and Wojak's books also contain "Eichmann quotes" that are actually quotes from Langer, Sassen, or Alvensleben. In particular, recent large-scale works on Rudolf Kasztner, and the people forced to become Eichmann's Jewish negotiating partners, were also written without the four "missing" tapes on this very topic. This is the case for Ladislaus Lob, *Reszö Kasztner* (London, 2009); Anna Porter, *Kasztner's Train: The True Story of an Unknown Hero of the Holocaust* (New York, 2007), p. 324; and Christian Kolbe, "'Und da begann ich zu überlegen': Adolf Eichmanns zwiespältige Erinnerungen an sein ungarisches 'Meisterstück,'" in *Im Labyrinth der Schuld: Täter, Opfer, Ankläger: Jahrbuch 2003 zur Geschichte und Wirkung des Holocaust,* ed. Fritz Bauer Institut (Frankfurt am Main and New York, 2003), pp. 65–93.

144. The Ludwigsburg film copy displays much of the same damage as the Israel copy, which suggests that the Ludwigsburg film and the Israel copy come from the same line of copies.

145. Tape 7 did not exist, according to one of Sassen's notes, and was probably typed up under tape 8 by accident—a possibility suggested by the number of pages there. The transition from tapes 6 to 8 shows that there is no missing text.

146. The short piece obviously belongs with tape 61. Sassen apparently started recording using the wrong tape but quickly realized his error.
147. These are filed with the Eichmann papers, and their real author was overlooked. Probably not even Sassen remembered, as he took all the rest of his notes out of the papers.
148. Isser Harel, *The House on Garibaldi Street* (New York, 1997).
149. They can be found under shelfmark B206/1986.
150. In January 2011 I was able to see the file collection in the context of this case. Here I would like to thank Hans-Wilhelm Saure, his lawyer Christoph Partsch, and Rosa Stark for an intensive and enjoyable weekend of work in Berlin, and the opportunity to cross-check my book. All quotes from the file are with the kind permission of Christoph Partsch.
151. You must forgive a dedicated academic this observation, but academics don't like to be told by someone with other interests why files on their topic, which has not interested anyone else until this point, cannot be important, because everything that has been found "has only marginal relevance for the information interests of the claimant [Gaby Weber seeking information on the Eichmann case]" (p. 9). Only someone currently pursuing a research project can determine what is interesting for it, not anyone else: not the staff of a national institution, and in many cases not even other subject specialists.
152. Most are documents from the Israeli police and prosecutors, which haven't been made public because they weren't used by the prosecution in the trial. On the practice of blacking out, and the construction and extent of the files presented, see Bettina Stangneth, "Kurzgutachten zu den Akten BVerwG 7A 15.10. aufgrund der Sichtung der Beiakten zum Verfahren BVerwG 7A 15.10 mit den Signaturen 100 470, 100 471, 121 082, 121 099 am 21. und 22. Januar 2011" (Hamburg, January 25, 2011), seven pages, with document appendix.
153. I expressly refuse to entertain the idea that a Federal German intelligence service could have made efforts to keep Adolf Eichmann a free man, for the psychological reason that I would find it unbearable.
154. As Gaby Weber is demonstrably one of these resourceful researchers, the argument can't be made that this statement was not written for public consumption.
155. Even Zvi Aharoni, who tracked down Eichmann in Argentina and was part of the abduction team, said that he had tried in vain to get Eichmann to talk about Mengele. This remarkable refusal is all the more surprising when you consider that Aharoni was one of Mossad's most feared interrogation specialists, whose nickname was "the Grand Inquisitor." In later years, he even managed to persuade Willem Sassen to help in the search for Mengele, in an interview that lasted over ten hours. See Aharoni and Dietl, *Operation Eichmann*; Zvi Aharoni, interview by Dan Setton for *Josef Mengele: The Final Account* (SET Productions, 2007); Wilhelm Dietl, interview by Roelf van Til for *Willem Sassen* (KRO, 2005).

156. Erich Schmidt-Eenboom, *BND: Der deutsche Geheimdienst im Nahen Osten: Geheime Hintergründe und Fakten* (Munich, 2007), p. 94.

157. *Deutscher Bundestag, Stenografischer Bericht, 83. Sitzung,* January 19, 2011. http://dip21.bundestag.de/dip21/btp/17/17083.pdf. Thanks to Jerzy Montag's office.

158. Supplementary file to case BVerwG 7A 15.10, *Saure vs. BND,* BND files 121 099, 1665.

159. Willem Sassen, interview broadcast on *Edicion plus* (Telefe Buenos Aires, 1991).

160. Willem Sluyse (Willem Sassen), *Die Jünger und die Dirnen* (Buenos Aires, 1954), pp. 51–53. The text is slightly abridged here.

161. According to Saskia and Francisca Sassen, their father left no incomplete manuscripts.

Sources

Document Collections

Archiv des Bundes der Verfolgten des Naziregimes, Berlin
Deutsche Reichspartei Collection

Archiv der Forschungsstelle für Zeitgeschichte (The Research Centre for Contemporary History in Hamburg, Archive), Hamburg

Archiv der Sozialen Demokratie, Bonn
Fritz Bauer Estate

Archiv der Universität, Vienna
Doktorandenlisten (list of doctorate degrees)

Archiv für Zeitgeschichte, Eidgenössische Technische Hochschule Zürich
Avner W. Less Estate
JUNA Archive

Berlin Hoppegarten
Die Bundesbeauftragte für die Unterlagen des Staatssicherheitsdienstes der ehemaligen Deutschen Demokratischen Republik (Federal Commissioner for the Records of the State Security Service of the Former GDR)
Archive material HA IX/11 1933–45

Bundesarchiv Berlin-Lichterfelde
BDC-Bestände (formerly U.S. Berlin Document Center)

Bundesarchiv Koblenz
Alliierte Prozesse (All. Proz. 6), Servatius papers, Eichmann Trial
N/1497 Eichmann Estate
R/58 RSHA

Bundesarchiv Ludwigsburg/Zentrale Stelle
Eichmann Trial files
Central Office of the State Justice Administrations for the Investigation of National Socialist Crimes

General files III, Correspondence Tuviah Friedman
Trial report by Dietrich Zeug for the Central Office

Central Archives of the History of the Jewish People, Jerusalem
A/W IKG-Archiv Collection, Vienna

Centre de Documentation Juive Contemporaine, Paris

Central Zionist Archive, Jerusalem

Deutsches Literatur Archiv, Marbach
Hans Grimm Estate (Correspondence with Eberhard Fritsch)
Ernst Kernmayr Estate (Correspondence with Eberhard Fritsch)

Deutsches Rotes Kreuz Archiv, Berlin

Deutsches Rundfunkarchiv, Frankfurt am Main
Eine Epoche vor Gericht

Hamburger Institut für Sozialforschung
Schwend Collection

Hessisches Hauptstaatsarchiv, Wiesbaden
Section 461

Holocaust Memorial, Washington, D.C.
Uki Goñi Collection

Institut für Stadtgeschichte, Frankfurt
Arnold Buchthal Estate

Israel State Archives
"Götzen" (Idols)

Niedersächsisches Landesarchiv, Hanover, Magazin Pattensen
Adolf von Thadden Estate

Österreichisches Staatsarchiv, Vienna
E/1797 Hermann Langbein Estate

Rheinische Landesbibliothek Koblenz
Werner Beumelburg Estate (Correspondence with Eberhard Fritsch)

Russian State Military Archive
Formerly the Central State Archive of the Soviet Army, Moscow

Simon Wiesenthal Archive, Vienna
Correspondence

Státní oblastní archiv Litomerice (National Area Archive in Litomerice), Czech Republic
MLS (International Law Collection), Lsp 441/47
Karl Rahm

Stadtarchiv Bergen (Bergen City Archive)
Eversen Register, Shelf 585, No. 2

Stadtarchiv Salzburg (Salzburg City Archive)
Meldekartei (Record Office Card Index)

Státní ússtreédní archive Praha (Prague National Central Archive), Czech Republic
AGK Warsaw

Syracuse University, New York, Special Collections
Francis Biddle Papers

U.S. National Archives
RG 263, CIA Name Files
RG 319, Dossier XE 004471, Adolf Eichmann

Yad Vashem Archive
O–1 K. J. Ball-Kaduri Collection
O–3 Verbal Witness Statements Collection
O–51 Nazi Document Collection (DN)
Tr. 3 Documents from the Eichmann Trial (numbered B06/xxx)

Interviews

With many thanks for interviews to Uki Goñi, Martin Haidinger, Raymond Ley, Roelf van Til, and Natasja de Winter: Altensalzkoth, Buenos Aires, Coronel Suárez, 2009 and 2010, Rafael Eitan, Wilhelm Höttl, José Moskovits, Pedro Pobierzym, Inge Schneider, and Saskia Sassen.

1978 (*Erscheinungsform Mensch*): Simon Wiesenthal, Isser Harel, Avner Less, Zwi Wohlstein, Israel Gutman, David Franko, Gideon Hausner, Gabriel Bach, Benjamin Halevi, Shlomo Kulcsár, Willem Sassen.

Adolf Eichmann's Texts (in Chronological Order)

Pre-1945

"Das Weltjudentum: Politische Aktivität und Auswirkung seiner Tätigkeit auf die in Deutschland ansässigen Juden" (World Jewry: Political Activities and Impact of Its Activities on Jews Resident in Germany), 1937.

Lecture at the conference of SD Advisers on Jewish Affairs on November 1, 1937, in SD Main Office, Berlin. (Rossiiskii gosudarstvennyi voennyi arkhiv—Russian State Military Archive, Moscow 500/3/322.) Published in Michael Wildt, ed., *Die Judenpolitik des SD 1935 bis 1938: Ein Dokumenation* (Munich, 1995), document 19, pp. 133–38.

Argentina Papers

Marginal notes in books
A few originals in Eichmann Estate, BA Koblenz, N/1497. Others quoted in *Stern*, June 26, 1960. Commentary in Interrogation, pp. 1026–35.

Commentaries on books
Originals and notes typed by Sassen in Eichmann Estate, BA Koblenz, N/1497; others in BA Ludwigsburg (B162).

"Die anderen sprachen, jetzt will ich sprechen!" (The Others Spoke, Now I Want to Speak!)
A large manuscript. Original handwritten pages, partial typed copies, films and copies distributed among: Eichmann Estate, BA Koblenz, N/1497; Servatius Estate, BA Koblenz, All. Proz. 6; and BA Ludwigsburg (B162), folder labeled "Diverses" (Miscellaneous).

Part of the manuscript is entitled "Betrifft: Meine Feststellungen zur Angelegenheit 'Judenfragen und Maßnahmen der nationalsozialistischen deutschen Reichsregierung zur Lösung dieses Komplexes in den Jahren 1933 bis 1945'" (Re: My Findings on the Matter of the Jewish Question and Measures Taken by the National Socialist Government of the German Reich Toward the Solution of This Complex in the Years 1933 to 1945). This was originally planned as an open letter to Konrad Adenauer.

There is a poor-quality copy of the sixty-nine-page handwritten text "Betrifft: Meine Feststellungen zur Angelegenheit 'Judenfragen und Maßnahmen der nationalsozialistischen deutschen Reichsregierung zur Lösung dieses Komplexes in den Jahren 1933 bis 1945'" (prosecution document T/1393), identical with Servatius Estate, BA Koblenz, All. Proz. 6/95-111. So-called File 17, (incorrectly) dated February 19, 1959. The text is occasionally taken to be a commentary written in jail but clearly belongs to the Sassen interviews and was written before Eichmann was captured.

General Essays, Notes, and Speech Texts, 1956–57

Circa two hundred pages extant, including handwritten originals, copies, Sassen's typed versions and microfilms in several archives: Eichmann Estate and Servatius Estate, BA Koblenz,; BA Ludwigsburg, "Miscellaneous" folder, and film.

"Tucumán Roman" (Tucumán Novel)

Manuscript, still privately owned by the family and inaccessible. Probably written in 1958–59 for Eichmann's children. Said to be 260 handwritten pages. We cannot rule out some overlap with "The Others Spoke."

Sassen Interviews

TAPES

Audio material in Eichmann Estate, BA Koblenz, N/1497. Ten tapes (29.5 hrs.), audiocassettes (K) (32 hrs.), and DAT cassettes (DAT) (32 hrs.) (Shelf mark Ton 1367, 6-1 to 6-10). Not all tapes are originals from Argentina but are later copies, as traces of more modern recordings underneath the conversations reveal. Audio and DAT cassettes are copies of the originals and are largely identical. The audio material also contains some conversations that were not transcribed.

TRANSCRIPTS

Listed in the order they came to light.

Life. Copy of 600 transcript pages and a few copied pages of handwriting. Not accessible to researchers.

Stern. Copy of transcript pages and 80 pages of handwriting. Cannot be found in the publisher's archive.

Israel (Hagag)/Servatius. Israel State Archives 74/3156. Copy in Servatius Estate, BA Koblenz, All. Proz. 6/95-111, available for use in BA Koblenz since 1979. Transcript of 62 tapes (1–5, 11–67 with pages missing), with Eichmann's handwritten corrections on tapes 6, 7, 9–26, 31–39, 48–67, divided in Israel into 16 +1 files. Transcript is 713 pages in total; including File 17, it totals 795 pages (the official number of 798 is due to double paginations). No transcript of tapes 68–73.

Linz. Stolen from the office of Dr. Robert Eichmann in March 1961 and transferred to microfilm by Hermann Langbein. The copy comprises 900 pages (tapes 1–5, 11–67), also with pages missing, but different pages from the Israel copy. Extensive corrections by Eichmann and typed copies of these, as well as further Argentina Papers. Langbein gave copies to Henry Ormond, Thomas Harlan (used for *Polityka*), and other public offices. Harlan gave the remains of the Ormond copy, as his own was lost, to Irmtrud Wojak. One of the two copies in BA Ludwigsburg clearly also comes from the Linz copy.

Sassen. Original transcripts with original corrections, and Sassen's microfilm copy, which was given to the Eichmann family in 1979 and has now been deposited in BA Koblenz by a Swiss publisher, Eichmann Estate, N/1497. This copy is the most extensive, at 835 pages plus 78 pages of Eichmann's notes on the transcript. It includes tape transcripts 6–10 (except "7," which never existed), and the rest of 68–73, though without tape 29 and page 41:3.

Early Editing and Ordering of Argentina Papers
Based on the Sassen interviews:
> Aschenauer, Rudolf, ed. *Ich, Adolf Eichmann: Ein historischer Zeugenbericht.* Leoni am Starnberger See, 1980.
>> The composition, with its clearly revisionist tendencies, can now be analyzed: manuscript copy in Eichmann Estate, BA Koblenz, N/1497, 77–86.

From the Sassen interviews:
> *Life:* "Eichmann Tells His Own Damning Story," in *Life,* Chicago, November 28 and December 5, 1960. Reprinted as "Eichmann Tells His Own Damning Story." Part I: "I Transported Them to the Butcher," in *Life International* 30, no. 1 (January 9, 1961), pp. 9–19; part II: "To Sum It All Up, I Regret Nothing," in *Life International* 30, no. 3 (February 13, 1961), pp. 76–82 (prosecution document T/47).
> Licensed reprints:
>> "Das Geständnis des Adolf Eichmann," *Revue,* no. 8, 9, 10, Munich 1961.
>> *Paris Match,* May 6, May 13, May 20, 1960.
> *Polityka,* May 20–June 17, 1961, parts of the Linz copy with commentary.
> Gideon Hausner. Hausner used the Israel (Hagag) copy for his report on the trial, *Justice in Jerusalem.* He was the only author before 1979 who was able to draw on the Sassen transcript.

List of Eichmann's contemporary comments on the *Life* articles during the Sassen interviews: prosecution document T/1432.

"Erklärung zur Überstellung nach Israel" (Declaration on Transfer to Israel), May 1960 (T/3)

Israel Sources

"Meine Memoiren" (My Memoirs)
"Today, 15 years and one day after May 8, 1945 . . . ," dated "May 9 to June 16, 1960," but begun only after May 23. Comprises 128 pages of handwritten text, copied for the court files on June 16, 1960. Trial document B06-1492 (T/44).

Also published, without academic rigor and in a flawed transcription, in *Die Welt,* August 12–September 4, 1999. The text is also cited as "127 [*sic*] Eichmann-pages."

"Meine Flucht: Bericht aus der Zelle in Jerusalem" (My Escape: Report from the Cell in Jerusalem)
Alternative title: "Mein Fluchtbericht"; original title: "In einer Mainacht 1945" (On a May Night in 1945). Dated March 1961. The text wasn't used as evidence in the

trial. BA Koblenz, All. Proz. 6/247; NA, RG 263 CIA Name File Adolf Eichmann, vol. 1, document 72; a better copy is vol. 3, 76.

Handwritten text "Mein Fluchtbericht," Israel State Archives, published in the British magazine *People*, April 30–May 28, 1961.

Interrogations, May 29, 1960–January 15, 1961 (Tape 1–76) and February 2, 1961 (Tape 77). Trial documents (T/37 and T/41).
Seventy-six tapes from 38 days of interrogation, 270 hours, 3,564 typed pages, corrected by Eichmann.

First: Police D'Israel, Quartier General 6-ème Bureau (Commander A. Selinger), *Adolf Eichmann*, vols. 1–6, Mahana Iyar, February 3, 1961, facsimile.

Then: State of Israel, Ministry of Justice, *The Trial of Adolf Eichmann*. Statement made by Adolf Eichmann to the Israel Police prior to his trial in Jerusalem. Vols. 7–8, Jerusalem, 1995, facsimile.

Prison Notes, May 30–December 19, 1960. T/44; copies largely in Eichmann Estate, BA Koblenz, All. Proz. 6
Fourteen typewritten pages of comments on the *Life* articles, written in Israel (T/48-51).
Handwritten comments on the Sassen transcript (prosecution document T/1393). Various notes and handwritten essays from prison, even before the trial, including letters to his family.

Psychiatric and Psychological Evaluations, conducted by I. S. Klucsár (Israel), January 20–March 1, 1961
Seven sessions of around three hours, with the tests in use at that time (IQ, Rorschach, TAT, Object Relation Test, Wechsler, Bender, Drawing Test, Szondi).

The original report is still classified. A summary may be found in Shlomo Kulcsár, Shoshanna Kulcsár, and Lipot Szondi, "Adolf Eichmann and the Third Reich," in *Crime, Law and Corrections*, ed. Ralph Slovenko (Springfield, Ill., 1966), pp. 16–52. Pictures from the drawing test were published in *Spiegel* (1978), no. 2.

Trial Documents

State of Israel, Ministry of Justice, *The Trial of Adolf Eichmann*. Microfiche Copies of the Exhibits Submitted by the Prosecution and Defense, Vol. 9 (Jerusalem, 1995). Documents are cited by T/xx numbers.

A complete copy is housed in the Central Office for the Investigation of National Socialist Crimes, Ludwigsburg, now BA Ludwigsburg, B 162. Large parts of the copy are also held in the Servatius Estate, BA Koblenz, All. Proz. 6, and at Avner Less Estate, ETH Zurich.

Trial Transcripts
The Attorney General of the State of Israel vs. Adolf, son of Karl Adolf Eichmann. Jerusalem District Court, Criminal Case 40/61. April 2–August 14, 1961. Statements before the court. Transcript of sessions 1–121. Unrevised and uncorrected transcription (German translation). Complete transcript: Servatius Estate, Less Estate. State of Israel, Ministry of Justice, *The Trial of Adolf Eichmann: Record of Proceedings in the District of Jerusalem,* vols. 1–6, Jerusalem, 1992–94 (English translation). Film of the proceedings: Steven Spielberg Jewish Film Archive/Hebrew University of Jerusalem.

"Götzen" (Idols)
Consisting of 1,206 pages, 676 of which are marked for publication, dated September 1961. Released on February 27, 2000, as evidence in the Irving-Lipstadt trial, London. Israel State Archives.

According to Servatius, Eichmann's working titles were "Recollections for Generations to Come" and "Versailles."

Prison Writings from the Start of the Trial to the Execution
Numerous notes, letters, dossiers, sketches, organizational charts, and larger manuscripts. These include the "Verhaftungsbericht" (Arrest Report), "Vorgeschichte der Entführung" (Background to the Abduction), "Auch hier im Angesicht des Galgens . . ." (Even Here, Facing the Gallows . . .), Eichmann's positions on the sentence and the appeal, various drafts of his concluding statement, correspondence with his family, associates, lawyer, foreign inquiries, the *Paris Match* questionnaire, and so on. Most of it is now in the Eichmann Estate, BA Koblenz, All. Proz. 6; Eichmann Trial Collection, Israel State Archives; and some in the family's possession (not accessible).

Theological Letters
"Conversion discussions" with Rev. William Hull. William L. Hull, *Kampf um eine Seele, Gespräche mit Eichmann in der Todeszelle* (Wuppertal, 1964), reproduces three letters from Eichmann, with (problematic) transcripts from memory of thirteen visits between April 11 and May 31, 1962.

Select Bibliography

With the wider body of source material and studies that has now become available, this book departs all the more frequently from previous works—though without pointing out every error made in these books. This sort of destructive text is not a joy to read, and the following titles are still indispensible to anyone making an intensive study of Eichmann, as I was. A complete list of the Eichmann literature used here is naturally impossible, as it extends to more than eight hundred titles. More references for further reading can be found in the endnotes. Randolph L. Braham's Eichmann bibliography remains essential reading: *The Eichmann Case: A Source Book* (New York, 1969).

Books and Articles

Adler, H. G. "Adolf Eichmann oder die Flucht aus der Verantwortung." *Tribüne* 1 (1962), pp. 122–34.

"Adolf Eichmann, Novelist." *Time and Tide* (London) 42, no. 25 (1961), p. 1009.

Aharoni, Zvi, and Wilhelm Dietl. *Operation Eichmann: The Truth About the Pursuit, Capture, and Trial.* Translated by Helmut Bögler. New York, 1997.

Aly, Götz. *"Endlösung": Völkerverschiebung und der Mord an den europäischen Juden.* Frankfurt am Main, 1995.

———. "Die späte Rache des Adolf Eichmann." *Österreichische Zeitschrift für Geschichtswissenschaften* 11, no. 1 (2000), pp. 186–91.

Aly, Götz, and Christian Gerlach. *Das letzte Kapitel: Realpolitik, Ideologie und der Mord an den ungarischen Juden 1944/1945.* Stuttgart and Munich, 2002.

Anderl, Gabriele. "Emigration und Vertreibung." In *Vertreibung und Neubeginn: Israelische Bürger österreichischer Herkunft.* Edited by Erika Weinzierl and Otto D. Kulka. Vienna, 1992.

Anderl, Gabriele, and Dirk Rupnow. *Die Zentralstelle für jüdische Auswanderung als Beraubungsinstitution.* Vienna, 2004.

Anderson, Jack. "Nazi War Criminals in South America." *Parade*, November 13, 1960, pp. 6–9.

Arendt, Hannah. *Eichmann in Jerusalem: A Report on the Banality of Evil.* 1963; reprint New York, 1994.

———. "Thinking and Moral Considerations: A Lecture." *Social Research* 38, no. 3 (Autumn 1971), pp. 417–46.

"Arendt in Jerusalem." *History and Memory* 8, no. 2 (Fall–Winter 1996), special issue.

Aronson, Shlomo. *Reinhard Heydrich und die Frühgeschichte von Gestapo und SD.* Stuttgart, 1971.

Arnsberg, Paul. "Eichmann—The Germans Don't Care." *Jewish Observer and Middle East Review* 10, no. 15 (April 14, 1961).

Ausschuß für deutsche Einheit, ed. *Eichmann: Henker, Handlanger, Hintermänner: Eine Dokumentation.* East Berlin, 1961.

Avni, Haim. "Jewish Leadership in Times of Crisis: Argentina During the Eichmann Affair (1960–1962)." *Studies in Contemporary Jewry* 11 (1995), pp. 117–35.

Bach, Gabriel. "Gespräch mit Herrn Gabriel Bach, stellvertretender Ankläger im Prozess gegen Adolf Eichmann, anlässlich des 65. Jahrestages der Wannsee-Konferenz vom 20. Januar 1942 am 18. Januar 2007 im Haus der Wannsee-Konferenz." In Haus der Wannseekonferenz, ed., *Newsletter* 8 (December 2007), pp. 2–21.

————. "Adolf Eichmann and the Eichmann Trial." In *Holocaust: Israel Pocket Library.* Jerusalem, 1974.

Bar-Nathan, Moshe. "Background to the Eichmann Trial." *Jewish Frontier* 28, no. 5 (May 1961), pp. 4–7.

Bar-On, A. Zvie. "Measuring Responsibility." *Philosophical Forum* 16, nos. 1–2 (1984–85), pp. 95–109.

Bar-On, Dan. "Steckt in jedem von uns ein Adolf Eichmann?" *Die Welt*, August 19, 1999.

Bar-Zohar, Michel. *Les vengeurs.* Paris, 1968. English: *The Avengers.* New York, 1968.

Bascomb, Neal. *Hunting Eichmann: How a Band of Survivors and a Young Spy Agency Chased Down the World's Most Notorious Nazi.* Boston and New York, 2009.

Bauer, Yehuda. *Freikauf von Juden? Verhandlungen zwischen dem nationalsozialistischen Deutschland und jüdischen Repräsentanten 1933–1945.* Frankfurt am Main, 1996.

————. "Wir müssen jetzt die richtigen wissenschaftlichen Fragen stellen." Interview in *Die Welt*, August 12, 1999.

————. "Das Böse ist niemals banal." Interview in *Spiegel*, August 16, 1999.

Baumann, Jürgen. "Die Psychologie des bürokratisch organisierten Mordes." *Frankfurter Hefte: Zeitschrift für Kultur und Politik* 21 (1966), pp. 199–205.

Beatty, Joseph. "Thinking and Moral Considerations: Socrates and Arendt's Eichmann." *Journal of Value Inquiry* 10 (1976).

Beier, Lars-Olav. "Anatomie eines Mörders." *Frankfurter Allgemeine Zeitung*, February 17, 1999.

Ben Natan, Asher. *The Audacity to Live: An Autobiography.* Tel Aviv, 2007.

Bergman, Monika. "Transporttechnische Angelegenheiten." *Die Zeit*, February 11, 1999.

Bernstein, Richard J. "*The Banality of Evil* Reconsidered." In *Hannah Arendt and the Meaning of Politics.* Edited by Craig Calhoun and John McGowan. Minneapolis, 1997.

————. "Responsibility, Judging, and Evil." *Revue Internationale de Philosophie* 53, no. 2 (June 1999), pp. 155–72.

Bethke. "Der Antisemitismus im Glaskasten. Zum Eichmann-Prozeß." In *Glaube und Gewissen*. Halle a. d. Saale 7, 1961.

Bettelheim, Bruno. "Eichmann—Das System—Die Opfer." In *Erziehung zum Über-leben: Zur Psychologie der Extremsituationen*. Munich, 1982.

Biss, Andreas. *Der Stopp der Endlösung: Kampf gegen Himmler und Eichmann in Budapest*. Stuttgart, 1966.

Biuletyn glownej komsji badania zbrodni Hitleowskich w Polsce (Bulletin of the Com-mission for Investigation of Hitlerite Crimes in Poland). Warsaw, 1960. Eich-mann documents: vols. 12 and 13.

Böll, Heinrich. "Befehl und Verantwortung. Gedanken zum Eichmann-Prozeß." In *Aufsätze, Kritiken, Reden*. Cologne and Berlin, 1967.

Botz, Gerhard. *Nationalsozialismus in Wien: Machtübernahme und Herrschafts-sicherung, 1938–1939*. Buchloe, 1988.

Braham, Randolph. *Eichmann and the Destruction of Hungarian Jewry: A Documen-tary Account*. New York, 1963.

————. *The Politics of Genocide: The Holocaust in Hungary*. New York, 1994.

Brandt, Willy. *Deutschland, Israel und die Juden: Rede des Regierenden Bürgermeis-ters von Berlin vor dem Herzl-Institut in New York am 19. März 1961*. Berlin, 1961.

Brand, Joel. *Adolf Eichmann: Fakten gegen Fabeln*. Munich and Frankfurt, 1961.

Brand, Joel, and Alex Weissberg. *Advocate for the Dead: The Story of Joel Brand*. London, 1958.

Brayard, Florent. "'Grasping the Spokes of the Wind of History': Gerstein, Eichmann and the Genocide of the Jews." *History and Memory* 20 (2008), pp. 48–88.

Brechtken, Magnus. *"Madagaskar für die Juden": Antisemitische Idee und politische Praxis 1885–1945*. Munich, 1998.

————. "Apologie und Erinnerungskonstruktion—Zum zweifelhaften Quellen-wert von Nachkriegsaussagen zur Geschichte des Dritten Reiches. Das Beispiel Madagaskar-Plan." *Jahrbuch für Antisemitismusforschung* 9 (2000), pp. 234–52.

Breitman, Richard David, and Shlomo Aronson. "The End of the 'Final Solution'? Nazi Plans to Ransom Jews in 1944." *Central European History* 25, no. 2 (1992), pp. 177–203.

Breitman, Richard, ed. *U.S. Intelligence and the Nazis*. Washington, D.C., 2004.

Breton, Albert, and Ronald Wintrope. "The Bureaucracy of Murder Revisited." *Journal of Political Economy* 94, no. 5 (October 1986), pp. 905–26.

Brochhagen, Ulrich. *Nach Nürnberg: Vergangenheitsbewältigung und Westintegra-tion in der Ära Adenauer*. Hamburg, 1994.

Brockdorff, Werner (alias Alfred Jarschel, former Nazi youth leader). "XVII. Karl [!] Adolf Eichmann." In *Flucht vor Nürnberg: Pläne und Organisation der Fluchtwege der NS-Prominenz im "Römischen Weg."* Munich-Wels, 1969 (sum-mary of Eichmann's delusional alternative biography).

Browder, George C. *Hitler's Enforcers: Gestapo and the SS Security Service in the Nazi Revolution.* New York, 1996.

Browning, Christopher. *The Path to Genocide: Essays on Launching the Final Solution.* Cambridge, 1992.

———. *Judenmord: NS-Politik, Zwangsarbeit und das Verhalten der Täter.* Frankfurt am Main, 2001.

Brunner, José. "Eichmann, Arendt and Freud in Jerusalem: On the Evils of Narcissism and the Pleasures of Thoughtlessness." *History and Memory* 8 (1996), pp. 61–88.

———. "Eichmann's Mind: Psychological, Philosophical and Legal Perspectives." *Theoretical Inquiries in Law* 1 (2000), pp. 429–63.

Buechler, Yeshoshua Robert. "Document: A Preparatory Document for the Wannsee 'Conference.'" *Holocaust and Genocide Studies* 9, no. 1 (Spring 1995), pp. 121–29.

Camarasa, Jorge. *Odessa al Sur: La Argentina Como Refugio de Nazis y Criminales de Guerra.* Buenos Aires, 1995.

Cantorovich, Nati. "Soviet Reactions to the Eichmann Trial: A Preliminary Investigation, 1960–1965." *Yad Vashem Studies* 35 (2007), pp. 103–41.

Carmichael, Joel. "Reactions in Germany." *Midstream* 7, no. 3 (Summer 1961), pp. 13–27.

Cesarani, David. *Eichmann: His Life and Crimes.* London, 2005.

Cesarani, David, ed. *Genocide and Rescue: The Holocaust in Hungary, 1944.* Oxford, 1997.

———. *After Eichmann: Collective Memory and the Holocaust Since 1961.* London, New York, 2005.

Clarke, Comer. *Eichmann—The Man and His Crimes.* New York, 1960.

Cohen, Ahiba, Tamor Zemach-Maron, Jürgen Wolke, and Birgit Schenk. *The Holocaust and the Press: Nazi War Crimes Trials in Germany and Israel.* New Jersey, 2002.

Cohen, Richard J. "Breaking the Code: Hannah Arendt's *Eichmann in Jerusalem* and the Public Polemic: Myth, Memory and Historical Imagination." In *Michael: The Diaspora Research Institute,* edited by Dina Porat and Shlomo Simonsohn (Tel Aviv, 1993) pp. 13:29–85.

Conze, Eckart, Norbert Frei, Peter Hayes, and Moshe Zimmermann. *Das Amt und die Vergangenheit: Deutsche Diplomaten im Dritten Reich und in der Bundesrepublik.* Munich, 2010.

Crossman, Richard H. S. "The Faceless Bureaucrat." *New Statesman,* March 31, 1961.

Diamant, Manus. *Geheimauftrag: Mission Eichmann.* Vienna, 1995.

Donovan, John. *Eichmann: Man of Slaughter.* New York, 1960.

"Eichmann and the German Government." *Jewish Chronicle* (London), March 17, 1961, p. 31.

"Eichmann's Ghost Writer: A Dutch Friend in Argentina." *Wiener Library Bulletin* 15, no. 1 (1961), p. 2.

Einstein, Siegfried. *Eichmann: Chefbuchhalter des Todes.* Frankfurt am Main, 1961.

Enzensberger, Hans Magnus. "Reflexionen vor einem Glaskasten." In *Politik und Verbrechen: Neun Beiträge.* Frankfurt am Main, 1964.

Felstiner, Mary. "Alois Brunner: 'Eichmann's Best Tool.'" *Simon Wiesenthal Center Annual* 3 (1986), pp. 1–46.

Friedman, Tuviah. *The Hunter.* New York, 1961.

———. *Die Ergreifung Eichmanns: Dokumentarische Sammlung.* Haifa, 1971.

Friedman, Tuviah, ed. *We Shall Never Forget: An Album of Photographs, Articles and Documents.* Haifa Documentation Centre, undated (1965).

Garner, Reuben. "Adolph Eichmann: The Making of a Totalitarian Bureaucrat." In *The Realm of Humanitas: Responses to the Writing of Hannah Arendt.* New York, 1990.

Gellhorn, Martha. "Eichmann and the Private Conscience." *Atlantic Monthly* 209, no. 2 (February 1962), pp. 52–59.

Gerlach, Christian. "The Eichmann Interrogations in Holocaust Historiography." *Holocaust and Genocide Studies* 3 (2001), pp. 428–52.

Giefer, Rena, and Thomas Giefer. *Die Rattenlinie: Fluchtwege der Nazis: Eine Dokumentation.* Frankfurt am Main, 1991.

Gilbert, G. M. "The Mentality of SS-Murderous Robots." *Yad Vashem Studies* 5 (1963), pp. 35–41.

Glock, Charles Y., Gertrude J. Selznick, and Joe L. Spaeth. *The Apathetic Majority: A Study Based on Public Responses to the Eichmann Trial.* New York, 1966.

Goldfarb, Jack. "The Eichmann Mailbag." *Congress Bi-Weekly* 29, no. 3 (February 5, 1962), pp. 8–9.

Goñi, Uki. *The Real Odessa: How Perón Brought the Nazi War Criminals to Argentina.* Rev. ed. London, 2003.

Goshen, Seev. "Eichmann und die Nizko Aktion im Oktober 1939. Eine Fallstudie zur NS-Judenpolitik in der letzten Etappe vor der 'Endlösung.'" *Vierteljahrshefte für Zeitgeschichte* 29 (1981), pp. 74–96.

———. "Nisko—Ein Ausnahmefall unter den Judenlagern der SS." *Vierteljahrshefte für Zeitgeschichte* 40 (1992), pp. 95–106.

Gottlieb, Roger S., ed. *Thinking the Unthinkable: Meanings of the Holocaust.* New York, 1990.

Gourevitch, Lev, and Stéphane Richey. *Agents Secrets Contre Eichmann.* Paris, 1961.

Gross, Raphael. *Anständig geblieben: Nationalsozialistische Moral.* Frankfurt am Main, 2010.

Große, Christina. *Der Eichmann-Prozeß zwischen Recht und Politik.* Frankfurt am Main, Berlin, et al., 1995.

Haas, Peter Jerome. "What We Know Today That We Didn't Know Fifty Years Ago: Fifty Years of Holocaust Scholarship." *CCAR Journal* 42, no. 2 (Summer–Fall 1995), pp. 1–15.

Halberstam, Joshua. "From Kant to Auschwitz." *Social Theory and Practice* 14, no. 1 (1988), pp. 41–54.

Harel, Isser. *The House on Garibaldi Street: The Capture of Adolf Eichmann.* London, 1975.

Hausner, Gideon. *Justice in Jerusalem.* New York, 1966.

Heiman, Leo. "Eichmann and the Arabs: The Untold Story of the Nazis and the Grand Mufti." *Jewish Digest* 6, no. 9 (June 1961), pp. 1–6.

Herbert, Ulrich. "Weltanschauungseliten. Ideologische Legitimation und politische Praxis der Führungsgruppe der nationalsozialistischen Sicherheitspolizei." *Potsdamer Bulletin für zeithistorische Studien* 9 (1997), pp. 4–18.

Herbert, Ulrich, ed. *Nationalsozialistische Vernichtungspolitik 1939–1945: Neue Forschungen und Kontroversen.* 2 vols. Frankfurt am Main, 2002.

Hesselbach. "Er schrieb Adolf Eichmanns Memoiren. Die abenteuerliche Geschichte des Willem Sassen." *Kölnische Rundschau*, December 16, 1960.

Hilberg, Raul. *Die Vernichtung der europäischen Juden: Die Gesamtgeschichte des Holocaust.* 3 vols. Frankfurt am Main, 1990.

———. "Eichmann war nicht banal." *Die Welt*, August 28, 1999.

Hillel, Marc, and Richard Caron. *Operation Eichmann.* Paris, 1961.

Horkheimer, Max. "Zur Ergreifung Eichmanns (1960/1967)." In *Zur Kritik der instrumentellen Vernunft: Aus Vorträgen seit Kriegsende.* Edited by Alfred Schmidt. (Frankfurt, 1967).

Hull, William L. *Kampf um eine Seele: Gespräche mit Eichmann in der Todeszelle.* Wuppertal, 1964.

Huth, Werner. "Adolf Eichmann. Ein Fall von pathologischer Ideologie." In *Glaube, Ideologie und Wahn: Das Ich zwischen Realität und Illusion.* Munich, 1984.

Jäger, Herbert. *Verbrechen unter totalitärer Herrschaft: Studien zur nationalsozialistischen Gewaltkriminalität.* 1967; reprinted Frankfurt am Main, 1982.

———. *Makrokriminalität: Studien zur Kriminologie kollektiver Gewalt.* Frankfurt am Main, 1989.

Jansen, Hans. *Der Madagaskar-Plan: Die beabsichtigte Deportation der europäischen Juden nach Madagaskar.* Munich, 1997.

Jaspers, Karl. Television interview by Thilo Koch, March 10, 1960 (broadcast on August 10). *Frankfurter Allgemeine*, August 17, 1960.

———. "Die grundsätzlich neue Art des Verbrechens." In *Wohin treibt die Bundesrepublik?* Munich, 1966.

Kárny, Miroslav. "Nisko in der Geschichte der 'Endlösung.'" *Judaica Bohemiae* 23, no. 2 (1987), pp. 69–84.

Kaul, Friedrich Karl. *Der Fall Eichmann.* East Berlin, 1963.

Kelen, Emery. "Bureaucrat or Beelzebub?" *Atlas* 2, no. 2 (August 1961), pp. 125–27.

Kempner, R. M. W. *Eichmann und Komplizen: Mit Dokumentenfaksimiles.* Zurich, Stuttgart, and Vienna, 1961.

Klarsfeld, Serge. *Vichy—Auschwitz: Die Zusammenarbeit der deutschen und französischen Behörden bei der "Endlösung der Judenfrage" in Frankreich.* Nördlingen, 1989.

Knopp, Guido. *Hitlers Helfer: Die Täter: Adolf Eichmann, Martin Bormann, Joachim von Ribbentrop, Roland Freisler, Baldur von Schirach, Josef Mengele.* Munich, 1996.

Kogon, Eugen. "Nicht der Einzige—Nur eine Anmerkung zum Fall Eichmann." *Frankfurter Hefte* 15, no. 7 (1960).

Kolbe, Christian. "'Und da begann ich zu überlegen.' Adolf Eichmanns zwiespältige Erinnerungen an sein ungarisches 'Meisterstück.'" In *Im Labyrinth der Schuld: Täter, Opfer, Ankläger.* Edited by Fritz Bauer Institut. Frankfurt am Main and New York, 2003, pp. 65–93. (A yearbook on the history and impact of the Holocaust.)

Koning, Ines de. *A Study of Adolf Eichmann (1906–1962): Adolf Hitler's Expert in Jewish Affairs.* Newton, Mass., 1964. (Self-published by Diss Newton College of the Sacred Heart; highly speculative and a fund of Eichmann legends.)

Krause, Peter. *Der Eichmann-Prozeß in der deutschen Presse.* Frankfurt am Main and New York, 2002.

Krummacher, Friedrich A., ed. *Die Kontroverse: Hannah Arendt, Eichmann und die Juden.* Munich, 1964.

Kühnrich, Heinz. *Judenmörder Eichmann: Kein Fall der Vergangenheit.* East Berlin, 1961.

Kulcsár, Shlomo. "The Psychopathology of Adolf Eichmann." In *Proceedings of the IVth World Congress of Psychiatry.* Madrid, 1966.

———. "De Sade and Eichmann." *Mental Health and Society* 3 (1976), pp. 102–13.

Kulcsár, Shlomo, Shoshanna Kulcsár, and Lipot Szondi. "Adolf Eichmann and the Third Reich." In *Crime, Law and Corrections.* Edited by Ralph Slovenko. Springfield, Ill., 1966.

Lamm, Hans. *Der Eichmann-Prozeß in der deutschen öffentlichen Meinung.* Frankfurt am Main, 1961.

Landau, Ernest, ed. *Der Kastner-Bericht über Eichmanns Menschenhandel in Ungarn.* Munich, 1961.

Lang, Berel. *Act and Idea in the Nazi Genocide.* Chicago and London, 1990.

———. *The Future of the Holocaust: Between History and Memory.* Ithaca, N.Y., and London, 1999.

Lang, Jochen von. *Das Eichmann-Protokoll: Tonbandaufzeichnungen der israelischen Verhöre. Mit einem Nachwort von Avner W. Less.* Berlin, 1982.

Lauryssens, Stan. *De fatale vriendschappen van Adolf Eichmann.* Leuven, 1998.

Lawson, Colin. "Eichmann's Wife Speaks." *Daily Express,* December 12, 1961.

LeBor, Adam. "Eichmann's List: A Pact with the Devil." *Independent,* August 23, 2000.

Levai, Jenö. *Abscheu und Grauen vor dem Genocid in aller Welt . . . Diplomaten und Presse als Lebensretter: Dokumentationswerk anhand der "streng geheim" bezeichneten Akten des Reichsaussenministeriums.* New York, 1968.

Levai, Jenö, ed. *Eichmann in Ungarn: Dokumente.* Budapest, 1961.

Levine, Herbert S.. "Politik, Persönlichkeit und Verbrechertum im Dritten Reich. Der Fall Adolf Eichmann." In *Geschichte als politische Wissenschaft: Sozialökonomische Ansätze, Analyse politikhistorischer Phänomene, politologische*

Fragestellungen in der Geschichte. Edited by J. Bergman, Kl. Megerle, and P. Steinbach. Stuttgart, 1979.

Linze, Dewey W. "LIFE and Eichmann." *Newsweek*, December 5, 1960.

Longerich, Peter. *Der ungeschriebene Befehl: Hitler und der Weg zur "Endlösung."* Munich and Zurich, 2001.

Lozowick, Yaacov. "Malice in Action." *Yad Vashem Studies* 27 (1999), pp. 287–330.

———. *Hitlers Bürokraten: Eichmann, seine willigen Vollstrecker und die Banalität des Bösen.* Zurich and Munich, 2000.

Malkin, Peter Z., and Harry Stein. *Ich jagte Eichmann.* Munich and Zurich, 1990.

Man, Peter, and Uri Dan. *Capturer Eichmann: Temoignage d'un agent du Mossad.* Paris, 1987.

Meding, Holger. *Flucht vor Nürnberg? Deutsche und österreichische Einwanderung in Argentinien 1945–1955.* Cologne, 1992.

———. *"Der Weg": Eine deutsche Emigrantenzeitschrift in Buenos Aires 1947–1957.* Berlin, 1997.

Miale, F. R., and M. Selzer. *The Nuremberg Mind: The Psychology of the Nazi Leader.* New York, 1975.

Mikellitis, Edith. "Der verlorene Sohn. Anmerkungen zum Fall Eichmann." *Zeitschrift für Geopolitik* (Heidelberg) 32 (1961), pp. 269–70.

Milotová, Jaroslava. "Die Zentralstelle für jüdische Auswanderung in Prag. Genesis und Tätigkeit bis zum Anfang des Jahres 1940." In *Theresienstädter Studien und Dokumente*, no. 4 (1997).

Moser, Jonny. "Nisko. The First Experiment in Deportation." *Simon Wiesenthal Center Annual* 2 (1985), pp. 1–30.

———. "Die Zentralstelle für jüdische Auswanderung in Wien." In *Der Pogrom 1938: Judenverfolgung in Österreich und Deutschland.* Edited by Kurt Schmid and Robert Streibel. 2nd ed. Vienna, 1990.

Mulisch, Harry. *Criminal Case 40/61, the Trial of Adolf Eichmann: An Eyewitness Account.* Philadelphia, 2009.

Naftali, Timothy. "The CIA and Eichmann's Associates." In *U.S. Intelligence and the Nazis.* Edited by Richard Breitman. Washington, D.C., 2004.

———. *New Information on Cold War: CIA Stay-Behind Operations in Germany and on the Adolf Eichmann Case.* Nazi War Crimes Interagency Working Group. Washington, D.C., 2006.

Nellessen, Bernd. *Der Prozess von Jerusalem: Ein Dokument.* Düsseldorf and Vienna, 1964.

Nicosia, Francis R.. "Revisionism Zionism in Germany II. Georg Kareski and the Staatszionistische Organisation, 1933–1938." In *Yearbook of the Leo Baeck Institute* 32 (1987), pp. 247ff.

———. "Ein nützlicher Feind. Zionismus im nationalsozialistischen Deutschland 1933–1939." *Vierteljahrshefte für Zeitgeschichte* 37 (1989), pp. 367–400.

Onfray, Michel. *Le songe d'Eichmann: Précédé de'un kantien chez les nazis.* Paris, 2008.

Oppenheimer, Max. *Eichmann und die Eichmänner: Dokumentarische Hinweise auf den Personenkreis der Helfer und Helfershelfer bei der "Endlösung."* Ludwigsburg, 1961.

Orth, Karin. "Rudolf Höß und die 'Endlösung der Judenfrage.'" *Werkstatt Geschichte* 18 (1997), pp. 45–57.

Paetzold, Kurt, and Erika Schwarz. *"Auschwitz war für mich nur ein Bahnhof": Franz Novak—der Transportoffizier Adolf Eichmanns.* Berlin, 1994.

Paul, Gerhard. "'Kämpfende Verwaltung.' Das Amt IV des Reichssicherheitshauptamtes als Führungsinstanz der Gestapo." In *Die Gestapo im Zweiten Weltkrieg: "Heimatfront" und besetztes Europa.* Edited by Gerhard Paul and Klaus-Michael Mallmann. Darmstadt, 2000.

———. "Von Psychopathen, Technokraten des Terrors und 'ganz normalen Deutschen.'" In *Die Täter der Shoah: Fanatische Nationalsozialisten und ganz normale Deutsche?* Edited by Gerhard Paul. Göttingen, 2002.

Pearlman, Moshe. *Die Festnahme des Adolf Eichmann.* Frankfurt am Main, 1961. (Published before the trial and by Pearlman's own admission unsupportable in places.)

———. *The Capture and Trial of Adolf Eichmann.* New York, 1963. (Heavily revised after the 1961 edition.)

Pendorf, Robert. *Mörder und Ermordete: Eichmann und die Judenpolitik des Dritten Reiches.* Hamburg, 1961.

Pohl, Dieter. *Nationalsozialistische Judenverfolgung in Ostgalizien 1941–1944: Organisation und Durchführung des Massenverbrechens.* Munich, 1996.

———. "Die Ermordung der Juden im Generalgouvernement." In *Nationalsozialistische Vernichtungspolitik 1939–1945: Neue Forschungen und Kontroversen.* Edited by Ulrich Herbert. Frankfurt am Main, 1998.

Poliakov, Léon. "Adolf Eichmann ou le rêve de Caligula." *Le Monde Juif.* Paris, June 4, 1949.

———. *Harvest of Hate: Background to the Eichmann Story Introduced by Lord Russell of Liverpool.* London, 1960.

Proces Eichmanna: Sprawy Miedzynarodowe. Warsaw, vol. 14, no. 8, 1961.

Rabinovici, Doron. *Instanzen der Ohnmacht: Wien 1938–1945: Der Weg zum Judenrat.* Frankfurt am Main, 2000.

Ranasinghe, Nalin. "Ethics for the Little Man: Kant, Eichmann, and the Banality of Evil." *Journal of Value Inquiry* 36 (2002), pp. 299–317.

Rappaport, Ernest A. "Adolf Eichmann: The Travelling Salesman of Genocide." *International Review of Psycho-Analysis* 3 (1976), pp. 111–19.

Rein, Raanan. *Argentina, Israel, and the Jews: Peron, the Eichmann Capture and After.* Bethesda, Md., 2003.

Reitlinger, Gerald. *The Final Solution: Hitler's Attempt to Exterminate the Jews of Europe, 1939–1945.* London, 1987.

Reyna, Mariano. "El caso Eichmann." *Todo es Historia* (Buenos Aires) 116 (January 1977), pp. 6–20.

Reynolds, Quentin. "Adolf Eichmann, Henker von Millionen." *Sie und Er* (Zofingen) 37 (January 5–March 30, 1961), pp. 1–13.

Reynolds, Quentin, Ephraim Katz, and Zwy Aldouby. *Minister of Death: The Adolf Eichmann Story.* London, 1961.

Ritzler, B. A., and L. Saradavian. "Sadism and the Banality of Evil as Factors in Nazi Personalities: A Rorschach Analysis." Paper presented at the American Psychological Association Convention. Washington, D.C., August 1986.

Robinson, Jacob. *And Crooked Shall Be Made Straight: The Eichmann Trial, the Jewish Catastrophe and Hannah Arendt's Narrative.* Philadelphia, 1965.

Rosenkranz, Herbert. *Verfolgung und Selbstbehauptung: Die Juden in Österreich 1938–1945.* Vienna and Munich, 1978.

Rotenstreich, Nathan. "Can Evil Be Banal?" *Philosophical Forum* 16, nos. 1–2 (1984–85), pp. 50–62.

Sachs, Ruth. *Adolf Eichmann: Engineer of Death*, New York, 2001.

Safrian, Hans. *Die Eichmann-Männer.* Vienna, 1993.

———. "Adolf Eichmann. Organisator der Judendeportation." In *Die SS: Elite unter dem Totenkopf.* Edited by Ronald Smelser. Paderborn, 2000.

Sandkühler, Thomas. "Eichmann war kein Subalterner, der nur Befehle ausführte." Interview in *Die Welt*, August 16, 1999.

Schechtman, Joseph B. "The Mufti-Eichmann Team." *Congress Bi-Weekly*, November 7, 1960, pp. 5–7.

Scheffler, Wolfgang. "Hannah Arendt und der Mensch im totalitären Staat." *Aus Politik und Zeitgeschichte* 45 (1964), pp. 19–38.

———. "Diese Notizen sind der Versuch, sich verständlich zu machen." Interview in *Die Welt*, August 14, 1999.

Schmidt, Regina, and Egon Becker. *Reaktionen auf politische Vorgänge: 3 Meinungsstudien aus der Bundesrepublik.* Frankfurt am Main, 1967.

Schneppen, Heinz. *Odessa und das Vierte Reich: Mythen der Zeitgeschichte.* Berlin, 2007.

Schubert, Günter. "Post für Eichmann." *Jahrbuch für Antisemitismusforschung* 15 (2006), pp. 383–93.

Schüle, Erwin. "Die strafrechtliche Aufarbeitung des Verhaltens in totalitären Systemen. Der Eichmann-Prozeß aus deutscher Sicht." In *Möglichkeiten und Grenzen für die Bewältigung historischer und politischer Schuld in Strafprozessen.* Edited by Karl Forster. Würzburg, 1962.

Schwelien, Joachim. *Jargon der Gewalt.* Frankfurt am Main, 1961.

Segev, Tom. *Simon Wiesenthal: The Life and Legends.* New York, 2010.

Selzer, Michael. "On Nazis and Normality." *Psychohistory Review* 5, no. 4 (March 1977), pp. 34–36.

———. "The Murderous Mind: Psychological Results of Tests Administered to Adolf Eichmann." *New York Times Magazine*, November 27, 1977, pp. 35ff.

———. "Ein Angreifer, zu nackter Grausamkeit fähig." *Der Spiegel*, February 1978.

Servatius, Robert. "Exclusiv-Interview mit Eichmann-Verteidiger." *Allgemeine Jüdische Wochenzeitung*, April 21, 1961.

Smith, Gary, ed. *Hannah Arendt Revisited: "Eichmann in Jerusalem" und die Folgen.* Frankfurt am Main, 2000.

Sommer, Theo. "Adolf Eichmann, Ostubaf. a. D. Der Mann am Schalthebel der Hitlerschen Vernichtungsmaschine." *Die Zeit*, June 3 1960.

Sontag, Susan. "Reflections on 'The Deputy.'" In *Against Interpretation*. London, 1994.

Sösemann, Bernd. "Viele NS-Quellen sind schlecht ediert." Interview in *Die Welt*, August 18, 1999.

Stangneth, Bettina. "Antisemitische und antijudaistische Motive bei Immanuel Kant? Tatsachen, Meinungen, Ursachen." In *Antisemitismus bei Kant und anderen Denkern der Aufklärung*. Edited by Horst Gronke et al. Würzburg, 2001.

———. "Adolf Eichmann interpretiert Immanuel Kant." Lecture at the University of Marburg, 2002 (unpublished).

Steinacher, Gerald. *Nazis on the Run: How Hitler's Henchmen Fled Justice*. Oxford, 2011.

Steur, Claudia. "Eichmanns Emissäre. Die 'Judenberater' in Hitlers Europa." In *Die Gestapo im Zweiten Weltkrieg: "Heimatfront" und besetztes Europa*. Edited by Gerhard Paul and Klaus Michael Mallmann. Darmstadt, 2000.

Strasser, Peter. *Verbrechermenschen: Zur kriminalwissenschaftlichen Erzeugung des Bösen*. Frankfurt am Main and New York, 1984.

Szondi, Leopold. "Blindanalyse der Triebteste Adolf Eichmanns." In *Kain: Gestalten des Bösen*. Bern, 1969. (A blind analysis of the test performed on Eichmann by Szondi.)

Vogel, Rolf, ed. *Der deutsch-israelische Dialog: Dokumentation eines erregenden Kapitels deutscher Außenpolitik*. Vols. 1–3. Munich, 1987–88.

Volk, Christian. "'Wo das Wort versagt und das Denken scheitert.' Überlegungen zu Hannah Arendts Eichmann-Charakterisierung." *ASCHKENAS—Zeitschrift für Geschichte und Kultur der Juden* 16 (2006), pp. 195–227.

Wassermann, Heinz P. "'Lang lebe Deutschland, lang lebe Argentinien, lang lebe Österreich . . .'– Der Prozeß gegen Adolf Eichmann: Eine Analyse historischer Bewußtseinsbildung durch die Tagespresse." *Zeitgeschichte* 20, nos. 7–8 (July–August 1993), pp. 249–59.

Weber, Gaby. *Daimler-Benz und die Argentinien-Connection: Von Rattenlinien und Nazigeldern*. Berlin and Hamburg, 2004.

Weibel-Altmeyer, Heinz. "Jagd auf Eichmann." *Neue Illustrierte*, June–July 8, 1960.

Weinke, Annette. "Die SED-Begleitkampagne zum Jerusalemer Eichmann-Prozeß." In *Die Verfolgung von NS-Tätern im geteilten Deutschland: Vergangenheitsbewältigung 1949–1969 oder: Eine deutsch-deutsche Beziehungsgeschichte im Kalten Krieg*. Paderborn, Munich, Zurich, and Vienna, 2002.

Weitz, Yehiam. "The Holocaust on Trial: The Impact of the Kasztner and Eichmann Trials on Israeli Society." *Israel Studies* 1, no. 2 (December 1996), pp. 1–26.

———. "The Founding Father and the War Criminal's Trial: Ben Gurion and the Eichmann Trial." *Yad Vashem Studies* (2008), 211–52.

Wiesenthal, Simon. *Großmufti—Großagent der Achse*. Salzburg and Vienna, 1947.

———. *Ich jagte Eichmann: Tatsachenbericht*. Gütersloh, 1961.

Wieviorka, Annette. *Procès de Eichmann—1961.* Brussels, 1989.

Wighton, Charles. *Eichmann: His Career and Crimes.* London, 1961.

Wildt, Michael. *Die Judenpolitik des SD 1935–1938: Eine Dokumentation.* Munich, 1995.

———. "Eichmanns Götzen." *Die Zeit,* March 23, 2000.

———. *Generation des Unbedingten: Das Führungskorps des Reichssicherheitshauptamtes.* Hamburg, 2003.

Wildt, Michael, ed. *Nachrichtendienst, Politische Elite und Mordeinheit: Der Sicherheitsdienst des Reichsführer SS.* Hamburg, 2003.

Winkler, Willi. *Der Schattenmann: Von Goebbels zu Carlos: Das mysteriöse Leben des François Genoud.* Berlin, 2011.

Witte, Peter. "Warum Eichmann bewußt Details verschweigt." *Die Welt,* August 21, 1999.

———. "Adolf Eichmann unterschlägt bewußt entscheidende Fakten. Der Judenreferent deportiert zielstrebig für seinen Führer." *Die Welt,* August 24, 1999.

Wojak, Irmtrud. "Über Eichmann nichts Neues." Interview in *Frankfurter Rundschau,* August 11, 1999.

———. *Eichmanns Memoiren: Ein kritischer Essay.* Frankfurt am Main, 2001.

———. *Fritz Bauer: 1903–1968: Eine Biographie.* Munich, 2009.

Wolfmann, Alfred. *Eichmannprozeß: Berichte aus Jerusalem.* Düsseldorf, c. 1962.

Wucher, Albert. *Eichmanns gab es viele: Ein Dokumentarbericht über die Endlösung der Judenfrage.* Munich and Zurich, 1961.

Wyss, P. "*Eichmann in Jerusalem.*" In Karl Jaspers, *Provokationen: Gespräche und Interviews.* Edited by Hans Saner. Munich, 1969.

Yablonka, Hanna. *The State of Israel vs. Adolf Eichmann.* New York, 2004.

Yahil, Leni. "'Memoirs' of Adolf Eichmann." *Yad Vashem Studies* 18 (1987), pp. 133–62.

———. *Die Shoah: Überlebenskampf und Vernichtung der europäischen Juden.* Munich, 1998.

Zachodnia Agencja Prasowa, ed. *Eichmann.* Poznan, 1960.

Zimmermann, Moshe. "An Eichmanns Aufzeichnungen kommt kein Historiker vorbei." *Die Welt,* August 17, 1999.

———. "Aufzeichnungen eines Mörders." *Allgemeine Jüdische Wochenzeitung,* March 16, 2000.

Documentaries

Bogart, Paul, director. *Engineer of Death: The Eichmann Story.* United States: Robert E. Costello, Talent Associates, CBS, New York, 1960.

Defrank, Rolf, director. *Erscheinungsform Mensch: Adolf Eichmann.* Hamburg: Aurora Television Productions, 1978–79.

Glynn, Clara, director. *Adolf Eichmann—Begegnungen mit einem Mörder.* BBC/NDR, 2002. English version: *I Met Adolf Eichmann.*

Graham, William A., director. *The Man Who Captured Eichmann.* United States, Argentina: Butcher's Run Films, Stan Margolies Company, Turner Pictures, 1996.

Gribowsky, Peter Schier, director. *Eine Epoche vor Gericht.* Germany: NDR 1961.

Keutner, Sabine, director. *Der Fall Adolf Eichmann: 40 Jahre Entführung und Verhaftung.* Mainz, Germany: ZDF, 3sat, 2000.

Knopp, Guido, director. *Eichmann: Der Vernichter.* Munich: BMG Video/ Universum-Film München, 1998. English version: *Hitler's Henchmen II. Adolf Eichmann: The Exterminator.*

Ley, Raymond, director. *Eichmanns Ende.* Hamburg: docstation for NDR, SWR, 2010.

Mossek, Nissim, director. *Adolph Eichmann: The Secret Memoirs.* Israel, Netherlands: Biblical Productions, EO Television, 2002.

Sandler, Michael, director. *I Captured Eichmann.* Belgium: Belbo Film Productions BV, 1980.

Setton, Dan, director. *Eichmann: The Nazi Fugitive/Lechidato shel Adolf Eichmann.* Israel: SET Productions, Jerusalem, 1994.

———. *Josef Mengele: The Final Account.* Israel: SET Productions, Jerusalem, 2002.

Sivan, Eyal, director. *Der Spezialist.* Germany, France, Belgium, Austria, Israel, 1998.

Wallace, Mike, interviewer. *The Devil Is a Gentleman.* United States: CBS New York, 1983.

Index